GROUPS AT WORK:
THEORY AND RESEARCH

Applied Social Research
Marlene Turner and Anthony Pratkanis, Series Editors

GROUPS AT WORK:
THEORY AND RESEARCH

Edited by

Marlene E. Turner
San Jose State University

LEA

LAWRENCE ERLBAUM ASSOCIATES, PUBLISHERS
2001   Mahwah, New Jersey   London

#42476714

Copyright © 2001 by Lawrence Erlbaum Associates, Inc.
   All rights reserved. No part of this book may be reproduced in
   any form, by photostat, microform, retrieval system, or any other
   means, without the prior written permission of the publisher.

Lawrence Erlbaum Associates, Inc., Publishers
10 Industrial Avenue
Mahwah, New Jersey 07430

Library of Congress Cataloging-in-Publication Data

Groups at work : theory and research / edited by Marlene Turner.
       p.   cm.
   Includes bibliographical references and index.
   ISBN 0-8058-2078-7 (c : alk. paper) — ISBN 0-8058-2079-5 (p : alk. paper)
   1. Teams in the workplace.   I. Turner, Marlene E.

   HD66.G758 1999
   658.4'02—dc21   99-049323

Books published by Lawrence Erlbaum Associates are printed on acid-free
paper, and their bindings are chosen for strength and durability.

Printed in the United States of America
10 9 8 7 6 5 4 3 2 1

For Tony,
who makes every group a joy

Contents

Introduction

Why do we find groups at once so tantalizing and yet, so disturbing? This paradoxical perspective on groups is perhaps due to our recognition of their potential to amplify the range of individual achievement. On the one hand, groups enthrall us for they allow us to aspire far greater heights than any individual might attain. Conversely, groups trouble us for they are responsible for some of our greatest devastation.

Explaining how and why these outcomes occur has long been a fascinating, yet thorny topic for social and organizational researchers. Understanding how groups function, why they work and how they work in organizational settings are crucial topics that have profound implications for both the design of groups and the fundamental research on groups. Interestingly, however, perspectives on groups arising from organizational and social psychological research all too frequently develop almost independently.

As such, this book has two purposes. First, it is most fundamentally about groups at work. It is about groups both as they attempt to accomplish their goals (whatever those goals might be) and as they operate in organizational settings. To that end, the book meets its second goal by drawing together group researchers from social psychological and organizational studies. Each chapter focuses on a central issue regarding groups as they work and examines that issue by drawing, where possible, from both social psychological and organizational research. Thus, the book at once centers on the convergence and divergence of these two fields.

Theoretical perspectives offering descriptive and prescriptive models of group behavior have long traditions in these disciplines (see, for example, Cartwright & Zander, 1968; Davis, 1969; Hackman, 1990; Homans, 1950; Lewin, 1948; Maier, 1952; Steiner, 1972; see Campion, Medsker, & Higgs, 1993; Guzzo & Shea, 1992; and Shaw, 1981 for reviews). These models vary widely in their emphasis on group characteristics and processes. Yet, despite this diversity, many share certain assumptions. Most importantly, these models highlight the importance of understanding not only the intragroup processes but also the context in which the group is embedded. Intragroup processes and attributes including socialization, motivation, creativity, power, and learning are, in many ways, inextricably interweaved with contextual factors such as institutionalized norms, organizational settings, cultural norms such as racial bias, environmental events such as threat, and technological aspects of the group environment. Indeed, the chapters in this book reflect this duality. They at once recognize that both the attributes of the group itself and the characteristics of the group context exert powerful influences on group processes and outcomes.

Part one of the book examines theoretical perspectives on groups. Fuller and Aldag examine conceptual issues regarding group problem solving and decision making. Their perspective is useful in that it simultaneously treats the intragroup processes impacting decision making and the political and organizational matters that affect groups as they engage in these tasks. John Turner and Haslam examine social identity theory and its implications for organizational settings. Their analysis of leadership processes from a social identity perspective provides a forceful documentation of the explanatory and prescriptive power of this approach.

Part two begins the exploration of intragroup processes and treats social and motivational processes in groups. Moreland and Levine examine socialization processes from both a group and an organizational standpoint. Using a multilevel perspective, they further discuss the role of the work group in accomplishing both group and organizational socialization. Karau and Williams provide a compelling look into the thorny issue of individual motivation in group settings. Their collective effort model has profound implications for understanding how groups accomplish tasks. Cropanzano and Schminke underscore the role of justice in designing work groups. They thoughtfully examine theoretical and empirical evidence on distributive and procedural justice and develop implications for both research and practice. Kramer, Hanna, Su, and Wei discuss the interplay between group identification and trust. They present an intriguing framework for conceptualizing how identification influences trust-related judgment and decision making and develop the implications of that framework for understanding groups at work. Finally, Wageman explores the conceptual foundations of interdependence in groups. Differentiating between structural and behavioral interdependence, this interpretation is especially important because it facilitates both descriptive and prescriptive propositions regarding the design of organizations to appropriately create interdependent structures and the specification of the impacts of those structures on interaction.

Part three continues this theme and also examines contextual influences on groups by centering on the issues of conflict and power relevant to group settings. Thompson and Fox focus a multilevel lens on intragroup and intergroup negotiations in organizations. Using this viewpoint, they analyze dyadic, multiparty, intermediary, intragroup, and intergroup relations, examining both obstacles to and effective interventions for dispute resolution. An integration of descriptive, explanatory, and prescriptive theory of conflict in group settings is the goal of Van de Vliert and Janssen. To that end, they present their approach to conglomerated conflict behavior and develop its implications for theory building, research, and implementation. Finally, Owens and Sutton examine the role of meetings in negotiating and maintaining status and power distributions within groups.

Part four expands the focus to examine creativity, innovation, and learning as they develop in various group settings. Brainstorming is the focus of the chapter by Paulus, Leary, and Dzindolet. They review conceptual and empirical work on brainstorming, develop conditions under which productivity losses are likely to occur, and present strategies for enhancing creativity in groups and teams. Eisenhardt, Schoonhoven, and Lyman examine the role of top management teams in fostering organizational innovation. Specifically, they explore when young organizations are likely to form technology sharing and joint product ventures. Argote, Gruenfeld, and Naquin integrate the literatures on group and organizational learning. They examine how these processes occur in the central domains of group work including construction and establishment of the group, operation (pursuit of group activities), reconstruction (modifications to the group, task, and so forth that occur as a result of project completion), and external relations.

Part five treats liabilities for groups as they work. Dovidio, Gaertner, and Bachman review the literature on aversive racism and develop its implications for bias in group settings. Moreover, they employ this perspective to develop useful recommendations for combatting bias in group settings and for facilitating group and organizational accomplishment. Turner and Horvitz examine the issue of how groups perform in the face of an external threat. They review the relevant social and organizational literature and develop intervention tactics for enhancing group effectiveness under threat. Brief, Buttram, and Dukerich develop a process model of collective corruption in groups by drawing on an intriguing array of literature including that on collective violence. They examine why groups and organizations sanction corruption, comply with pressures to engage in corruption, and institutionalize those practices. The final chapter reminds us that, despite the crucial importance of groups, individuals yet remain the building blocks of our social structures. Locke, Tirnauer, Roberson, Goldman, Latham, and Weldon discuss the importance of the individual, of intellectual independence, and the very real dangers that arise from inappropriate use of groups in decision making. They caution us to use groups not as a panacea but as a thoughtful tool appropriately applied to fit the requirements of the situation.

In sum, the chapters in this book echo the duality associated with groups. Groups can indeed allow us to achieve unprecedented aspirations. But, they can also have tragic consequences. The chapters in this book also provide a look into how groups can be effectively designed to facilitate their advantages while limiting their disadvantages, and they point out areas for new research. To do so, they underscore the importance of acknowledging that groups indeed are social entities that are profoundly affected by the context in which they are embedded. It is by discerning how these separate yet interrelated factors interplay that we can indeed further our understanding of groups at work.

REFERENCES

Campion, M. A., Medsker, G. J., & Higgs, A. C. (1993). Relations between work group characteristics and effectiveness: Implications for designing effective work groups. *Personnel Psychology, 46*, 823–850.

Cartwright, D., & Zander, A. (1968). *Group dynamics: Research and theory* (3rd ed.). New York: Harper & Row.

Davis, J. H. (1969). *Group performance*. Reading, MA: Addison-Wesley.

Guzzo, R. A., & Shea, G. P. (1992). Group performance and intergroup relations in organizations. In M. D. Dunnette & L. M. Hough (Eds.), *Handbook of industrial and organizational psychology* (pp. 269–313). Palo Alto, CA: Consulting Psychologists Press.

Hackman, J. R. (1990). *Groups that work (and those that don't): Creating conditions for effective teamwork*. San Francisco: Jossey-Bass.

Homans, G. C. (1950). *The human group*. New York: Harcourt Brace.

Lewin, K. (1948). *Resolving social conflicts: Selected papers in group dynamics*. New York: Harper & Row.

Maier, N. R. F. (1952). *Principles of human relations*. New York: Wiley.

Shaw, M. E. (1981). *Group dynamics* (3rd ed.). New York: McGraw-Hill.

Steiner, I. D. (1972). *Group process and productivity*. New York: Academic Press.

Part I

THEORETICAL
PERSPECTIVES

Chapter 1

The GGPS Model:
Broadening the Perspective
on Group Problem Solving

Sally Riggs Fuller
University of Washington

Ramon J. Aldag
University of Wisconsin–Madison

Models of group problem solving must reflect the emerging, and often disquieting, realities of the modern workplace. This brave new world of work is uncertain, political, and dynamic. Often, peers lead peers, the traditional hierarchy has no meaning, the implicit psychological contract between workers and organizations has been nullified, and measures of group effectiveness are multiple and sometimes conflicting. Simple deterministic models of group problem-solving processes, however appealing, cannot begin to capture the richness of group processes in these boundaryless, stressful, turbulent times.

An adequate model of the new reality of group processes would have to be able to address questions such as the following: When might group leaders be expected to pursue political goals and when might they focus on other outcomes, such as member motivation or group effectiveness? How do the roles of variables such as cohesiveness and leader impartiality vary over the life of the group? When do leaders choose to make use of outside experts and develop contingency plans, and when do they shun them? What factors determine when a preferred solution will emerge, and which solution will be chosen? How do the organization's political norms and members' political motives moderate the roles of decision process characteristics? What factors influence whether a leader will choose to make future use of a problem-solving group?

We don't believe development of the group problem-solving literature has achieved its potential over the past two decades. In general, researchers have not adopted a broad, comprehensive perspective when examining organizational group problem solving. We see this failure as stemming from two related tendencies. First, we believe the narrow focus is a direct consequence of an overemphasis on the groupthink phenomenon (Janis, 1971, 1972, 1982). Although anchors sometimes serve useful roles, clinging to an anchor can be constraining, especially if the anchor itself is suspect. Elsewhere, we have argued that the groupthink phenomenon has become an unfortunate anchor on the group decision-making literature (Aldag & Fuller, 1993; Fuller & Aldag, 1998). Second, research on group decision making has often been framed in relative isolation, without appropriate links to the broader problem-solving literatures.

Using the broad group problem-solving literature and a variety of related literatures as guides, we developed the general group problem solving (GGPS) model (Aldag & Fuller, 1993). The GGPS model provides a relatively comprehensive, and correspondingly complex, framework including many factors known to be important to group problem solving. This framework is intended to allow examination of a broad range of research questions. Two general characteristics of our model should be noted. First, the model presents each element in a value-neutral manner. Such an orientation is important both conceptually and in terms of future empirical analyses. Second, the GGPS model includes factors representing a political orientation to recognize the political realities of group processes.

In this chapter, we first present an overview of the GGPS model, highlighting key features. We then offer implications for research, including illustrative propositions, suggested methodologies for testing the model, and a variety of other implications. We conclude with implications for practice.

AN OVERVIEW OF THE GGPS MODEL

The GGPS model (Fig. 1.1) is intended to be realistic rather than deterministic, comprehensive rather than concise. As such, it provides a broad framework for assessment of group problem solving, specifying potentially relevant contingency variables. We initially presented the GGPS model as a richer, value-neutral alternative to the groupthink model (Aldag & Fuller, 1993). However, any elements shared with the groupthink model are included in the GGPS model because they are legitimate, previously recognized factors in group problem solving rather than (or despite) their presence in the groupthink model. Indeed, we have argued (Aldag & Fuller, 1993) that the groupthink model is an overly deterministic and unrealistically restrictive depiction of the group problem-solving process.

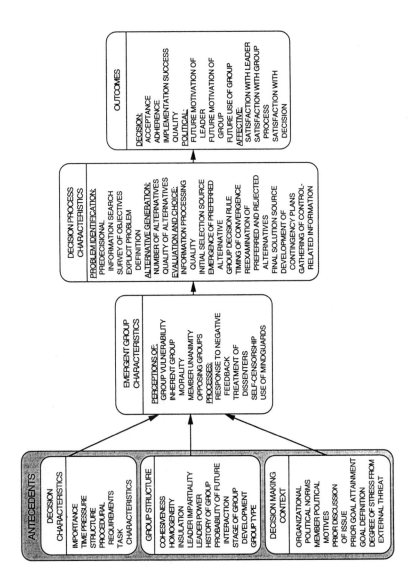

FIG. 1.1. General group problem solving (GGPS) model.

ANTECEDENTS

DECISION CHARACTERISTICS

IMPORTANCE
TIME PRESSURE
STRUCTURE
PROCEDURAL REQUIREMENTS
TASK CHARACTERISTICS

GROUP STRUCTURE

COHESIVENESS
HOMOGENEITY
INSULATION
LEADER IMPARTIALITY
LEADER POWER
HISTORY OF GROUP
PROBABILITY OF FUTURE INTERACTION
STAGE OF GROUP DEVELOPMENT
GROUP TYPE

DECISION MAKING CONTEXT

ORGANIZATIONAL POLITICAL NORMS
MEMBER POLITICAL MOTIVES
PRIOR DISCUSSION OF ISSUE
PRIOR GOAL ATTAINMENT
GOAL DEFINITION
DEGREE OF STRESS FROM EXTERNAL THREAT

EMERGENT GROUP CHARACTERISTICS

PERCEPTIONS OF:
GROUP VULNERABILITY
INHERENT GROUP MORALITY
MEMBER UNANIMITY
OPPOSING GROUPS
PROCESSES:
RESPONSE TO NEGATIVE FEEDBACK
TREATMENT OF DISSENTERS
SELF-CENSORSHIP
USE OF MINDGUARDS

DECISION PROCESS CHARACTERISTICS

PROBLEM IDENTIFICATION:
PREDECISIONAL INFORMATION SEARCH
SURVEY OF OBJECTIVES
EXPLICIT PROBLEM DEFINITION
ALTERNATIVE GENERATION:
NUMBER OF ALTERNATIVES
QUALITY OF ALTERNATIVES
EVALUATION AND CHOICE:
INFORMATION PROCESSING QUALITY
INITIAL SELECTION SOURCE
EMERGENCE OF PREFERRED ALTERNATIVE
GROUP DECISION RULE
TIMING OF CONVERGENCE
REEXAMINATION OF PREFERRED AND REJECTED ALTERNATIVES
FINAL SOLUTION SOURCE
DEVELOPMENT OF CONTINGENCY PLANS
GATHERING OF CONTROL-RELATED INFORMATION

OUTCOMES

DECISION:
ACCEPTANCE
ADHERENCE
IMPLEMENTATION SUCCESS
QUALITY
POLITICAL:
FUTURE MOTIVATION OF LEADER
FUTURE MOTIVATION OF GROUP
FUTURE USE OF GROUP
AFFECTIVE:
SATISFACTION WITH LEADER
SATISFACTION WITH GROUP
PROCESS
SATISFACTION WITH DECISION

Antecedent Conditions

Our framework includes three sets of antecedents shown by broad problem-solving research to be important in influencing group processes and outcomes. The first set contains relevant decision characteristics. These include the importance of the decision, time pressure, structure, procedural requirements, and task characteristics. The task, for example, is important for several reasons. Whether a task is simple or complex affects the requirements for member inputs and the need for a directive leader. Also, given a task in which a single correct answer becomes immediately obvious once insight is achieved by any group member, protracted group interaction will be limited, thus lessening the chance to observe certain characteristics that might emerge over time (Callaway & Esser, 1984; Steiner, 1976; Weldon & Gargano, 1985). Also important are whether the task requires a pooling of inputs, or interaction at all, distribution of information (Gladstein & Reilly, 1985), and the importance of individual ability (Locke, Tirnauer, Roberson, Goldman, Latham, & Weldon, this volume).

The second set of antecedents contains the following nine group structure factors; cohesiveness, members' homogeneity, insulation of the group, leader impartiality, leader power, history of the group, probability of future interaction, stage of group development, and type of group. We will highlight the importance of several of these factors.

A powerful leader can have a crucial impact on the group's functioning by strongly influencing members' behavior. For example, the emergent group characteristic of self-censorship may result from the exercise of influence by a powerful leader.

The organizational power and politics literature suggests that many decisions are influenced by ongoing political activity and reflect shifting power of various coalitions. Therefore, an important antecedent is the probability of future interaction of the group. If group members do not anticipate future interaction, some types of political influence may be lessened. The stage of group development is included for a variety of reasons. It may, for instance, moderate the influence of group cohesiveness on various group process factors. As discussed by Leana (1985) and Longley and Pruitt (1980), the members of a fairly cohesive group in the mature stage are likely to be secure enough in their roles to challenge one another and to have developed ways to reach agreement. In this case, cohesiveness could result in an effective decision-making process and in positive outcomes.

Group type is a critical factor because, for example, we would expect an advisory group, as opposed to an ongoing decision group that was responsible for implementation, to legitimately approach the problem-solving issue differently. Some negative characteristics of group problem-solving may be evident primarily in ongoing, fixed-membership, self-contained groups.

The third set of antecedents includes the following factors that address the decision-making context; organizational political norms, member political motives, prior discussion of the issue, prior goal attainment, goal definition, and degree of stress from external threat. Organizational political norms is included to recognize that the assumption of rationality is invalid where political influence is a prevalent part of the decision-making process (Pfeffer, 1981). Members' political motives are also relevant. Individuals may have a vested interest in certain alternatives, or there may be one or more strong coalitions present; both of these will affect behavior in the group decision-making process.

Whether group members discussed the issue prior to the decision-making meeting can also impact the problem-solving process. Members could have previously discussed which solution best serves organizational goals, or could have made deals, making the decision essentially a political one. Also, various alternatives could have been explored before the meeting, thereby shortening the observable problem-solving process and giving a false sense of premature closure to observers.

Another important antecedent is goal definition. To apply a rational model of decision making, there must be agreement on a unitary goal for the group. Instead, however, group members may have multiple, discrepant and/or ill-defined goals, thus violating the rational assumption.

Emergent Group Characteristics

In our GGPS framework, we categorize emergent group characteristics as group perceptions and processes. The former include group members' perceptions of the group's vulnerability, the inherent morality of the group, member unanimity, and views of opposing groups. Important processes are the group's response to negative feedback, treatment of dissenters, self-censorship, and use of mindguards.

Decision Process Characteristics

We group decision process characteristics in terms of the first three stages of the problem-solving process; problem identification, alternative generation, and evaluation and choice. We do not explicitly include the implementation and control stages here because they follow the actual decision, although we do include variables that prepare for those stages (i.e., development of contingency plans and gathering of control-related information).

Problem identification factors are predecisional information search, survey of objectives, and explicit problem definition. Group members may fail to explicitly define the problem because a focus on the problem is uncomfortable, because they are anxious to move on to choice, or for other reasons. However, failure to adequately define the problem may result in an "error of the third kind," solving the wrong problem. If a problem has been inadequately defined, the "solution" cannot be adequate (Elbing, 1978).

Alternative generation requires consideration of both the quantity and quality of alternatives. Processes that enhance alternative quantity will not necessarily enhance alternative quality. Although some group processes, such as brainstorming (Osborn, 1963), are based on the premise that a large quantity of alternatives improves the prospects for identification of a superior alternative, it is conceivable that defective processes may result in the generation of large numbers of hastily considered, low-quality alternatives. This could both complicate choice making and lead to poor decision outcomes. Paulus, Larey, and Dzindolet (this volume) present conditions for increasing the effectiveness of group brainstorming.

The following nine decision process characteristics are included in the evaluation and choice section; information processing quality, the source of the initial selection of a preferred alternative, emergence of preferred alternative, group decision rule, timing of convergence, reexamination of preferred and rejected alternatives, source of the final solution, development of contingency plans, and gathering of control-related information.

Here, we highlight the relevance of several of these factors. The source of the initially preferred solution is important because group member reaction to the alternative may vary considerably depending on factors such as whether it was selected by the leader, mandated by a person external to the group, or used in the past. Whether a preferred alternative emerges early in the process or the group converges on a solution much later must be known in order to evaluate the process. The group decision rule is also important. A decision rule identified early could influence other decision process characteristics. For instance, with a consensus decision rule, each member recognizes that dissent may preclude, or at least jeopardize, problem resolution. With a majority decision rule, such dissent may be more acceptable.

The timing of convergence is also critical. Consensus-seeking behavior should not always be considered negative. Indeed, the choice stage of problem solving is inherently convergent; reaching a consensus is the goal. We noted earlier that the source of the initial selection may be relevant. Similarly, the source of the final solution, which may or may not be the same as the initial selection, should be important. The problem-solving literature suggests that the source of the final solution should influence outcomes such as decision acceptance and implementation success. For instance, solutions proposed by group members during group discussion will likely result in greater understanding and acceptance of the decision and greater likelihood of implementation success.

Outcomes

The GGPS model includes an array of decision, political, and affective outcomes. Decision outcomes include acceptance of the decision by those affected by it and/or by those who must implement it, adherence to the decision (that is, whether the decision is subsequently overturned), implementation success, and decision quality. The political outcomes include future motivation of the leader and group and future use of the group. Finally, the affective outcomes include satisfaction with the leader, the group process, and the decision. The model makes no assumptions concerning the relationships among these outcomes.

The group problem-solving literature suggests these outcomes, recognizing that a "good" decision is not only one that appears so from an objective, rational evaluation immediately following the decision. Rather, it is also necessary to consider whether the decision is functional to the organization in the long term. Important outcomes such as trust, decision commitment, and attachment to the group, for example, reflect group members' perceptions of fairness in the group process (Cropanzano & Schminke, this volume). Including an array of outcomes is essential to explicitly recognize that group members may bring a variety of goals to the problem situation, that affective reactions may influence future group functioning, and that basically political outcomes (such as the likelihood that the group leader will refuse to use the group process in the future, or that the group's decision will subsequently be unilaterally reversed by the leader) may be critical.

IMPLICATIONS FOR RESEARCH

Future research on group problem solving should adopt a broad, value-neutral perspective, should explicitly recognize the role of political factors in group problem solving, and should avoid a priori assumptions about the pathology of particular characteristics or processes. Here, we present propositions and suggest research methodologies for addressing issues raised by our discussion and model. We then provide additional implications for research.

Illustrative Propositions

The following propositions are illustrative of those that can be addressed by the GGPS model. It becomes clear in reflecting on these propositions that the neat causal sequence from antecedent conditions to outcomes illustrated in the model represents a necessary oversimplification. For instance, we argue that some so-called antecedent conditions may also play moderating roles later in the model, and that there are interrelationships among variables within sets. While these propositions serve to give some sense of the breadth of issues that may be addressed by the GGPS model, they are obviously far from exhaustive.[1]

Propositions Relating to Power and Politics

The first four propositions address power and politics in group problem solving. Of particular importance here are the amount of power the group leader possesses, political norms within the organization, political norms and motives within the group, and antecedents to political behavior.

Proposition 1.   Increases in leader power will result in enhanced likelihood of self-censorship, and, in the increased probability that the leader will be the source of the final solution.

Self-censorship is the result in part of concerns about the potentially punitive reaction of a powerful leader to disquieting information. As such, as leader power and associated follower concerns about the leader's reactions increase, self-censorship should increase. The finding of increased distortion and filtering in the face of growing recipient power has been documented elsewhere, and this extrapolation to the leader as the recipient seems natural. In turn, reduced input from group members other than the leader increases the likelihood that the final solution will originate with the leader. Further, even in the absence of self-censorship, members may simply be more likely to "go along" with what they know to be the wishes of a powerful leader.

Proposition 2.   Organizational political norms will moderate the relationships of decision process characteristics to selected outcomes. For instance, in organizations that permit open political activity, decision process characteristics such as failure to reexamine selected and rejected alternatives will be positively associated with future use of the group and satisfaction with the group process. In organizations in which norms proscribe political activity, the opposite pattern of relationships will be evidenced.

This proposition makes explicit the fact that decision processes occur, and are interpreted, in a social context. Those characteristics consistent with group and organizational norms and rewards will be positively reinforced, and vice versa. As such, for instance, reexamination of selected and rejected alternatives is consistent with the expectations and demands

---

[1]It is important to note that none of these propositions would be suggested by the groupthink model.

of a setting in which politics are discouraged, but may be inconsistent with the attainment of a political agenda.

Proposition 3.　Member political motives will moderate the relationships between decision process characteristics and outcomes. For instance, if the group leader has political motives for use of the group, failure to use experts or to develop contingency plans will be associated with an increased probability of future use of the group and with high future leader motivation. If the group leader does not have political motives for use of the group, these decision process characteristics will be associated with decreased probability of future use of the group and with low future leader motivation.

Quite simply, use of expert inputs and explicit consideration of contingencies will make political activity more visible and render manipulation of the group process for political ends more difficult and use of the group more problematic. As such, a leader with political motives for the group will find the absence of those decision process characteristics to be desirable, and will be motivated to continue use of the group in their absence. Conversely, a leader lacking political motives for the group will use expert inputs and explicitly consider contingencies to maximize decision quality.

Proposition 4.　Explicit problem definition, increased predecisional information search, and increased survey of objectives will reduce the incidence of political behavior.

That is, because political activity feeds on uncertainty, ambiguity-reducing activities such as explicit problem definition, predecisional information search, and survey of objectives should dampen political activity.

Propositions Relating to Group Development and Group Type

The next five propositions deal with the stage of group development and the type of group, including whether it is an ongoing group in which the members would expect future interaction.

Proposition 5.　Stage of group development will moderate the relationship of leader impartiality to decision process characteristics. For instance, groups with a history of working together will exhibit a more positive constellation of decision process characteristics in the absence of leader impartiality than will ad hoc groups.

Leader impartiality helps ensure that member inputs are fairly elicited and weighted, and that outcomes reflect those inputs. In the absence of impartiality, alternative mechanisms, such as group norms and established procedures, are necessary to achieve these results. Because the existence of defined norms and procedures occurs only after the group has some history of interaction, leader impartiality should be more pivotal early in the group's life.

Proposition 6. Stage of group development will moderate the relationships of group cohesiveness to members' self-censorship and to perceived unanimity. For example, cohesiveness will have a more positive relationship to divergence of members' stated opinions in the mature stage of group development than in earlier stages.

Members of a cohesive group in the mature stage may feel sufficiently secure in their roles to challenge one another. As such, self-censorship should decrease and, because more divergent views will be openly expressed, perceived unanimity of opinions should also decline.

Proposition 7. Group type will affect emergent group characteristics. For example, perceived member unanimity will be lower in an advisory group than in a group given final decision-making responsibility.

In general, group leader and member time and other resources will be allocated in ways that best achieve desired outcomes. Because unanimity may be less critical in an advisory group than in a group that was responsible for making, and perhaps implementing, the decision, the group leader may feel correspondingly less need to devote resources to seeking agreement and closure.

Proposition 8. Group type will affect decision process characteristics. For example, an advisory group may give less attention to development of contingency plans and gathering of control-related information than would a group having the responsibility for implementing the decision.

Although it may seem obvious that an advisory group may feel that development of contingency plans and attention to control are outside its responsibilities, this proposition serves to highlight the fact that statements concerning a variety of decision process characteristics can be confidently presented only with knowledge of the group type.

Proposition 9. As probability of future group interaction increases, the degree of self-censorship and perceived unanimity will increase.

Likelihood of future interaction will, among other things, enhance salience of others' approval and concerns about future retribution for disagreement.

Other Propositions

The remaining propositions address a variety of other relationships within our framework.

Proposition 10. Cohesiveness and member homogeneity will result in enhanced member satisfaction and increased probability of future use of the group.

Group cohesiveness and homogeneity have regularly been shown to be associated with enhanced member satisfaction, and cohesiveness is also associated with greater group goal attainment. Because successful groups are more attractive to their members and leaders, cohesiveness and homogeneity should be associated with continued use. This proposition reflects the assertion that political and affective outcomes are important considerations in group functioning. As such, it is important to recognize that, whatever the impacts of cohesiveness and homogeneity on decision quality, those impacts will not be the sole determinants of reactions to, and the probability of future use of, the group.

Proposition 11. As leader impartiality increases, the emergence of a preferred alternative will occur later in the problem-solving process.

Leader partiality will result in attempts to steer the group toward a preferred solution. Understandably, a leader favoring a particular solution will discourage the generation and consideration of additional alternatives and push toward early closure. Conversely, an impartial leader will allow the group to spend more time in the earlier stages of the decision process.

Proposition 12. The group decision rule will influence the degree to which decision process characteristics are oriented toward convergence. For example, there will be more pressure for convergence with a consensus decision rule than with a majority decision rule.

Again, leaders expend energy and other resources in ways that best yield desired outcomes. Because full convergence on a desired solution is less important with a majority decision rule than with a consensus decision rule, pressure for such convergence should also be less.

Proposition 13. As member perceived unanimity increases, there will be less attention to reexamination of preferred and rejected alternatives, to development of contingency plans, and to gathering control-related information. ·

Quite simply, perceived unanimity will increase confidence in decision quality and thus reduce the need for further scrutiny and for follow-up activities and alternatives.

Proposition 14. When the leader's initially preferred solution is rejected by the group, such that the final solution is not the leader's preference, there will be reductions in the probability that the leader will adhere to the decision, the future motivation of the leader, and the probability of future use of the group by the leader.

Although it is not surprising that a leader will be inclined to reject a decision he or she finds undesirable, and will be less likely to make continued use of a group that has generated that decision, this proposition again encourages consideration of multiple outcomes. A group that is willing and able to arrive at a decision other than that desired by the leader may also be less prone to dysfunctional illusions and tendencies, but these benefits may be achieved at the cost of continued member participation in group decision processes. To the extent that opportunities for such participation are valued, disagreements with the leader may thus be muted.

Proposition 15. Solutions that were initially proposed by group members, rather than by the leader or a source external to the group, will be associated with greater member acceptance of the decision; with implementation success; with future motivation of the group; with member satisfaction with the group process; and with satisfaction with the decision.

This proposition is consistent with the common finding that participation in decision making enhances satisfaction with, and acceptance of, decision outcomes and processes, and increases motivation to implement the decision.

As previously mentioned, these propositions are certainly not exhaustive, but rather represent the variety of important group problem-solving issues that can be addressed within our framework. However, even this brief sampling of illustrative propositions makes it clear that deterministic models of group decision processes, whatever their intuitive appeal, are simplistic. Below we discuss methodologies for examining these and related research questions.

Suggested Methodologies for Use With the GGPS Model

We have argued against the continued heavy reliance on anecdotal evidence in group problem-solving research (Aldag & Fuller, 1993). Further, while laboratory experiments may be useful for exploring many aspects of group decision processes, we have presented reasons why they must, at least, be complemented by other methodologies. For example, laboratory experiments would be entirely appropriate for testing elements of the GGPS model; certain of the propositions presented earlier could be directly addressed by such experiments.

Even Irving Janis, in his work on groupthink, explicitly recognized the dangers of reliance on anecdote, and searched for alternative methodologies. For instance, he discussed a "modus operandi" approach, initially described by Scriven (1976). This approach, Janis wrote, is used by many coroners, detectives, and structural engineering troubleshooters in attempts to find "ways of determining the probable cause of undesirable events with high certainty even though the data available to them do not come from controlled experiments or even quasi-experiments" (1985, p. 79). The approach involves formulating all the known causal sequences that might account for an observed outcome and then attempting to find which of them appears to be implicated. According to Janis (1985):

> This requires careful scrutiny of every shred of evidence that might provide telltale signs indicating the step-by-step ways in which each of the alternative causes is most likely to operate. Thus, the modus operandi approach involves looking for a particular configuration that corresponds to a known causal chain. Working backwards from the observed effect, the investigator watches for a pattern of indicators of mediating processes that connect antecedent conditions with the observed outcome. (pp. 79–80)

Janis suggested that more than one causal sequence may be found to play contributory roles as sources of error, and that if none of them fits the case at hand, it would suggest that other causal sequences remain to be discovered. Although this modus operandi approach is intriguing, it continues to focus only on sources of error, and, because many causal sequences may lead to similar consequences, expected causal sequences may be "confirmed" when other, unexamined, sequences are actually playing roles. Nevertheless, this methodology appears to offer benefits beyond traditional case analysis because it moves toward "strong inference" (Platt, 1964), seeking to explicitly test competing explanations for an observed phenomenon.

Perhaps the ideal method for examination of the issues we have raised would be to study actual problem solvers in ongoing real-world decision settings. However, it would be necessary to go considerably beyond the sort of one-case situation that has, for instance, typified groupthink studies. For example, the research would have to consider—among other things—decision fiascoes and decision triumphs, "hot" decision situations and "cool" decision situations, and decision situations in which particular group characteristics are present and those in which they are absent. Issues of access, time constraints, obtrusiveness of observation and measurement, and other factors contribute to render this scenario challenging.

In the short run, however, other more limited methodologies may provide insights. As one example, the recalled problems methodology could be used with actual problem solvers dealing with real-world problems. Individuals could be asked to recall important group problem-solving situations in which they have been involved in the past. They could be asked, for instance, to recall a group problem situation that turned out "well" and one that turned out "badly," and then to both provide a general, written, "thick" description of the situation and to respond to scales developed to assess the elements of the GGPS model. The recalled problems methodology was used by Vroom and Jago (1974) to assess the degree to which decision makers adhered to the Vroom and Yetton (1973) model and by Vroom and Jago (1978) to examine the consequences of such adherence. There are some notable benefits and limitations of such a methodology. Among strengths are the fact that problem solvers are asked to recall actual problem situations and can be queried about various aspects of the situations, including subsequent developments regarding problem implementation, outcomes, group member responses, and so on. On the other hand, there are obvious problems of recall, including memory lapses and perceptual distortion. However, it appears that such problems are most acute when individuals are asked to recall specific details concerning the frequency or timing of events (Rossi, Wright, & Anderson, 1983; Turner & Martin, 1984) or when they are asked to recall events that occurred long ago. Accuracy of recall can be improved by asking a number of questions about an event and by reducing the period of time about which respondents are asked to report (Fowler, 1984).

Another potentially useful methodology is behavioral simulation. Behavioral simulation would facilitate a more thorough examination of process and permit the use of outside, "objective" ratings of some variables of interest. Such a simulation might be modeled after such currently popular behavioral simulations as Looking Glass, Inc. (Kaplan, Lombardo, & Mazique, 1985; McCall & Lombardo, 1982) and the Financial Services Industry Simulation (Stumpf, Mullen, Hartman, Dunbar, & Berliner, 1983). If such a simulation is employed, the timing of measurement of variables is important. For instance, it would be useful to track certain key emergent group process variables and decision process characteristics over the course of the simulation.

A simulation of the sort we are proposing differs from those employed, for instance, by Moorhead and Montanari (1986) and by Gladstein and Reilly (1985). In the case of the Moorhead and Montanari simulation, subjects completed the Space Tower Exercise, "a structured, timed task requiring group planning and assembly." This exercise involves subjects in a brief, artificial task. In the Tycoon simulation used by Gladstein and Reilly, groups interacted for 6 days. They first developed a strategy and structure and then made decisions regarding raw materials orders, production schedules, finances, and the like. Decisions were input into computers that then, according to a priori decision rules, controlled the game. Although elements of the Gladstein and Reilly simulation are desirable, we are proposing a simulation in which subjects are continually involved in the task, for which the simulation realistically captures elements of the subjects' daily work experiences, and for which a variety of decision outcomes are considered. The Financial Services Industry Simulation, in particular, satisfies these criteria. Subjects role play decision situations over a period of 3 days. They engage in the simulation not just for a discrete time period each day, but throughout the days and evenings. Subjects are currently employed decision makers performing tasks in their fields, and they are provided inputs in the forms of memos, in-basket exercises, and the like, which carefully simulate the decision context. They receive feedback not only about financial performance but also about whether their actions were consistent with the goals they set, whether they took advantage of opportunities, whether factors associated with actions taken and not taken were fully examined, which members made or did not make contributions, the nature of the group work climate, distribution of power and influence within the decision group, and the nature of information management. Such variables, and many others assessed by the simulation, focus directly on central issues in group problem solving.

The recalled problems methodology and behavioral simulation could serve as complements. The recalled problems methodology may be subject to memory lapses and perceptual distortion, but it involves actual decisions and permits questioning regarding subsequent developments, such as changes in use and composition of the group, as well as subsequent decision implementation and acceptance. Behavioral simulation introduces problem solvers to a hypothetical situation but permits actual observation of group process.

Finally, we believe research on group problem solving could profit from the incorporation of other innovative methodologies. Although our discussion, and in particular our critiques of anecdotal evidence and case studies, may suggest that we are simply calling for use of more rigorous quantitative methodologies, we are not arguing that qualitative methodologies are inappropriate. To the contrary, we feel that, properly applied, such methodologies may be not only valuable but necessary. That is, the subtleties of many critical aspects of group process may only be revealed by qualitative methodologies. In addition, such methodologies have the advantage of using problem solvers in real-world settings making actual decisions as subjects. These methods are particularly appropriate for research questions about processes, especially those with many interactions. Strategies such as participant observation and interviews would allow researchers to assess the "how" and "why" of the group decision process, and therefore, to go beyond simply counting the frequency of certain behaviors. Qualitative research could answer questions such as "How were specific decisions made?" and "Why did the processes occur?" In the case of political explanations for consensus-seeking behaviors, qualitative research is best suited, if not necessary, for illuminating that which is going on beneath the surface of the group. Qualitative and quantitative methodologies should not necessarily be thought of as competing strategies; they can and should be effectively integrated. Indeed, qualitative methods are often used to explain reasons behind phenomena that were identified through quantitative research.

In sum, we are suggesting that, for examination of the GGPS model, a full range of methodologies may prove useful. In general, this use of multiple, complementary methodologies permits triangulation (e.g., Denzin, 1978; Jick, 1979). This strategy allows researchers to improve the accuracy of their judgments by viewing the same issue from various perspectives. If several distinct methods yield comparable data, the results can be more confidently accepted.

Other Implications for Research

Along with illustrative propositions and suggested research methodologies, a variety of other implications for research flow from the GGPS model and the literature and logic underlying its development. Some of these are drawn from Aldag and Fuller (1993).

Potential for Disconfirmation.   Perhaps most important, we consider it critical to approach examination of group decision processes with an open mind. Starting with a statement such as the Janis (1982) definition of groupthink (i.e., "Groupthink refers to a deterioration of mental efficiency, reality testing, and moral judgment that results from in-group pressures," p. 9) invites the search for confirming evidence. Disconfirmation is the stuff of science. Greenwald, Pratkanis, Leippe, and Baumgardner (1986) stress the dangers of research that is theory confirming, rather than theory testing, and warn against the conduct of studies in which the researcher holds a strong prior belief about the outcome.

Rational and Political Perspectives.   Group processes are seldom purely rational. Our discussion suggests that it may be inappropriate to ignore the political aspects of group functioning, and artificial to treat the rational and political perspectives as mutually exclusive. Our integrative perspective of group problem solving sees the two aspects as coexisting, and views political behaviors as entirely rational in some situations (and vice versa). Most organizations may "operate under the guise of rationality with some elements of power and politics thrown in" (Pfeffer, 1981, p. 344). Therefore, there may be more going on than meets the "objective" eye. This clear recognition of political realities suggests that any research that leans solely on the rational perspective is fated to be limited and limiting.

Typology of Problem Types.   A typology of problem types would help to foster a more systematic appraisal of group problem solving. Some dimensions of that typology—not necessarily independent—have been suggested by our discussion to this point; crisis versus noncrisis, recurring versus nonrecurring, important versus unimportant, and successful versus unsuccessful. The need for such a typology is evident from the groupthink literature. Case support for groupthink has been drawn largely from crisis, nonrecurring, important, unsuccessful decisions. Conversely, many group problems, such as decisions by individuals at high levels in organizations, may be noncrisis, important, recurring or nonrecurring, successful or unsuccessful.

Others have called for and developed typologies of problem types. For instance, to illustrate the failure of psychological experiments to fully and adequately address the domain of intellectual tasks, Edwards (1983) presented a taxonomy of intellectual tasks and their performers. It included dimensions such as easy versus difficult, realistic versus unrealistic, time pressures versus lack of time pressures, tools available versus tools unavailable, and laboratory versus job versus life. Several other task typologies have been proposed (e.g., de Vries-Griever & Meijman, 1987; Fleishman, 1982; Shaw, 1973; Steiner, 1972) focusing on dimensions such as information-processing requirements, coordination requirements, required task behaviors, and ability requirements. However, such typologies have not been constructed specifically for application to group problem solving, and we feel they fail to incorporate important dimensions.

Decision Outcomes. The GGPS model suggests that a true understanding of group problem solving is futile without an understanding of leader and member goals. In any attempt to gauge process adequacy, goals must somehow be assessed. Ideally, such assessment would be made in ways that minimize the potential for distortion due to self-serving attributions (e.g., stating goals that are most consistent with achieved outcomes) and related biases. This may require, for example, assessing goals prior to the onset of the decision process or selecting situations for which goals are unambiguous (e.g., situations in that goals are externally dictated).

Longitudinal Designs. Furthermore, it is common practice to call for longitudinal studies of a phenomenon of interest; we do so here. Such studies would permit more adequate examination of the group problem-solving process, including timing of convergence to a group decision. They could, for instance, permit differentiation between convergence, which is inherent in the choice-making stage of the problem-solving process, and premature convergence, which may be pathological. Additionally, longitudinal research would allow examination of outcomes such as decision implementation and future use of the group.

Focus on Implicit Theories. Finally, we have suggested that implicit theories may help explain the appeal of the groupthink phenomenon (Aldag & Fuller, 1993). It would be instructive to directly address implicit theories of group problem solving, perhaps through use of cognitive mapping procedures (Aldag & Stearns, 1988; Bougon, 1983; Jones, 1986). This would permit examination of how antecedent conditions, emergent group characteristics, decision process characteristics, and outcomes are associated in such implicit theories.

IMPLICATIONS FOR PRACTICE

The GGPS model has many implications for practice, a few of which we suggest here. Some implications flow directly from casual observation of the model. For example, the GGPS model makes it clear that group problem solving is much more complex and less deterministic than might have been suggested by previous models. Although complexity of a model per se may not be valued by a practitioner, it is a necessary and important reflection of reality. The GGPS model attempts to explicitly recognize that complexity, and to give it structure. Further, we would ask practitioners to accept, and recognize the worth of, the model's use of value-neutral terminology. By avoiding leading language, we seek to discourage blinders and restrictive assumptions. The GGPS model's value-neutral terminology encourages recognition, for example, that cohesiveness may be desirable, that directive leader behaviors may sometimes be appropriate, and that political behaviors may have a rich variety of causes and consequences.

Choice of Prescriptions for Effective Group Functioning

Our discussion suggests that prescriptions for appropriate group functioning must consider cost, feasibility, and scope. For example, some of the remedies that have been proposed for groupthink may be costly or infeasible. As noted by Luechauer (1989), once groups have begun to engage in dysfunctional modes, it may be too late for the recommendations to be used because the groups will simply not perceive a need for them. In addition, regardless of the objective value of application of these remedies, they will not be used if the group decision process is consciously being manipulated for political ends.

Perhaps most important, a focus on specific remedies for specific decision situations may be misguided. It may be more appropriate to assess and potentially alter organizational culture or contingencies of reinforcement rather than to implement specific techniques in the hopes of overcoming the consequences of the group's decision environment. This suggests the need for explicit consideration of systemic changes.

Leader Behavioral Repertoire

The GGPS model encourages recognition of a broad repertoire of potential leader behaviors; rational, political, and their intersect. This is consistent with current views that many important leader roles may be symbolic rather than, or as well as, substantive. Further, the model emphasizes that leader and member political motives and organizational political norms may suffuse the entire group problem-solving process. These political aspects do more than just somehow taint an otherwise pristine rational process; they are real, relevant, and pervasive. Recognition that leaders may be engaging in political behaviors also serves to highlight the need to assess such behaviors on multiple levels. That is, leader agenda setting, use of outside experts, selection of decision criteria and group decision rules, coalition formation, and use of committees may all be politically motivated (consistent with the views of Pfeffer, 1981), and must be responded to accordingly.

Emphasis on Multiple Outcomes

Our discussion of the GGPS model stresses the need to consider many outcomes of group problem solving. As Pfeffer (1981) pointed out, "In ongoing organizations, implementation of and commitment to the decision may be as important, if not more so, than the decision itself" (p. 156). Additionally, we have argued that future motivation of the group and leader, future use of the group, and affective responses may also be important outcomes for groups and/or group members. As such, the GGPS model, through its emphasis on multiple goals, has a variety of practical implications. For one, as noted earlier, the model makes it clear that it is impossible to judge decision quality without knowledge of goals. If short-term decision quality is the assumed goal, a leader's behavior may seem misguided; however, this behavior may in fact represent brilliant leadership if the true goal is future motivation of the group or enhanced satisfaction with the group process.

Similarly, recognition of multiple goals forces corresponding recognition of tradeoffs. There may be cases, for instance, in which short-term decision quality can appropriately be subordinated to goals such as maintenance of member satisfaction or the potential for future use of the group. Any assumption of a neat congruence of alternative goals is both simplistic and contrary to most evidence.

Conversely, the GGPS model suggests that the process employed may provide clues concerning implicit goals. That is, because leaders may be pursuing one or more of multiple goals, and may not be open in revealing those goals, it may be necessary to examine the leaders' behaviors to infer goals.

Encouragement of Dissent

It is important to recognize that the GGPS model is silent concerning the importance of dissent. Although the dangers of lack of dissent have been recognized for more than half a century, the assumption that all concurrence seeking is undesirable is naive. Rather, the GGPS models leaves the leader with the difficult but critical task of determining whether the situation is one that calls for increased dissent and then of choosing appropriate actions.

CONCLUSION

We offer the GGPS model as a relatively comprehensive framework for the assessment of group problem solving. The GGPS model recognizes multiple—and perhaps conflicting—outcomes, accepts political realities, and makes no a priori assumptions about the desirability of its elements. The GGPS model does not provide a neat, deterministic causal sequence. Rather, it accepts the complexity of organizational reality. As suggested by our illustrative propositions, complexity faced straight on offers fertile ground for the examination of group problem solving.

We expect that practitioners may find the intricacy of the GGPS model to be troubling. Our response, as noted earlier, is simply that organizational life is complex, and tools that ignore that complexity are no bargain. Models are useful for guidance, but they become dangerous if they lead to deceptively simple prescriptions. The lesson, of course, is that skill, good judgment, and a critical eye are the keys to effective leadership, not blind adherence to a deterministic model.

REFERENCES

Aldag, R. J., & Fuller, S. R. (1993). Beyond fiasco: A reappraisal of the groupthink phenomenon and a new model of group decision processes. *Psychological Bulletin, 113*, 533–552.

Aldag, R. J., & Stearns, T. M. (1988). Issues in research methodology. *Journal of Management, 14*, 253–276.

Bougon, M. (1983). Uncovering cognitive maps: The self-Q technique. In G. Morgan (Ed.), *Beyond method: Strategies for social research* (pp. 173–188). Newbury Park, CA: Sage.

Callaway, M. R., & Esser, J. K. (1984). Groupthink: Effects of cohesiveness and problem-solving procedures on group decision making. *Social Behavior and Personality, 12*, 157–164.

de Vries-Griever, A. H., & Meijman, T. F. (1987). The impact of abnormal hours of work on various modes of information processing: A process model of human costs of performance. *Ergonomics, 30*, 1287–1299.

Denzin, N. K. (1978). *The research act.* New York: McGraw-Hill.

Edwards, W. (1983). Human cognitive capabilities, representativeness, and ground rules for research. In P. Humpreys, O. Svenson, & A. Vari (Eds.), *Analyzing and aiding decision processes* (pp. 507–513). Amsterdam: North-Holland.

Elbing, A. (1978). *Behavioral decisions in organizations* (2nd ed.). Glenview, IL: Scott, Foresman.

Fleishman, E. A. (1982). Systems for describing human tasks. *American Psychologist, 37*, 821–834.

Fowler, F. J., Jr. (1984). *Survey research methods.* Newbury Park, CA: Sage.

Fuller, S. R., & Aldag, R. J. (1998). Organizational tonypandy: Lessons from a quarter century of the groupthink phenomenon. *Organizational Behavior and Human Decision Processes, 73*, 163–184.

Gladstein, D. L., & Reilly, N. P. (1985). Group decision making under threat: The Tycoon game. *Academy of Management Journal, 28*, 613–627.

Greenwald, A. G., Pratkanis, A. R., Leippe, M. R., & Baumgardner, M. H. (1986). Under what conditions does theory obstruct research progress? *Psychological Review, 93*(2), 216–229.

Janis, I. L. (1971, November). Groupthink. *Psychology Today, 5*, 43–46, 74–76.

Janis, I. L. (1972). *Victims of groupthink.* Boston: Houghton Mifflin.

Janis, I. L. (1982). *Groupthink* (2nd ed.). Boston: Houghton Mifflin.

Janis, I. L. (1985). International crisis management in the nuclear age. *Applied Social Psychology Annual, 6*, 63–86.

Jick, T. D. (1979). Mixing qualitative and quantitative methods: Triangulation in action. *Administrative Science Quarterly, 24*, 602–611.

Jones, S. (1986). Addressing internal politics: A role for modeling in consultant-client interaction. *Small Group Behavior, 17*, 67–82.

Kaplan, R. E., Lombardo, M. M., & Mazique, M. S. (1985). A mirror for managers: Using simulation to develop management teams. *Journal of Applied Behavioral Science, 21*, 241–253.

Leana, C. R. (1985). A partial test of Janis' groupthink model: Effects of group cohesiveness and leader behavior on defective decision making. *Journal of Management, 11*, 5–17.

Longley, J., & Pruitt, D. G. (1980). Groupthink: A critique of Janis' theory. In L. Wheeler (Ed.), *Review of personality and social psychology* (pp. 507–513). Beverly Hills: Sage.

Luechauer, D. L. (1989, August). *Groupthink revisited: A dramaturgical approach.* Paper presented at the meetings of the Academy of Management, Washington, DC.

McCall, M. W., & Lombardo, M. M. (1982). Using simulation for leadership and management research: Through the looking glass. *Management Science, 28*, 533–549.

Moorhead, G., & Montanari, J. R. (1986). An empirical investigation of the groupthink phenomenon. *Human Relations, 39*, 399–410.

Osborn, A. F. (1963). *Applied imagination* (3rd ed.). New York: Scribner's.

Pfeffer, J. (1981). *Power in organizations.* Marshfield, MA: Pitman Publishing.

Platt, J. R. (1964, October 16). Strong inference. *Science, 146*, 347–353.

Rossi, P. H., Wright, J. D., & Anderson, A. B. (1983). *Handbook of survey research.* San Diego, CA: Academic Press.

Scriven, M. (1976). Maximizing the power of causal investigations: The modus operandi method. *Evaluation Studies Review Annual, 1*, 101–118.

Shaw, M. E. (1973). Scaling group tasks: A method for dimensional analysis. *JSAS: Catalog of Selected Documents in Psychology, 3*, (8, Ms. No. 294).

Steiner, I. D. (1972). *Group process and productivity.* San Diego, CA: Academic Press.

Steiner, I. D. (1976). Task-performing groups. In J. W. Thibaut, J. T. Spence, & R. C. Carson (Eds.), *Contemporary topics in social psychology* (pp. 393–422). Morristown, NJ: General Learning Press.

Stumpf, S. A., Mullen, T., Hartman, K., Dunbar, R., & Berliner, W. (1983). *Financial Services Industry Simulation.* New York: New York University.

Turner, C. F., & Martin, E. (Eds.). (1984). *Surveying subjective phenomena* (Vol. 1). New York: Russell Sage Foundation.

Vroom, V. H., & Jago, A. G. (1974). Decision making as a social process: Normative and descriptive models of leader behavior. *Decision Sciences, 5,* 743–769.

Vroom, V. H., & Jago, A. G. (1978). On the validity of the Vroom–Yetton model. *Journal of Applied Psychology, 63,* 151–162.

Vroom, V. H., & Yetton, P. W. (1973). *Leadership and decision making.* Pittsburgh: University of Pittsburgh Press.

Weldon, E., & Gargano, G. M. (1985). Cognitive effort in additive task groups: The effects of shared responsibility on the quality of multiattribute judgments. *Organizational Behavior and Human Decision Processes, 36,* 348–361.

Chapter 2

Social Identity, Organizations, and Leadership

John C. Turner
S. Alexander Haslam
The Australian National University

This chapter focuses on the role that group memberships play in shaping social life. It attempts to show the relevance of a social identity perspective to issues and processes of interest to organizational psychologists. We argue that to understand how group relationships affect social interaction in an organizational context, it is important to consider how these are bound up with individuals' *social identities*, their definitions of themselves in terms of their group memberships.

Traditionally, psychological theories of organizational behavior have tended to take the individual as the primary unit of analysis and see the group simply as one of many (extra-individual) contextual elements that impact on the individual (e.g., see Jackson et al., 1991, p. 675). This is particularly true in the area of leadership where analysis of the leader's individual attributes has been emphasized at the expense of considering the group of which the leader is a part. Our view is that group memberships are not simply a context for individual behavior but are a *part of the psychology of the individual* that critically shape the way he or she perceives and interacts with other people in the organization. Where theories of leadership often see the individual *qua* individual as the fundamental building block for theoretical and practical development, we argue that explanations of leadership need to give more emphasis to the way in which the psychology of individuals is structured by group life and its distinctive psychological and social realities.

The chapter begins with a summary of the social identity perspective. We then briefly comment on its general relevance to the organizational domain. Finally, we focus on one important area, the study of leadership, to illustrate its relevance in more detail. We develop and distinguish a social identity analysis of leadership from classic and contemporary approaches.

A reading of almost any organizational text illustrates that it is possible to approach leadership (like almost any issue in organizational psychology) from an assumption that group relationships work only to hinder accurate cognition and rational action. This may be because leaders are judged likely to be corrupted, cognitively and morally, by the demands of leadership and the power they wield (cf. Kipnis, 1972) or because they may become subservient to these varied and potentially capricious demands (Philips & Lord, 1981). In contrast, a major theme of the present chapter is to suggest that the structuring of psychology by group life—the cognitive redefining of self as "we" and "us" rather than as just "I" and "me"—is a precondition of people's ability to engage in meaningful, productive, and prosocial organizational behavior.

THE SOCIAL IDENTITY PERSPECTIVE

The social identity perspective on group psychology is now some 25 years old. It is rich theoretically and has stimulated a vast amount of research in many different areas. In this brief summary, we can do no more than sketch some of the major themes. To complicate matters, what is often called "social identity theory" in fact comprises two related but distinct theories, social identity theory proper and self-categorization theory. The former began with an analysis (Tajfel, 1972; Turner, 1975) of the processes at work in the "minimal group paradigm" of Tajfel, Flament, Billig, and Bundy (1971). It was then developed by Tajfel (1978) into a theory of intergroup conflict and social change in macrosocial contexts and systematized by Tajfel and Turner (1979, 1986) along these lines. Self-categorization theory developed from the late 1970s onward (Turner, 1981, 1982, 1985; Turner, Hogg, Oakes, Reicher, & Wetherell, 1987) as an explanation of the basis and effects of psychological group formation in terms of the social identity concept. The focus of social identity theory, therefore, is on intergroup relations, especially ingroup bias and social conflict; whereas self-categorization theory, initially at least, focused on the psychological group and related processes of social cohesion, cooperation, and influence. More recently, the latter theory has taken social identity ideas into the realm of social cognition, providing analyses of social stereotyping and the self-concept (Oakes, Haslam, & Turner, 1994; Turner, Oakes, Haslam, & McGarty, 1994). What both theories have in common is the central notion that individuals' behavior is qualitatively transformed by their definition of themselves in terms of their group memberships.

Social Identity Theory

In their well-known minimal group paradigm, Tajfel et al. (1971) produced evidence that *social categorization alone*—the mere perception by subjects that they belonged to one group rather than to another—was sufficient under certain conditions to elicit ingroup bias (i.e., discriminatory behavior and attitudes in favor of the ingroup and at the expense of the outgroup).

In these studies, schoolboys were assigned to one of two groups, ostensibly on the basis of trivial criteria but in fact, randomly. There was no social interaction at all either between or within the groups and subjects did not even know who was in their group and who was in the other group, because membership was anonymous. The groups were neither positively nor negatively interdependent, they had no history of hostility, and members' self-interest was not linked to their group membership. The groups were truly "minimal," simply perceptual or cognitive categories. Nevertheless, when asked to allocate small sums of money to other individuals identified only by a code number and their group membership, subjects tended to award more money to ingroup than outgroup members. In fact, they tended to be more concerned with getting more than the outgroup than with getting as much as possible for the ingroup.

A number of further experiments replicated, clarified, and elaborated these basic findings (see Oakes et al., 1994, for a review). It appears that virtually any basis for social categorization can lay the foundations for ingroup favoritism. There is also evidence that variables that psychologically activate or make *salient* the social categorization are important determinants of bias. Factors that enhance category salience, such as intergroup conflict, are likely to enhance ingroup bias, whereas factors that reduce the salience of category boundaries, such as individuating information or the presence of a superordinate group identity, are likely to reduce bias.

After 25 years, the results of the minimal group studies appear sound and reliable. They have not been persuasively reinterpreted in terms of methodological artifact or the "normal" causes of intergroup discrimination (see Turner & Bourhis, 1996, for a recent discussion). The findings imply that ingroup biases appear in intergroup relations under conditions where they cannot be easily explained in terms of personal self-interest, realistic conflict of interests, interpersonal relationships, individual prejudices, or personality factors. Social identity theory emerged initially as an attempt to make sense of these data.

Tajfel (1972) argued that subjects in the minimal group paradigm invested the situation with meaning by creating distinctions between their own and the other group. He pointed out (1972, 1978) that social categorization allows the perceiver to structure the social environment as a guide to action. Importantly, it also provides a system of orientation for *self-reference*, creating and defining the individual's own place in society. Individuals use social categorizations to define themselves in the social context. This definition of the self in terms of cognitively represented social group memberships was described by Tajfel (1972) as one's *social identity*—"that part of an individual's self-concept which derives from his [or her] knowledge of his [or her] membership of a social group (or groups) together with the value and emotional significance attached to that membership" (p. 273).

He went on to argue that people are motivated to evaluate themselves positively, and that insofar as a group membership becomes significant to their self-definition, they will be motivated to evaluate that group positively. In other words, people seek a *positive social identity*. Because the value of any group membership depends on comparison with other relevant groups, positive social identity is achieved through the establishment of *positive distinctiveness* of the ingroup from relevant outgroups. Turner (1975) then used this analysis to argue that discrimination in the minimal group paradigm could be understood as a form of "social competition," based on the need for positive social identity, rather than instrumental competition, reflecting conflicting group interests. Having identified with the minimal categories, subjects compared their ingroup and the outgroup in terms of the only available dimensions (the reward allocations or evaluative ratings, depending on the response format) and sought positive distinctiveness for their own group by awarding it more money or points, or by favoring it in other ways.

Studies have established that ingroup bias is by no means an automatic product of social categorization. Consistent with social identity theory, it is a function, *inter alia*, of (1) the degree to which subjects identify with the relevant ingroup, (2) the salience of the relevant social categorization in the setting, (3) the importance and relevance of the comparative dimension to ingroup identity, (4) the degree to which the groups are comparable on that dimension (similar, close, ambiguously different), including, in particular, (5) the ingroup's relative status and the character of the perceived status differences between the groups. Studies have demonstrated that *outgroup* favoritism will eventuate where an outgroup is perceived as superior to the ingroup on a relevant dimension of comparison, providing that the status difference is consensually secure (e.g., Ellemers & van

Knippenberg, 1997) or where the dimension is unimportant for an ingroup's social identity (Mummendey & Schreiber, 1984; Mummendey & Simon, 1989).

Social identity theory, however, is not simply an analysis of psychological processes in intergroup discrimination. Tajfel (1979) described the theory as a "conceptual tripod" of which the psychological analysis, focused on the processes of "social categorization–social identity–social comparison" (p. 184) leading to the search for positive ingroup distinctiveness, was only one leg. There are two other important themes (Tajfel & Turner, 1979, 1986). Firstly, there is the idea of an "interpersonal–intergroup continuum," and secondly, there is the idea that real-life intergroup relations and attitudes are always a function of an interaction between people's collective psychology as group members and the perceived social structure of status differences between groups.

The former idea refers to Tajfel's (1974, 1978) distinction between *interpersonal* and *intergroup* behavior. He suggested that social behavior varied along a continuum from interpersonal to intergroup. At the "intergroup" extreme, all of the behavior of two or more individuals toward each other is determined by their membership of different social groups or categories (i.e., by group affiliations and loyalties to the exclusion of individual characteristics and interpersonal relationships). The "interpersonal" extreme refers to any social encounter in which all the interaction that takes place is determined by the personal relationships between the individuals and their individual characteristics (i.e., idiosyncratic personal qualities are the overriding causal influences). Tajfel used the interpersonal–intergroup continuum to explain when social identity processes were likely to come into operation and how social interaction differed qualitatively between the extremes. He argued that as behavior becomes more intergroup, attitudes toward the outgroup within the ingroup tend to become more uniform and consensual and outgroup members tend to be seen more as homogeneous and undifferentiated members of their social category.

Shift along the continuum was a function of an interaction between psychological and social factors. He emphasized, in particular, the degree to which group members shared an ideology of "individual mobility" or "social change" and saw the social system as characterized by rigid and intense social stratification. He suggested that subjective and objective barriers to moving between groups, the perceived impermeability of group boundaries, tend to be associated with a "social change" belief system, a view that people cannot resolve their identity problems through individual action and mobility but can only change their social situation by acting collectively in terms of their shared group membership. Impermeable group boundaries and the social change belief system are key fac-

tors in shifting behavior along the continuuum toward the intergroup
pole and therefore play a central role in determining collective reactions
by group members to low or insecure status in the social system.

The theory's third leg related to how the need for positive social identity interacts with groups members' collective beliefs about the nature of
the intergroup status differences within a society to generate different
individual and collective strategies. Tajfel (1979) stated that, "'Social reality' can be described or analysed in terms of socio-economic, historical or
political structures. Such descriptions or analyses are not within the competence of the social psychologist," (p. 186) but he or she *can* ascertain the
"shared interpretations of social reality" held by group members. Such
shared perceptions of intergroup relations as being secure or insecure,
legitimate or illegitimate, stable or unstable, and so on, in combination
with the perceived location of groups within the particular system, can
then be used to formulate specific hypotheses. The resulting hypotheses
are summarized by Tajfel and Turner (1979). Essentially, they outline the
different social strategies available to high- and low-status group members
whose social identity is threatened in order to maintain, preserve, or
restore a positive social identity and they specify the different social and
psychological conditions within a status-stratified social system under
which the different strategies might be pursued.

Thus, for example, low-status groups that see their status as secure (stable and legitimate) and group boundaries as permeable are likely to adopt
an individual mobility strategy; secure low-status groups that perceive
group boundaries as impermeable are likely to adopt a social creativity
strategy that redefines their attributes as positive but does not change
their objective social position; low-status group members who see their
status position as insecure (unstable and/or illegitimate) and who identify
strongly with their group are likely to engage in social competition with
the outgroup (i.e., adopt a competitive and ethnocentric orientation
toward the outgroup). Similarly, high-status groups will also be motivated
to adopt varying strategies in order to *preserve* their positive social identity where it is under threat. A high-status group, for example, that sees its
position as legitimate but unstable, under threat from the outgroup, will
be likely to demonstrate a strongly competitive bias in its own favor. There
is good supportive evidence for many of these ideas (e.g., Ellemers, 1993;
Tajfel, 1978, 1982).

Overall, then, social identity theory emphasizes the subtlety of the discrimination process and its sensitivity to the realities of the societal context and intergroup relations. Tajfel and Turner did not see ingroup bias
as an inevitable and automatic product of social categorization, as some
have inferred (e.g., see Duckitt, 1992). On the contrary, they argued that,
in addition to social categorization, a process of social identification,

accompanied by motives for positive self-evaluation and intergroup distinctiveness, underlie intergroup discrimination and that this psychological sequence itself interacts with conflicts of interest and the larger social context. Whether or not intergroup relations are characterized by ingroup bias or by some other strategy for positive social identity is seen as the complex product of a variety of social and psychological factors.

Self-Categorization Theory

During the 1950s and 1960s, a relatively individualistic conception of the social group took hold in social psychology. Influential concepts such as *interdependence* and *cohesiveness* originally had a *Gestalt* quality, implying that groups were dynamic social systems with emergent *whole-properties*. By the 1970s, however, interdependence had been redefined from membership in a "functional whole," which psychologically changed individuals into group members, to a purely instrumental relationship between separate persons for the satisfaction of their individual needs. *Group relations were no longer seen as qualitatively different from interpersonal relationships* (Turner et al., 1987).

It was argued, for example, that group cohesion could be completely equated with *interpersonal* attraction and that there were no such things as *properties of the group as a whole* separate from the properties of individual members (Lott & Lott, 1965). A group was nothing more than a collection of mutually rewarding individuals in relatively stable relationships of interpersonal attraction, cooperation, and influence. The idea that the relations between group members might be mediated psychologically by their membership in a joint social unit was discarded. If the psychological group were no more than a redescription of interpersonal relations and processes, then it was superfluous from an explanatory point of view. There was no specific group process to be understood.

However, this "interpersonal interdependence" model of the group is problematic both empirically and theoretically (see Turner, 1984, 1985, 1991; Turner & Oakes, 1989). Turner (1982) noted that the findings of the minimal group studies were as inconsistent with the interpersonal model of group membership as they were with the realistic conflict analysis of discrimination. Minimal social categorization appeared capable of producing all the usual symptoms of psychological group formation (ingroup bias, mutual attraction, altruism, etc.) even though the paradigm was designed to exclude all its orthodox theoretical determinants (interpersonal interdependence, attraction, similarity, etc.). The subjects did not even know which other persons were in their group. Group formation did not seem to reflect but to *cause* attraction between people: People liked others not as *individuals* but as members of the same *group*. Theory and data in the areas of social cooperation and influence were also incompatible with an individualized model of the group (Turner et al., 1987).

Building on the social categorization data in particular, Turner (1982, 1984) proposed a social identity theory of group behavior. He distinguished social identity (self-definitions in terms of social category memberships) from personal identity (self-descriptions in terms of personal or idiosyncratic attributes), and pointed to evidence of situational variations in self-concept functioning to suggest that "social identity is sometimes able to function to the relative exclusion of personal identity" (1984, p. 527). It was hypothesized that "the adaptive function of social identity . . . is to produce group behaviour and attitudes, . . . it is the cognitive mechanism which makes group behaviour possible" (1984, p. 527).

The basic process postulated is *self-categorization*, leading to *self-stereotyping* and the *depersonalization* of self-perception. It was argued that where people define themselves in terms of a shared social category membership, there is a perceptual accentuation of intragroup similarities and intergroup differences on relevant correlated dimensions. People stereotype themselves and others in terms of salient social categorizations, leading to an enhanced perceptual identity between self and ingroup members and an enhanced perceptual contrast between ingroup and outgroup members. Where social identity becomes relatively more salient than personal identity, people see themselves less as differing individual persons amd more as the similar, prototypical representatives of their ingroup category. There is a depersonalization of the self; a "cognitive redefinition of the self—from unique attributes and individual differences to shared social category memberships and associated stereotypes" (Turner, 1984, p. 528)— and it is this process that transforms individual into collective behavior as people perceive and act in terms of a shared, collective conception of self. "The identity perspective . . . reinstates the group as a psychological reality and not merely a convenient label for describing the outcome of interpersonal processes and relations" (1984, p. 535). This was an important shift: Instead of seeing social identity as a reflection of group affiliations and intergroup behaviour, it was now seen as the process that changed interpersonal into intergroup behavior, which produced movement along Tajfel's continuum.

Self-categorization theory continued to develop during the 1980s and 1990s (see Hogg, 1992; Oakes et al., 1994; Turner, 1985, 1991; Turner et al., 1987). In its current form, the theory is concerned with variation in how people categorize themselves, in the antecedent conditions of such variation and its effects. In particular, it focuses on the conditions under which people categorize themselves more as social groups and less as individual persons, more in terms of social identity and less in terms of personal identity.

It assumes that self-conception reflects self-*categorization*, the cognitive grouping of the self as identical to some class of stimuli in contrast to some other class of stimuli. As is the case with all systems of natural categories, self-categorizations can exist at different *levels of abstraction* related by *class inclusion*. That is, a given self-category (e.g., "scientist") is seen as more abstract than another (e.g., "biologist") to the extent that it can contain, but cannot be contained by, the other; all biologists are scientists, but not all scientists are biologists. Self-categories can be both more or less inclusive than personal and social identity, but these are the most important levels for understanding group behavior.

Personal identity refers to self-categories that define the individual as a unique person in terms of their individual differences from other (ingroup) persons. *Social identity* refers to social categorizations of self and others, self-categories that define the individual in terms of his or her shared similarities with members of certain social categories in contrast to other social categories. Social identity refers to the social categorical self (e.g., "us" vs. "them," ingroup vs. outgroup, us women, men, whites, blacks, etc.). It is a more inclusive level of self-perception than personal identity in the sense that the category "scientist" is more inclusive than "biologist."

The theory proposes that when we think of and perceive ourselves as "we" and "us" as opposed to "I" and "me," this is ordinary and normal self-experience in which the self is defined in terms of others who exist outside of the individual person doing the experiencing and therefore cannot be reduced to purely personal identity. At certain times the subjective self is defined and experienced as identical, equivalent, similar to, or interchangeable with a social class of people in contrast to some other class. Psychologically, the social collectivity becomes self.

The theory's central hypothesis, as already noted, is that as shared social identity becomes salient, individual self-perception tends to become *depersonalized*. That is, individuals tend to define and see themselves less as differing individual persons and more as the interchangeable representatives of some shared social category membership. For example, when an individual man tends to categorize himself as a man in contrast to women, then he (subjectively "we") tends to accentuate perceptually his similarities to other men (and reduce his idiosyncratic personal differences from other men) and enhance perceptually his stereotypical differences from women (Hogg & Turner, 1987). His self changes in level and content and his self-perception and behavior become depersonalized. Depersonalization of the self is the subjective stereotyping of the self in terms of the relevant social categorization.

Why is it that sometimes we define ourselves as social groups and at other times as individual persons? What determines this variation in the salient level of self-categorization? The theory explains such variation as a function of an interaction between the relative accessibility of a particular self-category (or "perceiver readiness," the readiness of a perceiver to use a particular categorization) and the fit between category specifications and the stimulus reality to be represented (the match between the category and reality). Relative accessibility reflects a person's past experience, present expectations, and current motives, values, goals, and needs. It reflects the active selectivity of the perceiver in being ready to use categories that are relevant, useful, and likely to be confirmed by the evidence of reality. One important factor affecting a person's readiness to use a social category for self-definition in specific situations is the extent of their identification with the group, the degree to which it is central, valued, and ego-involving (e.g., Doosje & Ellemers, 1997).

Fit has two aspects, comparative fit and normative fit (Oakes, 1987). Comparative fit is defined by the principle of *meta-contrast*, which states that a collection of stimuli is more likely to be categorized as an entity (a higher order unit) to the degree that the average differences perceived between them are less than the average differences perceived between them and the remaining stimuli that comprise the frame of reference. Stated in this form, the principle defines fit in terms of the emergence of a focal category against a contrasting background. It can also be used to define fit for the salience of a dichotomous classification. For example, any collection of people will tend to be categorized into distinct groups to the degree that the intragroup differences perceived within the relevant comparative context are smaller on average than the perceived intergroup differences.

Normative fit refers to the content aspect of the match between category specifications and the instances being represented. For example, to categorize a group of people as Catholics as opposed to Protestants, they must not only differ (in attitudes, actions, etc.) from Protestants more than from each other (comparative fit), but must also do so in the *right direction* on *specific content dimensions* of comparison. Their similarities and differences must be consistent with our normative beliefs about the substantive social meaning of the social category (Oakes, Turner, & Haslam, 1991).

The theory emphasises the fact that categorization is a dynamic, context-dependent process, determined by *comparative relations within a given context*. The meta-contrast principle indicates that, to predict categorization, the entire range of stimuli under consideration, rather than isolated stimulus characteristics, must be considered. By proposing that categories form so as to ensure that the differences between them are larger than the differences within them, meta-contrast contextualizes categorization, tying it to an on-the-spot judgement of *relative differences*. For example, we might categorize an individual as "Australian" to the extent that, in the current comparative context, the differences between individual Australians (Paul, Kylie, Rolf, etc.) are *less than* the differences between Australians and Americans. Alternatively, the salient category might be "English speaking" in a context where the difference between various English-speaking groups (such as Americans and Australians) is *less than* the difference between English and non-English speakers. These ideas can be expressed in terms of a *meta-contrast ratio*, that is, the average perceived intercategory difference divided by the average perceived intracategory difference. The higher this ratio for some social category such as Australian, the more likely it is that individual Australians will be perceived in terms of their shared national identity (Haslam & Turner, 1992, 1995).

Note, however, that the meta-contrast principle provides only a partial account of categorization. It describes the *comparative relations* between stimuli that lead them to be represented by a category, but it is also always important to take into account the *social meaning* of differences between people in terms of the normative and behavioral content of their actions, and the relative accessibility of particular categorizations.

The emphasis on categorization as highly variable and context-dependent produces a concomitant emphasis on the context-dependence of perceived similarity and difference, the major *outcome* of categorization. People who are categorized and perceived as different in one context (e.g., "biologists" and "physicists" within a science faculty) can be recategorized and perceived as similar in another context (e.g., as "scientists" rather than "social scientists" within a university) *without any actual change in their own positions*. Categorization is a cognitive grouping process that transforms differences into similarities (and *vice versa*). Whether people see themselves as similar or different, and the extent to which they do so, is not a fixed, absolute given, but varies with how, and the level at which, people categorize themselves and others. Arising from the comparisons specified in the meta-contrast principle, self-categorization subjectively transforms people's relations into similarities and differences, and from perceived similarities and differences flow, the theory hypothesizes, perceptions of attraction and dislike, agreement and disagreement, cooperation and conflict. In sum, *self-categorization provides the fundamental basis of our social orientation toward others*.

The concept of depersonalization implies that there tends within the same psychological situation to be an inverse relationship between self-perception as a unique individual and as an ingroup category: The more an individual perceives herself as similar to other ingroup members, the harder it will be for her to be aware of her personal, idiosyncratic differences from them (and vice versa). Thus, self-categorization theory maintains the idea of an interpersonal–intergroup continuum, but changes the underlying conceptualization, hypothesizing that shift along it is the result of the varying outcome of a continual conflict between the effects of personal and social identity, as they vary in relative salience.

In sum, as an account of the group, the theory's key ideas are 1) that the level and kind of identity used to represent self and others vary with one's motives, values, and expectations, one's background knowledge and theories, and the social context within which comparison takes place; 2) that the salience of shared social identity leads to the depersonalization of self-perception; and 3) that depersonalization produces group behavior.

The evidence that salient social identity depersonalizes the perception of self and others is now quite extensive (e.g., Oakes et al., 1994; Spears, Oakes, Ellemers, & Haslam, 1997; Turner et al., 1994). Research illustrating the role of depersonalization in group behavior has been pursued in the areas of group cohesion, social cooperation, social influence, crowd behavior, "deindividuation," the perception of ingroup and outgroup homogeneity, and intergroup biases (e.g., Anastasio, Bachman, Gaertner, & Dovidio, 1997; Brewer & Schneider, 1990; Caporael, Dawes, Orbell, & van de Kragt, 1989; Haslam, Oakes, Turner, & McGarty, 1996; Hogg, 1992; Reicher, 1987; Reicher, Spears, & Postmes, 1995; Turner, 1984, 1991). The fundamental principle that follows from self-categorization theory is that psychological group formation is an adaptive process that produces socially unitary, collective behavior and makes possible group relations of mutual attraction, cooperation, and influence between members. Factors that in a given social setting tend to create and make salient shared group membership, shared social identity, tend to produce a mutual orientation of attraction, cooperation, and influence as members define and react to each other in terms of their common social category membership rather than as differing individual persons. Group formation is not merely an effect of interpersonal relationships, it actively determines people's attitudes and behaviors toward each other.

SOCIAL IDENTITY AND THE ORGANIZATIONAL DOMAIN

There are three basic features of many, if not most, organizations that suggest the general relevance of social identity principles to explaining organizational behavior: (a) that organizations are a complex form of social group, which may represent a superordinate group identity for members; (b) that part of their complexity derives from the fact they are "mini-social systems," that is, they comprise a system of different, less inclusive groupings (subgroups, units, roles, etc.) that stand in a socially structured relationship to each other; and (c) that at both the superordinate and subgroup level the activities of members are more or less strongly regulated by a consensual structure of social norms, values, and roles (i.e., there are normative values, goals, rules, standards, procedures, customs, etc., that prescribe appropriate behavior in differing locations and within the organization as a whole).

These features paint an "ideal type" or prototypical instance. There are inevitably exceptions and variations. Organizations and subgroups may be *membership* rather than *reference* groups. Intraorganizational relations and subgroup identities may be ambiguous, fluid, and conflicted. The social structure of norms, values, and roles may not be consensual, but, rather, there may be disagreement about appropriate goals and values within the organization or within subgroups. There is no value in creating an axiomatic definition of an organization prior to careful study of the concrete features of any specific organizational context. The point is to gain some idea in terms of basic theory of the kind of group or institution we tend to describe as an organization. Our suggestion is that theoretically, *the organization is a complex social group characterized by a differentiated, normative social structure, the presence of subgroupings, and an internal system of intergroup relations.*

From this viewpoint, the relevance of the social identity perspective is extensive, because it provides analyses of (a) intergroup relations within a social structure, (b) the nature and effects of psychological group formation, and (c) the role of social categorizations of self and others in mediating basic organizational processes such as social influence, cohesion, and cooperation. Social identity theory, for example, can be applied more or less directly to inter and intraorganizational relations. To the degree that people identify with the organization as a whole, their self-attitudes and identity-relevant behavior will be affected by the relations between their own and other relevant organizations. The extent to which they are attached to the organization, seek to leave individually or collectively, are motivated to redefine its identity or engage in competitive rivalry with other organizations, will all be affected by prestige differences between organizations and the related social structural variables discussed by social identity theory. (e.g., see Haslam, in press).

Perhaps more importantly, the same analysis can also be applied to the internal functioning of organizations, pinpointing the social psychological consequences of subgroup relationships. Subgroup relations are commonly associated with differences in status and prestige within the organization and with perceptions of the legitimacy and stability of those differences and the permeability of group boundaries. The theory is relevant to understanding when such relations are likely to threaten the cohesiveness of the organization as a whole by producing destructive, competitive tendencies and to indicating, alternatively, the kinds of conditions under which positive subgroup identity can coexist with cooperative and positive social contact between different subgroups. A great deal of recent work on the "contact hypothesis" has drawn on social identity and self-categorization theories to this end (e.g., Anastasio et al., 1997; Hewstone & Brown, 1986).

A particular advantage of social identity theory for organizational studies, compared to virtually all other other psychological approaches to intergroup relations, is its focus on the interplay between social identity processes and perceived social structure. It is a genuinely *social* psychological theory, which resists simple-minded extrapolation from purely abstract psychological processes to real-life group action and considers instead how their effects are shaped by and interact with the macrosocial context. It is therefore ideally suited to studying intergroup relations within real-life organizational contexts. Tajfel focused on society at large, but the "mini-social system" of the organization reproduces many of the same issues and processes. Another advantage, which follows from this perspective, is the capacity of the theory to predict a variety of different strategies of social action and change other than solely social conflict and ingroup bias. The theory is not simply about social conflict, but about collective behavior more generally.

Self-categorization theory probably has an even more fundamental relevance, focusing directly on the individual–group relationship as a dynamic psychological process. Instead of a view of groups as fixed, static, sociological entities, which form and persist as external constraints on the behavior of the individual, it considers group phenomena as the outcome of an active self-categorizing process on the part of the individual. It takes for granted that multiple organizational identifications can exist at different levels of inclusiveness, that they become psychologically salient as a function of an interaction between perceiver motives and beliefs and the specific social setting, that almost any significant social differentiation within the organization can become the basis for psychological group membership under appropriate conditions, and that group memberships can be in conflict, overlap, or reinforce each other. In focusing on the group as a *process* rather than a reified *thing*, it integrates neo-Lewinian concepts of interdependence, cohesiveness, common fate, proximity, and so forth as bases of group formation, with more recent research on the social categorization of self and others. It shows how the awareness of a shared social identity arises in specific social settings and how it produces mutually positive social orientations between group members and facilitates the acceptance of organizational norms, values, and goals as one's own.

There is now a good body of research evidence relevant to the role of self-categorization in producing social cohesion within groups and between (sub-)groups (e.g., Anastasio et al., 1997; Hogg, 1992; Turner,

1984). There is also a clear picture of its role in cooperation and of its complementary relationship to functional interdependence (Turner & Bourhis, 1996). It has been proposed that the perceived interdependence of people can function as both a cause and an effect of psychological group formation (Turner, 1981, 1982, 1985). Any variable such as common fate, shared threat, proximity, similarity, shared interests, cooperative interaction, or positive interdependence that can function *cognitively as a criterion of social categorization to produce an awareness of shared social identity* can lead to group formation. We can define ourselves as a distinct we-group on the basis of our shared interests in contrast to others. Similarity of fate, shared goals, and so forth can directly create a group through social identification prior to any experience of positive outcomes mediated by group membership. Conversely, group formation can produce perceived interdependence:

> [T]he social group can be an independent variable in the perception of cooperative and competitive interdependence . . . we can derive from the social identity principle the hypothesis that . . . social categorization *per se* should cause individuals to perceive their interests as cooperatively linked within groups and competitively linked between groups . . . the formation of a common or superordinate group tends to induce and stabilize cooperative behaviour in the same way that an ingroup-outgroup division elicits competitive tendencies: not merely through the need for positive distinctiveness, but more basically, because social categorization directly influences individuals' perceptions of their goals. . . . The fundamental point is that the processes implicated in group-formation *per se* may also tend to dictate the cooperative and competitive orientations characteristic respectively of intra-group and intergroup relations. (Turner, 1981, pp. 97–99)

It is assumed that in depersonalizing the self, salient social identity also depersonalizes self-interest, transforming differing personal self-interests into a collective we-group interest (Turner, 1985; Turner et al., 1987). The disagreement between self-categorization theory and interpersonal interdependence theory is *not* about the empirical importance of interdependence *but its theoretical role*. Is perceived interdependence the necessary and sufficient causal basis for psychological group formation? Does group belongingness represent the development of mutual cooperation and social cohesion between persons based on the mutual satisfaction of their individual needs? Self-categorization theory holds that interdependence, like many other variables, *can* lead to group formation, but only where it leads to mutual social identification. It proposes that the underlying psychological process is the emergence of shared social identity, not the development of reward-based cohesiveness. Goal interdependence, therefore, is neither necessary nor sufficient for cooperation and group formation, but *once a group is formed* (and one *empirical* factor could be the awareness of interdependent goals or of a common fate), it will directly affect how people perceive their interests and, in particular, will lead to the development of collective, shared interests.

> What seems to matter for cooperation, the decisive condition, is the intervention of social psychological variables—that produce a mutually cooperative relationship. If one looks carefully at the relevant variables—a shared self-definition as partners, being oriented to the common interest, shared goals and experiences, similarity, reduced social distance and increased social contact, empathy and trust, mutual attraction, the salience of shared norms and values, acting in "public" (a shared social field) as opposed to as an isolated private individual, etc.—there is a strong implication that the general process underlying mutually cooperative intentions and expectations is the extent to which players come to see themselves as a collective or joint unit, to feel a sense of "we-ness" . . . the fundamental process is one of becoming a psychological group. . . .Instead of social cooperation producing the group, it may well be that, psychologically, the group is the basis of cooperation. (Turner et al., 1987, p. 34)

Probably most work applying self-categorization theory to group processes has looked at social influence (Turner, 1991). As with cooperation, the theory argues that shared social identity is the basis of mutual influence between people. It is assumed that depersonalization, the creation of mutually perceived similarity between ingroup members, not only leads to more consensual behavior in terms of the norms and values that define one's group, but that it also produces shared expectations of agreement between ingroup members. Where the latter are disconfirmed (i.e., where there is disagreement within the group), subjective uncertainty about the validity (appropriateness, correctness, etc.) of one's judgments is produced, which has to be resolved. The uncertainty is created by individuals' implicit awareness that people who are similar and who are judging a similar (shared, publicly invariant) stimulus situation *ought* to agree (i.e., react in the same way). Furthermore, where they do so agree, the agreement provides evidence that ingroup members' responses reflect an external, objective reality, rather than personal biases or idiosyncrasies. If some response to the stimulus situation is depersonalized, shared with similar others, if it is consensual and normative for the group, then it can be attributed to external reality and it provides information about reality. In fact, the response is experienced as subjectively valid and appropriate precisely because it is perceived as in some sense "objectively demanded" by reality. By the same token, disagreement within the group raises basic questions to do with the perceived cause of one's response, which amount to the experience of uncertainty: Do we differ in some relevant way after all, are we confronting the same reality, approaching it from the same perspective, am I or are they wrong?

Thus, the basic ideas are that (a) shared social identity is the precondition of mutual influence, (b) disagreement within the ingroup creates uncertainty, which must be resolved, and (c) one's own judgment or behavior is subjectively validated (as correct, desirable, appropriate, informative of reality) to the degree that it participates in and exemplifies an ingroup norm. The traditional distinction between informational and normative influence is rejected in this formulation. It is assumed that ingroup norms induce private acceptance rather than merely public compliance because they provide information about appropriate behavior. They define congruent reponses as *informationally valid* for members, as shared within the ingroup and hence as reflecting reality rather than personal bias or the incompetence and/or prejudice of outgroups. Informational influence is influence as a function of the perceived validity of information, and here, perceived validity is a function of the degree to which the message (judgment, response, etc.) is consensual (i.e., normative) within the ingroup. Thus, for self-categorization theory, informational and (ingroup) normative influence represent the same process. On the other hand, compliance or going along with social norms as a function of the social power of the source, rather than its capacity for persuasive influence, is seen specifically as a reaction to the norms and power of an outgroup.

Several hypotheses follow from this analysis (see Turner et al., 1987; Turner & Oakes, 1989), but the one most relevant to the issue of leadership, to be discussed in the next section, is the idea that group members will differ in their relative persuasiveness as a function of the degree to which they embody the ingroup and its norm. The notion that people vary in the extent to which they represent the group as a whole is operationalized by means of the concept of relative prototypicality (in turn based on the meta-contrast principle). To the degree that, on average, an individual differs more from outgroup members and less from ingroup members on some dimension or attribute than other ingroup members, the more he or she can be defined as *relatively prototypical* of the ingroup (compared to other ingroup members); that is, the more he or she will be perceived as representative of the ingroup as a whole in this intergroup context, and the more influential will he or she be within the ingroup:

> In self-categorization theory, the expert/leader is the individual who best represents the group consensus. . . . The theory uses the concept of "prototypicality" derived from research on categorization (Rosch, 1978) to explain how there can be differences between category members in the degree to which they represent categorical identity. Thus there can be individual differences between members in the degree to which they exemplify the group as a whole . . . and a person can be perceived as *different from one's individual self in better expressing one's shared social identity*. The idea of levels of self-iden-

tity clarifies that [a leader] may be different from one's personal self at the same time as being (and indeed just because they are) more similar to our shared social categorical self. (Turner, 1991, pp. 164–165)

This notion that there is variation within groups in the degree to which particular individuals and subgroups represent the group as a whole, and the additional notion that the relative prototypicality of extremist and moderate members varies as a function of the social context within which the ingroup is defined, have been used to explain group polarization and minority influence (David & Turner, 1992, 1996; Turner, 1991). In the next section these ideas are applied to the issue of leadership.

A SELF-CATEGORIZATION ANALYSIS OF LEADERSHIP

A Brief Overview of Leadership Research

Lord and Maher (1991, p. 129) noted that the study of leadership is probably "the most important topic in the realm of organizational behavior." The sheer amount of research in the area (see Smith, 1995, for a summary) makes it difficult to provide more than a partial review. Nevertheless, some overview must be attempted in order to outline the contribution offered by self-categorization theory.

Broadly speaking, since the very first inquiries into leadership—which date back at least as far as the writings of Plato—approaches to the topic have sought to examine the extent to which successful leadership is a product either (a) of specific characteristics of the leader, (b) of features of the situation in which those qualities (or others) are exercised, or (c) of some combination of these elements. In this vein, trait-based approaches (exemplified by the "great man" theory) have argued that leaders are set apart from followers by their possession of distinctive intellectual and social characteristics, which lead to their being inherently more adept at directing, managing, and inspiring others. On the other hand, situationalist approaches (e.g., Cooper & McGaugh, 1963) have argued that effective leadership is largely determined by features of the context in which leaders operate, and hence, that successful leaders are distinguished more by being in "the right place at the right time" than by their personal qualities.

Dissatisfaction with both these "main-effect" approaches was soundly founded on a range of theoretical and empirical problems, including, most tellingly, a failure to find evidence of any single attribute that reliably distinguished leaders from nonleaders together with a general lack of predictive power (e.g., Mann, 1959). In consequence, most developments of these theories have argued that leadership is an interactive product of *both* personal and situational characteristics. Most contemporary approaches to leadership are of this type.

Four approaches are worth singling out as having been particularly influential, and as being representative of distinct perspectives on the topic. Despite this, it is clear that the opportunities for theoretical synthesis are considerable—a fact confirmed by the number of recent attempts to integrate different approaches (e.g., Fiedler & House, 1995; Hollander, 1993; House & Shamir, 1993). As Fiedler and House (1995, p. 107) observed, of the dozen or so theories of leadership that have widespread currency, "there has been a notable complementarity and convergence in recent years."

Most aligned with the early trait-based theories is the theory of *charismatic leadership* (after Weber, 1921/1946, but recently revitalized by, among others, Burns, 1978), which suggests that effective leaders are those whose personal qualities enable them to articulate a vision for a given (typically large) group. A considerable part of this charisma is considered to derive from the leader's ability to set an example that provides a behavioral model for others, enabling them to contribute to the vision's realization and to an associated group mission. Studies have demonstrated some agreement between raters in assigning leaders to charismatic and noncharismatic categories (e.g., among historians describing U.S. presidents; Donley & Winter, 1970), but the precise nature of "charisma" has proved somewhat difficult to elucidate. Nonetheless, the argument is made that, whatever their exact nature, charismatic leaders (e.g., Gandhi, Martin Luther King, Steve Biko) achieve their success through an ability to impact on the self-concept and self-esteem of followers and thereby redefine group norms and objectives (House & Shamir, 1993).

Probably the most prominent approach to leadership over the past 40 or so years has been Fiedler's *contingency model* (e.g., Fiedler, 1964, 1978; Fiedler & Garcia, 1987). This considers successful leadership to be a product of the match between the characteristics of the leader (specifically, whether they are relationship- or task-motivated) and features of the situation (specifically, the quality of relations between the leader and other group members, the degree to which the leader has power, and the extent to which the group task is structured). Stated most simply, the theory predicts that task-motivated leaders are most effective when features of the situation are all either favorable (i.e., when relations are good, the task is structured, and the leader has power) or all unfavorable, but that relationship-motivated leaders are more effective in situations of intermediate favorableness.

According somewhat higher status to the quality of relations between leader and other group members, *transactional* approaches to leadership, derived in part from social exchange theories, argue that effective leadership flows from a maximization of the mutual benefits that leaders and followers potentially afford each other. Hollander's (1958, 1995) work is most associated with this idea, pointing among other things (a) to the role that the group plays in validating and licensing the leader (partly through the leader's accumulation of group-given "idiosyncrasy credits") and (b) to the importance of "followership" as the necessary concomitant of leadership. There are strong parallels, too, between this perspective and House's *trans-formational* approach, exemplified by his (1971) path-goal theory, which asserts that the key to leaders' success lies in their ability to identify and ulti-mately provide the path for satisfaction of subordinates' goals, while at the same time ensuring that those goals are compatible with those of the group as a whole. Despite differences in complexity and emphasis (see Bass, 1985; Hollander, 1995), in both Hollander's and House's treatments, leaders and followers engage in reward-based transactions, the implementation (or emergence) of which is ultimately for the greater good of the whole group. A significant elaboration of these approaches is provided by work that has argued because the effectiveness of leadership is not entirely under the con-trol of leaders, a range of factors—including high group cohesiveness and an intrinsically motivating task—can act as leadership substitutes (Howell, Dorf-man, & Kerr, 1986; Kerr & Jermier, 1978), whereas other factors—including organizational indifference and low leader power—can act as leader neu-tralizers (Yukl, 1981).

Finally, one comparatively new development in leadership research is provided by Lord's *leadership categorization theory* (Lord, Foti, & De Vader, 1984; Lord, Foti, & Phillips, 1982; Lord & Maher, 1991). Derived from cognitive theories of categorization (e.g., Rosch, 1978), this argues that a leader's effectiveness is determined in large part by others' perceptions of him or her, and that these are based primarily on fixed, preformed lead-ership prototypes. These prototypes are hierarchically organized (with prototypes at lower levels being more specific) and, like stereotypes, are believed to provide perceivers with a set of expectations regarding a per-son's appropriate traits and behaviors. In these terms, leadership itself is defined as "the process of being perceived by others as a leader" (Lord & Maher, 1991, p. 11), and its success depends on the ability of leaders to embody their followers' expectations. One important problem noted by advocates of the model arises when leaders attempt to move from one behavioral domain to another (e.g., from sport into politics). Lord and Maher argued that because different expectations are typically associated with different domains (depending on their degree of "family resem-blance"), leader mobility is restricted and leadership is therefore neces-sarily situationally contingent (as argued by Fiedler and others).

Social Identity and Leadership

A number of the themes in the above review are addressed by self-categorization theory. Turner (1987, 1991) argued against trait-based approaches that suggest that particular personality characteristics determine a person's suitability for leadership. Like Fiedler, self-categorization theory suggests that different types of leaders will be better suited for different tasks, but it suggests that the reasons for this lie not so much in the variable match between the leader's characteristics and structural features of the leadership context as in the variable definition of the group per se. For example, it would attribute the common observation that different types of national leaders fare better in different international climates more to the fact that war or peace would change the overall interests and definition of the group than to the fact that they impact on leader–follower relations, leader power, and task structure (although the latter are undoubtedly affected by changes in intergroup relations and group identity).

In this regard, the theory has most in common with Hollander's work on followership in suggesting that the analysis of leaders cannot be divorced from consideration of the group of which they are part and that they represent:

> It is therefore important that the leader, by his [or her] behavior, manifest a loyalty to the needs and aspirations of group members. These things must matter to him [or her] in ways that are accessible to view because such evidences of good faith and sincere interest serve to elicit greater acceptance of influence. (Hollander, 1964, p. 231; see also 1995)

Hollander suggests that in order for groups to function as effectively as possible, "the leader needs to be attuned to the needs of followers, their perceptions and expectancies" (1995, p. 75). In essence, it can be argued that if a group is to function *as* a group rather than just an aggregate of individuals, its leader must represent the interests of, and be a representative of, the collective as a whole rather than just him- or herself.

In this sense, leadership is intimately bound up with the concerns of followers. The point was expressed succinctly when Ledru-Rollin remarked of his political supporters, "I must follow them; I am their leader" (a statement also attributed to Bonar Law) and was equally apparent in Bergen Evans' observation that "for the most part our leaders are but followers out in front; they do but marshal us in the way we are going." This idea was also emphasized by Rost (1991, p. 109) in the claim that "followers and leaders develop a relationship wherein they influence one another as well as each other, and that is leadership." Emphasizing the higher order nature of leadership as a

group phenomenon, von Cranach (1986) also noted that the behavior of
leaders and the perceptions of their behavior by other group members are
necessarily bound up with issues relating to the social identity that they share,
and that leaders play a central role in defining:

> Groups have an identity that originates from the members' cognitions and
> emotions as a system of mutual feedback on the group level. It serves as a
> source of unity and stability and forms an important part, in turn, of mem-
> bers' social identity. . . . The leader is likely to form the nucleus of this struc-
> ture. (von Cranach, 1986, p. 128)

Consistent with this perspective, one important way in which self-categorization theory conceptualizes the leader (the group member who is
likely to exercise most influence in any given instance) is as the *ingroup prototype*, the member who is most representative in a given context of the
shared social identity and consensual position of the group (Turner, 1987,
1991). The (most) prototypical group member best epitomizes (in the dual
sense of both *defining* and *being defined by*) the social category of which he
or she is a member. An important point of divergence between this idea
and that of Lord and his colleagues is that prototypicality is not considered to be a fixed property of a given stimulus category, but rather is a
variable feature of the definition of the social category in context. As
Turner (1987) put it:

> The relative prototypicality of an individual varies with the dimension(s) of
> comparison and the categories employed. The latter too will vary with the
> frame of reference (the psychologically salient pool of people compared)
> and the comparative dimension(s) selected. These phenomena are relative
> and situation-specific, not absolute, static and constant. Also, unlike in Rosch
> (1978), categories are not defined simply by "prototypes" or "best exemplars"
> . . . prototypes are [also] defined by the given categories, in turn a function
> of the relevant dimensions selected for comparison. (p. 80)

The variability of relative prototypicality follows from the principle of
meta-contrast. Meta-contrast predicts that any particular stimulus will be
perceived as more prototypical of a category to the extent that it is less different from other members of that category than from other stimuli that
are salient in a given context (Haslam & Turner, 1992, 1995; Turner &
Oakes, 1989). A critical implication is that *the prototypicality of exactly the
same exemplar for exactly the same category will vary as a function of the social
context within which categorization takes place*.

As an example, one can think of the most extreme left- and right-wing
members (L and R) as well as the most moderate member (M) of a hypo-

TABLE 2.1
Example of Prototypicality According to Meta-Contrast

										Prototypicality (MCR)		
										L	M	R
Case 1	o	o	o	L	M	R	o	o	o	2.0	3.0	2.0
Case 2				L	M	R	o	o	o	2.7	3.0	1.3
Case 3	o	o	o	L	M	R				1.3	3.0	2.7
Scale values:	1	2	3	4	5	6	7	8	9			
		left wing			centre			right wing				

Notes. Meta-contrast ratio (MCR) of a given stimulus = $\dfrac{\text{mean interclass difference}}{\text{mean intraclass difference}}$

So, for L in Case 2, MCR $= \dfrac{(3 + 4 + 5) / 3}{(1 + 2) / 2} = 2.7$

thetical centrist political group represented in capitals in Table 2.1 (where o indicates the positions of individuals in other groups).

On the basis of the meta-contrast principle, self-categorization theory predicts that where this centrist group is considered in context of the broad political spectrum (i.e., Case 1), L and R would tend to be equally prototypical of the group as a whole but that M would clearly be most prototypical. However, the prototypicality of L relative to R would increase (making them almost as prototypical as M) where the group was compared with a right-wing group (Case 2) and would decrease in comparison to a left-wing group (Case 3). This is because in Case 2, the left-wing member is associated with a greater interclass difference than the right-wing member, whereas this pattern is reversed in Case 3. Thus, if, as self-categorization theory suggests, the extent of a person's relative influence and hence their ability to lead, or at least to be perceived as a leader, is determined by relative prototypicality, then the moderate's authority would be most secure where the group was defined relative to groups occupying the full political spectrum (as in Case 1). However, the same person would be more open to challenge from an extreme left-wing group member if the party confronted only right-wing opponents (Case 2), whereas they would be more likely to face a challenge from a right-winger in the context of conflict with a left-wing group (Case 3).

Nonetheless, just as meta-contrast is only a partial determinant of *which* categories perceivers use to represent a given stimulus array—the normative fit and relative accessibility of the categorization also always being inseparably involved—so too is it only an interactive determinant of the internal structure of those categories (Haslam, Oakes, McGarty, Turner, & Onorato, 1995b, pp. 510–512). This analysis, then, like contingency theories (e.g., Fiedler, 1964) is intended only to present a part of the explanation of why different leaders (or different leadership styles) are appropriate for different situations. (We must also leave aside in this chapter issues to do with legitimate authority, formal power, etc., that we might characterize as to do with social structural complications rather than basic process). Unlike most of the accounts presented in mainstream leadership theory, however, the properties of the individual associated with this variation derive not from qualities inherent in the person *as an individual* (e.g., their personality) but from features of the individual *as representative of a contextually defined social category*. As an example, one can consider the emergence of Norman Schwarzkopf as an American leader of some national stature during the 1990–1991 war in the Persian Gulf (see Haslam et al., 1995). This, we would argue, arose not from the fact that his personality was appropriate for the task, but from the fact that in the specific intergroup relationship, the particular values and goals he espoused and the facets of American identity he projected were congruent with and epitomized Americans' feelings about, intentions toward, and strategic aims in relation to Iraq at the time (e.g., commitment to a strong military reaction to Saddam Hussein rather than a negotiated solution to the conflict). In this sense, Schwarzkopf's emerging authority as a leader derived not from his personality, but from the group whose values he came to represent. A similar process can be seen to underpin his ultimate retreat into the political shadows at the conflict's conclusion.

All this is not to suggest that the emergence of a leader is an entirely passive process, dictated purely by the whims of the group and the tides of changing circumstance. Under the above conceptualization, the leader is an *active* constituent of the group, who is simultaneously defining of and defined by the group. Where a would-be leader espouses views that are not representative of their group (e.g., L's views in Case 1), they may be expected as one strategy to seek to restructure the social context that defines the group, to make their own views more prototypical—either through a process of argumentation and engaging in political rhetoric (see Reicher & Hopkins, 1996) or, more boldly, by seeking conflict with a relevant outgroup. The latter strategy is consistent with the behavior of desperate extremist political leaders faced with internal dissent (e.g., the actions of Mrs. Thatcher and President Galtieri in launching and taking advantage of the 1982 war in the South Atlantic). Three empirical studies reported by Rabbie and Bekkers (1978) support this idea; they showed that leaders whose positions within their group were unstable were more likely to choose to engage in rather than avoid intergroup conflict than leaders whose positions were secure.

This analysis is also consistent with the argument that charismatic leaders achieve their impact largely through an ability to redefine a group's objectives and hence both the self-concept of its members and their own relative influence (as proposed by House & Shamir, 1993). Here, though, charisma is seen to be an *emergent product* of the social categorization process and the definition of the group and its leader in context: It is an expression of the underlying causes of leadership success rather than an independent determinant. Even though, in both lay and psychological theory, charisma is typically attributed purely to the individual (being seen as inherent in the leader's personality and fundamental to organizational success), we argue that it is actually an expression of the leader–group relationship as perceived by group members in a specific social context and is thus conferred by them as a function of how they define the leader and themselves. Hence, charisma, we argue, is essentially a social psychological or social relational rather than a personality phenomenon. Such a view helps to explain why the death of a leader (particularly at the hands of the outgroup or an outgroup member) so often powerfully *adds to* rather subtracts from a leader's charismatic appeal.

Empirical Support for the Self-Categorization Analysis

The previously discussed ideas have been most widely tested in the domain of experimental social psychology. Research has applied the self-categorization analysis of social category salience, and in particular the principles of category fit and relative prototypicality, to, among other things, the study of stereotyping (Oakes et al., 1994), perceived group homogeneity (Haslam et al., 1996), social attribution (Oakes et al., 1991), group polarization (Hogg, Turner, & Davidson, 1990; McGarty, Turner, Hogg, David, & Wetherell, 1992; Turner, 1991; Turner et al., 1987), group cohesiveness (Hogg, 1992), social judgment (Haslam & Turner, 1992, 1995; McGarty & Turner, 1992), conformity and minority influence (Abrams,Wetherell, Cochrane, Hogg, & Turner, 1990; David & Turner, 1992, 1996; Turner, 1991), and the self-concept (Turner et al., 1994). Two recent experiments conducted in our laboratory serve to illustrate the general point that the perceived prototypicality of group members, and their overall representativeness for a given group, varies as a function of the social context (Haslam et al., 1995b).

In the first of these studies, subjects were asked to watch a video of a woman proposing that the viewers should lobby the government to do more to improve road safety. The social category membership of the presenter was varied across a number of conditions. She was identified as either an ingroup member—someone who wanted to improve road safety—or an outgroup member—someone who wanted to ban the sale and consumption of alcohol. Both her position relative to other members of her group (she was said to be either extreme or moderate) and the salience of subjects' own social identity (high or low) were also varied orthogonally. In high salience conditions, subjects had to indicate whether they agreed with the goals of the group of which the woman was said to be a member. In low salience conditions, they were not so required.

Following the arguments presented earlier, it was predicted that the woman would be perceived as most representative of the outgroup (and by extension more likely to be seen as a leader rather than a follower) in the condition where she was believed to be an extremist and group membership was salient, and most representative of the ingroup when group membership was salient and she was a moderate. The first of these predictions was based on the fact that the former condition would render the intergroup features of the study most salient and hence, in this context, an extremist—who maximized the difference between ingroup and outgroup—would be seen as most representative of the outgroup's position. On the other hand, in the intragroup context where only the ingroup was mentioned, a moderate position would maximize intragroup similarity. Both these predictions were supported.

Along similar lines, a second study asked subjects to judge the extent to which two people—one who espoused moderately proauthority views and one who espoused extremely proauthority views—were representative of a group that in the course of a videotaped discussion generated relatively hard-line solutions to a range of social problems (e.g., agreeing that the best way to solve the drug problem was to make the laws more strict). The (generally antiauthority) subjects completed this task in one of three conditions, which again manipulated the salience of the intergroup division (between the antiauthority subjects and the proauthority target group). In a high salience condition, viewing of the videotape was preceded by a lecture on authoritarianism, after which all subjects completed a personality inventory (based on Adorno, Frenkel-Brunswik, Levinson, & Sanford's, 1950, F-scale) that indicated that they were all antiauthoritarian. In a moderate salience condition, they completed the inventory without the lecture; and, in a low salience condition, they simply watched the video, without either the lecture or completion of the personality scale. As predicted, it was found that the extreme member was perceived to be relatively more representative of the target group than the moderate member to the extent that the intergroup nature of the task was rendered more salient.

Both these studies suggest that the prototypicality of a person in relation to a particular group (and by extension, their perceived fitness as leader of it) is a much more dynamic process than envisaged by the work of Lord and his colleagues. That is, prototypicality appears not to be based simply on "a match of the characteristics of the person to abstractions or features common to category members." Neither is the evidence consistent with the idea that "perceivers use degree of match to this ready-made structure to form leadership perceptions" (Lord & Maher, 1991, p. 132). On the contrary, judgments of prototypicality appear to be context-sensitive and to be structured on-the-spot by, among other things, the intergroup realities of the situation (Oakes, Haslam, & Turner, 1998). In other words, prototypical "leadership material" in any sphere is unlikely simply to reflect the matching of a given candidate with a stored set of requisite attributes, but is more likely to reflect the extent to which the candidate is representative of the group as it is currently defined in a given social context.

Lord and Maher (1991, p. 132) used the domain of politics to illustrate their argument, stating that here "someone seen as wanting peace, having strong convictions, being charismatic, and a good administrator would be labelled as a leader." Yet, such a rigid and prescriptive approach seems incompatible with on-the-ground realities where the demand for these qualities clearly varies as a function of social circumstance. This point is illustrated in the response of Steve Biko when asked in 1977 (shortly before his death in detention) if he was going to lead black South Africans down a path of conflict or of nonviolence:

> It is only, I think when black people are so dedicated and united in their cause that we can effect the greatest results. And whether this is going to be through the form of conflict or not will be dictated by the future. I don't believe for a moment we are going willingly to drop our belief in the nonviolent stance—as of now. But I can't predict what will happen in the future, inasmuch as I can't predict what the enemy is going to do in the future. (Biko, 1978, p. 168)

A legitimate reaction to the studies we have described so far is that they pertain to issues of leadership prototypicality only indirectly and then largely in perceptions of an outgroup. In order to examine whether leadership prototypes really are as flexible as a self-categorization analysis would suggest, we conducted two additional studies in which subjects were asked to identify the desirable characteristics of different types of leaders under conditions that manipulated (a) the salience of subjects' social identity (Haslam, 1995, Experiment 1) and (b) features of comparative context (Experiment 2).

In the first study, Australian students in independent conditions were asked to rate a list of 12 attributes in terms of their importance as qualities that they thought either national leaders, sporting leaders, or business leaders should possess. All but one of the attributes were taken from the 12 identified by Lord et al. (1984) as most commonly selected to describe basic level leadership categories (the exception being that "patriotic" was included instead of "well-dressed"). The three leadership categories were also selected on the basis of Lord et al.'s finding that there was minimal overlap in the attributes associated with each (mean $r = .10$). The key experimental manipulation here was of the salience of subjects' national identity, which was achieved simply by asking half the subjects to indicate whether or not they were Australian prior to responding. The basic prediction was that this manipulation would impact prototypical beliefs relating to the different leadership categories, so that their underlying meaning would change as a function of being apprehended from a different social perspective (Turner et al., 1994).

Factor analysis was conducted on responses to the 12 trait dimensions and this identified three primary factors, which (based on the highest loading trait) were labeled dedicated, patriotic, and aggressive. Analysis of these scores as a function of leadership category revealed a main effect for leadership category on only the second of these factors (patriotic). Importantly, as shown by Fig. 2.1, this effect was conditioned by a significant interaction with national identity salience. It is apparent that in standard conditions (conceptually similar to those used by Lord et al., 1984), patriotism was seen to be much more important for national leaders than for sports or business leaders. However, in a context where subjects' national identity was made salient, this attribute was seen to be equally appropriate for all three groups.

It is possible to explain the pattern in high salience conditions in terms of subjects' aversion to overly patriotic Australian politicians, and their sensitivity to the lack of patriotism among Australian businessmen. This aside, however, the study makes the point that the notion of an ideal leader in any domain is necessarily conditioned by the social vantage point of the perceiver and the salience of a set of norms, values, and beliefs associated with a given ingroup membership. The random assignment of subjects to conditions here precludes there having been any sys-

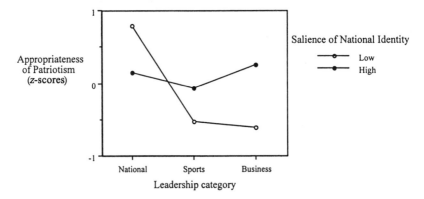

FIG. 2.1.   Perceived appropriateness of patriotism for leadership as a function of the salience of subjects' national identity and leadership category.

tematic differences in subjects' experience-based "cognitive knowledge structure" (Lord & Maher, 1991, p. 132), and yet their beliefs about desirable leadership attributes clearly did vary systematically and dramatically as a result of a relatively straightforward manipulation of identity salience.

It could be argued that what this study accessed in high-identity salience conditions were lower level (i.e., more specific) leadership prototypes than those in no salience conditions (i.e., the prototype for an Australian business leader rather than just a business leader). In this way, it is possible to defend a belief in leadership prototypes as fixed structures by claiming that there are an infinite number of prototypes associated with an infinite number of leadership categories of differing specificity. However, this argument seems relatively circular and likely to prove highly unparsimonious.

Nonetheless, we conducted a second study that sought to demonstrate variation in the content of leadership prototypes simply by manipulating comparative context. In different conditions, subjects were asked to describe each of the three leader types (national, sports, and business) either alone or at the same time as another category of leader. In this manner there were six independent conditions (national alone, sports alone, business alone, national and sports, national and business, and sports and business) and each leadership category was rated three times. Leadership categories were rated on the three dimensions corresponding to the three trait factors identified in Experiment 1 (dedicated, patriotic, and aggressive).

There was no evidence of variation in the perceived appropriateness of dedication for leadership as a function of either leadership category or comparative context. However, as shown by Fig. 2.2, these variables did influence the perceived appropriateness of patriotism and aggressiveness. As in the first study, there was evidence that patriotism was more important for national leaders than for business or sports leaders when these groups were judged alone, and this difference was largely preserved across manipulations of comparative context. However, once again, the perceived appropriateness of patriotism also varied as a function of an interaction between the independent variables. Patriotism was seen as more important for national leaders when they were compared with sporting leaders than when considered alone, more appropriate for sporting leaders when compared with business leaders than when considered alone, and more important for business leaders when compared with sporting leaders than when considered alone or when compared with national leaders. Despite evidence that when categories were judged alone, patriotism was seen as more appropriate for national that other types of leaders, this was not the case under all judgmental conditions. Patriotism was seen as just as important for sporting as for national leaders when each was compared with business leaders.

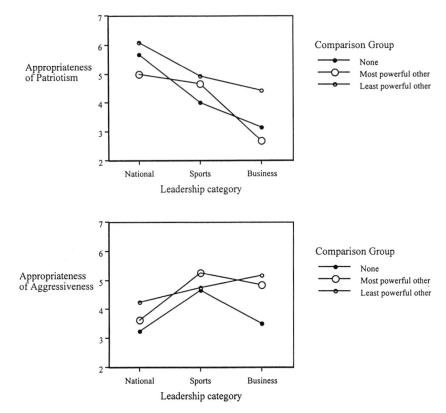

FIG. 2.2.   Perceived appropriateness of patriotism and aggressiveness for leadership as a function of leadership category and comparative context. Rating of 7 = extremely appropriate, 1 = not at all appropriate. "Most powerful other" refers to comparison with national leader for sports and business leaders, comparison with business leaders for national leaders (i.e., this is not part of a factorial design).

Evidence of similar variation was found for ratings of aggressiveness (see Fig. 2.2). Thus, although aggressiveness was generally seen as more appropriate for sporting leaders than for national leaders, it was also seen as more important for national leaders when compared with sporting leaders than when considered alone, and more important for business leaders when compared with either sporting or national leaders than when considered alone.

The general finding is that there appears to be no absolute level of a given trait that is inherently fitting for a given leadership category. So the idea that to become an effective national leader, for example, a person should simply aim to be seen by others as extremely patriotic and quite unaggressive (cf. Lord & Maher, 1991, p. 132) might well prove problematic if he or she were perceived in a business context or in a context where Australian norms (of perhaps greater aggressiveness and less patriotism) were salient. The point is more significant because these studies involved relatively weak manipulations of judgmental context. To our mind, it seems highly likely that the perceived appropriateness of given attributes would change much more dramatically in the context of real-world fluctuations in the character of intergroup relations (as alluded to in the words of Steve Biko).

Evidence that leader prototypes vary with context can be considered important insofar as it makes the case for a more dynamic analysis of the role of the cognitive aspects of leadership than is provided by Roschian theory (the limitations of which are now widely accepted by cognitive theorists; e.g., Barsalou, 1987; Medin, 1989). Nonetheless, it would also appear important to show that social categorical processes of the sort described by self-categorization theory impact on actual leadership emergence. To this end, a study by Burton (1993) examined how group members' choice of a leader varied in the face of different intergroup tasks.

At the start of the study, undergraduate students (who participated in the study in groups of four) completed a bogus inventory that served to identify them as either "idealistic" or "pragmatic." Subjects were informed that they were going to take part in a debate with a group that, in some cases, was identified as extremely proauthority and pragmatic and, in others, as antiauthority and idealistic. The subjects then watched a video in which this outgroup discussed a range of issues related to crime and punishment (in the first condition, the video was actually the same as that used in Haslam et al., 1995b, Experiment 2). After having seen the video, subjects were informed that before they took part in the debate, they needed to elect a leader for their own group and that the best way to do this was to find out what each other's views were and make a decision on that basis. The subjects were ushered into separate cubicles to perform this task in which they completed items constructed so that they tended to give idealistic responses (where subjects had been assigned to an idealistic group) or pragmatic responses (where subjects had been assigned to a pragmatic group). They then received feedback supposedly emanating from the other group members. In fact, the feedback was false and had been manipulated by the experimenter to suggest that the group members differed in the extent to which they were idealistic or pragmatic. Thus, for subjects assigned to the pragmatic group, one other group member espoused extremely pragmatic views, one espoused moderately pragmatic views and one espoused only slightly pragmatic views (with a similar pattern for members of the idealistic group).

After receiving this feedback, subjects were asked to divide 10 votes among the three group members, being told that the person who obtained the most votes would be appointed group leader. The chief prediction here was that leadership selection would vary as a function of the specific group that subjects expected to face, due to the role that this outgroup would play in redefining ingroup prototypicality (as per the working example described earlier). Variation in leader choice was thus expected across conditions where the characteristics of the ingroup (its internal relations and structure) remained constant and hence, where none would be anticipated by standard contingency theories (e.g., Fiedler, 1964).

The pattern of results supported this hypothesis and partially confirmed specific predictions derived from self-categorization theory. Thus, although there was no significant variation in votes assigned to members of the pragmatic group across conditions (a result that posttest measures indicated was due to a lack of identification with this proauthority ingroup), subjects assigned to the idealistic group cast significantly more votes supporting the extremely idealistic candidate when they believed they were going to encounter a pragmatic group rather than an idealistic one. Indeed, when their group was set to confront pragmatists, these idealistic subjects gave most votes to the extreme idealist ($M = 3.6$), but when set to confront other idealists, they allocated most votes to the moderate (3.8) and fewest to the extremist (2.5). In other words, when confronted by the clearly different outgroup, those subjects who identified with their group were more likely to vote for the candidate who maximized intercategory difference—this being the candidate who was most representative of the group's distinctive qualities in the anticipated intergroup encounter.

It is worth noting that as well as being incompatible with contingency theories, which accord no status to the intergroup dimensions of a given context, the results are also inconsistent with situationalist accounts, which seek to explain leadership emergence in terms of the demands of the task at hand (cf. Cooper & McGaugh, 1963). Under this model, one might argue that subjects' interpretation of the upcoming task varied as a function of the outgroup they were due to debate, seeing the encounter with the like-minded group as cooperative and that with the very different group as competitive. However, as Burton (1993) remarked, that being the case, one would actually expect subjects to have selected the most hard-nosed candidate (i.e., the *least* idealistic group member) to lead the group through the competitive task. Again, then, we are led to conclude that the leader emerges as someone qualified for the job not by virtue of his or her purely personal qualities (that could be appreciated in isolation from the group) but by virtue of being contextually representative of the essence of the group and of what differentiates "us" from "them."

One implication of this analysis is that to the extent that group activities and interaction serve to emphasise what makes the leader different from other ingroup members, their leadership may be undermined and rendered less effective. This point fits with observations by Hollander (1995) that group productivity can suffer where structural or other factors mark leaders out as distinct from those they lead (e.g., where, as in examples he discusses, some managers get paid more than 100 times the wages of workers). By the same token, if it is the case that the leadership selection procedure serves to emphasise intragroup differences (e.g., by focusing on individual differences in competence or qualification), then it follows from the principle of comparative fit that this may undermine a group's shared social identity. This in turn might be expected to impact negatively on the two main indices of group productivity identified by Cartwright and Zander (1960, p. 496), namely "(a) the achievement of some specific group goal [and] (b) the maintenance or strengthening of the group itself."

In order to examine these ideas, we conducted a series of studies testing the counterintuitive hypothesis that the process of seeking to identify the "best" leader for a small group task might serve to undermine rather than enhance group performance (Haslam et al., 1998). Our objective was not to demonstrate that the process of systematically selecting group leaders is *generally* counterproductive. Rather, on the basis of previous research, we hypothesized that this could be the case under a specific and restricted set of conditions, in particular, where, in the absence of a leader being chosen, the group *already has* a salient social identity and is already oriented to a well-defined shared goal.

In an initial study, small groups of subjects (containing between 3 and 5 members) had to imagine that they were survivors from a plane that had crashed in a frozen wilderness and had to formulate a rational strategy for rescuing potentially useful items from the plane wreckage (the "winter survival task" developed by Johnson & Johnson, 1991). The study manipulated the method of *group selection* so that in *systematic* conditions, groups decided among themselves who should be leader by whatever means they considered appropriate, whereas in *random* conditions, the leader was simply the person whose name appeared first in the alphabet. We also manipulated *leadership style* by instructing half the leaders to lead their group in an *autocratic* manner (leading "from the front" and imposing their views on other members of the group) and half to lead in a *democratic* manner (involving all group members in the process of making consensual decisions; cf. Lewin, Lippitt, & White, 1939). The dependent measures of interest (corresponding to group goal and group maintenance functions respectively) were (a) the quality of the strategy individuals ultimately decided on (as measured relative to expert ratings) and (b) the extent to which the strategy chosen by individuals *deviated* from the one on which their group had previously agreed. Less deviation, suggesting that individuals were bound more to the group and its original decision, is evidence of a stronger orientation to group maintenance.

Our main prediction was that individual group members would make better decisions where the leader of their group was randomly rather than systematically selected. The method of leader selection was also expected to have relatively small impact on groups led in an autocratic manner (which might generally tend to have a comparatively low level of shared social identification), but was expected to have a stronger effect on groups that were led democratically (where there was greater potential for a reduction in shared identification and hence, group-based cohesiveness and productivity). The pattern of results supported these predictions, with individuals in groups with random leaders tending to arrive at better solutions to the exercise than those from groups with systematically selected leaders, a pattern that was particularly marked for groups whose leader adopted a democratic style. Although there were no significant effects for group maintenance, there was also evidence that individuals from groups with randomly chosen leaders identified more strongly with their group.

This basic pattern of results was replicated in a second study that contained three conditions in which the leader always adopted a democratic leadership style. As well as the *random* and *informal* (labeled *systematic* earlier) leadership selection conditions of the first study, an additional *formal* condition sought to select a group leader by means of an externally imposed selection procedure. This involved group members completing a short "leadership selection inventory" in which they rated their own ability in areas that Ritchie and Moses (1983) identified as being positively correlated with long-term managerial success (e.g., being flexible in approaching tasks, having broad-ranging interests). Again, our central prediction was that on both group goal and group maintenance measures, the responses of subjects in groups where the leader was randomly chosen would be superior to those of subjects in groups involving a systematic (i.e., nonrandom) leadership selection process. Results on both measures supported the predictions.

These findings serve to question the belief that the process of systematic leadership selection is always in the interest of better group performance. This assumption is more or less implicit in many organizational settings (and in the self-justificatory pronouncements of senior executives; see Hollander, 1995), and yet, there are strong theoretical grounds for believing that the procedure can be counterproductive where the act of attempting to select the best leader may undermine a strong sense of shared identity and purpose by drawing attention to properties and entitlements that are not shared within the group as a whole. To the extent that a group can realistically assert that "united we stand, and divided we fall," it follows that where leadership selection brings to light and even engenders intragroup division, it may presage poor group performance and ultimately disintegration (cf. Jackson, 1992; Worchel, 1994; Worchel, Coutant-Sassic, & Grossman, 1992).

It is important to note, however, that in presenting these arguments, we are claiming neither that the process of seeking to select the best group leader always reduces individual performance, nor that random leader selection always enhances it. We believe that the pattern of findings obtained in the previously discussed studies are likely to hold only for particular groups performing particular tasks. Broadly speaking, random leader selection might only ever be advantageous where the group (a) has a clearly defined shared goal, (b) is disposed or able to behave in a relatively democratic manner (involving shared decision making, division of labor and responsibility, etc.), and therefore (c) in the *absence of a leader being appointed*, would already have a strong sense of shared social identity. These circumstances are not especially common and will typically be restricted to small groups performing well-defined tasks (cf. Howell et al., 1986).

Although under such circumstances, random leadership selection might engender greater identity-based group cohesiveness, it is not the case that this will necessarily manifest itself in superior performance. A large body of research on the phenomenon of "groupthink" (Janis, 1972) has testified to this point, as has other research showing that there is no simple relationship between group cohesiveness and group productivity or performance (Hogg, 1992; Mullen, Anthony, Salas, & Driscoll, 1994). In part, this is because the latter variables are difficult to define and highly negotiable (Pritchard, 1990). A key issue here is the extent to which the judged value of the group product is commensurate with the contextually defined goals and values of the group itself; only where it is would we expect greater cohesiveness to enhance performance (see Haslam, in press).

These speculations aside, the major theoretical point made by these studies and the research described in this section as a whole, is that, to the extent that leadership research focuses on the properties of leaders as differentiated individuals, it may actually be neglecting the essence of the leadership process. In contrast to the focus of contingency and categorization theories on the possession (or perceived possession) of specific traits that equip a person for effective leadership, we suggest that effective leadership is always a product of the interaction between the individual and their social environment. We hypothesize that effective leaders are those whose individuality is *transformed* by group membership in such a way that they come to articulate, embody, and direct social identity-based interests. These higher order, group-level attributes of the leader cannot be reduced to enduring personality characteristics, any more than the collective interests of the group represented by the leader can be equated with his or her personal self-interest.

This does not in any way deny the distinctiveness of effective or charismatic leadership, but rather argues that, although it may seem paradoxical, researchers need to look for its basis in the character of the group and group life, and in the match of the leader to the group, at least as much as in any intrinsic personal qualities of the leader.

CONCLUSION

In this chapter, we tried to do three things: (a) summarize some of the main ideas of the social identity approach, (b) indicate briefly why it is of general relevance to organizational behavior, and (c) provide one detailed example, by looking at leadership, of how self-categorization theory generates a distinctive analysis of a classic issue in organizational research. The social identity approach provides a new theoretical perspective on basic social psychological processes in inter- and intragroup relations, social cognition, and the self. It is the first really new way of thinking about group phenomena since the group dynamics tradition and its derivatives, and it has the particular advantage of building a bridge between the group preoccupations of much classic social psychology and the cognitive perspective that has been so influential in contemporary research. In this sense, it provides a set of theoretical resources for organizational psychology rather than a limited, ready-made list of hypotheses about specific domains of behavior (see, too, Ashforth & Mael, 1989). What, ultimately, it has to say about organizational behavior is likely to prove as varied as the problems that define the field and to which it can be applied. There seems little doubt, however, that organizational contexts—where loyalties and hostilities, cooperation and conflict, influence and power, all collide and intersect as a function of group identifications and social structure—should provide a natural home for the social identity approach.

REFERENCES

Abrams, D., Wetherell, M. S., Cochrane, S., Hogg, M. A., & Turner, J. C. (1990). Knowing what to think by knowing who you are: A social identity approach to norm formation, conformity and group polarization. *British Journal of Social Psychology, 29,* 97–119.

Adorno, T. W., Frenkel-Brunswik, E., Levinson, D. J., & Sanford, R. N. (1950). *The authoritarian personality.* New York: Harper & Row.

Anastasio, P., Bachman, B., Gaertner, S., & Dovidio, J. (1997). Categorization, recategorization and common ingroup identity. In R. Spears, P. J. Oakes, N. Ellemers, & S. A. Haslam (Eds.), *The social psychology of stereotyping and group life* (pp. 236–256). Oxford, England: Blackwell.

Ashforth, B. E., & Mael, F. (1989). Social identity theory and the organization. *Academy of Management Review, 14,* 20–39.

Barsalou, L. W. (1987). The instability of graded structure: Implications for the nature of concepts. In U. Neisser (Ed.), *Concepts and conceptual development: Ecological and intellectual factors in categorization* (pp. 101–140). Cambridge, England: Cambridge University Press.

Bass, B. M. (1985). *Leadership and performance beyond expectations*. New York: Free Press.

Biko, B. S. (1988). *I write what I like*. London: Penguin. (Original work published 1978)

Brewer, M. B., & Schneider, S. K. (1990). Social identity and social dilemmas: A double-edged sword. In D. Abrams & M. A. Hogg (Eds.), *Social identity theory: Constructive and critical advances*. London: Harvester Wheatsheaf.

Burns, J. M. (1978). *Leadership*. New York: Harper & Row.

Burton, J. (1993). *The social contextual basis of leadership perceptions*. Unpublished honors thesis, Australian National University, Canberra, Australia.

Caporael, L. R., Dawes, R. M., Orbell, J. M., & van de Kragt, A. J. C. (1989). Selfishness examined: Cooperation in the absence of egoistic incentives. *Behavioral and Brain Sciences, 12*, 683–699.

Cartwright, D., & Zander, A. (1960). Leadership and group performance: Introduction. In D. Cartwright & A. Zander (Eds.), *Group dynamics: Research and theory* (pp. 487–510). Evanston, IL: Row Peterson.

Cooper, J. B., & McGaugh, J. L. (1963). Leadership: Integrating principles of social psychology. In C. A. Gibb (Ed.) *Leadership: Selected readings* (pp. 97–116). Baltimore: Penguin

David, B., & Turner, J. C. (1992, July). *Studies in self-categorization and minority conversion*. Paper presented at the joint EAESP/SESP Meeting, Leuven/Louvain-la-Neuve, Belgium.

David, B., & Turner, J. C. (1996). Studies in self-categorization and minority conversion: Is being a member of the outgroup an advantage? *British Journal of Social Psychology, 35*, 179–199.

Donley, R. E., & Winter, D. G. (1970). Measuring the motives of public officials at a distance: An exploratory study. *Behavioral Science, 15*, 227–236.

Doosje, B., & Ellemers, N. (1997). Stereotyping under threat: The role of group identification. In R. Spears, P. J. Oakes, N. Ellemers, Haslam (Eds.), *The social psychology of stereotyping and group life*. Oxford, England: Blackwell.

Duckitt, J. (1992). *The social psychology of prejudice*. New York: Praeger.

Ellemers, N. (1993). The influence of socio-structural variables on identity enhancement strategies. *European Review of Social Psychology, 4*, 27–57.

Ellemers, N., & van Knippenberg, A. (1997). Stereotyping in social context. In R. Spears, P. J. Oakes, N. Ellemers, & S. A. Haslam (Eds.), *The social psychology of stereotyping and group life* (pp. 208–235). Oxford, England: Blackwell.

Fiedler, F. E. (1964). A contingency model of leader effectiveness. In L. Berkowitz (Ed.), *Advances in experimental social psychology* (Vol. 1, pp. 149–190). New York: Academic Press.

Fiedler, F. E. (1978). The contingency model and the dynamics of the leadership process. In L. Berkowitz (Ed.), *Advances in experimental social psychology* (Vol. II). New York: Academic Press.

Fiedler, F. E., & Garcia, J. E. (1987). *New approaches to effective leadership*. New York: Wiley.

Fiedler, F. E., & House, R. J. (1995). Leadership theory and research: A report of progress. In C. L. Cooper & I. T. Robertson (Eds.), *Key reviews in managerial psychology* (pp. 97–116). New York: Wiley.

Haslam, S. A. (in press). *Psychology in organizations: The social identity approach*. London and Thousand Oaks, CA: Sage.

Haslam, S. A. (1995). *Contextual variation in leadership prototypes*. Unpublished manuscript, Australian National University, Canberra, Australia.

Haslam, S. A., McGarty, C., Eggins, R. A, Morrison, B. E., Brown, P. M., & Reynolds, K. J. (1998). Inspecting the emperor's clothes: Evidence that randomly-selected leaders can enhance group performance. *Group Dynamics: Theory, Process and Research, 2*, 168–184.

Haslam, S. A., Oakes, P. J., McGarty, C., Turner, J. C., & Onorato, R. (1995). Contextual shifts in the prototypicality of extreme and moderate outgroup members. *European Journal of Social Psychology, 25*, 509–530.

Haslam, S. A., Oakes, P. J., Turner, J. C., & McGarty, C. (1996). Social identity, self-categorization, and the perceived homogeneity of ingroups and outgroups: The interaction between social motivation and cognition. In R. M. Sorrentino, & E. T. Higgins (Eds.), *Handbook of motivation and cognition: Vol. 4. The interpersonal context* (pp. 182–222). New York: Guilford.

Haslam, S. A., & Turner, J. C. (1992). Context-dependent variation in social stereotyping: II. The relationship between frame of reference, self-categorization and accentuation. *European Journal of Social Psychology, 22*, 251–277.

Haslam, S. A., & Turner, J. C. (1995). Context-dependent variation in social stereotyping: III. Extremism as a self-categorical basis for polarized judgement. *European Journal of Social Psychology, 25*, 341–371.

Hewstone, M., & Brown, R. J. (Eds.). (1986). *Contact and conflict in intergroup encounters*. Oxford, England: Basil Blackwell.

Hogg, M. A. (1992). *The social psychology of group cohesiveness: From attraction to social identity*. Hemel Hempstead, England: Harvester Wheatsheaf.

Hogg, M. A., & Turner, J. C. (1987). Intergroup behaviour, self-stereotyping and the salience of social categories. *British Journal of Social Psychology, 26*, 325–340.

Hogg, M. A., Turner, J. C., & Davidson, B. (1990). Polarized norms and social frames of reference: A test of the self-categorization theory of group polarization. *Basic and Applied Social Psychology, 11*, 77–100.

Hollander, E. P. (1958). Conformity, status, and idiosyncrasy credit. *Psychological Review, 65*, 117–127.

Hollander, E. P. (1964). *Leaders, groups, and influence*. New York: Oxford University Press.

Hollander, E. P. (1993). Legitimacy, power, and influence: A perspective on relational features of leadership. In M. M. Chemers & R. Ayman (Eds.), *Leadership theory and research: Perspectives and directions* (pp. 29–47). Orlando, FL: Academic Press.

Hollander, E. P. (1995). Organizational leadership and followership. In P. Collett & A. Furnam (Eds.), *Social psychology at work* (pp. 69–87). London: Routledge.

House, R. J. (1971). A path-goal theory of leader effectiveness. *Administrative Science Quarterly, 16*, 321–339.

House, R. J., & Shamir, B. (1993). Toward the integration of transformational, charismatic, and visionary theories. In M. M. Chemers & R. Ayman (Eds.), *Leadership theory and research: Perspectives and directions* (pp. 81–107). Orlando, FL: Academic Press.

Howell, J. P., Dorfman, P. W., & Kerr, S. (1986). Moderator variables in leadership research. *Academy of Management Review, 11*, 88–102.

Jackson, S. E. (1992). Team composition in organizational settings: Issues in managing an increasingly diverse workforce. In S. Worchel, W. Wood, & J. A. Simpson (Eds.), *Group processes and productivity* (pp. 136–180). Newbury Park, CA: Sage.

Jackson, S. E., Brett, J. F., Sessa, V. I., Cooper, D. M., Julin, J. A., & Peyronnin, K. (1991). Some differences make a difference: Individual dissimilarity and group heterogeneity as correlates of recruitment, promotions and turnover. *Journal of Applied Psychology, 76*, 675–689.

Janis, I. (1972). *Victims of groupthink*. Boston: Houghton-Mifflin.

Johnson, D. W., & Johnson, F. P. (1991). *Joining together: Group theory and group skills*. Englewood Cliffs, NJ: Prentice-Hall.

Kerr, S., & Jermier, J. M. (1978). Substitutes for leadership: Their meaning and measurement. *Organizational Behavior and Human Performance, 22*, 375–403.

Kipnis, D. (1972). Does power corrupt? *Journal of Personality and Social Psychology, 24*, 33–41.

Lewin, K., Lippitt, R., & White, R. (1939). Patterns of aggressive behavior in experimentally created "social climates." *Journal of Social Psychology, 10*, 271–299.

Lord, R. G., Foti, R., & De Vader, C. L. (1984). A test of leadership categorization theory: Internal structure, information processing and leadership perceptions. *Organizational Behavior and Human Performance, 34*, 343–378.

Lord, R. G., Foti, R., & Phillips, J. S. (1982). A theory of leadership categorization. In J. G. Hunt, V. Sekaran & C. Schriesheim (Eds.), *Leadership: Beyond established views.* Carbondale, IL: South Illinois University Press.

Lord, R. G., & Maher, K. J. (1991). *Leadership and information processing: Linking perceptions and performance.* London: Unwin Hyman.

Lott, A. J., & Lott, B. E. (1965). Group cohesiveness as interpersonal attraction: A review of relationships with antecedent and consequent variables. *Psychological Bulletin, 64*, 259–309.

Mann, R. D. (1959). A review of the relationship between personality and performance in small groups. *Psychological Bulletin, 56*, 241–270.

McGarty, C., & Turner, J. C. (1992). The effects of categorization on social judgement. *British Journal of Social Psychology, 31*, 253–268.

McGarty, C., Turner, J. C., Hogg, M. A., David, B., & Wetherell, M. S. (1992). Group polarization as conformity to the prototypical group member. *British Journal of Social Psychology, 31*, 1–20.

Medin, D. L. (1989). Concepts and conceptual structure. *American Psychologist, 44*, 1469–1481.

Mullen, B., Anthony, T., Salas, E., & Driscoll, J. E. (1994). Group cohesiveness and quality of decision making: An integration of tests of the groupthink hypothesis. *Small Group Research, 25*, 189–204.

Mummendey, A., & Schreiber, H. J. (1984). Different just means better: Some obvious and some hidden pathways to ingroup favouritism. *British Journal of Social Psychology, 23*, 363–368.

Mummendey, A., & Simon, B. (1989). Better or just different? III: The impact of comparison dimension and relative group size upon intergroup discrimination. *British Journal of Social Psychology, 28*, 1–16.

Oakes, P. J. (1987). The salience of social categories. In J. C. Turner, M. A. Hogg, P. J. Oakes, S. D. Reicher, & M. S. Wetherell, *Rediscovering the social group: A self-categorization theory* (pp. 117–141). Oxford, England: Blackwell.

Oakes, P. J., Haslam, S. A., & Turner, J. C. (1994). *Stereotyping and social reality.* Oxford, England: Blackwell.

Oakes, P. J., Haslam, S. A., & Turner, J. C. (1998). The role of prototypicality in group influence and cohesion: Contextual variation in the graded structure of social categories. In S. Worchel, J. F. Morales, D. Páez, & J.-C. Deschamps (Eds.), *Social identity: International perspectives* (pp. 75–92). London: Sage.

Oakes, P. J., Turner, J. C., & Haslam, S. A. (1991). Perceiving people as group members: The role of fit in the salience of social categorizations. *British Journal of Social Psychology, 30*, 125–144.

Philips, J. S., & Lord, R. G. (1981). Causal attributions and perceptions of leadership. *Organizational Behavior and Human Performance, 28*, 143–163.

Pritchard, R. D. (1990). *Measuring and improving organizational productivity: A practical guide.* New York: Praeger.

Rabbie, J. M., & Bekkers, F. (1978). Threatened leadership and intergroup competition. *European Journal of Social Psychology, 8*, 9–20.

Reicher, S. (1987). Crowd behaviour as social action. In J. C. Turner, M. A. Hogg, P. J. Oakes, S. D. Reicher, & M. S. Wertherell, *Rediscovering the social group: A self-categorization theory* (pp. 171–202). Oxford, England: Blackwell.

Reicher, S., & Hopkins, N. (1996). Self-category constructions in political rhetoric: An analysis of Thatcher's and Kinnock's speeches concerning the British Miners' Strike (1984–1985). *European Journal of Social Psychology, 26*, 353–372.

Reicher, S., Spears, R., & Postmes, T. (1995). A social identity model of deindividuation phenomena. *European Review of Social Psychology, 6*, 161–198.

Ritchie, R. J., & Moses, J. L. (1983). Assessment center correlates of women's advancement into middle-management. *Journal of Applied Psychology, 68*, 227–231.

Rosch, E. (1978). Principles of categorization. In E. Rosch & B. B. Lloyd (Eds.), *Cognition and categorization* (pp. 28–49). Hillsdale, NJ: Lawrence Erlbaum Associates.

Rost, J. C. (1991). *Leadership for the twenty-first century*. Westport, CN: Praeger.

Smith, P. M. (1995). Leadership. In A. S. R. Manstead & M. R. C. Hewstone (Eds.), *The Blackwell dictionary of social psychology* (pp. 358–362). Oxford, England: Blackwell.

Spears, R., Oakes, P. J., Ellemers, N., & Haslam, S. A. (1997). *The social psychology of stereotyping and group life*. Oxford, England: Blackwell.

Tajfel, H. (1972). La catégorisation sociale (Social categorization). In S. Moscovici (Ed.), *Introduction à la psychologie sociale* (pp. 272–302). Paris: Larouse.

Tajfel, H. (1974). Social identity and intergroup behaviour. *Social Science Information, 13*, 65–93.

Tajfel, H. (1978). *Differentiation between social groups*. London: Academic Press.

Tajfel, H. (1979). Individuals and groups in social psychology. *British Journal of Social and Clinical Psychology, 18*, 183–190.

Tajfel, H. (1982). *Social identity and intergroup relations*. Cambridge: Cambridge University Press and Paris: Éditions de la Maison des Sciences de l'Homme.

Tajfel, H., Flament, C., Billig, M. G., & Bundy, R. F. (1971). Social categorization and intergroup behaviour. *European Journal of Social Psychology, 1*, 149–177.

Tajfel, H., & Turner, J. C. (1979). An integrative theory of intergroup conflict. In W. G. Austin & S. Worchel (Eds.), *The social psychology of intergroup relations* (pp. 33–47). Monterey, CA: Brooks/Cole.

Tajfel, H., & Turner, J. C. (1986). The social identity theory of intergroup behaviour. In S. Worchel & W. G. Austin (Eds.), *Psychology of intergroup relations* (2nd ed., pp. 7–24). Chicago: Nelson-Hall.

Turner, J. C. (1975). Social comparison and social identity: Some prospects for intergroup behaviour. *European Journal of Social Psychology, 5*, 5–34.

Turner, J. C. (1981). The experimental social psychology of intergroup behaviour. In J. C. Turner & H. Giles (Eds.), *Intergroup behaviour* (pp. 66–101). Oxford, England: Basil Blackwell.

Turner, J. C. (1982). Towards a cognitive redefinition of the social group. In H. Tajfel (Ed.), *Social identity and intergroup relations* (pp. 15–40). Cambridge, England: Cambridge University Press; Paris: Éditions de la Maison des Sciences de l'Homme.

Turner, J. C. (1984). Social identification and psychological group formation. In H. Tajfel (Ed.), *The social dimension: European developments in social psychology* (Vol. 2, pp. 518–538). Cambridge, England: Cambridge University Press and Paris: Éditions de la Maison des Sciences de l'Homme.

Turner, J. C. (1985). Social categorization and the self-concept: A social cognitive theory of group behaviour. In E. J. Lawler (Ed.), *Advances in group processes* (Vol. 2, pp. 77–122). Greenwich, CT: JAI.

Turner, J. C. (1987). The analysis of social influence. In J. C. Turner, M. A. Hogg, P. J. Oakes, S. D. Reicher, & M. S. Wetherell, *Rediscovering the social group: A self-categorization theory* (pp. 68–88). Oxford, England: Blackwell.

Turner, J. C. (1991). *Social influence*. Milton Keynes, England: Open University Press.

Turner, J. C., & Bourhis, R. Y. (1996). Social identity, interdependence and the social group: A reply to Rabbie et al. In W. P. Robinson (Ed.) *Social groups and identities: Developing the legacy of Henri Tajfel* (pp. 25–63). Oxford, England: Butterworth Heinemann.

Turner, J. C., Hogg, M. A., Oakes, P. J., Reicher, S. D., & Wetherell, M. S. (1987). *Rediscovering the social group: A self-categorization theory*. Oxford, England: Blackwell.

Turner, J. C., & Oakes, P. J. (1989). Self-categorization theory and social influence. In P. B. Paulus (Ed.), *The psychology of group influence* (2nd ed., pp. 233–275). Hillsdale, NJ: Lawrence Erlbaum Associates.

Turner, J. C., Oakes, P. J., Haslam, S. A., & McGarty, C. A. (1994). Self and collective: Cognition and social context. *Personality and Social Psychology Bulletin, 20,* 454–463.

von Cranach, M. (1986). Leadership as a function of group action. In C. F. Graumann & S. Moscovici (Eds.), *Changing conceptions of leadership* (pp. 115–134). New York: Springer-Verlag.

Weber, M. (1946). The sociology of charismatic authority. In H. H. Gerth & C. W. Milles (Eds.), *Max Weber: Essays in sociology* (pp. 245–252). New York: Oxford University Press. (Original work published 1921)

Worchel, S. (1994). You can go home again: Returning group research to the group context with an eye on developmental issues. *Small Group Research, 25,* 205–223.

Worchel, S., Coutant-Sassic, D., & Grossman, M. (1992). A developmental approach to group dynamics: A model and illustrative research. In S. Worchel, W. Wood, & J. A. Simpson (Eds.), *Group processes and productivity* (pp. 181–202). Newbury Park, CA: Sage.

Yukl, G. A. (1981). *Leadership in organizations*. Englewood Cliffs, NJ: Prentice-Hall.

Part II

SOCIAL AND MOTIVATIONAL PROCESSES

Chapter 3

Socialization in Organizations and Work Groups

Richard L. Moreland
John M. Levine
University of Pittsburgh

Socialization is a process of mutual adjustment that produces changes over time in the relationship between a person and a group. Because socialization occurs in groups of many kinds, it has been analyzed by scholars from many disciplines and professions (Bell & Price, 1975; Putallaz & Wasserman, 1990; Scott & Scott, 1989). Much of the best work, though, has been done by organizational psychologists. The purpose of this chapter is to offer a fresh perspective on that work by emphasizing the role of work groups in the socialization process. We begin with a brief review of recent theory and research on organizational socialization, focusing on the tactics used by organizations and their employees, and on commitment, the emotional bond that links organizations and employees to one another. Next, we make two surprising claims about organizational socialization, namely that it occurs largely in work groups, and that it is less important than work group socialization. These claims reflect clear evidence that much of what organizations and employees know about each other is learned in the context of work groups, and that work groups have a stronger influence than organizations on the behavior of most employees. Finally, we describe a model of group socialization (Moreland & Levine, 1982) that is relevant to work groups and could thus enhance many analyses of organizational socialization. Theoretical and empirical work on that model is reviewed, and some issues regarding the model's application to work groups is discussed.

ORGANIZATIONAL SOCIALIZATION:
A BRIEF REVIEW

Several good reviews of theory and research on organizational socialization are available (e.g., Anderson & Thomas, 1996; Ashford & Taylor, 1990;
Bauer, Morrison, & Callister, 1998; Fisher, 1986; Saks & Ashforth, 1997;
Wanous & Colella, 1989), so we focus here on three topics that seem especially important. First, what tactics do organizations use during the socialization process, and how successful are they at achieving their socialization
goals? Second, what tactics do new employees use during the socialization
process, and how successfully are their socialization goals achieved? Finally, what is commitment, how does it arise, and how does it affect employees' behavior?

Organizational Tactics

Many socialization tactics can be used by organizations. One way to study
such tactics is to consider the underlying strategies that they reflect. This
can be accomplished by first examining the relationships among socialization tactics and then considering their strategic implications. Several studies of this sort can be found (e.g., Allen & Meyer, 1990; Ashforth & Saks,
1996; Baker, 1995; Baker & Feldman, 1990; Black & Ashford, 1995; Jones,
1986; Mignerey, Rubin, & Gorden, 1995; Zahrly & Tosi, 1989). In this work,
descriptions by new employees of the socialization tactics used in their
organizations were analyzed using a set of dimensions proposed by Van
Maanen and Schein (1979; see also Van Maanen, 1978). Those dimensions
are collective versus individual, formal versus informal, sequential versus
random, fixed versus variable, serial versus disjunctive, and investiture versus divestiture. Collective tactics provide newcomers with shared experiences during socialization, whereas individual tactics allow socialization
experiences to vary from one newcomer to another. Formal tactics involve
structured training that occurs outside the workplace, whereas informal
tactics involve unstructured training that occurs while newcomers are on
the job. Sequential and fixed tactics, as opposed to random and variable
tactics, clarify for newcomers what steps socialization requires and how
long the process takes. Serial tactics use oldtimers to train newcomers for
familiar jobs, whereas disjunctive tactics force newcomers to learn about
unfamiliar jobs on their own. Finally, investiture tactics affirm newcomers
by suggesting that they are already valuable to the organization, whereas
divestiture tactics challenge newcomers by suggesting that their value
depends on completing the socialization process successfully.

    These dimensions are interdependent, and their relationships can be
informative. Jones (1986), for example, identified two clusters of social-

ization tactics that may reflect distinct organizational strategies. When *institutional tactics* (collective, formal, sequential, fixed, serial, and investiture) are used by an organization, newcomers are more likely to adopt a custodial role orientation, viewing socialization as a process requiring personal rather than organizational change (see Nicholson, 1984). But when an organization uses *individual tactics* (individual, informal, variable, random, disjunctive, and divestiture), newcomers are more likely to adopt an innovative role orientation, viewing socialization as a process that requires some organizational change as well. The available evidence confirms these role orientation effects and suggests that institutional tactics can also improve the organizational commitment and job attitudes of newcomers. However, these and other effects are often weak, depend on just a few tactics within each cluster, and fade over time. And there is little evidence that other important outcomes, such as job performance, absenteeism, or turnover, are affected by the use of institutional versus individual tactics.

A more direct way to study the tactics that organizations use during socialization is to focus on specific tactics and examine their effects. Much of this work involves four tactics: orientation sessions, training programs, mentoring, and information dissemination. In many organizations, special orientation sessions are held to welcome newcomers, educate them about the organization, and perhaps strengthen their organizational commitment. These are often formal, ritualistic events (Trice & Beyer, 1984), but they can be informal as well, and they need not be pleasant. Initiations are orientations of a sort, for example, and they can be traumatic (see Rohlen, 1973). Orientation sessions seem to be a common socialization tactic, yet employees do not view such sessions as helpful, nor is there much evidence for their benefits (see Louis, Posner, & Powell, 1983; Nelson & Quick, 1991; Posner & Powell, 1985; Saks, 1994; Wanous, 1993). And although there are good reasons to believe that initiating newcomers could be useful, perhaps by strengthening organizational commitment through the resolution of cognitive dissonance, the evidence is again weak. For example, Feldman (1977) asked hospital employees to recall events during socialization that they regarded as initiations into their jobs or their work groups. Employees who experienced initiations were no more likely than others to feel competent at their jobs or accepted by their work groups. There is even some evidence that stressful initiations can weaken commitment to a group (Lodewijkz & Syroit, 1997).

Training programs are designed primarily to help employees acquire or improve job skills, a goal that is often achieved (Grant, 1995; Guzzo, Jette, & Katzell, 1985). But as Feldman (1989) and others have noted, training can play a role in socialization as well, whether it is meant to or not. Training has some symbolic value—the resources spent on training send messages to newcomers about their potential value to an organization and can thus affect their organizational commitment. And newcom-

ers can learn much about their organization from the ways in which it
trains them. Is the training well organized? Who are the trainers? How
challenging is the training? What does the organization expect from
employees, and what happens if its expectations are not met? Finally,
when a training program succeeds, newcomers' job skills improve, so they
feel less anxious, more self-confident, and so on. These changes could
also affect the socialization process and its outcomes. How important are
training programs for socialization? Most organizations offer their employees no training at all, and employees who are trained seldom view that
experience as helpful (Louis et al., 1983; Nelson & Quick, 1991). However, some studies suggest that training can be a useful socialization tactic
(Saks, 1995, 1996; Tannenbaum, Mathieu, Salas, & Cannon-Bowers,
1991). Saks (1996), for example, asked new accountants from several companies how much training they received and how helpful it was to them.
Both of these variables had beneficial effects on such socialization outcomes as organizational commitment, job satisfaction, and turnover intentions. Training also helped newcomers to feel less anxious, which may
explain why it improved some of their other outcomes. Few of these effects
were strong, but they do show that training programs can be useful socialization tools.

Mentoring occurs when older employees (mentors) develop special
helping relationships with younger employees (protégés). Mentors can
help their protégés in many ways (Kram, 1988). For example, they can
provide training, reveal hidden aspects of an organization, interpret ambiguous work experiences, act as advocates or guardians, and offer sym-
pathy. Such help makes new employees more likely to succeed (see, for
example, Whitely & Coetsier, 1993), in part by improving their socialization. Although mentoring is a natural phenomenon, there are ways in
which it might be managed by organizations. When these management
attempts succeed, mentoring becomes a socialization tactic. For example,
an organization can encourage mentoring by educating employees about
its benefits, by providing models of successful mentor/protégé relationships, by rewarding mentors for their helpfulness, and so on (Kram,
1985). A more direct approach is to match protégés with mentors and
then try to regulate their relationships with one another. Guidelines for
mentoring programs can be found in several sources (e.g., Lawrie, 1987;
Phillips-Jones, 1983; Zey, 1985), along with descriptions of some actual
programs (e.g., Geiger-Dumond & Boyle, 1995). These programs raise
complex issues, such as who should participate, how protégés and mentors are best matched, what mentoring activities to prescribe, and how to
respond if mentoring relationships fail. If such issues are not resolved, a
mentoring program will be ineffective and may even do more harm than
good. Mentoring programs *can* succeed (Noe, 1988), of course, but a

revealing study by Chao, Walz, and Gardner (1992) suggested that informal mentoring relationships may be more helpful to newcomers than formal relationships that are created through mentoring programs (see also
Kizilos, 1990). In fact, doubts about the value of such programs have led
Kram (1985) and others to argue that most organizations should just
encourage mentoring, rather than trying to regulate it.

Finally, the dissemination of information to new employees is another
socialization tactic that can be used by organizations. Through newslet-
ters, bulletin boards, mailings (paper or electronic), manuals, and special
reports, organizations can distribute information of several kinds, including news, announcements of organizational policies and goals, descriptions of employee benefits or services, suggestions for improving job performance, and so on. Few researchers have studied the effects of such
information on newcomers (see Jablin, 1987), but the available evidence
is not encouraging. Jablin (1984), for example, found that new employees
in nursing homes wanted more information about their jobs than they
actually received. And even when organizations provide information to
newcomers, it may not be very helpful. Burke and Bolf (1986) asked
employees from several organizations to recall how valuable information
obtained from different sources was for learning their jobs. The information that employees received from their organizations (e.g., reports, manuals, public relations materials) was evaluated less positively than information from other sources, such as supervisors and coworkers. Similar
results were later reported by Ostroff and Kozlowski (1992) and Kramer
(1993a).

Several socialization tactics are thus available to organizations, but just
how successful are most organizations at achieving their socialization
goals? Research on the socialization strategies and tactics used by organizations indicates that their impact on new employees is weak. Other evidence also suggests that organizations are not socializing their employees
effectively. For example, Reichheld (1996) argued that years of downsizing have produced a loyalty crisis in many American corporations—
employees no longer feel very committed to the organizations for which
they work. Robinson and Rousseau (1994), in fact, showed that soon after
most employees are hired, they come to believe that the implicit contracts
governing their employment were violated. They lose trust in their organizations as a result and may decide to break such contracts themselves.
Finally, many organizations struggle to cope with high levels of turnover
among new employees (see Chao, 1988; Wanous, 1992), who may well mis-
behave before they leave by indulging in absenteeism, substance abuse,
sabotage, or theft (Crino, 1994; DuPont, 1989; Jones & Boye, 1994). An
organization can always modify its socialization tactics, of course, in an
effort to achieve better outcomes. Wanous (1993) and Kram (1985), for

example, have offered suggestions for improvements in orientation sessions and mentoring, respectively. But given the apparent difficulty of socializing new employees effectively, it may be wiser for most organizations to emphasize recruiting instead (Chatman, 1991; Schneider, Goldstein, & Smith, 1995; see also Mulford, Klonglan, Beal, & Bohlen, 1968; Mulford, Klonglan, & Warren, 1972), searching for workers who already have whatever qualities are desired. Recent work on how to identify workers whose experiences or personalities incline them to become more committed to organizations reflects this alternative (see, for example, James & Cropanzano, 1994; Lee, Ashford, Walsh, & Mowday, 1992; Mael & Ashforth, 1995).

Tactics of New Employees

Because new employees tend to be younger, less experienced, and lower in status than other workers, one might assume that they have little influence on the socialization process, but that would be a mistake (see Bell & Staw, 1989; Jablin, 1984). In fact, newcomers can influence socialization in both unintentional and intentional ways (see Levine, Moreland, & Choi, in press). Unintentional influence occurs when organizations change their socialization tactics to accommodate newcomers of different types, or when different types of newcomers respond to the same socialization tactics in distinct ways. Effects of both kinds could involve many personal characteristics (e.g., sex, prior job experience, status), but most researchers have focused on newcomers' personalities. Self-efficacy, for instance, can apparently influence socialization by shaping the role orientations of newcomers (Brief & Aldag, 1981; Jones, 1986; Saks, 1994; 1995). Jones found that the use of institutional tactics by organizations was more likely to produce custodial role orientations among newcomers with lower levels of self-efficacy. Similarly, Saks (1994) found that training had stronger effects on newcomers' coping abilities, job performance, and turnover intentions when their levels of self-efficacy were lower. Other personality characteristics, such as a tolerance for ambiguity (Ashford & Cummings, 1985; Reichers, 1987) or self-monitoring (Snyder, 1995), might influence the socialization process as well. For example, newcomers with higher self-monitoring levels may know more about what organizations want from them and may be more willing or able to provide it (cf. Zaccaro, Foti, & Kenny, 1991).

New employees can also influence the socialization process intentionally through their own tactics. Several complex analyses of these socialization tactics can be found (Ashford & Taylor, 1990; Comer, 1991; Feldman & Brett, 1983; Miller & Jablin, 1991), but for our purposes, a simple summary may be sufficient—newcomers can engage in surveillance or feedback seeking, encourage mentoring by oldtimers, or collaborate with one another.

A careful surveillance of people and events in an organization can be very helpful to new employees (see Gundry & Rousseau, 1994). Newcomers who watch what happens to other workers, for example, can often benefit from observational learning, acquiring new behaviors and accepting those most likely to be rewarded. Anyone can serve as a model for newcomers, but they tend to observe and imitate people who appear competent or successful (Weiss, 1977). Surveillance also allows for social comparison, especially with other newcomers who seem particularly successful (upward comparisons) or unsuccessful (downward comparisons). Either type of comparison can be encouraging or discouraging, depending on the target person. Upward comparisons are encouraging, and downward comparisons are discouraging, if newcomers identify with that person and thus believe that they could experience similar outcomes. But upward and downward comparisons have the opposite effects if newcomers do not identify with the target person. Finally, surveillance helps newcomers to develop and test mental models of the workplace (see Cannon-Bowers, Tannenbaum, Salas, & Volpe, 1995; Louis, 1980). As those models improve, they generate more accurate predictions about life at work, building newcomers' confidence and helping them adjust to their jobs.

Surveillance is relatively easy and tends to be covert, so that newcomers can hide their lack of knowledge about the organization from others. A more dangerous tactic, but one that often provides more information, is feedback seeking. Newcomers can and do ask a variety of questions during socialization. Miller and Jablin (1991) asserted that newcomers seek answers to three types of questions, namely referent (*What does it take to succeed?*), appraisal (*Am I successful?*), and relational (*Am I accepted?*). Unfortunately, there may be costs associated with asking these and other questions (Ashford & Cummings, 1983). For example, Morrison and Bies (1991) suggested that the mere act of asking appraisal questions can affect how newcomers are viewed by others. Under some conditions, they may seem ignorant and insecure, whereas under other conditions, they may seem conscientious and eager to improve. And of course, the answers to appraisal questions are important as well. If newcomers receive negative feedback, for example, their reputations can be damaged, along with their self-esteem. Information, in other words, usually comes at a price. Miller and Jablin described some ways in which newcomers can make feedback seeking less costly. These include asking questions indirectly, starting and/or joining casual conversations about work (which might produce answers to questions not yet asked), and talking with outsiders who are familiar with the organization (e.g., customers, suppliers, union officials).

As noted earlier, mentoring can also help new employees to succeed, but some workers (especially women and minorities) may have trouble finding older colleagues who are willing and able to become their mentors. That is one reason why many organizations have tried to develop formal mentoring programs. Is there anything that newcomers could do to attract mentors on their own? If so, then mentoring could become a socialization tactic for them. Unfortunately, the development of mentoring relationships is rarely studied, so very little is known about this tactic. Kram (1983) interviewed mentors and protégés in a public utility firm and found that their relationships often began when young workers fantasized about working closely with older colleagues whom they admired and respected. If opportunities for such collaboration later arose, a mentoring relationship often developed, especially when the senior person seemed interested in his or her partner and was asked for advice or aid by that person. Additional insights into the development of mentoring relationships may come from work on leader–member exchange theory (see Dienesch & Liden, 1986; Scandura & Schriesheim, 1994). Leaders can relate to followers in different ways—"outgroup" relationships are much less collegial than "ingroup" relationships, which resemble mentoring relationships. Several studies have shown that leaders tend to develop ingroup relationships with followers who seem competent, similar to themselves, and likable (Deluga & Perry, 1994; Dockery & Steiner, 1990; Liden, Wayne, & Stilwell, 1993; Wayne & Ferris, 1990; see also Tepper, 1995). In a study of employees in several organizations, for example, Deluga and Perry found that better quality relationships arose between supervisors and their subordinates when the latter workers performed their jobs well and used various ingratiation tactics, such as flattering supervisors and agreeing with their opinions. These findings suggest that new employees may indeed use mentoring as a socialization tactic, if older colleagues who would make good mentors are available and newcomers can impress them favorably.

Finally, when several new employees enter an organization at about the same time, they can collaborate with one another to make the socialization process easier. Newcomers may, for example, offer one another information, advice, encouragement, aid, and protection. In these and other ways, they can become "mentors" for one another, especially when regular mentors are unavailable (Kram & Isabella, 1985; Ostroff & Kozlowski, 1993). Collaboration is not inevitable—newcomers who believe they are competing for acceptance by oldtimers may treat one another harshly. But more often, newcomers seem willing to help each other, perhaps because the fact that they are all "new" is so salient (see Moreland, 1985). When newcomers are similar to one another, spend much time together, and are treated alike by oldtimers, they could form a group of their own, embedded in the organization (Feldman, 1989). Such a group can be valuable, because its members are especially likely to help one another (Dornbusch, 1955). But a group of newcomers might also develop its own special culture, which may be incongruent with that of the organization and thus interfere with the socialization process. In fact, if a group of newcomers becomes cohesive and its members are sufficiently disenchanted with the organization, they may even work together to demand that it change (see Dunham & Barrett, 1996).

New employees, like the organizations for which they work, thus have access to several socialization tactics, but how successful are most newcomers at achieving their socialization goals? The evidence we mentioned earlier, indicating that turnover and misbehavior among employees are serious problems in many organizations, implies that newcomers often fail to adjust to work. The socialization tactics used by newcomers may contribute to this problem—research suggests that those tactics are seldom effective. Ostroff and Kozlowski (1992), for example, found that although surveillance (observing others and experimentation) was a popular tactic among newcomers, its use was unrelated to their organizational commitment, job satisfaction, work adjustment, or turnover intentions. Moreover, newcomers who used that tactic experienced greater stress than those who did not. Many researchers have also studied how feedback seeking affects newcomers' socialization outcomes. Although some studies suggest that this tactic is beneficial (Morrison, 1993a, 1993b), its effects are rather weak, and other studies show no benefits at all (Ashford & Black, 1996; Brett, Feldman, & Weingart, 1990; Mignery et al., 1995). Kramer (1993a) actually found that the adjustment of transferred employees improved only when they received feedback that was unsolicited! Mentoring is obviously useful, but only for those few newcomers lucky enough to become protégés. There is little evidence as yet that mentoring can be tactical—even competent and likable newcomers may have difficulty establishing mentoring relationships. Finally, collaboration among newcomers can be problematic as well. Newcomers may have limited contact with one another, for example, or believe that it is better to compete rather than cooperate. Even when collaboration is possible, it may be unwise for newcomers to rely on each other for advice or information, because they usually know far less than other employees about the organization. In fact, when researchers ask newcomers to evaluate their socialization experiences, collaboration is not described as very helpful (Louis et al., 1983; Nelson & Quick, 1991; see also Settoon & Adkins, 1997).

Commitment

Commitment plays a vital role in socialization because it links organizations to employees emotionally and thus provides the conduit through which influence flows in either direction. Perhaps for that reason, commitment has become a very popular topic, producing far more theoretical and empirical work than we can consider here. Guest (1992), Mathieu and

Zajac (1990), Morrow (1993), and Randall (1990) offer summaries of that work. Commitment is generally regarded as a characteristic of employees rather than organizations; researchers study how employees feel about their organizations, not how organizations feel about their employees. Much of the interest in commitment also appears to be pragmatic; researchers study commitment because of its potential value to organizations. When employees feel more committed to an organization, they are more likely to act in ways that could help that organization achieve its goals. Evidence suggests that employee commitment is indeed an asset for organizations because it is related to several desirable outcomes, such as higher levels of motivation, satisfaction, and prosocial behavior; better job performance; and less tardiness, absenteeism, and turnover. Two caveats regarding this evidence should be noted, however. First, commitment has much weaker effects on some outcomes (e.g., job performance) than on others (e.g., satisfaction), and its effects often seem inconsistent, varying from one setting to another (see Randall, Fedor, & Longenecker, 1990). Second, commitment is more complex than it once appeared. It is now clear that there are different components (dimensions) of organizational commitment, that someone could be committed to many groups in and around an organization, and that commitment to an organization can change in important ways over time. Each of these discoveries deserves some discussion.

Early analyses of commitment (see Mowday, Steers, & Porter, 1979) implied that it was a unidimensional construct, but most theorists now see it as multidimensional. O'Reilly and Chatman (1986), for example, argued that compliance, identification, and internalization are three bases for the attachment of employees to organizations. Compliance involves a desire for the extrinsic rewards of employment, identification involves a desire to affiliate with the organization and other employees, and internalization involves congruence between personal and organizational values. There is some evidence that these are indeed distinct aspects of commitment (see Harris, Hirschfeld, Feild, & Mossholder, 1993), although identification and internalization can be difficult to distinguish. These three aspects of commitment do seem to have different antecedents and consequences as well. Caldwell, Chatman, and O'Reilly (1990), for example, found that identification and internalization reflect rigorous recruitment and selection procedures and value systems in organizations, whereas compliance reflects strong career and reward systems. And the effects of identification and internalization on such employee outcomes as job satisfaction, prosocial behavior, and turnover are more positive than the effects of compliance on those same outcomes (Becker, 1992; Becker, Randall, & Riegel, 1995; Harris et al., 1993). Another analysis, by Meyer and Allen (1991), distinguished among affective, continuance, and normative commitment. Affective commitment involves emotional attachment to, identification with, and involvement in an organization. Continuance commitment involves the perceived costs of leaving an organization. Normative commitment involves feelings of obligation to stay in an organization. There is evidence that these three aspects of commitment are also distinct (Dunham, Grube, & Castaneda, 1994; Hackett, Bycio, & Hausdorf, 1994; Meyer, Allen, & Gellatly, 1990) and that they have separate antecedents and consequences as well (Meyer, Bobocel, & Allen, 1991; Meyer, Paunonen, Gellatly, Goffin, & Jackson, 1989; Randall et al., 1990). For example, affective commitment reflects positive work experiences, continuance commitment reflects investments (e.g., pension contributions) or employment alternatives, and normative commitment reflects personal values (e.g., loyalty). Job performance relates positively to affective commitment and negatively to continuance commitment, whereas prosocial behavior relates positively to both affective and normative commitment, but not to continuance commitment.

Although Meyer and Allen's (1991) analysis of commitment has generated more research than O'Reilly and Chatman's (1986) analysis, it would be difficult to choose which approach is "best" at this point. Each approach has its critics (see Jaros, Jermier, Koehler, & Sincich, 1993; Vandenberg, Self, & Seo, 1994), and there are several other analyses of commitment that also seem worthy of consideration. For example, some analysts view commitment as a set of positive employee behaviors that reflect efforts to cope with the decision to work for one organization rather than another (see Salancik, 1977). This approach, based loosely on cognitive dissonance theory, suggests that commitment should be stronger when decisions about jobs are made publicly and voluntarily and seem irrevocable. These factors do appear to influence commitment in these ways (Kline & Peters, 1991). In contrast, Rusbult and her colleagues analyzed commitment from the perspective of social exchange theory. According to their approach, commitment to an organization is stronger when work satisfaction is high (employment generates more rewards than costs), employment alternatives are unattractive, and large investments have been made. Investments are resources that an employee could not recover if he or she left the organization; they may be intrinsic to work (e.g., time and energy spent on the job) or extrinsic (e.g., friendships with other employees). Evidence for this analysis of commitment can also be found (Farrell & Rusbult, 1981; Rusbult & Farrell, 1983; Rusbult, Farrell, Rogers, & Mainous, 1988). Finally, Ashforth and Mael (1989; see also Dutton, Dukerich, & Harquail, 1994) suggested that organizational identification may be more important than commitment for predicting many employee outcomes. Their analysis, drawn from social identity and self-categorization theory, emphasizes cognitive rather than emotional processes, especially the tendency for some employees to incorporate distinctive characteristics of organizations into their self-concepts. Research exploring the causes and effects of organizational identification has produced intriguing results (see Mael & Ashforth, 1995; Mael & Tetrick, 1992).

The discovery that commitment to an organization can take different forms, each with its own effects on employees' outcomes, is clearly important. Another discovery that may be just as important had its origins in a paper by Reichers (1985), who argued that multiple commitments can affect the outcomes of many employees. Employees may feel committed not only to the organization where they work, but also to other entities in and around that organization, such as work groups, supervisors, top management, clients, unions, friends or family members, and so on. A particular outcome, such as turnover, can thus depend not only on organizational commitment, but also on these other commitments. This suggests a need to develop *commitment profiles* for employees, so that better predictions can be made about their outcomes. Becker and his colleagues created such profiles and used them successfully in a series of studies (Becker, 1992; Becker & Billings, 1993; Becker, Billings, Eveleth, & Gilbert, 1996; Becker et al., 1995). Becker (1992), for example, found that commitments to work groups, supervisors, and top management were related to a variety of employee outcomes, including job satisfaction, prosocial behavior, and interest in quitting, even after organizational commitment was taken into account. The existence of multiple commitments also suggests a need to explore the ways in which they are related to one another. Reichers (1986) noted that such commitments can create both psychological and social conflicts for employees and that work outcomes may well depend on how those conflicts are resolved. The complex relationships among commitments to organizations and other entities have been studied recently by some researchers (e.g., Hunt & Morgan, 1994; Yoon, Baker, & Ko, 1994). We will discuss that work later, as it applies to the feelings of employees about organizations versus work groups.

Finally, it is essential to realize that commitment changes in important ways over time. This discovery may seem prosaic at first, because an employee's commitment is probably always rising or falling in response to events at work. But consider how complex changes in commitment might become in the context of the other discoveries just discussed. Over time, different aspects of commitment could change independently, some rising and others falling (Allen & Meyer, 1993). In fact, changes could even occur in the whole structure of commitment, making it difficult to compare an employee's feelings about an organization at different points in his or her career (see Meyer et al., 1990; Vandenberg & Self, 1993). Similarly, commitments to different entities could change independently (Gregersen, 1993), and the number or kinds of entities to which someone feels committed could change too, altering the relative impact of that person's organizational commitment on various work outcomes. The implications of these and other changes for socialization are just beginning to be explored, but they seem important.

SOCIALIZATION IN WORK GROUPS

As this brief review suggests, much has been learned about organizational socialization, especially in recent years. This progress reflects a general willingness among researchers to acknowledge the problems apparent in earlier work and then modify their methodologies in ways that help to solve those problems. For example, a common feature of earlier work on organizational socialization was a narrow *temporal perspective* that led most researchers to focus on the entry experiences of new employees. These experiences are important, of course, but they are only part of a larger socialization process and thus should be analyzed in broader and more complex ways. Fortunately, this problem has become less serious as more longitudinal studies of organizational socialization are performed. Several examples of such studies can now be found (e.g., Bauer & Green, 1994; Nelson, Quick, & Eakin, 1988; Nelson & Sutton, 1990; Settoon & Adkins, 1997; Vandenberg & Self, 1993), and their results provide insights into the socialization process. Another problematic feature of earlier work on organizational socialization was a narrow *social perspective* that led most researchers to study how organizations influence new employees, rather than how new employees try to influence their organizations. But this problem has also become less serious, as more researchers study newcomers' efforts to control the socialization process (e.g., Ashford & Black, 1996; Fagenson, 1988; Wanous, 1989), and more theorists analyze ways in which that process can change work groups and organizations (see Feldman, 1994; Levine & Moreland, 1985; Levine et al., in press; Sutton & Louis, 1987).

Despite these and other improvements, organizational socialization research still suffers from several problems. An especially serious problem, in our opinion, is that the *contexts* in which such socialization occurs are ignored by many researchers. In particular, there is too little work on the important role that small work groups (formal or informal) can play in the socialization process (Anderson & Thomas, 1996). Although some theorists (e.g., Feldman, 1981, 1989; Van Maanen & Schein, 1979) have discussed that role, their remarks have not led to much research. We would like to make two claims about organizational socialization, claims that may seem surprising at first, but that are supported by considerable evidence. First, we believe that the socialization process occurs primarily in work groups, which can control what and how organizations and employees learn about one another. Second, we believe that work group socialization has a stronger impact than organizational socialization on the behavior of most employees.

Work Groups as Contexts for Organizational Socialization

Where does organizational socialization occur? Research on the socialization process is often decontextualized—contexts are either ignored or are assumed to have trivial effects. Organizations and their employees seem to influence one another directly in such research, as if each worker were involved in a close, personal relationship with his or her organization. But in most organizations, this is simply impossible. Instead, the relationships between an organization and its employees are usually more distant and impersonal. Such relationships can thus be shaped by various contextual factors. Small work groups, formal and informal, seem especially important in this regard. In fact, much evidence suggests that the process of organizational socialization occurs primarily within such groups.

A series of studies by Ancona and her colleagues (Ancona, 1990; Ancona & Caldwell, 1988, 1992) provide some evidence relevant to this claim. These studies investigate how work groups try to manage the flow of information and resources across their boundaries with other groups and individuals from the same organization. Boundary management can be accomplished in various ways, but many groups develop special activities and roles for this purpose. In a study of new product development teams, for example, Ancona and Caldwell (1988) found that *scout, ambassador, sentry,* and *guard activities* occurred more often in more successful teams and that workers from those teams were more likely to play *immigrant, captive,* and *emigrant* roles. Scouts gathered information for a group about the organization in which it operated, whereas ambassadors provided (favorable) information about the group to that organization. Sentries and guards controlled both the amount and type of information that entered or left a group, respectively. Finally, both immigrants and captives were employees from other parts of the organization who were brought into the group to reduce levels of uncertainty or dependence, whereas emigrants were employees sent out of the group to work elsewhere in the organization for similar reasons. These and other efforts by work groups to manage their boundaries (see also Sundstrom, deMeuse, & Futrell, 1990) have important implications for organizational socialization. To some extent, every group can control what the organization learns about an employee and what he or she learns about the organization by regulating the person's contacts with workers outside the group and restricting what information the person and the organization receive about each other (Feldman, 1981).

Another set of relevant findings comes from research on social information processing theory (see Salancik & Pfeffer, 1978; Zalesny & Ford, 1990). According to that theory, an employee's opinion about a job is often influenced by the opinions of his or her coworkers. Such influence can be direct, as when one group member persuades another to share his or her opinion about a job, or more indirect, as when someone in the group calls attention to specific job characteristics, offers explanations for events at work, reminds everyone about past events or generates expectations for future events, and so forth. It would not be surprising if employees' opinions about organizations were affected in similar ways. Organizations can be difficult to understand, making employees (especially newcomers) susceptible to social influence as they search for meaning in their work experiences (Louis, 1980). Even when work groups cannot control the flow of information across their boundaries, they can still alter the interpretation of that information and thereby influence the socialization process (Feldman, 1981). Messages from an organization to its employees, efforts to create new organizational programs or practices, and even evaluations of an organization by outsiders can thus vary considerably in their meaning or importance for employees in different work groups. Consider, for example, research by Fulk and her colleagues (Fulk, 1993; Schmitz & Fulk, 1991) on reactions to new communication technologies. After surveying scientists and engineers from several organizations, Fulk (1993) found that work group memberships were powerful predictors of attitudes and behavior toward electronic mail. Similar results involving other aspects of organizational life can be found in studies by Baba (1995) and Rentsch (1990).

Finally, there is good evidence that most of the tactics used by organizations and their employees during the socialization process depend on work groups. In some organizations, socialization is neglected, forcing employees to acquire whatever information they may need from other sources, such as coworkers or outsiders (Chao, 1988). And many organizations, using the socialization tactics described earlier, provide employees with information that is not very useful, because it is irrelevant, vague, or erroneous (Comer, 1991; Darrah, 1994; Dirsmith & Covaleski, 1985). Employees in such organizations must again depend on other sources, such as coworkers, for the information that they need. Organizational socialization tactics *can* provide employees with useful information, of course, but that information is usually delivered by supervisors and coworkers during work group interactions. Many new employees, for example, undergo work group initiations designed to test their commitment to those groups (see Vaught & Smith, 1980). And training in most organizations is rather informal, occurring while new employees are working at their jobs (Moreland, Argote, & Krishnan, 1998). Mentoring usually involves efforts by supervisors to help new employees who work for them (Kram, 1988), and information dissemination is often "aided" by social networks among employees (Noon & Delbridge, 1993). The socialization tactics used by new employees, including surveillance, feedback seeking, mentoring, and collaboration, also tend to occur in work groups, because they often involve supervisors or coworkers. Several researchers have surveyed new employees about their socialization experiences to discover which experiences were most helpful (Burke & Bolf, 1986; Comer, 1991; Louis et al., 1983; Nelson & Quick, 1991; Ostroff & Kozlowski, 1992, 1993). A very common finding in such research is that interactions with supervisors and coworkers are more helpful than experiences involving the organization as a whole. Many other studies (e.g., Chatman, 1991; Dansky, 1996; George & Bettenhausen, 1990; Kram & Isabella, 1985; Kramer,1993a; 1993b; Morrison, 1993b) also show that coworkers are an integral part of the socialization process. Taken altogether, this work suggests that organizational socialization takes place largely in work groups.

Work Group Socialization Is the Key

An organization can be viewed as a collection of allied work groups whose activities and outcomes are interdependent. This perspective reveals an important aspect of organizational socialization, namely that it can involve the passage of an employee through several groups, from the organization itself to the various work groups (formal and informal) that it contains. In a *holographic* organization (Albert & Whetten, 1985), work groups resemble one another because they embody the organization's central features, so socialization is relatively simple. An employee can relate to different groups (and they can relate to that person) in similar ways. But in an *ideographic* organization, work groups tend to be more distinctive, making socialization more complex. Some theorists believe every work group is unique (see Levine & Moreland, 1991, 1999), but a more common claim is that the work groups in most organizations can be sorted into clusters or *subcultures*, each with a different approach to organizational life. Several analyses of organizational subcultures can be found (see Johns & Nicholson, 1982; Louis, 1983; Van Maanen & Barley, 1985), focusing on why they develop and how they affect organizations and employees. And several studies of organizational subcultures (e.g., Baba, 1995; Fulk, 1993; Gregory, 1983; Rentsch, 1980; Sackman, 1992) offer clear evidence for their existence and importance. Baba, for example, studied how employees in a large manufacturing corporation reacted to proposed changes in procedures for developing new products. Those reactions varied from one work group to another, and much of that variability reflected the "ecological zones" in which groups operated. Adaptations to local operating conditions apparently led groups from each zone to interpret the new procedures differently and to react to them accordingly.

All of this suggests that organizational socialization and work group socialization can be distinct processes for many employees. While organizations and employees are adjusting to one another, analogous adjustments are also occurring in work groups. This raises an interesting question: Which process is more important? Work group socialization seems more important to us for two related reasons. First, employees are generally more committed to their work groups than they are to their organizations. Second, work groups often have more influence on employees than do organizations. So, if the goal of studying socialization in organizations is to predict and/or control how employees think, feel, and act, then work groups and their members clearly deserve more attention.

Are employees really more committed to their work groups than to their organizations? There are several good reasons to suspect that work group commitment is stronger. Much of an employee's time, especially in this era of teamwork (see Lawler, Mohrman, & Ledford, 1992), is spent in work groups whose members become familiar and attractive as a result (Moreland & Beach, 1992). And in many organizations, employee compensation systems now take work group performance into account, making outcome dependence among group members a salient issue. Work groups are also more likely than organizations to satisfy the psychological needs of employees. These include the need to belong (Baumeister & Leary, 1995; see also Riordan & Griffeth, 1995), the need to be distinctive (Brewer, 1993), and the need to exert control (Lawler, 1992). Lawler, for example, noted that people typically have more control over group than organizational events, so they often feel more attached to groups than to organizations. Finally, organizational socialization can be stressful (Katz, 1985; Louis, 1980; Nelson, 1987), and coworkers, especially work group members, are an important source of encouragement, advice, and aid for employees who seek social support (Nelson et al., 1988; see also Nelson, Quick, & Joplin, 1991). We focused here on employees' commitment to work groups versus organizations, but work groups are probably more committed than organizations to employees as well, for many of the same reasons.

Few researchers have measured how committed employees are to both work groups *and* organizations, but the available evidence suggests that work group commitment is stronger. Zaccaro and Dobbins (1989), for example, found that group commitment was stronger than organizational commitment among college students in a military training program. Becker (1992) studied the employees of a military supply company, measuring their commitments (both levels and types) to the organization, its top management, and their supervisors and work groups. Commitment to work groups was stronger than commitment to supervisors, top management, or the organization. In a similar study of hospital workers, Gregersen (1993) found that their commitment to customers and coworkers was stronger than their commitment to supervisors, top management, or the organization. Finally, Barker and Tompkins (1994) found that employees in a small manufacturing organization were more committed to their work groups (self-managed teams) than to the organization as a whole.

More research of this sort is clearly needed, especially concerning whether different *types* of commitment link employees to work groups and organizations. A related issue is how work group and organizational commitment are related to one another. Commitment to a work group could strengthen or weaken an employee's commitment to the organization in which that group is embedded. Or work group and organizational commitment could be unrelated, with distinct causes and effects. The available evidence, although complex and often difficult to interpret, suggests that work group and organizational commitment are indeed independent in many settings (see Becker & Billings, 1993; Hunt & Morgan, 1994; Mathieu, 1991; Meyer & Allen, 1988; Randall & Cote, 1991; Wright, 1990; Yoon et al., 1994; Zaccaro & Dobbins, 1989; see also Mathieu & Zajac, 1990; Reichers, 1986). Apparently, commitment to work groups has little impact on the organizational commitment of most employees and vice versa.

Are employees really more influenced by their work groups than by their organizations? The fact that work group commitment is often stronger than organizational commitment is one reason to suspect that they are. Another reason is that coworkers, because they have more contact with an employee than anyone else in the organization, are more capable of monitoring that person's behavior and taking corrective action when necessary. Finally, some theorists (Ashforth & Mael, 1989; Feldman, 1981; Fisher, 1986; Katz, 1985; see also Feldman, 1976; Ostroff & Kozlowski, 1992) argue that adjusting to work groups is an early, critical step in organizational socialization. There is much to learn about every work group (see Cannon-Bowers et al., 1995; Chao, O'Leary-Kelly, Wolf, Klein, & Gardner, 1994; Levine & Moreland, 1991, 1999), and employees who neglect this task are often rejected by coworkers. Regardless of how well they relate to the organization as a whole, such employees are thus less likely to succeed at their jobs. Once again, we focused here on how employees are influenced by work groups versus organizations, but it seems likely that employees also have more influence on work groups than they do on organizations.

Many studies indicate that work groups indeed have more influence on employees than do organizations. These studies can be sorted into two categories. The first category contains studies showing that employees from different work groups in the same organization often think, feel, and act in distinct ways. Some of the studies cited earlier on social information processing and organizational subcultures belong in this category, along with studies of the differences among work groups in such employee behaviors as job performance (George & Bettenhausen, 1990; Joyce &

Slocum, 1984); prosocial behavior (Becker et al., 1995; George, 1990; George & Bettenhausen, 1990; see also Brief & Motowidlo, 1986); tardiness (Becker et al., 1995); and absenteeism (George, 1990; Markham & McKee, 1995; see also Johns & Nicholson, 1982; Nicholson & Johns, 1985). The second category contains studies showing that work group norms are good predictors of employee behaviors (e.g., Baratta & McManus, 1992; Blau, 1995; Kidwell, Mossholder, & Bennett, 1997; Lusch, Boyt, & Schuler, 1996; Martocchio, 1994; Mathieu & Kohler, 1990). In a study of public transit authority drivers, for example, Mathieu and Kohler found that the average levels of work group absenteeism were related to individual absenteeism levels, even after demographic characteristics, prior absenteeism records, job involvement and satisfaction, and organizational commitment were taken into account. More dramatic evidence for the power of work groups could be found in situations where organizations and groups make conflicting demands on employees (see Bearman, 1991; Roethlisberger & Dickson, 1939). When employees choose to act in ways that please their coworkers, but displease the organization, the importance of work group socialization becomes quite clear. Of course, work groups are not omnipotent, and some employees may be less sensitive than others to their influence. These include marginal group members, who are not strongly committed to their groups, and employees with experience in several groups, who often have a more "cosmopolitan" perspective on their work.

A MODEL OF GROUP SOCIALIZATION

We have made two claims about organizational socialization, namely that it occurs largely in work groups and that it is less important than work group socialization for employees. If these claims are correct, then much of the work on organizational socialization is misguided because it has ignored the critical role of work groups in the socialization process. Perhaps that is why so much research on organizational socialization has produced results that seem weak or inconsistent. A better understanding of the socialization process may thus require a familiarity with theory and research on small groups (Feldman, 1989). A general model of group socialization would be especially helpful; fortunately, one is already available.

We have developed a model (Moreland & Levine, 1982) that both describes and explains the process of group socialization. In that model, the relationship between a group and an individual is assumed to change in systematic ways over time, and both parties are viewed as potential influence agents. The model applies best to small, autonomous, and voluntary groups whose members interact regularly, are behaviorally interdependent, have feelings for each other, and share a common perspective on the world. Groups of many kinds, including work groups, sports teams, self-help groups, or cults, can thus be analyzed using the model.

Basic Processes

Our model is built around three psychological processes—*evaluation, commitment*, and *role transition*. Evaluation involves attempts by the group and the individual to assess and maximize one another's rewardingness. Evaluation produces feelings of commitment, which rise and fall over time. When commitment reaches a critical level (decision criterion), a role transition occurs. The relationship between the group and the individual is transformed, and both parties begin to evaluate one another again, often in different ways than before. Thus, a cycle of socialization activity is created, one that propels the individual through the group.

For the group, evaluation involves assessing individual contributions to the achievement of group goals. This includes identifying the goals to which a person can contribute and the behavioral dimensions on which such contributions will be measured, developing normative expectations for each of those dimensions, and finally comparing the person's expected and actual behavior. If someone fails to meet a group's expectations, attempts may be made to modify his or her behavior. A similar evaluation process is carried out by the individual, who focuses on group contributions to the satisfaction of personal needs. Through their mutual evaluations, both the group and the individual develop a general sense of the rewardingness of their relationship.

Evaluations are not limited to the present. The group and the individual may also recall how rewarding their relationship was in the past and speculate about how rewarding it will be in the future. Evaluations can extend to alternative relationships (actual or potential) as well—other individuals are evaluated by the group, and other groups are evaluated by the individual. All of these evaluations can influence commitment through three comparisons. For either the group or the individual, commitment is stronger to the extent that (a) their past relationship was more rewarding than other relationships in which they were or could have been involved; (b) their present relationship is more rewarding than other relationships in which they are or could be involved; and (c) their future relationship is expected to be more rewarding than other relationships in which they will or can be involved. A more detailed analysis of how these three comparisons combine to produce an overall feeling of commitment can be found in Moreland and Levine (1982). Our approach to commitment is simpler than those of many organizational psychologists (whose work we reviewed earlier) because we have not distinguished among different types of commitment. But simplicity is often a virtue, and our approach is flexible enough to capture (as rewards or costs of group membership) most of the sources of commitment identified by organizational psychologists. A more detailed analysis of these matters can also be found in Moreland and Levine (1982).

Commitment has important consequences for both the group and the individual. When a group is strongly committed to an individual, it is likely to accept that person's needs, work hard to satisfy them, feel warmly toward the person, and try to gain (or retain) the person as a member. And when an individual is strongly committed to a group, he or she is likely to accept that group's goals, work hard to achieve them, feel warmly toward the group, and try to gain or maintain membership. Problems can arise if commitment levels diverge. Such divergence occurs when the group's commitment to the individual grows stronger than his or her commitment to the group, or vice versa. Because of these problems, each party may monitor the other's commitment (see Eisenberger, Fasolo, & Davis-LaMastro, 1990; Shore & Wayne, 1993) and respond to any divergence by changing its own commitment or trying to change the commitment of its partner.

Changes in commitment are also important, because they can transform the relationship between a group and an individual. These transformations are governed by *decision criteria*, or specific levels of commitment that mark the boundaries between different membership roles the person could play in the group. The group will try to initiate a role transition when its commitment to an individual reaches its decision criterion. And the individual will make a similar effort when his or her commitment to a group reaches a personal decision criterion. Role transitions often involve ceremonies or other activities (see Trice & Beyer, 1984) that signify these changes in the relationship between the group and the individual.

After a role transition, the group and the individual relabel their relationship and may well change their expectations for one another's behavior. Evaluations continue, producing more changes in commitment and maybe other role transitions. In this way, the individual can go through five distinct phases of group membership (investigation, socialization, maintenance, resocialization, remembrance), separated by four transitions (entry, acceptance, divergence, exit). Figure 3.1 provides a typical example of how the relationship between a group and an individual might change over time.

Passage Through a Group

Group membership begins with a period of investigation. During investigation, the group engages in recruitment, searching for individuals who can contribute to the achievement of group goals. The individual, as a

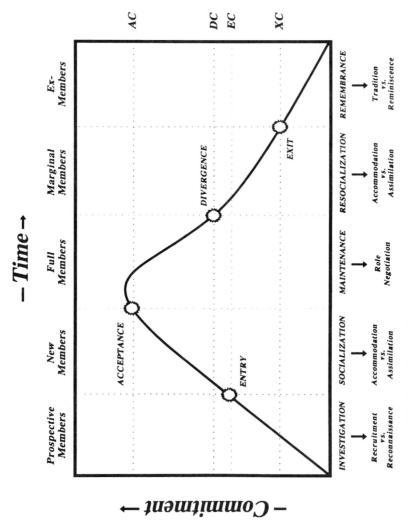

FIG. 3.1. The socialization process for a typical group member.

prospective member, engages in reconnaissance, searching for groups that can contribute to the satisfaction of personal needs. If the commitment levels of both parties rise to their respective entry criteria (EC), entry occurs and the person becomes a new group member.

Entry marks the end of investigation and the beginning of socialization. The group and the individual try during socialization to change one another in ways that might make their relationship more rewarding (Moreland & Levine, 1989). The group wants the individual to contribute more to the achievement of its goals, whereas the individual wants the group to contribute more to the satisfaction of his or her needs. To the extent that these efforts succeed, the individual experiences assimilation and the group experiences accommodation. If the commitment levels of both parties rise to their respective acceptance criteria (AC), acceptance occurs and the person becomes a full member of the group.

Acceptance marks the end of socialization and the beginning of maintenance. The group and the individual negotiate during maintenance about functional roles (e.g., leader) for the individual that might maximize both the achievement of group goals and the satisfaction of personal needs. If role negotiation succeeds, the commitment levels of both parties rise and maintenance continues, perhaps indefinitely. But if role negotiation fails, commitment levels fall. If they reach the respective divergence criteria (DC) of both parties, divergence occurs and the individual becomes a marginal member of the group.

Divergence marks the end of maintenance and the beginning of resocialization. During resocialization, the group and the individual try again to change one another so that the group's goals are more likely to be achieved and the individual's needs are more likely to be satisfied. If enough assimilation and accommodation occur, the commitment levels of both parties may rise again to their respective divergence criteria. This produces a special role transition (*convergence*) that allows the individual to regain full membership. Convergence is rare, however. Commitment levels usually continue to fall (as in Fig. 3.1) until they reach the respective exit criteria (XC) of the group and the individual. Exit then occurs and the individual becomes an ex-member of the group.

Group membership ends with a period of remembrance, when both parties look back at their relationship. The group recalls the individual's contributions to the achievement of its goals, whereas the individual recalls the group's contributions to the satisfaction of his or her needs. Some of these memories may be incorporated into group traditions and/or individual reminiscences. If they still have an influence on one another's outcomes, then both parties may also evaluate their current relationship. Over time, feelings of commitment between the group and the individual eventually stabilize, often at a low level.

Figure 3.1 is an idealized representation of how the relationship between a group and an individual might change over time and thus masks several complexities (see Moreland & Levine, 1982). For example, group and individual commitment levels may undergo sudden shifts, rather than changing gradually. Group and individual decision criteria are sometimes unstable, and changes in decision criteria could affect how long individuals spend in various membership phases. If two adjacent criteria are similar, for example, the membership phase they demarcate will be short, and it will not occur at all if the criteria are identical. Some decision criteria can also vary in their relative positions, which would change the order in which related role transitions occur. There are situations, for instance, in which exit might occur during the investigation or socialization phase of membership. And finally, the figure suggests that the group and the individual have the same set of decision criteria and are equally committed to one another throughout their relationship. When decision criteria or commitment levels diverge, conflict is likely to occur.

Exploring the Model

We have explored our model of group socialization in several ways. Much of this work, which includes both theoretical and empirical papers, is reviewed in Levine and Moreland (1994). In some of our theoretical papers, we expanded the model by analyzing its basic processes in more detail. In an early paper on role transitions (Moreland & Levine, 1984), we analyzed the strains associated with anticipating, scheduling, producing, and then adjusting to these events. Role transitions are simplest when the group and the individual have the same decision criteria and are equally committed to one another. But what if decision criteria and/or commitment levels differ? Role transitions then become more complicated and might produce strain. Imagine, for example, that neither the group nor the individual is ready for a role transition. They may still anticipate that transition by developing expectations about whether it will occur at all, how and when it might occur, and so on. Group and individual expectations can differ considerably when the commitment level of one party is much closer to its decision criterion. Strain may arise as a result, and it should increase with the difference in the distances separating the commitment levels of the group and the individual from their decision criteria. Now imagine that either the group *or* the individual, but not both, is ready for a role transition. Strain may arise around issues of scheduling, as one party tries to hasten the role transition while the other tries to delay it. Strain should now increase with the *sum* of the distances separating the commitment levels of the group and the individual from their decision criteria. Finally, imagine that the group and the individual are both ready for a role transition. Producing a role transition requires decisions about where that event will occur, who will participate in it, how they should act, and so on. And after a role transition ends, the group and the individual must both adjust to their new relationship. Producing and adjusting to a role transition can be difficult if the commitment level of one party is much closer to its decision criterion, so strain may again arise. As before, that strain should increase with the difference in the distances separating the commitment levels of the group and the individual from their decision criteria.

A later paper (Moreland, Levine, & Cini, 1993) focused on commitment. Although social exchange theory guided our original analysis of commitment, other theories may be relevant too and could reveal different aspects of that process. Self-categorization theory (see Hogg & McGarty, 1990; Turner, 1985), for example, has been applied to a related phenomenon, namely group cohesion. Hogg (1987) argued that cohesion depends on how well a group's members match its *prototype*—a shared mental image of someone with the characteristics that make the group unique. Cohesion is stronger insofar as group members seem (to one another) to match that prototype more closely. Perhaps an analogy to commitment can be made. A group's commitment to an individual may depend on how prototypical the person seems to other group members. And an individual's commitment to a group may depend on the person's self-perceived prototypicality, or on how prototypical the other group members seem to him or her. This analysis suggests that commitment can change because of shifts in a group's prototype. Such shifts might involve changes in who belongs to the ingroup or relevant outgroups, or changes in which outgroups are most salient. Shifts of either sort would alter the perceived prototypicality of everyone in the group and thereby change the group's commitment to each individual and each individual's commitment to the group. Identity theory (Stryker, 1987; Stryker & Serpe, 1982) may also be relevant to commitment. According to that theory, social roles (e.g., group memberships) are often incorporated into the self as *identities*. Commitment to an identity depends on the number, intensity, and value of whatever personal relationships would be lost if the relevant role were no longer played. As the overall damage associated with the loss of those relationships increases, commitment grows stronger. A group's commitment to an individual may thus reflect its members' beliefs about how their relationships (with one another and outsiders) would be affected if that person moved further into or out of the group. And similarly, an individual's commitment to a group may reflect that person's beliefs about how such movement would affect his or her own relationships. This analysis suggests that changes in commitment are sometimes caused by shifts in the social networks that surround and permeate most groups. These shifts, which might occur if the composition of a network changed or if its participants developed new relationships with one another, would alter the interpersonal consequences of membership for everyone in the group. Each individual's commitment to the group, and the group's commitment to each individual, would be influenced as a result.

Besides expanding our model of group socialization by analyzing such processes as role transitions and commitment in more detail, we have also extended the model to other small group phenomena. In an early paper, for example, we explored how group socialization can affect minority influence, or innovation (Levine & Moreland, 1985). Innovation was defined as any significant change an individual produces in the structure, dynamics, or performance of a group. Each of the basic processes in our model offers some general insights into this phenomenon. An analysis of commitment, for example, clarifies when innovation attempts will be made and whether they will succeed. Attempts to change a group are more likely to occur when someone's commitment to the group is weak, although very weak commitment can cause a person to give up on a group entirely. And if someone makes an innovation attempt, it is more likely to succeed when the group's commitment to the person is strong. Success is especially likely when the group is more committed to the person than he or she is to the group. Our model offers some specific insights into innovation as well, revealing a variety of ways in which it might occur during each phase of group membership. Attempts to change a group by prospective members during investigation, and by ex-members during remembrance, are particularly interesting because people who do not belong to a group are often ignored as potential innovators. Innovation during investigation can be unintentional, as when prospective members ask questions about a group that lead members to consider making changes in it (see Feldman, 1994; Sutton & Louis, 1987), or intentional, as when prospective members demand changes from a group (*anticipatory accommodation*) before they will join it. Conceding to these demands can have serious consequences for a group, beyond attracting new members. For example, the group may have trouble retaining those members if the changes they were promised are not made. And if those changes are made, other group members may feel alienated because their own recruitment was less rewarding or angry because they dislike how the group has changed. Innovation during remembrance can also be unintentional, as when someone's departure from a group changes its dynamics or performance (see Staw, 1980), or when fond memories of an ex-member lead a group to evaluate current members more harshly or to raise its decision criteria. Intentional innovation can also occur, as when successful ex-members improve a group's performance by offering advice or aid. Recently, we have offered a detailed analysis of how newcomers can produce innovation in the groups they have entered (Levine et al., in press).

In another paper (Moreland & Levine, 1988), we examined the relationship between group socialization and group development. These phenomena are identical in dyads, where there is just one relationship changing over time. In larger groups, socialization and development are related, but distinct. Group socialization involves temporal changes in the relationships between a group and each of its members, whereas group development involves temporal changes in the group as a whole. Each phenomenon can affect the other in various ways. Consider the possible effects of group socialization on group development. Socializing new members and resocializing marginal members could interfere with a group's development by absorbing valuable resources. And if new or marginal members produce accommodation in a group, its development could be affected by whatever changes are made. Although they do not belong to a group, prospective or ex-members could affect its development as well. For example, prospective members can facilitate development by demanding improvements in a group before they join, whereas ex-members can delay development by demanding that a group remain as it was when they belonged. The possible effects of group development on group socialization should also be considered. If development indeed occurs in a series of stages, as many theorists have argued (see Tuckman, 1965; Tuckman & Jensen, 1977), some socialization activities simply may not occur during certain stages of development. During the forming stage, for example, investigation activities may be common, but socialization, maintenance, and resocialization activities are unlikely because they depend on norms that have not yet developed. Remembrance activities are also unlikely when someone leaves a group during its forming stage. When a socialization activity occurs during more than one developmental stage, it may also vary from one stage to another. For example, compared to a group in the performing stage, a group in the adjourning stage often feels less secure, and may thus demand less assimilation from new or marginal members, lower acceptance and divergence criteria for them, and permit them to produce more accommodation.

The role of group socialization in maintaining work group cultures was examined in yet another paper (Levine & Moreland, 1991). A group's culture, we argued, includes socially shared knowledge and related customs. In work groups, shared knowledge provides the answers to questions that employees often ask about their group (*Are we successful?*), its members (*Who is best at what?*), and the work they perform (*Which tasks really matter?*). Customs, which include routines (everyday procedures), accounts (stories about important issues), jargon (unusual words or gestures), rituals (ceremonies marking important events), and symbols (objects with special meanings), embody this shared knowledge, often in very subtle ways. All of this suggests that someone entering a work group may have much to

learn, and that acceptance is likely to be delayed until the person understands, appreciates, and participates in the group's culture. The transfer
of cultural information from oldtimers to newcomers is an important socialization activity, and our model is helpful in identifying variables that
can affect that process. These variables include the personal characteristics of newcomers and oldtimers and the socialization tactics that they
employ. For example, some newcomers may already be familiar with a
work group because of prior contact with the group or its members. And
when further information is required, newcomers who are more motivated (stronger commitment to the group) or capable (better social skills) are
more likely to seek and obtain it. Experience, motivation, and ability are
important characteristics among oldtimers as well. Oldtimers are more
likely to provide helpful information about the group, for example, when
they have dealt with similar newcomers in the past, when they want current newcomers to gain acceptance, and when they understand the
group's culture well (perhaps because they helped to shape it). Whatever
their personal characteristics, newcomers and oldtimers can also improve
the transfer of cultural information through various socialization tactics.
Newcomers' tactics include evoking help from oldtimers by behaving in
role-congruent ways (e.g., anxious and dependent), developing close relationships with oldtimers who might be helpful, and collaborating with one
another. Oldtimers' tactics include training newcomers, "encapsulating"
newcomers by making them spend most of their time (on and off the job)
with group members, and testing what newcomers have learned about the
group's culture, then rewarding or punishing them accordingly. We have
also analyzed how organizations can improve the socialization practices of
work groups that are embedded within them (Levine & Moreland, 1999).

Finally, in a recent paper (Levine, Moreland, & Ryan, 1998), we explored the influence of group socialization on intergroup relations. Conflict is common between groups, especially when there is competition for
scarce resources. Because members are a scarce resource for many groups,
some conflicts are related to efforts by groups to gain and retain members.
One situation where such conflicts often arise is when two groups are
recruiting the same prospective member. Each group can focus on its own
relationship with that individual and try to raise the person's commitment
or lower the person's entry criterion. But each group can also focus on the
individual's relationship with its competitor and attempt to lower the person's commitment to that group or raise the person's entry criterion for
that group. The latter tactics are difficult and can be risky. A prospective
member may be suspicious of one group's efforts to disparage another, so
subtlety is often required. A group may pretend, for example, to be
unaware that the individual is being recruited by a competitor, so that its
criticism of that group seems less self-serving. Or a group may arrange for

outsiders (with no apparent links to either group) to make pointed comparisons between the groups that favor itself. Whatever tactics are used, the group's competitor may well learn about them (perhaps from the prospective member) and then retaliate. As a result, both groups might lose the prospective member, and they could be harmed in other ways as well. Another situation where conflicts arise is when a group recruits someone who is already in another group, but cannot belong to both groups. In this case, the group must somehow weaken the prospective member's relationship with its competitor, maybe by lowering the person's commitment to that group or raising the person's exit criterion for that group. But achieving those goals may be even more dangerous than before. Resistance to the group's recruiting efforts can come from both the individual (who may view the group as an "outgroup," or worry that changing groups will seem like a betrayal) and from the group to which he or she already belongs. That group may again retaliate, perhaps by trying to turn the tables and recruit someone from its competitor. Finally, conflicts can also arise in situations where groups share a member. Competition here involves efforts to control the individual's time, energy, and other assets, rather than to persuade the person to stay in one group and leave the other. A group may become anxious if someone's commitments seem to be changing in ways that favor another group. Responses to such changes can vary widely, depending on the group's own commitment to that person. A group will probably work harder to improve its relationship with someone to whom it is strongly committed. Compromises might even be made with the other group if the alternative is losing that member. But if these efforts fail, then anxiety can turn to anger, directed at both the individual and the group that he or she prefers.

Our exploration of the model is not limited to theoretical work—we have also collected and analyzed data on the socialization process in many kinds of small groups. Most of this empirical work focused on the first two phases of group membership, namely investigation and socialization, and rather than testing the model directly, we have often used it instead as a tool for generating interesting hypotheses about socialization activities. In one project (Pavelchak, Moreland, & Levine, 1986), we studied the influence of earlier group memberships on later reconnaissance activities. During summer orientation sessions, all of the students entering our university were asked to complete a questionnaire assessing their experiences in high school groups and expectations about college groups. Later on, a representative sample of students was interviewed by telephone about their behavior at an activities fair, which the university offered at the start of the fall term to help new students learn more about campus groups. Three reconnaissance activities were explored using these data. Reconnaissance begins with efforts by the individual to identify potentially desirable groups. We found that such efforts often depended on earlier experiences in other groups—students whose high school group experiences were more positive (enjoyable and important) could name more college groups that they might join, and were more likely to have already chosen a group that they would join. These effects were mediated, however, by the belief that memberships in college groups were valuable for achieving the students' goals. After some prospective groups have been identified, the individual must evaluate how rewarding it might be to belong to those groups. Once again, earlier experiences (especially in similar groups) proved to be important. Students who had already chosen a college group to join were optimistic overall, expecting the rewards of membership to far outweigh its costs, but weaker optimism was found among students who belonged to similar groups in high school (see Premack & Wanous, 1985), and the levels of optimism among these students reflected the positivity of their experiences in those groups. Finally, when commitment to any group reaches the individual's entry criterion, he or she will attempt to join that group. There is evidence (see Fazio & Zanna, 1981) that attitudes formed on the basis of direct experience affect behavior more strongly than do attitudes formed in other ways. Among the students who wanted to join a specific college group, we thus expected greater effort to actually join that group by students who belonged to a similar group in high school. That is indeed what we found. When students were interviewed about the activities fair, those who had direct experience with their chosen group (through membership in a high school analog) were more likely than others to state that they went to the fair to visit that group, visited the group at the fair, and left their names with the group to encourage further contact.

One of the most remarkable findings from the project just described was how optimistic prospective members were about the groups they wanted to join. Many students could not (or would not) name a single cost of group membership, and when such costs were named, they were regarded as less probable and powerful than the rewards of group membership. Such optimism can be dangerous, because it often leads to disappointment and leaves many newcomers poorly prepared for the problems of group life (see Wanous, Poland, Premack, & Davis, 1992). It would be helpful to learn *why* prospective members are so optimistic, so in a later project (Brinthaupt, Moreland, & Levine, 1991), we studied three potential sources of optimism in college students' evaluations of campus groups they were about to join. These were (a) recruiting efforts by those groups; (b) feelings of cognitive dissonance about joining groups that might be unsatisfying; and (c) an illusion that the future will generally be better for the self than for others (Taylor & Brown, 1988; Weinstein, 1980). Students planning to join a campus group were given a questionnaire that measured their expectations about that group and experiences with it. For example, they were asked to name the possible rewards and costs of group membership, for both themselves and for the average student, and then to evaluate every reward and cost for probability and strength. We also asked students about their group's recruiting activities (e.g., Was the group described by its members primarily in positive terms?), and any reasons they might have for feeling dissonant about joining the group (e.g., Did you devote much time and energy to the group as a prospective member?). As in our earlier project, students were very optimistic about their chosen groups, naming more rewards than costs of membership and evaluating the rewards as more probable and powerful than the costs. There was little evidence that this optimism was due to recruiting efforts or cognitive dissonance. With some exceptions, students reported weak recruiting efforts by their chosen groups and few reasons for feeling dissonant about becoming group members. Neither of these factors was strongly related to students' optimism levels either. However, illusions about the self did seem to be an important source of optimism. Students expected group membership to be much better for themselves than for the average student, even when the same rewards and costs were evaluated.

Aside from studying the socialization activities of individuals, we have also studied such activities by groups. For example, one project (Cini, Moreland, & Levine, 1993) investigated how staffing levels can affect the behavior of groups toward prospective and new members. This project reflected an interest in research showing that members of understaffed groups work harder at a wider variety of tasks, and thus feel more important and involved, than do members of groups that are optimally staffed or overstaffed (see Schoggen, 1989). We were interested in whether staffing differences produce differential treatment of prospective and new group members. When understaffing occurs, a group may try to cope by altering its socialization practices in ways that make it easier for people to enter the group and then become full members. To explore this possibility, we interviewed the leaders of nearly 100 student groups at our university. We asked them several questions related to staffing levels, such as how large their groups actually were, how big or small those groups could become before problems occurred, what those problems were and how they might be solved, and so on. We also asked leaders questions about the typical socialization practices in their groups, especially the ways in which their prospective and new members were treated. Regarding staffing levels, we found that most leaders believed their groups were understaffed and that leaders were more concerned about understaffing than overstaffing. The most common problems associated with understaffing were poor group performance, fatigue and burnout, a loss of resources (from stakeholders), and member homogeneity. Such problems were typically solved by simply recruiting more members or by reorganizing the group.

The most common problems associated with overstaffing were apathy and boredom, alienation, disorganization, strained resources, and clique formation. These problems were most often solved by building commitment among group members, recruiting fewer or better members, punishing deviates more harshly, or subdividing the group. Regarding socialization tactics, we found that prospective and new members were indeed treated more favorably by groups with lower staffing levels. Those groups wanted more new members, sought fewer special qualities in prospective members, had lower entry criteria, and tended to allow entry at any time. Groups with lower staffing levels also demanded less from new members. In these groups, newcomers' behavior was evaluated less carefully, they were treated more leniently when problems arose, and acceptance criteria were lower.

CONCLUSIONS

We began this chapter with a brief review of recent work on organizational socialization. That review focused on the tactics used by organizations and their new employees during socialization and on the commitment of new employees to their organizations. Much has been learned about the socialization process in organizations, but the results are somewhat discouraging. Many socialization tactics used by organizations and employees seem to be ineffective, and although some employees do become committed to their organizations, the impact of that commitment on their outcomes is modest. Moreover, many organizations suffer high levels of turnover (especially among new employees) and employee misbehavior of various sorts. The socialization process in these organizations is apparently failing and must somehow be improved.

We think that it is time to analyze organizational socialization in a different way. In our opinion, much of the work in this area ignores the critical role of small work groups in the socialization process. There is now good evidence that organizational socialization occurs primarily within such groups and that work group socialization is more important for many employees than is organizational socialization. This suggests a need for new research, guided by a general model of group socialization, that investigates the socialization process in work groups. We have developed such a model and used it (in a series of papers) to explore not only socialization, but other group phenomena as well.

As a tool for analyzing organizational socialization, our model has four major strengths. First, and most importantly, it focuses on small groups. If our claims about work group socialization are correct, and it really is the key to understanding how new employees and organizations adjust to one another, then our model provides a useful theoretical approach. Second, our model has two features that should help to expand the temporal and social perspectives of psychologists who study organizational socialization. It acknowledges that the relationship between a group and an individual often extends over a long period of time, from investigation (when both parties speculate about their future relationship) through remembrance (when both parties remember their past relationship). And it acknowledges that the group and the individual are both sources and targets of influence throughout their relationship with one another—the individual can affect the group, just as it can affect him or her. Third, our model has proven useful in exploring several phenomena that are relevant to organizational socialization and that have already been analyzed by others in that context. These phenomena include innovation by new group members (see Levine & Moreland, 1985; Levine et al., in press; Nicholson, 1984), and unrealistic optimism in prospective group members (see Brinthaupt et al., 1991; Pavelchak et al., 1986; Wanous, 1992). Finally, an emphasis on work group socialization may reveal new ways in which the socialization process could be improved for new employees and their organizations. Nelson, Quick, and Eakin (1988), for example, suggested that team building and social support interventions in work groups could help make socialization less stressful for new employees.

Of course, our model may also have weaknesses that could limit its value for analyzing organizational socialization. For example, the model was not developed specifically for that purpose, and insofar as work groups have special characteristics, it may become necessary to stretch the model accordingly. One potential problem in this regard is that work groups are seldom wholly autonomous or voluntary—groups cannot always choose who to admit or eject, and workers are not always free to enter or leave a group. This suggests some interesting ways in which organizational socialization might shape work group socialization. By hiring and firing different kinds of employees, for example, an organization may force its work groups to allow the entry of people who evoke only weak commitment or the exit of people who evoke strong commitment. Jackson, Stone, and Alvarez (1993) analyzed the former phenomenon and its impact on group socialization in the context of recent efforts by many organizations to improve the diversity of their workforce. When minority workers enter a work group, its level of relational dissimilarity rises, and this may alter the ways in which newcomers and oldtimers relate to one another. Jackson and her colleagues argued, for example, that as relational dissimilarity rises, socialization becomes less open and direct, inhibiting both assimilation and accommodation and thereby delaying acceptance. Recent efforts by many organizations to downsize their workforce may have an impact on work group socialization as well. Research in both of these areas could be very fruitful. Another possible weakness in our model is its approach to commitment, which is simpler than those found in most recent work on organizational socialization. It may be necessary to consider how different dimensions of commitment, and multiple commitments to entities in and out of work groups, influence the socialization process. Finally, because empirical work on our model has lagged behind theoretical work, several of the model's assumptions (e.g., the effects of group and individual decision criteria in producing role transitions) have not yet been tested.

In our opinion, these weaknesses are clearly outweighed by the model's strengths, and so we urge those who study the process and outcomes of organizational socialization to consider how socialization in smaller groups might be relevant. Organizational psychology is already the source for much of the best work on other small group processes (see Levine & Moreland, 1990; 1998; Sanna & Parks, 1997). It is now time to include socialization as one of those processes.

ACKNOWLEDGMENTS

We would like to thank Linda Argote, Thomas Becker, Daniel Feldman, Marlene Turner, and John Wanous for their comments on an earlier version of the chapter. Copies of this or other papers we have written on group socialization can be obtained from either author at the Psychology Department, University of Pittsburgh, Pittsburgh, Pennsylvania, 15260.

REFERENCES

Albert, S., & Whetten, D. A. (1985). Organizational identity. In L. L. Cummings & B. M. Staw (Eds.), *Research in organizational behavior* (Vol. 7, pp. 263–295). Greenwich, CT: JAI.

Allen, N. J., & Meyer, J. P. (1990). Organizational socialization tactics: A longitudinal analysis of links to a newcomer's commitment and role orientation. *Academy of Management Journal, 33*, 847–858.

Allen, N. J., & Meyer, J. P. (1993). Organizational commitment: Evidence of career stage effects? *Journal of Business Research, 26*, 49–61.

Ancona, D. G. (1990). Outward bound: Strategies for team survival in an organization. *Academy of Management Journal, 33*, 334–365.

Ancona, D. G., & Caldwell, D. F. (1988). Beyond task and maintenance: Defining external functions in groups. *Group and Organization Studies, 13*, 468–494.

Ancona, D. G., & Caldwell, D. F. (1992). Bridging the boundary: External activity and performance in organizational teams. *Administrative Science Quarterly, 37*, 634–665.

Anderson, A., & Thomas, H. D. C. (1996). Work group socialization. In M. A. West (Ed.), *Handbook of work group psychology* (pp. 423–450). Chichester, England: Wiley.

Ashford, S. J., & Black, J. S. (1996). Proactivity during organizational entry: The role of desire for control. *Journal of Applied Psychology, 81*, 199–214.

Ashford, S. J., & Cummings, L. L. (1985). Feedback as an individual resource: Personal strategies of creating information. *Organizational Behavior and Human Performance, 32,* 370–398.

Ashford, S. J., & Taylor, M. S. (1990). Adaptation to work transitions: An integrative approach. In G. R. Ferris & K. M. Rowland (Eds.), *Research in personnel and human resources management* (Vol. 8, pp. 1–39). Greenwich, CT: JAI.

Ashforth, B. E., & Mael, F. (1989). Social identity theory and the organization. *Academy of Management Review, 14,* 20–39.

Ashforth, B. E., & Saks, A. M. (1996). Socialization tactics: Longitudinal effects on newcomer adjustment. *Academy of Management Journal, 39,* 149–178.

Baba, M. L. (1995). The cultural ecology of the corporation: Explaining diversity in work group responses to organizational transformation. *Journal of Applied Behavioral Science, 31,* 202–233.

Baker, H. E., & Feldman, D. C. (1990). Strategies of organizational socialization and their impact on newcomer adjustment. *Journal of Managerial Issues, 2,* 198–212.

Baker, W. K. (1995). Allen and Meyer's 1990 longitudinal study: A reanalysis and reinterpretation using structural equation modeling. *Human Relations, 48,* 169–186.

Baratta, J. E., & McManus, M. A. (1992). The effect of contextual factors on individuals' job performance. *Journal of Applied Social Psychology, 22,* 1702–1710.

Barker, J. R., & Tompkins, P. K. (1994). Identification in the self-managing organization: Characteristics of target and tenure. *Human Communication Research, 21,* 223–240.

Bauer, T. N., & Green, S. G. (1994). Effects of newcomer involvement in work-related activities: A longitudinal study of socialization. *Journal of Applied Psychology, 79,* 211–223.

Bauer, T. N., Morrison, E. W., & Callister, R. R. (1998). Organizational socialization: A review and directions for future research. In G. R. Ferris (Ed.), *Research in personnel and human resources management* (Vol. 16, pp. 149–214). Stamford, CT: JAI.

Baumeister, R. F., & Leary, M. R. (1995). The need to belong: Desire for interpersonal attachments as a fundamental human motivation. *Psychological Bulletin, 117,* 497–529.

Bearman, P. S. (1991). Desertion as localism: Army unit solidarity and group norms in the U.S. Civil War. *Social Forces, 70,* 321–342.

Becker, T. E. (1992). Foci and bases of commitment: Are they distinctions worth making? *Academy of Management Journal, 35,* 232–244.

Becker, T. E., & Billings, R. S. (1993). Profiles of commitment: An empirical test. *Journal of Organizational Behavior, 14,* 177–190.

Becker, T. E., Billings, R. S., Eveleth, D. M., & Gilbert, N. L. (1996). Foci and bases of employee commitment: Implications for job performance. *Academy of Management Journal, 39,* 464–482.

Becker, T. E., Randall, D. M., & Riegel, C. D. (1995). The multidimensional view of commitment and the theory of reasoned action: A comparative evaluation. *Journal of Management, 21,* 617–638.

Bell, C. G., & Price, C. M. (1975). *The first term: A study of legislative socialization.* Beverly Hills, CA: Sage.

Bell, N. E., & Staw, B. M. (1989). People as sculptors versus sculpture: The role of personality and personal control in organizations. In M. B. Arthur, D. T. Hall, & B. S. Lawrence (Eds.), *The handbook of career theory* (pp. 232–251). Cambridge, England: Cambridge University Press.

Black, J. S., & Ashford, S. J. (1995). Fitting in or making jobs fit: Factors affecting mode of adjustment for new hires. *Human Relations, 48,* 421–437.

Blau, G. (1995). Influence of group lateness on individual lateness: A cross-level examination. *Academy of Management Journal, 38,* 1483–1496.

Brett, J., Feldman, D. C., & Weingart, L. R. (1990). Feedback-seeking behavior of new hires and job changers. *Journal of Management, 16,* 737–749.

Brewer, M. (1993). The role of distinctiveness in social identity and group behavior. In M. A. Hogg & D. Abrams (Eds.), *Group motivation: Social psychological perspectives* (pp. 1–16). New York: Harvester Wheatsheaf.

Brief, A. P., & Aldag, R. J. (1981). The "self" in work organizations: A conceptual review. *Academy of Management Review, 6*, 75–88.

Brief, A. P., & Motowidlo, S. J. (1986). Prosocial organizational behaviors. *Academy of Management Review, 11*, 710–725.

Brinthaupt, T. M., Moreland, R. L., & Levine, J. M. (1991). Sources of optimism among prospective group members. *Personality and Social Psychology Bulletin, 17*, 36–43.

Burke, R. J., & Bolf, C. (1986). Learning within organizations: Sources and content. *Psychological Reports, 59*, 1187–1198.

Caldwell, D. F., Chatman, J., & O'Reilly, C. A. (1990). Building organizational commitment: A multifirm study. *Journal of Occupational Psychology, 63*, 245–261.

Cannon-Bowers, J. A., Tannenbaum, S. I., Salas, E., & Volpe, C. E. (1995). Defining competencies and establishing team training requirements. In R. Guzzo & E. Salas (Eds.), *Team effectiveness and decision making in organizations* (pp. 333–380). San Francisco: Jossey-Bass.

Chao, G. T. (1988). The socialization process: Building newcomer commitment. In M. London & E. Mone (Eds.), *Career growth and human resource strategies* (pp. 31–47). Westport, CT: Quorum Press.

Chao, G. T., O'Leary-Kelly, A. M., Wolf, S., Klein, H. J., & Gardner, P. D. (1994). Organizational socialization: Its content and consequences. *Journal of Applied Psychology, 79*, 730–743.

Chao, G. T., Walz, P. M., & Gardner, P. D. (1992). Formal and informal mentorships: A comparison on mentoring functions and contrast with nonmentored counterparts. *Personnel Psychology, 45*, 619–636.

Chatman, J. A. (1991). Matching people and organizations: Selection and socialization in public accounting firms. *Administrative Science Quarterly, 36*, 459–484.

Cini, M., Moreland, R. L., & Levine, J. M. (1993). Group staffing levels and responses to prospective and new group members. *Journal of Personality and Social Psychology, 65*, 723–734.

Comer, D. R. (1991). Organizational newcomers' acquisition of information from peers. *Management Communication Quarterly, 5*, 64–89.

Crino, M. D. (1994). Employee sabotage: A random or preventable phenomenon? *Journal of Managerial Issues, 6*, 311–330.

Dansky, K. H. (1996). The effect of group mentoring on career outcomes. *Group and Organization Management, 21*, 5–21.

Darrah, C. (1994). Skill requirements at work: Rhetoric versus reality. *Work and Occupations, 21*, 64–84.

Deluga, R. J., & Perry, J. T. (1994). The role of subordinate performance and ingratiation in leader–member exchanges. *Group and Organization Management, 19*, 67–86.

Dienesch, R. M., & Liden, R. C. (1986). Leader–member exchange model of leadership: A critique and further development. *Academy of Management Review, 11*, 618–634.

Dirsmith, A. J., & Covaleski, M. A. (1985). Informal communications, nonformal communications, and mentoring in public accounting firms. *Accounting, Organizations, and Society, 10*, 149–169.

Dockery, T. M., & Steiner, D. D. (1990). The role of the initial interaction in leader–member. *Group and Organization Studies, 15*, 395–413.

Dornbusch, S. M. (1955). The military academy as an assimilating institution. *Social Forces, 33*, 316–321.

Dunham, R. B., Grube, J. A., & Castaneda, M. B. (1994). Organizational commitment: The utility of an integrative definition. *Journal of Applied Psychology, 79*, 370–380.

Dunham, R. S., & Barrett, A. (1996, January 29). The house freshmen. *Business Week*, pp. 24–31.

DuPont, R. L. (1989). Never trust anyone under 40: What employers should know about drugs in the workplace. *Policy Review, 48*, 52–57.

Dutton, J. E., Dukerich, J. M., & Harquail, C. V. (1994). Organizational images and member identification. *Administrative Science Quarterly, 39*, 239–263.

Eisenberger, R., Fasolo, P., & Davis-LaMastro, V. (1990). Perceived organizational support and employee diligence, commitment, and innovation. *Journal of Applied Psychology, 75*, 51–59.

Fagenson, E. A. (1988). The power of a mentor: Protégés and nonprotégés' perceptions of their own power in organizations. *Group and Organization Studies, 13*, 182–194.

Farrell, D., & Rusbult, C. E. (1981). Exchange variables as predictors of job satisfaction, job commitment, and turnover: The impact of rewards, costs, alternatives, and investments. *Organizational Behavior and Human Performance, 28*, 78–95.

Fazio, R. H., & Zanna, M. P. (1981). Direct experience and attitude–behavior consistency. In L. Berkowitz (Ed.), *Advances in experimental social psychology* (Vol. 14, pp. 161–202). New York: Academic Press.

Feldman, D. C. (1976). A contingency theory of socialization. *Administrative Science Quarterly, 21*, 433–452.

Feldman, D. C. (1977). The role of initiation activities in socialization. *Human Relations, 11*, 977–990.

Feldman, D. C. (1981). The multiple socialization of organization members. *Academy of Management Review, 6*, 309–318.

Feldman, D. C. (1989). Careers in organizations: Recent trends and future directions. *Journal of Management, 15*, 135–156.

Feldman, D. C. (1994). Who's socializing whom? The impact of socializing newcomers on insiders, work groups, and organizations. *Human Resource Management Review, 4*, 213–233.

Feldman, D. C., & Brett, J. M. (1983). Coping with new jobs: A comparative study of new job hires and job changers. *Academy of Management Journal, 26*, 258–272.

Fisher, C. D. (1986). Organizational socialization: An integrative review. In G. R. Ferris & K. M. Rowland (Eds.), *Research in personnel and human resources management* (Vol. 4, pp. 101–145). Greenwich, CT: JAI.

Fulk, J. (1993). Social construction of communication technology. *Academy of Management Journal, 36*, 921–950.

Geiger-Dumond, A. H., & Boyle, S. K. (1995, March). Mentoring: A practitioner's guide. *Training and Development*, 51–54.

George, J. M. (1990). Personality, affect, and behavior in groups. *Journal of Applied Psychology, 75*, 107–116.

George, J. M., & Bettenhausen, K. (1990). Understanding prosocial behavior, sales performance, and turnover: A group-level analysis in a service context. *Journal of Applied Psychology, 75*, 698–709.

Grant, L. (1995, May 22). A school for success. *U.S. News and World Report*, pp. 53–55.

Gregersen, H. B. (1993). Multiple commitments at work and extra-role behavior during three stages of organizational tenure. *Journal of Business Research, 26*, 31–47.

Gregory, K. L. (1983). Native-view paradigms: Multiple cultures and culture conflicts in organizations. *Administrative Science Quarterly, 28*, 359–376.

Guest, D. E. (1992). Employee commitment and control. In J. F. Hartley & G. M. Stephenson (Eds.), *Employment relations: The psychology of influence and control at work* (pp. 111–135). Oxford, England: Basil Blackwell.

Gundry, L. K., & Rousseau, D. M. (1994). Critical incidents in communicating culture to newcomers: The meaning is the message. *Human Relations, 47*, 1063–1088.

Guzzo, R. A., Jette, R. D., & Katzell, R. A. (1985). The effects of psychologically based intervention programs on worker productivity: A meta-analysis. *Personnel Psychology, 38*, 275–291.

Hackett, R. D., Bycio, P., & Hausdorf, P. A. (1994). Further assessments of Meyer and Allen's (1991) three-components model of organizational commitment. *Journal of Applied Psychology, 79*, 15–23.

Harris, S. G., Hirschfeld, R. R., Feild, H. S., & Mossholder, K. W. (1993). Psychological attachment: Relationships with job characteristics, attitudes, and preferences for newcomer development. *Group and Organization Management, 18*, 459–481.

Hogg, M. A. (1987). Social identity and group cohesiveness. In J. C. Turner, M. A. Hogg, P. J. Oakes, S. D. Reicher, & M. S. Wetherell (Eds.), *Rediscovering the social group: A self-categorization theory* (pp. 89–116). Oxford, England: Basil Blackwell.

Hogg, M. A., & McGarty, C. (1990). Self-categorization and social identity. In D. Abrams & M. A. Hogg (Eds.), *Social identity theory: Constructive and critical advances* (pp. 10–27). New York: Springer-Verlag.

Hunt, S. D., & Morgan, R. M. (1994). Organizational commitment: One of many commitments or key mediating construct? *Academy of Management Journal, 37*, 1568–1587.

Jablin, F. M. (1984). Assimilating new members into organizations. In R. N. Bostrom (Ed.), *Communication yearbook* (Vol. 8, pp. 594–626). Newbury Park, CA: Sage.

Jablin, F. M. (1987). Organizational entry, assimilation, and exit. In G. M. Goldhaber & G. A. Barnett (Eds.), *Handbook of organizational communication* (pp. 679–740). Norwood, NJ: Ablex.

Jackson, S. E., Stone, V. K., & Alvarez, E. B. (1993). Socialization amidst diversity: Impact of demographics on work team oldtimers and newcomers. In L. L. Cummings & B. M. Staw (Eds.), *Research in organizational behavior* (Vol. 15, pp. 45–109). Greenwich, CT: JAI.

James, K., & Cropanzano, R. (1984). Dispositional group loyalty and individual action for the benefit of an ingroup: Experimental and correlational evidence. *Organizational Behavior and Human Decision Processes, 60*, 179–205.

Jaros, S. J., Jermier, J. M., Koehler, J. W., & Sincich, T. (1993). Effects of continuance, affective, and moral commitment on the withdrawal process: An evaluation of eight structural equation models. *Academy of Management Journal, 36*, 951–995.

Johns, G., & Nicholson, N. (1982). The meaning of absence: New strategies for theory and research. In B. M. Staw & L. L. Cummings (Eds.), *Research in organizational behavior* (Vol. 4, pp. 127–172). Greenwich, CT: JAI.

Jones, G. R. (1986). Socialization tactics, self-efficacy, and newcomers' adjustment to organizations. *Academy of Management Journal, 29*, 262–279.

Jones, J. W., & Boye, M. W. (1994). Job stress, predisposition to steal, and employee theft. *American Journal of Health Promotion, 8*, 331–333.

Joyce, W. F., & Slocum, J. W. (1984). Collective climate: Agreement as a basis for defining aggregate climates in organizations. *Academy of Management Journal, 27*, 721–742.

Katz, R. (1985). Organizational stress and early socialization experiences. In T. Beehr & R. Bhagat (Eds.), *Human stress and cognition in organizations: An integrative perspective* (pp. 117–139). New York: Wiley.

Kidwell, R. E., Mossholder, K., & Bennett, N. (1997). Cohesiveness and organizational citizenship behavior: A multilevel analysis using work groups and individuals. *Journal of Management, 23*, 775–793.

Kizilos, P. (1990, April). Take my mentor, please! *Training*, 49–55.

Kline, C. J., & Peters, L. H. (1991). Behavioral commitment and tenure of new employees: A replication and extension. *Academy of Management Journal, 34*, 194–204.

Kram, K. W. (1983). Phases of the mentor relationship. *Academy of Management Journal, 26*, 608–625.

Kram, K. E. (1985). Improving the mentoring process. *Training and Development Journal, 39*, 40–43.

Kram, K. E. (1988). *Mentoring at work: Developmental relationships in organizational life.* Lanham, MD: University Press of America.

Kram, K. E., & Isabella, L. A. (1985). Mentoring alternatives: The role of peer relationships in career development. *Academy of Management Journal, 28*, 110–132.

Kramer, M. W. (1993a). Communication after job transfers: Social exchange processes in learning new roles. *Human Communication Research, 20,* 147–174.

Kramer, M. W. (1993b). Communication and uncertainty reduction during job transfers: Learning and joining processes. *Communication Monographs, 60,* 178–198.

Lawler, E. E., Mohrman, S. A., & Ledford, G. E. (1992). *Employee involvement and total quality management.* San Francisco: Jossey-Bass.

Lawler, E. J. (1992). Affective attachments to nested groups: A choice process theory. *American Sociological Review, 57,* 327–339.

Lawrie, J. (1987). How to establish a mentoring program. *Training and Development Journal, 41,* 25–27.

Lee, T. W., Ashford, S. J., Walsh, J. P., & Mowday, R. T. (1992). Commitment propensity, organizational commitment, and voluntary turnover: A longitudinal study of organizational entry processes. *Journal of Management, 18,* 15–32.

Levine, J. M., & Moreland, R. L. (1985). Innovation and socialization in small groups. In S. Moscovici, G. Mugny, & E. Van Avermaet (Eds.), *Perspectives on minority influence* (pp. 143–169). Cambridge, England: Cambridge University Press.

Levine, J. M., & Moreland, R. L. (1990). Progress in small group research. *Annual Review of Psychology, 41,* 585–634.

Levine, J. M., & Moreland, R. L. (1991). Culture and socialization in work groups. In L. B. Resnick, J. M. Levine, & S. D. Teasley (Eds.), *Perspectives on socially shared cognition* (pp. 257–279). Washington, DC: APA.

Levine, J. M., & Moreland, R. L. (1994). Group socialization: Theory and research. In W. Stroebe & M. Hewstone (Eds.), *European review of social psychology* (Vol. 5, pp. 305–336). Chichester, England: Wiley.

Levine, J. M., & Moreland, R. L. (1998). Small groups. In D. Gilbert, S. Fiske, & G. Lindzey (Eds.), *The handbook of social psychology* (4th ed., Vol. 2, pp. 415–469). Boston: McGraw-Hill.

Levine, J. M., & Moreland, R. L. (1999). Knowledge transmission in work groups: Helping newcomers to succeed. In L. Thompson, J. Levine, & D. Messick (Eds.), *Shared cognition in organizations: The management of knowledge* (pp. 267–296). Mahwah, NJ: Lawrence Erlbaum Associates.

Levine, J. M., Moreland, R. L., & Choi, H-S. (in press). Group socialization and newcomer innovation. In M. Hogg & S. Tindale (Eds.), *Blackwell handbook in social psychology (Vol. 3): Group processes.* Oxford: Blackwell.

Levine, J. M., Moreland, R. L., & Ryan, C. S. (1998). Group socialization and intergroup relations. In C. Sedikides, J. Schopler, & C. A. Insko (Eds.), *Intergroup cognition and intergroup behavior* (pp. 283–308). Mahwah, NJ: Lawrence Erlbaum Associates.

Liden, R. C., Wayne, S. J., & Stilwell, D. (1993). A longitudinal study on the early development of leader–member exchanges. *Journal of Applied Psychology, 78,* 662–674.

Lodewijkz, H., & Syroit, J. (1997). Severity of initiation revisited: Does severity of initiation increase attractiveness in real groups? *European Journal of Social Psychology, 27,* 275–300.

Louis, M. R. (1980). Surprise and sense-making: What newcomers experience in entering unfamiliar organizational settings. *Administrative Science Quarterly, 25,* 226–251.

Louis, M. R. (1983). Organizations as culture-bearing milieux. In L. R. Pondy, P. J. Frost, G. Morgan, & T. C. Dandridge (Eds.), *Organizational symbolism* (pp. 39–54). Greenwich, CT: JAI.

Louis, M. R., Posner, B. Z., & Powell, G. N. (1983). The availability and helpfulness of socialization practices. *Personnel Psychology, 36,* 857–866.

Lusch, R. F., Boyt, T., & Schuler, D. (1996). Employees as customers: The role of social controls and employee socialization in developing patronage. *Journal of Business Research, 35,* 179–187.

Mael, F. A., & Ashforth, B. E. (1995). Loyal from day one: Biodata, organizational identification, and turnover among newcomers. *Personnel Psychology, 48,* 309–333.

Mael, F. A., & Tetrick, L. E. (1992). Identifying organizational identification. *Educational and Psychological Measurement, 52,* 813–824.

Markham, S. E., & McKee, G. H. (1995). Group absence behavior and standards: A multi-level analysis. *Academy of Management Journal, 38,* 1174–1190.

Martocchio, J. J. (1994). The effects of absence culture on individual absence. *Human Relations, 47,* 243–262.

Mathieu, J. E. (1991). A cross-level nonrecursive model of the antecedents of organizational commitment and satisfaction. *Journal of Applied Psychology, 76,* 607–618.

Mathieu, J. E., & Kohler, S. S. (1990). A cross-level examination of group absence influences on individual absence. *Journal of Applied Psychology, 75,* 217–220.

Mathieu, J. E., & Zajac, D. M. (1990). A review and meta-analysis of the antecedents, correlates, and consequences of organizational commitment. *Psychological Bulletin, 108,* 171–194.

Meyer, J. P., & Allen, N. J. (1988). Links between work experiences and organizational commitment during the first year of employment: A longitudinal analysis. *Journal of Occupational Psychology, 61,* 195–209.

Meyer, J. P., & Allen, N. J. (1991). A three-component conceptualization of organizational commitment. *Human Resources Management Review, 1,* 61–89.

Meyer, J. P., Allen, N. J., & Gellatly, I. R. (1990). Affective and continuance commitment to the organization: Evaluation of measures and analysis of concurrent and time-lagged relations. *Journal of Applied Psychology, 75,* 710–720.

Meyer, J. P., Bobocel, D. R., & Allen, N. J. (1991). Development of organizational commitment during the first year of employment: A longitudinal study of pre- and post-entry influences. *Journal of Management, 17,* 717–733.

Meyer, J. P., Paunonen, S. V., Gellatly, I. R., Goffin, R. D., & Jackson, D. N. (1989). Organizational commitment and job performance: It's the nature of the commitment that counts. *Journal of Applied Psychology, 74,* 152–156.

Mignerey, J. T., Rubin, R. B., & Gorden, W. I. (1995). Organizational entry: An investigation of newcomer communication behavior and uncertainty. *Communication Research, 22,* 54–85.

Miller, V. C., & Jablin, F. M. (1991). Information seeking during organizational entry: Influences, tactics, and a model of the process. *Academy of Management Review, 16,* 92–120.

Moreland, R. L. (1985). Social categorization and the assimilation of "new" group members. *Journal of Personality and Social Psychology, 48,* 1173–1190.

Moreland, R. L., Argote, L., & Krishnan, R. (1998). Training people to work in groups. In R. S. Tindale, L. Heath, J. Edwards, E. J. Posavac, F. B. Bryant, Y. Suarez-Balcazar, E. Henderson-King, & J. Meyers (Eds.), *Theory and research on small groups* (pp. 37–60). New York: Plenum.

Moreland, R. L., & Beach, S. R. (1992). Exposure effects in the classroom: The development of affinity among students. *Journal of Experimental Social Psychology, 28,* 255–276.

Moreland, R. L., & Levine, J. M. (1982). Group socialization: Temporal changes in individual–group relations. In L. Berkowitz (Ed.), *Advances in experimental social psychology* (Vol. 15, pp. 137–192). New York: Academic Press.

Moreland, R. L., & Levine, J. M. (1984). Role transitions in small groups. In V. L. Allen & E. Van de Vliert (Eds.), *Role transitions: Explorations and explanations* (pp. 181–195). New York: Plenum.

Moreland, R. L., & Levine, J. M. (1988). Group dynamics over time: Development and socialization in small groups. In J. McGrath (Ed.), *The social psychology of time: New perspectives* (pp. 151–181). Newbury Park, CA: Sage.

Moreland, R. L., & Levine, J. M. (1989). Newcomers and oldtimers in small groups. In P. Paulus (Ed.), *Psychology of group influence* (pp. 143–186). Hillsdale, NJ: Lawrence Erlbaum Associates.

Moreland, R. L., Levine, J. M., & Cini, M. (1993). Group socialization: The role of commitment. In M. A. Hogg & D. Abrams (Eds.), *Group motivation: Social psychological perspectives* (pp. 105–129). New York: Harvester Wheatsheaf.

Morrison, E. W. (1993a). Longitudinal study of the effects of information seeking on new-comer socialization. *Journal of Applied Psychology, 78,* 173–183.

Morrison, E. W. (1993b). Newcomer information seeking: Exploring types, modes, sources, and outcomes. *Academy of Management Journal, 36,* 557–589.

Morrison, E. W., & Bies, R. J. (1991). Impression management in the feedback seeking process: A literature review and research agenda. *Academy of Management Review, 16,* 522–541.

Morrow, P. C. (1993). *The theory and measurement of work commitment.* Greenwich, CT: JAI.

Mowday, R. T. L., Steers, R. M., & Porter, L. W. (1979). The measurement of organizational commitment. *Journal of Vocational Behavior, 14,* 224–227.

Mulford, C. L., Klonglan, G. E., Beal, G. N., & Bohlen, J. M. (1968). Selectivity, socialization, and role performance. *Sociology and Social Research, 53,* 68–77.

Mulford, C. L., Klonglan, G. E., & Warren, R. D. (1972). Socialization, communication, and role performance. *Sociological Quarterly, 13,* 74–80.

Nelson, D. L. (1987). Organizational socialization: A stress perspective. *Journal of Organizational Behavior, 8,* 311–324.

Nelson, D. L., & Quick, J. C. (1991). Social support and newcomer adjustment in organizations: Attachment theory at work? *Journal of Organizational Behavior, 12,* 543–554.

Nelson, D. L., Quick, J. C., & Eakin, M. E. (1988). A longitudinal study of newcomer role adjustment in U.S. organizations. *Work & Stress, 2,* 239–253.

Nelson, D. L., Quick, J. C., & Joplin, J. R. (1991). Psychological contracting and newcomer socialization: An attachment theory foundation. *Journal of Social Behavior and Personality, 6,* 55–72.

Nelson, D. L., & Sutton, C. (1990). Chronic work stress and coping: A longitudinal study and suggested new directions. *Academy of Management Journal, 33,* 859–869.

Nicholson, N. (1984). A theory of work role transitions. *Administrative Science Quarterly, 29,* 172–191.

Nicholson, N., & Johns, G. (1985). The absence culture and the psychological contract—who's in control of absence? *Academy of Management Review, 10,* 397–407.

Noe, R. A. (1988). An investigation of the determinants of successful assigned mentoring relationships. *Personnel Psychology, 41,* 457–479.

Noon, M., & Delbridge, R. (1993). News from behind my hand: Gossip in organizations. *Organization Studies, 14,* 23–36.

O'Reilly, C. A., & Chatman, J. (1986). Organizational commitment and psychological attachment: The effects of compliance, identification, and internalization on prosocial behavior. *Journal of Applied Psychology, 71,* 492–499.

Ostroff, C., & Kozlowski, S. W. J. (1992). Organizational socialization as a learning process: The role of information acquisition. *Personnel Psychology, 45,* 849–874.

Ostroff, C., & Kozlowski, S. W. J. (1993). The role of mentoring in the information-gathering processes of newcomers during early organizational socialization. *Journal of Vocational Behavior, 42,* 170–183.

Pavelchak, M., Moreland, R. L., & Levine, J. M. (1986). Effects of prior group memberships on subsequent reconnaissance activities. *Journal of Personality and Social Psychology, 50,* 56–66.

Phillips-Jones, L. (1983). Establishing a formalized mentoring program. *Training and Development Journal, 37,* 38–42.

Posner, B. Z., & Powell, G. N. (1985). Female and male socialization experiences: An initial investigation. *Journal of Occupational Psychology, 58,* 81–85.

Premack, S. L., & Wanous, J. P. (1985). A meta-analysis of realistic job preview experiments. *Journal of Applied Psychology, 70,* 706–718.

Putallaz, M., & Wasserman, A. (1990). Children's entry behavior. In S. R. Asher & J. D. Coie (Eds.), *Peer rejection in childhood* (pp. 60–89). New York: Cambridge University Press.

Randall, D. M. (1990). The consequences of organizational commitment: A methodological investigation. *Journal of Organizational Behavior, 11,* 361–378.

Randall, D. M., & Cote, J. (1991). Interrelationships of work commitment constructs. *Work & Occupations, 18,* 194–211.

Randall, D. M., Fedor, D. B., & Longenecker, C. O. (1990). The behavioral expression of organizational commitment. *Journal of Vocational Behavior, 36,* 210–224.

Reichers, A. E. (1985). A review and reconceptualization of organizational commitment. *Academy of Management Review, 10,* 465–476.

Reichers, A. E. (1986). Conflict and organizational commitments. *Journal of Applied Psychology, 71,* 508–514.

Reichers, A. E. (1987). An interactionist perspective on newcomer socialization rates. *Academy of Management Review, 12,* 278–287.

Reichheld, F. (1996). *The loyalty effect.* Cambridge, MA: Harvard Business School Press.

Rentsch, J. R. (1990). Climate and culture: Interaction and qualitative differences in organizational meanings. *Journal of Applied Psychology, 75,* 668–681.

Riordan, C. M., & Griffeth, R. W. (1995). The opportunity for friendship in the workplace: An underexplored construct. *Journal of Business and Psychology, 10,* 141–154.

Robinson, S. L., & Rousseau, D. M. (1994). Violating the psychological contract: Not the exception but the norm. *Journal of Organizational Behavior, 15,* 245–259.

Roethlisberger, F. J., & Dickson, W. J. (1939). *Management and the worker.* Cambridge, MA: Harvard University Press.

Rohlen, T. P. (1973). "Spiritual education" in a Japanese bank. *American Anthropologist, 75,* 1542–1562.

Rusbult, C. E., & Farrell, D. (1983). A longitudinal test of the investment model: The impact on job satisfaction, job commitment, and turnover of variations in rewards, costs, alternatives, and investments. *Journal of Applied Psychology, 68,* 429–438.

Rusbult, C. E., Farrell, D., Rogers, G., & Mainous, A. G. (1988). Impact of exchange variables on exit, voice, loyalty, and neglect: An integrative model of responses to declining job satisfaction. *Academy of Management Journal, 31,* 599–627.

Sackman, S. A. (1992). Culture and subcultures: An analysis of organizational knowledge. *Administrative Science Quarterly, 37,* 140–161.

Saks, A. M. (1994). Moderating effects of self-efficacy for the relationship between training method and anxiety and stress reactions of newcomers. *Journal of Organizational Behavior, 15,* 639–654.

Saks, A. M. (1995). Longitudinal investigation of the moderating and mediating effects of self-efficacy on the relationship between training and newcomer adjustment. *Journal of Applied Psychology, 80,* 211–225.

Saks, A. M. (1996). The relationship between the amount and helpfulness of entry training and work outcomes. *Human Relations, 49,* 429–451.

Saks, A. M., & Ashforth, B. E. (1997). Organizational socialization: Making sense of the past and present as a prologue for the future. *Journal of Organizational Behavior, 51,* 234–279.

Salancik, G. R. (1977). Commitment and the control of organizational behavior and belief. In B. M. Staw & G. R. Salancik (Eds.), *New directions in organizational behavior* (pp. 1–74). Chicago: St. Clair Press.

Salancik, G. R., & Pfeffer, J. (1978). A social information processing approach to job attitudes and task design. *Administrative Science Quarterly, 23,* 224–253.

Sanna, L. J., & Parks, C. D. (1997). Group research trends in social and organizational psychology: What ever happened to intragroup research? *Psychological Science, 8,* 261–267.

Scandura, T. A., & Schriesheim, C. A. (1994). Leader–member exchange and supervisor career mentoring as complementary constructs in leadership research. *Academy of Management Journal, 37,* 1588–1602.

Schoggen, P. (1989). *Behavior settings: A revision and extension of Roger G. Barker's ecological psychology.* Stanford, CA: Stanford University Press.

Scott, W. A., & Scott, R. (1989). *Adaptation of immigrants: Individual differences and determinants.* Oxford, England: Pergamon.

Schmitz, J., & Fulk, J. (1991). Organizational colleagues, media richness, and electronic mail: A test of the social influence model of technology use. *Communication Research, 18,* 487–523.

Schneider, B., Goldstein, H. W., & Smith, D. B. (1995). The ASA framework: An update. *Personnel Psychology, 48,* 747–774.

Settoon, R. P., & Adkins, C. L. (1997). Newcomer socialization: The role of supervisors, coworkers, friends, and family members. *Journal of Business and Psychology, 11,* 507–526.

Shore, L. M., & Wayne, S. J. (1993). Commitment and employee behavior: Comparison of affective commitment and continuance commitment with perceived organizational support. *Journal of Applied Psychology, 78,* 774–780.

Snyder, M. (1995). Self-monitoring: Public appearances versus private realities. In G. G. Brannigan & M. R. Merrens (Eds.), *The social psychologists: Research adventures* (pp. 35–50). New York: McGraw-Hill.

Staw, B. (1980). The consequences of turnover. *Journal of Occupational Behavior, 1,* 253–273.

Stryker, S. (1987). Identity theory: Developments and extensions. In K. Yardley & T. Honess (Eds.), *Self and identity: Psychosocial perspectives* (pp. 89–103). New York: Wiley.

Stryker, S., & Serpe, R. T. (1982). Commitment, identity, salience, and role behavior: Theory and research example. In W. Ickes & E. S. Knowles (Eds.), *Personality, roles, and social behavior* (pp. 199–218). New York: Springer-Verlag.

Sundstrom, E., deMeuse, K. P., & Futrell, D. (1990). Work teams: Applications and effectiveness. *American Psychologist, 45,* 120–133.

Sutton, R. I., & Louis, M. R. (1987). How selecting and socializing newcomers influences insiders. *Human Resource Management, 26,* 347–361.

Tannenbaum, S. I., Mathieu, J. E., Salas, E., & Cannon-Bowers, J. A. (1991). Meeting trainees' expectations: The influence of training fulfilment on the development of commitment, self-efficacy, and motivation. *Journal of Applied Psychology, 76,* 759–769.

Taylor, S. E., & Brown, J. D. (1988). Illusion and well-being: A social psychological perspective on mental health. *Psychological Bulletin, 103,* 193–210.

Tepper, B. J. (1995). Upward maintenance tactics in supervisory mentoring and nonmentoring relationships. *Academy of Management Journal, 38,* 1191–1205.

Trice, H. M., & Beyer, J. M. (1984). Studying organizational cultures through rites and ceremonials. *Academy of Management Review, 9,* 653–669.

Tuckman, B. W. (1965). Developmental sequence in small groups. *Psychological Bulletin, 63,* 384–399.

Tuckman, B. W., & Jensen, M. A. C. (1977). Stages of small-group development revisited. *Group & Organization Studies, 2,* 419–427.

Turner, J. C. (1985). Social categorization and the self-concept: A social cognitive theory of group behavior. In E. J. Lawler (Ed.), *Advances in group process* (Vol. 2, pp. 77–122). Greenwich, CT: JAI.

Vandenberg, R. J., & Self, R. M. (1993). Assessing newcomers' changing commitments to the organization during the first six months of work. *Journal of Applied Psychology, 78,* 557–568.

Vandenberg, R. J., Self, R. M., & Seo, J. H. (1994). A critical examination of the internalization, identification, and compliance commitment measures. *Journal of Management, 20,* 123–140.

Van Maanen, J. (1978). People processing: Strategies of organizational socialization. *Organizational Dynamics, 7,* 18–36.

Van Maanen, J., & Barley, S. R. (1985). Cultural organization: Fragments of a theory. In P. J. Frost, L. F. Moore, M. R. Louis, C. C. Lundberg, & J. Martin (Eds.), *Organizational culture* (pp. 31–53). Beverly Hills, CA: Sage.

Van Maanen, J., & Schein, E. (1979). Toward a theory of organizational socialization. In B. M. Staw (Ed.), *Research in organizational behavior* (Vol. 1, pp. 209–264). Greenwich, CT: JAI.

Vaught, C., & Smith, D. L. (1980). Incorporation and mechanical solidarity in an underground coal mine. *Sociology of Work and Occupations, 7,* 159–187.

Wanous, J. P. (1989). Impression management at organizational entry. In R. A. Giacalone & P. Rosenfeld (Eds.), *Impression management in the organization* (pp. 253–267). Hillsdale, NJ: Lawrence Erlbaum Associates.

Wanous, J. P. (1992). *Organizational entry: Recruitment, selection, orientation, and socialization of newcomers.* Reading, MA: Addison-Wesley.

Wanous, J. P. (1993). Newcomer orientation programs that facilitate organizational entry. In H. Schuler, J. L. Farr, & M. Smith (Eds.), *Personnel selection and assessment: Individual and organizational perspectives* (pp. 125–139). Hillsdale, NJ: Lawrence Erlbaum Associates.

Wanous, J. P., & Colella, A. (1989). Organizational entry research: Current status and future research directions. In K. M. Rowland & G. R. Ferris (Eds.), *Research in personnel and human resources management* (Vol. 7, pp. 59–120). Greenwich, CT: JAI.

Wanous, J. P., Poland, T. D., Premack, S. L., & Davis, K. S. (1992). The effects of met expectations on newcomer attitudes and behaviors: A review and meta-analysis. *Journal of Applied Psychology, 77,* 288–297.

Wayne, S. J., & Ferris, G. R. (1990). Influence tactics, affect, and exchange quality in supervisor–subordinate dyads. *Journal of Applied Psychology, 75,* 487–499.

Weinstein, N. D. (1980). Unrealistic optimism about future life events. *Journal of Personality and Social Psychology, 39,* 806–820.

Weiss, H. M. (1977). Subordinate imitation of supervisor behavior: The role of modeling in organizational socialization. *Organizational Behavior and Human Performance, 19,* 89–105.

Whitely, W. T., & Coetsier, P. (1993). The relationship of career mentoring to early career outcomes. *Organization Studies, 14,* 419–441.

Wright, P. L. (1990). Teller job satisfaction and organization commitment as they relate to career orientations. *Human Relations, 43,* 369–381.

Yoon, J. K., Baker, M. R., & Ko, J. (1994). Interpersonal attachment and organizational commitment: Subgroup hypothesis revisited. *Human Relations, 47,* 329–351.

Zaccaro, S. J., & Dobbins, G. H. (1989). Contrasting group and organizational commitment: Evidence for differences among multilevel attachments. *Journal of Organizational Behavior, 10,* 267–273.

Zaccaro, S. J., Foti, R. J., & Kenny, D. A. (1991). Self-monitoring and trait-based variance in leadership: An investigation of leader flexibility across multiple group situations. *Journal of Applied Psychology, 76,* 308–315.

Zahrly, J., & Tosi, H. (1989). The differential effect of organizational induction process on early work role adjustment. *Journal of Organizational Behavior, 10,* 59–74.

Zalesny, M. D., & Ford, J. K. (1990). Extending the social information processing perspective: New links to attitudes, behaviors, and perceptions. *Organizational Behavior and Human Decision Processes, 47,* 205–246.

Zey, M. G. (1985). Mentor programs: Making the right moves. *Personnel Journal, 64,* 53–57.

Chapter 4

Understanding Individual Motivation in Groups: The Collective Effort Model

Steven J. Karau
Southern Illinois University at Carbondale

Kipling D. Williams
University of New South Wales

Much of the world's work is accomplished in groups, and many groups perform collective tasks that require the pooling of individual members' inputs. At a societal level, sports teams, juries, rock groups, quality circles, policy committees, symphony orchestras, construction crews, government assemblies, and research teams provide but a few examples of groups that combine the efforts of individual members into a single group product or outcome. In organizational settings, the issue of group effectiveness has acquired special relevance in recent years with a dramatic increase in the use of work team, participative management, self-management, continuous quality improvement (CQI), and total quality management (TQM) approaches (e.g., Guzzo & Salas, 1995; Hackman & Wageman, 1995; Sundstrom, De Meuse, & Futrell, 1990).

Given the vital importance of groups to both organizations and society, it is not surprising that social and organizational psychologists have devoted considerable effort to understanding group processes and group effectiveness, with special attention to the issue of group performance. It is widely acknowledged that the motivation level of individual group members is often a key determinant of group performance (cf. Hackman, 1987). But how does working in a group affect the motivation of individual members? Although intuition might suggest that individuals would be energized to work especially hard in groups, research has shown that they often reduce their efforts when working collectively—a phenomenon known as *social loafing*. However, social loafing is not inevitable, and a number of factors have been found to reduce or eliminate the effect.

Recently, we developed a model of individual motivation in groups, the Collective Effort Model (CEM), that we believe successfully explains and integrates the existing research on social loafing, and that has important implications for a variety of naturally occurring groups and work teams. In this chapter, we (a) provide an historical survey of research on the issue of individual motivation in groups, (b) consider several prior theories of social loafing, (c) introduce the CEM and consider its ability to account for existing research findings and generate novel hypotheses for work groups in organizations, and (d) discuss several implications of the model for both research and practice. Of course, a complete review of all research and theory relevant to the CEM is beyond the scope of this chapter. We seek instead to provide a good understanding of the model, a feel for how it might be applied to organizational settings, and a few detailed examples of how specific implications of the model lend themselves to research with clear applications for work groups.

HISTORICAL BACKGROUND

Scientific interest in the issue of how working with others influences our motivation and performance is hardly new. Somewhere between 1882 and 1887, in what may have been the first experimental studies in social psychology, Ringelmann asked male volunteers in groups of various sizes to pull on a rope as hard as they could (see Kravitz & Martin, 1986). He found that as group size increased, there was a marked decrease in the total force exerted over what would have been expected on the basis of individuals' performances. This raised the possibility that working in a group on a collective task might be demotivating for the individual members, although motivation loss could not be separated from simple incoordination among group members on the task (Steiner, 1972).

Although research on other aspects of group dynamics flourished in the middle part of this century, it wasn't until 1974 that Ringelmann's findings were replicated (Ingham, Levinger, Graves, & Peckham, 1974). However, a great deal of interest in motivation loss in groups was stimulated by an inventive study by Latané, Williams, and Harkins (1979). While blindfolded and wearing headphones that masked the noise, college men shouted as loudly as they could both in actual groups, and in pseudogroups in which they shouted alone but believed they were shouting with others. A performance decrease was found for both actual groups and pseudogroups. Thus, Latané and colleagues demonstrated that a substantial portion of the performance decrease in groups was attributable to motivation loss, as distinct from coordination loss. They also coined the term social loafing for the demotivating effects of working in groups and described it as a type of social disease, having "negative consequences for individuals, social institutions, and societies" (p. 831). This provocative statement and the creative study on which it was based set the stage for more than 90 studies that have compared individuals' efforts on coactive tasks with individuals' efforts on collective tasks. Coactive tasks, in which the participant works individually in the presence of others working on the same task, are used as the individual control condition to keep group size constant across comparison conditions, thus removing arousal, distraction, and evaluation apprehension as alternative explanations for any observed differences.

Social loafing has been found for a wide variety of tasks. These include physical tasks, such as shouting, swimming, and rope pulling; cognitive tasks, such as generating ideas, navigating mazes, and identifying signals on a simulated radar screen; evaluative tasks, such as rating the quality of poems, editorials, and clinical therapists; creative tasks, such as thought listing and song writing; and work-related tasks, such as in-basket exercises, typing, and evaluating job candidates. Finally, although differences do occasionally emerge across samples, a number of studies have found significant social loafing regardless of participants' gender, nationality, or age. Thus, social loafing generalizes across tasks, as well as across most subject populations.

Although social loafing research has been conducted in field settings (usually classroom project groups or sports teams), with similar results emerging across contexts, almost no research has been conducted in business organizations. In fact, we are currently aware of only three such studies. The first, conducted by Faulkner and Williams (1996), examined factory assembly-line workers who were told either that they were responsible only for their individual performance or for their groups' performance. This study replicated the social loafing pattern found in previous research. The second and third, conducted by George (1992, 1995), examined only perceptions of social loafing among salespersons and their supervisors. These studies generally found results consistent with prior research on actual effort levels—namely, that perceptions of loafing increased when workers believed their inputs were less readily identifiable, that this relationship was strongest when intrinsic involvement with one's work was low, and that performance-contingent reward reduced perceived levels of loafing. Although these studies provide initial evidence that social loafing research from the laboratory and from a variety of field settings may indeed be applicable to business organizations, there is a great need for additional research examining motivation within ongoing work teams and other groups within organizations. We are hopeful that this chapter, and the integrative model it discusses, may serve as an impetus for more of this type of research.

THEORIES OF SOCIAL LOAFING

Several researchers have offered theories of social loafing. Although all of these theories have some limitations, each has inspired useful research and provided valuable insights into the nature and causes of social loafing. We have also incorporated elements of these theories into our own integrative model. Therefore, we consider briefly five of the most prominent views.

Social Impact Theory

Social Impact Theory (Latané, 1981) proposes that people can be viewed as either sources or targets of social influence. When individuals work collectively, the demands of an outside source of social influence (e.g., one's boss or an experimenter) to work hard are diffused across multiple targets (i.e., across all of the group members), leading to reduced social impact and decreased effort. On individual tasks, no such diffusion takes place, and individuals work hard. The division of social influence is thought to be a function of the strength, immediacy, and number of sources and targets present. This division of influence is also predicted to follow an inverse power function, with a exponent having an absolute value less than 1. Thus, using the number construct as an example, each new group member will have less additional influence as group size increases.

Arousal Reduction

Jackson and Williams (1985) proposed a drive explanation to accompany a social impact theory perspective on social loafing. Research on social facilitation has suggested that the presence of other coactors increases arousal. This arousal facilitates dominant responses, thereby enhancing performance on simple or well-learned tasks (in which the dominant response is likely to be correct), but reducing performance on complex, unfamiliar tasks (in which the dominant response is likely to be in error; Zajonc, 1980). Note that social facilitation is easily distinguished from social loafing by the nature of the comparison—social loafing compares individual performance on collective tasks to that on coactive tasks, whereas social facilitation compares individual performance when working alone to performance on coactive tasks. Jackson and Williams (1985) argued that the presence of other coworkers is actually *drive reducing* when these others serve as cotargets of an outside source of social influence. They found support for this view in an experiment that combined features of the social loafing and social facilitation paradigms. Participants completed simple and complex computer mazes either alone, coactively, or collectively. On simple tasks, participants performed better coactively than collectively. On complex tasks, however, subjects performed better collectively than coactively. These findings suggest that social loafing might actually lead to enhanced performance on complex or unfamiliar tasks. Other studies have produced similar results (Griffith, Fichman, & Moreland, 1989; Sanna, 1992).

Evaluation Potential

Several interpretations of social loafing invoke the concept of evaluation (e.g., Harkins, 1987; Williams, Harkins, & Latané, 1981). These viewpoints suggest that social loafing occurs because working collectively often makes each group member's inputs difficult to identify and evaluate. Thus, working collectively may allow individuals to "hide in the crowd" (Davis, 1969) and avoid taking the blame for a poor group performance. Working collectively may also lead individuals to feel "lost in the crowd" (Latané et al., 1979) so that they cannot receive their fair share of credit for a good group performance. Research by Harkins and colleagues (Harkins, 1987; Harkins & Jackson, 1985; Harkins & Szymanski, 1988, 1989; Williams et al., 1981) has suggested that when individuals' collective inputs can be evaluated by anyone (including oneself), this alone may be enough to eliminate social loafing in many situations. This research has also shown that two criteria must be met for evaluation of inputs by any source (one's boss, one's coworkers, or oneself) to be possible: (1) The participants' output must be known or identifiable, and (2) there must be a standard (personal, social, or objective) with which this output can be compared.

Dispensability of Effort

Dispensability views suggest that people exert less effort when working collectively because they feel that their inputs are not needed in order for the group to perform well. Kerr and his colleagues (Kerr, 1983; Kerr & Bruun, 1983) found that individuals tend to reduce their collective efforts on threshold tasks that follow a disjunctive rule whereby if any group member reaches the performance criterion, the entire group succeeds. These reductions have been found even though each group member's contribution is made identifiable to themselves, their coworker, and the experimenter. Thus, on some tasks, individuals may not be willing to work hard if they feel that their efforts will have little impact on the final group product.

Self-Efficacy

Sanna (1992) proposed that self-efficacy theory (Bandura, 1986) can account for findings from both the social loafing and social facilitation paradigms. According to this view, individuals will work hardest when they perceive high levels of self-efficacy at the task and expect their performance to be evaluated (i.e., when working alone or coactively rather than collectively). In contrast, individuals will be less likely to work hard when they perceive low levels of self-efficacy at the task, especially if they expect their performance to be evaluated. This latter point is compelling, because it suggests that evaluation may undermine performance in some situations (see also Szymanski & Harkins, 1992). Sanna and others found initial support for the self-efficacy perspective in a series of recent studies (e.g., Earley, 1994; Sanna, 1992; Sanna & Pusecker, 1994).

Discussion

Support has been found for all five of these theories, but they have also been criticized on various grounds (see Karau & Williams, 1993). For example, social impact theory appears to predict the effects of group size quite well, but has been criticized for not specifying the underlying psychological processes that it describes. Similarly, a number of experiments have clearly documented that evaluation processes can be very important in collective contexts, yet other experiments have found social loafing even when individuals' inputs to a collective task can be fully identified and evaluated.

The most significant limitation common to all five views is that each offers explanations and makes predictions about social loafing within a restricted domain. For example, the evaluation potential, dispensability, and efficacy views all provide excellent analyses of the roles that those specific factors play in social loafing, but none of these theories explains nor attempts to explain the operation of the entire range of variables that have been found to influence social loafing. Indeed, several of the key factors are associated with their own separate theory that explains only one possible cause of loafing. Given the wealth of research and theory that is available on social loafing, individual motivation in organizational and work group contexts, and the impact of individual performance on group performance, we feel that an integrative framework that can account for most or all of the findings relevant to individual motivation in groups is long overdue. We now present the key elements of a theory that not only accounts for the wide range of findings in the social loafing literature, but also offers compelling predictions for future research and practice relevant to a variety of group settings.

THE COLLECTIVE EFFORT MODEL (CEM)

The CEM integrates key elements of traditional expectancy-value models of effort with recent research and theory on social identity and self-evaluation processes in groups. The synergistic blend of these two orientations provides unique insights into motivation and has important implications for both research and practice. In this section, we (a) provide an overview of the central features of the CEM and discuss how it extends the basic implications of expectancy-value and self-evaluation theories to the specific realm of motivation on collective tasks, (b) consider the general implications of the CEM for understanding individual motivation in groups, (c) present an overview of the results of a recent meta-analysis of social loafing and highlight its linkages with the CEM, and (d) discuss specific implications of the CEM for enhancing individual motivation within organizational work groups.

Central Features

The key features of the CEM are shown in Fig. 4.1. The model suggests that individuals will be willing to exert effort on a collective task only to the degree that they expect their efforts to be instrumental in obtaining outcomes that they value personally. When those outcomes tied to the collective situation or to the group's performance are not perceived as important, meaningful, or intrinsically satisfying, individuals are unlikely to work hard. Moreover, even when the relevant outcomes are highly valued, individuals are unlikely to work hard if their effort is not expected to lead to performance that will be instrumental in obtaining those outcomes.

Like traditional expectancy-value models of effort (e.g., Heckhausen, 1977; Porter & Lawler, 1968; Vroom, 1964), the CEM assumes that individuals attempt to maximize the expected utility of their actions. In Vroom's (1964) original model, individuals' motivational force is determined by three factors; (a) *expectancy*, or the degree to which high levels of effort are expected to lead to high levels of performance, (b) *instrumentality*, or the degree to which high-quality performance is perceived as instrumental in obtaining an outcome, and (c) *valence* of the outcome, or the degree to which the outcome is viewed as desirable. The CEM expands on this logic by specifying that instrumentality on collective tasks is determined by three factors; (a) the perceived relationship between individual performance and group performance, (b) the perceived relationship between group performance and group outcomes, and (c) the perceived relationship between group outcomes and individual outcomes. Thus, the model suggests that working on a collective task poses additional barriers to peoples' perceptions that their efforts will be instrumental in obtaining valued outcomes. Stated another way, we believe that social loafing occurs because there is usually a stronger perceived contingency between individual effort and valued outcomes when working individually. When working collectively, factors other than the individual's

SOCIAL LOAFING

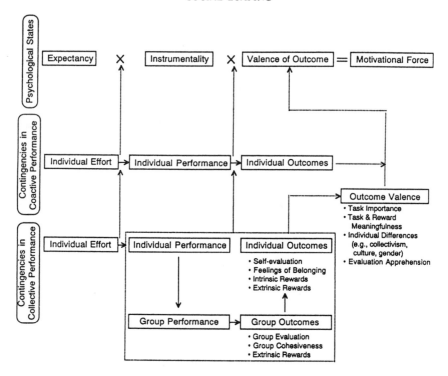

FIG. 4.1. The Collective Effort Model (CEM). From "Social Loafing: A Meta-Analytic Review and Theoretical Integration," by S. J. Karau and K. D. Williams, 1993, *Journal of Personality and Social Psychology, 65*, p. 685. Copyright © 1993 by the American Psychological Association. Reprinted with permission.

effort frequently determine performance, and valued outcomes are often divided among all of the group members.

But what outcomes are individuals likely to value? Valued outcomes can consist of either objective outcomes such as pay or subjective outcomes such as enjoyment, satisfaction, feelings of group cohesiveness and belonging, and feelings of self-worth. However, it is the individual's evaluation of the outcome rather than the outcome itself that determines its valence (e.g., Deci, 1975). Because the CEM is focused primarily on group phenomena, it places special emphasis on group-level outcomes that have implications for the individual's self-evaluation. Research has repeatedly demonstrated that individuals are motivated to maintain a favorable self-evaluation (e.g., Brown, Collins, & Schmidt, 1988; Greenwald & Pratkanis, 1984; Suls & Miller, 1977; Tesser, 1988). Group performance settings produce the potential for self-evaluation from a variety of relevant sources (Breckler & Greenwald, 1986; Crocker & Luhtanen, 1990; Leary & Forsyth, 1987). The CEM suggests that collective settings that provide clear information relevant to self-evaluation, whether from oneself, one's coworkers, one's boss, important reference groups, or others, should have stronger implications for motivation than situations that do not provide such information or that make it less potent or ambiguous.

Similar implications emerge from social identity theory and group-level variations of social comparison theory. Social identity theory (e.g., Tajfel & Turner, 1986) proposes that individuals gain positive self-evaluation by identifying with the positive attributes and accomplishments of groups and social categories to which they belong, and research evidence provides good support for this view (Abrams & Hogg, 1990; Banaji & Prentice, 1994; Brewer, 1991; Cialdini et al., 1976; Fiske & Taylor, 1991). Indeed, Smith and Henry (1996) found that ingroup traits may actually be incorporated into one's personal identity: They found that participants responded more quickly when making speeded self-descriptiveness judgments that matched, rather than mismatched, those of a salient ingroup. In addition, several recent analyses suggest that some social motivations, such as a need for belonging or a need for social interaction and communication, can only be fulfilled in a collective setting (e.g., Brewer, 1991; Caporael, Dawes, Orbell, & van de Kragt, 1989). Moreover, Baumeister and Leary (1995) proposed that the need to belong and to establish and maintain strong interpersonal bonds is one of the most fundamental, pervasive, and motivating aspects of the human social condition.

Recent group-level revisions of social comparison theory further illustrate the importance of group outcomes to individual motivation. Goethals and Darley (1987) suggested that individuals obtain self-evaluation information not only by comparing themselves with other individuals, but also by comparing the groups to which they belong with other groups. They further stated that individuals seek group-level comparison information both to obtain self-knowledge (information about the actual level of one's performance compared with others) and self-validation (information that one's level of performance is superior to that of others). Thus, recent research and theory from a variety of perspectives converges and agrees on the importance of self-evaluation processes within groups and social categories and suggests that collective settings that provide a great deal of information (especially if likely to be positive) relevant to one's self-evaluation and self-validation should be more motivating to individuals than settings that provide less information. These perspectives also suggest that self-evaluation information can come from a variety of sources and that information relevant to one's role in valued reference groups may be especially influential.

The CEM is largely a cognitive model of motivation because of its focus on both perceived contingencies (rather than on actual contingencies) and its assumption that individuals either consciously or subconsciously select a level of effort to exert on the task. However, the model is not intended to imply a deliberative process within individuals. In most settings, people are unlikely to systematically process all of the available information about the task performance setting. Tendencies to process only as much information as necessary, such as the "cognitive miser" effect (Fiske & Taylor, 1991), as well as repeating process cycles (e.g., Sundstrom et al., 1990) and habitual routines (Gersick & Hackman, 1990) in group settings, strengthen the likelihood that information will often be processed in a relatively automatic or nondeliberative manner. Systematic processing is only likely when situational constraints or individual differences increase one's motivation to consider information carefully. Thus, some situations may lead individuals to respond automatically to a preexisting effort script, whereas other situations may lead individuals to strategically increase or decrease their effort on collective tasks. The "free-rider" and "sucker" effects described by Kerr (1983) may provide examples of this latter kind of strategic loafing. When it is made salient to individuals that their group will succeed regardless of their personal efforts (the free-rider effect) or that their individual success will cause other, unworthy group members who are loafing to succeed at their expense (the sucker effect), they may make a conscious decision to relax and not work hard on the collective task. Strategic analysis of the performance setting could also lead to enhanced motivation in cases where individuals' valued outcomes are more reliant on their own performances collectively rather than coactively (e.g., Williams & Karau, 1991).

Of course, the notion that expectancy-value models can be used to shed light on individual motivation in group contexts is not entirely new. Several researchers have used expectancy-value models to organize and explain the findings of studies on social loafing and social dilemmas (e.g., Kerr, 1983; Olson, 1965; Shepperd, 1993; Williams & Karau, 1991) and well as on group behavior in organizational settings (Naylor, Pritchard, & Ilgen, 1980). Similarly, several previous researchers have discussed the relationship between self-evaluation processes and motivational issues in collective contexts (e.g., Baumeister & Leary, 1995; Goethals & Darley, 1987; Taylor & Brown, 1988; Tesser, 1988). The CEM, however, is unique in specifying additional contingencies between effort and outcomes that are unique to collective contexts, and in using group-level social comparison and self-evaluation theories to identify which specific factors should influence individual motivation within groups. This combination allows for the identification of a range of threats to collective motivation in a manner that is not restricted to mere task performance outcomes.

Implications

The CEM generates a number of specific predictions regarding individual motivation in groups. First, the model suggests that collective work settings are highly susceptible to social loafing because individuals' outcomes frequently depend less on their efforts when working collectively than when working coactively. Second, the CEM suggests that individuals will work harder on a collective task when they expect their effort to be instrumental in obtaining valued outcomes. Therefore, holding other factors constant, social loafing should be reduced (and group members should be willing to work harder) when individuals (a) believe that their collective performance can be evaluated by their boss, their coworkers, themselves, or other people; (b) work in smaller rather than larger groups; (c) perceive that their contributions to the collective product are unique, rather than redundant with the inputs of other group members; (d) are provided a standard with which to compare their group's performance; (e) work on tasks that are either intrinsically interesting, meaningful to them, important to valued reference groups or to valued causes, or high in personal involvement; (f) work with respected people or in a situation that activates a salient group identity; (g) expect their coworkers to perform poorly; (h) have a dispositional tendency to view favorable collective outcomes as valuable and important; and (i) have feelings of high self-efficacy and high collective efficacy for their group on the task. Combinations of factors influencing the perceived value of outcomes and the perceived likelihood of obtaining valued outcomes lead to additional, more complex predictions. As just one example, individuals may be willing to work harder when they expect their coworkers to perform poorly, but only if they expect their performance to be useful to the final outcome, view the task or outcome of the task as meaningful, and value the group or at least do not find it distasteful to temporarily devote more than their fair share of effort to the task.

The CEM and Social Loafing Research: Findings
From a Recent Meta-Analysis

One test of the adequacy of the CEM is to compare its central tenets and predictions with the patterns of results in the existing literature on social loafing. Recently, we conducted a meta-analysis of 78 published and unpublished studies that were available as of 1991 (Karau & Williams, 1993). We were able to both estimate the magnitude and consistency of social loafing, and examine the degree to which each of a number of factors moderated social loafing across the large body of studies in the existing literature. Across all studies, there was a statistically reliable and moderately strong (a mean weighted effect size of $d = 0.44$) social loafing effect: People produced lower effort levels when working collectively than when working coactively. Subjects' self-reports of their efforts, however, tended to fail to acknowledge this difference.

In addition, a number of factors were found to moderate social loafing across studies. These moderating variables suggest a number of strategies that might be useful for reducing or overcoming social loafing in intact work groups. A summary of some of the more interesting results of the moderator analysis is presented in Table 4.1. Within each class of a variable in the table, a signficant social loafing effect is indicated by a positive mean effect size with a confidence interval that does not include zero. As shown in the table, a number of variables had a significant influence on the magnitude of the

TABLE 4.1
Selected Moderators of Social Loafing

Variable and Class	n	Mean Weighted Effect Size (d_{i+})	95% CI Lower	95% CI Upper
Evaluation potential[a]				
None	5	−0.12	−0.33	0.08
Coactive condition only	115	0.59	0.55	0.64
Coactive and collective conditions	27	0.08	−0.01	0.17
Unclear	16	0.32	0.20	0.45
Task meaningfulness				
High	30	−0.10	−0.22	0.02
Moderate or unclear	128	0.49	0.45	0.54
Low	5	0.90	0.57	1.22
Expectations of coworker performance				
High	14	0.33	0.14	0.53
Moderate	141	0.45	0.41	0.50
Low	8	−0.17	−0.45	0.10
Uniqueness of individual inputs				
Unique	8	0.03	−0.18	0.24
Potentially redundant	64	0.49	0.41	0.56
Completely redundant	91	0.44	0.39	0.49
Complexity of task				
Simple	133	0.47	0.42	0.51
Complex	7	−0.11	-0.37	0.14
Unclear	23	0.36	0.25	0.47
Opportunity for group-level evaluation				
Present	12	0.03	−0.10	0.16
Absent	151	0.48	0.44	0.52
Type of cover story used				
Effort or performance related	112	0.39	0.34	0.44
Other	51	0.52	0.46	0.59
Setting of study				
Laboratory	140	0.47	0.43	0.51
Field	23	0.25	0.16	0.35

(Continued)

TABLE 4.1. *(Continued)*

Variable and Class	n	Mean Weighted Effect Size (d_{i+})	95% CI	
			Lower	Upper
Relationship among group members				
Friends or teammates	9	−0.17	−0.41	0.08
Mere acquaintances	11	0.25	0.08	0.42
Strangers	127	0.50	0.46	0.55
Unknown or unclear	16	0.28	0.18	0.38
Culture of subjects[b]				
Eastern	15	0.19	0.06	0.32
Western	148	0.46	0.42	0.50
Sex of subjects[c]				
Men	39	0.57	0.48	0.65
Women	23	0.22	0.13	0.32
Both	113	0.44	0.39	0.49

Note. Adapted from "Social Loafing: A Meta-Analytic Review and Theoretical Integration," by S. J. Karau and K. D. Williams, 1993, *Journal of Personality and Social Psychology, 65,* p. 698. Copyright © 1993 by the American Psychological Association. Adapted with permission. All results presented in this table are from statistically significant categorical models. A description of the statistical procedures and coding criteria used in the meta-analysis is provided in Karau and Williams (1993). Information on the general meta-analytic approach used is provided in Hedges and Olkin (1985). CI = 95% confidence interval; *n* refers to the number of coactive/collective comparisons available in each class. Such comparisons included both entire studies and subdivided study units.

[a]Refers to the conditions under which individual outputs could be evaluated.

[b]Eastern cultures included Japan, Taiwan, and China. Western cultures included the United States and Canada.

[c]This analysis included effect sizes that were, whenever possible, partitioned by sex of subject within each separate study unit.

effect sizes, suggesting a number of strategies for reducing or eliminating social loafing. Additional analysis showed that the magnitude of social loafing also increased significantly with increases in group size. The observed patterns correspond quite well with the logic and implications of the CEM. Indeed, in nearly every case, the CEM successfully accounted for the empirical status of the moderating variables. Finally, it is worth noting that since the publication of our meta-analysis, several recent studies produced results that provide additional support for the CEM. We offer several examples throughout this chapter.

The CEM and Work Groups in Organizations

Because the CEM incorporates elements from a variety of prior theories in areas such as social influence, social identity, general human motivation, and work motivation, it represents an integrative model that should have applications to a wide variety of groups, including organizational work groups. Indeed, each of the moderators of social loafing identified in our meta-analysis suggests a clear strategy for enhancing individual group members' efforts on collective tasks. But how does a leader or manager select the best strategies for his or her group?

In general, the CEM suggests that member motivation can be enhanced by strengthening members' expectations that their efforts will be instrumental in obtaining valued individual and group outcomes, and by increasing the value or importance attached to those outcomes. When attempting to enhance work group effectiveness, the leader or manager can influence group members' perceptions, expectations, and motivation either by carefully designing work groups or by carefully designing or changing the work group's physical and social environment. A useful procedure for selecting the best intervention strategies would be to identify all possible barriers to members' perceptions that their efforts will be useful in obtaining valued outcomes. Once the barriers specific to the work group's setting have been identified, it may be possible to remove them or to minimize their influence by restructuring the group, the task, or the environment. Separately examining each of the contingencies in collective performance specified by the CEM helps identify some of the key barriers to motivation. We have already discussed some of the factors influencing the value, or outcome valence, component of the CEM, but it may be useful to provide some examples of factors that influence expectancy and instrumentality on collective tasks.

Expectancy.   An individual's expectancy that his or her efforts will be useful in producing successful performance is likely influenced by a variety of factors, including the nature of the task, member skills and abilities, goal setting, self-efficacy, self-esteem, an understanding of the requirements for successful performance, the provision of necessary resources to succeed at the task, and a match between individual personality and the social requirements of the task. Thus, the expectancy link may be strengthened through a variety of strategies that tap into these constructs, including careful selection of members and matching of members to appropriate tasks based on their skills and personality (Argyris, 1974; Driskell, Hogan, & Salas, 1988; Wanous, Reichers, & Malik, 1984), training in key basic skills, as well as in the unique attributes of the task or role (Tannebaum & Yukl, 1992), setting challenging, realistic, goals that are accompanied by regular, diagnostic feedback (Klein, 1989; Locke & Latham, 1990; White, Kjelgaard, & Harkins, 1995), providing opportunities to practice skills in a nonevaluative atmosphere (Kanter, 1985), providing needed resources and support functions (Hackman & Wageman, 1995), and creating an environment conducive to developing and enhancing self-efficacy and self-esteem, or for encouraging those aspects of the individual's personality to be expressed (Bandura, 1986; Brockner, 1988).

Instrumentality. Because it identifies additional contingencies relevant to collective tasks (see Fig. 4.1), the CEM is especially useful for identifying obstacles to perceived instrumentality. Regarding the link between individual and group performance, a number of factors influence this relationship and how it is perceived by group members. Group dynamicists have long recognized the importance of task type for performance (McGrath, 1984), and tasks also have strong influences on motivation (Steiner, 1972). If the method of combining individual inputs into a group product makes members feel that their inputs will have little to do with group performance, motivation is likely to suffer. For example, Kerr and Bruun (1983) demonstrated that conjunctive tasks are usually more motivating to low ability members than to high ability members, whereas disjunctive tasks are more motivating to high ability members than to low ability members. Tasks that are perceived as overwhelmingly difficult may also decrease one's feelings of efficacy and undermine motivation or performance (Kelly, Futoran, & McGrath, 1990). Group size may also undermine efficacy because as the group gets larger, a single individual's inputs are likely to have less actual or perceived impact on group outcomes (e.g., Latané, 1981; Kerr, 1989). Research has also documented that when one's inputs are redundant with those of other group members, social loafing is more likely (Harkins & Petty, 1982), pointing to the importance of group members perceiving that they are making unique and valuable contributions (cf. Hackman & Oldham, 1980). Expectations of coworker performance also likely interact with task type to influence the perceived contingency between one's own work and group outcomes. If others are expected to perform poorly, one's own inputs may become especially important to group success (Williams & Karau, 1991). In contrast, when others are expected to do well, one's own inputs are less vital to group success on many tasks (Kerr, 1983). Finally, training both in basic group processes and on how the group must coordinate its efforts in order to be successful at its tasks are also likely to enhance the perception that individual efforts will be related to group performance (e.g., Argote, Insko, Yovetch, & Romero, 1995; Hirokawa, 1988; Liang, Moreland, & Argote, 1995). Group planning and goal setting may also enhance this perception by clarifying to members how and why their inputs are unique and important to the group (e.g., Weldon, Jehn, & Pradhan, 1991).

Regarding the links between group performance and group outcomes, and between group outcomes and individual outcomes, these relationships and how they are perceived are often influenced by internal group norms, organizational features, and other elements of the environment. If the group does not expect to be recognized, evaluated, or rewarded for good performance, this can undermine motivation (Hackman & Lawler, 1971; Hackman & Oldham, 1980; Vroom, 1964). Consistent with this idea, Harkins and Szymanski (1989) found that providing a group-level comparison standard eliminated social loafing. Similarly, if individuals do not expect to be recognized, evaluated, or rewarded for their contributions to the group, motivation may be undermined (Williams et al., 1981), unless individuals value the group outcome in and of itself, or value the impact successful performance has on the group's cohesiveness or on their own personal feelings of belonging or identification with a successful group (e.g., Abrams & Hogg, 1990; Baumeitser & Leary, 1995). Finally, we note that sometimes high motivation levels may exist even in the absence of any tangible group or individual outcomes. If an individual finds the task or group environment intrinsically meaningful (Deci, 1975), or becomes absorbed in the sheer joy of their work or the group experience (Csikszentmihalyi, 1990), they may work very hard or persist at the task for a long time, even in the absence of any tangible outcomes, rewards, or potential for evaluation.

SELECTED IMPLICATIONS AND FUTURE DIRECTIONS

Group Cohesiveness and Social Identification

The CEM suggests that enhancing the importance of collective outcomes and their relevance to individuals' self-evaluation should decrease or eliminate social loafing. One strategy for achieving both of these outcomes may be to increase the cohesiveness of the group or the degree to which individuals socially identify with the group. People are more likely to be concerned with the welfare of other group members and to feel that the evaluation of the group is important to their own self-evaluation when working in cohesive, rather than noncohesive, groups. Members of cohesive groups may also be more attentive to the fact that the group's performance and resulting outcomes are partially dependent on their own individual performances. The impact of group cohesiveness and social identification on member motivation also has enormous implications for intact work groups, in which members are likely to form social attachments and in which team-building exercises are often used in the expectation that performance increases will result (e.g., Liebowitz & De Meuse, 1982).

Although researchers have traditionally overlooked the effects of group cohesiveness, recent evidence shows that it can have a positive impact on member motivation. First, in our recent meta-analysis (Karau & Williams, 1993) we found that the relationship between group members does seem to have an impact on social loafing. Specifically, the magnitude of loafing was highest when the group was composed of strangers, somewhat lower (although still significant) when the group was composed of acquaintances, and not significant (with a tendency toward a motivation gain) when the group was composed of friends or was otherwise high in cohesiveness or social identity (see bottom portion of Table 4.1). However, these results must be interpreted with caution given their correlational nature and the limited sample size.

Second, we obtained more direct evidence in a series of recent studies. Two of these studies (Karau & Williams, 1997) compared groups of friends to groups of strangers. In Experiment 1, secretarial students worked on a typing task both individually and collectively in simulated word-processing pools composed of either friends or strangers. Typing rate tended to decrease in noncohesive collectives composed of strangers, but tended to increase in cohesive collectives composed of friends. In Experiment 2, dyads composed of either friends or strangers worked either coactively or collectively on an idea-generation task. As predicted, participants socially loafed when working with strangers, but worked just as hard collectively as coactively when working with friends. However, friends and strangers likely differ in a number of attributes other than cohesiveness. Thus, in a third experiment (Karau & Hart, 1998) cohesiveness was manipulated directly among groups of previously unacquainted participants by asking them to discuss controversial issues on which they either agreed strongly (high cohesiveness), disagreed strongly (low cohesiveness), or disagreed mildly (control) before they worked either coactively or collectively on an idea-generation task. Members of low cohesiveness and control groups engaged in social loafing, whereas members of high cohesiveness groups worked just as hard collectively as coactively. Taken as a whole, these three studies provide converging evidence for the hypothesis that social loafing can be reduced or eliminated among cohesive groups.

Another related strategy for enhancing individuals' concern with group outcomes and their own, related self-evaluations would be to enhance or make salient individuals' social identification with the group. Social identity theory suggests that the outcomes of important or valued groups or social categories have major implications for one's own self-esteem and self-evaluation (e.g., Abrams & Hogg, 1990; Banaji & Prentice, 1994). Indeed, Hogg (1992) suggested that the construct of group cohesiveness is best conceptualized in terms of social identity, and argued that social identification processes may account for group-related outcomes such as performance and attitudes more directly than traditionally conceptualized cohesiveness in the form of interpersonal attraction (Hogg, Cooper-Shaw, & Holzworth, 1993; Hogg & Turner, 1985). According to this perspective, group cohesiveness resides within individuals in the form of their identification with groups and social categories.

In considering how specific aspects of the social self may map onto motivational processes, Breckler and Greenwald (1986) identified three distinct motivational facets of the self that correspond with three evaluative audiences. They distinguish between a private self that responds primarily to internal values, a public self that responds mainly to others' evaluations, and a collective self that is sensitive primarily to fulfilling one's role within the context of the goals of important reference groups. Most prior social loafing research has focused on the motivation produced by the experimenter's evaluation of performance, which is most relevant to the public self (for exceptions, see Harkins & Szymanski, 1988, 1989). However, Breckler and Greenwald (1986) suggested that individuals can be motivated by appeals to any of the three motivational facets of the self, including the collective. They suggested that "achieving the internalized goals of a reference group (the collective self's ego task) can be accomplished by cooperating in group endeavors or by behaving in accordance with a reference group's norms and expectations" (pp. 151–152). Considering that typical reference groups may consist of "coworkers, religious organizations, clubs, athletic teams, and family" (p. 148), this suggests that enhancing social identification with the group may motivate individuals to work hard by appealing to a desire for self-validation as manifested through the collective facet of the self.

Recently, we conducted three studies examining the effects of social identification on social loafing (Karau, Williams, Ostrom, & Hitlan, 1999). In all three studies, participants worked either coactively or collectively on an effortful task (either generating ideas, finding hidden items in a picture, or identifying simulated radar signals). Social identification was manipulated by either enhancing or not enhancing the salience of a personally relevant, preexisting social category and comparison with an outgroup. Thus, participants in the high identification conditions were told that their scores would be compared with those of students at an arch-rival university (Experiment 1) or with those of students of the opposite gender (Experiments 2 and 3). In all three studies, participants in the low identification condition engaged in social loafing, whereas participants in the high identification condition worked just as hard collectively as coactively.

Taken as a whole, our research provides strong initial evidence that enhancing members' attraction to the group and activating members' social identification with the group may increase their efforts on collective tasks. However, the CEM suggests that enhancing cohesiveness and social identification will only enhance individual effort when the task is seen as important or meaningful, and when members feel that they can make valuable contributions to the group product. Considering the literatures on individual motivation and work group performance, in addition to the social loafing research cited earlier, team building and group development initiatives may be most successful in enhancing member motivation when they make members personally accountable (e.g., Harkins, 1987; Williams et al., 1981), enhance commitment to commonly shared group goals (e.g., Hackman, 1987; Weldon et al., 1993), foster development of a salient and easily activated social identity for the group that can be contrasted with a salient outgroup comparison (e.g., Abrams & Hogg, 1990; Harkins & Szymanski, 1989; James & Greenberg, 1989; Karau et al., 1999), and enhance the meaningfulness and personal relevance of the task for its members (e.g., Brickner, Harkins, & Ostrom, 1986; Hackman & Oldham, 1980; Williams & Karau, 1991).

Individual Differences in the Importance Attached to Collective Outcomes

According to the CEM, individuals who have either a dispositional or situational tendency to view collective outcomes as important should be less likely to engage in social loafing than those who do not value collective outcomes or who place primary emphasis on their own individual outcomes. The relative importance attached to collective outcomes could be influenced by one's personal commitment to the group, attraction to the group, or degree of social identification with the group, as discussed earlier. But the perceived importance of collective outcomes is also likely influenced by a range of other factors, including culture, gender, personality and individual differences, group norms, and organizational culture. Such individual differences, whatever their source, are also likely to interact with task and situational variables to determine one's effort on collective tasks.

Most of the research on social loafing has been conducted in the United States. Given the tendency for American society to reward and encourage individual achievement and to emphasize competition, it is possible that social loafing might be less of a problem for other societies that emphasize more communal aspects of life. Consistent with this reasoning, research suggests that Western or American culture is very individualistically oriented, whereas Eastern or Oriental culture is more group or socially oriented (Triandis, 1989; Wheeler, Reis, & Bond, 1989). Because individuals from Eastern cultures are more likely to view performing well on collective tasks as important and valuable, they may be less likely to engage in social loafing. Interestingly, despite important exceptions (e.g., Earley, 1993), studies examining social loafing in a variety of countries ranging in their relative emphasis on individualism or collectivism have often found that social loafing is robust across cultures. However, the magnitude of loafing is often lower in Eastern cultures. Indeed, in our recent meta-analysis (Karau & Williams, 1993), a significant social loafing effect was found within both Eastern and Western culture studies, although the magnitude of the effect was lower in Eastern studies (see bottom portion of Table 4.1).

However, this does not necessarily suggest that social loafing is inevitable in all cultures. A fairly small number of studies has been conducted outside of the United States, with only a few studies within each Eastern country of interest, and many cultural differences have yet to be explored. Examining the individual studies, we also find variability in outcomes and in what variables were of prime interest to researchers. It is likely that cultural factors interact with situational factors in ways that may suggest unique levers for enhancing motivation within each culture. It is especially noteworthy that most studies in Eastern cultures have examined groups of strangers, possibly neutralizing the participants' natural tendencies to value the collective outcome. Following the logic of the CEM, we might predict that motivation gains would be found in Eastern cultures when the group is personally important to members and their inputs are seen as vital to the group's success at a meaningful task. In contrast, the absence of one or more of these factors could lead participants either to view the outcome of the group task as unimportant or to see little utility to their efforts, possibly leading to motivation loss even though collective contexts are still valued in general. A similar analysis could be made for other sources of cultural influences, including regional culture, organizational culture, and group norms: Those cultures emphasizing the value, importance, and meaningfulness of collective activity and outcomes may be less conducive to social loafing, relative to more individualistic cultures.

Gender is another key factor that is likely to affect one's perception of the importance of collective tasks and outcomes. Gender research suggests that women tend to be more collectively oriented than men. For example, research on gender stereotypes, behavior in small groups settings, leadership behavior, and other aspects of social behavior has found that men tend to possess agentic qualities, such as being independent and assertive, whereas women tend to possess communal qualities, such as being friendly, cooperative, and concerned with the reactions and outcomes of others (e.g., Bakan, 1966; Broverman, Vogel, Broverman, Clarkson, & Rosenkrantz, 1972; Eagly, 1987). These findings suggest that men are more likely to be oriented toward individualistic and competitive concerns, whereas women are more likely to be oriented toward interpersonal and cooperative concerns. Thus, we might expect women to be less likely to socially loaf than men and to be more responsive to group settings that provide the potential for contributing to a positive collective outcome that reflects favorable on individual members. Indeed, in our recent meta-analysis (Karau & Williams, 1993), we found that although women and men both engaged in social loafing across studies, the magnitude of loafing was significantly lower for women (see bottom portion of Table 4.1).

Similar analyses can be made of other factors such as personality, group norms, and organizational culture. Regarding personality, the CEM predicts that individual difference variables may influence effort through both the value attached to collective outcomes and the perception that one's efforts will be useful in obtaining such collective outcomes. The more individuals value group work and collective outcomes, the less likely they will be to loaf on a collective task and the more likely they will be to respond in a favorable manner to opportunities to make unique contributions to a collective outcome. A number of individual differences variables may tap into this tendency to value collective outcomes, including individualism/collectivism, self-monitoring, and Protestant work ethic. Individual difference variables also likely influence the meaningfulness or intrinsic value attached to various collective tasks. Such relevant individual difference variables may include need for cognition, affect intensity, need for affiliation, need for control, and need for power. Similarly, the more individuals perceive that their efforts will be useful in obtaining valued outcomes, the more likely they will be to work hard on a collective task. Individual difference variables that may influence this perception may include self-efficacy, self-esteem, and locus of control. In addition, combinations of personality variables and situational factors that enhance both perceptions that efforts will be useful in obtaining collective outcomes and the value of those outcomes should be most useful in enhancing effort.

Our theory-driven analysis of personality factors and individual motivation in groups is somewhat speculative at this point, given that few studies have directly explored personality influence on social loafing. Yet, results from several recent studies have produced data consistent with this analysis. First, situationally induced self-efficacy has been found to enhance individual effort on collective tasks when participants are identified and evaluated (Sanna, 1992). It would be intriguing to examine whether individual differences in self-efficacy have similar effects or to examine whether collective efficacy enhances individuals' efforts on collective tasks when the group output is identified and evaluated. Second, Earley (1993) found that individuals in collectivist cultures actually worked harder in a group context than individually, but only when working with an ingroup rather than an outgroup. Third, another intriguing study by Earley (1994) found that individualism/collectivism had a strong impact on which training regimens were most useful for enhancing individual and group feelings of efficacy and resulting performance. Self-focused training had the most positive impact on individualists, whereas group-focused training had the most positive impact on collectivists. These results were consistent within each of three samples comprised of managers from the United States, Hong Kong, and the People's Republic of China, lending further credence to the notion that it is the relative level of collectivism/individualism residing within the individual, rather than cultural background per se, that is the primary influence on motivation in collective settings. Fourth, Petty, Cacioppo, and Kasmer (1985) found that participants high in need for cognition did not engage in social loafing when working on a cognitive task, consistent with the logic of the CEM.

The Potential for Motivation Gains in Groups

Researchers have focused their attention on identifying factors that reduce or eliminate social loafing. Almost no studies have examined factors that increase social loafing, and only a handful of studies have examined the potential for motivation gains to emerge in groups. Viewing social loafing mainly as a problem and a barrier to productivity, researchers have, quite reasonably, chosen to examine moderating variables that may suggest strategies for preventing motivation losses. This emphasis is consistent with Latané et al.'s (1979) characterization of social loafing as a "social disease." However, the CEM suggests that making members' valued outcomes more reliant on their inputs collectively than coactively can create motivation gains in some situations. Indeed, this potential was recognized by Latané et al. (1979) when they suggested that ". . . the cure [to social loafing] will come from finding ways of channeling social forces so that the group can serve as a means of intensifying individual responsibility rather than diffusing it." We agree with this general sentiment and extend it beyond individual responsibility to include a range of factors that would enhance expectations of favorable, valued outcomes as a result of working hard in a group.

Consider a situation in which an individual is reliant on the group for an important and valued outcome, but expects that the other group members will not perform well at the task. This creates a situation in which the individual's efforts are suddenly very important to their own outcomes, possibly even more so than if they had been working on their own. A classic example is the class project in which students must work together in groups and share a single grade for the project. It is not uncommon for a serious, highly capable student who desires an A to do much of the work for an entire group of less serious, less capable, or less grade-motivated students. If the serious student perceives that he or she is actually capable of covering up for the less serious students (expectancy) and producing a good group outcome largely on their own (instrumentality), wants or needs the A badly enough (value), and doesn't find it more repellent to cover up for the others and get an A than to also slack off and share a lower grade (value), he or she may well work extremely hard on the task.

In a recent series of studies, we demonstrated conditions under which people may actually work harder in a collective setting than in a coactive setting in order to compensate for the others in their group (Karau & Williams, 1997; Williams & Karau, 1991). We refer to this phenomenon as "social compensation." One factor that might produce social compensation is the expectation that other group members will perform at insufficient levels for the group to succeed. Compensating for others could be done either to maintain the success or long-term viability of the group, or to maintain one's own favorable outcomes (such as evaluation) that result from a successful group performance. The expectation that one's coworkers will perform poorly could arise from a variety of sources, including feedback or direct knowledge of poor performance on previous related tasks, inabilities, perceptions of general motivation and work ethic or motivation specific to the group task, statements made by others, and a general distrust of other peoples' reliability.

However, consistent with the CEM, the expectation that others will perform poorly is not sufficient, in and of itself, to produce higher levels of effort. Individuals must also perceive that their increased efforts will make a difference, or will lead to performance that will be instrumental in the group's success and the benefits associated with it. In addition, the group product, the group's success, or individual consequences related to the group's success, must be important or valued by the individual: If the task or group product is seen as meaningless, then there is no need to compensate because it doesn't matter to the individual how well or how poorly the group does.

We initially examined these ideas in a series of three studies (Williams & Karau, 1991). In each experiment, participants worked either coactively or collectively on an idea-generation task that was designed to be viewed as meaningful. Expectations of coworker performance were either inferred from interpersonal trust scores (Experiment 1) or were manipulated via a confederate coworker's statement of either effort (Experiment 2) or ability (Experiment 3). We hypothesized that, when working on a task that was considered meaningful, participants would compensate for a coworker whom they expected to perform poorly and would actually work harder collectively than coactively. The results from all three experiments supported this hypothesis. Experiment 3 also showed that participants were not willing to compensate for a poor-performing coworker when the task was low in meaningfulness, consistent with the CEM. The social compensation effect was also replicated in a recent study in which ability expectations were manipulated using a bogus note-passing technique (Karau & Williams, 1997, Experiment 2).

Taken as a whole, these studies all provide compelling support for the social compensation hypothesis, and demonstrate that there are conditions under which people will exert more effort on a collective task than on a coactive task, even when their individual inputs cannot be monitored collectively. These studies also illustrate how the CEM can be used to generate predictions regarding how a range of situational, personality, and group structual factors may interact to influence individual's efforts in collective contexts. Social compensation was only found on meaningful tasks and among relatively small groups. In larger groups, expectations that compensation would produce a favorable outcome would likely be diminished on many tasks. Social compensation might also be unlikely to persist over time, unless reciprocated in some form. Feelings of equity and fairness may influence long-term success, as has been found in studies of interpersonal relationships (e.g., Walster, Walster, & Berscheid, 1978). It would be interesting to examine the potential for motivation gains, even in larger groups, on disjunctive tasks in which a single member can determine the group's success.

CONCLUDING OBSERVATIONS

Understanding individual motivation on collective tasks is central to developing more effective work groups. Given the widespread and growing use of work groups and teams in business and health care organizations, it is vital to understand the dynamics of group members' motivation. Member effort is a major influence on group performance, and it is important to separate effort from other performance-related factors to determine how best to utilize the organization's physical and personnel resources. Organizational psychologists have developed large literatures on individual motivation and on work group performance, but generally have not studied individuals' efforts on collective tasks. Social psychologists have developed a large literature on social loafing among ad hoc laboratory groups (and occasionally among classroom project groups or sports teams), but generally have not studied social loafing among intact organizational groups. However, when the knowledge emerging from both the social and organizational arenas is integrated, a rich framework for understanding individual motivation within work groups begins to emerge.

In this chapter, we presented a model, the CEM, that we believe successfully integrates the theoretical and empirical strengths of a variety of perspectives and makes clear predictions for research and practice. We documented the usefulness of the model for explaining and integrating the research on social loafing (Karau & Williams, 1993), and the inclusion of key assumptions from well-tested motivational theories enhances the likelihood of the model's applicability to everyday work groups. We also discussed a general strategy for applying the model and identified a number of specific implications for work groups in organizations. In our analysis, we suggested that leaders and managers may often be able to enhance motivation within work groups by identifying the social, situational, and perceptual factors that may decrease individuals' expectations that their efforts will be useful in obtaining valued outcomes in a collective setting. Thus, barriers to motivation can often be uncovered by considering how individual differences, task characteristics, group structural variables, and other group and individual processes may influence expectancy and instrumentality, as well as the value that members attach to the various outcomes associated with collective tasks. The CEM is a useful tool for performing such a diagnosis because it identifies unique contingencies created by collective tasks that can create barriers to motivation, and considers the importance of self-evaluation and other social processes on motivation in groups.

For researchers, a vital next step is to conduct controlled studies on intact organizational groups that directly test the effectiveness of the strategies suggested by the CEM. Until a fair amount of such work has been done, we must acknowledge that our guidelines for practice are somewhat tentative. Research on organizational work groups that tests the CEM would be very useful in helping leaders and managers identify the best tools and resources for keeping group members motivated, as well as for identifying when less than desirable group performance is a motivational issue rather than a problem of resources, tasks, or systems design. The CEM, as well as the social loafing research discussed in this chapter, provide future researchers with a firm foundation for future work. The CEM also provides an example of the vast potential for greater integration of knowledge and communication across the subdisciplines of social and organizational psychology. As this entire book documents, some of this integration has already taken place. Yet, the potential for additional integration and cross-disciplinary communication is vast.

REFERENCES

Abrams, D., & Hogg, M. (1990). *Social Identity Theory: Constructive and critical advances.* New York: Springer-Verlag.

Argote, L., Insko, C. A., Yovetch, N., & Romero, A. A. (1995). Group learning curves: The effects of turnover and task complexity on group performance. *Journal of Applied Social Psychology, 25,* 512–529.

Argyris, C. (1974). Personality vs. organization. *Organizational Dynamics, 3*(2), 2–17.

Bakan, D. (1966). *The duality of human existence: An essay on psychology and religion.* Chicago: Rand McNally.

Banaji, M. R., & Prentice, D. A. (1994). The self in social contexts. *Annual Review of Psychology, 45,* 297–332.

Bandura, A. (1986). *Social foundations of thought and action: A social cognitive theory.* Englewood Cliffs, NJ: Prentice-Hall.

Baumeister, R. F., & Leary, M. R. (1995). The need to belong: Desire for interpersonal attachments as a fundamental human motivation. *Psychological Bulletin, 117,* 497–529.

Breckler, S. J., & Greenwald, A. G. (1986). Motivational facets of the self. In R. M. Sorrentino & E. T. Higgins (Eds.), *Handbook of motivation and cognition* (Vol. 1, pp. 145–164). New York: Guilford.

Brewer, M. B. (1991). The social self: On being the same and different at the same time. *Personality and Social Psychology Bulletin, 17,* 475–482.

Brickner, M. A., Harkins, S. G., & Ostrom, T. M. (1986). Effects of personal involvement: Thought-provoking implications for social loafing. *Journal of Personality and Social Psychology, 51,* 763–769.

Brockner, J. (1988). *Self-esteem at work: Research, theory, and practice.* Lexington, MA: Lexington Books.

Broverman, I. K., Vogel, S. R., Broverman, D. M., Clarkson, F. E., & Rosenkrantz, P. S. (1972). Sex-role stereotypes: A current appraisal. *Journal of Social Issues, 28*(2), 59–78.

Brown, J. D., Collins, R. L., & Schmidt, G. W. (1988). Self-esteem and direct versus indirect forms of self-enhancement. *Journal of Personality and Social Psychology, 55,* 445–453.

Caporael, L., Dawes, R., Orbell, J., & van de Kragt, A. (1989). Selfishness examined: Cooperation in the absence of egoistic incentives. *Behavioral and Brain Sciences, 12,* 683–699.

Cialdini, R. B., Borden, R. J., Thorne, A., Walker, M. R., Freeman, S., & Sloan, L. R. (1976). Basking in reflected glory: Three (football) field studies. *Journal of Personality and Social Psychology, 34,* 366–375.

Crocker, J., & Luhtanen, R. (1990). Collective self-esteem and ingroup bias. *Journal of Personality and Social Psychology, 58,* 60–67.

Csikszentmihalyi, M. (1990). *Flow: The psychology of optimal experience.* New York: Harper & Row.

Davis, J. H. (1969). *Group performance.* Reading, MA: Addison-Wesley.

Deci, E. L. (1975). *Intrinsic motivation.* New York: Plenum.

Driskell, J. E., Hogan, R., & Salas, E. (1988). Personality and group performance. *Review of Personality and Social Psychology, 14,* 91–112.

Eagly, A. H. (1987). *Sex differences in social behavior: A social-role interpretation.* Hillsdale, NJ: Lawrence Erlbaum Associates.

Earley, P. C. (1993). East meets West meets Mideast: Further explorations of collectivistic and individualistic work groups. *Academy of Management Journal, 36,* 319–348.

Earley, P. C. (1994). Self or group? Cultural effects of training on self-efficacy and performance. *Administrative Science Quarterly, 39,* 89–117.

Faulkner, S. L., & Williams, K. D. (1996, May). *A study of social loafing in industry.* Paper presented at the annual meeting of the Midwestern Psychological Association, Chicago.

Fiske, S. T., & Taylor, S. E. (1991). *Social cognition* (2nd ed.). New York: Random House.

George, J. M. (1992). Extrinsic and intrinsic origins of perceived social loafing in organizations. *Academy of Management Journal, 35,* 191–202.

George, J. M. (1995). Asymmetrical effects of rewards and punishments: The case of social loafing. *Journal of Occupational and Organizational Psychology, 68,* 327–338.

Gersick, C. J., & Hackman, J. R. (1990). Habitual routines in task-performing groups. *Organizational Behavior and Human Decision Processes, 47,* 65–97.

Goethals, G., & Darley, J. (1987). Social comparison theory: Self-evaluation and group life. In B. Mullen & G. Goethals (Eds.), *Theories of group behavior* (pp. 21–47). New York: Springer-Verlag.

Greenwald, A. G., & Pratkanis, A. R. (1984). The self. In R. S. Wyer & T. K. Srull (Eds.), *Handbook of social cognition* (pp. 129–178). Hillsdale, NJ: Lawrence Erlbaum Associates.

Griffith, T. L., Fichman, M., & Moreland, R. L. (1989). Social loafing and social facilitation: An empirical test of the cognitive-motivational model of performance. *Basic and Applied Social Psychology, 10,* 253–271.

Guzzo, R. A., & Salas, E. (Eds.). (1995). *Team effectiveness and decision making in organizations.* San Francisco: Jossey-Bass.

Hackman, J. R. (1987). The design of work teams. In J. Lorsch (Ed.), *Handbook of organizational behavior* (pp. 315–342). Englewood Cliffs, NJ: Prentice-Hall.

Hackman, J. R., & Lawler, E. E., III. (1971). Employee reactions to job characteristics. *Journal of Applied Psychology, 55,* 259–285.

Hackman, J. R., & Oldham, G. R. (1980). *Work redesign.* Reading, MA: Addison-Wesley.

Hackman, J. R., & Wageman, R. (1995). Total quality management: Empirical, conceptual, and practical issues. *Administrative Science Quarterly, 40,* 309–342.

Harkins, S. G. (1987). Social loafing and social facilitation. *Journal of Experimental Social Psychology, 23,* 1–18.

Harkins, S. G., & Jackson, J. M. (1985). The role of evaluation in eliminating social loafing. *Personality and Social Psychology Bulletin, 11,* 575–584.

Harkins, S. G., & Petty, R. E. (1982). Effects of task difficulty and task uniqueness on social loafing. *Journal of Personality and Social Psychology, 43,* 1214–1229.

Harkins, S. G., & Szymanski, K. (1988). Social loafing and self-evaluation with an objective standard. *Journal of Experimental Social Psychology, 24,* 354–365.

Harkins, S. G., & Szymanski, K. (1989). Social loafing and group evaluation. *Journal of Personality and Social Psychology, 56,* 934–941.

Heckhausen, H. (1977). Achievement motivation and its constructs: A cognitive model. *Motivation and Emotion, 1,* 283–329.

Hedges, L. V., & Olkin, I. (1985). *Statistical methods for meta-analysis.* San Diego: Academic Press.

Hirokawa, R. Y. (1988). Group communication and decision-making performance: A continued test of the functional perspective. *Human Communication Research, 14,* 487–515.

Hogg, M. A. (1992). *The social psychology of group cohesiveness: From attraction to social identity.* London: Harvester Wheatsheaf.

Hogg, M. A., Cooper-Shaw, L., & Holzworth, D. W. (1993). Group prototypicality and depersonalized attraction in small interactive groups. *Personality and Social Psychology Bulletin, 19,* 452–465.

Hogg, M. A., & Turner, J. C. (1985). When liking begets solidarity: An experiment on the role of interpersonal attraction in psychological group formation. *British Journal of Social Psychology, 24,* 267–281.

Ingham, A. G., Levinger, G., Graves, J., & Peckham, V. (1974). The Ringelmann effect: Studies of group size and group performance. *Journal of Personality and Social Psychology, 10,* 371–384.

Jackson, J. M., & Williams, K. D. (1985). Social loafing on difficult tasks: Working collectively can improve performance. *Journal of Personality and Social Psychology, 49,* 937–942.

James, K., & Greenberg, J. (1989). In-group salience, intergroup comparison, and individual performance and self-esteem. *Personality and Social Psychology Bulletin, 15,* 604–616.

Kanter, R. M. (1985). Managing the human side of change. *Management Review, 74*(4), 52–56.

Karau, S. J., & Hart, J. W. (1998). Group cohesiveness and social loafing: Effects of a social interaction manipulation on individual motivation within groups. *Group Dynamics: Theory, Research, and Practice, 2,* 185–191.

Karau, S. J., & Williams, K. D. (1993). Social loafing: A meta-analytic review and theoretical integration. *Journal of Personality and Social Psychology, 65,* 681–706.

Karau, S. J., & Williams, K. D. (1997). The effects of group cohesiveness on social loafing and social compensation. *Group Dynamics: Theory, Research, and Practice, 1,* 156–168.

Karau, S. J., Williams, K. D., Ostrom, M. A., & Hitlan, R. T. (1999). *Social identification and social loafing.* Manuscript in progress.

Kelly, J. R., Futoran, G. C., & McGrath, J. E. (1990). Capacity and capability: Seven studies of entrainment of task performance rates. *Small Group Research, 21,* 283–314.

Kerr, N. L. (1983). Motivation losses in small groups: A social dilemma analysis. *Journal of Personality and Social Psychology, 45,* 819–828.

Kerr, N. L. (1989). Illusions of efficacy: The effects of group size on perceived efficacy in social dilemmas. *Journal of Experimental Social Psychology, 25,* 287–313.

Kerr, N. L., & Bruun, S. E. (1983). Dispensability of member effort and group motivation losses: Free-rider effects. *Journal of Personality and Social Psychology, 44,* 78–94.

Klein, H. J. (1989). An integrated control theory model of work motivation. *Academy of Management Review, 14,* 150–172.

Kravitz, D. A., & Martin, B. (1986). Ringelmann rediscovered: The original article. *Journal of Personality and Social Psychology, 50,* 936–941.

Latané, B. (1981). The psychology of social impact. *American Psychologist, 36,* 343–356.

Latané, B., Williams, K., & Harkins, S. (1979). Many hands make light the work: The causes and consequences of social loafing. *Journal of Personality and Social Psychology, 37,* 822–832.

Leary, M. R., & Forsyth, D. R. (1987). Attributions of responsibility for collective endeavors. *Review of Personality and Social Psychology, 8,* 167–188.

Liang, D. W., Moreland, R., & Argote, L. (1995). Group versus individual training and group performance: The mediating factor of transactive memory. *Personality and Social Psychology Bulletin, 21,* 384–393.

Liebowitz, S. J., & De Meuse, K. P. (1982). The application of team building. *Human Relations, 35,* 1–18.

Locke, E. A., & Latham, G. P. (1990). *A theory of goal setting and task performance.* Englewood Cliffs, NJ: Prentice-Hall.

McGrath, J. E. (1984). *Groups: Interaction and performance.* Englewood Cliffs, NJ: Prentice-Hall.

Naylor, J. C., Pritchard, R. D., & Ilgen, D. R. (1980). *A theory of behavior in organizations.* San Diego, CA: Academic Press.

Olson, M. (1965). *The logic of collective action: Public goods and the theory of groups.* Cambridge, MA: Harvard University Press.

Petty, R. E., Cacioppo, J. T., & Kasmer, J. A. (1985, May). *Individual differences in social loafing on cognitive tasks.* Paper presented at the annual meeting of the Midwestern Psychological Association, Chicago.

Porter, L. W., & Lawler, E. E. (1968). *Managerial attitudes and performance.* Homewood, IL: Dorsey.

Sanna, L. J. (1992). Self-efficacy theory: Implications for social facilitation and social loafing. *Journal of Personality and Social Psychology, 62,* 774–786.

Sanna, L. J., & Pusecker, P. A. (1994). Self-efficacy, valence of self-evaluation, and performance. *Personality and Social Psychology Bulletin, 20,* 82–92.

Shepperd, J. A. (1993). Productivity loss in performance groups: A motivation analysis. *Psychological Bulletin, 113,* 67–81.

Smith, E. R., & Henry, S. (1996). An in-group becomes part of the self: Response time evidence. *Personality and Social Psychology Bulletin, 22,* 635–642.

Steiner, I. D. (1972). Group process and productivity. San Diego, CA: Academic Press.

Suls, J. M., & Miller, R. L. (Eds.). (1977). *Social comparison processes: Theoretical and empirical perspectives.* Washington, DC: Hemisphere.

Sundstrom, E., De Meuse, K. P., & Futrell, D. (1990). Work teams: Applications and effectiveness. *American Psychologist, 45,* 120–133.

Szymanski, K., & Harkins, S. G. (1992). Self-evaluation and creativity. *Personality and Social Psychology Bulletin, 18,* 259–265.

Tajfel, H., & Turner, J. (1986). The social identity theory of intergroup behavior. In S. Worchel & W. Austin (Eds.), *Psychology of intergroup relations* (pp. 33–48). Chicago: Nelson-Hall.

Tannebaum, S. I., & Yukl, G. (1992). Training and development in work organizations. *Annual Review of Psychology, 43,* 399–441.

Taylor, S. E., & Brown, J. D. (1988). Illusion and well-being: Some social psychological contributions to a theory of mental health. *Psychological Bulletin, 103,* 193–210.

Tesser, A. (1988). Toward a self-evaluation maintenance model of social behavior. In L. Berkowitz (Ed.), *Advances in experimental social psychology* (Vol. 21, pp. 181–227). San Diego, CA: Academic Press.

Triandis, H. C. (1989). The self and social behavior in differing cultural contexts. *Psychological Review, 96,* 506–520.

Vroom, V. H. (1964). *Work and motivation.* New York: Wiley.

Walster, E., Walster, G. W., & Berscheid, E. (1978). *Equity: Theory and research.* Boston: Allyn & Bacon.

Wanous, J. P., Reichers, A. E., & Malik, S. D. (1984). Organizational socialization and group development: Toward an integrative perspective. *Academy of Management Review, 9,* 670–683.

Weldon, E., Jehn, K. A., & Pradhan, P. (1991). Processes that mediate the relationship between a group goal and improved group performance. *Journal of Personality and Social Psychology, 61,* 555–569.

Wheeler, L., Reis, H. T., & Bond, M. H. (1989). Collectivism–individualism in everyday social life: The middle kingdom and the melting pot. *Journal of Personality and Social Psychology, 57,* 79–86.

White, P. H., Kjelgaard, M. M., & Harkins, S. G. (1995). Testing the contributions of self-evaluation to goal-setting effects. *Journal of Personality and Social Psychology, 69,* 69–79.

Williams, K., Harkins, S., & Latané, B. (1981). Identifiability as a deterrent to social loafing: Two cheering experiments. *Journal of Personality and Social Psychology, 40,* 303–311.

Williams, K. D., & Karau, S. J. (1991). Social loafing and social compensation: The effects of expectations of coworker performance. *Journal of Personality and Social Psychology, 61,* 570–581.

Zajonc, R. B. (1980). Compresence. In P. B. Paulus (Ed.), *Psychology of group influence* (pp. 35–60). Hillsdale, NJ: Lawrence Erlbaum Associates.

Chapter 5

Using Social Justice to Build Effective Work Groups

Russell Cropanzano
Colorado State University

Marshall Schminke
University of Central Florida

What does a business mean when it says that it wants "effective" work groups? Generally speaking, it seems that effectiveness has at least two parts. First, its members must hold together as a unit, and second, the work group should effectively perform some necessary tasks. The first challenge is that of maintenance. All other things being equal, a harmonious group has a better chance at maintenance than one that is riddled with conflict. The second challenge is that of performance. A variety of things can impact performance, including the skills of members, suitability of the social structure (e.g., does it allow for the free flow of necessary information), and sequential dependencies with other groups. Although we do not deny the importance of these factors, we emphasize that individuals are likely to be motivated on behalf of the organization when the organization is motivated on behalf of them. As we discuss, organizations can build group effectiveness by meeting these twin challenges.[1]

---

[1]The research literature on these topics is exceedingly large. To make our task manageable, we limit ourselves to the individual level of analysis within existing work groups. That is, we focus on the reactions and performance of individual group members. For example, in the studies we discuss, harmony and maintenance are operationalized mostly by workers' evaluations of their group or organization (e.g., job satisfaction, organizational commitment, supervisory trust, and so on) and also by their desire to remain part of the collective (e.g., turnover and turnover intentions). Performance refers to actual ratings of in-role job performance and, where noted, to organizational citizenship behaviors. These limitations are all necessary for a practical reason. Research on organizational justice has been dominated by the individual level of analysis (cf. Cropanzano & Greenberg, 1997; Greenberg, 1990). Another level of analysis would misrepresent the current literature.

The remaining question is one of means. How is effectiveness to be achieved? We can sum up the perspective taken by this chapter in a single sentence: *Treat people fairly*. We maintain that justice provides one platform on which effective groups are launched (Kirkman, Shapiro, Novelli, & Brett, 1996). However, the matter is more complicated than this. Most researchers argue that there are at least two types of justice—distributive and procedural. The first refers to the outcomes rendered, the second to the means by which these outcomes are assigned. To articulate this position, we explain these concepts. But there is another issue as well. Sometimes these two types of justice work together. A group may be high on both, low on both, or high on one and low on the other.

To address these considerations, this chapter proceeds in four steps. First, we review the literature on distributive justice, discussing how outcome fairness can promote both group harmony (by providing equal allocations to all members) and performance (by rewarding members based on merit or equity). Second, we examine procedural justice, noting how process fairness relates to both harmony and performance. Third, we discuss the manner in which procedures and outcomes work together to promote effective work groups by considering an additive theory called the "two-factor model." This model might be taken to suggest that procedural justice is more central to group maintenance than is distributive justice. We review and critique this perspective. Fourth and last, we turn our attention to recent research emphasizing the statistical interaction between process and outcomes. We critique the so-called two-stage model and conclude by noting several points of debate in the current literature.

PART I: DISTRIBUTIVE JUSTICE

A distribution refers to the outcomes of allocations that result from some decision. For example, when one applies for a job, the individual may or may not be selected. A job offer is the outcome of the selection decision (cf. Gilliland, 1993, and Singer, 1993 for reviews of this literature). Individuals do not accept their distributions passively. Quite the contrary, when an outcome is important, people tend to evaluate it carefully. Generally speaking, individuals will compare what they receive to some referent standard (Kulik & Ambrose, 1992). These referents come from a variety of sources, although social referents (i.e., the distributions obtained by other people) have probably received the most attention (e.g., Austin, 1977; Crosby, 1976; 1984; Martin, 1981; Pettigrew, 1967).

When the referent standard differs from the individual's actual allocations, then one is apt to feel that his or her outcomes were unfair. This judgment is one of *distributive* injustice, because it is based on a person's allocations (Flinder & Hauenstein, 1994; Schwarzald, Koslowsky, & Shalit, 1992; Stepina & Perrewe, 1991; Summers & Hendrix, 1991; Sweeney, McFarlin, & Inderrieden, 1990). Both under and overreward can spur a sense of distributive injustice, but this evaluation is more pronounced when the individual is relatively disadvantaged. Individuals are somewhat more tolerant when the comparison is in their favor (Deustch, 1985). For this reason, we limit ourselves to the case of underreward inequity. The reader is referred to Greenberg (1982, 1988) and Harder (1992) for information on overreward.

This brief overview provides a sampling of the three main ideas in distributive justice research. First, fairness is a judgment that is based on someone's perceptions—not on any objective standards. Second, the object of this judgment is one's outcomes with respect to a particular decision. Third, judgments of distributive justice are ultimately relative. The allocation is neither fair nor unfair by itself. Rather, justice is determined with respect to some referent standard. If such a standard is lacking, then one cannot ascertain the appropriateness of a given outcome.

Allocation Rules and Inequity

Thus far, we have evaded a larger question. We have said that individuals compare their outcomes to a standard and then decide whether these outcomes are appropriate. Although this comparison is said to be the basis for distributive justice judgments, it necessitates some rule or rules by which the allocations should be made. For example, within a work team, some have suggested that organizations should divide rewards equally so as not to create unhealthy intragroup competition (Deming, 1986). Under an equality rule, one would formulate a distributive justice judgment by comparing one's allocations to those of any other group member. If both sets of outcomes were equivalent, then one is being treated fairly (i.e., in accordance with an equality rule).

Others have suggested that distributions could be allocated based on need (Rawls, 1971). Under a need rule, one would first require an accounting of at least two sets of exigencies—those of the self and those of the referent other. One would further require a second accounting. This time the perceiver would have to gather information regarding each person's outcomes. If one's outcomes were appropriate for one's needs, while the referent individual's outcomes were likewise appropriate, then distributive fairness would prevail. It is easy to see how equality and need distributions differ. When using a need rule, it is acceptable for a referent other to obtain more goods than you if he or she needed them more. However, this would not be acceptable according to an equality rule. In a later section, we say more concerning equality and need. For now, however, we should note they have not received as much attention as another allocation rule.

In modern justice research, the most widely studied allocation rule is that of equity (Cropanzano & Greenberg, 1997; Greenberg & Cohen, 1982). In fact, Walster and Walster (1975) went so far as to maintain that all allocation rules reduce to equity. However, this point is disputed by most contemporary theorists (Deustch, 1985; Greenberg & Cohen, 1982; James, 1993).[2] In any case, the equity rule has garnered the most research attention. According to the equity principle, one's outcomes should be proportional to one's inputs (Chen, 1995; Homans, 1961). In short, those who contribute more to the group should reap most of the benefits. To decide whether or not an allocation is inequitable, one compares his or her input/outcome ratio to the input/outcome ratio of some referent other (Adams, 1965; Adams & Freedman, 1976). When these ratios are nonequivalent, one judges the allocation to be unfair. Subsequently, individuals will experience a feeling of negative emotion and dissatisfaction with their outcomes (Cropanzano & Randall, 1993). They will likely alter their inputs, perhaps even lowering job performance, in order to realign the errant ratios (Greenberg, 1982; 1988).

Allocation Rules, Group Harmony, and Performance

Armed with this review of allocation rules, it is now suitable for us to ask how these rules impact group effectiveness. In fact, the evidence is very limited, particularly in regard to need (cf. James, 1993; Greenberg & Cohen, 1982). However, more evidence is available with regard to equality and, especially, equity. Generally speaking, the use of equity rules tends to boost individual performance but may sometimes threaten group harmony. As Deming (1986) suspected, equity sometimes increases individual performance, but it also promotes competition among group members. Dividing rewards equally seems to have more beneficial results for maintaining group harmony, although individual performance can suffer somewhat. These points have already been noted by several reviewers (e.g., Cropanzano & Greenberg, 1997; Deustch, 1975, 1985; Ferris, Frink, Beehr, & Gilmore, 1995; James, 1993; Kabanoff, 1991; Kerr & Slocum, 1987), although we shall see that some caveats are in order.

Within work teams, we can most easily demonstrate the contrast between equity and equality rules by examining recent research on salary dispersion. Salary dispersion is the amount of variance in pay within some specified

---

[2]It is noteworthy that other researchers have argued that all allocation rules reduce to equality. Messick and Sentis (1983) and Rutte and Messick (1995) maintain that fair allocations are always equal. However, equality must be understood with respect to some dimensions, and outcomes can vary on this. For example, to reward each according to his or her contribution (equity) is tantamount to saying that all people with a given level of performance receive equal rewards. Likewise, need distributions refer to giving everyone with the same exigency the same outcome.

work group. To the extent that one abides by norms of equality, salary dispersion tends to be low. Equity distributions tend to produce wider levels of dispersion. In one large-scale study, Pfeffer and Davis-Blake (1992) gathered data on thousands of university administrators from hundreds of different schools. These researchers found that when salary dispersion was wide, turnover dropped for those at the high end of the pay scale, whereas it increased for those at the low end. Pfeffer and Langton (1993) followed up this study by examining salary dispersion within academic departments. Generally speaking, as salary dispersion increased, job satisfaction, research productivity, and the number of collaborative projects all fell off. It should be noted that various factors moderated these relationships.

Earlier, we maintained that equity rules can sometimes serve to increase job performance. From our brief description, however, the Pfeffer and Langton (1993) study would seem to contradict our claim regarding performance. A closer analysis shows that this is not the case. Using an equity distribution rule, an unequal allocation can boost performance only if the recipient of the low payment agrees that his or her inputs are minimal. In other words, we can tolerate earning less if we believe that we are also contributing less (van Dijk & Wilke, 1993). However, if an individual believes that he or she has earned less while contributing the same amount (or more) than a referent other, a mismatch between the input/outcome ratios will occur. Consequently, the individual will perceive distributive injustice and (if not constrained by the situation, see Harder, 1992) may lower performance to compensate. Put differently, an unequal allocation that is judged to be distributively fair will likely boost performance, but an unequal allocation that is judged to be distributively unfair will likely lower performance (Cropanzano & Greenberg, in press; Harder, 1992).

A closer look at the Pfeffer and Langton (1993) study provides evidence for this. Some academic disciplines have widely accepted scientific paradigms (e.g., physics). There is less consensus in others (e.g., literature). A well-defined paradigm makes it easier for professors to agree as to what constitutes a scholarly contribution and what does not. Under these conditions, one would expect more consensus as to appropriate inputs and, therefore, less ill will in the face of salary dispersion. This is exactly what Pfeffer and Langton (1993) discovered. In those disciplines with a widely accepted paradigm, salary dispersion had weaker relationships to the outcome variables.

When managing work groups, organizations use equity at their own risk. If employees believe that their low earnings are justifiable, then so much the better—performance should improve. However, if employees do not believe this, then they are apt to be less cooperative and less productive. Thus, when using equity distributions it would behoove work teams and organizations to make sure that everyone understands and agrees to the standards. According to two studies by Cooper, Dyck, and Frohlich (1992), participation offers much promise as a mechanism for solving this problem.

How Groups Use Distributive Justice to Build
Performance and Harmony

Assuming that agreed upon performance standards either do exist or can be formulated, our observations raise a dilemma for work teams. If they utilize a pure equality distribution (i.e., pay everyone equally) then they lose the performance-enhancing effects of equity. On the other hand, if the team opts for a pure equity distribution, then many individuals will likely show lower levels of cooperation. The work group will be less harmonious. In addition, given the popularity of equity rules in different cultures (e.g., Chen, 1995; James, 1993; Kabanoff, 1991; Kim, Park, & Suzuki, 1990; Martin & Harder, 1994), it is by no means a foregone conclusion that group members will judge pure equality to be distributively fair. Some individuals will likely be operating under an equity rule, in which equal allocations would be viewed as unjust. Many, especially the group's higher performers (cf. Greenberg & Bies, 1992), may prefer allocations based on equity because these would maximize their profits.

This would seem to place work teams between the proverbial rock and a hard place. The solution, of course, is to realize that no one needs to compulsively stick to one rule or the other. In fact, few groups are "pure," if by that we mean that they allocate rewards in only one way (cf. Kabanoff, 1991). For example, in a series of studies conducted by Frohlich, Oppenheimer, and Eavy (1987a; 1987b), groups of research subjects were given the opportunity to allocate rewards according to a variety of justice rules. The only stipulation was that each work team had to come to an agreement on a rule before working together on an experimental task. The most common policy was to maintain a minimum payment for every member, while distributing rewards above this minimum utilizing equity. Similar findings were obtained by Lissowski, Tyszka, and Okrasa (1991) using two samples of Polish undergraduates. At least for these temporary work groups, a mixed allocation rule was preferred.

Another approach to resolving this dilemma was investigated by Martin and Harder (1994). Martin and Harder (1994) argued that different distribution rules can be used for different types of outcomes. Managers, therefore, can match the rule to the allocation in question. Consistent with this, Martin and Harder (1994) found that American managers tend to prefer equity rules for concrete, economic benefits (such as pay), but equality distributions for social benefits.

The allocation strategy discovered by Martin and Harder (1994) has an interesting implication. Allocating social outcomes through equality does not reduce the absolute discrepancy in economic earnings. The egalitarian social benefits serve as a mathematical constant that is added to each individual's outcome score. Therefore, if one individual earns $150 per week more than a fellow team member, then offering both workers praise and respect will not alter this wage gap. However, suppose that social allocations, like their economic counterparts, have some value. If this is so (and evidence suggests that it is; see Lind & Tyler, 1988; Tyler, 1990, 1991), then social rewards can cause the wage differential to become a smaller *proportion* of each individual's total benefits. Consequently, the Martin and Harder (1994) study suggests that when individuals compare themselves to some referent, it is not the absolute size of the difference (that is, the difference between one's outcomes and the outcomes of a referent other) that triggers perceptions of distributive injustice. Rather, it is the size of the difference as a percentage of their obtained outcomes. Although plausible, to our knowledge this idea has never been investigated, nor even stated, within the justice literature.

PART II: PROCEDURAL JUSTICE

Outcomes do not simply materialize into existence. Rather, they are the result of some series of events. We refer to these instrumental events as the "process," "means," or "procedures" that cause the distribution. As one might expect, individuals make decisions regarding the fairness of these processes. We term these evaluations judgments of "procedural fairness" (Folger & Greenberg, 1985; Greenberg, 1990, 1996; Greenberg & Folger, 1983; Lind & Tyler, 1988; Tyler, 1990, 1991; Tyler & Lind, 1992). As with distributive justice, procedural justice is phenomenological (Cropanzano & Greenberg, in press). That is, what is fair or unfair is decided by the individual. When discussing procedural justice, there is another important issue to note. Whereas certain outcomes may be circumspect and well-defined, processes are often general and amorphous. For this reason, some theorists have divided procedures into subtypes; structural and social processes (Greenberg, 1993a, 1993b; Tyler & Bies, 1990). For completeness, we briefly define each.

A structural or formal procedure is an aspect of the environmental context in which a decision is made. This term refers to the specified work policies that lead to a decision outcome (Cropanzano & Greenberg, 1997; Greenberg, 1993b). According to Leventhal (1976, 1980), for a structural procedure to be judged as fair, it should conform to six criteria: It should be applied consistently to all, bias free, be as accurate as possible, correctable, representative of all viewpoints, and ethical. Research generally supports Leventhal's (1976, 1980), ideas. However, recent theorists have enlarged and refined this list in order to apply it to specific contexts (see Cropanzano & Greenberg, 1997).

A social procedure refers to the interpersonal treatment that an individual receives during the course of an allocation decision. A given formal procedure can be enacted in a variety of ways. For example, two groups may all participate, but in one, the opinions of subordinates are greeted with respectful debate, whereas in the other, they are subjected to derision. In each case, the structural policy remains constant. However, the interpersonal treatment varies. People evaluate the justice of this treatment (Bies, 1987; Bies & Moag, 1986; Folger & Bies, 1989; Greenberg, 1993b; Tyler & Bies, 1990).

According to Brockner and Wiesenfeld (1996) and Tyler and Bies (1990), social procedural justice has two aspects. First, individuals want to be treated with dignity and respect. We refer to this as interpersonal sensitivity. It is sometimes termed interactional justice (Bies & Moag, 1986) or interpersonal justice (Greenberg, 1993b). It should come as no surprise to learn that insensitive treatment has corrosive effects on interpersonal relationships (e.g., Baron, 1988, 1990, 1993; Preskitt & Olson-Buchanan, 1996). Second, people want an explanation or reason as to why a decision was made. We refer to these explanations as social accounts or justifications (Bies, 1987). Judgments concerning the fairness of these accounts form the basis of informational justice (Greenberg, 1993b). When appropriate explanations are provided, individuals respond more favorably—even when they receive negative outcomes (e.g., Bies & Shapiro, 1988; Bobocel, Agar, Meyer, & Irving, 1996; Bobocel & Farrell, 1996; Shapiro, Buttner, & Barry, 1994).

Consequences of Procedural Justice for Group Effectiveness

Together, structural and social procedural justice are extremely important predictors of group outcomes (for reviews, see Cropanzano & Greenberg, in press; Greenberg, 1990, 1996; Lind & Tyler, 1988; Tyler & Lind, 1992). For one thing, fair procedures make it easier to maintain a group. When individuals perceive themselves to be treated fairly, they report fewer intentions to leave (Dailey & Kirk, 1992; Konovsky & Cropanzano, 1991) and higher levels of commitment (Daly & Geyer, 1995; Folger & Konovsky, 1989; Konovsky, Folger, & Cropanzano, 1987; McFarlin & Sweeney, 1992; Sweeney & McFarlin, 1993). Moreover, procedural justice makes individuals less likely to take hostile actions against their coworkers, such as suing (Sitkin & Bies, 1993) or stealing (Greenberg, 1993a). Indeed, when workers believe that they have been fairly treated, they are more trusting of authority (Brockner & Siegel, 1995; Konovsky, Elliott, & Pugh, 1995; Konovsky & Pugh, 1994; Siegel, Brockner, & Tyler, 1995) and more likely to accept its dictates (Lind,

1995; Lind & Earley, 1992; Lind & Tyler, 1988; Tyler, 1990; Tyler & Dawes, 1993; Tyler & Lind, 1992).

There is also evidence that fair procedures can promote performance, although these findings are more mixed. With respect to job performance, the results suggest only a possible link. In two laboratory experiments, Earley and Lind (1987) found that undergraduate subjects showed higher performance when they were treated with procedural fairness. Gilliland (1994) found similar results in a field experiment, and Konovsky and Cropanzano (1991) reported consistent findings from a cross-sectional survey. However, other studies are not entirely consistent. In two laboratory experiments, Cropanzano and Randall (1995) failed to obtain a significant correlation between procedural justice and performance. Even worse, Kanfer, Sawyer, Earley, and Lind (1987) found that procedural fairness produced *lower* performance.

As we can see, the relationship between procedural justice and job performance is complex. This complexity is perhaps best illustrated in a field study by Baldwin, Magjuka, and Loher (1991). Baldwin and his colleagues conducted a field experiment in which employees were either given voice as to the training program they would receive, given voice but did not get the program they desired, or given no voice at all. The group that was given voice and obtained the program they wanted were the most motivated and showed the most learning. The no voice group was intermediate. Finally, the lowest performance came from those who had voice but did not get their preferred program. Sometimes a fair procedure boosted performance, and sometimes it hampered it.

Perhaps the best evidence for a relationship between procedures and performance comes from work on organizational citizenship behavior (OCB). OCB is discretionary actions that are beyond formal role requirements. Employees perform OCB even though they are not directly compensated for them. Instead, these behaviors are performed out of a sense of helpfulness and supportiveness for one's employer and teammates. Considerable evidence suggests that procedurally fair treatment increases the amount of OCB that individuals are willing to perform (Ball, Treviño, & Sims, 1994; Deluga, 1994; Farh, Podsakoff, & Organ, 1990; Konovsky & Folger, 1991; Konovsky & Pugh, 1994; Konovsky & Organ, in press; Lee, 1995; Moorman, 1991; Niehoff & Moorman, 1993; Organ & Moorman, 1993).

Taken together, we find that as procedural justice perceptions increase, employees become more committed, less likely to leave, less likely to take acrimonious actions, more trusting, more accepting, and more willing to sacrifice on behalf on their team members. Based on this evidence, procedural justice would seem to promote effective work teams.

As an example, let us consider some research on strategic planning groups. In one experiment, Korsgaard, Schweiger, and Sapienza (1995) had managers from an executive training program form teams. Each team was responsible for formulating a hypothetical strategic plan. Korsgaard and her colleagues (1995) found that when group members were able to influence the team's decisions, and when their opinions were taken into consideration, perceived procedural justice was high. As team participants perceived fairer processes, they also reported heightened feelings of trust, decision commitment, and attachment to the group.

Procedural justice effects have also been obtained in actual work groups. Kim and Mauborgne (1991) surveyed managers from sundry multinational companies. They found that when planning was done in a fashion seen as procedurally just, the managers reported more commitment, trust, social harmony, and satisfaction with the plan. These findings were replicated in a later longitudinal study by Kim and Mauborgne (1993). Once again, research seems to suggest that procedural fairness pulls groups together. Injustice, on the other hand, seems to pull people apart.

Why Procedural Justice?

According to procedural justice researchers, how one is treated during an allocation decision seems to matter as much as what one receives. For those social scientists who are steeped in the rational person perspective, these effects could seem counterintuitive. Despite this, there are good reasons for anticipating the importance of process, although they might not be apparent at first glance. These reasons have been discussed in terms of two models, each of which complements the other.

The first perspective is the *instrumental model*. The instrumental model accepts the rational person premise that group members wish to maximize their outcomes. However, it adds one important caveat. The instrumental model maintains that individuals take a long-term view of social relationships. Thus, employees may accept the fact that a particular outcome went awry, so long as they can be confident of receiving their due over time. That is, the instrumental model argues that people are willing to trade short-term losses for long-term gains. According to the instrumental model, process is important because it provides an indication of people's long-term opportunities. When the procedures are fair, people are eventually likely to earn what they deserve. There is good evidence for the instrumental model (Shapiro, 1993; Shapiro & Brett, 1993; Thibaut & Walker, 1975). However, there are other considerations that affect procedural justice judgment as well (Cropanzano & Greenberg, 1997; Greenberg, 1990; Lind, Kanfer, & Earley, 1990; Lind & Tyler, 1988; Tyler & Lind, 1992).

A second model focuses less on concrete outcomes and more on the nature of the relationship between individuals. According to the *relational model,* individuals are concerned with their status and dignity within a given group. Thus, people prefer to affiliate with those who affirm their basic worth, rather than with those who tear it down. Decision makers can meet this goal by providing status recognition, benevolence, and neutrality (Lind, 1995). These three qualities are termed "relational concerns" (Lind & Tyler, 1988; Tyler, 1990). When their relational concerns are met, people feel that their dignity and worth have been affirmed. As such, they perceive the process to be fair (Tyler, 1991, 1994; Tyler & Degoey, 1995).

This brief review should serve to underscore the complementary nature of the instrumental and relational models. In both cases, procedures serve some larger end because they allow the individual to achieve desired personal goals (Cropanzano & Ambrose, 1996). However, for each model, the end result is different. The instrumental model emphasizes those consequences that "have a consummatory facet . . . [and] can be enjoyed immediately" (as Lind, 1995, p. 96, put it in a somewhat different context). Conversely, the relational model stresses consequences that "are valued because they have greater implications for feelings of inclusion and social identity" (Lind, 1995, p. 96). We term the first class of outcomes "economic" and the second class "socioemotional."

People join groups to meet these twin sets of needs. What is less clear from the literature is whether procedural and outcome fairness are equally proficient at meeting these goals. Some researchers have suggested that procedural justice may be relatively more effective than distributive justice at addressing the socioemotional needs. As such, process may be the more important consideration for understanding group maintenance. On the other hand, outcome fairness may be more important for understanding satisfaction with and reactions toward particular organizational decisions. In the next section, we examine the evidence for this claim. We conclude by noting caveats and limitations with this perspective and discussing the need for a new conceptual framework.

PART III: DISTRIBUTIVE AND PROCEDURAL JUSTICE TOGETHER—THE TWO-FACTOR MODEL

Many contemporary researchers have argued that procedural and distributive justice have somewhat different effects (e.g., Brockner & Wiesenfeld, 1996; Cropanzano & Greenberg, 1997; Folger & Konovsky, 1989; Fryxell & Gordon, 1989; Tyler, 1991). Some evidence suggests that attitudes toward a particular outcome or decision (e.g., pay satisfaction) show a relatively high correlation with distributive justice and a relatively low correlation with procedural justice. Conversely, attitudes toward a social group (e.g., commitment) or toward an authority figure (e.g., trust) show a relatively high correlation with procedural justice and a relatively low correlation with distributive justice (for reviews see Greenberg, 1990; Lind & Tyler, 1988; van de Bos, 1996). Sweeney and McFarlin (1993) dubbed this phenomena the "two-factor" model.

The two-factor model follows from our earlier observations. If we suppose that individuals join groups to fulfill economic and social motives, then it is reasonable to believe that distributive justice (which emphasizes the allocation of economic outcomes) is more intimately associated with the manner in which people respond to those outcomes. Procedural justice, on the other hand, examines both economic (the instrumental model) and socioemotional (the relational model) concerns. However, when considering a particular economic outcome, the relationship to process fairness is temporally distal. This is because the instrumenal model is largely concerned with outcomes that are likely to occur sometime in the future. Thus, although outcome reactions will show some relationship with procedural justice, this relationship should be smaller than that between these responses and distributive fairness. On the other hand, procedural fairness emphasizes the manner in which individuals are treated. Consequently, it is reasonable to argue that process justice will show a tighter link to socioemotional responses, such as one's attitude toward group authority.

The two-factor model has profound implications for the management of work teams. According to this framework, procedures are more closely connected to employees' socioemotional responses than are outcomes. This makes procedural justice a more critical cause of social harmony. Distributive justice is still important, but primarily because it predicts more circumscribed responses to various decisions, such as pay satisfaction. Such things are less consequential to maintaining group solidarity. Thus, to the extent that the two-factor model provides an appropriate understanding of group dynamics, organizations can afford to be relatively inattentive to resource allocations without seriously risking group maintenance. However, firms must carefully respect the processes by which these decisions are made.

In some respects, it would be a good thing if the two-factor model were found to be accurate. Certainly, it would simplify the task of work group management. Because harmony would be heavily based on procedures, organizations could concentrate their attention on process fairness, perhaps by utilizing Leventhal's (1976, 1980) rules and by maintaining social sensitivity and the free flow of information. Less effort would have to be directed toward the distribution of benefits. However, if outcomes are also important, then a strict application of the two-factor model would fail to consider the role of distributive fairness and thereby damage group solidarity. We take up this possibility in the next section.

Limitations of the Two-Factor Model

As we have seen, research strongly attests to the important of procedural justice. However, given the evidence reviewed earlier in this chapter, we also believe that a strong statement of the two-factor model underestimates the importance of distributive fairness for the maintenance of group harmony. Procedures are important, but outcomes are important as well. In the following sections, we discuss some important caveats regarding the two-factor model.

The Difference Between Procedures and Outcomes Is Relative. The first caveat is probably the most obvious. The two-factor model does not maintain that perceptions of outcome fairness are uncorrelated with social appraisals, only that these associations are somewhat smaller than those for procedural justice. In fact, several studies have found that outcome fairness can predict group relevant criteria such as commitment (e.g., Folger & Konovsky, 1989; Lowe & Vodanovich, 1995; McFarlin & Sweeney, 1992), some aspects of OCB (Konovsky et al., 1995; Konovsky & Pugh, 1994; Lee, 1995; Moorman, 1991), and supervisory trust (Konovsky et al., 1995; Konovsky & Pugh, 1994). Although procedural justice tends to show a stronger relationship, distributive fairness may also be significantly associated with these variables.

It should be emphasized that these relationships were not obtained in every study that examined them. For instance, Fryxell and Gordon (1989) and Konovsky, Folger, and Cropanzano (1987) failed to obtain significant associations between distributive justice and commitment. Nevertheless, the corpus of available research would suggest that one's reaction to social groups is at least sometimes related to outcome fairness. It seems unlikely that individuals show commitment to groups that they believe do not compensate them fairly. Although processes matter, it does not follow that work teams can neglect distributive fairness altogether.

Outcome Favorability Causes Perceptions of Procedural Justice. Implicit in the two-factor model is a sort of horse race between procedural and distributive justice. It is as if there is competition to see which accounts for the lion's share of variance in each criteria. This might be taken to suggest that procedural and distributive justice are independent. In fact, they are not. Several researchers have observed that when outcomes are seen as fair (or at least favorable), then procedures are correspondingly seen as fair as well (e.g., Ambrose, Harland, & Kulik, 1991; Brunning, Keup, & Cooper, 1996; Conlon, 1993; Conlon & Fasolo, 1990; Conlon & Ross, 1993; Flinder & Hauenstein, 1994; Krzystofiak, Lillis, & Newman, 1995; Lind et al., 1990; Lind, Kulik, Ambrose, & de Vera Park, 1993; Lowe & Vodanovich, 1995). Once again, the findings are not completely unanimous (e.g., Giacobbe-Miller, 1995; Lind, 1995) and other things certainly predict procedural fairness judgments as well or better than do outcome appraisals (Lind, 1995; Tyler, 1989, 1990). Nonetheless, it seems reasonable to conclude that judgments of procedural fairness are partially influenced by self-interest. If one receives a fair outcome, then one is more apt to conclude that the procedure that provided that outcome is fair as well. If this is so, then it may not be possible for organizations to disregard outcomes in favor of processes. For if firms do not attend to distributive justice, then perceptions of procedural justice are likely to suffer as well. In short, unfair outcomes will likely be a cause of procedural injustice.

It is interesting to note that a causal relationship of this kind could explain another phenomenon as well. When procedures and outcomes are both used to predict organizationally relevant criteria, process fairness typically explains a good proportion of variance above and beyond that accounted for by outcomes. Allocations, however, typically explain little if any variability above that accounted for by process (e.g., Lind & Tyler, 1988; Tyler, 1990, 1991, 1994; Tyler & Degoey, 1995; Tyler & Lind, 1992). This pattern of relationships might be expected if one assumed that procedural justice is partially caused by outcome appraisals (cf. Baron & Kenny, 1986). However, more research is needed to test this proposition.

Outcomes Are Often Allocated by an Equity Rule; Procedures by an Equality Rule.   Most research on the two-factor model has operationalized distributive justice as some approximation of the equity allocation rule (e.g., Ambrose et al., 1991; Cropanzano & Folger, 1989; Flinder & Hauenstein, 1994; Greenberg, 1987; Lind et al., 1990; Taylor, Moghaddam, Gamble, & Zellerer, 1987). In many of these investigations, an allocation that was distributively unfair was more or less synonymous with one that was inequitable. By extension, we can say that most work on the two-factor model has not compared procedural justice to distributive justice per se. More accurately, it has compared procedural justice to equitable treatment.

This plot thickens when one examines the allocation of procedures. Historically, researchers have assumed that a fair procedure treats everyone consistently (Leventhal, 1976, 1980; van den Bos, 1996). In other words, all employees get the same process—an equality allocation rule. If outcomes are allocated based on equity and procedures are allocated based on equality, then each type of justice is confounded with the rule by which it is allocated. It may not be the outcome or process, per se, that is important. Rather, it may be the means by which the outcome or process is distributed.

What would happen, however, if procedures were allocated based on merit? For instance, supervisors might more readily solicit participation from those individuals who were proven performers. Assuming participation is desirable, and for many this is likely the case, then this would entail the allocation of a process (voice) based on an equity rule (more voice to the higher performers). On the face of it, at least, this does not seem to be (procedurally) unfair. However, would procedural equity do as much to promote group harmony as the procedural equality favored by researchers? We suspect that it would not, although the data are not available for a conclusive test.

As we have already noted, research on allocation decisions suggests that equity distributions do less well than equality in promoting group harmony (except perhaps among those who are the most favorably compensated). It could be that some tests of the two-factor model have engaged in an unfair comparison (cf. Cooper & Richardson, 1986). In certain cases, they may have pitted procedural equality against distributive equity—the one variety of distributive justice that was least likely to be related to group relevant criteria, such as commitment and self-sacrifice. Within teams where an equality norm reigns, distributive justice may be less highly associated with outcome satisfaction and more highly associated with group harmony and attachment. This is consistent with previous work (e.g., James, 1993; Kabanoff, 1991; Kerr & Slocum, 1987). Although we are speculating here, it could be that in teams where processes are allocated based on equity, then procedural justice might be less highly associated with harmony and more highly associated with responses to relevant outcomes.

Conclusions

None of these observations disprove the two-factor model. There may indeed be relative differences in the manner in which procedures and allocations correlate to sundry criteria. (Although we would have more confidence in this if research had considered need and equality distributions in addition to equity.) In any case, it does not seem to be the case that procedures only predict group level reactions whereas allocations only predict reactions to economic outcomes. Instead, both types of criteria seem to be associated with both types of justice. With respect to what they predict, the differences between process and allocation do not appear fundamental, rather they seem to be a matter of degree. This raises an interesting prospect: There may be some previously unexplored commonalities between procedures and outcomes. Although the two-factor model does not completely rule out such similarities, it certainly does little to emphasize them (Cropanzano & Ambrose, 1996).

PART IV: DISTRIBUTIVE AND PROCEDURAL JUSTICE TOGETHER AGAIN—THE INTERACTION OF PROCESSES AND OUTCOMES

The two-factor model tacitly assumes that procedures and allocations have independent and additive effects. Although this may be so, it seems likely that the two also interact. One simple account of this interaction is provided by Cropanzano and Folger (1991). They argued that when outcomes were favorable, individuals were content, regardless of the process. On the other hand, a negative event, such as an unfavorable outcome, triggers a search for an explanation. If the procedures are judged to be fair, the discontent is mitigated. However, if the procedures are unfair, then discontent is high. In essence, the two-stage model maintains that outcomes moderate the effect of processes (i.e., processes only predict judgments of unfairness when outcomes are poor). Or, to state the matter differently, injustice is mostly a problem when both procedures and outcomes are seen as unjust.

Brockner and Wiesenfeld (1996) offer a more detailed and complete reckoning. They noted that this Process × Interaction can be described in one of two ways. From one point of view, outcomes moderate processes, but it is equally accurate to maintain that processes moderate the effect of outcomes. That is, one could say that outcomes only predict when processes are poor. This follows from our earlier comments. If the process is judged to be fair, then individuals will always respond positively to the treatment they receive, regardless of the fairness (or favorability) of the outcomes. It is only an unfair process, coupled with an unfavorable outcome, that produces ill will. Obviously this is an important topic. It suggests that human beings are not all that cantankerous, as their anger and hostility can be alleviated by either fair outcomes or fair treatment. The problem, of course, is that the matter is not as simple as that. There are several questions that need to be answered before we can fully understand this interaction.

On the Nature of the Interaction

What Interacts With Processes? Is It Fair or Favorable?   At times, justice researchers have treated outcome "fairness" as interchangeable with the notion of outcome "favorability." The two are different. As we have already discussed, an unfavorable outcome (or even a favorable one, for that matter) is only unfair after it is compared to some referent standard. This ambiguity is especially acute among those who primarily study procedural justice or the process by outcome interaction (e.g., Brockner & Wiesenfeld, 1996; Cropanzano & Folger, 1991). Outcome fairness and outcome favorability are correlated. When this fact is considered, then the interaction becomes much less clear. We assume that processes are interacting with something. But is that "something" outcome fairness, favorability, or both?

What Interacts With Outcomes? Is It Procedural Justice or Is It Trust? In a recent work, Brockner and Siegel (1995) made a suggestion regarding the process term in the interaction. Perhaps procedural fairness is not what is at issue. They argued that when individuals trust decision makers, they become more likely to accept unfavorable/unfair outcomes. Thus, the crucial interaction could be between outcomes and trust, and not between outcomes and processes. Procedural fairness is only an incidental variable that happens to be a major cause (and therefore a correlate) of trust.

We know of only a single study that has tested this new model. Brockner and Siegel (1995) had workers recall a disagreement they once had with their supervisors. Brockner et al. (1995) found that outcomes interacted with both trust and procedures. However, when the Trust × Outcome interaction was entered into the regression model first, it accounted for all of the variance due to the Process × Outcome interaction. The reverse was not true. This provides promising support for the model, but it is still very preliminary.

When the Brockner and Siegel (1995) model is juxtaposed with our uncertainty regarding fairness and favorability, it becomes clear how little we understand about this important interaction. Basically, all we know is that *something is happening*. Process or trust is interacting with outcome fairness or favorability.

What Causes the Interaction?: The Fairness Heuristic. Leaving aside this conceptual confusion, recent work has also attempted to understand the causes of the Process × Outcome interaction. When individuals enter into a situation, they carefully try to assess the amount of fairness. Over time, they go so far as to build a justice heuristic (or rules of thumb) to make their search strategies more efficient (Lind, 1994, 1995). According to van den Bos (1996), these justice heuristics may have implications for how we understand the Process × Outcome interaction.

Van den Bos (1996) argued that an unfavorable event triggers a more profound attributional search than does a favorable event. When something positive occurs, individuals have a reduced need for an explanation; when something negative occurs, individuals try to understand it. These ideas are consistent with the work of Cropanzano and Folger (1991) and of Brockner and Wiesenfeld (1996), only van den Bos (1996) took them one step further. He argued that the form of the interaction depends on the initial event. Because van den Bos' (1996) reasoning is illustrated more easily than it is described, let's consider the initial events one at a time.

Under some conditions, people receive information about the process before receiving information about the outcome. In this case, a positive process colors subsequent perceptions and thereby engenders positive reactions. However, a negative process causes the individual to search for more data. If a favorable outcome is forthcoming, then the individual reacts positively (i.e., the initial negative perception gets revised). On the other hand, if a negative outcome is forthcoming, this confirms the initial impression and results in discontent. Van den Bos (1996, Study 3) tested these ideas in a role-playing experiment. He presented subjects with a vignette in which they took the role of an applicant for a new job. They were told either that the selection procedure was very thorough and accurate (i.e., used all nine parts of a comprehensive evaluation) or that it was not especially accurate (i.e., used only one of the nine parts). They were then instructed that they had either received the job (favorable) or had not received the job (unfavorable). Van den Bos (1996, Study 3) had two criterion variables; perceived procedural justice and perceived distributive justice. As expected, both procedural and distributive fairness were predicted by an interaction between test accuracy and outcome favorability. These are shown in Fig. 5.1. Figure 5.1 shows the interaction for procedural justice and Fig. 5.2 for distributive. In each case, we displayed the

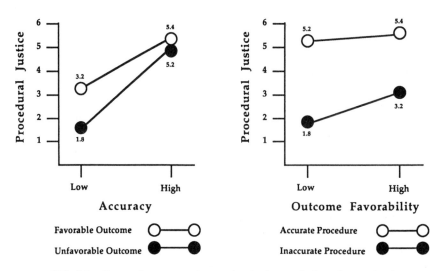

FIG. 5.1. Process by outcome interaction in the prediction of procedural justice. In this experiment, the process information was presented before outcome information. Adapted from "Procedural Justice and Conflict," by K. van den Bos, Study 3, 1996, unpublished doctoral dissertation.

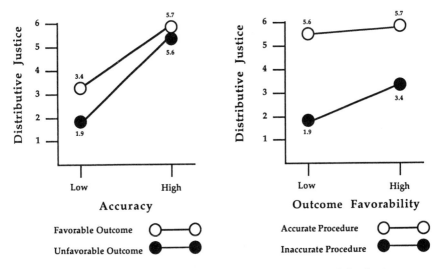

FIG. 5.2.   Process by outcome interaction in the prediction of distributive justice. In this experiment, the process information was presented before outcome information. Adapted from "Procedural Justice and Conflict," by K. van den Bos, Study 3, 1996, unpublished doctoral dissertation.

same interaction from two different perspectives. In the first panel of each figure, accuracy is on the x-axis. In the second panel, the x-axis shows favorability. The reason for doing this will be apparent shortly.

Let us begin by examining the first panels in Fig. 5.1 and Fig. 5.2. Keep in mind that in this experiment, the process information (accurate vs. inaccurate) was received prior to the outcome information (favorable vs. unfavorable). As one can see, when accuracy was high, the subjects believed that they were treated with both procedural and distributive justice—regardless of the outcome. However, when accuracy was low, then both procedural and distributive justice were low, and this was especially true when an unfavorable outcome was paired with a lack of accuracy. The second panels in Figs. 5.1 and 5.2 display the same interaction but from a different vantage point. In this case, we can again see that procedural and distributive justice were maintained, so long as the procedure was accurate. However, when an inaccurate procedure was used, both types of justice were compromised. Once more, this was especially true when an inaccurate procedure was coupled with an unfavorable outcome. In short, a favorable procedure seems to have colored subsequent perceptions of the outcome. These data are consistent with the notion that favorable process information can lead to more positive reactions, whereas unfavorable processes trigger an attributional search. If the search produces an advantageous consequence, the discontent is partially mitigated.

However, this is only part of the story. Van den Bos (1996, Study 4) ran a very similar experiment. The only difference was that in this case, the outcome information was presented to the subject prior to the process information. The results are displayed in Figs. 5.3 and 5.4.

These experiments also produced an interaction. In each case, processes and outcomes qualified one another. But closer scrutiny of the different figures and panels shows that the interaction reversed itself. Let us start with perceived procedural justice. When the outcome is favorable, procedural justice is always high, regardless of the accuracy of the procedure (Fig. 5.3, panel 1). Thus, it seems that the initial presentation of outcome information influenced the subjects' perceptions of the process. For this reason, the form of the interaction in Fig. 5.3, panel 1, is virtually identical to the interaction in Fig. 5.1, panel 2. It seems that in the first experiment (Fig. 5.1, panel 2), initial favorable procedures kept reactions high, whereas in the second experiment (Fig. 5.3, panel 1), the initial favorable outcomes kept reaction high. There is an interaction in both studies, but it is of a slightly different form.

We can now turn our attention to distributive justice perceptions. We are still considering van den Bos' (1996) Experiment 4, where the outcome information was presented prior to the procedural information. We can see that favorable outcomes led to more positive subject reactions, even when the process was inaccurate (Fig. 5.4, panel 1). Once again, the initial presentation of outcome information overshadowed the process. The reader should compare these findings to those of Experiment 3 (Fig. 5.2, panel 2). In that case, the process information influenced perceptions of the outcomes. That is, in Experiment 3, when subjects learned of the process before hearing about the outcome, individuals reported high distributive justice so long as the procedures were accurate. Van den Bos' (1996, Studies 3–4) findings qualify the earlier work of Cropanzano and Folger (1991). This suggests that there are actually *two* different Process Outcome interactions, and they change in form depending on which type of information is received first.[3]

And What of Self-Esteem?   In all of the research we have discussed thus far, the Process × Outcome interaction was being used to predict a judgment about something external to the individual. For example, a respondent was asked to judge a particular procedure or outcome. Recently,

---

[3]Van den Bos (1996) actually did four studies on this interaction effect, not two (van den Bos, 1996, Studies 3–6). We have limited ourselves to the first two to make our discussion simpler. It should be noted that although van den Bos' Studies 2 and 4 used a role-playing methodology (possessing the requisite limitations of this design), the findings were replicated in Studies 5 and 6. In these latter two experiments, subjects actually experienced the experimental manipulations.

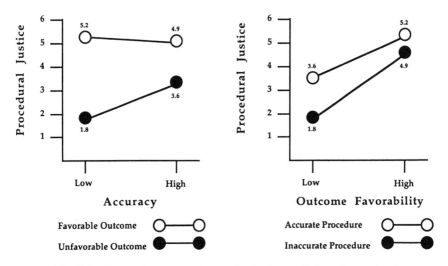

FIG. 5.3.   Process by outcome interaction in the prediction of procedural justice. In this experiment, the outcome information was presented before process information. Adapted from "Procedural Justice and Conflict," by K. van den Bos, Study 3, 1996, unpublished doctoral dissertation.

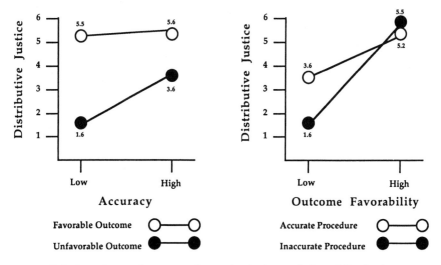

FIG. 5.4.   Process by outcome interaction in the prediction of distributive justice. In this experiment, the outcome information was presented before process information. Adapted from "Procedural Justice and Conflict," by K. van den Bos, Study 3, 1996, unpublished doctoral dissertation.

Brockner and Wiesenfeld (1996) reviewed evidence suggesting that the form of the interaction may change if one uses a different class of criterion variables. In particular, when self-evaluations are involved (self-esteem and self-efficacy), the pattern of data changes.

In two experiments, Koper, Van Knippenberg, Bouhuijs, Vermunt, and Wilke (1993) had students complete a test of basic ability. The test was either graded accurately or it was not. Afterwards, Koper and his colleagues gave these participants performance feedback. This feedback was either high or low. When a fair grading procedure was used, positive feedback improved self-esteem. When an unfair grading procedure was in force, the feedback did not alter self-esteem. Similar results were obtained in a field study of job applicants conducted by Gilliland (1994). When a job-related test was used, the hiring decision impacted self-efficacy. That is, self-efficacy was lower when the decision was unfavorable and higher when the decision was favorable. On the other hand, when the test was not job related, the hiring decision did not impact self-efficacy. Individuals only reacted to the job-related assessment instrument.

It is not yet clear precisely why these findings occurred. So far, two explanations have been proposed. Tyler and Degoey (1995) suggested that fair processes boost self-evaluations, because they boost a person's status and sense of worth. Although this makes sense, it does not fully account for the Koper et al. (1993) and Gilliland (1994) findings. In these studies, people receiving an unfavorable outcome felt as good or better about themselves when the process was *unfair*. In response to this, Cropanzano and Greenberg (1997) offered a second model. We suggested that procedural fairness, at least as operationalized here, can serve to make information more reliable and believable. Hence, fair feedback has a greater diagnostic value and is likely to be accepted. (This assumes that the fairness manipulation is one that promotes accuracy.) On the other hand, unfair information is less valuable and more suspect. For this reason, it can be safely ignored.

CONCLUSIONS

In this chapter, we have tried to articulate the important role that justice plays in helping to build group effectiveness. We first discussed two types of justice—distributive and procedural—and reviewed evidence that each of these can impact peoples' responses to their groups. It seems clear from this work that a manager who wishes to build an effective team should start with justice. Fairly treated individuals tend to stay with their groups.

We then considered procedures and outcomes simultaneously. We noted that the two-factor model suggests that distributive justice primarily impacts reactions to outcomes and particular decisions, whereas procedural justice is the primary determinant of reactions to the social group and to group authority. This model was discussed and critiqued at length. It was concluded that some serious limitations still exist, although future work could possibly address them. Finally, we discussed the interaction of procedural and distributive justice. We noted that contemporary research suggests several needs, including distinguishing between fairness and favorability, clarifying the role of trust, integrating research on the justice heuristic, and identifying the different interactions that occur for self-referent cognitions.

Despite the ever present need for new knowledge, we feel it is best to close by emphasizing what we now know. Treating people with both distributive and procedural justice seems to bolster their commitment to the group and increase their desire to remain. Additionally, fair treatment seems also to increase workers' willingness to perform well and engage in helpful citizenship behaviors that benefit their employers and coworkers. In this light, the particulars of the two-factor and two-stage models seem to matter less. The bottom line remains: *Treat people fairly.*

REFERENCES

Adams, J. S. (1965). Inequity in social exchange. In L. Berkowitz (Ed.), *Advances in experimental social psychology* (Vol. 2, pp. 267–299). New York: Academic Press.

Adams, J. S., & Freedman, S. (1976). Equity theory revisited: Comments and annotated bibliography. In L. Berkowitz (Ed.), *Advances in experimental social psychology* (Vol. 9, pp. 43–90). New York: Academic Press.

Ambrose, M. L., Harland, L. K., & Kulik, C. T. (1991). Influence of social comparisons on perceptions of organizational fairness. *Journal of Applied Psychology, 76*, 239–246.

Austin, W. (1977). Equity theory and social comparison processes. In J. M. Suls & R. M. Miller (Eds.), *Social comparison processes* (pp. 279–306). Washington, DC: Hemisphere.

Baldwin, T. T., Magjuka, R. J., & Loher, B. T. (1991). The perils of participation: Effects of choice of training on trainee motivation and learning. *Personnel Psychology, 44*, 51–65.

Ball, G. A., Treviño, L. K., & Sims, H. P., Jr. (1994). Just and unjust punishment: Influences on subordinate performance and citizenship. *Academy of Management Journal, 37*, 299–322.

Baron, R. A. (1988). Negative effects of destructive criticism: Impact on conflict, self-efficacy, and task performance. *Journal of Applied Psychology, 73*, 199–207.

Baron, R. A. (1990). Countering the effects of destructive criticism: The relative efficacy of four potential interventions. *Journal of Applied Psychology, 75*, 235–245.

Baron, R. A. (1993). Criticism (informal negative feedback) as a source of perceived unfairness in organizations: Effects, mechanisms, and countermeasures. In R. Cropanzano (Ed.), *Justice in the workplace: Approaching fairness in human resource management* (pp. 155–170). Hillsdale, NJ: Lawrence Erlbaum Associates.

Baron, R. M., & Kenny, D. A. (1986). The moderator–mediator distinction in social psychological research: Conceptual, strategic, and statistical considerations. *Journal of Personality and Social Psychology, 51*, 1173–1182.

Bies, R. J. (1987). The predicament of injustice: The management of moral outrage. In L. L. Cummings & B. M. Staw (Eds.), *Research in organizational behavior* (Vol. 9, pp. 289–319). Greenwich, CT: JAI.

Bies, R. J., & Moag, J. S. (1986). Interactional justice: Communication criteria of fairness. In R. J. Lewicki, B. H. Sheppard, & M. Bazerman (Eds.), *Research on negotiation in organizations* (Vol. 1, pp. 43–55). Greenwich, CT: JAI.

Bies, R. J., & Shapiro, D. L. (1988). Voice and justification: Their influence on procedural and fairness judgments. *Academy of Management Journal, 31*, 676–685.

Bobocel, D. R., Agar, S. E., Meyer, J. P., & Irving, P. G. (1996, April). *Managerial accounts and fairness perceptions in third-party conflict resolution: Differentiating the effects of shifting responsibility and providing a justification.* Paper presented at the annual meeting of the Society of Industrial and Organizational Psychology, San Diego, CA.

Bobocel, D. R., & Farrell, A. C. (1996). Sex-based promotion decisions and perceptions of interactional fairness: Investigating the role of managerial accounts. *Journal of Applied Psychology, 81*, 22–35.

Brockner, J., & Siegel, P. (1995). Understanding the interaction between procedural and distributive justice. In R. M. Kramer & T. R. Tyler (Eds.), *Trust in organizations* (pp. 390–413). Thousand Oaks, CA: Sage.

Brockner, J., & Wiesenfeld, B. M. (1996). An integrative framework for explaining reactions to decisions: The interactive effects of outcomes and procedures. *Psychological Bulletin, 120*, 189–208.

Brunning, N. S., Keup, L., & Cooper, C. L. (1996, April). *Justice perceptions and outcomes in a restructured organization: A longitudinal study.* Paper presented at the annual meeting of the Society of Industrial and Organizational Psychology, San Diego, CA.

Chen, C. C. (1995). New trends in rewards allocation preferences: A Sino–U.S. comparison. *Academy of Management Journal, 38*, 408–428.

Conlon, D. E. (1993). Some tests of the self-interest and group-value models of procedural justice: Evidence from an organizational appeal procedure. *Academy of Management Journal, 36*, 1109–1124.

Conlon, D. E., & Fasolo, P. M. (1990). Influence of speed of third-party intervention and outcome on negotiator and constituent fairness judgments. *Academy of Management Journal, 33*, 833–846.

Conlon, D. E., & Ross, W. H. (1993). The effects of partisan third parties on negotiator behavior and outcome perceptions. *Journal of Applied Psychology, 78*, 280–290.

Cooper, C. L., Dyck, B., & Frohlich, N. (1992). Improving the effectiveness of gainsharing: The role of fairness and participation. *Administrative Science Quarterly, 37*, 471–490.

Cooper, W. H., & Richardson, A. J. (1986). Unfair comparisons. *Journal of Applied Psychology, 71*, 179–184.

Cropanzano, R., & Ambrose, M. A. (1996, April). *Distributive and procedural justice are more similar than you think: A monistic view and a research agenda.* Paper presented at the annual meeting of the Society for Industrial and Organizational Psychology, San Diego, CA.

Cropanzano, R., & Folger, R. (1989). Referent cognitions and task decision autonomy: Beyond equity theory. *Journal of Applied Psychology, 74*, 293–299.

Cropanzano, R., & Folger, R. (1991). Procedural justice and worker motivation. In R. M. Steers & L. W. Porter (Eds.), *Motivation and work behavior* (5th ed., pp. 131–143). New York: McGraw-Hill.

Cropanzano, R., & Greenberg, J. (1997). Progress in organizational justice: Tunneling through the maze. In C. L. Cooper & I. T. Robertson (Eds.), *International review of industrial and organizational psychology* (pp. 317–372). New York: Wiley.

Cropanzano, R., & Randall, M. L. (1993). Injustice and work behavior. In R. Cropanzano (Ed.), *Justice in the workplace: Approaching fairness in human resource management* (pp. 3–20). Hillsdale, NJ: Lawrence Erlbaum Associates.

Cropanzano, R., & Randall, M. L. (1995). Advance notice as a means of reducing relative deprivation. *Social Justice Research, 8*, 217–238.

Crosby, F. (1976). A model of egoistical relative deprivation. *Psychological Review, 83*, 85–113.

Crosby, F. (1984). Relative deprivation in organizational settings. In B. M. Staw & L. L. Cummings (Eds.), *Research in organizational behavior* (Vol. 6, pp. 51–93) Greenwich, CT: JAI.

Dailey, R. C., & Kirk, D. J. (1992). Distributive and procedural justice as antecedents of job dissatisfaction and intent to turnover. *Human Relations, 45*, 305–317.

Daly, J. P., & Geyer, P. D. (1995). Procedural fairness and organizational commitment under conditions of growth and decline. *Social Justice Research, 8*, 137–151.

Deluga, R. J. (1994). Supervisor trust building, leader–member exchange and organizational citizenship behaviour. *Journal of Occupational and Organizational Psychology, 67*, 315–326.

Deming, W. E. (1986). *Out of crisis.* Cambridge, MA: MIT Press.

Deutsch, M. (1975). Equity, equality, and need: What determines which value will be used as the basis of distributive justice? *Journal of Social Issues, 31*, 137–149.

Deutsch, M. (1985). *Distributive justice: A social psychological perspective.* New Haven, CT: Yale University Press.

Earley, P. C., & Lind, E. A. (1987). Procedural justice and participation in task selection: The role of control in mediating justice judgments. *Journal of Personality and Social Psychology, 52*, 1148–1160.

Farh, J., Podsakoff, P. M., & Organ, D. W. (1990). Accounting for organizational citizenship behavior: Leader fairness and task scope versus satisfaction. *Journal of Management, 16*, 705–721.

Ferris, G. R., Frink, D. D., Beehr, T. A., & Gilmore, D. C. (1995). Political fairness and fair politics: The conceptual integration of divergent constructs. In R. Cropanzano & M. K. Kacmar (Eds.), *Organizational politics, justice, and support: Managing the social climate of the workplace* (pp. 21–36). Westport, CT: Quorum Books.

Flinder, S. W., & Hauenstein, M. A. N. (1994). *Antecedents of distributive and procedural justice perceptions.* Unpublished manuscript, Virginia Polytechnic Institute and State University, Blacksburg, Virginia.

Folger, R., & Bies, R. J. (1989). Managerial responsibilities and procedural justice. *Employee Responsibilities and Rights Journal, 2*, 79–90.

Folger, R., & Greenberg, J. (1985). Procedural justice: An interpretive analysis of personnel systems. In K. Rowland & G. Ferris (Eds.), *Research in personnel and human resources management* (Vol. 3, pp. 141–183). Greenwich, CT: JAI.

Folger, R., & Konovsky, M. (1989). Effects of procedural and distributive justice on reactions to pay raise decisions. *Academy of Management Journal, 32*, 115–130.

Frohlich, N., Oppenheimer, J. A., & Eavy, C. L. (1987a). Laboratory results on Rawls's distributive justice. *British Journal of Political Science, 17*, 1–21.

Frohlich, N., Oppenheimer, J. A., & Eavy, C. L. (1987b). Choice of principles of distributive justice in experimental groups. *American Journal of Political Science, 45*, 606–636.

Fryxell, G. E., & Gordon, M. E. (1989). Workplace justice and job satisfaction as predictors of satisfaction with unions and management. *Academy of Management Journal, 32*, 851–866.

Giacobbe-Miller, J. (1995). A test of the group-values and control models of procedural justice from competing perspectives of labor and management. *Personnel Psychology, 48*, 115–142.

Gilliland, S. W. (1993). The perceived fairness of selection systems: An organizational justice perspective. *Academy of Management Review, 18*, 694–734.

Gilliland, S. W. (1994). Effects of procedural and distributive justice on reactions to a selection system. *Journal of Applied Psychology, 79*, 691–701.

Greenberg, J. (1982). Approaching equity and avoiding inequity in groups and organizations. In J. Greenberg & R. L. Cohen (Eds.), *Equity and justice in social behavior* (pp. 389–435). New York: Academic Press.

Greenberg, J. (1987). Reactions to procedural injustice in payment decisions: Do the means justify the ends? *Journal of Applied Psychology, 72*, 55–61.

Greenberg, J. (1988). Equity and workplace status: A field experiment. *Journal of Applied Psychology, 73*, 606–613.

Greenberg, J. (1990). Organizational justice: Yesterday, today, and tomorrow. *Journal of Management, 16*, 399–432.

Greenberg, J. (1993a). Stealing in the name of justice: Informational and interpersonal moderators of theft reactions to underpayment inequity. *Organizational Behavior and Human Decision Processes, 54*, 81–103.

Greenberg, J. (1993b). The social side of fairness: Interpersonal and informational classes of organizational justice. In R. Cropanzano (Ed.), *Justice in the workplace: Approaching fairness in human resource management* (pp. 79–103). Hillsdale, NJ: Lawrence Erlbaum Associates.

Greenberg, J. (1996). *The quest for justice on the job: Essays and experiments.* Thousand Oaks, CA: Sage.

Greenberg, J., & Bies, R. J. (1992). Establishing the role of empirical studies of organizational justice in philosophical inquiries into business ethics. *Journal of Business Ethics, 11*, 433–444.

Greenberg, J., & Cohen, R. L. (1982). Why justice? Normative and instrumental interpretations. In J. Greenberg & R. L. Cohen (Eds.), *Equity and justice in social behavior* (pp. 437–469). New York: Academic Press.

Greenberg, J., & Folger, R. (1983). Procedural justice, participation, and the fair process effect in groups and organizations. In P. B. Paulus (Ed.), *Basic group processes* (pp. 235–256). New York: Springer-Verlag.

Harder, J. W. (1992). Play for pay: Effects of inequity in pay-for-performance context. *Administrative Science Quarterly, 37*, 321–335.

Homans, G. C. (1961). *Social behavior: Its elementary forms.* New York: Harcourt Brace.

James, K. (1993). The social context of organizational justice: Cultural, intergroup, and structural effects on justice behaviors and perceptions. In R. Cropanzano (Ed.), *Justice in the workplace: Approaching fairness in human resource management* (pp. 21–50). Hillsdale, NJ: Lawrence Erlbaum Associates.

Kabanoff, B. (1991). Equity, equality, power, and conflict. *Academy of Management Review, 16*, 416–441.

Kanfer, R., Sawyer, J., Earley, P. C., & Lind, E. A. (1987). Participation in task evaluation procedures: The effects of influential opinion expression and knowledge of evaluative criteria on attitudes and performance. *Social Justice Research, 1*, 235–249.

Kerr, J., & Slocum, J. W. (1987). Managing corporate culture through reward systems. *Academy of Management Executive, 1*, 98–108.

Kim, K. I., Park, H-J., & Suzuki, N. (1990). Reward allocations in the United States, Japan, and Korea: A comparison of individualistic and collectivistic cultures. *Academy of Management Journal, 33*, 188–198.

Kim, W. C., & Mauborgne, R. A. (1991). Implementing global strategies: The role of procedural justice. *Strategic Management Journal, 12*, 125–143.

Kim, W. C., & Mauborgne, R. A. (1993). Procedural justice, attitudes, and subsidiary top management compliance with multinationals' corporate strategic decisions. Academy of Management Journal, 36, 502–526.

Kirkman, B . L., Shapiro, D. L., Novelli, L., Jr., & Brett, J. M. (1996). Employee concerns regarding self-managing work teams: A multidimensional justice perspective. *Social Justice Research, 9*, 47–67.

Konovsky, M. A., & Cropanzano, R. (1991). The perceived fairness of employee drug testing as a predictor of employee attitudes and job performance. *Journal of Applied Psychology, 76*, 698–707.

Konovsky, M. A., Elliott, J., & Pugh, S. D. (1995, August). *The dispositional and contextual predictors of citizenship behavior in Mexico.* Paper presented at the annual meeting of the Academy of Management, Vancouver, BC, Canada.

Konovsky, M. A., & Folger, R. (1991, August). *The effects of procedural and distributive justice on organizational citizenship behavior.* Paper presented at the annual meeting of the Academy of Management, Miami Beach, FL.

Konovsky, M., Folger, R., & Cropanzano, R. (1987). Relative effects of procedural and distributive justice on employee attitudes. *Representative Research in Social Psychology, 17,* 15–24.

Konovsky, M. A., & Organ, D. W. (in press). Dispositional and contextual determinants of organizational citizenship behaviors. *Journal of Organizational Behavior.*

Konovsky, M. A., & Pugh, S. D. (1994). Citizenship behavior and social exchange. *Academy of Management Journal, 37,* 656–669.

Koper, G., Van Knippenberg, D., Bouhuijs, F., Vermunt, R., & Wilke, H. (1993). Procedural fairness and self-esteem. *European Journal of Social Psychology, 23,* 313–325.

Korsgaard, M. A., Schweiger, D. M., & Sapienza, H. J. (1995). Building commitment, attachment, and trust in strategic decision-making teams: The role of procedural justice. *Academy of Management Journal, 38,* 60–84.

Krzystofiak, F. J., Lillis, M., & Newman, J. M. (1995, August). *Justice along the scarcity continuum.* Paper presented at the annual meeting of the Academy of Management, Vancouver, BC, Canada.

Kulik, C. T., & Ambrose, M. L. (1992). Personal and situational determinants of referent choice. *Academy of Management Review, 17,* 212–237.

Lee, C. (1995). Prosocial organizational behaviors: The roles of workplace justice, achievement striving, and pay satisfaction. *Journal of Business and Psychology, 10,* 197–206.

Leventhal, G. S. (1976). The distribution of rewards and resources in groups and organizations. In L. Berkowitz & E. Walster (Eds.), *Advances in experimental social psychology* (Vol. 9, pp. 91–131). New York: Academic Press.

Leventhal, G. S. (1980). What should be done with equity theory? In K. J. Gergen, M. S. Greenberg, & R. H. Willis (Eds.), *Social exchange: Advances in theory and research* (pp. 27–55). New York: Plenum.

Lind, E. A. (1994, June). *Procedural justice and procedural preferences: Evidence for a fairness heuristic.* Paper presented at the annual meeting of the International Association of Conflict Management, Minneapolis, MN.

Lind, E. A. (1995). Justice and authority relations in organizations. In R. Cropanzano & M. K. Kacmar (Eds.), *Organizational politics, justice, and support: Managing the social climate of the workplace* (pp. 83–96). Westport, CT: Quorum Books.

Lind, E. A., & Earley, P. C. (1992). Procedural justice and culture. *International Journal of Psychology, 27,* 227–242.

Lind, E. A., Kanfer, R., & Earley, P. C. (1990). Voice, control, and procedural justice: Instrumental and noninstrumental concerns in fairness judgments. *Journal of Personality and Social Psychology, 59,* 952–959.

Lind, E. A., Kulik, C. A., Ambrose, M., & de Vera Park, M. V. (1993). Individual and corporate dispute resolution: Using procedural fairness as a decision heuristic. *Administrative Science Quarterly, 38,* 224–251.

Lind, E. A., & Tyler, T. R. (1988). *The social psychology of procedural justice.* New York: Plenum.

Lissowski, G., Tyszka, T., & Okrasa, W. (1991). Principles of distributive justice: Experiments in Poland and America. *Journal of Conflict Resolution, 35,* 98–119.

Lowe, R. H., & Vodanovich, S. H. (1995). A field study of distributive and procedural justice as predictors of satisfaction and organizational commitment. *Journal of Business and Psychology, 10,* 99–114.

Martin, J. (1981). Relative deprivation: A theory of distributive injustice for an era of shrinking resources. In B. M. Staw & L. L. Cummings (Eds.), *Research in organizational behavior* (Vol. 3, pp. 53–107). Greenwich, CT: JAI.

Martin, J., & Harder, J. W. (1994). Bread and roses: Justice and the distribution of financial and socioemotional rewards in organizations. *Social Justice Research, 7*, 241–264.

McFarlin, D. B., & Sweeney, P. D. (1992). Distributive and procedural justice as predictors of satisfaction with personal and organizational outcomes. *Academy of Management Journal, 35*, 626–637.

Messick, D. M., & Sentis, K. P. (1983). Fairness, preference, and fairness biases. In D. M. Messick & K. S. Cook (Eds.), *Equity theory: Psychological and sociological perspectives* (pp. 61–94). New York: Praeger.

Moorman, R. H. (1991). Relationship between organizational justice and organizational citizenship behaviors: Do fairness perceptions influence employee citizenship? *Journal of Applied Psychology, 76*, 845–855.

Niehoff, B. P., & Moorman, R. H. (1993). Justice as a mediator of the relationship between methods of monitoring and organizational citizenship behavior. *Academy of Management Journal, 36*, 527–556.

Organ, D. W., & Moorman, R. H. (1993). Fairness and organizational citizenship behavior: What are the connections? *Social Justice Research, 6*, 5–18.

Pettigrew, T. (1967). Social evaluation theory. In D. Levine (Ed.), *Nebraska symposium on motivation* (Vol. 15). Lincoln, NE: University of Nebraska Press.

Pfeffer, J., & Davis-Blake, A. (1992). Salary dispersion, location in the salary distribution, and turnover among college administrators. *Industrial and Labor Relations Review, 45*, 753–763.

Pfeffer, J., & Langton, N. (1993). The effects of wage dispersion on satisfaction, productivity, and working collaboratively: Evidence from college and university faculty. *Administrative Science Quarterly, 38*, 382–407.

Preskitt, S. K., & Olson-Buchanan, J. B. (1996, April). *Impact of interactional justice on fairness in organizational conflict resolution*. Paper presented at the annual meeting of the Society of Industrial and Organizational Psychology, San Diego, CA.

Rawls, J. (1971). *A theory of justice*. Cambridge, MA: Harvard University Press.

Rutte, C. G., & Messick, D. M. (1995). An integrated model of perceived unfairness in organizations. *Social Justice Research, 8*, 239–261.

Schwarzwald, J., Koslowsky, M., & Shalit, B. (1992). A field study of employees' attitudes and behaviors after promotion decisions. *Journal of Applied Psychology, 77*, 511–514.

Shapiro, D. L. (1993). Reconciling theoretical differences among procedural justice researchers by re-evaluating what it means to have one's view "considered": Implications for third-party managers. In R. Cropanzano (Ed.), *Justice in the workplace: Approaching fairness in human resource management* (pp. 51–78). Hillsdale, NJ: Lawrence Erlbaum Associates.

Shapiro, D. L., & Brett, J. M. (1993). Comparing three processes underlying judgments of procedural justice: A field study of mediation and arbitration. *Journal of Personality and Social Psychology, 65*, 1167–1177.

Shapiro, D. L., Buttner, E. H., & Barry, B. (1994). Explanations for rejection decisions: What factors enhance their perceived adequacy and moderate their enhancement of justice perceptions? *Organizational Behavior and Human Decision Processes, 58*, 346–368.

Siegel, P., Brockner, J., & Tyler, T. (1995, August). *Revisiting the relationship between procedural and distributive justice: The role of trust*. Paper presented at the Annual Meeting of the Academy of Management, Vancouver, BC, Canada.

Singer, M. S. (1993). *Fairness in personnel selection*. Aldershot, New Zealand: Avebury.

Sitkin, S. B., & Bies, R. J. (1993). The legalistic organization: Definitions, dimensions, and dilemmas. *Organization Science, 4*, 345–351.

Stepina, L. P., & Perrewe, P. L. (1991). The stability of comparative referent choice and feelings of inequity: A longitudinal field study. *Journal of Organizational Behavior, 12*, 185–200.

Summers, T. P., & Hendrix, W. H. (1991). Modeling the role of pay equity perceptions: A field study. *Journal of Occupational Psychology, 64*, 145–157.

Sweeney, P. D., & McFarlin, D. B. (1993). Workers' evaluations of the "ends" and the "means": An examination of four models of distributive and procedural justice. *Organizational Behavior and Human Decision Processes, 55*, 23–40.

Sweeney, P. D., McFarlin, D. B, & Inderrieden, E. J. (1990). Using relative deprivation theory to explain satisfaction with income and pay level: A multistudy examination. *Academy of Management Journal, 33*, 423–436.

Taylor, D. M., Moghaddam, F. M., Gamble, I., & Zellerer, E. (1987). Disadvantaged group responses to perceived inequity: From passive acceptance to collective action. *Journal of Social Psychology, 127*, 259–272.

Thibaut, J., & Walker, L. (1975). *Procedural justice: A psychological analysis*. Hillsdale, NJ: Lawrence Erlbaum Associates.

Tyler, T. R. (1989). The psychology of procedural justice: A test of the group-value model. *Journal of Personality and Social Psychology, 57*, 830–838.

Tyler, T. R. (1990). *Why people obey the law: Procedural justice, legitimacy, and compliance*. New Haven, CT: Yale University Press.

Tyler, T. R. (1991). Using procedures to justify outcomes: Testing the viability of a procedural justice strategy for managing conflict and allocating resources in work organizations. *Basic and Applied Social Psychology, 12*, 259–279.

Tyler, T. R. (1994). Psychological models of the justice motive: Antecedents of distributive and procedural justice. *Journal of Personality and Social Psychology, 67*, 850–863.

Tyler, T. R., & Bies, R. J. (1990). Beyond formal procedures: The interpersonal context of procedural justice. In J. S. Carroll (Ed.), *Applied social psychology and organizational settings* (pp. 77–98). Hillsdale, NJ: Lawrence Erlbaum Associates.

Tyler, T. R., & Dawes, R. M. (1993). Fairness in groups: Comparing self-interest and social identity perspectives. In B. A. Mellers & J. Baron (Eds.), *Psychological perspectives on justice: Theory and applications* (pp. 87–108). New York: Cambridge University Press.

Tyler, T. R., & Degoey, P. (1995). Collective restraint in social dilemmas: Procedural justice and social identification effects on support for authorities. *Journal of Personality and Social Psychology, 69*, 482–497.

Tyler, T. R., & Lind, E. A. (1992). A relational model of authority in groups. In M. P. Zanna (Ed.), *Advances in experimental social psychology* (Vol. 25, pp. 115–191). San Diego, CA: Academic Press.

van den Bos, K. (1996). *Procedural justice and conflict*. Unpublished doctoral dissertation, University of Leiden, the Netherlands.

van Dijk, E., & Wilke, H. (1993). Differential interests, equity, and public good provision. *Journal of Experimental Social Psychology, 29*, 1–16.

Walster, E., & Walster, G. W. (1975). Equity and social justice. *Journal of Social Issues, 31*, 21–44.

Witt, L. A. (1995). Influences of supervisor behaviors on the levels and effects of workplace politics. In R. Cropanzano & K. M. Kacmar (Eds.), *Organizational politics, justice, and support: Managing social climate at work* (pp. 37–54). Westport, CT: Quorum Books.

Chapter 6

Collective Identity, Collective Trust, and Social Capital: Linking Group Identification and Group Cooperation

Roderick M. Kramer
Benjamin A. Hanna
Steven Su
Jane Wei
Stanford University

In recent years, there has been a resurgence of interest by organizational scholars in groups and teams. Although sometimes noting the liabilities of group processes, much of this literature celebrates the virtues of groups, arguing that they contribute to more effective organizational learning, decision making, and problem solving (Bennis, 1997; Goodman, 1986; Hackman, 1990). Bennis (1997) provided perhaps the most enthusiastic analysis of what groups can accomplish over individuals: "In these creative alliances," he suggested, "the leader and the team are able to achieve something together that neither could achieve alone. The leader finds greatness in the group. And he or she helps the members find it in themselves" (p. 3).

Irrespective of where one stands on the issue of the relative merits of individual versus group decision making, it seems clear that realization of any benefits from group process depends on the willingness of group members to cooperate fully with other group members. Thus, group members are expected to share useful information with other group members, especially critical information others might not possess (Bonacich & Schneider, 1992); they are expected to exercise responsible restraint when using valuable but limited group resources (Kramer, 1991; Tyler & Degoey, 1995); and they are expected to allocate their fair share of time and attention toward the achievement of the group's collective goals (Latané, 1986; Murnighan, Kim, & Metzger, 1994; Olson, 1965). Such constructive actions constitute, in one sense, the productive "social capital" that resides within a group (cf. Putnam, 1993).

Although most group members recognize that failure to engage in such cooperative actions can contribute to suboptimal processes and outcomes—even outright failure—they also realize that isolated, individual acts of cooperation are unlikely to have much impact on the group's outcome. Moreover, unilateral actions can be quite costly, because the individual who engages in cooperative behaviors of this sort bears all of the burdens of cooperation, while the benefits are enjoyed by each of the group members. In the absence of some basis for thinking that other group members will reciprocate, therefore, individual group members may find it hard to justify such actions themselves. The inexorable logic of collective action leading to the unravelling of cooperative relations is well known (Olson, 1965) and need not be elaborated. Suffice it to say that, as Pfeffer and Salancik (1978) once laconically observed, "Interdependence is the reason why nothing works out quite the way one wants it to"(p. 34).

Recognizing this difficulty, researchers have frequently argued that trust plays a prominent role in the emergence of cooperation within groups (e.g., Dawes, 1980; Edney, 1980; Golembiewski, & McConkie, 1975; Kramer & Brewer, 1984; Messick & Brewer, 1983; Messick et al., 1983). In particular, they have proposed that individuals' willingness to cooperate with other group members is conditioned, at least partially, on their belief or expectancy that other members of a group will do the same (Brann & Foddy, 1988; Kramer, 1991; Messick et al., 1983).

Although its importance is readily apparent, the contours of trust in group contexts are much less obvious. On what basis is the decision to trust in group contexts predicated? Under what circumstances are individuals likely to assume that other members of a group will act in a trustworthy fashion? When are they willing to engage in trusting behavior themselves? These are the central questions we explore in this chapter. In doing so, we articulate a perspective that links individuals' level of psychological identification with other group members to their willingness to contribute toward the achievement of collective goals.

IDENTITY-BASED TRUST AND COLLECTIVE ACTION IN GROUPS

Contemporary theory and research on trust provides a number of useful perspectives on such questions. For example, a number of studies highlight the role that social networks play in the emergence and maintenance of trust within groups and organizations (e.g., Burt & Knez, 1995; Granovetter, 1985; Powell, 1990; Putnam, 1993) and imply the efficacy of various institutional mechanisms and governance structures that contribute to the production of collective trust (e.g., Powell, 1995; Sitkin & Roth, 1993; Yamagishi & Sato, 1986; Zucker, 1986).

The present chapter examines the role *group identification* plays in trust-related judgment and decision-making processes in work group contexts. We argue that the willingness of individuals to engage in trust behavior in situations requiring collective action is tied to the salience and strength of their identification with a group and its members. This approach is derived from recent social psychological theory and research on the relationship between group identification and cooperation (Brewer, 1981; Brewer & Kramer, 1986; Brewer & Schneider, 1990; Dawes, van de Kragt, & Orbell, 1988, 1990; Kramer, 1991; Kramer & Brewer, 1984, 1986; Kramer & Goldman, 1995; Tyler & Dawes, 1993; Tyler & Degoey, 1995).

Extrapolating from this work, we propose that psychological and social processes associated with group identification increase individuals' propensity to confer trust on other group members and their willingness to engage in trusting behavior themselves. We also use this conceptual framework to motivate an analysis of why trust sometimes fails. In particular, we argue that when individuals find their status within a group problematic or uncertain, trust based on group identification becomes problematic.

To advance these general arguments, our chapter is organized as follows. First, we explore the anatomy of the decision to trust in group contexts, describing some of the essential and also distinctive problems surrounding trust in such settings. Next, we introduce a framework for conceptualizing how group identification influences trust-related judgment and decision-making processes. Using this framework, we describe several distinct forms of identity-based trust behavior. We conclude by considering some of the implications of an identity-based conception of trust for understanding groups at work.

THE DECISION TO TRUST IN DYADIC TRUST DILEMMAS

When individuals decide to engage in trust behavior, they create for themselves both opportunity and vulnerability. The opportunity surrounds the perceived gains that accrue to both individual and group if and when their acts of trust are reciprocated by others. The vulnerabilities derive from the potential individual and collective costs associated with misplaced trust. From a judgment and decision-making perspective, such behavior is interesting because it entails a more or less conscious decision by individuals to expose themselves to risk. A central question in trust research, accordingly, is the basis on which individuals are willing to assume risks in trust dilemmas.

There are two types of decision errors possible in a trust dilemma; *misplaced trust* (engaging in trust behavior when the other doesn't) and *misplaced distrust* (failing to engage in trust behavior when the other person either does or would have). Each of these errors entails potential costs, some of which are fairly immediate and some of which are delayed. In the case of misplaced trust, the individual endures the immediate costs associated with their willingness to engage in trusting behavior when the other person failed to reciprocate. These include all of the opportunity costs associated with trust. For example, the individual may have squandered scarce attentional resources on a joint venture, while the other person devoted his or her time and effort toward pursuit of personal goals. The erosion of confidence in others that attends the experience of misplaced trust may have pervasive and long-lasting effects. For example, the psychological residues of misplaced trust may inhibit individuals' willingness to initiate cooperative actions in future encounters where such actions might have been reciprocated.

The potential costs associated with misplaced distrust are no less attractive, however. Individuals who routinely distrust others forgo many opportunities for gains. For example, presumptive distrust reduces the likelihood that the incremental benefits of reciprocal exchange will have an opportunity to materialize (cf. Axelrod, 1984; Bendor, Kramer, & Stout, 1991; Lindskold, 1978) because, after all, those who distrust invite distrust in return. Further, individuals who regularly engage in distrust, even if motivated by purely defensive concerns, expose themselves to reputational damage. Being labeled by others as distrustful can lead to exclusion from important networks, both formal and informal, within the organization.

The Role of Expectations in Trust Dilemmas

Much of this analysis, of course, simply reiterates the familiar observation that the decision to trust is largely about decision makers' anticipations of the benefits and risks associated with social acts—anticipations that are shrouded, in turn, in significant uncertainties. In situations where collective trust is high, the benefits of presumptive action may loom large in such anticipations. In situations where suspicion casts its shadow over the expectational landscape, the prospect of both immediate losses and future vulnerabilities may loom large, inhibiting risk taking.

Regardless of their particular form, such anticipations direct our attention to the critical role that individuals' expectations play in the emergence of trust within groups. Ultimately, the decision to trust is tied to individuals' expectations, not only about what others will do, but about the expected consequences of their own acts as well. But what form do such expectations take and where do they come from? One answer to this question, although incomplete, is provided by empirical work on the development of trust in interpersonal relationships. A fairly substantial body of empirical data suggests trust development can be conceptualized as a history-dependent process (Lindskold, 1978; Rotter, 1980). According to this evidence, individuals act much like intuitive Bayesians whose judgments about others' trustworthiness are calibrated on the basis of their cumulative experience with them. Boyle and Bonacich (1970) provided a representative view, asserting that expectations about trustworthy behavior will change "in the direction of experience and to a degree proportional to the difference between this experience and the initial expectations applied to them" (p. 130). In addition to these a priori expectations, other research suggests that the causal attributions individuals make about other's actions and inactions play a critical role in the process of deciding whether they can be trusted and, if so, how much. These attributions become, in a sense, the grist from which inferences about others' trust-related intentions, motives, and dispositions are formed (Deutsch, 1973).

THE DECISION TO TRUST IN GROUP CONTEXTS

In dyadic relationships, all of the "arithmetic" of trust—including the calibration of expectations, the aggregation of perceived benefits, and the calculation of risks—is facilitated by the fact that there usually exists a relatively detailed and precise history of interaction with a specific interaction partner. The trustworthiness of this person has been revealed, more or less fully, over the course of numerous exchanges and transactions. Thus, even allowing for occasional misperceptions and misunderstandings, the relevant history is comparatively fixed and bounded.

In contrast, in group settings, the relevant history about others' behavior is often incomplete (e.g., for newly formed groups, for situations in which a new individual comes into an existing group, or when an existing group's purposes and/or activities change significantly). This uncertainty about others' trustworthiness compounds considerably the inferential difficulties that individuals confront in the process of solving trust dilemmas. For example, the task of drawing reasonable inferences about the *distribution* of trust within a group is far from easy because it is more difficult to interact with and know each group member. Relatedly, the process of updating or recalibrating expectations about the trustworthiness of the group as a whole can be difficult. For example, to what extent should trust in the group be increased when some, but not all, of its members act in a trustworthy fashion? Similarly, to what extent should individuals reduce trust in the group when evidence becomes available that a few, but not all, group members have violated that trust?

As we argue in the next section, many of these questions can be approached from a perspective that links individuals' perceptions of the group's trustworthiness to their psychological identification with the group. To animate this argument, it is important to draw a distinction between the objective representation of a collective trust dilemma, and a given individual's subjective construal of that dilemma. People seldom respond to trust dilemmas purely as they are given. Instead, they respond in terms of how they subjectively interpret or construe those situations.

This relationship between the objective bases of interdependence, defined in terms of the explicit incentive structure linking social actors, and their subjective representations of that interdependence, was conceptualized by Kelley (1979) using the notion of *psychological transformations*. According to Kelley, when individuals encounter choice dilemmas they do not act directly in response to the objective or "given" payoff matrix. Instead, this matrix is transformed, via the operation of a variety of psychological processes, into an *effective matrix*. It is this effective matrix, he argued, that is most closely linked to their actual choice behavior.

In social psychological terms, this effective matrix can be viewed as the end result of a complex process of construal (or, more precisely, reconstrual) of a choice dilemma. This transformation process proceeds, it should be emphasized, largely outside individuals' awareness (i.e., it is not assumed they consciously transform a matrix in their minds; rather, the transformed matrix is an expression of their values, motives, goals, and dispositions). In this sense, the transformation process is revealed through behavior, and must be inferred rather than observed directly.

Kelley's formulation of the relationship between the objective and subjective representations of interdependence structures invites the question, "What psychological processes govern this transformation process?" Most of the research to date bearing on this question has focused on individual differences that drive the transformation process (see McClintock & Liebrand, 1988 for a recent review). In several previous articles, however, we argued that social group and organizational identification contribute to transformations (Kramer, 1991; Kramer, 1994; Kramer & Brewer, 1986; Kramer & Goldman, 1995). Extrapolating from this work, we argue next that identity-based transformations also play an important role in the decision to trust because they affect individuals' beliefs and expectations about the consequences of their own and other's actions.

LINKING GROUP IDENTIFICATION AND TRUST

The central thesis of this chapter is that individual group members' level of identification with the group influences their beliefs about the consequences of trust and distrust of the group and its members, and then they make decisions about whether to engage in trusting behavior based on those beliefs. In this section, we elaborate on this framework for understanding how individuals decide to trust or not to trust in group contexts.

Construal of the Decision

In group contexts, the central question faced by group members is whether to engage in trusting behavior toward the collective as a whole. An individual's level of identification with the group affects how the individual construes the payoffs to trust or distrust in the situation. Psychological transformations to the payoff matrix occur based on particular, salient characteristics of the situation and individuals respond based on these transformed matricies (Kelly, 1979). To articulate in more concrete terms how identity-based transformations affect group members' beliefs about the consequences of trust and distrust, we must first describe the specific form these transformations take. To do so, it is useful to draw a distinction between cognitive, motivational, and affective bases of transformations.[1]

Cognitive Bases of Identity Transformations

The cognitive transformations associated with organizational identification derive primarily from the effects of categorization on social perception and judgment (see Wilder & Cooper, 1981 for a review). Categorization processes affect not only how individuals perceive other individuals, often referred to as *social categorization effects* (Tajfel, 1969, 1982), but also how they perceive themselves, which have been characterized as *self-categorization effects* (Turner, 1987).

There are several ways in which social categorization processes influence individuals' judgments about the prospects for collective trust. The first has to do with the effects of social categorization on individuals' perceptions of other people's trustworthiness. Research on ingroup bias (Brewer, 1979) has shown that people tend to perceive members of their own social groups in relatively positive terms. Ingroup members are typically viewed, for example, as being more cooperative, more honest, and more trustworthy than members of other groups. Thus, all else equal, people expect more positive behavior from those with whom they share group membership compared to outsiders.

Second, there is evidence that social categorization enhances perceived similarity among individuals who share membership in a social category (Tajfel, 1969). Because of this enhanced perception of similarity, individuals may presume that other members of a collective perceive a given trust dilemma in similar terms and will act in similar fashion. In other words, common categorization may inflate judgments of consensus about how a dilemma will be construed by other members of the group. These assump-

---

[1]Although we feel that these processes are distinct enough to warrant independent acknowledgment, we do not assume that they are independent of each other.

tions of similarity and consensus thus provide a basis for presumptive action by reducing the perceived risk that one will be the only person thinking and acting in collective terms (i.e., the only "sucker" in the group).

Third, research on psychological contracts (Rousseau, 1989) suggests that group members often possess a variety of more or less tacit understandings regarding the norms, obligations, duties, and rights that govern their relationships with other group members. Thus, group membership may be taken as prima facie evidence that other members of the group are willing to live by the codes of conduct that bind them together. This may be especially true with respect to those groups that maintain strong cultures, that create significant barriers to entry, and that impose substantial socialization costs on their members.

The presumption that a psychological contract is in force helps individual group members solve an important psychological barrier to presumptive action—namely, the fear of exploitation. As Rotter (1980) observed, concerns about fear and gullibility, often more than greed or temptation, underlie the reluctance to trust. Thus, the belief that other group members will not willingly violate the psychological contract may reduce individuals' fears that unilateral initiatives on their part will leave them "exposed" (i.e., at risk of ending up with the sucker's payoff).

In this respect, social categorization creates cognitive benefits that can operate as substitutes for other mechanisms on which trust is more usually predicated. For example, individuals may perceive less of a need to verify or "negotiate" trust before engaging in exchanges or transactions with other organizational members. As Brewer (1981) proposed in this respect:

> Common membership in a salient social category can serve as a rule for defining the boundaries of low-risk interpersonal trust that bypasses the need for personal knowledge and the costs of negotiating reciprocity with individual others. As a consequence of shifting from the personal level to the social group level of identity, the individual can adopt a sort of "depersonalized trust" based on category membership alone. (p. 356)

Social categorization also affects individuals' causal attributions about other's dispositions, motives, and intentions—important considerations when determining the risks of engaging in trusting behavior. Research has shown, for example, that individuals are more likely to attribute ingroup members' negative behaviors to external, unstable factors, whereas the same behavior by an outgroup member is more likely to be attributed to stable, internal factors (see Brewer & Kramer, 1985; Hewstone, 1992; Pettigrew, 1979; and Weber, 1994 for reviews). Because of these attributional biases, individuals tend to give other ingroup members the benefit of the doubt when confronted with information that might otherwise be viewed as diagnostic of a lack of trustworthiness. By discounting such data, trust within the ingroup remains intact.

Complementing this evidence that social categorization influences individuals' expectations and attributions about other ingroup members' behaviors is evidence that similar processes are at work when individuals view themselves. Turner (1987) characterized these as *self-categorization* effects. When an individual's identification moves from the personal level to the collective level, he noted, there is a "shift towards the perception of self as an interchangeable exemplar of some social category and away from the perception of self as a unique person" (p. 253). In support of these arguments, research has demonstrated that when individuals are categorized in terms of group or social identities, they are likely to think and act in collective terms. When categorized in terms of more distinctive personal or individualistic identities, however, they are likely to act more self-interestedly (Brewer & Kramer, 1986).

Such findings suggest that self-categorization processes may affect the utility or weight that individuals afford to their own versus others' outcomes (Kramer & Brewer, 1986; Kramer & Goldman, 1995). This line of argument draws attention to the possibility that there are motivational as well as cognitive underpinnings to identity-based transformations.

Motivational Bases of Transformations

Several motivational bases of transformations seem plausible. First, to the extent that common categorization enhances perceptions of similarity with others, it may also reduce perceived social distance between the self and other group members. As a consequence, decision makers may afford more psychological significance to the impact of their actions on others. As Brewer (1979) suggested in this regard, "The reduced differentiation between one's own and other's outcomes associated with ingroup formation provides one mechanism for increasing the weight given to collective outcomes in individual decision making" (p. 322). As a result of common categorization, individuals may draw a less sharp distinction between their own and others' outcomes.

There are additional benefits one can imagine. In discussing the motivational bases of transformations, Kelley (1979) noted that behavior in interdependent situations is important not only insofar as it materially affects the tangible outcomes that individuals derive from their actions (represented in the given matrix as payoffs), but it also affects a variety of less tangible but nonetheless important psychological benefits. He proposed, for example, that interdependence dilemmas afford individuals—as social actors—a setting in which to display to others valued interpersonal orientations and behavioral dispositions.

From the standpoint of individuals who identify with an organization and its members, public affirmations and displays of trust serve a number of important social motives. Individuals may use these opportunities to signal socially important characteristics to other group members (Goffman, 1959). For example, public affirmations and displays of trust provide a way for individuals to affirm the importance or value that they associate with their membership in their organization (cf. Lind & Tyler, 1988), to communicate respect and liking for other group members by acting as if they trust other group members, and to signal to others the importance they assign to preservation of the collective trust. From this perspective, the psychological significance of choice in collective trust dilemmas resides not only in the calculus of risks and benefits, but also in the social opportunities such situations afford individuals. Thus, a complete theory regarding the decision to trust in collective contexts requires that we take account not only of the direct and obvious benefits of such behavior, but also the less visible but no less important self-presentational motives and expressive needs such behavior serves.

Affective Bases of Transformations

One important implication of our arguments regarding the psychological benefits of identification with others is that individuals in organizations may derive substantial hedonic benefits from engaging in collective behavior. For example, to the extent that individuals perceive trust behavior as a mechanism for affirming cherished social identities and positive relationships with others, such affirmations are likely to be perceived as intrinsically pleasurable and self-rewarding. Such linkages, moreover, open the door for powerful secondary reinforcers to come into play.

For example, individuals may experience additional pleasure when they subsequently learn that presumptive actions predicated on trust in others have been validated. When individuals learn that their own voluntary restraint in a resource crisis has been met by others, they may derive satisfaction from knowing that the risks they willingly assumed ex ante have, in a sense, paid off.[2] Similarly, violated expectations generate emotions (Lazarus, 1984). Learning that other group members engaged in trusting behavior despite original expectations to the contrary is a positive violation of expectations and will generate positive emotions.

In this sense, presumptive acts made on the basis of these positive hedonic anticipations may be self-reinforcing and eventually internalized.

---

[2]Interestingly, although researchers are often quick to point out the aversiveness of the sucker's payoff (and its motivating potential), they tend to ignore the possibility that *not* obtaining this outcome might be quite satisfying and motivating as well.

As Simon (1991) observed in this regard, "Identification with the 'we,' which may be a family, a company, a city, a nation, or the local baseball team, allows individuals to experience satisfactions (to gain utility) from successes of the unit thus selected. Thus, organizational identification becomes a motivation for employees to work actively for organizational goals" (p. 36).[3] And note that such self-control may be pushed back up the temporal chain of action because our ability, as cognitively complex "self managers," enables us to anticipate and engineer such affective outcomes. As a consequence, they have a chance to influence our *ex ante* calculations regarding the perceived benefits associated with engaging in them.[4] Elster and Loewenstein (1992) argued that anticipatory cognitions of this sort can exert a potent effect on the self-management of behavior:

> Like memory, anticipated experiences affect current utility through the consumption and contrast effects. Through the consumption effect we are able to, in effect, consume events before they occur through anticipation . . . [our capacity to savor events] acts as multipliers of experience, causing individuals to experience the hedonic impact of events repeatedly before they occur. . . . Anticipated experiences also affect current well-being via the contrast effect, by serving as a reference point against which current consumption is measured. When the future is expected to be superior to the present, the comparison leads to a denigration of the present. (p. 225)

Within the context of the present arguments, consumption and contrast imply socially adaptive cognitive mechanisms that may tip the balance toward presumptive action.

The hedonic consequences associated with identity-based trust, and their behavioral implications, are worth highlighting, we feel, because previous work on trust has remained, for the most part, silent about the positive emotional dimensions of trust behavior. Instead, it has focused almost exclusively on negative affective reactions associated with violations of trust. For example, clinical social psychologists (e.g., Janoff-Bulman, 1992) and organizational theorists (e.g., Bies & Tripp, 1995) have afforded considerable attention to the intense emotional reactions that

---

[3]Simon goes on to note that,

Of course, identification is not an exclusive source of motivation; it exists side by side with material rewards and enforcement mechanisms that are part of the employment contract. But a realistic picture of how organizations operate must include the importance of identification in the motivations of employees. (p. 36)

[4]There is an additional motivational "kicker" associated with such acts. By engaging in them, individuals not only have an opportunity to affirm the value they attach to organizational membership, they also have a chance, via downward social comparison, to feel morally superior to those who fail to do so.

follow the betrayal of trust. By contrast, the positive emotional consequences that might attend affirmations of trust in social contexts have been largely neglected.

The cognitive, motivational, and affective transformations described thus far can be regarded as important primarily with respect to their influence on individuals' expectations and calculations regarding the consequences (risks and benefits) that are likely to attend their decisions to trust or not to trust. We now elaborate on the logic of this argument, postulating that individuals' willingness to expose themselves to the risks of trust are conditioned on three distinct, but related, types of expectations. We characterize these as expectations of reciprocity, perceptions of efficacy, and expectations regarding hedonic reinforcement or consequences.

Expectations of Reciprocity. Expectations of reciprocity reflect individuals' a priori beliefs regarding the likelihood that other group members will reciprocate acts of trust. Evidence that generalized expectations of reciprocity play a role in individuals' willingness to trust comes from several sources (see Brann & Foddy, 1988; Lindskold, 1978; Messick et al., 1983). In one demonstration, Messick et al. (1983) found that individuals' willingness to exercise personal restraint when consuming resources from a rapidly depleting common pool were correlated with their belief that others would do so as well.

Although necessary, merely thinking that one's own actions will be reciprocated by others does not necessarily provide sufficient justification for the decision to trust in collective contexts. As Arrow (1974) suggested, "Collective undertakings of any kind . . . become difficult or impossible not only because A may betray B *but because even if A wants to trust B he knows that B is unlikely to trust him*" (p. 26, italics added). Gambetta (1988) made a similar point in arguing that, "it is necessary not only to trust others before acting cooperatively, but also to believe that one is trusted *by* others" (p. 216, emphasis in original).

In the case of collective contexts, therefore, one must be confident that others also entertain similar expectations—and enough others to make a difference. In this respect, trust in collective contexts depends on what Schelling (1960) aptly characterized as the familiar "spiral of reciprocal expectations" (p. 87). These reciprocal expectations make up the fragile cognitive chain linking perceptions of own and others' actions, a chain that may "tip" the collective towards trust.

Perceptions of Efficacy. Perceptions of efficacy reflect individuals' beliefs regarding the agency of their actions (i.e., the extent to which their actions can influence a particular outcome; see, e.g., Kaufman & Kerr, 1993; Kerr, 1989, 1992). In the case of collective trust dilemmas, they reflect individuals' judgments regarding the extent to which their own trusting behavior will make a difference in terms of actually influencing the final outcome of the dilemma.

Logically, there are two distinct but related ways in which individuals might conceptualize the links between their own actions and collective outcomes. The first way can be characterized as a form of *causal efficacy*. Causal efficacy has to do with the presumed impact of one's own behavior on a collective dilemma itself (e.g., my belief that exercising personal restraint during a water shortage will actually help reduce the scarcity, rather than be merely an inconsequential drop in the bucket).

The second form of efficacy has to do with the anticipated impact of one's own actions on other group members. With respect to trust, this form of efficacy reflects individuals' beliefs regarding the extent to which they can induce others to engage in trusting behavior by first modeling such behavior themselves. As such, it represents a form of perceived social influence.

Although perceptions of efficacy have received little attention from trust researchers, we think such perceptions may play a critical role in the decision to trust in collective contexts.

Hedonic Expectations. One important consequence of assuming that decisions about trust are viewed by group members as, at least partially, social decisions is that individuals may be able to anticipate hedonic benefits from engaging in such acts. Decisions about trust in collective contexts are not only about the calculation of individual risks and profits, they are also about identity and image (cf. March, 1994). Following the work of Tyler and his colleagues (Lind & Tyler, 1988; Tyler, 1993; Tyler & Degoey, 1995), we assume individuals generally care about their standing in social groups. As a consequence, they are likely to care not only about the material benefits they associate with a decision to trust, but also its self-presentational implications. These hedonic anticipations function to discipline and constrain their more self-interested impulses.

As social acts, decisions about trust may also, although not always or necessarily, become linked to group members' perceptions of their obligation to protect cherished group norms and values. For example, individuals may feel the decision to trust is mandated by moral imperatives that dominate or override other, more parochial concerns. It is important to note that, in making this argument, we do not intend to suggest (nor do we need to invoke) a principalistic account of social action (cf. Batson, 1994). To explain why individuals engage in such behavior, a purely hedonic argument is more than adequate: The hedonic bases of social acts, and the underlying motivating potential of moral imperatives linked to them, derive from two sources. First, in a positive sense, individuals' ability to anticipate the pleasurable states associated with prosocial, principalistic behavior when interacting with people within one's social boundaries. Relatedly, our capacity to anticipate the negative hedonic states (guilt and fear) that may attend personal acts that violate the collective trust push us in the same direction.

In terms of the standard payoff matrix, of course, such anticipations are purely exogeneous or "extrarational" considerations (cf. Elster, 1989). From the perspective of the transformed matrix, however, they can be construed as anticipations that individuals, as social decision makers, routinely incorporate in their calculus.

The social character of identity-based trust, and its importance, emerges most clearly when consideration is given, first, to the distinct ways in which the decision to trust in collective settings can be construed by individuals, and, second, to the implications of such differences with respect to their influence on individuals' willingness to engage in trust behavior. In particular, the identity framework advanced in this chapter suggests several distinct motives for engaging in trust behavior, which we will characterize as (1) reciprocity-based trust, (2) elicitative trust, (3) compensatory trust, and (4) noncontingent or moralistic trust.

Reciprocity-Based Trust. The logic of reciprocity-based trust is simply, "I will engage in trust behavior *because* I believe you are likely to do the same." It is explicitly tied to, and thus contingent on, individuals' expectations of reciprocity. In this respect, it is a form of calculative trust not unlike those encounterd in a number of recent economic and game theoretic treatments (see notably Williamson, 1993).

The strongest evidence for reciprocity-based trust is found in experimental research on interpersonal trust (Lindskold, 1978) and trust in social dilemma situations (Messick et al., 1983). As noted earlier, these studies demonstrate that individuals' expectations of reciprocity influence their willingness to engage in cooperative behavior themselves (although see Tyler & Degoey, 1995 for a discussion of evidence that expectations of reciprocity alone are not always sufficient). Thus, individuals strongly identified with a group are likely to have higher expectations for reciprocity and therefore engage in more reciprocity-based trust than individuals not strongly identified with the group.

Elicitative Trust Behavior. Elicitative trust behavior is motivated by the belief or expectation that, by engaging in acts of trust themselves, one may be able to induce others to do the same. Elicitative behavior entails an expectation of reciprocity, but an expectation that is linked to individuals' perceptions of personal efficacy (i.e., their belief that their actions will influence others, especially those who might be reticent to engage in trust because of fear of being the only one to do so). It is thus predicated on individuals' expectation that they can *create* a climate of reciprocal trust through unilateral initiatives. In elicitative trust, the individual acts as "first mover" or "missing hero" (Schelling, 1978), an important role if the failure of collective trust is viewed as a problem of volunteer's dilemma (cf. Murnighan et al., 1994) or motivated by fear of ending up with the sucker's payoff.

The notion of elicitative trust behavior is suggested by empirical research on the development of trust (Pilisuk & Skolnick, 1968) and the evolution of cooperation (Axelrod, 1984). Extrapolating from this research, we might expect that elicitative trust behavior is most likely to be observed in situations where expectations of reciprocity are initially low but perceptions of personal agency are high.

Compensatory Trust Behavior. Perhaps one of the most important implications of our analysis of the effects of organizational identification on individual judgment and decision making is that, through the transformation process, collective trust itself may come to be construed as a public good in its own right. If the collective trust is perceived by organizational members as a valuable shared resource worth protecting, then individuals may be willing to engage in compensatory actions to offset the behavior of other individuals they think might threaten its stability or survival.

Compensatory trust behavior is predicated on the recognition that some, but not all, of the other members of a collective may fail to engage in the needed presumptive behavior. Because most individuals are sophisticated enough to realize that the solution to many collective action problems requires only cooperation from some critical mass or minimal set of decision makers (Schelling, 1978; van de Kragt, Orbell, & Dawes, 1983), compensatory acts (if "replicated" by sufficient others) can offset the harm of anticipated free riders. Some evidence of such compensatory behavior has been observed in social dilemma experiments (e.g., Brewer, 1985; Brewer & Schneider, 1990).

In making this argument, it is critical to emphasize here, as before, that we are not assuming that individuals who engage in compensatory acts necessarily view such behavior as altruistic. As Lieberman (1964) noted, "Many views of trust have overlooked what appears to be an essential ingredient in the analysis of trust . . . [For example] we trust other nations, but this trust is not based primarily on moral considerations or any notion of the building of positive feelings; (rather) *it is based on a sophisticated notion of self-interest*" (p. 272, italics added). Thus, it is not necessary to presuppose that decision makers who engage in compensatory acts in collective contexts ipso facto perceive themselves as forfeiting their own self-interests on behalf of their group. Instead, we argue, the shift in identity from the personal to the collective level may serve, more simply, to enhance individuals' perception of the tight coupling that exists between their interests and the collective welfare, especially if a sufficiently long-term horizon is adopted. Behavior of this sort reveals, in other words, individuals' willingness to incur personal costs in the near-term in order to protect a valuable resource that they expect will pay dividends later. In this respect, decisions predicated on compensatory motives resemble calculative trust, but they are more forward looking (i.e., made with the "shadow of the future" in mind; Axelrod, 1984).

Compensatory behaviors may get even more bite, from a motivational standpoint, vis-à-vis their impact on the cognitive links between self-perception and commitment (cf. Cialdini, 1983). As Boulding (1988) suggested:

> A very important dynamic in the building up of community is what I have called the "sacrifice trap." Once people are coerced, or even better, persuaded, into making sacrifices, *their identity becomes bound up with the community organization for which the sacrifices were made* [italics added]. Admitting to one's self that one's sacrifices were in vain is a deep threat to identity and is always sharply resisted. (p. 288)

Thus, compensatory acts may lead to self-reinforcing changes in individuals' perceptions not only of themselves, but also of their relationship to the collective. In this respect, compensatory behaviors not only solve the individual's immediate decisional dilemma (to engage in collective action this time), they also help resolve a more vexing and recurrent commitment dilemma by breeding attachment to the group.

Moralistic Trust Behavior.   Moralistic trust constitutes a fourth kind of identity-based trust behavior. Moralistic trust takes the form of "I will act in a trusting and trustworthy fashion irrespective of what others in the group do or don't do." The notion of moralistic trust was originally suggested by Rotter (1980), who argued that trust behavior sometimes reflects an individual's "belief in the moral rightness of trust [rather than] an expectancy of risk in trusting others" (p. 4). In contrast with the first three motives for engaging in trust behavior, which are clearly contingent on various forms of social or causal expectation, we view moralistic trust as noncontingent.[5] It is presumed to be explicately predicated not on calculations of risks and benefits, but

---

[5]Having said this, it is important to be clear about the sense in which moralistic trust should be construed noncontingent. By noncontingent, we mean that individuals do not view their actions as conditioned on the expectation they will reciprocated; nor do they think that they can induce others to follow suit by engaging in trust. Instead, they act in a trustworthy fashion because they believe that's what good group members do. However, there is a sense in which moralistic behavior may be contingent, insofar as the need for such behavior might be most salient in situations where one expects trust to fail. For example, a kind of moral outrage over the failure of others to act in a trustworthy fashion may impel individuals toward acts of moralistic trust.

rather on general ethical convictions and intrinsic values that individuals associate with group membership.

Within Rotter's framework, we should note, moralistic trust is conceptualized as an individual difference variable. As such, it is presumably linked to individuals' social values and dispositions. By contrast, an identity-based conception of moralistic trust emphasizes its ties to individuals' beliefs about what responsible membership in a social group entails. Moralistic trust is about the identities and images that attend being a "good" group member and one who cares about maintaining that good standing.

Summary

In this section, we've elucidated the process by which individuals' identification with a group affects their construal of a trust dilemma. We've described several ways in which identification affects cognitive, motivational, and affective transformations of the perceived payoffs from engaging in trusting behavior, and how these transformations affect derived expectations of reciprocity, efficacy, and potential hedonic consequences. At the end of this process, the decision to trust is framed in terms of several motives that are expected to shape whether or not the individual ultimately engages in trusting behavior.

SOME IMPLICATIONS OF AN IDENTITY-BASED CONCEPTION OF GROUP TRUST

As with other forms of trust, the utility of an identity-based conception of trust in groups can be judged from the standpoint of the resilience or fragility of trust it implies. Social scientists have often noted that forms of trust can be "thick" or "thin," "weak" or "strong," or "fragile" or "resilient" (see, e.g., Bernard, 1988; Meyerson, Kramer, & Weick, 1995; Putnam, 1993). And therein, to a large degree, lies their efficacy. Gambetta (1988) most sharply engaged this issue when he asked pointedly, "To what extent can we, and should we, 'trust' trust to make a difference?" (p. 261). If, for example, the cognitive and social processes that produce and sustain identity-based trust are themselves fragile, why not go around such trust? In other words, why not turn to other, more robust routes to cooperation?

In approaching this question, we would note first that it is not necessary to assume, as might appear at first glance, that a particularly strong or cohesive bond need exist among group members in order for identity-based trust to take hold. It is only necessary to assume that collective identity provides *some* credible basis for individuals to believe that engaging in trusting behavior does not entail unacceptable levels of risk. As Deutsch (1958) observed in this regard, "Mutual trust can occur even under circumstances where the people involved are not overly concerned with each other's welfare, *provided that the characteristics of the situation are such as to lead one to expect one's trust to be fulfilled*" (p. 279, italics added).

Thus, our arguments about identity-based trust are not predicated on the assumption that people necessarily care about what happens to others (although we have implied there is some of that present in most social groups). Instead, the cognitive, motivational, and affective processes associated with group identification give rise to a number of distinct motives for engaging in acts of trust in collective contexts. To the extent that these psychological factors converge to produce trust behavior, identity-based trust can be characterized as an *overdetermined* form of trust. Overdeterminedness alone obviously does not guarantee resilience. The extent to which identity-based trust is fragile or hardy depends also on numerous, often quite subtle, group actions, cues, and contexts. Identity-based trust can be viewed as by-products of a variety of factors, including the extent to which socialization practices create strong collective identities, the effectiveness of a group leaders' symbolic management activities at reinforcing those identities, and the power of the group's culture to nurture and sustain them. Identity-based trust, like group identity itself, is a socially constructed product.

Of course, organizations are often mindful of this fact, as evidenced by their willingness to allocate substantial organizational resources to foster positive identities—identities they hope will forge the necessary perceptual links between individual actions and collective outcomes (cf. Albert & Whetten, 1985; Ashforth & Mael, 1989; Dutton, Dukerich, & Harquail, 1994; Elsbach & Kramer, 1995; Mael & Ashforth, 1992; March, 1994).

Our arguments about the overdeterminedness of identity-based trust draw attention to the ambiguous nature of trust behavior, especially as they are enacted in group settings. We observe others' acts, but the motive or motives underlying those acts are usually far from clear. Because of this inherent ambiguity, observers can never know for sure what to make of others' trust-like behavior, that is, what it "means" or reveals about them. For example, it is often hard to know whether an observed act of trust is predicated on the other's confidence that he or she won't be exploited (i.e., an example of reciprocal trust), or whether it is intended to move others toward trust (an example of elicitative trust). Thus, it is often difficult to infer whether an instance of trust behavior is indicative of another's confidence, fear, hope, or resignation.

To the extent that individuals recognize that inferring motives and intentions from others' behavior is problematic, they are likely to become more attentive and attuned to the nuances of others' actions and inactions. In other words, the ambiguities that surround trust in collective contexts should invite a form of adaptive vigilance (Kramer, 1994). Individuals become willing to pay attention to others' behavior, and how much they are willing to pay (the degree of vigilance) increases as the costs of misplaced trust increase. Thus, we assume individuals do not respond passively to the vulnerabilities and uncertainties they encounter in collective action situations. Rather, they proactively seek information to reduce their preceived vulnerability and uncertainty.

Additionally, to the extent that they realize that similar ambiguities attend their own actions (i.e., that their behavior creates interpretive predicaments for others), individuals often proactively undertake initiatives to clarify those actions. In other words, just as people understand the need to obtain reassurance, they also recognize the need to *provide* it. Accordingly, we assume that, as with many forms of social behavior, acts of trust are often accompanied by verbal accounts that are aimed at reducing their ambiguity.

Some economists and game theorists argue, of course, that "cheap talk" of this sort is meaningless and should be discounted. Certainly, when the costs of misplaced trust cross some salient threshold, cheap talk should be discounted (for example, in arms races, actions do speak louder than words). However, in more benign group contexts, cheap talk serves a variety of useful social functions, including the reduction of ambiguity and the provision of partial, even if incomplete, reassurance. Thus, although such talk may be cheap, it is often far from worthless.

We further assume that the emergence and maintenance of collective trust is linked to positive and mutually reinforcing cycles of action–reaction among interdependent players (Kahn & Kramer, 1990). In other words, collective trust should be viewed as the end product of a reciprocal influence process, in which individual actions not only affect collective outcomes, but feedback about collective behavior, in turn, influences individual decisions.

Such dynamics arise, at least in part, from the self-reinforcing properties of cooperative behavior. As Putnam (1993) noted, trust within social communities not only "lubricates cooperation [but] cooperation itself breeds trust" (p. 171). And it is this "steady accumulation of social capital," he suggested, that plays a fundamental role in the development of collective trust and cooperation.[6] Cast in terms of the present analysis, we would argue that it is thus the *perception* of common identification—and also the perception that the perception is common—that provides the critical cognitive glue that binds interdependent players together and, at

---

[6]Although Putnam's arguments were aimed at understanding the evolution of cooperation among Italian civic communities, they seem just as relevant to understanding the emergence of trust in large, complex organizations as well. Such organizations resemble, in more ways than we often like to admit, such fiercely competitive tribes and parochial communities.

the same time, provides a lubricant that enables presumptive actions to diffuse and reverberate throughout the collective.

Miller (1992) offered an excellent example of this kind of socially constructed and self-reinforcing dynamic. In recounting the philosophy of Hewlett-Packard (HP) founder Bill Hewlett, he noted that the HP way

> consists of the policies and actions that flow from the belief that men and women want to do a good job, a creative job, and that if they are provided with the proper environment they will do so. The reality of cooperation . . . is suggested by the open lab stock policy, which not only allows engineers access to all equipment, but encourages them to take it home for personal use . . . the open door symbolizes and demonstrates management's trust in the cooperativeness of the employees. . . . The elimination of time clocks and locks on equipment room doors is *a way of building a shared expectation among all the players that cooperation will most likely be reciprocated creating a shared "common knowledge" in the ability of the players to reach cooperative outcomes.* (p. 197, italics added)

Because such acts are so manifestly predicated on confidence in other group members, they tend to breed confidence in turn. As a consequence, collective trust becomes over time institutionalized (at the macro level) and internalized (at a micro level). In this respect, collective trust becomes a potent form of "expectational asset" that group members can rely on to help solve problems of cooperation and coordination (cf. Camerer & Knez, in press). They become, in other words, expectations that bind (Kramer & Goldman, 1995).

REFERENCES

Albert, S., & Whetten, D. A. (1985). Organizational identity. In B. M. Staw & L. L. Cummings (Eds.), *Research in organizational behavior* (Vol. 7, pp. 263–295). Greenwich, CT: JAI.

Arrow, K. (1974). *The limits of organization.* New York: Norton.

Ashforth, B. E., & Mael, F. (1989). Social identity theory and the organization. *Academy of Management Review, 14,* 20–39.

Axelrod, R. (1984). *The evolution of cooperation.* New York: Basic Books.

Barnard, C. I. (1968). *The functions of the executive.* Cambridge: Harvard University Press (Original work published 1938)

Batson, C. (1994). Why act for the public good? Four answers. *Personality and Social Psychology Bulletin, 20,* 603–610.

Bernard, W. (1988). Formal structures and social reality. In D. Gambetta (Ed.), *Trust: Making and breaking cooperative relations.* Cambridge, MA: Basil Blackwell.

Bendor, J., Kramer, R. M., & Stout, S. (1991). When in doubt: Cooperation in a noisy prisoner's dilemma. *Journal of Conflict Resolution, 35,* 691–719.

Bennis, W. (1997). *Organizing genius: The secrets of creative collaboration.* Menlo Park, CA: Addison-Wesley.

Bies, R., & Tripp, T. (1995). Beyond distrust: Getting even and the need for revenge. In R. M. Kramer & T. R. Tyler (Eds.), *Trust in organizations*. Thousand Oaks, CA: Sage.

Bonacich, P., & Schneider, S. (1992). Communication networks and collective action. In W. G. Liebrand, D. M. Messick, & H. A. M. Wilke (Eds.), *A social psychological approach to social dilemmas*. Oxford, England: Pergamon.

Boulding, K. E. (1988). Commons and community: The idea of a public. In G. Hardin & J. Baden (Eds.), *Managing the commons*. San Francisco: Freeman.

Boyle, R, & Bonacich, P. (1970). The development of trust and mistrust in mixed-motives games. *Sociometry, 33*, 123–139.

Brann, P., & Foddy, M. (1988). Trust and the consumption of a deteriorating resource. *Journal of Conflict Resolution, 31*, 615–630.

Brewer, M. B. (1979). In group bias in the minimal intergroup situation: A cognitive-motivational analysis. *Psychological Bulletin, 86*, 307–324.

Brewer, M. B. (1981). Ethnocentrism and its role in interpersonal trust. In M. B. Brewer & B. E. Collins (Eds.), *Scientific inquiry in the social sciences*. San Francisco: Jossey-Bass.

Brewer, M. B. (1995). In group favoritism: The subtle side of intergroup discrimination. In D. M. Messick & A. Tenbrunsel (Eds.), *Behavioral research and business ethics*. New York: Russell Sage.

Brewer, M. B., & Kramer, R. M. (1985). The psychology of intergroup attitudes and behavior. *Annual Review of Psychology, 36*, 219–243.

Brewer, M. B., & Kramer, R. M. (1986). Choice behavior in social dilemmas: Effects of social identity, group size, and decision framing. *Journal of Personality and Social Psychology, 50*, 543–549.

Brewer, M. B., & Schneider, S. (1990). Social identity and social dilemmas: A double-edged sword. In D. Abrams & M. A. Hogg (Eds.), *Social identity theory: Constructive and critical advances*. New York: Springer-Verlag.

Burt, R., & Knez, M. (1995). Third-party gossip and trust. In R. M. Kramer & T. R. Tyler (Eds.), *Trust in organizations*. Thousand Oaks, CA: Sage.

Camerer, C. F., & Knez, M. (in press). Creating "expectational assets" in the laboratory: "Weakest link" coordination games. *Strategic Management Journal*.

Cialdini, R. (1993). *Influence* (3rd ed.). New York: HarperCollins.

Dawes, R. M. (1980). Social dilemmas. *Annual Review of Psychology, 31*, 169–193.

Dawes, R. M., van de Kragt, A. J. C., & Orbell, J. M. (1988). Not me or thee but we: The importance of group identity in eliciting cooperation in dilemma situations: Experimental manipulations. *Acta Psychologica, 68*, 83–97.

Dawes, R. M., van de Kragt, A. J. C., & Orbell, J. M. (1990). Cooperation for the benefit of us—not me, or my conscience. In J. Mansbridge (Ed.), *Beyond self-interest*. Chicago: University of Chicago Press.

Deutsch, M. (1958). Trust and suspicion. *Journal of Conflict Resolution, 2*, 265–279.

Deutsch, M. (1973). *The resolution of conflict*. New Haven, CT: Yale University Press.

Dutton, J., Dukerich, J. M., & Harquail, C. V. (1994). Organizational images and member identification. *Administrative Science Quarterly, 39*, 239–263.

Edney, J. J. (1980). The commons problem: Alternative perspectives. *American Psychologist, 35*, 131–150.

Elsbach, K. D., & Kramer, R. M. (1995). Members' responses to organizational identity threats: Encountering and countering the *Business Week* rankings. *Administrative Science Quarterly, 41*, 442–476.

Elster, J. (1989). *The cement of society*. Cambridge, England: Cambridge University Press.

Elster, J., & Loewenstein, G. (1992). Utility from memory and anticipation. In G. Loewenstein & J. Elster (Eds.), *Choice over time*. New York: Russell Sage.

Gambetta, D. (1988). Can we trust trust? In D. Gambetta (Ed.), *Trust: Making and breaking cooperative relations*. Cambridge, MA: Basil Blackwell.

Goffman, E. (1959). *The presentation of self in everyday life*. New York: Anchor Books.

Golembiewski, R. T., & McConkie, M. (1975). The centrality of interpersonal trust in group processes. In C. L. Cooper (Ed.), *Theories of group processes* (pp. 131–185). London: Wiley.

Goodman, P. (1986). *Designing effective work groups*. San Francisco: Jossey-Bass.

Granovetter, M. (1985). Economic action and social structure: The problem of embeddedness. *American Journal of Sociology, 91*, 481–510.

Hackman, R. (1990). *Groups that work and those that don't: Creating conditions for effective teamwork*. San Francisco: Jossey-Bass.

Hardin, G., & Baden, J. (1988). *Managing the commons*. San Francisco: Freeman.

Hewstone, M. (1992). The "ultimate attribution error"? A review of the literature on intergroup causal attribution. *European Journal of Social Psychology, 20*, 311–335.

Janoff-Bulman, R. (1992). *Shattered assumptions: Towards a new psychology of trauma*. New York: Free Press.

Kahn, R., & Kramer, R. M. (1990). Untying the knot: Deescalatory processes in international conflict. In R. L. Kahn & M. Zald (Eds.), *Organizations and nation-states: New perspectives on conflict and cooperation*. San Francisco: Jossey-Bass..

Kaufman, C. M., & Kerr, N. L. (1993). Small wins: Perceptual focus, efficacy, and cooperation in a stage-conjunctive social dilemma. *Journal of Applied Social Psychology, 23*, 3–20.

Kelley, H. H. (1979). *Personal relationships*. Hillsdale, NJ: Lawrence Erlbaum Associates.

Kerr, N. L. (1989). Illusions of efficacy: The effects of group size on perceived efficacy and group motivation losses: Free rider effects. *Journal of Personality and Social Psychology, 44*, 78–94.

Kerr, N. L. (1992). Efficacy as a casual and moderating variable in social dilemmas. In W. B. G. Liebrand, D. M. Messick, & H. A. M. Wilke (Eds.), *Social dilemmas* (pp. 59–80). New York: Pergamon.

Kramer, R. M. (1991). Intergroup relations and organizational dilemmas: The role of categorization processes. In L. L. Cummings & B. M. Staw (Eds.), *Research in organizational behavior* (Vol. 13, pp. 191–227). Greenwich, CT: JAI.

Kramer, R. M. (1994). The sinister attribution error: Paranoid cognition and collective distrust in organizations. *Motivation and Emotion, 18*, 199–230.

Kramer, R. M., & Brewer, M. B. (1984). Effects of group identity on resource use in a simulated commons dilemma. *Journal of Personality and Social Psychology, 46*, 1044–1057.

Kramer, R. M., & Brewer, M. B. (1986). Social group identity and the emergence of cooperation in resource conservation dilemmas. In H. A. M. Wilke, D. M. Messick, & C. G. Rutte (Eds), *Experimental social dilemma*. Frankfurt: Peter Lang.

Kramer, R. M., & Goldman, L. (1995). Helping the group or helping yourself? In D. Schroeder (Ed.), *Social dilemmas*. New York: Praeger.

Latané, B. (1986). Responsibility and effort in organizations. In P. S. Goodman (Ed.), *Designing effective work groups* (pp. 147–162). San Francisco: Jossey-Bass.

Lazarus, R. S. (1984). *Stress, appraisal, and coping*. New York: Springer.

Lieberman, R. (1964). Three notions about trust. *Journal of Conflict Resolution, 13*, 261–278.

Lind, E. A., & Tyler, T. R. (1988). *The social psychology of procedural justice*. New York: Plenum.

Lindskold, S. (1978). Trust development, the GRIT proposal, and the effects of conciliatory acts on conflict and cooperation. *Psychological Bulletin, 85*, 772–793.

Mael, F., & Ashforth, B. E. (1992). Alumni and their alma mater: A partial test of the reformulated model of organizational identification. *Journal of Organizational Behavior, 13*, 103–123.

March, J. G. (1994). *A primer on decision making*. New York: Free Press.

McClintock, C. G., & Liebrand, W. B. G. (1988). Role of interdependence structure, individual value orientation, and another's strategy in social decision making: A transformational analysis. *Journal of Personality and Social Psychology, 55,* 396–409.

Messick, D. M., & Brewer, M. B. (1983). Solving social dilemmas: A review. *Review of Personality and Social Psychology, 4,* 11–44.

Messick, D. M., Wilke, H., Brewer, M. B., Kramer, R. M., Zemke, P. E., & Lui, L. (1983). Individual adaptations and structural change as solutions to social dilemmas. *Journal of Personality and Social Psychology, 44,* 294–309.

Meyerson, D., Kramer, R., & Weick, K. (1995). Swift trust and temporary groups. In R. M. Kramer & T. R. Tyler (Eds.), *Trust in organizations.* Thousand Oaks, CA: Sage.

Miller, G. J. (1992). *Managerial dilemmas.* New York: Cambridge University Press.

Murnighan, J. K., Kim, J. W., & Metzger, A. R. (1994). The volunteer dilemma. *Administrative Science Quarterly, 38,* 515–538.

Olson, M. (1965). *The logic of collective action.* New Haven, CT: Yale University Press.

Pettigrew, T. F. (1979). The ultimate attribution error: Extending Gordan Allport's cognitive analysis of prejudice. *Personality and Social Psychology Bulletin, 5,* 461–477.

Pfeffer, J., & Salancik, G. R. (1978). *The external control of organizations.* New York: Harper & Row.

Pilisuk, M., & Skolnick, P. (1968). Inducing trust: A test of the Osgood proposal. *Journal of Personality and Social Psychology, 8,* 121–133.

Powell, W. (1990). Neither markets nor hierarchy: Network forms of social organization. In B. M. Staw & L. L. Cummings (Eds.), *Research in organizational behavior* (Vol. 12). Greenwich, CT: JAI.

Powell, W. (1995). Trust in governance structures. In R. M. Kramer & T. R. Tyler (Eds.), *Trust in organizations.* Thousand Oaks, CA: Sage.

Putnam, R. (1993). *Making democracy work.* Princeton, NJ: Princeton University Press.

Rousseau, D. M. (1989). Psychological and implied contracts in organizations. *Employee Responsibilities and Rights Journal, 2,* 121–139.

Rotter, J. B. (1980). Interpersonal trust, trustworthiness, and gullibility. *American Psychologist, 35,* 1–7.

Schelling, T. C. (1960). *The strategy of conflict.* New Haven, CT: Yale University Press.

Schelling, T. C. (1978). *Micromotives and macrobehavior.* New York: Norton.

Simon, H. A. (1991). Organizations and markets. *Journal of Economic Perspectives, 5,* 34–38.

Sitkin, S. B., & Roth, N. L. (1993). Explaining the limited effectiveness of legalistic "remedies" for trust/distrust. *Organizational Science, 4,* 367–392.

Tajfel, H. (1969). Cognitive aspects of prejudice. *Journal of Social Issues, 25,* 79–97.

Tajfel, H. (1982). *Social identity and intergroup relations.* Cambridge, England: Cambridge University Press.

Turner, J. C. (1987). *Rediscovering the social group: A self-categorization theory.* Oxford, England: Basil Blackwell.

Tyler, T. R. (1993). The social psychology of authority. In J. K. Murnighan (Ed.), *Social psychology in organizations: Advances in theory and practice* (pp. 141–160). Englewood Cliffs, NJ: Prentice-Hall.

Tyler, T. R., & Dawes, R. (1993). Fairness in groups: Comparing the self-interest and social identity perspectives. In B. Mellers & J. Baron (Eds.), *Psychological perspectives on justice: Theory and applications.* Cambridge, England: Cambridge University Press.

Tyler, T. R., & Degoey, P. (1995). *Collective restraint in a social dilemma situation: The influence of procedural justice and community identification on the empowerment and legitimation of authority.* Unpublished manuscript, University of California, Berkeley.

van de Kragt, A. J. C., Orbell, J., & Dawes, R. (1983). The minimal contributing set as a solution to public goods problems. *American Political Science Review, 77,* 112–122.

Weber, J. (1994). The nature of ethnocentric attribution bias: Ingroup protection or enhancement? *Journal of Experimental Social Psychology, 30,* 482–504.

Wilder, D. A., & Cooper, W. E. (1981). Categorization into groups: Consequences for social perception and attribution. In J. H. Harvey, W. Ickes, & R. F. Kidd (Eds.), *New directions in attribution research* (pp. 79–92). Hillsdale, NJ: Lawrence Erlbaum Associates.

Williamson, O. (1993). Calculativeness, trust, and economic organization. *Journal of Law and Economics, 34,* 453–502.

Yamagishi, T., & Sato, K. (1986). Motivational bases of the public goods problem. *Journal of Personality and Social Psychology, 50,* 67–73.

Zucker, L. G. (1986). Production of trust: Institutional sources of economic structure, 1840–1920. In B. M. Staw & L. L. Cummings (Eds.), *Research in organizational behavior* (Vol. 8, pp. 53–111).

Chapter 7

The Meaning of Interdependence

Ruth Wageman
Dartmouth College

There has been increasing attention to promoting interdependence in organizations recently, from self-managing front line teams, to cross-functional task forces, to process complete departments, and so on. The hope for these structures is that getting people to operate interdependently for collective outcomes will improve the quality, timeliness, and/or originality of those outcomes. The data are still out about how well interdependence can produce such outcomes. It is by no means a simple and straightforward task to create interdependence where there has been none before, as many organizations implementing total quality management (TQM) have discovered (Hackman & Wageman, 1995). Indeed, if managers draw from long experience to create well-designed individual work, they may well be better off than those organizations that attempt to create teams but end up with poorly structured interdependent work.

One of the impediments to both the use and the analysis of interdependence is that the concept is something of a projective test—different people mean different things by it. This chapter seeks to clarify the different types of interdependence among people who perform work, to summarize research evidence about the dynamics and consequences of interdependence, and to point to some potentially constructive future directions for both research and practice regarding interdependence in task-performing teams in organizations.

TYPES OF INTERDEPENDENCE

The term "interdependence" has been used to convey a wide variety of meanings in the organizational and social psychological literature, from an inherent property of relationships between organizational units (e.g., Thompson, 1967; Van de Ven & Ferry, 1980) to the extent of cooperation between individuals in performing a task (e.g., Shea & Guzzo, 1987) to unit- or organization-based performance measures. This variety of meanings associated with the term creates confusion for scholars and practitioners who seek to understand the antecedents and consequences of interdependence. To understand how to create interdependence—indeed, to understand why one would wish to create it—it is necessary to clarify just what interdependence *is*.

To begin with, it is important to distinguish between two important types of interdependence—what is *structured in* versus how people *actually behave*. I refer to these two concepts throughout this chapter as structural and behavioral interdependence, respectively. This distinction allows us to ask the question: What design features of organizations can be manipulated to create interdependent structures; and what are the effects of such structures on how individuals interact—behavioral interdependence—in organizations? Presumably, behavioral interdependence will occur more often when structural interdependence is present; but, as will be seen, the link is far from direct. Below, first structural interdependence is defined, and three conceptual and researchable issues raised about structural interdependence in groups.

Structural Interdependence

Structural interdependence refers to elements outside the individual and his or her behavior—that is, features of the context—that define a relationship between entities such that one affects (and is affected by) the other. These elements can include features of the work itself, how goals are defined, how rewards are distributed, and so forth. Structural interdependence can be further differentiated into interdependence around work inputs and interdependence around work outcomes. I refer to these as "task interdependence" and "outcome interdependence."

Task Interdependence Defined. Task interdependence refers to features of inputs into the work itself that require multiple individuals to complete the work. Various scholars have identified multiple sources and types of task interdependence. Some social psychologists (e.g., Johnson & Johnson, 1989) have referred to "means interdependence," specifically, interdependence in which the actions of individual members elicit and constrain the actions of others (e.g., the movement down court of a basketball team). They have distinguished this from "resource interdependence," in which critical resources such as information and materials are distributed among members such that the whole task is not complete until each member has completed his or her part (e.g., an advertising design team made up of writers, artists, etc.).

Thompson (1967), by contrast, specified three types of interdependence, in increasing order of the complexity of the coordination required among unit members; (1) pooled interdependence, in which subtasks are performed separately and in any sequence (no coordination required); (2) sequential interdependence, in which subtasks are completed in a specified sequence with no return to earlier steps (linear coordination); and (3) reciprocal interdependence, in which the completed subtask of one unit member becomes input for the second, and the second's completed subtask becomes input for the first, and so forth (complex coordination). These distinctions describe different processes by which inputs can be combined to complete a whole piece of work. They were intended to describe forms of interdependence between large units (such as divisions or departments) of entire organizations; they overlap with, but are not identical to, characterizations of task interdependence in small groups. For example, pooled interdependence among individuals is essentially the absence of any means interdependence. Individuals whose work requires only pooled interdependence with others are nontask interdependent coactors—individuals working independently, usually in the same setting, such as a roomful of telephone salespeople— whose output is measured collectively (i.e., who are goal interdependent, see following). Sequential interdependence among individuals can exist on an assembly line. In neither of these cases would we typically define these sets of individuals as a group—people who collectively perform a whole task. Rather, they are individuals operating largely independently. Moreover, "reciprocal interdependence" or that in which the work of one becomes the input for another is not the only observable form of true task interdependence among group members. For example, a quality group collectively analyzing and solving a problem produces a single output—a solution or recommendation—has no obvious reciprocal qualities among inputs. The usefulness of Thompson's typology for defining the task interdependence of groups in organizations is thus relatively limited. Van de Ven, Delbecq, and Koenig (1976) noted this limitation, and added a fourth category of interdependence types—"team interdependence." Little work has been done to define precisely what team interdependence is, or how it varies in groups operating in organizations.

Nevertheless, there are four particular task structures that are frequently manipulated or described in research on task interdependence.

These four elements are: (1) How the task is defined to the group. The task may be defined to members as a task for which the team as a collective is responsible; alternatively, particular tasks (perhaps subparts of the whole task) may be the responsibility of particular individuals; (2) Rules/instructions about process. Instructions about task process can convey that group members are expected to share resources and work together for at least part of the task; alternatively, they can convey that individuals are expected to work alone, or, of course, they can convey nothing about the level of joint action expected of members; (Although process itself—how team members behave in coordinating their work—is sometimes used as a type or source of interdependence, I include actual process in behavioral interdependence later); (3) Physical technology of the task. The task technology can either demand simultaneous action by individuals, creating interdependence (e.g., one a person alone cannot play a quartet), or it can prevent it (e.g., if the defined task is "writing a report," the physical technology of using a computer prevents simultaneous action by individuals); and (4) The degree to which resources necessary for the work, such as skills, information, and materials, are distributed among individuals. The role of resource distribution in creating structural task interdependence (contrary to common claims; e.g., Johnson & Johnson, 1989) is not straightforward; rather, it depends on the task definition and/or the technology of the task. For example, the task for a team composed of individuals each of whom has unique and necessary skills for the work may be either highly interdependent, or completely independent, depending on the nature of the task definition. Copywriters, graphic artists, and account managers may each have skills others do not, but their task is only interdependent if defined as "collectively producing an ad campaign." If, however, tasks are defined to members specifically as their set of subtasks—for example, "writing the copy"—these same individuals have independent tasks. Moreover, when individuals have all possible skills and information needed to do a particular task, the current task technology may prevent complete independence. Imagine, for example, a fully "cross-trained" surgeon attempting to manage anesthesia while performing surgery. Thus, the degree of skill and resource distribution among individuals in a team does not independently define the level of task interdependence; rather, it operates jointly with task definition and technology.

These four elements together define the level of structural task interdependence among group members. They determine whether whole tasks are designed to be done by groups versus individuals. Generally, the more of these elements that are highly interdependent, the greater the need for collaboration and cooperative behavior in the group to complete the task (Galbraith, 1987). The combination of these elements creates a contingent relationship between the behavior of performers—whether or not, and how much, they cooperate—and their task accomplishment. Thus, these elements of task interdependence may influence the degree to which group members actually cooperate in executing the task. The conditions under which strong cooperation does arise are discussed under behavioral interdependence. For the present, we continue the discussion of structural interdependence.

Outcome Interdependence Defined.   Outcome interdependence refers to the degree to which shared significant consequences of work are contingent on collective performance of the task(s). Here we include reward interdependence or tangible outcomes that accrue to the group as a whole, and goal interdependence, which refers to the measurement of collective output, regardless of whether rewards are attached to goal attainment.

Reward interdependence refers to the extent to which the rewards that accrue to an individual depend on the performance of coworkers. The most interdependent reward scheme is one based exclusively on collective performance, such as a group-based gain-sharing system. Rewards accrue to the group, and are distributed among members in shares that are independent of the performance of specific individuals in the team. The least interdependent rewards, by contrast, are earned by members based solely on individual performance, such as a commission for an individual salesperson.

Goal interdependence is a function of how performance is measured—as team performance, individual performance, or some combination of these. The term goal interdependence has sometimes been used synonymously with task interdependence (typically pooled task interdependence; e.g., Van de Ven & Ferry, 1980). However, goal interdependence (like reward interdependence) can exist without any interdependence in the task inputs (e.g., a room full of telemarketers may be held accountable for a collective goal, but they complete individual tasks). One can also establish individual, noninterdependent goals for members of a group with an interdependent task (e.g., hours billed by a member of a consulting team.) In this chapter, I use the term outcome interdependence to refer to interdependence of any significant outcomes (including feedback about goal attainment) that are contingent on collective performance.

In sum, task interdependence refers to interdependence that derives from task inputs, including task definition, task technology, the distribution of task resources among individuals, and the instructions about how to carry out the work. That is, the task is interdependent when multiple individuals must act to complete it. Under conditions of no interdependence, a task can be executed entirely by one person. A highly interdependent task, by contrast, requires every group member to contribute something to the collective output; the overall task is not accomplished until each has contributed his or her part. Outcome interdependence refers to the degree to which outcomes such as goal attainment and tangible rewards are contingent on collective performance. Noninterdependent outcomes are those that accrue to individuals independent of others, whereas maximally interdependent outcomes accrue to the group as a whole based exclusively on the performance of the collective.

With structural interdependence defined, we can now address three researchable issues about task and outcome interdependence among organization members. These three issues, as will be seen, have been studied to different degrees; they have implications for both theory about the effects of interdependence, and for organizational practice. They are (1) whether structural interdependence is a continuum, or a set of discrete forms; (2) the joint effects of task and outcome interdependence on performers; and (3) the relative malleability of task and outcome interdependence.

Levels of Structural Interdependence

Are structural task and outcome interdependence continuous, or are there discrete forms of tasks and outcomes (e.g., "true group tasks" vs. "individual tasks")? If task interdependence is determined by multiple elements then, logically, total task interdependence ought to be continuous—ranging from none (all four elements are independent), to very high (all four elements are interdependent). Moreover, certain ones of these four might themselves be continua, for example, process instructions that convey the expectation of some solo and some simultaneous action, suggest a form of "moderate" interdependence. Or, partial cross-training of individuals creates a distribution of skills that allows a certain, but not perfect, degree of independence among team members.

Such middle-range forms of interdependence have not been much studied. But one mixed form of interdependence does appear to exist—a "hybrid" design, in which some task elements are highly interdependent, demanding a real team, whereas others are highly independent (Wageman, 1995). Hybrid tasks require groups to act sometimes as groups, sometimes as individuals. One example of such a design is a collection of researchers in a development laboratory, each of whom pursues individual projects and at the same time collaborates on a larger, shared enterprise. In such circumstances, it is possible for the individuals to spend much of their time on their own pursuits and thus to avoid the constraints of interdependence. Hybrid rewards exist, as well, in systems that sometimes reward group performance and at other times reward individual performance. Groups experiencing hybrids—tasks or outcomes—perform very poorly.

Because hybrid groups have only half the opportunity to learn to become teams that highly interdependent groups have, they have less time to develop norms, work through process problems, and develop collective strategies. Such hybrid groups have not been much studied, but examples of problems with hybrid groups are easy to find in organizations. Task forces often turn their group tasks into hybrid tasks by meeting once and dividing subtasks among individuals, and people proceed independently, with little contact with other members of the group. In the interests of saving time, they may not meet again as a group until their individual contributions must be combined. Such teams often run into disasters because some members have not done their part to acceptable standards or have taken disparate views of what the group was trying to accomplish—problems that the group could not deal with during its life, because after initial meetings it never met or acted as a group.

Hybrids are at least conceptually distinct from truly moderate forms of structural interdependence. True moderate forms, rather than combining several highly interdependent with several highly independent task elements, would combine middle-range versions of all task elements. But little research has addressed these true moderate forms. What little evidence exists is mixed; some forms of moderate rewards have been shown to undermine performance regardless of task type (Rosenbaum et al, 1980) whereas others have been shown to enhance performance (Gumpert et al., 1994). At present, it is not known how team members behave or how well teams perform when all structural task elements are moderately interdependent; nor do we know much about the outcomes of such tasks when combined with moderately interdependent outcomes.

Interactions of Task and Outcome Interdependence

Task and outcome interdependence have both been cited as important influences on the degree of helping behavior in teams (Hamblin, Hathaway, & Wodarsky, 1971; Hayes, 1976; Shaw, 1973), member attitudes (Mesch, Lew, Johnson, & Johnson, 1988), and team performance (Shea & Guzzo, 1987). They have thus been seen as substitutes for one another in their effects on teams; that is, increasing either task or outcome interdependence is expected to produce greater collective action. This view of the relative effects of the two forms of structural interdependence suggests that their joint effects might be additive. Alternatively, some researchers have argued that the two interact to influence team outcomes (Miller & Hamblin, 1963; Saavedra, Earley, & Van Dyne, 1993). What is the nature of the joint effects of the two forms of interdependence, and what happens to team performance when the two are at different levels?

The most strongly stated case for an additive effect of interdependence on performance comes from a meta-analysis of the effects of cooperative versus individualistic and competitive forms of interdependence (Johnson & Johnson, 1989). In this work, the authors argued for the benefits of high total interdependence, citing positive effects on learning, achievement, cognitive complexity of thought, and interpersonal relations. In a similar vein, Mesch et al., (1988) found that high task interdependence in classrooms enhanced learning relative to an independent task structure, and this effect became even more pronounced when a group reward was added to the interdependent task. Two problems arise in extrapolating from these findings to group performance in general. First, both the Johnsons' (1989) meta-analysis and Mesch et al.'s (1988) work focused on groups in classrooms, where the task is learning, rather than on working groups in organizations. Second, in Mesch et al.'s study, no comparison group experienced an interdependent task with rewards based on individual performance. It may be that adding any performance-contingent reward, even a noninterdependent one, enhances interdependent learning. To test for an additive effect of task and outcome interdependence on working groups, tasks with different levels of interdependence must be combined with both independent and interdependent outcomes, as was done in several studies of the interaction effects of task and outcome interdependence.

Findings from several of these studies about the joint effects of outcome and task interdependence have led some researchers to the conclusion that tasks and outcomes that are congruent, that is, equally interdependent, enhance performance relative to tasks and outcomes that are incongruent (Earley & Northcraft, 1987; Miller & Hamblin, 1963). A number of other studies have detected a significant positive interaction effect of task and outcome interdependence on group performance. Rosenbaum and his colleagues (1980), for example, offered individual or group rewards to subjects working on interdependent and independent tasks. Subjects were asked to construct towers of blocks, either jointly producing a single tower (the interdependent condition) or separately producing their own towers (the independent condition). They were rewarded either for the total number of blocks used by all members (group rewards) or for the number of blocks used by them personally (individual rewards). Subjects receiving group incentives for an interdependent task outperformed those receiving individual rewards. But reward system design had no effect on performance of the individual task. Wageman and Baker (1997) found a similar interaction effect for pairs of subjects working on a copyediting task, such that the greater the task interdependence, the greater the positive effect of reward interdependence on performance. However, although group rewards greatly enhanced performance over individual rewards for interdependent tasks, the degree of reward interdependence did not influence the performance of dyads with independent tasks. Negative effects of group rewards for individual tasks are not frequently found, and occur in those circumstances in which individuals have no opportunity for observation of or interaction with the other individuals with whom their outcomes are interdependent (Williams, Harkins, & Latané, 1981). Thus, "free-riding" in the presence of interdependent rewards—the

principal argument against group rewards for individual tasks—seems limited to individuals isolated from each other.

What happens at moderate levels of interdependence? Findings here
are highly mixed, and much in need of further exploration. Whereas Rosenbaum et al. (1980) found that moderate reward interdependence
undermined performance of both group and individual tasks, Wageman
and Baker (1997) found that moderately interdependent rewards were
most effective for moderately interdependent tasks. And Gumpert et al.
(1994) found that their moderately interdependent "Rawlsian" reward
design, one that split high performers' earnings between the team and the
individual, outperformed all other rewards for an interdependent task,
including fully interdependent ones. By contrast, Wageman (1995) found
that both hybrid outcomes (ones that sometimes rewarded individuals and
sometimes groups) and tasks (ones that called sometimes for individual
and sometimes for collective action) undermined performance in task-
performing teams in organizations relative to all other combinations of
task and outcome interdependence. Such hybrid forms performed worse
even than teams with highly interdependent tasks and individual rewards.

Part of the confusion here almost certainly comes from the different operationalizations of moderate interdependence. In many cases (e.g., Wageman & Baker, 1997; Rosenbaum et al., 1980; Gumpert et al., 1994), moderate interdependence refers to rewarding group performance and also
especially rewarding those individuals who contributed most to the group's
product. Hybrids, by contrast, refer to designs that *sometimes* reward individuals (or cue individual action), and sometimes reward groups (or cue collective action). Nevertheless, the reasons for differing effects of moderately
interdependent designs, and their interaction with individual and group
designs, remain a important puzzle for future research.

Thus, the argument that tasks and outcomes must be congruent is too
simple. For individualistic task designs, outcome interdependence appears not to matter, so long as individuals work in settings where they
have direct contact with each other. Moreover, hybrid designs appear to
undermine group performance, regardless of whether tasks and outcomes
are congruent. The clearest implication of these many findings is that
when groups perform highly interdependent tasks, highly interdependent
outcomes are essential to good group performance.

Malleability of Tasks and Outcomes

In various papers, conversations with colleagues, and reviews, I have often
encountered the view that task interdependence is less manipulable—indeed
it may even be an inherent property of particular tasks—than is outcome
interdependence. Reward systems, after all, are frequently modified by

organizations to respond to changing environments and to produce different incentives; changing goal interdependence is merely a matter of communicating different goals and performance metrics. Such a view of tasks is highly consequential for our view of organizations; it suggests that there are strong limits on our ability to create cooperative work systems. Why has outcome interdependence often been viewed (perhaps unwisely) as the more manipulable of the two forms of structural interdependence?

Historical practice, what has most often been done before, may be part of the reason for this belief. Historically, tasks have been taken as given and rewards designed to fit with them. That historical emphasis by practitioners, however, does not provide an intellectual basis for asserting that task interdependence cannot be, or should not be, modified. Indeed, with so many organizations creating work teams these days, one cannot dismiss changes in task interdependence as "generally not done." Rather than being excluded from consideration by scholars on a priori grounds, therefore, the matter merits conceptual and empirical attention.

Two different meanings of the word "inherent" underlie beliefs about the malleability of task interdependence. First is the view that certain tasks cannot be made structurally independent, or, alternatively, cannot be made structurally highly interdependent. Some oft-cited examples of inherent levels of interdependence are a comparison of basketball versus baseball, sales versus manufacturing, and many others. Part of the conviction that task interdependence is inherent may derive from reliance on such examples to reflect on task interdependence (e.g., Fry, Kerr, & Lee, 1986; Harder, 1992; Jones, 1974; Keidel, 1985; Pratt & Eitzen, 1989). Let us look at sports, in particular. Because of sports' familiarity (and our cultural attachments to various games) we take their rules as given. Changing the level of interdependence among players would alter, as some have put it, the very nature of the sport. Basketball might be made a less interdependent, for example, with a change of rules about carrying and a smaller basketball court (a change in technology)—individuals could much more easily score a basket without the inputs and skills of teammates. Serious enthusiasts might be appalled at the example, and say "That's not basketball!" Such changes in the rules do alter task interdependence, and thereby, the nature of the sport. But sports *are* their rules in ways that most organizational tasks are not (even though some of us would say that the essence of basketball is getting a large orange ball through a net). Tasks can appear fixed because organizations have historical attachments to particular rules and technologies, but rules and technologies are themselves changeable. To change task interdependence, which is to change the rules of the game, is by no means trivial a either for sports fans or for organizational members. But the same "inherent" task can, in most cases, be accomplished with greater or lesser interdependence among those who perform it.

Aside from the familiarity of particular task forms, there is a second strong influence on common views of the inherence of interdependence: Thompson's highly influential 1967 work is the starting point for most later discussions of interdependence in organizations. His distinction between pooled, sequential, and reciprocal interdependence is invariably cited in discussions of interdependence in groups, in spite of the fact that it was designed to describe relations among various units of whole organizations. Thompson developed propositions about the relationship between these forms of interdependence, means of organizing (e.g., departmentalization), and organization performance. Interdependence is treated as a given, whereas only organizational responses to different forms of interdependence, through different organizational structures, are treated as managerial choice variables. Thus, Thompson's original classification of forms of interdependence set the stage for taking interdependence as given, and designing the rest of the organization to meet demands of whatever form it was stuck with.

There also exists a second meaning of inherent levels of task interdependence—that is, the level of *efficiency* associated with group versus individual versions of the same task. Some scholars have argued that although most tasks may be manipulated to alter their levels of structural interdependence, there is nevertheless a particular level at which the task is most efficiently executed. This claim, at least, is an empirical question. And to the extent that level of interdependence is related to the motivational properties of work, we do indeed see that performance seems to be better for some tasks when they are designed to be done highly interdependently, rather than as a set of independent subtasks (Hackman & Oldham, 1980). But some so-called inherent levels we might discover may be performed better by groups (or by individuals) not because of the nature of the task, but because of other organizational features (e.g., characteristics of individuals doing the work, nature of the culture in which they operate). Thus the efficiency of levels of interdependence for different tasks may best be studied as a function not merely of the task itself, but of the broader context in which it is performed. For researchers and practitioners alike, this means relaxing assumptions about "right ways" to design particular tasks, and instead, asking what the conditions are that can best support a particular version of a task, independent or interdependent—including reward interdependence.

BEHAVIORAL INTERDEPENDENCE

Behavioral interdependence refers to the amount of task-related interaction *actually engaged in* by group members in completing their work. The distinction between structural and behavioral interdependence is important because, as will be seen, (a) just because there are structures that are supposed to foster such behavior does not necessarily mean that it will be observed, and (b) even when there are not structural imperatives to behave interdependently, people sometimes do anyway (e.g., coactors with individual work and individual rewards who, nevertheless help each other out). We look here at what gives rise to, and what gets in the way of, behavioral interdependence. As with structural interdependence, three researchable issues are posed and discussed, noting what has and has not been addressed in studies of interdependence in organizations. These issues are (1) whether behavioral interdependence is a continuum or a set of discrete forms; (2) the role of perceptions of interdependence in the link between structure and behavior; and (3) moderators of the relationship between structural and behavioral interdependence.

Levels of Behavioral Interdependence

Behavioral interdependence may vary from none (i.e., individuals execute their tasks without help, input, or cooperation from coworkers) to very high (i.e., team members complete a whole piece of work in interaction together throughout the task). As with structural interdependence, the question arises: Is behavioral interdependence a continuous variable, or a discontinuous one? That is, do we typically observe the whole range of behavioral interdependence from no interaction, to a little, through a great deal? Behavioral interdependence is often conceptually treated as continuous, but perhaps empirically it behaves more like a step function. Rather than displaying a range of "cooperativeness," from negative cooperation (active obstruction) to extreme cooperativeness, the behavior of teams members may fall into one of three discrete patterns. That is, members (1) do their work alone, (2) do the work as a group, or (3) work largely alone, with loose coordination happening at periodic team meetings. If this categorization of behavioral interdependence is valid, it raises important questions about the relationships between structural and behavioral interdependence. In particular, if the aim of team interventions in organizations is to develop high behavioral interdependence among individuals doing a task, it is important to identify the conditions that lead to "teamlike behavior" or working together to complete a task.

Both structural task and structural outcome interdependence have been cited as means of creating incentives for strong cooperation (Hayes, 1976; Kelley & Thibaut, 1978; Slavin, 1983; Thomas, 1957). Miller and Hamblin (1963) argued that the congruence of task and reward interdependence, especially at high levels, is essential to team performance because the presence of interdependent outcomes creates incentives that lead to the "facilitative behaviors" that are needed for the task. In general, outcome interdependence is assumed to have direct behavioral effects on team members, whereas tasks are more behaviorally inert; they require certain kinds of behavior to be performed well, but may not affect behavior directly (e.g., Saavedra et al., 1993).

Recent evidence, however, suggests otherwise. Whereas *negative* outcome interdependence—competitive rewards and performance measures—does actively undermine cooperative behavior (Deutsch, 1949), positive outcome interdependence alone does not elicit it. Rather, it is structural *task* interdependence that directly influences cooperative behavior. Wageman and Baker (1997) and Wageman (1995) observed the same pattern in field and laboratory settings. The presence of any significant task-based interdependence elicited high levels of cooperative behavior from subjects, regardless of reward interdependence. Group rewards had no direct influence on amount of cooperative behavior or types of cooperative strategies that group members chose.

What, then, is the role of outcome interdependence, if not to increase the level or alter the type of behavioral interdependence via incentives for cooperation? In the above- cited studies, while cooperation was a function of task interdependence, that cooperation resulted in superior performance only in the presence of highly interdependent rewards. Reward outcomes appear to affect the character of members' motivation—their effort levels—rather than to influence group behavior directly. Effort and behavioral interdependence are two distinct processes. What is often measured through behavioral observations is the number and frequency of cooperative interactions, and whether individuals work together or independently to complete the task (e.g., Chatman & Barsade, 1995; Rosenbaum et al., 1980). It may be that whereas task design elicits cooperative or independent behavior for completing the work, reward system design influences the effort levels of performers, a relatively more difficult to observe phenomenon.

Moreover, behavioral interdependence appears to operate as a step function—both moderate and high levels of task interdependence can result in strong cooperation—rather than a linear process of more and more cooperation that matches the proportion of structural task interdependence (Wageman & Baker, 1997). When sufficiently high levels of interdependence are structured into the task, teams engage in teamlike behavior, rather than mere loose coordination. An exception to this relationship appears to be hybrid task designs, which lead to periodic loose coordination, rather than strong cooperation in teams.

One important difference between moderate levels of task interdependence and hybrid tasks (which sometimes call for team action and sometimes for individual action) is the kind of behavioral interdependence they motivate, and the appropriateness of that behavior for meeting task demands. Hybrids, at times, require real teams, as when the team must use collective intelligence to solve a team problem, for the work to be done effectively. Yet the mixed signals that come from such task designs appear to cue only loose coordination, with individuals working largely independently of each other. Among individuals with little experience of interdependence, such a design appears to result not in separate periods of strong cooperation and complete independence (as the task requires), but rather in largely independent action. This misfit between the behavioral demands of hybrid tasks and the actual behavior that occurs in such teams may account for the poor performance associated with such designs.

The Questionable Role of Individuals' Perceptions of Interdependence

Certain accounts of the effects of task and outcome structures on behavioral interdependence have a strong cognitive flavor: They suggest that interdependent structures influence group members' perceptions that they need one another in order to perform effectively or to receive valued outcomes (Deutsch, 1962; Johnson, 1974; Johnson & Johnson, 1982, 1989; Tjosvald, 1988). These perceptions, in turn, lead to instrumental behavior that is cooperative, that is, behavioral interdependence. This is a relatively common model of how structures and context operate; humans are seen as interpreting the demands of their environment and acting instrumentally to meet those demands. Without clear and correct perceptions, the structure–behavior link becomes more random. But is it actually necessary for people to perceive their work or outcomes as interdependent to elicit interdependent behavior or might such behavior happen fairly automatically in the presence of "interdependent structures?

An alternative account of the structure–behavior relationship is evidenced in the work design literature: The core characteristics elicit internal motivation regardless of whether people perceive their jobs as having those characteristics (Hackman & Oldham, 1980). This pattern implies an alternative version of the structure–behavior relationship. Structures provide direct stimuli to which humans respond behaviorally; they may or may not make interpretations of that structure, and those interpretations are not necessary for the behavior to occur. Indeed, perceptions may come much later in the causal chain; structures lead to behavior, and individuals interpret their own behavior (Bem, 1972), developing their perceptions from self-observations, rather than from examination of the structures themselves. Thus, group members may cooperate directly in response to the presence of structural task and outcome interdependence, observe their cooperative behavior, and then come to experience themselves as needing each other for important outcomes.

To demonstrate empirically that perceptions mediate the relationship between structures and behavior, three essential relationships must be demonstrated; (1) that perceptions of interdependence are indeed influenced by task and outcome structures, (2) that perceptions of high interdependence are associated with greater levels of behavioral interdependence, and (3) that in the absence of perceived interdependence, structures do not influence behavior (at least to the same degree).

Empirical evidence to date supports the first two requirements; that structures influence perceptions, and perceptions are related to behavior. Several studies have shown that perceived task and reward interdependence varies with structural interdependence (Fry et al., 1986; Wageman, 1995), such that the more interdependent the task or outcomes, the more group members perceive themselves as needing others to perform well or to attain important outcomes. Interestingly, the presence of structural task interdependence appears to influence both perceptions of task interdependence—that the task requires cooperative effort—and perceptions that rewards are interdependent. Structural outcome interdependence, by contrast, influences only perceived outcome interdependence (Wageman, 1995). Behavioral interdependence and perceptions of interdependence also appear to covary. Several studies have assessed perceptions of interdependence, and shown that cooperation is indeed greater when group members perceive their tasks or rewards to be highly interdependent (Berkowitz, 1957; Deutsch & Gerard, 1955).

The final condition—that when structural interdependence is high but individuals perceive relatively little interdependence, behavioral interdependence is low—remains relatively unexamined. Only in one study was structural interdependence varied and both perceived and behavioral interdependence assessed (Wageman, 1995). In this research, although both perceptions and behavior did vary with structural interdependence, perceptions did not mediate the relationship between structure and behavior. This is, of course, only one study, and it provided no data about the relative timing of the development of perceptions and behavior.

Perceptions thus may operate independently of behavior; that is, they may operate merely as another outcome, along with behavior, of the presence of structural interdependence. Alternatively, they may come last in the causal chain, after structures have elicited behavior for group members to interpret.

In either case, the evidence suggests that it is fruitless to attempt to elicit behavioral interdependence through manipulations of perceptions alone. Relying on social cues and exhortations about how interdependent group members are without attention to structural interdependence may influence nothing but perceptions, and perhaps not even that.

Moderators of the Relationship Between Structural and Behavioral Interdependence

I noted earlier that even in the presence of task interdependence, some team members may operate independently; at the same time, even when individuals are structurally independent, they may choose to cooperate. What factors moderate the relationship between structure and behavior? Two variables in particular may play an especially important role in how team members actually behave under varying conditions of structural interdependence: individual differences and cultural context. Certain individuals are predisposed toward cooperative relationships, whereas others are predisposed toward individualism. And certain social contexts (both particular organizations and particular national cultures) contain deeply embedded values about collective versus individual goals and actions (Triandis, 1988).

Measures of cultural tendencies around collectivism and individualism vary; nonetheless, several features are common across these many definitions of culture. Individualistic cultures emphasize values of self-interest, differentiation of individuals from their group memberships, and independent action. Collectivist cultures, by contrast, emphasize values of collective, group, or societal interest, strong ingroup memberships, collective action and performance (e.g., Hofstede, 1980; Triandis, 1989). Cooperative behavior within groups is far more central to the values of collectivist cultures than to individual cultures, and thus behavioral interdependence is more likely to be fostered in such contexts than in individualistic ones.

Individuals also vary in the degree to which they hold cooperative versus individualistic tendencies. A range of measures has been developed for assessing individual differences in personal dispositions on these dimensions. Those with cooperative tendencies prefer working toward a common goal to working alone (McClintock & Liebrand, 1988), believe in the importance of cooperation (Triandis, McCusker, & Hui, 1990) and given a choice, elect to work in collectivist organizations (Chatman & Barsade, 1995). Individualists, by contrast, prefer to work alone, value individual accomplishment above group outcomes, and choose individualistic over collectivist contexts (Argyle, 1991). Even within strong organizational and national cultural contexts, individuals vary widely on these dimensions.

What are the joint effects of cultural context, individual dispositions, and structural interdependence? A combination of collectivist values, high structural interdependence, and cooperative individuals clearly creates high levels of behavioral interdependence (Chatman & Barsade, 1995). And individualistic cultures, combined with low task interdependence and strong individualists results in minimal behavioral interdependence (Spence, 1985). What is less clear are the effects of mismatches among individuals, structures, and cultural context. It might be expected that individuals with strong cooperative tendencies will cooperate more than individualists, even in the absence of structural interdependence and collectivist cultural values; likewise, collectivist cultural values might produce higher levels of cooperation than individualistic ones, even when members are individualists and tasks are noninterdependent. Interestingly, Chatman and Barsade (1995) showed that culture and personal tendencies did not have a simple additive relationship in influencing cooperativeness. They studied cooperative and individualistic individuals under different cultural contexts, working at a structurally independent task. Members with individualistic dispositions responded less to the demands of culture than did those with cooperative dispositions. That is, individualists did not change their behavior to meet the demands of collectivist cultural values—they did not cooperate much—as much as collectivists responded to the demands of individualistic cultural values by reducing their levels of helping and interaction with others.

The authors argued that responsiveness to the social context is a value embedded in the disposition to cooperate. Indeed, other accounts of individual differences in collectivism or interdependent self-construal (e.g., Markus & Kitayama, 1991; Singelis, 1994) describe such responsiveness to social norms as a central element of such dispositions, as contrasted with more individualistic tendencies. Thus, the behavior of cooperative individuals is more influenced by social cues than is that of individualists. An individualistic culture is therefore sufficient to reduce the cooperativeness of those predisposed to display such behavior, whereas a cooperative culture is insufficient to radically increase the cooperative behavior of individualists.

The implication for organizations of these findings, taken by themselves, is that behavioral interdependence will be extraordinarily difficult to achieve in individualistic contexts. Organization members who have strong individualist tendencies are relatively unresponsive to values and cues that promote cooperation. Moreover, the cooperative tendencies of collectivists are readily undermined by strong individualistic organizational values. The presence of a minority of individuals predisposed to cooperate offers little leverage to change the behavior of the individualists around them.

However, what was examined in Chatman and Barsade's (1995) research were the effects of broader social context (organizational culture) without attention to the more immediate contextual demands—the interdependence built into the task. The task structure in this study was largely independent: Although individuals were assigned group memberships, and told that they were playing roles in the same organization, each had independent tasks to complete. Structural interdependence places strong demands for cooperative behavior, just as do collectivist cultures. Thus, an interesting set of questions remains unexplored: Do people with particular dispositions around cooperation respond more to the immediate demands of a team task, or to the surrounding cultural context?

Recent work on the joint effects of situations and dispositions on individuals' behavior suggests that when situations are "strong," they tend to dominate individual dispositions in influencing behavior. By contrast, in weak situations, individual differences become much better predictors of behavior (Wright & Mischel, 1987). A highly structurally interdependent task combined with group rewards may be a strong situation in its demands for behavioral interdependence.

There is some evidence that the immediate team context, that is, strong structural interdependence, can override the effects of individual dispositions. One field study (Wageman, 1995), predicted that highly interdependent groups composed largely of individuals with strong individual preferences would perform less well and show lower levels of cooperation and individual satisfaction than highly interdependent groups composed of individuals who prefer cooperation. This moderating effect of individual dispositions did not occur; rather, individuals in highly structurally interdependent teams *changed* in their autonomy preferences over time, and exhibited equally high levels of cooperative behavior regardless of the personal dispositions of members. Thus, personal dispositions are themselves malleable, and respond to experience with structural interdependence. Perhaps the strong behavioral demands of immediate structures are sufficient to establish cooperative behavior, and reflection on that behavior, in turn, alters personal attitudes and dispositions toward cooperation. Future research should address whether behavioral interdependence may be created even among individualists, and sustained among collectivists, when the immediate task and reward structures as well as the cultural values in the organizational context promote cooperation.

CONCLUSION

The relationships among behavior, structural interdependence, personal characteristics, and culture are complex and dynamic: Individuals, when they can, choose their organizational context. They respond behaviorally to the culture of that organization to different degrees, depending on their personal predispositions. Their behavior responds to the nature of immediate task and reward structures. And their personal predispositions are themselves shaped by their experiences with interdependence. Moreover, given the latitude to shape their immediate task and reward structures, individuals very likely act according to their personal preferences—

building individual or group tasks and reward systems to suit their dispositional tendencies. And the demands of particular structures, especially tasks, may lead them to alter other structures to bring them into congruence. Teams with group tasks have been known, for example, to change individualistic rewards to group ones by dividing all rewards equally among members. The relationships among all these factors—structures, personal predispositions, behavior, and culture—may thus be a self-reinforcing spiral.

Organizations operating in individualistic cultures are built by individualistic people, who create structures that promote independent behavior. Such independent experiences further enhance members' individualism, and the strength with which individualistic values are held in the organization. This pattern underlines the difficulty organizations face in attempting to change the level of interdependence among members. Cultures and individuals are slow to change. Indeed, the commitment of leaders of individualistic organizations to creating real interdependence may be low, given their own values and preferences. And one risk of such change efforts is that in attempting to enhance interdependence in individualistic organizations, managers may go only halfway, creating hybrids that undermine performance. The likely learning for such organizations is that interdependence does not work, thus reinforcing the individualist values in the organization.

Because systems operate as stable and self-maintaining spirals, real change in interdependence can only occur in one of two ways. Change can occur with a radical alteration in the system, such as new technology that renders old routines irrelevant, or an entirely new workforce. With such radical alterations, the old stability of the system is violated, because the very things maintaining that stability, the people or their routines, are eliminated.

Change in interdependence can also occur if all influenceable aspects of the system—tasks, rewards, values, and individuals—are altered via persistent and long-term changes. This kind of change requires simultaneously redesigning the immediate context in which people operate, the task and the reward system, and allowing the individuals themselves to be shaped by their new experiences over time, until the new system reaches its own level of stable, self-maintaining congruence.

REFERENCES

Argyle, M. (1991). *Cooperation: The basis of sociability*. London: Routledge.

Bem, D. (1972). Self-perception theory. In L. Berkowitz (Ed.), *Advances in experimental social psychology* (Vol. 6). New York: Academic Press.

Berkowitz, L. (1957). Effects of perceived dependency relations upon conformity to group expectations. *Journal of Abnormal and Social Psychology*, *55*, 350–354.

Chatman, J. A., & Barsade, S. G. (1995). Personality, organizational culture, and cooperation: Evidence from a business simulation. *Administrative Science Quarterly, 40,* 423–443.

Deutsch, M. (1949). An experimental study of the effects of cooperation and competition upon group process. *Human Relations, 2,* 129–152.

Deutsch, M. (1962). Cooperation and trust: Some theoretical notes. In M. R. Jones (Ed.), *Nebraska Symposium on Motivation* (pp. 275–319). Lincoln, NE: University of Nebraska Press.

Deutsch, M., & Gerard, H. (1955). A study of normative and informational social influences upon individual judgment. *Journal of Abnormal and Social Psychology, 51,* 629–636.

Earley, P. C., & Northcraft, G. B. (1987). Goal-setting, resource interdependence, and conflict management. In M. A. Rahim (Ed.), *Managing conflict.* NY: Praeger.

Fry, L. W., Kerr, S., & Lee, C. (1986). Effects of different leader behaviors under different levels of task interdependence. *Human Relations, 39,* 1067–1082.

Galbraith, J. R. (1987). Organization design. In J. Lorsch (Ed.), *Handbook of organizational behavior.* Englewood Cliffs, NJ: Prentice-Hall.

Gumpert, P., Gordon, F. M., Welch, K. R., Offringa, G., & Katz, N. (1994). *The importance of hybrid systems of distributive justice.* Manuscript under review.

Hackman, J. R., & Oldham, G. R. (1980). *Work redesign.* Reading, MA: Addison-Wesley.

Hackman, J. R., & Wageman, R. (1995). Total quality management: Empirical, conceptual and practical issues. *Administrative Science Quarterly, 40,* 309–342.

Hamblin, R. I., Hathaway, C., & Wodarsky, J. (1971). Group contingencies, peer tutoring, and accelerating academic achievement. In E. A. Ramp & B. L. Hopkins (Eds.), *A new direction for education: Behavior analysis 1971.* Lawrence: University of Kansas Press.

Harder, J. (1992). Play for pay: Effects of inequity in a pay for performance context. *Administrative Science Quarterly, 37,* 321–335.

Hayes, L. A. (1976). The use of group contingencies for behavioral control: A review. *Psychological Bulletin, 83,* 628–648.

Hofstede, G. (1980). *Culture's consequences: International differences in work-related values.* Beverly Hills, CA: Sage.

Johnson, D. W. (1974). Communication in conflict situations: A critical review of the research. *International Journal of Group Tensions, 3,* 46–67.

Johnson, D. W., & Johnson, R. T. (1982). Effects of cooperative and individualistic instruction on handicapped and non-handicapped students. *Journal of Social Psychology, 118,* 257–268.

Johnson, D. W., & Johnson, R. T. (1989). *Cooperation and competition: Theory and research.* Edina, MN: Interaction Book Company.

Jones, M. B. (1974). Regressing group on individual effectiveness. *Organizational Behavior and Human Performance, 11,* 426–451.

Keidel, R. W. (1985). Team sports models as a generic organizational framework. *Human Relations, 40,* 592–612.

Kelley, H. H., & Thibaut, J. W. (1978). *Interpersonal relations: A theory of interdependence.* New York: Wiley.

Markus, H. R., & Kitayama, S. (1991). Culture and the self: Implications for cognition, emotion, and motivation. *Psychological Review, 98,* 224–253.

McClintock, C. G., & Liebrand, W. B. G. (1988). Role of interdependence structure, individual value orientation, and another's strategy in social decision-making. *Journal of Personality and Social Psychology, 55,* 398–409.

Mesch, D., Lew, M., Johnson, D. W., & Johnson, R. T. (1988). Impact of positive interdependence and academic group contingencies on achievement. *Journal of Social Psychology, 128,* 345–352.

Miller, L., & Hamblin, R. (1963). Interdependence, differential rewarding, and productivity. *American Sociological Review, 28,* 768–778.

Pratt, S. R., & Eitzen, D. S. (1989). Contrasting leadership styles and organizational effectiveness: The case of athletic teams. *Social Science Quarterly, 70,* 311–322.

Rosenbaum, M. E., Moore, D. L., Cotton, J. L., Cook, M. S., Hieser, R. A., Shovar, M. N., & Gray, M. J. (1980). Group productivity and process: Pure and mixed reward structures and task interdependence. *Journal of Personality and Social Psychology, 39,* 626–642.

Saavedra, R., Earley, P. C., & Van Dyne, L. (1993). Complex interdependence in task-performing groups. *Journal of Applied Psychology, 78,* 61–72.

Shaw, M. E. (1973). Scaling group tasks: A method for dimensional analysis. *JSAS Catalogue of Selected Documents in Psychology, 3* (MS No. 294).

Shea, G. P., & Guzzo, R. A. (1987). Groups as human resources. In G. R. Ferris & K. M. Rowlands (Eds.), *Research in personnel and human resources management* (Vol. 5, pp. 323–356). Greenwich, CT: JAI.

Singelis, T. M. (1994). The measurement of independent and interdependent self-construals. *Personality and Social Psychology Bulletin, 20,* 580–591.

Slavin, R. (1983). *Cooperative learning.* New York: Longman.

Spence, J. (1985). Achievement American style: The rewards and costs of individualism. *American Psychologist, 40,* 1285–1295.

Thomas, E. J. (1957). Effects of facilitative role interdependence on group functioning. *Human Relations, 10,* 347–366.

Thompson, J. D. (1967). *Organizations in action.* New York: McGraw-Hill.

Tjosvald, D. (1988). Effects of shared responsibility and goal interdependence on controversy and decision-making between departments. *Journal of Social Psychology, 128,* 7–18.

Triandis, H. C. (1988). Collectivism and individualism: A reconceptualization of a basic concept in cross-cultural psychology. In C. Bagley & G. Verma (Eds.), *Personality, cognition, and values: Cross-cultural perspectives of childhood and adolescence.* London: Macmillan.

Triandis, H. C. (1989). The self and social behavior in different cultural contexts. *Psychological Review, 96,* 506–520.

Triandis, H. C., McCusker, C., & Hui, H. C. (1990). Multimethod probes of individualism and collectivism. *Journal of Personality and Social Psychology, 59,* 1006–1020.

Van de Ven, A. H., Delbecq, A. L., & Koenig, R. (1976). Determinants of coordination modes within organizations. *American Sociological Review, 41,* 322–328.

Van de Ven, A. H., & Ferry, D. L. (1980). *Measuring and assessing organizations.* New York: Wiley.

Wageman, R. (1995). Interdependence and group effectiveness. *Administrative Science Quarterly, 40,* 145–180.

Wageman, R., & Baker, G. P. (1997). Incentives and cooperation: The joint effects of task and reward interdependence on group performance. *Journal of Organizational Behavior, 18,* 139–158.

Willliams, K., Harkins, S. G., & Latané, B. (1981). Identifiability as a deterrent to social loafing: Two cheering experiments. *Journal of Personality and Social Psychology, 40,* 303–311.

Wright, J. C., & Mischel, W. (1987). A conditional approach to dispositional constructs: The local predictability of social behavior. *Journal of Personality and Social Psychology, 53,* 1159–1177.

Part III

CONFLICT AND POWER
IN GROUPS

Chapter 8

Negotiation Within and Between Groups in Organizations: Levels of Analysis

Leigh Thompson
Northwestern University

Craig R. Fox
Duke University

Groups are the building blocks of organizations (Ancona, 1987; Hackman, 1987; Kramer, 1991; Thompson, 2000). As a central structure of organizations, groups play an increasingly important role in the development, planning, and production of organizational services and products. For an organization to be effective and competitive, the groups that comprise it must be effective. However, organizational groups face a number of challenges that threaten effective functioning. Members of groups in organizations often have disparate interests and objectives, which can lead to conflict. Organizational productivity, personal satisfaction, and interpersonal harmony all hinge on the effective resolution of conflict among organizational actors.

The increasing use of decentralized organizational structures moves the control and regulation of conflict from higher levels of management to the group. Group members may use any number of means of resolving conflict, ranging from inaction, withdrawal, and absenteeism to aggression, ostracism, and threats. In this chapter, we focus on an increasingly common and especially important means of resolving conflict between organizations and within decentralized organizational structures: negotiation, a joint decision-making process by which interdependent parties mutually allocate scarce resources.

The term "group negotiation" has been used in reference to a number of different types of activities among and between organizational actors. It has been used to describe the interaction of organization members operating as a negotiating team (e.g., O'Connor, 1996; Thompson, Peterson, & Brodt, 1996), the effects of social identity among group members negotiating in the context of other groups (e.g., Kramer, 1991) and the interactions among several interdependent principals in which coalitions can form (e.g., Weingart, Hyde, & Prietula, 1996). Unfortunately, this generous use of the term has led to conceptual confusion. The goal of this chapter is to provide a tool for analyzing negotiation within and between organizations that isolates distinct dynamics within and between groups in organizations. Section II introduces this analytical framework, which begins with the behavior of individuals, expands to consider dyads, then multiparty ("polyad") dynamics, intermediaries and collateral relationships, intragroup dynamics, and finally intergroup dynamics. Our central premise is that group negotiations may be analyzed from any or all of these perspectives. Section III presents a brief overview of the decision analytic approach to negotiation (e.g., Raiffa, 1982). The approach in this chapter is primarily descriptive in nature, with a special attention to factors that can thwart the effectiveness of negotiators. Section IV discusses obstacles to the efficient resolution of conflict at each level of analysis. Attention to these factors will suggest how negotiation situations may be structured to promote more desirable outcomes. Section V summarizes the levels of analysis approach and offers some conclusions.

II. LEVELS OF ANALYSIS

Negotiations within and between organizations are embedded in an intricate web of interdependent relationships and interests. The level of analysis is the lens through which one scrutinizes a negotiation. It determines the aspects of the interaction to which one attends and the aspects that one neglects. For example, by restricting one's attention to the principals in a dispute, the influence of peripheral players may be ignored; by treating a negotiation team as a homogeneous entity, important aspects of the social interaction within the team may be overlooked.

Just as a complete understanding of human anatomy requires analysis at the levels of cell chemistry, tissues, organs, and organ systems, a complete understanding of negotiation within and between organizations requires analysis at several levels. In this chapter we identify and describe seven levels of analysis, as depicted in Fig. 8.1: the *individual*, the *dyad*, the *polyad*, the third party *intermediary*, *collateral relationships*, the *intragroup*, and the *intergroup*. These seven levels of analysis parse the social context common to virtually all group negotiation situations.

The basic level of analysis is that of the individual. An understanding of the beliefs and values of the individual negotiator provides a founda-

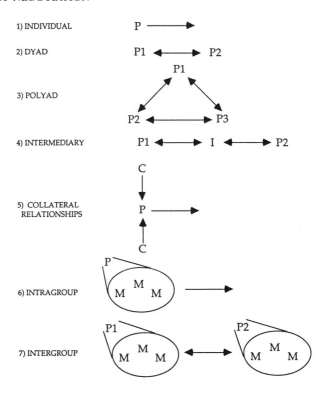

FIG. 8.1.   Levels of analysis in negotiation. P = Principal; I = Intermediary; C = Collateral Party; M = Group Member

tion for understanding dyadic processes. In turn, an understanding of dyadic processes in negotiations is essential for examining multiparty dynamics.[1] Each successive analysis provides new insights into the dynamics of a negotiation, providing breadth of understanding without compromising precision. Obviously, an analysis of all seven levels is not always feasible for the researcher, who may focus on a particular phenomenon of interest. However, an awareness of all levels of analysis may remind the researcher of factors that have been neglected and suggest promising avenues for follow-up research.

We acknowledge that various researchers and practitioners have different goals when analyzing negotiations. In particular, they may be interested in understanding what constitutes rational negotiation (normative

---

[1]Others have taken a similar approach, although usually on a smaller scale. For example, in their classic treatment of groups, Kelley and Thibaut (1969) examined dyadic processes as a basis for developing a theory of triads.

analysis), how people actually negotiate (descriptive analysis), or how people can improve their negotiation process and outcomes (prescriptive analysis). For those interested in what constitutes rational behavior, normative analysis at each level will be the first and final step. For those interested in predicting how people actually negotiate, normative analysis is necessary because it provides a yardstick against which one can detect and measure departures from rationality observed at each level. For those interested in improving negotiation, normative analysis is required to discover what constitutes an "optimal" outcome, and descriptive analysis is required to discover common barriers to achieving such outcomes. Hence, descriptive analysis relies on normative analysis, and prescriptive analysis relies on both normative and descriptive analysis. Whether one's interest is normative, descriptive, or prescriptive, we argue that all applicable levels of analysis should be considered.[2]

The Levels of Analysis Approach: An Illustration

To introduce the seven levels of analysis depicted in Fig. 8.1 and to illustrate how the levels of analysis approach may be applied to an interorganizational dispute, consider the following example:[3]

Film Gate (FG), a new television production company, pitched a number of ideas for one-hour television specials to the three major networks. The executives at ABC liked one of the ideas and began negotiations with FG to develop the series. Because FG had never produced a network special, ABC insisted that FG coproduce the special with Tri-Color (TC), an experienced television production company. Both FG and TC were represented by the same Hollywood agent (HA); in fact, TC was one of HA's largest and most established clients.

The FG negotiating team was composed of the president, chief financial officer, and head of production. Privately, each member of the team found the prospect of working with TC aversive. After some discussion the team was staunchly opposed to the plan. However, because there was no obvious alternative they proceeded to negotiate. The key issues to be addressed were: (1) credit for the program as listed in the titles; (2) monetary compensation; and (3) the option of follow-up programming with ABC. FG was most concerned with credit and the option of future programming so that they could establish a reputation within the industry. However, FG felt pressure to please their major shareholder (SH) in the negotiations. SH was most concerned with the short-term profitability of FG, and was unwilling to continue staking FG unless it would show a profit in the near future. FG

---

[2]For further discussion of descriptive, normative, and prescriptive interactions in decision making, see Bell, Raiffa, and Tversky (1988).

[3]We are indebted to Alan Fox for providing the details of this negotiation.

decided therefore that money would be as important as credit in the negotiation with ABC and TC.

Working through HA, the three principals (ABC, FG, and TC) arrived at a deal that gave top billing and generous compensation to FG. However, HA later sent a memo to ABC stating that the production would be credited to "TC in association with FG," and that ABC's future options would be exercised, if at all, solely through TC. FG was infuriated by HA's apparent betrayal, and found a new agent. Furthermore, FG threatened to sue HA; this threat proved ineffective, as both FG and HA were convinced that a jury would side with them. Finally, FG explored the possibility with ABC of collaborating with Unicorn Productions (UP), another established production company. In light of this development, HA and TC relented and the deal went through under the original terms.

Analysis

The first step in the analysis of this complex negotiation is to identify the parties, the roles they play, and the structure of their relationships, as illustrated in Fig. 8.2. There are four types of parties in negotiations: principals, intermediaries, collaterals, and group members. Each party may be an individual or a *monolithic* group of individuals that acts as a single unit, with the same values and beliefs (cf. Raiffa, 1982). Of course, individuals comprising a group seldom act as one; however, it will be convenient at some levels of analysis to treat them as if they do, and postpone an exploration of the within-group heterogeneity and interactions for other levels of analysis.

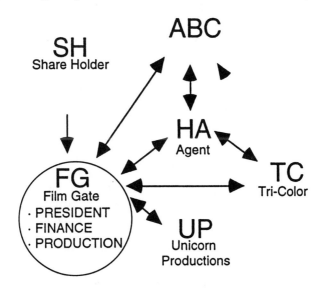

FIG 8.2. Film Gate negotiation structure.

The most fundamental party is a *principal* in a dispute (*P* in Fig. 8.1). A principal is a party with a direct stake in the outcome of a negotiation and at least some influence in its process. In our example, there are three principals: Film Gate, ABC, and Tri-Color. Additionally, Unicorn Productions is a potential principal.

An *intermediary* (*I* in Fig. 8.1) is a party who serves as agent or intervenes in some way between two or more principals. An intermediary usually has some stake in the outcome (e.g., a real estate agent earns a commission on the sale of a home); however, it is the perceived conflict of interests of the principals that motivates negotiation. In the present example, the Hollywood Agent acts as an intermediary between Film Gate and ABC, and also between Tri-Color and ABC.

A *collateral party* is ostensibly on the "same side" as a principal, but exerts an independent influence on the outcome through the principal. We distinguish three varieties of collateral parties: A *superior* is a party with some authority over a principal and to whom the principal is accountable; a *subordinate* is a party over whom the principal has some authority and for whom the principal is responsible; a *constituent* is a party whom the principal has been selected to represent—that is, for whom the principle is responsible and to whom the principal is accountable (these collateral parties are represented by the letter *C* in Fig. 8.1). In our example, Film Gate has a collateral relationship with their major shareholder, who acts in some ways as a superior.

Finally, a group *member* (*M* in Fig. 8.1) is a party within a *multilithic* group. Each member of the group might have different values and beliefs, but ultimately they must act in concert with other members as a decision-making unit. In our example, Film Gate is represented by a three-member negotiating team consisting of the president, the chief financial officer, and the head of production.

The second step in our approach is to undertake a normative, descriptive, and/or prescriptive analysis at each of the seven levels depicted in Fig. 8.1. We now discuss some descriptive aspects of the Film Gate negotiation at each level of analysis.

Individual Level. The most basic level of analysis is that of the *individual* within an organization. An individual level analysis examines the beliefs and preferences of each party, and the way in which parties act on the basis of these judgments. For example, a well-known phenomenon in the behavioral decision-making literature is the tendency for losses to be more painful than forgone gains (Kahneman & Tversky, 1979). After the initial verbal agreement, Film Gate assumes that they will receive top billing and a generous sum of money; the proposed changes would be viewed as a loss relative to this reference point. An analysis of the individuals comprising the

Film Gate team predicts that they will bargain more aggressively for top billing than they would have had this been the initial offer.[4]

Dyad Level. With an understanding of the individual negotiators' decision-making processes, we can proceed to a simple situation in which one party interacts with another. This is the level of the *dyad*, which includes a normative analysis of potential agreements, as well as a descriptive treatment of cognitive biases specific to negotiations, emotions, power, fairness, relationships, emotions, and social influence tactics. In the present example, the threat of a lawsuit by Film Gate is ineffective, as both Film Gate and the Hollywood Agent are convinced that they would prevail if such a case went to court. This is consistent with the egocentric bias phenomenon, in which parties in a dispute tend to overestimate, on average, the degree to which a neutral third party will agree with their position (Babcock, Loewenstein, Issacharoff, & Camerer, 1995; Thompson & Loewenstein, 1992).

Polyad Level. The involvement of more than two principals in this negotiation complicates the interaction enormously. As the number of principals increases, social interactions become more complex, information-processing demands increase exponentially, and coalition formation becomes a possibility. These issues are explored at the level of the *polyad*. A polyad analysis explores social dilemmas, and how the communication network and potential synergies within an environment affect the coalitions that are likely to develop. In our example, a consortium will include Film Gate, ABC, and either Tri-Color or Unicorn Productions. Film Gate successfully pressures Tri-Color to concede on the terms of the agreement by dramatizing the realistic alternative of collaborating with Unicorn Productions.

Intermediary Level. A third party may intervene in a dispute between two principals. The third party may serve as an agent, mediator, arbitrator, adjudicator, or a combination of these roles. Also, the press may play a role by stirring up sentiment in a public dispute. Analysis of *intermediaries* includes a treatment of principal–agent issues, an evaluation of various forms of alternative dispute resolution, and the effects of media involvement. In our example, intermediary analysis might explore the conflicts of interest that the Hollywood Agent experiences by simultaneously representing two production companies in the negotiations with ABC. In particular, the longer standing and more lucrative relationship with Tri-Color leads the agent to place the interests of that company ahead of the interests of Film Gate.

---

[4]In addition to loss aversion, the tendency to be risk seeking when facing losses of moderate probability would predict aggressive bargaining here (Kahneman & Tversky, 1979).

Collateral Relationship Level.   When a negotiating party is embedded within an organization, there are often several peripheral players ostensibly on the same "side" who have an indirect stake in the outcome and influence the negotiation process through the principals. An analysis of *collateral relationships* examines the relationship between parties and their superiors, subordinates, and constituents. In our example, Film Gate is accountable to the major shareholder, who is ostensibly on their side, but who has interests of her own. The shareholder's strong expressed interest in short-term profitability leads Film Gate to weigh the issue of financial compensation more heavily than they otherwise would have in this negotiation.

Intragroup Level.   *Intragroup* analysis examines the benefits and shortcomings of teamwork, and the influence that individuals exert on group decisions. In our example, Film Gate is represented by a negotiating team of three people. Although these individuals must operate as a decision-making unit, they each have disparate interests and exert a unique and not necessarily symmetric influence on the team. In our example, the Film Gate negotiating team is more averse to collaboration than is the average member of the team itself, consistent with the group polarization effect (Isenberg, 1986).

Intergroup Level.   When members of a particular organization or division negotiate in the presence of another organization or division, group identification becomes salient. The *intergroup* level of analysis examines the effects of social identity on the negotiation process and outcomes. Each of the key players identifies with his or her organization and regards other players to be outgroup members. The identification of ingroups and outgroups often leads to the ingroup bias effect, where members of outgroups are negatively compared with ingroup members. For example, Film Gate considered Tri-Color to be competitive and untrustworthy. Further, once an ingroup and an outgroup is established, people tend not to distinguish individuals but rather, make group-level attributions.

We have only explored a few descriptive aspects of the Film Gate negotiation. We argue that all levels are necessary to fully understand the dynamics of this dispute. For example, had we restricted our analysis merely to the level of the interaction between the principals, we would have failed to detect the conflict of interests of the Hollywood Agent and the role of group polarization and outgroup stereotyping in Film Gate's reluctance to work with Tri-Color. Had we focused instead on the intergroup processes, we would have failed to understand the role of framing in Film Gate's aggressive bargaining position and how egocentric bias could render the threat of a lawsuit ineffective.

Strengths and Limitations of the Levels of Analysis Approach

The levels of analysis approach to group negotiation in organizations has several advantages. First, it provides a systematic means of organizing one's thinking about a particular dispute and can aid the researcher or practitioner in understanding the nature of the problem in its full structural context. In this sense, the levels of analysis approach provides both a micro and a macro understanding of negotiator behavior. Second, it provides an efficient method for investigating the causes of conflict and the potential consequences of various courses of action. Third, this framework organizes the research literature around structural themes. Currently, there is no overarching model of group negotiation; we believe our approach integrates the vast majority of research relevant to negotiation. Finally, by providing a means of understanding the structure, dynamics, and research literature relevant to a particular negotiation, the levels of analysis approach may facilitate the discovery of prescriptions for resolving disputes within and between organizations.

Of course, the levels of analysis may sometimes be difficult to apply. First, there will sometimes be overlap between levels of analysis. For example, a superior can act as a mediator in an intraorganizational dispute—thus acting as both a collateral party and an intermediary. Second, our mapping of the research literature onto distinct levels of analysis is somewhat subjective. For example, we discuss generic cognitive biases at the level of the individual, but we discuss biases of negotiator cognition (i.e., biases in the perception of one's counterpart) at the level of the dyad. Finally, although the levels of analysis approach may provide a comprehensive understanding of a particular negotiation, it may not be practical to attend to all levels of analysis simultaneously in designing most empirical studies.

III. THE DECISION ANALYTIC APPROACH TO NEGOTIATION

To understand the negotiation process and evaluate negotiated outcomes, it is necessary to abstract key features common to all negotiations from a normative perspective. An understanding of these basic features seldom allows us to prescribe a single, "correct" or optimal division of resources, but it does allow us to evaluate the efficiency of a negotiated outcome and determine how a settlement might be improved for all parties (for more extensive treatments, see Raiffa, 1982; Neale & Bazerman, 1991; Thompson, 1998).

Key Elements of Negotiation

The key elements of a negotiation situation include the principals, the issues, the principals' interests, their beliefs about future states of the world, the communication that occurs among principals, and the outcomes of the negotiation (see Thompson & Hastie, 1990, for a more complete discussion).

The *issues* are the resources to be divided or items to be agreed upon. For example, a commercial lease negotiation might include discussion of rent to be paid, the duration of the lease, and improvements to be made by the landlord.

The *interests* of parties are the underlying values that are being served. The parties' interests determine their preferences for the issues in question, and their priorities among these issues. For example, a tenant's interest in a commercial property is to have a profitable business. This may manifest itself as a preference for lower rent and more improvements. The landlord is also interested in profit. Hence, she may prefer higher rent and fewer improvements. Both parties might prefer a longer lease. In terms of priorities, the tenant might be most interested in improvements; the landlord might be most interested in rent.

Often the desirability of a particular agreement hinges on the parties' disparate *beliefs* about future states of the world. For example, commercial leases often include clauses in which the tenant agrees to pay the landlord a fixed percentage of sales exceeding a particular level. Obviously, each party's forecast will influence his or her perception of the attractiveness of such a clause.

In most negotiation situations, people do not have complete, perfect information concerning the interests of the other parties. People may exchange information about their interests, but they may not ultimately verify, with certainty, the other person's preferences. The *communication* that occurs among negotiators may be restricted or unrestricted and may either be direct or filtered through one of many organizational gatekeepers. For example, the landlord and tenant might discuss terms in person, over the phone, via electronic mail, or through an agent.

Finally, a critical element of negotiation is the *outcome*. Negotiations may end in mutual agreement or impasse. Mutual agreements may be evaluated in terms of their joint profitability and in terms of the individual parties' outcomes.

Bargaining Zone

One of the most important questions to address in any dispute situation is whether an agreement is feasible. In other words, is it possible for parties to reach a settlement, and is it wise for them to do so? The answer to this question depends on the *reservation point* of each principal; that is, the least desirable outcome that is acceptable (Raiffa, 1982). A party's reservation point is based on their best alternative to a negotiated agreement, also known as their *BATNA* (Fisher, Ury, & Patton, 1991). The overlap among principals' reservation points determines what is called the *bargaining zone,* or *zone of possible agreement* (Raiffa, 1982). Hence, the possibility of a settlement is equivalent to the existence of a positive bargaining zone.

Consider a negotiation situation between a sales group and a distributor. The sales group has determined that the lowest price they will sell their product to the distributor is $3 per unit; the distributor has determined that the highest price at which they are willing to purchase the product is $3.10 per unit. In this case, the bargaining zone is positive: Any price settlement between $3 and $3.10 per unit is viable and it is in both parties' interests to reach an agreement.

Distributive and Integrative Dimensions

The bargaining zone only tells us if it is possible for parties to agree. It does not pinpoint which agreement will be reached. Obviously, it is in each party's interest to reach a settlement that is closer to the other party's reservation point and further from their own reservation point. The *distributive* dimension of negotiation refers to how parties allocate fixed resources among themselves.

Most negotiation situations involve multiple issues for which the principals hold different priorities. In this case, there exists an *integrative* dimension, which is the total amount of resources that parties identify or create. Most negotiation situations are not purely fixed sum. Through a variety of mechanisms, people can expand the total amount of resources to be divided (see Thompson, 1998).

Negotiated outcomes may be assessed in terms of their efficiency, which is a measure of the extent to which all possible resources were utilized. An outcome is deemed *pareto efficient* if none of the parties can be made better off without making at least one other party worse off. It is often in the best interests of the principals to continue to search for pareto-improving outcomes by negotiating "post-settlement settlements" after a mutually acceptable agreement has been reached (Bazerman, Russ, & Yakura, 1987; Raiffa, 1982).

An Example

To illustrate the notion of creating resources in integrative bargaining, consider the following example. Three managers in an organization, Abbott, Barnes, and Costello, have a stake in the allocation of three scarce organizational resources: computer equipment, network communications, and secretarial assistance. Presumably, each manager would prefer to have most of the available resources in all three areas. Obviously, it is not possible for all three managers to achieve this. One potential resolution to the conflict is to allocate each manager one-third of the available resources in these areas. However, suppose that the three managers have differing preferences for the organizational resources: Abbott has pressing computer needs, Barnes has immediate network needs, and Costello is in dire need of secretarial support. A more efficient solution would be to allocate Abbott the computer resources, Barnes the network abilities, and Costello the secretarial support. Thus, by assessing each party's underlying interests, a resolution is reached that all parties prefer to the compromise agreement.

Expanding the amount of resources to be divided serves a number of useful purposes. First, it means that people get more of what they want and are therefore more satisfied. Second, it makes it more likely that the outcome will exceed the principals' reservation points so that an impasse can be avoided. Third, it means that resources are not unnecessarily wasted. Two fundamental questions for the scholar interested in group conflicts in organizations are whether integrative agreements are possible, and if so, how they may be achieved.

We believe that integrative agreements are possible in virtually all organizational disputes because parties seldom have completely opposed interests on all of the issues to be negotiated. Furthermore, it is unlikely that parties have the same risk preferences and beliefs about the future. These differences in beliefs, interests, and attitudes provide the potential for the development of integrative agreements. There are several means to expand the pie of resources besides making tradeoffs. For example, parties can bring additional resources to the negotiating table or find creative ways to address underlying interests that may not be included among the issues formerly under discussion (cf. Lax & Sebenius, 1986; Pruitt & Carnevale, 1993). The question is seldom whether it is possible for parties to reach integrative agreements, but how much value may be added.

IV. DESCRIPTIVE FEATURES OF NEGOTIATION IN ORGANIZATIONAL GROUPS

Using the levels of analysis framework we introduced earlier, we now consider the key challenges and obstacles that negotiators face when attempting to resolve disagreements efficiently. We begin at the level of the individual and work our way up the hierarchy. Our review highlights what we believe to be some of the most important themes in the research literature; it is not meant to represent an exhaustive summary of this research.

Individual

The analysis of groups interacting in an organizational setting begins with an examination of the judgment and decision-making process of the individuals that comprise those groups. People's beliefs about potential consequences of their actions and the value that they place on those consequences determine how they choose among options. The classical economic model of decision making under uncertainty (Savage, 1972; von Neumann & Morgenstern, 1947) assumes that people form internally consistent beliefs and choose among options in a way that maximizes their self-interest and does not depend on the way in which those options are described. Modern behavioral decision theory, however, has documented severe and systematic violations of these assumptions in individual behavior (see e.g., Camerer, 1995). Several of these judgment and decision-making biases have important manifestations in the negotiation process (for an overview, see Neale & Bazerman, 1991, chap. 3). We briefly describe three of the most pervasive biases: anchoring, positive illusions, and framing effects.

Anchoring. When people judge an uncertain quantity with which they have little familiarity, they often begin with a salient, focal value and adjust from there. Because they are "anchored" on this focal value, people tend to make insufficient adjustments. For example, Kahneman and Tversky (1974) asked people to judge the percentage of African countries that were members of the United Nations. The experimenters spun a "wheel of fortune" to determine a threshold number, and asked respondents if they thought the true number was above or below that value. Next, participants were asked to estimate the true percentage. Despite the fact that the focal number was apparently determined at random and therefore completely nondiagnostic of the true number of countries, responses were dramatically influenced by the starting point. When the number from the wheel was 10, the median guess was 25%, whereas when the number from the wheel was 65, the median guess was 45%. Similarly, Northcraft and Neale (1987) asked experienced real estate brokers to report the lowest price they would accept for a house if they were selling, and the investigators found that they could influence responses by manipulating the alleged listing price: Higher listing prices resulted in higher reservation prices.

Negotiations in organizations often require parties to judge uncertain values. What is a fair amount to compensate an employee who was wrongfully terminated? What is the value of a joint venture with another company? How long should it take to complete a construction project? Often, past precedents serve as anchor values; other times, a shrewd negotiator will exploit his or her counterpart's lack of knowledge by anchoring on an extreme initial offer.

Positive Illusions.   Positive illusions refer to the fact that most people consider themselves to be "above average" and more likely to fall into good fortune compared to others (Taylor & Brown, 1988). For example, people tend to overestimate the probability that their predictions are correct, at least for items of moderate to extreme difficulty (see Lichtenstein, Fischhoff, & Phillips, 1982). Overconfidence can inhibit negotiated settlements because if parties are overoptimistic that they can secure a favorable outcome, they may set extreme reservation points. Indeed, Neale and Bazerman (1985) found that overconfident negotiators were less concessionary and completed fewer deals than well-calibrated negotiators. Also, in final-offer arbitration, negotiators consistently overestimated the probability that their offer would be favored by the arbiter (Bazerman & Neale, 1982; Neale & Bazerman, 1983).

Another variety of positive illusions is the tendency to maintain overly positive views of one's own attributes and motives. For example, most people think that they are more intelligent (Wylie, 1979) and better drivers (Svenson, 1981) than others. Similarly, 94% of university professors believe that they do a better job than their average colleague (Cross, 1977). More to the point, most negotiators believe themselves to be more flexible, more purposeful, more fair, more competent, more honest, and more cooperative than their counterparts (Kramer, Pommerenke, & Newton, 1993). Obviously, such self-enhancing views can inflate expectations and inhibit negotiated settlements.

Framing Effects and the Psychology of Value.   The classical theory of decision making assumes that the value that a person attaches to an outcome is a function of its impact on his or her state of wealth and should not vary as a function of the way in which the outcome is described. Modern behavioral decision theory, however, has documented systematic violations of this assumption (see, e.g., Kahneman & Tversky, 1984). In particular, prospect theory (Kahneman & Tversky, 1979; Tversky & Kahneman, 1992) assumes that people adapt to their present state of wealth and are sensitive to changes from that endowment. Second, prospect theory suggests that people exhibit diminishing sensitivity to both gains and losses. For example, receiving an initial $100 is more pleasurable than receiving a second $100 in addition to the first; in other words, receiving $100 brings more than half as much pleasure as receiving $200. Similarly, paying an initial $100 is more painful than paying a second $100; in other words, paying $100 brings more than half as much pain as paying $200. One key implication of this pattern is that people prefer to receive $100 for sure rather than face a 50–50 chance of receiving $200 or nothing (i.e., they are risk averse for medium probability gains); however, they prefer to risk a 50–50 chance of losing $100 or losing nothing to losing $200 for sure (i.e., they are risk seeking for medium probability losses).[5] Third, prospect theory asserts that loss-es have more impact on choices than do equivalent gains. For example, most people do not think that a 50% chance of gaining $100 is sufficient to compensate a 50% chance of losing $100.

Taken together, the way in which a problem is framed in terms of losses or gains dramatically affects behavior in negotiations. First, loss aversion contributes to a bias in favor of the status quo (see Samuelson & Zeck-hauser, 1988), which may inhibit pareto-improving tradeoffs with counter-parts (cf. Kahneman, 1992). Second, both loss aversion and the pattern of risk seeking for losses may lead to more aggressive bargaining when the task is viewed as minimizing losses rather than maximizing gains. Indeed, in laboratory studies, negotiators whose payoffs are framed in terms of gains tend to be more risk averse than those whose payoffs are framed in terms of losses: They tend to be more concessionary and complete more transactions (Bazerman, Magliozzi, & Neale, 1985). Although participants whose payoffs are framed in terms of losses tend to complete fewer deals, the terms of these deals tend to be more favorable (see also, Neale & Ba-zerman, 1985; Neale, Huber, & Northcraft, 1987; Neale & Northcraft, 1986). Third, people tend to categorize gains and losses on particular issues into "mental accounts" (Thaler, 1985), which may influence the attractiveness of agreements. For example, if a negotiator wants to present a proposed agreement in its best possible light to a counterpart, he or she should attempt to incorporate each aspect of the agreement on which the counterpart stands to lose (because each additional loss when lumped together is less and less aversive) and segregate each aspect of the agree-ment on which the counterpart stands to gain (because each additional gain when lumped together would be less and less attractive). This is espe-cially important in logrolling, which by definition involves negotiators giv-ing up (incurring losses) on some issues in exchange for larger gains on other issues.

Dyads

The analysis of the dyad begins with the normative exploration of the issues, interests, beliefs, and bargaining zones, as outlined in section III. In addition, descriptive dyadic analysis includes an examination of the biases of negotiator cognition, and a host of other factors that influence negotiated outcomes, such as relationships between the parties and their perceptions of fairness.

---

[5]For low probability outcomes, people tend to be risk seeking on gains and risk averse on losses.

Biases of Negotiator Cognition

Probably the most serious hindrance to the development of mutually beneficial tradeoffs are the faulty perceptions people hold about the interests, motives, and reasonableness of their own position. This gives rise to the *fixed pie bias, reactive devaluation,* and *egocentric bias* in negotiation.

Fixed Pie Bias and Lose–Lose Agreements.   Most negotiators assume the "pie" of resources is fixed; that is, they perceive the other party's interests to be completely opposed to their own (Bazerman & Neale, 1983; Thompson & Hastie, 1990). This faulty perception is present at the outset of most negotiation situations (Thompson & Hastie, 1990) and is remarkably resistant to disconfirming information (Thompson & DeHarpport, 1994). Not only does fixed pie bias inhibit the identification of mutually beneficial tradeoffs; it can also inhibit the ability of negotiators to take full advantage of issues on which their interests are congruent so that they instead reach "lose–lose" agreements (Thompson & Hrebec, 1996). At least half the time that lose–lose agreements are reached in laboratory studies, people are not aware that they have unnecessarily wasted resources. Inefficient agreements such as this are costly not only for the parties involved, but also for the organization that pays the price of increased waste and underutilized human capital.

Reactive Devaluation.   The assumption that what is good for my counterpart must be bad for me may also contribute to an insidious bias called reactive devaluation, in which specific proposals are evaluated as less favorable by a negotiator after they have been offered by the negotiator's adversary (Lepper, Ross, Tsai, & Ward, 1994; Ross, 1995; Stillinger, Epelbaum, Keltner & Ross, 1990). For example, Stillinger and her colleagues examined students' evaluations of two university plans for divestment from South Africa: The first called for partial divestment; the second increased investments in companies that had left South Africa. Both plans, which fell short of the students' demand for full divestment, were rated by students before and after the university announced that it would adopt the partial divestment plan. The results were dramatic: Students rated the university plan less positively after it was announced by the university, and the alternative plan more positively. If negotiators routinely undervalue concessions made my their counterparts, it will inhibit their ability to exploit pareto-improving tradeoffs so that they can achieve more efficient, integrative agreements.

One-Sided Evidence and Egocentric Bias.   In general, people have difficulty divorcing themselves from their own perspective so that they can take an objective view of disputes in which they are involved. For example, people underestimate how persuasive arguments invoked by their counterparts will be to neutral third parties. In one study, Brenner, Koehler, and Tversky (in press) presented groups of people with background information about a legal dispute and either the plaintiff's or the defendant's arguments. Other groups were presented with background information only or background information plus both sides' arguments. Participants presented with only one side of the case tended to overestimate how compelling those arguments would be to jurors relative to the other two groups, who had a much more balanced view.

Even when negotiators are provided with complete information, they judge fairness in a self-interested, or "egocentric" manner. For example, Thompson and Loewenstein (1992) randomly assigned subjects roles in negotiation simulations involving a wage dispute between labor and management. Both groups were given identical background information on the dispute, and were asked to negotiate under the threat of a costly strike if they failed to reach an agreement. Prior to negotiating, both groups were asked what they thought was a "fair wage from the vantage point of a neutral third party." These judgments were biased in an self-interested direction; that is, participants believed the neutral third party would favor their own role. Moreover, the magnitude of the resulting discrepancy in views of a given dyad strongly predicted the length of strikes. Babcock and her colleagues replicated these effects with real money at stake in a simulated a legal dispute (Babcock et al., 1995; Loewenstein, Issacharoff, Camerer, & Babcock, 1993).

Factors Determining the Negotiated Outcome

Negotiators face two competing tasks in the development of negotiated agreements: creating and claiming value (Lax & Sebenius, 1986). Although one can invoke normative analysis to help identify integrative potential (i.e., the value that can be created in the negotiation), decision analysis does not speak to the issue of how to rationally divide resources (i.e., the value that is claimed by each party). Obviously, this distribution is influenced by the particular tactics that are employed by negotiators (see Pruitt & Carnevale, 1993). In addition, outcomes are affected by emotions, the power dynamic, perceptions of fairness, relationships, and social influence tactics employed by the parties.

Affect and Emotion in Negotiation

Most people would like to believe that they are not emotional and that their behavior is not servant to their affect. This pessimistic view of emotion derives from a misperception that emotions are primarily negative. The truth is that we are always in an emotional state; we may be calm, joyous, frustrated, or angry. Affect[6] in negotiation can have an adaptive function, such as when emotions signal the transgression of social–moral rules (Keltner & Robinson, 1994). For example, consider a negotiation situation in which a negotiator refers to an opponent by his first name; the opponent frowns, and the negotiator learns that he has violated a normative rule. Further, negotiators may seek or avoid circumstances promoting particular emotions (Frank, 1988). For example, a negotiator who realizes that he or she is more likely to make unattractive, unilateral concessions when in the presence of her coworkers (perhaps for impression management reasons) will arrange to meet the opponent in private. People in a positive mood help others more often (Isen, 1970), are more creative (Isen, 1983), and are more sociable (Isen, 1970), and reach more integrative agreements (Carnevale & Isen, 1986), than those in a neutral state. Emotional cues that accompany lying allow negotiators to potentially detect deception (Ekman, 1992; Frank 1988). However, emotion can have dysfunctional consequences, such as when negative affect is reciprocated (Deutsch, 1973). Furthermore, negative emotion may inhibit one's ability to detect integrative agreements For example, Kim and Thompson (1996) found that mediators were more likely to detect integrative opportunities when principals displayed positive, rather than negative affect.

Power

Bacharach and Lawler (1980) called power the essence of bargaining. Fisher (1983) equated negotiating power with "the ability to affect favorably someone else's decision" (p. 150) and defined six categories of power in negotiations. First on his list of power is skill and knowledge. Knowledge in advance about the people involved in a negotiation, their interests, and about the relevant facts gives a party an advantage in obtaining an attractive outcome. The second category of power is good relationships. Positive relationships promote, among other things, trust and good communication. Fisher's third category of power is a good alternative to negotiating. The better an alternative the more favorable an agreement one can credibly demand. The fourth category of power is an elegant solution. Fisher asserted that brainstorming enhances negotiating power by increasing the possibility that a negotiator devises a solution that satisfies the legitimate interests of all sides. The fifth category of power is legitimacy. By developing various objective criteria and standards of legitima-

---

[6]We use the term *affect* to refer to the broad constellation of feeling states, such as emotion and mood.

cy, negotiators can improve their power. Finally, Fisher identified the power of commitment. This includes positive commitments about terms to which a negotiator is willing to agree as well as negative commitments or threats about what a negotiator will do if his or her counterpart fails to agree. Obviously, all negotiators would like to improve their bargaining power. The most effective way to increase bargaining power is to improve one's reservation point, which of course means finding alternative options.

Fairness

A principal's willingness to accept a particular negotiated settlement is influenced by his or her subjective satisfaction with that settlement. Satisfaction with an agreement is a function of objective provisions and also of the perceived fairness of the process and outcome (Thompson, Valley, & Kramer, 1995). Concerns for fairness result in behavior that systematically differs from that predicted by the rational model.

Norms of Fairness. The most common norms of distribution that are invoked in negotiation include equality (Ashenfelter & Bloom, 1984), egalitarianism (Rawls, 1971), equity (Adams, 1963; Homans, 1961), need (Deutsch, 1985), and past practice or precedent (Bazerman, 1985; Kahneman, Knetsch, & Thaler, 1986a). Not only do people define what is fair in a self-interested manner (as we have seen in the case of egocentric bias), but they also tend to favor norms of fairness that benefit them most. For example, people in positions of high power tend to favor distributions based on equity norms, whereas those in positions of lower power favor equality norms (Komorita & Chertkoff, 1973; Shaw, 1981). Austin, McGinn, and Susmilch (1980) instructed pairs of people to complete a work task in which they received feedback on their performance. When participants outperformed strangers, they were more likely to divide compensation according to an equity norm, giving more to themselves; however, when the stranger outperformed them, participants tended to prefer an equality norm, splitting the money evenly.

Relative Versus Absolute Payoffs. The rational model predicts that people will maximize absolute payoffs to themselves and ignore relative payoffs to others. However, in practice, people are not so selfish nor as forgiving as classical economic theory predicts. For example, Kahneman, Knetsch, and Thaler (1986b) asked participants to play a "dictator" game in which they could split $20 with an anonymous other person one of two ways: either keep $10 and give $10, or keep $18 and give $2. Contrary to the rational model, 76% of participants split the money evenly. Moreover, participants were willing to hurt themselves in order to punish players who had been greedy: 74% of participants preferred to receive $5 and give $5 to a person who had split the original $20 evenly rather than receive $6 and give $6 to a person who had taken $18 of the original $20. Similarly, Guth and his colleagues conducted an "ultimatum" game in which a first player makes an offer on how to divide $100, and a second player decides whether to accept or reject that distribution. Contrary to the rational model, first players demanded on average less than 70% of the total, and as many as 20% of second players rejected a positive offer that gave more to player one (Guth, Schmittberger, & Schwartz, 1982). Finally, participants in ultimatum games are willing to hurt themselves in order to punish others who have behaved unfairly. Ochs and Roth (1989) constructed a version of the ultimatum game such that if player two rejected the offer of player one, he or she could make a counterproposal on how to split a smaller prize. In this game, 81% of offers that were rejected by player two were followed by counteroffers that gave less in absolute terms (but more in relative terms) to the rejecter.

It is clear from these examples that negotiators are sensitive not only to their own payoff, but also to the relative payoff to their counterpart. Indeed, in a study of symmetric distributive bargaining situations, participants report greater satisfaction with even distributions than with uneven distributions, regardless of whether the uneven distribution was in that person's own favor (Loewenstein, Thompson & Bazerman, 1989).

Past Precedents.   Not only do relative outcomes matter, but so does past precedent. The past tends to serve as a reference state against which the present agreements are framed. In a series of telephone surveys Kahneman, Knetsch, and Thaler (1986a) found that most people find it unfair for firms to impose a loss on customers, employees, or tenants by raising prices, cutting wages, or raising rents, unless firms do so to protect themselves from a threatened loss (see also Medvec, Valley, & Thaler, 1995).

Relationships

If parties are engaged in repeated distributive negotiations, integrative potential can be created by trading off concessions at different periods in time (Mannix, Tinsley & Bazerman, 1995). A static, transactional model of negotiation neglects such opportunities (Sheppard, 1995). Compared to negotiations with distant others, people are less competitive in their negotiations with close others (Halpern, 1992; Schoeninger & Wood, 1969), they exchange more information with close others (Greenhalgh & Chapman, 1995; Thompson & DeHarpport, 1994), they make more concessions (Halpern, 1992; Schoeninger & Wood, 1969), and joint outcomes are often *less* mutually beneficial (Fry, Firestone, & Williams, 1983) or at least not more integrative (Greenhalgh & Chapman, 1995; Schoeninger & Wood, 1969; Thompson & DeHarpport, 1994; Valley, Moag, & Bazerman, 1994).[7]

Relationships and Fairness. The relationship between negotiators is also an important moderator of their attitudes toward fairness. For example, earlier we cited a study by Austin and his colleagues (1980) in which participants chose a self-interested standard of fairness in dividing compensation with a stranger. In a different condition of that same study, participants were paired with their roommate rather than with a stranger. In this case, they were more likely to split the money evenly even if they had outperformed their roommates (see also Pinkley, Sondak, & Neale, 1992). Earlier we also mentioned a study by Loewenstein, Thompson, and Bazerman (1989) in which participants preferred even distributions to uneven distributions, regardless of whether or not the inequity was in participants' own favor. This pattern broke down when participants negotiated with people with whom they had a negative relationship. In that case, people were particularly dissatisfied with disadvantageous inequity and actually preferred advantageous inequity to an even distribution.

Social Influence Tactics

Negotiation is a game of mutual influence. There is a vast literature in social psychology that examines how individuals influence others to accede to their requests. Cialdini (1993) organized the literature into six principles of influence that we describe below.

1. *Reciprocation.* We should repay, in kind, what another person has provided us. Even uninvited favors and gifts leave people with a sense of indebtedness that they feel they must reciprocate. In negotiation, there is a strong norm that a party should respond to each concession that his or her counterpart makes with a concession of his or her own, even if the initial offer was rather extreme (see Cialdini et al., 1975).

2. *Commitment and Consistency.* Once we make a choice or make a stand, we encounter personal and interpersonal pressure to behave consistently with that commitment. In negotiation, a public commitment to a statement of principles or a criterion of fairness is difficult to later abnegate (cf. Deutsch & Gerard, 1955). After a negotiator gets his or her "foot in the door" by having his or her counterpart accede a small initial request, later cooperation becomes more likely (cf. Freedman & Fraser, 1966).

---

[7]It seems particularly ironic that our negotiations with close others should fall short. There are several differing views on why this is so (for an overview, see Thompson, 1996).

After investing time and energy in a lengthy and important negotiation, negotiators are likely to give in to last minute "low-ball" requests by their counterpart (cf. Cialdini, Cacioppo, Bassett, & Miller, 1978).

3. *Social Proof.* We view a behavior as correct in a given situation to the degree that we see others performing it (Festinger, 1950). This is the principle behind "canned" laughter on television, which has been shown to elicit more laughter in audiences and cause them to rate material as funnier than they do in its absence (Fuller & Sheehy-Skeffington, 1974; Smythe & Fuller, 1972). In general, people are more likely to follow the behavior of others when the situation is unclear or ambiguous or when people are unsure of themselves (Tesser, Campbell, & Minckler, 1983). Moreover, people are more likely to follow the example of others who they perceive to be similar to themselves (e.g., Hornstein, Fisch, & Holmes, 1968). In negotiation, people can exploit past precedents and examples of others who have accepted similar terms to gain compliance.

4. *Liking.* We prefer to say yes to people we know and like. Several factors that promote liking include physical attractiveness, similarity, compliments, familiarity (see Cialdini, 1993). Contrary to the popular belief that a successful negotiator ruthlessly intimidates and exploits his or her counterparts, a positive relationship can be more effective for achieving mutually beneficial outcomes (Thompson, Valley, & Kramer, 1995).

5. *Authority.* We are more likely to accede to the request of a perceived authority figure. The most well-known illustration of this principle is Milgram's (1974) studies that showed the willingness of ordinary people to administer what they thought were dangerous levels of electrical shocks to a person with an alleged heart condition merely because an "experimenter" in a white laboratory coat insisted that "the experiment requires that [they] continue." Equally sobering is the demonstration by Hofling and his colleagues (Hofling, Brotzman, Dalrymple, Graves, & Pierce, 1966) in which a researcher identified himself over the phone as a (fictitious) hospital physician and asked hospital nurses to administer a dangerous dose of an unauthorized drug to a specific patient; in this case, 95% of the nurses attempted to comply. Not only do titles tend promote compliance and deference, but so do uniforms (e.g., Bickman, 1974) and other trappings, such as fancy automobiles (e.g., Doob and Gross, 1968). Negotiators can improve their results by citing authorities, and by acting and dressing in a professional manner.

6. *Scarcity.* Opportunities often seem more valuable when they are less available. According to psychological reactance theory, people react against threats to their freedom to choose an item by desiring it more and working harder to obtain it (Brehm, 1966; Brehm & Brehm, 1981; Wicklund, 1974). This is the principle underlying the success of the ubiquitous "limited time offer" in consumer advertising. Threats to freedom can take the form of time

limits, supply limits, and competition. In negotiation, these tactics can be a particularly effective means for gaining compliance. Savvy negotiators can dramatize their BATNAs by entertaining competing bids, or they can strategically impose artificial time limits for negotiation.

Polyads

When we expand analysis from dyadic (two-party) negotiation to polyad (three-plus party) negotiation, the potential emerges for coalition formation and soscial dilemmas. In the dyadic case, parties are more interdependent because one cannot reach settlement without the consent of the other. In the case of the polyad, it is possible for parties to exclude individuals from an agreement. This introduces new tensions and constraints to the negotiation situation, which we now discuss.

We described a polyad as a collection of three or more principals in a dispute, each of whom represents their own interests and acts reasonably autonomously. The parties may be individuals, teams, or groups. Thus, polyad analysis focuses on how three or more individuals jointly reach agreement and does not focus on intraparty differences. In some cases, polyads are composed of independent entities who each make decisions that have repercussions for collective well-being, giving rise to social dilemmas. In other instances, polyads are composed of collaborating principals, who can make side agreements and form coalitions. We consider these cases in turn.

Individual Choice and Social Dilemmas

In some situations, each member of an organization (or firm in an industry) takes actions that have implications for the entire group. For example, consider a commons area in an organizational department that is shared by several members and is run on the principle of honesty, with organizational members obliged to pay for supplies and refreshments that are made publicly available. If all members elect to take a large number of supplies without paying for them, the commons supply is depleted and all suffer. However, if organizational members exercise restraint, the commons area is a self-sustaining resource for organizational members. The situation we have described is known as a social dilemma (Hardin, 1968), in which organizational members make independent decisions on whether to further their own interests or further the interests of the group (for more extensive discussions, see Messick & Liebrand, 1995; Parks, 1994). A dilemma arises because if each member decides to rationally pursue his or her own interests, the group as a whole suffers.

The most effective means for inducing cooperation and group-interested choice in social dilemma situations is communication. By allowing group members to talk with one another prior to their making independent choices, rates of cooperation have been shown to increase dramatically (for a review, see Sally, in press). Communication appears to be effective for two reasons. First, it allows members to develop a sense of group identity; people feel more committed to helping their group because group welfare is an extension of individual welfare (Dawes, 1980). Second, communication allows members to make commitments to one another. Even if the commitments that people make are not legally binding, they may be psychologically binding because people desire to follow through for intrinsic reasons rather than extrinsic sanctions (Kerr & Kaufman-Gilliland, 1994). In a sense, the commitments that members make to one another transform the situation from a noncooperative task to a cooperative task. Obviously, understanding the factors that promote repeated cooperation within and between organizational groups is important for organizational effectiveness.

Coalitions

Coalition formation is one way that group members may marshal a greater share of resources. A coalition is a (sub)group of two of more individuals who join together in using their resources to affect the outcome of a decision in a mixed-motive situation involving at least three parties (Gamson, 1964; for a recent review, see Komorita & Parks, 1994). Coalitions involve both cooperation and competition: Members of coalitions cooperate with one another in competition against other coalitions but compete against one another regarding the allocation of rewards the coalition obtains. Bargaining power (in terms of quality and feasibility of alternative solutions) is intimately involved in both the formation of coalitions and the allocation of resources among coalition members. Power imbalance among coalition members leads to a number of detrimental consequences. Compared to egalitarian power relationships, unbalanced power relationships produce more coalitions defecting from the larger group (Mannix, 1993), fewer integrative agreements (Mannix, 1993; McAlister, Bazerman, and Fader, 1986), greater likelihood of bargaining impasse (Mannix, 1993), and more competitive behavior (McClintock, Messick, Kahlman, & Campos, 1973). Power imbalance makes power issues salient to group members, whose primary concern is to protect their interests.

Intermediary

There are a number of ways in which a third party can intervene in a dispute. The intermediary can act as an agent by bringing parties together and representing the interests of one or more parties. Alternatively, the intermediary can attempt to facilitate the negotiation through mediation or impose a solution through arbitration, adjudication, or autocratic decision making (see Pruitt & Carnevale, 1993, chap. 12). In mediation, the third party aids disputants in resolving the dispute but has no power to impose a settlement. In arbitration, the principals present their case or final offer to a third party who has power to impose a solution. Arbitration can range from passive to inquisitive, and the arbiter can have full discretion to impose any kind of settlement or have constraints such as the requirement to choose one side's final offer.

Agency

There are many advantages to using agents to represent one's interests. Rubin and Sander (1988) observed that agents can provide substantive knowledge (e.g., a tax attorney), expertise in the negotiation process (e.g., a real estate agent), or special influence (e.g., a Washington lobbyist). Moreover, they can provide emotional detachment (e.g., a divorce attorney) and tactical flexibility. However, there are costs to agency. Because they are usually compensated for their services, agents diminish the potential resources to be divided among the principals. Second, ineffective agents may complicate the negotiation dynamic and thereby inhibit settlement. Most problematic, the agent's interests may be at odds with those of the principals (for an overview of principal–agent issues in economics, see Jensen & Meckling, 1976). For example, Valley, White, Neale, and Bazerman (1992) examined the impact of an agent's knowledge of the buyer's and/or the seller's reservation point in a residential real estate negotiation simulation. Their results suggested a distinct disadvantage for parties with agents: Selling price was lowest when the agent knew only the seller's reservation price and highest when the agent knew only the buyer's reservation price. In another study using a similar paradigm, the presence of an agent increased the impasse rate (Bazerman, Neale, Valley, Zajac, & Kim, 1992).

Arbitration and Mediation

There are a number of criteria on which one can judge the success of dispute resolution by a third party. An ideal procedure should (1) increase the likelihood that the parties reach an agreement if a positive bargaining zone exists; (2) promote a pareto efficient outcome; (3) promote outcomes that are perceived as "fair" to the disputants; and (4) improve the relationship between the parties.

However, there are a number of obstacles that may threaten the success of third-party intervention. First, there is no guarantee that third parties are neutral (Gibson, Thompson, & Bazerman, 1995). In fact, third parties evince many of the biases that plague principals (Carnevale, 1995). Even a neutral mediator may be mistakenly viewed as partial to one's adversary (Morris & Su, 1995). Second, third parties may have a bias to broker an agreement at any cost, which may be disadvantageous to the principals (Gibson et al., 1995). Finally, the threat of third-party intervention may inhibit settlement— for example if principals believe that an arbitrator is inclined to impose a compromise settlement (Farber & Bazerman, 1986). For this reason, final offer arbitration may be more effective than traditional arbitration (see also Chelius & Dworkin, 1980; cited in Raiffa, 1982, Table 4).

Managers are often called on to resolve disputes in organizations (Tornow & Pinto, 1976). In contrast to traditional arbitrators and mediators, managers may have a direct stake in the outcome and an ongoing relationship with the disputants. In addition, managers are more likely to have technical expertise and background knowledge about the dispute. Although several intervention techniques are available to managers, they tend to choose techniques that maximize their own control over the outcome (Karambayya & Brett, 1989; Sheppard, 1984). This may be less preferable to participants because it gives them less voice (Lind & Tyler, 1988).

Collateral Relationships

Collateral relationships refer to negotiations within organizations in which the negotiator is linked to other organizational actors, such as superiors, subordinates, or constituents. Walton and McKersie (1965) noted the importance of intraorganizational relationships when they formulated their intraorganizational bargaining model in which the negotiator in the organization faces two distinct sets of challenges; negotiating between organizations and within the organization.

Most of the research on collateral relationships has focused on the influence of constituents on negotiator behavior. In this paradigm, the organizational actor is accountable to a constituency who has a vested interest in the outcomes of the negotiation. There are two general models of the organizational actor who represents a constituency: the organizational agent and the organizational autocrat.

The *organizational agent* model is the one most often investigated by conflict theorists. The actor is viewed as an agent who is elected to serve the interests of the larger constituency and negotiates on behalf of the interests of his or her constituents. In its purest form, the organizational agent does not have decision control, but is dependent on approval of the constituency. To the extent that this is true, many of the agency issues described earlier will be relevant. For example, the lack of decision control can often give the agent increased power. The "my hands are tied" strategy is a common bargaining ploy of organizational agents who are able to extract larger concessions from opponents who do have decision control. In this sense, empowered negotiators are often in a weaker bargaining position than those without decision control.

In contrast to the organizational agent model, the *organizational autocrat* model views the actor as determining the welfare of his or her constituents. The actor has complete decision control and the constituency is dependent on the actions taken by the negotiator. The negotiator does not need to seek the approval of his or her constituency before enacting an agreement. Raiffa (1982) cautioned negotiators to determine in advance whether or not their counterpart has the power to ratify agreements. The issue of ratification power is more salient in the case where the negotiator is dealing with a subordinate (who is accountable to a superior) rather than with a superior.

Accountability

Accountability to collateral actors is an inevitable aspect of organizational life (Tetlock, 1985, 1992). There are at least two motivational processes that are triggered by accountability: decision-making vigilance and evaluation apprehension.

Decision-Making Vigilance.   According to Tetlock (1985, 1992), decision makers who are accountable for their actions tend to consider relevant information and alternatives more carefully. In this sense, accountability increases the use of thoughtful, deliberate processing of information and decreases automatic, heuristic processing (see also Chaiken, 1980; Fiske & Neuberg, 1990). Decision makers who believe that their decisions will be scrutinized by others are concerned with making a good decision that is supported by the available evidence. Viewed in this light, accountability would seem to uniformly improve the equality of decisions made by negotiators and increase the likelihood of integrative agreements.

Thompson (1995) reasoned that decision accountability may not always promote more thorough and unbiased processing of information if organizational actors were partisan to a particular view. In a series of studies, observers watched videotapes of organizational actors negotiating. In some instances, the observers were asked to assume an objective and impartial view of the situation; in other instances, observers were instructed to take the perspective of one of the parties. Further, some observers were told that they would be accountable for their actions and behaviors (they were told they would have to justify their decisions to others, an unspecified audience, who would question them). After watching the tape, observers made judgments about the interests of the organizational actors. Accountable partisans were more likely to fall prey to the fixed-pie assumption than were accountable nonpartisans. Thompson's explanation of this finding is that the partisan observers were motivated to reach a particular conclusion, and were therefore theory-driven; however, the nonpartisan observers were presumably motivated to reach whatever conclusion the data would allow and were therefore evidence-driven. Thus, accountability does not uniformly increase the accuracy of negotiators' judgments; the effects of accountability seem to depend on the negotiators' goals.

Evaluation Apprehension and Face Saving. A second motivational process triggered by accountability pressure is evaluation apprehension. Negotiators who are accountable for their behaviors are concerned with how they are viewed by relevant others. Evaluation apprehension leads negotiators to employ face-saving strategies and to make their actions appear more favorable to relevant others. Face-saving concerns may lead negotiators to be more aggressive and uncompromising in their bargaining so that they are not accused of being suckers or pushovers. In fact, negotiators who are accountable to constituents are more likely to maintain a tough bargaining stance, make fewer concessions, and hold out for more favorable agreements compared to those who are not accountable (see Carnevale & Pruitt, 1992).

Constituent Goals

Negotiators often face a conflict between their goals and those of their constituency. Peterson and Thompson (1994) examined the impact of different types of organizational accountability on negotiator effectiveness. Negotiations took place in teams of two people. Each team was told that they were to report to a manager who would brief them about the goals of the organization. In one condition, the manager was "profit oriented" and instructed the team to serve the interests of the group at all costs. In another condition, the manager was "people oriented" and instructed the team to maximize their interests while maintaining harmonious intergroup relations. In a control condition, the teams were not accountable to a manager. Teams who reported to the "profit" supervisor claimed a greater share of the resources than did teams who reported to the "people" supervisor and the nonaccountable teams, but only when team members were unacquainted. When team members were previously acquainted, there were no differences in relative profitability. The implication is that people are better able to focus on maximizing their profit (i.e., focusing on distributive negotiation) when they are given a clear profit maximization goal and they are not previously acquainted. For the manager interested in effective dispute resolution, it is not only important to understand the relationships negotiators share *across* the bargaining table, but it is important also to understand the *hidden* table of collateral relationships—that is, the relations within a party (see Kolb, 1983).

Intragroup

Thus far, we have treated each party in a negotiation as either an individual or a monolithic entity, in which each person comprising that party has identical beliefs, preferences, skills, and goals. Obviously, parties are often composed of individuals with differing beliefs, interests, skills and goals; in this sense, groups are *multilithic*. Intragroup analysis focuses on the internal dynamics of the team or group that must act as a single decision-making unit. We now consider two aspects of intragroup activity: decision making and task performance. (A more comprehensive treatment of intragroup conflict and negotiation is provided by Van de Vliert and Janssen in this volume.)

Group Decision Making

Voting and Majority Rule. The most common procedure used to aggregate preferences of team members is to vote using majority rule. Voting refers to the procedure of collecting individuals' preferences for alternatives on issues and selecting the most popular alternative as the group choice. Whereas majority rule appears democratic, it presents several problems with respect to the attainment of efficient negotiation settlements. First, voting ignores group members' strength of preferences for issues. Because strength of preference is a key component in the fashioning of integrative agreements, majority rule may hinder the development of mutually beneficial tradeoffs. Second, voting in combination with other decision aids, such as agendas, may be especially detrimental to the attainment of efficient outcomes because it prevents logrolling among issues (Mannix, Thompson, & Bazerman, 1989; Thompson, Mannix, & Bazerman, 1988). Finally, voting focuses the group on members' positions rather than on their underlying interests, hence inhibiting members' ability to identify pareto-improving solutions.

There are other problems with voting as well. First, group members may not agree on a method for voting. Some members may insist on unanimity; others may argue for a simple majority rule; still others may advocate a weighted majority rule. Second, even if a voting method is agreed upon, it may not yield a choice. For example, the group may not find a majority if there is an even split in the group. Finally, voting does not eliminate conflicts of interest, but rather provides a way for group members to live with conflicts of interest; hence group decisions may not be stable. In this sense, voting "hides" disagreement within groups, which may threaten long-term group and organizational effectiveness.

Arrow (1951) analyzed the problem of combining members' preferences among options to derive a common preference ordering. He proved the "impossibility theorem," which states that no such rule for combining members' preferences is possible if it must satisfy a minimal set of reasonable conditions (e.g., completeness, transitivity). The problem of indeterminacy of group choice is further compounded by the temptation for members to strategically misrepresent their true preferences so that a preferred option is more likely to be favored by the group (Chechile, 1984; Ordeshook, 1986; Plott, 1976; Plott & Levine, 1978). For example, a group member may vote for his or her second choice option in order to ensure that his or her last choice option does not receive the most votes. Furthermore, members may manipulate the order in which alternatives are voted on; when alternatives are voted on sequentially in pairs, those voted on later are more likely to win (May, 1982).

Consensus and Group Influence Tactics. Consensus agreements require the consent of all parties to the negotiation before an agreement is binding. These should be distinguished from unanimous agreements in which parties to the negotiation agree inwardly as well as outwardly. Consensus agreements imply that parties agree publicly to a particular settlement, though their underlying views about the situation may be in conflict.

Although consensus agreements are often most desirable, there are several problems with them in practice. First, they are time consuming because they require the consent of all members, who are often not in agreement. Second, they may lead to the development of compromise agreements where parties attempt to identify a lowest common denominator. Compromise agreements are a quick and easy method of reaching agreement and are compelling because they appear to be fair, but they are usually inefficient because they fail to exploit potential pareto-improving tradeoffs. However, consensus agreements tend to be more efficient than majority rule (Mannix et al., 1989; Thompson et al., 1988). As a general principle, groups should strive for consensus—at least initially.

As organizational actors attempt to build consensus, they may employ group influence tactics to persuade others to change their views or interests. There are several group influence tactics that organizational actors may use to persuade others within their group (see Deutsch & Gerard, 1955). We identify three.

1. *Normative influence.* Normative influence refers to the influence group members exert on one another due to each individual's desire to be liked and respected by members of his or her referent group. A group may

exert normative influence on a member by threatening to dismiss him or her from the group either physically or emotionally (i.e., ostracism). When members don't agree with the views of the group, the group will first attempt to persuade the member to change his or her mind, but if unsuccessful will ultimately reject the member (Schacter, 1959).

2. *Informational influence.* Informational influence refers to the influence attempts made by members that rely on facts and objective reasoning. That is, group members may attempt to persuade others of the virtue of their own positions by supporting their position with objective data, factual knowledge, summary reports, and the like.

3. *Values influence.* Values influence refers to the influence attempts made by members of groups that prey upon individual's desires to hold the "right" values. In many situations it is not acceptable for organizational members to advocate a position of self-interest. Rather, members use organizational values and goals in the service of justifying their own self-serving needs. Most organizational members want to view themselves and to be viewed by others as a good organizational citizen who espouses the appropriate values.

To illustrate the differences between these varieties of group influence tactics, consider a group member who is reluctant to go along with a new hire that all other group members prefer. The group has previously decided that consensus is needed before making a new hire. The group could exert normative influence by threatening to ostracize the dissenting member or exclude him or her from social outings. The group could exert informational influence by providing additional, corroborating information about the attractiveness and values of the potential new hire (e.g., letters of recommendation). Finally, the group could exert values influence by arguing that it is consistent with the culture and mission of their organization to hire this person.

Group Task Performance

Team Negotiation. A team negotiation is a situation in which two or more people act as a single party to determine allocation of resources with another party who is perceived to have some differing interests. Are teams better than individuals at exploiting integrative potential—in other words, are two or more heads better than one? To answer this question, Thompson et al. (1996) compared three types of negotiation configurations; team versus team, team versus solo, and solo versus solo negotiations. The presence of at least one team at the bargaining table dramatically increased the incidence of integrative agreement. Why are teams so effective? Apparently, teams promote information exchange about interests and alternatives that leads to the discovery of mutually beneficial tradeoffs.

It seems clear that the presence of a team at the bargaining table increases the integrativeness of joint agreements, but what about the distributive component? Do teams outperform their solo counterparts? The answer to this question is currently inconclusive, with teams earning more than their solo opponents in some investigations (e.g., O'Connor, 1996; Thompson et al., 1996, Experiment 2), but not in others (e.g., Thompson et al., 1996, Experiment 1). Even when solo negotiators claim less value relative to their team counterparts, they do not seem to suffer in an absolute sense because of the increased integrativeness of agreements.

Distributed Cognition.   Often organizational members negotiate as a team or a group because no single person has the requisite knowledge and expertise required to negotiate effectively. By combining the expertise of different members, the group will be more effective as a unit at the bargaining table. This is an appealing notion, but it is not clear how group members combine and share their expertise and knowledge. The study of how information is shared and tasks are divided is known as distributed cognition (Hutchins, 1991; Levine, Resnick, & Higgins, 1993). We now review the major components of the distributed cognition approach (see Thompson, Peterson, & Kray, 1995, for a review).

1. *Information processing.* The fundamental building block of the distributed cognition model is the individual information-processing system (for a review, see Anderson, 1990; Fiske & Taylor, 1991). The basic processes of the individual information-processing system include encoding, retention, and retrieval. In Wegner's (1986) transactive memory model, the model of the individual mind is extended to the group. For example, when an individual attempts to retrieve information, a search through long-term memory is instigated. In the group context, the search for a piece of information would occur on an individual level, but would also be manifested at the group level, with individuals treating other members of the group as storage locations to be searched, (e.g., "Hey Joe, do you remember the IBM salesperson's name?"). Similar processes operate for encoding (e.g., "You're the numbers person on this project. I am counting on you to know the financial end of this deal.").

2. *Communication.* In a group or team situation, each individual member serves as a storage receptacle for certain information. For a team to retrieve a given piece of information, the location of the information must be known and the person who stores the information must have stored the information with the same label as that used by other members of the group. As an example, consider a research and development group in a

company who is preparing for a negotiation with upper management concerning the distribution and sale of a new product. Key issues include the history of the development of the product, the initial agreement settled upon, the market viability of the product, and potential sales. The research and development group includes a member of the marketing group on their team to provide expertise about the market.

3. *Responsibility.* Teams not only deal with the recollection of stored information, but they also deal with the encoding and storage of new information. The issue of how teams decide who is responsible for storing and retaining which information is crucial to the effectiveness of the team. There are trade-offs involved in the storage of information. It is more efficient for each team member to be responsible for particular information so that each member is not overwhelmed by too much data. However, as the redundancy of storage decreases, so do the chances of successfully retrieving the desired information. Furthermore, groups are less likely to consider and discuss information that is only shared by a subset of its members; this is known as the *common information bias* (Gigone & Hastie, 1993; Stasser, Taylor, & Hanna, 1989).

In conflict situations, it cannot and should not be assumed that all members of a given group are privy to the same facts and information. The distributed cognition approach suggests that people often rely on others for information. In this sense, teams of individuals can be more efficient by dividing the labor. However, distributed cognition is risky because if a team loses one of its members, information may be lost to the entire group. Thus, any group faces a dilemma between spreading responsibility, thereby increasing the dependence of the group on each individual member of the team, and on sharing information.

Group Productivity

How productive are groups? Although a full treatment of this question is beyond the scope of this chapter (see Aldag & Fuller, 1993; Fuller & Aldag, this volume; Hoffman, 1978; Maier, 1950; Thompson, 2000), as a general rule, a group's productivity is equal to its potential productivity minus its process losses (Steiner, 1972). Process losses in groups can be divided into three categories: motivation losses, coordination losses, and conceptual losses. Each form of process loss affects the quality of negotiated agreements in groups. *Motivational losses* refer to the decreased motivation for group members to contribute to a group. When individuals feel that their contributions are not valued or that they are not positively rewarded for their efforts, their motivation may decrease (Latané, Williams, & Harkings, 1979). *Coordination losses* refer to the difficulties groups experience in coordinating effort. In this sense, groups are well intentioned, but may fall short of realizing their potential because they have not developed a system for communicating and working smoothly together (see Shaw, 1981). *Conceptual losses* refer to the inability of individuals to make effective decisions or contributions when in a group. This can occur because individuals are cognitively taxed in groups and because time spent interacting with others diverts attention from information processing.

An analysis of group productivity is useful because it provides a reasonable estimate of how effective a group or team might be. In this sense, it provides a normative benchmark of performance. Furthermore, it provides a means by which to locate the source of potential ineffectiveness. People often blame poor group performance on low motivation of others. However, group ineffectiveness can often be traced to coordination losses, which may often be easily corrected. For the manager interested in improving the efficiency of group negotiations, it is essential to understand the major threats to productivity.

Intergroup

We defined intergroup negotiation as negotiations between groups, which may involve groups within the same organization or different organizations within an industry. The focus of intergroup analysis is on the dynamics of group membership and relationships among group members. One of the most well-known social psychological findings is the bias for people to evaluate their own group more favorably than outgroups (Tajfel, 1974). Downward social comparison leads to the general perception that one's own group is superior to other groups. According to Ellemers (1993), people of high status, those of low status who have few alternatives, and those members of groups who have an opportunity to improve their group are most likely to identify with their group. Members of groups with lower perceived status display more ingroup bias than members of groups with higher perceived status (Ellemers, Van Rijswijk, Roefs, & Simons, in press). However, high-status group members show more ingroup bias on group-status-related dimensions whereas low-status group members consider the ingroup superior on alternative dimensions (Ellemers & Van Rijswijk, 1997).

Social Identity.   People derive self-esteem and identity through their memberships in groups (Tajfel & Turner, 1981), and group membership is a source of esteem and identity for organizational actors (Kramer, 1990). Group membership, however, is a fluid concept that may be defined in several different ways, depending on what features are salient in a particular situation. Kramer (1991) noted that within an organization, people may identify their existence at any of three major levels; the individual level, the group level, and the organizational level. Not surprisingly, level of identification has serious implications for how people negotiate. When people define their social identity at the level of the organization, they are more likely to make more organizationally beneficial choices than when social identity is defined at an individual or subgroup level. For example, Kramer and Brewer (1984) instructed group members to consider either features they had in common with another group or features they had that were distinct. When members were instructed to think of commonalties—thus highlighting the superordinate group, behavior toward outgroups was much more generous than when members focused on differences—thus highlighting the subgroup level.

Ingroup and Outgroup Negotiations. In some cases, social identity cannot be easily transformed and people are faced with task of negotiating with a member of an outgroup (i.e., a member of a different organization or subgroup within an organization). One question concerns how negotiations with outgroup members are different from those with members of one's own ingroup. Thompson (1993) examined negotiations with ingroup and outgroup members and did not find differences in the incidence of integrative agreements. However, group identity affected evaluations of others. As a general rule, when organizational actors anticipate negotiations with outgroup members, they are more likely to engage in downward social comparison (Wills, 1981). They evaluate the outgroup to be less attractive on a number of organizationally relevant dimensions (such as intelligence, competence, and trustworthiness) than their own ingroup. However, after negotiations with outgroups, intergroup relations improve and downward social comparison virtually disappears. Thompson's interpretation is that negotiation with outgroup members is threatening to organizational actors, but to the extent that integrative agreements are feasible, such negotiation has remarkable potential for improving intergroup relations.

Although initial expectations may be quite pessimistic, interactions with members of opposing groups often has a beneficial impact on intergroup relations if several key conditions are met, such as when members of different groups are mutually dependent, a common superordinate goal exists, and an egalitarian culture is present (see Aronson & Bridgeman, 1979). From a prescriptive standpoint, the most significant steps that may be taken to smooth and enhance intergroup relations are to allow members of groups to have voice or express views (Lind & Tyler, 1988), to develop a single document or text that attempts to integrate parties' interests (Raiffa, 1982), and encourage parties to interact with individual members of outgroups rather than with collectives.

Perceptions of Outgroups.   Our analysis of ingroup and outgroup negotiations assumes that the source of conflict lies in the attainment of scarce
resources that each group desires. However, there is another potential
source of conflict that threatens the effectiveness of intergroup negotiation;
misperception of beliefs. Ross and his colleagues (Robinson, Keltner, Ward,
& Ross, 1995; Ward & Ross, 1996) showed that in general, parties in conflict
do not have an accurate understanding of the views of the other party, and
they tend to exaggerate the position of the other side in a way that promotes
the perception of conflict. In a sense, each side views the other as holding
more extreme and opposing views than is really the case. For example,
Robinson et al. (1995) found that in a racial dispute, each side to the conflict had an exaggerated perception of the views of the other party, thereby
exacerbating the perception of a difference in opinion.

The "naive realism" perspective holds that people expect others to
hold similar views of the world as they themselves do. When conflict
erupts, people are initially inclined to provide the other party with evidence that they believe must be lacking. When this fails to bridge interests, people regard others who dissent as extremists who are out of touch
with reality.

V. CONCLUSIONS

We do not promote our levels of analysis framework as a theory per se.
Rather, we argue that a systematic analysis at all levels is a fruitful
approach for both the scholar and practitioner interested in understanding and improving negotiations within and between organizational
groups. The specific application of the levels of analysis approach will vary
according to the goals of the researcher or practitioner. One general tem-
plate for this analysis is summarized in Table 8.1.

The first step is to abstract the analytical structure of the negotiation.
This involves the identification of the key players and their relationships
to one another, the issues to be negotiated, and the interests and beliefs
of each party. This can guide the investigator in analyzing the bargaining
zone to determine what constitutes an efficient outcome. The second step
is to identify key obstacles to achieving efficient outcomes at each level of
analysis.

There is currently no theory of group negotiation. For this reason, it is
not surprising that the research literature on group negotiation is not
integrated or systematic. In short, it is a collection of disparate findings in
search of an overarching framework. We think there is a good reason why
no theory of group negotiation has emerged: Group negotiation has been
conceptualized in fundamentally different ways and at different levels of
analysis. It has been convenient for researchers to narrow their focus to

TABLE 8.1
A Framework for Negotiation Analysis

I. Abstract the analytical structure of the negotiation.
   A. Identify the key players and their relationship to one another.
      1) Identify principals and potential principals.
      2) Identify potential third parties and their roles.
         a) Are there superiors, subordinates, or constituents whose interests the principals have a motivation to represent or who can exert an influence on the outcome of the negotiation?
         b) Are there potential intermediaries (agents, mediators, arbitrators, adjudicators)?
      3) Are the principals monolithic? If not, identify the group members that comprise the principal in question.
   B. Identify the key elements of the negotiation.
      1) For the principals:
         a) Identify the issues under consideration.
         b) Identify each party's underlying interests, and determine their preferences and priorities; identify their beliefs regarding any relevant uncertainties.
         c) Identify each party's BATNA, and estimate reservation points.
      2) Identify the interests, beliefs, and attitudes of all group or team members and collateral parties.
      3) Identify the interest of third parties, and the nature of their influence on the negotiation process and outcome.
II. For each level of analysis, examine potential barriers to dispute resolution and factors that influence the outcome.
   A. Individuals
      1) Is there potential for anchoring bias?
      2) Do positive illusions play a role?
      3) Are there any framing effects?
   B. Dyads
      1) Are there any biases of negotiator cognition (fixed pie, lose–lose agreements, egocentric bias, reactive devaluation)?
      2) What role do emotions, power, fairness, and relationships play?
      3) How are social influence tactics used by the parties?
   C. Polyads
      1) Are there any social dilemmas?
      2) What potential coalitions may form, and how will this affect the dynamic?
   D. Intermediaries
      1) Is there potential for third-party intervention? What kind?
      2) How might the private interests of intermediaries promote or subvert the interests of each principal?
   E. Collateral relationships
      1) To whom is each principal accountable and whose interests is each responsible for representing?
      2) What specific interests of collateral players has the principal internalized?
   F. Intragroup
      1) Groups as decision-making units
         a) What is the mechanism by which preferences are aggregated?
         b) What are the implications of the voting rules?
         c) What group influence tactics are or might be brought to bear?
      2) Groups as action units/teams
         a) How are teams organized?
         b) What are the costs and benefits of this variety of teamwork?

(Continued)

TABLE 8.1.
(Continued)

G. Intergroup
   1) What social identities are salient in this context?
      How might this affect the behavior of groups toward one another?
   2) How does each group perceive the others?
      Are these views biased or polarized in any way?

---

the level of specific phenomena, but this may have been at the expense of understanding the broader context and important moderating variables.

In the past decade, social psychology and organizational behavior have become more concerned with exploring the role of social context in shaping behavior (Kramer & Messick, 1995). On a theoretical level, it is clear that the processes and outcomes of negotiation are critically dependent on the social context. However, the social context in many investigations often serves as a catch-all category that includes anything present in the situation that is not explicitly controlled by the experimenters. Often this means that the multiparty and organizational context is ignored in dyadic analysis; or conversely, that fundamental individual and dyadic processes are ignored at the level of intergroup processes. A levels of analysis approach may be a useful means of parsing the social context in negotiation.

Our levels of analysis point to the perils of approaching group negotiation from a single perspective. For example, to argue that group negotiation is fundamentally about coalition formation, social identity, or social influence is to unjustifiably constrain the focus of analysis. We believe the ultimate goal of the theoretician as well as the practitioner should be to seek a comprehensive understanding of groups as they negotiate.

Although we have touted the benefits of examining group negotiation at different levels of analysis, we have not addressed prescriptive issues in any detail. Our belief is that effective intervention programs can be derived from an understanding of rational negotiation (normative analysis) and common obstacles (descriptive analysis) at each of several structural levels. Probably our most significant contribution is to provide a more systematic means of parsing that context and suggesting a framework around which to organize the research literature.

A shortcoming of negotiation research in general, and group negotiation research in particular, is that it has generated few unique theoretical insights. Paradigms are often borrowed directly from the social psychology and group relations literatures. Our levels of analysis framework provides a generative theoretical function by identifying new concepts and new relationships to explore. For example, the analysis of relationships across and on the same side of the bargaining table are unique to negotiation contexts.

Probably the most common criticism voiced by practitioners is that negotiation research fails to provide a comprehensive view of negotiation. The abundant research on the topic is not especially useful because it seldom provides clear prescriptive advice for negotiating optimally. Researchers counter that such a "one size fits all" equation is not possible; the best we can hope to convey are useful ways of evaluating negotiated outcomes and a list of lessons learned from research on the topic. Most researchers have modest aims and value precision over comprehensiveness. As a result, the voluminous research relevant to negotiation can appear to be an intimidating morass of narrow phenomena disembodied from their broader, more natural context. It is our hope that the approach presented in this chapter (and others that follow in its spirit) provides the necessary context and can serve as an interface between theory and practice. For researchers, we hope that this chapter is useful in organizing the literature in a meaningful way to provide a clearer sense of how their work fits into the bigger picture of negotiation within and between organizations, and how it dovetails with other research on related topics. For practitioners, we hope this chapter provides a means of parsing the analysis of complex negotiations as well as a catalog of research that is useful in determining strategies that will produce more satisfactory outcomes.

Of course this early attempt at an overarching framework is only a starting point. To begin with, normative and prescriptive analytical perspectives are yet to be fleshed out more fully at all levels of analysis. And certainly, particular negotiation scenarios map onto this approach better than others. It is our hope that this first attempt will encourage other researchers to develop similar frameworks so that this approach evolves into a more useful method that can facilitate more systematic and thorough analysis of negotiations.

ACKNOWLEDGMENTS

Research for this chapter was supported in part by a grant from the National Science Foundation, #PYI 91-57447 and support from the Center for Advanced Study in the Behavioral Sciences, under NSF SBR 90-22192.

REFERENCES

Adams, J. S. (1963). Toward an understanding of unequity. *Journal of Abnormal and Social Psychology, 67,* 422–436.

Aldag, R. J., & Fuller, S. R. (1993). Beyond fiasco: A reappraisal of the groupthink phenomenon and a new model of group decision processes. *Psychological Bulletin, 113,* 533–552.

Ancona, D. (1987). Groups in organizations: Extending laboratory models. In C. Hendrick (Ed.), *Group processes and intergroup relations* (pp. 207–230). Beverly Hills: Sage.

Anderson, J. (1990). *Cognitive psychology and its implications.* New York: Freeman.

Aronson, E., & Bridgeman, D. (1979). Jigsaw groups and the desegregated classroom: In pursuit of common goals. *Personality and Social Psychology Bulletin, 5,* 438–446.

Arrow, K. (1951). *Social choice and individual values.* New York: Wiley.

Ashenfelter, O., & Bloom, D. (1984). Models of arbitrator behavior: Theory and evidence. *American Economic Review, 74,* 111–124.

Austin, W., McGinn, N. C., & Susmilch, C. (1980). Internal standards revisited: Effects of social comparisons and expectancies on judgments of fairness and satisfaction. *Journal of Experimental Social Psychology, 16,* 426–441.

Babcock, L., Loewenstein, G., Issacharoff, S., & Camerer, C. F. (1995). Biased judgments of fairness in bargaining. *American Economic Review, 85,* 1337–1343.

Bacharach, S., & Lawler, E. (1980). *Power and politics in organizations.* San Francisco: Jossey-Bass.

Bazerman, M. H. (1985). Norms of distributive justice in interest arbitration. *Industrial and Labor Relations Review, 38,* 558–570.

Bazerman, M. H., Magliozzi, T., & Neale, M. A. (1985). Integrative bargaining in a competitive market. *Organizational Behavior and Human Performance, 34,* 294–313.

Bazerman, M. H., & Neale, M. A. (1982). Improving negotiator effectiveness: The role of selection and training. *Journal of Applied Psychology, 67,* 543–548.

Bazerman, M. H., & Neale, M. A. (1983). Heuristics in negotiation: Limitations to effective dispute resolution. In M. H. Bazerman & R. J. Lewicki (Eds.), *Negotiating in organizations* (pp. 51–67). Beverly Hills: Sage.

Bazerman, M. H., & Neale, M. A. (1992). *Negotiating rationally.* New York: Free Press.

Bazerman, M. H., Neale, M. A., Valley, K. L., Zajac, E. J., & Kim, Y. M. (1992). The effect of agents and mediators on negotiation outcomes. *Organization Behavior and Human Decision Processes, 53,* 55–73.

Bazerman, M. H., Russ, L. E., & Yakura, E. (1987). Post settlement in dyadic negotiations: The need for renegotiation in complex environments. *Negotiation Journal, 3,* 283–297.

Bell, D. E., Raiffa, H., & Tversky, A. (1988). *Decision making: Descriptive, normative, and prescriptive interactions.* Cambridge, England: Cambridge University Press.

Bickman, L. (1974). The social power of a uniform. *Journal of Applied Social Psychology, 4,* 47–61.

Brehm, J. W. (1966). *A theory of psychological reactance.* New York: Academic Press.

Brehm, S. S., & Brehm, J. W. (1981). *Psychological reactance.* New York: Academic Press.

Brenner, L. A., Koehler, D. J., & Tversky, A. (in press). On the evaluation of one-sided evidence. *Journal of Behavioral Decision Making.*

Camerer, C. (1995). Individual decision making. In J. H. Kagel & A. E. Roth (Eds.), *The handbook of experimental economics* (pp. 587–703). Princeton, NJ: Princeton University Press.

Carnevale, P .J. (1995). Property, culture, and negotiation. In R. M. Kramer & D. M. Messick (Eds.), *Negotiation as a social process: New trends in theory and research* (pp. 309–323). Thousand Oaks, CA: Sage.

Carnevale, P. J., & Isen, A. (1986). The influence of positive affect and visual access on the discovery of integrative solutions in bilateral negotiations. *Organizational Behavior and Human Decision Processes, 37,* 1–13.

Carnevale, P. J., & Pruitt, D. G. (1992). Negotiation and mediation. *Annual Review of Psychology, 43,* 531–582.

Chaiken, S. (1980). Heuristic versus systematic information processing and the use of source versus message cues in persuasion. *Journal of Personality and Social Psychology, 39,* 752–766.

Chechile, R. (1984). Logical foundations for a fair and rational method of voting. In W. Swap (Ed.), *Group decision making* (pp. 97–114). Beverly Hills, CA: Sage.

Chelius, J. R., & Dworkin, J. B. (1980). An economic analysis of final-offer arbitration. *Journal of Conflict Resolution, 24,* 293–310.

Cialdini, R. B. (1993). *Influence: Science and practice* (3rd ed.). New York: HarperCollins.

Cialdini, R. B., Cacioppo, J.T., Bassett, R., & Miller, J. A. (1978). Low-ball procedure for producing compliance: Commitment then cost. *Journal of Personality and Social Psychology, 36,* 463–476.

Cialdini, R. B., Vincent, J. E., Lewis, S. K., Catalan, J., Wheeler, D., & Darby, B. L. (1975). Reciprocal concessions procedure for inducing compliance: The door-in-the-face technique. *Journal of Personality and Social Psychology, 31,* 206–215.

Cross, P. (1977). Not *can* but *will* teaching be improved? *New Directions for Higher Education.* Spring, No. 17, 1–15. Reported in D. G. Myers (1990) Social Psychology (3rd ed.) New York: McGraw-Hill.

Dawes, R. M. (1980). Social dilemmas. *Annual Review of Psychology, 31,* 169–193.

Deutsch, M. (1973). *The resolution of conflict.* New Haven, CT: Yale University Press.

Deutsch, M. (1985). *Distributive justice: A social-psychological perspective.* New Haven, CT: Yale University Press.

Deutsch, M., & Gerard, H. B. (1955). A study of normative and informational social influence upon individual judgment. *Journal of Abnormal and Social Psychology, 51,* 629–636.

Doob, A. N., & Gross, A. E. (1968). Status of frustrator as an inhibitor of horn-honking response. *Journal of Social Psychology, 76,* 213–218.

Ekman, P. (1992). *Telling lies.* New York: Norton.

Ellemers, N. (1993). The influence of socio-structural variables on identity management strategies. *European Management Review, 4,* 25–57.

Ellemers, N., & Van Rijswijk, W. (1997). Identity needs versus social opportunities: The use of group level and individual level identity management strategies. *Social Psychology Quarterly, 60*(1), 52–65.

Ellemers, N., Van Rijswijk, W., Roefs, M., & Simons, C. (in press). Bias in intergroup perceptions: Balancing group identity with social reality. *Personality and Social Psychology Bulletin.*

Farber, H. S., & Bazerman, M. H. (1986). The general basis of arbitrator behavior: An empirical analysis of conventional and final offer arbitration. *Econometrica, 54,* 1503–1528.

Festinger, L. (1950). Informal social communication. *Psychological Review, 57,* 271–282.

Fisher, R. (1983). Negotiating power. *American Behavioral Scientist, 27,* 149–166.

Fisher, R., Ury, W., & Patton, B. (1991). *Getting to yes: Negotiating agreement without giving in* (2nd ed.). Boston: Houghton Mifflin.

Fiske, S. T., & Neuberg, S. L. (1990). A continuum of impression formation, from category-based to individuating processes: Influences of information and motivation on attention and interpretation. In M. P. Zanna (Eds.), *Advances in experimental social psychology* (pp. 1–74). New York: Academic Press.

Fiske, S. T., & Taylor, S. E. (1991). *Social cognition.* New York: McGraw-Hill.

Frank, R. H. (1988). *Passions within reason: The strategic role of the emotions.* New York: Norton.

Freedman, J. L., & Fraser, S. C. (1966). Compliance without pressure: The foot-in-the door technique. *Journal of Personality and Social Psychology, 4,* 195–203.

Fry, W. R., Firestone, I., & Williams, D. (1983). Negotiation process and outcome of stranger dyads and dating couples: Do lovers lose? *Basic and Applied Social Psychology, 4,* 1–16.

Fuller, R. G. C., & Sheehy-Skeffington, A. (1974). Effects of group laughter on responses to humorous materials: A replication and extension. *Psychological Reports, 35,* 531–534.

Gamson, W. (1964). Experimental studies in coalition formation. In L. Berkowitz (Ed.), *Advances in experimental social psychology* (pp. 81–110). New York: Academic Press.

Gibson, K., Thompson, L., & Bazerman, M. (1995). Biases and rationality in the mediation process. In L. Heath, F. Bryant, J. Edwards, E. Henderson, J. Myers, E. Posavac, Y. Suarez-Balacazar, & S. Tindale (Eds.), *Application of heuristics and biases to social issues* (pp. 163–183). New York: Plenum.

Gigone, D., & Hastie, R. (1993). The common knowledge effect: Information sharing and group judgment. *Journal of Personality and Social Psychology, 65,* 959–974.

Greenhalgh, L., & Chapman, D. I. (1995). Joint decision making: The inseparability of relationships and negotiation. In R. M. Kramer (Ed.), *Negotiation as a social process: New trends in theory and research* (pp. 166–185). Thousand Oaks, CA: Sage.

Guth, W., Schmittberger, R., & Schwartz, B. (1982). An experimental analysis of ultimatum bargaining. *Journal of Economic Behavior and Organization, 3,* 367–388.

Hackman, J. R. (1987). The design of work teams. In J. W. Lorsch (Ed.), *Handbook of organizational behavior* (pp. 315–342). Englewood Cliffs, NJ: Prentice-Hall.

Halpern, J. (1992, August). *The effect of friendship on bargaining: Experimental studies of personal business transactions.* Paper presented at the Academy of Management, Las Vegas.

Hardin, G. (1968). The tragedy of the commons. *Science, 162,* 1243–1248.

Hoffman, L. R. (1978). Group problem solving. In L. Berkowitz (Ed.), *Group processes* (pp. 67–113). New York: Academic Press.

Hofling, C. K., Brotzman, E., Dalrymple, S., Graves, N., & Pierce, C. M. (1966). An experimental study of nurse–physician relationships. *Journal of Nervous and Mental Disease, 143,* 171–180.

Homans, G. (1961). *Social behavior: Its elementary forms.* New York: Harcourt Brace.

Hornstein, H. A., Fisch, E., & Holmes, M. (1968). Influence of a model's feeling about his behavior and his relevance as a comparison other on observers' helping behavior. *Journal of Personality and Social Psychology, 10,* 222–226.

Hutchins, E. (1991). The social organization of distributed cognition. In L. Resnick, J. Levine, & S. Teasdale (Eds.), *Perspectives on socially shared cognition* (pp. 283–307). Washington, DC: American Psychological Association.

Isen, A. (1970). Success, failure, attention, and reaction to others: The warm glow of success. *Journal of Personality and Social Psychology, 48,* 1413–1426.

Isenberg, D. J. (1986). Group polarization: A critical review and meta-analysis. *Journal of Personality and Social Psychology, 50,* 1141–1151.

Jensen, M. C., & Meckling, W. H. (1976). Theory of the firm: Managerial behavior, agency costs, and ownership structure. *Journal of Financial Economics, 3,* 305–360.

Kahneman, D. (1992). Reference points, anchors, norms, and mixed feelings. *Organizational Behavior and Human Decision Processes, 51,* 291–312.

Kahneman, D., Knetsch, J., & Thaler, R. H. (1986a). Fairness as a constraint on profit seeking: Entitlements in the market. *American Economic Review, 76,* 728–741.

Kahneman, D., Knetsch, J., & Thaler, R. H. (1986b). Fairness and the assumptions of economics. *Journal of Business, 59,* S285–S300.

Kahneman, D., & Tversky, A. (1974). Judgment under uncertainty: Heuristics and biases. *Science, 185,* 1124–1131.

Kahneman, D., & Tversky A. (1979). Prospect theory: An analysis of decision under risk. *Econometrica, 47,* 263–291.

Kahneman, D., & Tversky, A. (1984). Choices, values, and frames. *American Psychologist, 39,* 341–350.

Karambayya, R., & Brett, J. M. (1989). Managers handling disputes: Third party roles and perceptions of fairness. *Academy of Management Journal, 32,* 687–704.

Kelley, H., & Thibaut, J. (1969). Group problem solving. In G. Lindzey & E. Aronson (Eds.), *Handbook of social psychology* (pp. 33–51). New York: Random House.

Kerr, N., & Kaufman-Gilliland, C. (1994). Communication, commitment, and cooperation in social dilemmas. *Journal of Personality and Social Psychology, 66,* 513–529.

Kolb, D. (1983). *The mediators.* Cambridge, MA: MIT Press.

Komorita, S., & Chertkoff, J. (1973). A bargaining theory of coalition formation. *Psychological Review, 80,* 149–162.

Komorita, S., & Parks, C. (1994). *Social dilemmas.* Madison, WI: Brown & Benchmark.

Kramer, R. (1990). The effects of resource scarcity on group conflict and cooperation. In E. Lawler & B. Markovsky (Eds.), *Advances in group processes* (pp. 151–177). Hillsdale, NJ: JAI.

Kramer, R. (1991). The more the merrier? Social psychological aspects of multiparty negotiations in organizations. In M. H. Bazerman, R. J. Lewicki, & B. H. Sheppard (Eds.), *Research on negotiation in organizations: Handbook of negotiation research* (pp. 307–332). Greenwich, CT: JAI.

Kramer, R., & Brewer, M. (1984). Effects of group identity on resource use in a simulated commons dilemma. *Journal of Personality and Social Psychology, 46,* 1044–1057.

Kramer, R., & Messick, D. (Eds.). (1995). *Negotiation as a social process.* Beverly Hills, CA: Sage.

Kramer, R., Pommerenke, P., & Newton, E. (1993). The social context of negotiation: Effects of social identity and accountability on negotiator judgment and decision making. *Journal of Conflict Resolution, 37,* 633–654.

Latané, B., Williams, K., & Harkings, S. (1979). Many hands make light the work: The causes and consequences of social loafing. *Journal of Personality and Social Psychology, 37,* 822–823.

Lax, D. A., & Sebenius, J. K. (1986). *The manager as negotiator.* New York: Free Press.

Levine, J., Resnick, L., & Higgins, E. (1993). Social foundations of cognition. *Annual Review of Psychology, 44,* 585–612.

Lichtenstein, S., Fischhoff, B., & Phillips, L. D. (1982). Calibration of probabilities: The state of the art to 1980. In D. Kahneman & A. Tversky (Eds.), *Judgment under uncertainty: Heuristics and biases* (pp. 306–334). Cambridge, England: Cambridge University Press.

Lind, A. E., & Tyler, T. R. (1988). *The social psychology of procedural justice.* New York: Plenum.

Loewenstein, G., Issacharoff, S., Camerer, C. F., & Babcock, L. (1993). Self-serving assessments of fairness and pretrial bargaining. *Journal of Legal Studies, 22,* 135–159.

Loewenstein, G., Thompson, L. L., & Bazerman, M. H. (1989). Social utility and decision making in interpersonal contexts. *Journal of Personality and Social Psychology, 57,* 426–441.

Maier, N. R. F. (1950). The quality of group decisions as influenced by the discussion leader. *Human Relations, 3,* 155–174.

Mannix, E. (1993). Organizations as resource dilemmas: The effects of power balance on coalition formation in small groups. *Organizational Behavior and Human Decision Processes, 55,* 1–22.

Mannix, E., Thompson, L., & Bazerman, M. (1989). Negotiation in small groups. *Journal of Applied Psychology, 74,* 508–517.

Mannix, E., Tinsley, C., & Bazerman, M. (1995). Negotiating over time: Impediment to integrative solutions. *Organizational Behavior and Human Decision Processes, 62,* 241–251.

May, K. (1982). A set of independent, necessary and sufficient conditions for simple majority decisions. In B. Barry & R. Hardin (Eds.), *Rational man and irrational society* (pp. 297–303). Beverly Hills, CA: Sage.

McAlister, L., Bazerman, M., & Fader, R. (1986). Power and goal setting in channel negotiations. *Journal of Marketing Research, 23,* 238–263.

McClintock, C., Messick, D., Kuhlman, D., & Campos, F. (1973). Motivational bases of choice in three-choice decomposed games. *Journal of Experimental and Social Psychology, 9,* 572–590.

Messick, D. M., & Liebrand, W. B. G. (1995). Individual heuristics and the dynamics of cooperation in large groups. *Psychological Review, 102,* 131–145.

Milgram, S. (1974). *Obedience to authority.* New York: Harper & Row.

Morris, M. W., & Su, S. K. (1995). *The hostile mediator phenomenon: When each side perceives the mediator to be partial to the other.* Unpublished manuscript, Stanford University Graduate School of Business.

Neale, M. A., & Bazerman, M. H. (1983). The role of perspective-taking ability in negotiation under different forms of arbitration. *Industrial and Labor Relations Review, 36,* 378–388.

Neale, M. A., & Bazerman, M. H. (1985). The effects of framing and negotiator overconfidence on bargainer behavior. *Academy of Management Journal, 28,* 34–49.

Neale, M. A., & Bazerman, M. H. (1991). *Cognition and rationality in negotiation.* New York: Free Press.

Neale, M. A., Huber, V. L., & Northcraft, G. B. (1987). The framing of negotiations: Context versus task frames. *Organizational Behavior and Human Decision Processes, 39,* 228–241.

Neale, M., & Northcraft, G. (1986). Experts, amateurs, and refrigerators: Comparing expert and amateur negotiators in a novel task. *Organizational Behavior and Human Decision Processes, 38,* 305–317.

Northcraft, G. B., & Neale, M. (1987). Amateurs, experts, and real estate: An anchoring-and-adjustment perspective on property pricing decision. *Organizational Behavior and Human Decision Processes, 39,* 84–97.

Ochs, J., & Roth, A. E. (1989). An experimental study of sequential bargaining. *American Economic Review, 79,* 335–385.

O'Connor, K. M. (1996). *Groups and solos in context: The effects of accountability on team negotiation.* Unpublished manuscript, Kellogg Graduate School of Management, Northwestern University.

Ordeshook, P. (1986). *Game theory and political theory: An introduction.* Cambridge, England: Cambridge University Press.

Parks, C. D. (1994). The predictive ability of social values in resource dilemmas and public goods games. *Personality and Social Psychology Bulletin, 20,* 431–438.

Peterson, E., & Thompson, L. (1997). Negotiation teamwork: The impact of information distribution and accountability for performance depends on the relationship among team members. *Organization Behavior and Human Decision Processes, 72(3),* 364–383.

Pinkley, R., Sondak, H., & Neale, M. (1992). *Negotiating norms of justice.* Unpublished paper, Southern Methodist University, Dallas, TX.

Plott, C. (1976). Axiomatic social choice theory: An overview and interpretation. *American Journal of Political Science, 20,* 511–596.

Plott, C., & Levine, M. (1978). A model of agenda influence on committee decisions. *American Economic Review, 68,* 146–160.

Pruitt, D. G., & Carnevale, P. J. (1993). *Negotiation in social conflict.* Pacific Grove, CA: Brooks/Cole.

Raiffa, H. (1982). *The art and science of negotiation.* Cambridge, MA: Belknap.

Rawls, J. (1971). *A theory of justice.* Cambridge, MA: Harvard University Press.

Robinson, R., Keltner, D., Ward, A., & Ross, L. (1995). Actual versus assumed differences in construal: "Naive realism" in intergroup perception and conflict. *Journal of Personality and Social Psychology, 68,* 404–417.

Ross, L. (1995). Reactive devaluation in negotiation and conflict resolution. In K. Arrow, R. Mnookin, L. Ross, A. Tversky, & R. Wilson (Eds.), *Barriers to the negotiated resolution of conflict.* New York: Norton.

Ross, L., & Stillinger, C. (1991). Barriers to conflict resolution. *Negotiation Journal, 8,* 389–404.

Rubin, J. Z., & Sander, F. E. A. (1988, October). When should we use agents? Direct vs. representative negotiation. *Negotiation Journal,* 395–401.

Sally, D. F. (in press). Conversation and cooperation in social dilemmas: Experimental evidence from 1958 to 1992. *Rationality and Society.*

Samuelson, W., & Zeckhauser, R. (1988). Status quo bias in decision making. *Journal of Risk and Uncertainty, 1,* 7–59.

Savage, L. J. (1972). *The foundations of statistics.* New York: Dover.

Schacter, S. (1959). *The psychology of affiliation.* Stanford, CA: Stanford University Press.

Schoeninger, D., & Wood, W. (1969). Comparison of married and ad hoc mixed-sex dyads negotiating the division of a reward. *Journal of Experimental Social Psychology, 5,* 483–499.

Shaw, M. (1981). *Group dynamics: The psychology of small group behavior.* New York: McGraw-Hill.

Sheppard, B. H. (1984). Third-party intervention: A procedural framework. In B. M. Staw & L. L. Cummings (Eds.), *Research in organizational behavior* (Vol. 6, pp. 141–190). Greenwich, CT: JAI.

Sheppard, B. H. (1995). Negotiating in long-term mutually interdependent relationships among relative equals. *Research on Negotiations in Organizations, 5,* 3–44.

Smythe, M. M., & Fuller, R. G. C. (1972). Effects of group laughter on responses to humorous materials. *Psychological Reports, 30,* 132–134.

Stasser, G., Taylor, L., & Hanna, C. (1989). Information sampling in structured and nonstructured discussions of three- and six-person groups. *Journal of Personality and Social Psychology, 53,* 81–93.

Steiner, I. (1972). *Group process and productivity.* New York: Academic Press.

Svenson, O. (1981). Are we all less risky and more skillful than our fellow drivers? *Acta Psychologica, 47,* 143–148.

Tajfel, H. (1974). Social identity and intergroup behavior. *Social Science Information, 13,* 65–93.

Tajfel, H., & Turner, J. C. (1981). The social identity theory of intergroup behavior. In S. Worchel & W. G. Austin (Eds.), *Psychology of intergroup relations* (pp. 7–24). Chicago: Nelson-Hall.

Taylor, S. E., & Brown, J. D. (1988). Illusion and well-being: A social psychological perspective on mental health. *Psychological Bulletin, 103,* 193–210.

Tesser, A., Campbell, J., & Minckler, S. (1983). The role of social pressure, attention to the stimulus, and self-doubt in conformity. *European Journal of Social Psychology, 13,* 217–233.

Tetlock, P. (1985). Accountability: A social check on the fundamental attribution error. *Social Psychology Quarterly, 48,* 227–236.

Tetlock, P. (1992). The impact of accountability on judgment and choice: Toward a social contingency model. *Advances in Experimental Social Psychology, 25,* 331–376.

Thaler, R. H. (1985). Mental accounting and consumer choice. *Marketing Science, 4,* 199–214.

Thompson, L. (1993). The impact of negotiation on intergroup relations. *Journal of Experimental Social Psychology, 29,* 304–325.

Thompson, L. (1995). They saw a negotiation: Partisanship and involvement. *Journal of Personality and Social Psychology, 68,* 839–853.

Thompson, L. (1998). *The mind and heart of the negotiator.* Upper Saddle River, NJ: Prentice Hall.

Thompson, L. (2000). *Making the team: A guide for managers.* Upper Saddle River, NJ: Prentice Hall.

Thompson, L., & DeHarpport, T. (1994). Social judgment, feedback, and interpersonal learning in negotiation. *Organizational Behavior and Human Decision Processes, 58,* 327–345.

Thompson, L., & Hastie, R. (1990). Social perception in negotiation. *Organizational Behavior and Human Decision Processes, 47,* 98–123.

Thompson, L., & Hrebec, D. (1996). Lose–Lose agreements in interdependent decision making. *Psychological Bulletin, 120,* 396–409.

Thompson, L., & Kim, P. (in press). How the quality of third parties' settlement solutions are affected by the relationship between negotiators. *Journal of Experimental Social Psychology: Applied.*

Thompson, L., & Loewenstein, G. (1992). Egocentric interpretations of fairness and negotiation. *Organizational Behavior and Human Decision Processes, 51,* 176–197.

Thompson, L., Mannix, E., & Bazerman, M. (1988). Group negotiation: Effects of decision rule, agenda, and aspiration. *Journal of Personality and Social Psychology, 54,* 86–95.

Thompson, L., Peterson, E., & Kray, L. (1995). Social context in negotiation: An information processing perspective. In R. Kramer & D. Messick (Eds.), *Negotiation as a social process* (pp. 5–36). Beverly Hills, CA: Sage.

Thompson, L., Peterson, E., & Brodt, S. (1996). Team negotiation: An examination of integrative and distributive bargaining. *Journal of Personality and Social Psychology, 70,* 66–78.

Thompson, L., Valley, K., & Kramer, R. (1995). The bittersweet feeling of success: An examination of social perception in negotiation. *Journal of Experimental Social Psychology, 31,* 467–492.

Tornow, W. W., & Pinto, P. R. (1976). The development of a managerial job taxonomy. *Journal of Applied Psychology, 4,* 410–418.

Tversky, A., & Kahneman, D. (1992). Advances in prospect theory: Cumulative representation of uncertainty. *Journal of Risk and Uncertainty, 5,* 297–323.

Valley, K., Medvec, V. H., & Thaler, R. (1995). *Concession aversion: A story of loss and betrayal.* Working paper, Harvard Business School, Boston.

Valley, K., Moag, J., & Bazerman, M. (1994). *Away with the curse: Effects of communication on the efficiency and distribution of outcomes.* Unpublished manuscript, Harvard Business School.

Valley, K., White, S., Neale, M., & Bazerman, M. (1992). The effect of agent's knowledge on negotiator performance in simulated real estate negotiations. *Organizational Behavior and Human Decision Processes, 52,* 220–236.

von Neumann, J., & Morgenstern, O. (1947). *Theory of games and economic behavior* (2nd ed.). Princeton, NJ: Princeton University Press.

Walton, R. E., & McKersie, R. B. (1965). *A behavioral theory of labor relations.* New York: McGraw-Hill.

Ward, A., & Ross, L. (1996). Naive realism in everyday life: Implications for social conflict and misunderstanding. In E. Reed, E. Turiel, & T. Brown (Eds.), *Values and knowledge.* Mahwah, NJ: Lawrence Erlbaum Associates.

Wegner, D. (1986). Transactive memory: A contemporary analysis of the group mind. In B. Mullen & G. Goethals (Eds.), *Theories of group behavior* (pp. 185–208). New York: Springer-Verlag.

Weingart, L. R., Hyde, E., & Prietula, M. (1996). The effect of tactical descriptions on negotiation behavior and outcome. *Journal of Personality and Social Psychology, 70,* 1205–1217.

Wicklund, R. A. (1974). *Freedom and reactance.* Hillsdale, NJ: Lawrence Erlbaum Associates.

Wills, T. A. (1981). Downward comparison principles in social psychology. *Psychological Bulletin, 90,* 245–271.

Wylie, R. C. (1979). *The self-concept: Vol. 2.* Theory and research on selected topics. Lincoln, NE: University of Nebraska Press.

Chapter 9

Description, Explanation, and Prescription of Intragroup Conflict Behaviors

Evert Van de Vliert
Onne Janssen
University of Groningen, The Netherlands

Conflict-free groups do not exist. We especially detect conflict in the group members' actions: They avoid a reproach, accommodate a poor plan, negotiate on a price or a problem, fight an opponent on principle, and the like. Psychologists describe all such behaviors, try to explain them, and study the outcomes to recommend effective methods of conflict management. Consequently, there are descriptive, explanatory, and prescriptive theories of conflict behavior, as well as an assortment of combinations of these three types of scientific efforts. Note that this trichotomization of theories constitutes a very useful organizing principle for a broad-ranging literature. Indeed, the unique features of our viewpoint could serve as a model for reviewing many scholarly fields in terms of description, explanation, and prescription.

In the case of handling conflict, the descriptive theories identify main types of conflict behaviors, name them, and interrelate them by listing their characteristics. The explanatory theories propose a set of rules of correspondence between the conflict behaviors and their determinants or consequences. The prescriptive theories recommend courses of action on the basis of a set of rules of correspondence between the conflict behaviors and their consequences. Too often, however, these three qualitatively different types of theories are mixed up, causing a Babel-like confusion of tongues that hinders theoretical progress and practical application. To disentangle this tie in the present chapter on the management of intragroup conflict at work, we have chosen to review, integrate, and advance

descriptive theories of conflict behavior first, before we address their connections with explanatory and prescriptive theories, respectively.

DESCRIPTIVE THEORIES OF CONFLICT BEHAVIOR

Group members are in conflict when they are obstructed or irritated by one
or more other group members and react to it in a beneficial or costly way
(Van de Vliert, 1997, 1998a). Numerous behaviors are capable of handling
social conflict. For example, Roloff (1976) reported 44 conflict response
modes, and Wall (1985) listed and categorized 169 tactics. A question that
remains very much alive concerns the structure of classification underlying
the abundance of behaviors used in interpersonal and other small-group
conflicts (e.g., Daves & Holland, 1989; Psenicka & Rahim, 1989; Sternberg
& Dobson, 1987; Van de Vliert, 1990; Van de Vliert & Euwema, 1994).
Despite the research attention that has been paid to this, as yet no consensus has emerged regarding the most valid taxonomy.

In this section, we first review the following three pairs of factors used
to describe and compare conflict behaviors: concern for one's own and
others' goals, integration and distribution, mitigation–intensification and
passive–active. We conclude that these factors are typically used to
describe group members' conflict behaviors in terms of their causes or
consequences. This is a questionable activity, because it confounds independent and dependent variables, and it therefore hinders unambiguous
observations and theoretical progress. As suggested elsewhere (Van de
Vliert & Euwema, 1994), this problem may be overcome by adopting
agreeableness and activeness as more appropriate dimensions to describe
and compare modes of conflict handling. In addition, we argue that
agreeableness and activeness as common descriptors are suitable factors
to integrate not only widespread taxonomies of conflict behaviors but also
specific modes of conflict management. The ultimate implication of this
position is that each conflict behavior has to be conceptualized as a complex conglomeration of interrelated behavioral components instead of as
a manifestation of pure, singular behavior.

Concern for One's Own and Others' Goals

Blake and Mouton (1964, 1970) proposed two factors to describe and
explain conflict behaviors: "concern for the production of results" and
"concern for people." Their original model, which first appeared in 1964,
was restricted to managerial behavior, including managerial conflict
behavior. However, in 1970, Blake and Mouton claimed that the concerns
and the resulting styles of conflict management also apply to people other

than managers and to social conflicts other than managerial conflicts. That is, any reaction to a conflict—notably including avoiding, accommodating, compromising, problem solving, and competing—is assumed to result from what may be interpreted as concern for the production of results for self and concern for the production of results for other people (Van de Vliert, 1997).

Thomas (1976, 1988) labeled the dimensions as *assertiveness*, "attempting to satisfy one's own concerns," and *cooperativeness*, "attempting to satisfy other's concerns." He saw the concerns as behavioral features rather than antecedent variables. "The model . . . is purely a taxonomy. . . . It attempts to describe what the conflict modes are." (Thomas, 1988, pp. 432–433; for a similar view, see Shockley-Zalabak, 1988). In contrast, Rubin, Pruitt and Kim (1994) viewed the goal concerns as inner determinants of outward conflict behaviors. For example, a strong concern for both parties' goals leads to problem solving, whereas a strong concern for one's own goals but a weak concern for one's opponent's goals produces contending.

Because the concerns are intrapersonal and cannot be observed well by others, they are not unequivocal features of intended or displayed conflict behavior. Moreover, predictors such as the concerns are rarely good descriptors (Nicotera, 1993). The pair of concerns only indicates the preferred strategy of conflict behavior. "But for a strategy actually to be adopted, it must also be seen as minimally feasible. If not, another strategy will be chosen, even if it is less consistent with the current combination of concerns" (Rubin et al., 1994, p. 37). Overall, the common practice of using the concerns for one's own and for another's goals as descriptors of conflict behavior at work is not to be recommended at all. A similar critique holds for the common practice of mapping reactions to social conflict in terms of an integrative and a distributive dimension.

Integration and Distribution

Building on Walton and McKersie's (1965) work on labor negotiations, Thomas (1976; see also Putnam, 1990) suggested that the joint outcome space of a conflict party's strategic objectives can also be described with the help of an integrative and a distributive dimension. The integrative component of a particular strategy of conflict handling represents the extent to which that behavior is trying to maximize the total outcomes for the conflict parties together; the size of the joint pie is at stake, also called "creating value" (Lax & Sebenius, 1986). The distributive component of each strategy represents the extent to which that behavior is trying to maximize unequal outcomes for the respective conflict parties; the size of each party's proportion of the fixed pie is at stake, also called "claiming value" (Lax & Sebenius, 1986). Empirical support for the existence and the descriptive qualities of the integrative and distributive dimensions is claimed by Prein (1976) and Van de Vliert (1990).

Because integration and distribution are primarily defined in terms of aspired outcomes, they refer to more than the conflict behavior as such. The same conflict behavior may attempt to realize quite different allocations of outcomes. Furthermore, conflict behaviors and ultimate outcomes are far from perfectly correlated. Different modes of conflict behavior may have the same consequences under different circumstances, whereas the same modes of conflict behavior may lead to various benefits or costs in various situations. Thus, strictly speaking, a certain conflict behavior cannot be coded as more or less integrative and more or less distributive if the behavioral outcomes are as yet unknown. In other words, integration and distribution cannot validly serve as descriptors of conflict behavior. This is even more true for the pair of descriptive dimensions discussed next.

Mitigation–Intensification and Passive–Active

Sternberg and his coworkers (Sternberg & Dobson, 1987; Sternberg & Soriano, 1984) had students rate the extent to which each of 16 behavioral styles characterized their own and others' ways of dealing with conflict in a variety of situations. They then conducted several factor analyses, and interpreted their results to reflect two independent dimensions, namely mitigation–intensification and passive–active. The inferred rather than observed concept of mitigation was used to implicitly classify activities including "step down," "bargain/compromise," and "mutual discussion" as high on deescalation. Likewise, activities such as "withholding," "manipulate," and "verbal force" were incorrectly enriched by classifying them as high on intensification, the opposite pole of mitigation. Forms of passiveness included "avoid," "wait and see," and "give in," whereas forms of activeness included "discuss," "confront," and "force."

Because mitigation refers to deescalatory whereas intensification refers to escalatory consequences, these constructs have the disadvantage of referring to behavioral outcomes rather than to behaviors themselves. Recall that this is a problem because reactions to conflict and ultimate outcomes are far from perfectly correlated. For example, from many other studies we know that process- and issue-oriented competition may have constructive consequences in overly harmonious or protest-repressive groups (e.g., Bartunek, Kolb, & Lewicki, 1992; Robbins, 1974; Turner & Pratkanis, 1994, 1998), but destructive consequences in conflicts where the group members' personal identities are at stake (e.g., Amason, 1996; Amason & Schweiger, 1994; Jehn, 1994; Van de Vliert & De Dreu, 1994).

A more appropriate label than mitigation–intensification exists to capture Sternberg and Dobson's (1987) factual behavioral differences. This apt behavioral pendant of mitigating–intensifying consequences is Bales's (1950) observation category of showing agreement ("accepts, understands, concurs; tends to show tension release and solidarity") versus disagreement ("withholds help, shows formality, rejects; tends to show tension and antagonism"). Unlike mitigation–intensification, Sternberg and Dobson's (1987) passiveness and activeness are indeed restricted to behavioral descriptions as such. They are real and readable features of the group members' reactions, which make them suitable to distinguish among ways of conflict handling.

In conclusion, descriptions of conflict behaviors in terms of behavioral causes or consequences should be avoided as much as possible, because such descriptions confound independent and dependent variables. Descriptive dimensions that remain much closer to pure characteristics of conflict handling are agreeable–disagreeable and passive–active. Relying on Sternberg and Dobson's (1987) factor analyses, agreeableness and activeness may be conceptualized as orthogonal dimensions that every behavior has in common with other behaviors.

Agreeableness and Activeness as Descriptors of a Metataxonomy

Conflict behaviors are agreeable to the extent that they make a pleasant and relaxed rather than unpleasant and strainful impression; and they are active to the extent that they make a responsive and direct rather than inert and undirect impression. Viewed in these ways, agreeableness and activeness should have the potency to integrate a variety of as yet unrelated taxonomies of conflict behaviors into a metataxonomy. This will be subsequently shown for Deutsch's (1949, 1973) cooperation–competition dichotomy, Horney's (1945) moving away, moving toward, and moving against trichotomy, and the five-part taxonomy of avoiding, accommodating, compromising, problem solving, and competing (e.g., Hall, 1969; Rahim, 1992; Rubin et al., 1994; Thomas, 1988, 1992a, 1992b, who all built on the seminal work of Blake & Mouton, 1964, 1970). Because the five-part taxonomy can be criticized for underrepresenting relatively aggressive reactions, agreeableness and activity will also be used to formulate a more accurate as well as a more generally applicable eight-part taxonomy that includes four types of fighting.

Cooperation–Competition. Cooperation is typically seen as representing an agreeable activity, whereas competition constitutes a disagreeable activity (e.g., Axelrod, 1984; Johnson & Johnson, 1989; Thomas, 1976, 1988). However, this bifurcation is a rather undifferentiated division in which both cooperation and competition have passive and active behavioral variants. Cooperation varies from passive and sometimes hardly agreeable noncompetition, to active and preeminently agreeable resolution of the conflict issue (Van de Vliert, 1997). In fact, the dichotomy conceptualizes cooperation as a residual category of noncompetition ranging from passive to active cooperation.

Moving Away–Toward–Against. Horney's (1945) conceptual scheme of passively moving away or withdrawing from people and from confrontation, actively moving toward people, and aggressively moving against people can be seen as a result of refining the concept of noncompetition along the lines of passive and active cooperation. In organizational units, Lawrence and Lorsch (1967) found exactly these three modes of handling conflict outlined by Horney (1945). Highly similar empirical results have been reported by others (e.g., Weider-Hatfield, 1988; Wilson & Waltman, 1988). Putnam and Wilson (1982) described the three factors resulting from their factor analysis as nonconfrontation (moving away), solution orientation (moving toward), and control (moving against). Active cooperation or solution orientation, directed at a mutually acceptable or mutually satisfactory agreement between the conflict parties, has also been called *negotiation* (e.g., Gulliver, 1979; Pruitt, 1981; Wall, 1985).

Five-Part Taxonomy. The five-part taxonomy of avoiding, accommodating, compromising, problem solving, and competing (Blake & Mouton, 1964, 1970; Hall, 1969; Rahim, 1992; Thomas, 1988, 1992a, 1992b) can be understood in the light of the following two conceptual refinements of the foregoing trichotomy. In the first place, it makes sense to assume that avoiding and accommodating are different ways by which one can move away and refrain from a proactive stance (cf. Rubin et al., 1994). Nonconfrontation will tend to take the form of no signals of agreement or disagreement whatsoever if one avoids but of signals of agreement if one accommodates. So, less agreeable avoidance and more agreeable accommodation can well be subsumed under passive nonconfrontation.

Similarly, active cooperation by negotiation can be broken down into settling for a compromise through a less agreeable process of give and take and solving the problem through a more agreeable process of satisfying all parties' wishes completely (cf. Putnam & Wilson, 1989; Van de Vliert & Hordijk, 1989; Walton & McKersie, 1965). This further subdivision results in the five-part typology, which has repeatedly been supported empirically in organizational contexts (e.g., Prein, 1976; Rahim, 1983; Van de Vliert & Kabanoff, 1990; Van de Vliert & Prein, 1989).

Eight-Part Taxonomy. Of course, five is an arbitrary rather than the "right" number of behavioral categories. As we now argue, there are reasons to subdivide competition into two forms of indirect fighting (process controlling and resisting) and two forms of direct fighting (issue fighting and outcome fighting).

First of all, it makes sense to assume that competition varies on the continuum of activeness as well. We prefer the terms passive and active fighting to passive and active competition, because fighting does not necessarily restrict itself to a sportsmanlike contest in which the conflicting parties share the same interest and accept the same rules of play (cf. Filley, 1975). Although fighting is never as passive as nonconfrontation through avoiding or accommodating, two relatively inactive variants of indirect fighting do exist, one that is not and one that is disagreeable. Process controlling, the often masked domination of the adversary by dominating the group's procedures to one's own advantage (Putnam & Wilson, 1982; Sheppard, 1984), is not or is hardly disagreeable. It notably includes forcing the agenda and the rules of the game to one's will, often in such a way that the procedures are seen as fair (Lax & Sebenius, 1986; Lind & Tyler, 1988; Sheppard, Lewicki, & Minton, 1992). Its disagreeable counterpart covering devious ways of passive resistance and concealment, in particular, may be labeled *resisting* (Bisno, 1988; Glasl, 1980). If at all possible, face-to-face contacts are avoided while one obstructs the others' plans, talks behind the others' back, or forms a hidden alliance with initial outsiders.

In contrast to indirect fighting, direct fighting is the active and straightforward domination of the individual or collective opponent with regard to the content of the conflict (Sheppard, 1984; Volkema & Bergmann, 1989). It can be broken down into issue fighting that is not disagreeable, and outcome fighting that is disagreeable. *Issue fighting*, or confronting (Prein, 1976), refers to acts of demanding the opponent's attention to one's own frustrations and to unilateral acts of launching the conflict issue and taking initial positions, whereas *outcome fighting* refers to acts of winning ground and ultimately defeating the opponent.

Figure 9.1 summarizes the eight-part taxonomy in terms of agreeableness and activeness. The pattern of similarities and differences among the eight modes of conflict behavior in this metataxonomy was translated into the following two testable hypotheses. *Hypothesis 1:* Conflict behaviors are less positively or more negatively related to agreeableness in the following order of main types: (a) accommodating and problem solving; (b) avoiding and compromising; and (c) indirect fighting, issue fighting, and outcome fighting. *Hypothesis 2:* Conflict behaviors are less positively or more negatively related to activeness in the following order of main types: (a) issue fighting, outcome fighting, compromising, and problem solving; (b) indirect fighting; and (c) avoiding and accommodating.

Systematic observations of videotaped simulations by 82 male police sergeants handling a standardized escalating conflict with either a subordinate or a superior supported this metataxonomy (Van de Vliert & Euwe-

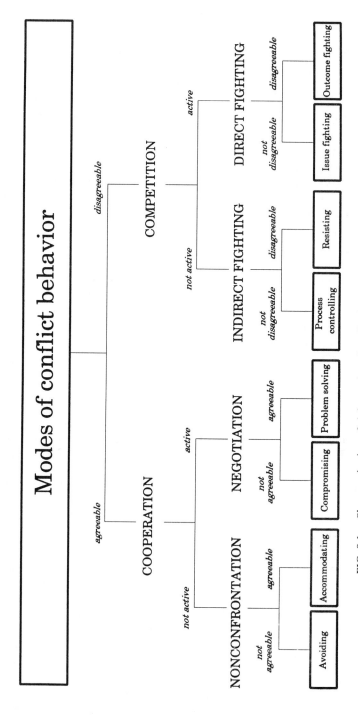

FIG. 9.1. Characterization of eight modes of conflict behavior in terms of agreeableness and activeness.

ma, 1994). That is, the hypothesized pattern of relations between the conflict behaviors and agreeableness as well as activeness was confirmed; this pattern even tended to be identical for sergeants in the respective roles of superior and subordinate. So, agreeableness and activeness seem to really pave the way for integration of heretofore separated descriptive theories of main reactions to social conflicts.

Complex Conflict Behavior

Obviously, agreeableness and activeness interrelate not only taxonomies but also specific modes of conflict behavior. For example, accommodating stands out as the opposite of outcome fighting, and compromising considerably overlaps issue fighting and problem solving. It implies that the field experiment in police organizations also supported a whole configuration of similarities and differences among avoiding, accommodating, compromising, problem solving, process controlling, resisting, issue fighting, and outcome fighting (Van de Vliert & Euwema, 1994). In other words, rather than being pure and mutually independent, as a rule, conflict behaviors are complex conglomerations of interrelated behavioral components (for the origins of this viewpoint, see Van de Vliert & Hordijk, 1989; Van de Vliert & Kabanoff, 1990; Van de Vliert & Prein, 1989).

Conglomerated conflict behavior refers to an aggregation of various degrees of several modes of conflict handling (Van de Vliert, 1997; Van de Vliert, Euwema, & Huismans, 1995). The behavioral components in a conglomeration may occur simultaneously or they may be sequentially linked to each other (Van de Vliert, Nauta, Giebels, & Janssen, 1999). For example, "tacit bargaining" is a merger of reactions in which one sticks to one's guns and withholds relevant information while revealing obligingness and real interests through nonverbal cues (Pruitt & Carnevale, 1993; Putnam, 1990). In contrast, Blake and Mouton's (1964) "paternalism" is a conglomeration of demanding compliance and subsequently offering security and well-being in return. Paternalism is just one illustration of fighting and problem solving, or even accommodating, operating in sequential juxtaposition (for additional and more complex examples, see Blake & Mouton, 1964; Putnam, 1990; Rubin et al., 1994; Van de Vliert, 1997).

A behavioral conglomeration can be described in terms of both the *intensity* with which each component occurs, and the *correlation* between each component and each of the other components. For all components together, this results in a configuration of relative degrees of occurrence, and a configuration of relative levels of covariation. For instance, indirect fighting to settle a disagreement in a task force in a fair way might be characterized by avoiding for 20%, compromising for 15%, process controlling for 40%, and resisting for 25%. In addition, this complex fight might yield the following six correlations: avoiding–compromising .05; avoiding–process controlling −.35; avoiding–resisting .15; compromising–process controlling .45; compromising–resisting −.25; process controlling–resisting .25. In this dual pattern of occurrence and covariation, process controlling, which occurs most, tends to be opposite to avoiding and clearly overlaps compromising.

Of course, the conceptualization of conflict behavior as complex and conglomerated instead of simple and pure, does not produce a parsimonious descriptive paradigm. However, this disadvantage is counterbalanced by several advantages. First of all, the patterns of occurrence and covariation mirror a person's behaviors much more adequately than the data on single types commonly reported. They do not ignore relevant forms of reaction that supplement the dominant response. Second, the patterns make a promising research device: The pattern of occurrence consists of a simple set of means, and the pattern of covariation consists of a simple set of correlations. Third, the pattern of covariation emphasizes that the components of conflict behavior are not independent. This is an important observation given the fact that designers of self-assessment instruments (e.g., Hall, 1969; Lawrence & Lorsch, 1967; Putnam & Wilson, 1982; Rahim, 1983; Thomas & Kilmann, 1974) attempt to construct factorially independent subscales, and that they do not control a subscale's relation with a validation criterion for the mutual relations among the subscales. Finally, with the help of multidimensional scaling techniques, the pattern of covariation of a conglomeration's behavioral components may be visualized. The resulting picture usually brings out behavioral features that are obscured in the numerical representation of the data (for examples, see Van de Vliert, 1990, 1997; Van de Vliert & Hordijk, 1989; Van de Vliert & Kabanoff, 1990).

Recapitulation

Agreeableness and activeness, which are appropriate descriptors of intragroup conflict behavior as they do not confound independent and dependent variables, appear to integrate dichotomies, trichotomies, and more extended taxonomies of conflict behavior. Additionally, they specify an empirically supported pattern of interrelations among avoiding, accommodating, compromising, problem solving, process controlling, resisting, issue fighting, and outcome fighting. This suggests that modes of conflict management are complex conglomerations of interrelated behavioral components rather than pure and mutually independent behaviors. Each conglomeration can be operationalized in terms of a pattern of occurrence and a pattern of covariation of its behavioral components. But why does particular conflict behavior occur in the first place?

EXPLANATORY THEORIES OF CONFLICT BEHAVIOR

So-called *structural models* are oriented toward rather stable conditions that determine how actors decide among the conflict behaviors; organization and group characteristics, the parties' relationship and their predispositions, the degree of mutual dependence and incompatibility of interests, pressure from others, rules and procedures, and so forth (Katz & Kahn, 1978; Lewicki, Weiss, & Lewin, 1992; Thomas, 1992b; Van de Vliert, 1998a). A good illustration are Mintzberg's (1979) propositions about how conflict is handled in organizations structured as rigid machine bureaucracies versus flexible adhocracies. In the machine bureaucracy, characterized by centralization, standardization of work processes, and external control, conflict is neither resolved nor battled out; rather it is bottled up so that the work can get done (cf. avoiding, accommodating, process controlling, resisting). In the adhocracy, characterized by decentralization, mutual adjustment, and expert control, conflict is not bottled up; rather it is channeled to productive ends to fuse the individualistic experts into smoothly functioning multidisciplinary teams (cf. compromising, problem solving, issue fighting, outcome fighting).

In contrast to structural models, *process models* are oriented toward the cyclical and dynamic antecedents of conflict behaviors including frustration, conceptualization of the issue, action, reaction, consequence, renewed frustration, and so forth (De Dreu, Nauta, & Van de Vliert, 1995; Filley, 1975; Lewicki et al., 1992; Rahim, 1992; Thomas, 1992b; Walton, 1987). Interpersonal theory, for example, proposes that a party's conflict behaviors constrain the other party's subsequent conflict behaviors (Kiesler, 1983; Orford, 1986, 1994; Pruitt, 1981; Tracey, 1994). The complementarity rule asserts that dominance pulls submission, and that submission pulls dominance. The reciprocity rule asserts that hostility pulls hostility, and that friendliness pulls friendliness, or in the words of Deutsch's (1973, p. 365) crude law of social relations, "the characteristic processes and effects elicited by a given type of social relationship . . . tend also to elicit that type of social relationship." Although more empirical evidence exists for the reciprocity rule than for the complementarity rule, there is no doubt that such "behavioral reflexes" account for some variance in interpersonal conflict behaviors.

Whereas structural models tend to neglect the dynamics and consequences of conflicts, process models tend to pay little attention to the more permanent causes of conflicts. Because intragroup conflicts typically place the group members in both a constellation of stable conditions (structural model) and a sequence of events (process model), an explanatory theory should integrate elements from the two types of models as much as possible. To date, at least one theory provides a parsimonious and sufficiently general set of rules of correspondence between structural characteristics of the environment and subsequent social-psychological processes, to wit: Deutsch's (1949, 1973) *goal interdependence theory*. However, this theory is insufficiently accurate in that it neglects each party's goal strength and predicts only constructive cooperation and destructive competition (Van de Vliert, 1998b). We therefore attempt to integrate the goal interdependence theory and the *dual goal concern theory* (Blake & Mouton, 1964, 1970), which predicts the five conflict behaviors from the five-part taxonomy discussed earlier. We describe the two theories, then list their commonalities and differences to finally present an integrative interdependence concerns theory.

Goal Interdependence Theory

According to Deutsch (1949, 1973), people pursue goals through the employment of activities. A dyadic conflict exists if one individual perceives that his or her activities are incompatible with those of another. The central thesis of the theory postulates that a party's conflict behavior is determined by the relation he or she perceives between his or her own goals and the opponent's goals, whereby both types of goals are based on the group structure, the personality structure, or both. Fundamentally, two types of goal linkages are formulated, positive or promotive versus negative or contrient goal interdependence. Some scholars sometimes refer to these goal linkages as cooperative versus competitive context or structure (e.g., Johnson, Maruyama, Johnson, Nelson & Skon, 1981; Tjosvold, 1991), which again should be discouraged because it confounds descriptors and predictors.

In the case of *positive interdependence*, a conflict party experiences not only incompatible activities but also a positive relation between the parties' goals, that is, each party can only reach its goals if the other party also reaches its goals ("sink or swim together"). Such perceptions may be found, for instance, in an ambience of teamwork against a background of rewards for the group as a whole, and in a situation of crisis that can be solved by joint effort only. Positive goal linkages foster the willingness to allow someone else's actions to be substituted for one's own (substitutability), the development of positive attitudes toward each other (positive cathexis), and the readiness to be influenced positively by one another (inducibility), which subsequently results in cooperative behavior, as is illustrated in Fig. 9.2. Considerable research supported the proposition that conflict parties under circumstances of greater positive interdependence cooperate more (Deutsch, 1973; Johnson & Johnson, 1989; Tjosvold, 1989, 1990).

By contrast, in case of *negative interdependence*, one experiences not only incompatible activities but also a negative relation between the respective

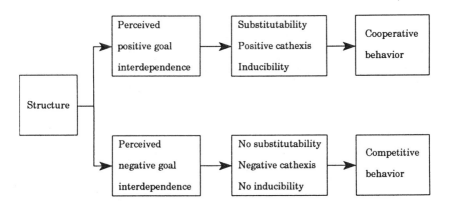

FIG. 9.2. Representation of conflict behavior as an indirect function of environmental structure and perceived goal interdependence.

goals, that is, each party can only achieve its goals if the other party does not attain its goals ("if one swims the other sinks"). Such perceptions especially occur when there are generally desired scarce resources including money, facilities, materials, space, manpower, information, status, power. Negative goal linkages foster unwillingness to allow the opponent's actions to be substituted for one's own (no substitutability), negative attitudes toward each other (negative cathexis), and resistance to be influenced by the adversary (no inducibility), which results in competitive conflict behavior (see Fig. 9.2). The aforementioned research also provides evidence in support of the claim that negative interdependence elicits the vigorous pursuit of one's own interests at the expense of the opponent's interests.

In intragroup conflicts, goal interdependence nearly always consists of a mix of positively and negatively interdependent goals, the so-called mixed motive situations (e.g., Deutsch, 1973; Lax & Sebenius, 1986). According to Deutsch (1973, p. 22), extrapolation from the "pure" situation to the more complex one is often self-evident, as the relative strengths of the perceived positive and negative goal linkages will determine the direction of the resulting processes. We believe that this view is rather simplistic. Instead, as is discussed later, we assume that mixed goal interdependencies elicit conglomerated rather than purely cooperative or competitive conflict behavior.

Dual Goal Concern Theory

Blake and Mouton (1964, 1970) defined conflict as differences in the ways people think and act. According to their dual goal concern theory—further developed by Rubin et al. (1994), and Van de Vliert (1997)—conflict behavior is determined by two elementary motives, concern about one's own goals (hereinafter self-concern), and concern about the others' goals (hereinafter other-concern), as is illustrated in Fig. 9.3. The importance of the dual goal concern theory in organizational psychology is underlined by the existence of the highly similar theory of social motives in social psychology (McClintock, 1976; Van de Vliert, 1997). The latter theory also postulates basic orientations toward one's own and others' outcomes when dealing with opponents. The weights assigned to one's own and other's outcomes then determine the more specific orientations of individualism, altruism, cooperation, competition, and aggression (for recent work in this tradition, see De Dreu & Van Lange, 1995; Kramer, McClintock, & Messick, 1986; McClintock & Allison, 1989; McClintock & Liebrand, 1988; Van Lange, 1992).

On the basis of the strength of each goal concern, the dual goal concern theory predicts a variety of conflict behaviors, including avoiding, accommodating, compromising, problem solving, and fighting. Equal concern about one's own and the other's goals results in avoiding in case of weak dual concern, in compromising in case of moderate dual concern, and in problem solving in case of strong dual concern. Strong one-sided

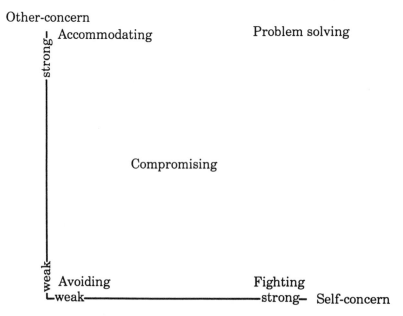

FIG. 9.3.   Representation of conflict behavior as a direct function of concern for one's own goals (self-concern) and concern for the others' goals (other-concern).

other-concern activates accommodating, whereas strong one-sided self-concern brings about fighting. The concerns can have both independent and interactive effects on the five behavioral modes.

Three experimental studies reported in Rubin et al. (1994), and a more recent study (Janssen & Van de Vliert, 1996), all indicated that self-concern and other-concern do indeed codetermine the conflict parties' behavior in line with the typological specifications of the dual goal concern theory. There is one noteworthy exception. Compromising appears to be located between accommodating and problem solving rather than in the middle of the other main modes of conflict management. It results from strong rather than moderate other-concern (Cosier & Ruble, 1981; Janssen & Van de Vliert, 1996; Kabanoff, 1987; Pruitt & Carnevale, 1993; Ruble & Thomas, 1976; Van de Vliert & Hordijk, 1989).

Commonalities and Differences

The interdependence theory as well as the dual goal concern theory restricts its explanation of conflict behavior to situations in which a conflict already exists. In addition, both theories restrain the clarification of conflict behavior to situations in which actors are not only aware of their own goals but also of the opponent's goals. Whereas the goal interdependence theory views the positive or negative linkage structure between one's own and the other's goals as the root of conflict behavior, the dual goal concern theory views the concerns for one's own and the other's goals as the behavioral roots. In view of these similarities, it is surprising that two theories that cover virtually the same object of study were never related to each other in a systematic way.

The first difference concerns the operationalization of conflict behavior. Whereas the interdependence theory uses the classical one-dimensional dichotomy of cooperation and competition, the dual goal concern theory addresses the more refined five-part taxonomy. Second, goal interdependence as the origin of behavior refers to the perception of goal linkage structures, whereas self-concern and other-concern are in essence two fundamental motives to create and distribute outcomes for oneself and the opponent. Compared to the perception of goal interdependence, the goal concerns are often embedded less in the environmental structure and more in the conflicting individuals themselves. Third, goal interdependence reflects the correlation between goals, whereas the goal concerns reflect the level of commitment to one's own and the other's goals. Fourth, positive and negative goal interdependence are mutually exclusive behavioral determinants. In contrast, self-concern and other-concern are two independent motivational dimensions. By implication, positive and negative goal interdependence evoke mutually exclusive cooperative and competitive behavior, respectively, whereas self-concern and other-concern codetermine at least five modes of conflict behavior. Finally, perceptions of goal interdependence elicit conflict behavior indirectly via the mediators of substitutability, cathexis, and inducibility (see Fig. 9.2), whereas the concerns codetermine conflict behavior in a direct way (see Fig. 9.3). With these commonalities and differences as a point of departure, we now propose an integration of the interdependence theory and the dual goal concern theory into an overarching theory.

Interdependence Concerns Theory

As outlined, in the interdependence theory, substitutability, cathexis, and inducibility function as mediators between perceptions of goal interdependence and conflict behavior. The core of our proposal for integration includes the replacement of these three mediators by dual concern for one's own and the others' goals. More specifically, we propose an integrated theory in which the effect of perceived goal interdependence on conflict behavior is mediated by self-concern and other-concern, as is portrayed in Fig. 9.4.

The elementary motives from the dual goal concern theory are theoretically more convenient mediators than substitutability, cathexis, and inducibility for at least three reasons. First, the explicitly independent mutual relation between self-concern and other-concern is clear, whereas the interrelations among substitutability, cathexis, and inducibility are unclear. Second, self-concern and other-concern introduce more differentiation into the mediating function of the variables between the parties' goals and con-

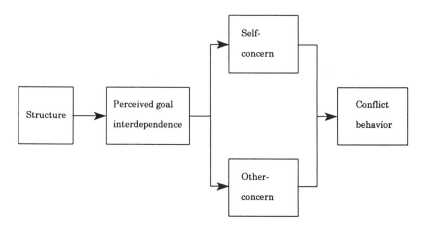

FIG. 9.4.   Interdependence concerns theory with self-concern and other-concern as mediators between perceived goal interdependence and conflict behavior.

flict behavior than do substitutability, cathexis, and inducibility. In case of positive or negative interdependence, self-concern and other-concern may change either in the same direction or in different directions, whereas substitutability, cathexis, and inducibility change *en bloc* in the same positive or negative direction. Third, the dual goal concern theory clearly states that self- and other-concern have a different impact when they codetermine the same conflict behavior, whereas the interdependence theory does not specify whether substitutability, cathexis, and inducibility have identical, independent, or joint behavioral effects.

Elsewhere (Janssen, Van de Vliert, Euwema, & Stroebe, 1996) we have reasoned out that positive goal interdependence tends to equalize group members' levels of self-concern and other-concern, whereas negative interdependence tends to produce opposite levels of strong self-concern versus low other-concern. Consequently, positive compared to negative interdependence will result in a stronger level of other-concern, which in turn will inhibit avoiding and outcome fighting, as well as activate accommodating, compromising, and problem solving. Predictions for process controlling, resisting, and issue fighting (see Fig. 9.1) were not developed yet. However, tests of descriptive theories (Van de Vliert, 1990, 1997) strongly suggest that process controlling and resisting result from moderate self-concern and low other-concern, whereas issue fighting results from strong self-concern and moderate other-concern.

To test the interdependence concerns theory, we conducted a scenario study and a simulation experiment, both with the conflict behaviors from the five-part taxonomy as dependent variables, and with student dyads as subjects. Positive relative to negative goal interdependence did indeed evoke more other-concern, which subsequently resulted in similar levels of avoiding, more accommodating, more compromising, more problem solving, and less outcome fighting. Other-concern rather than self-concern emerged as the main mediator between goal interdependence and conflict behavior. It implies that changes in other- rather than self-concern are key to processes of conflict deescalation or escalation (Janssen & Van de Vliert, 1996; Janssen et al., 1996; Van de Vliert, 1997). All this challenges the dominant paradigm in which self- rather than other-concern is seen as the paramount motivator of conflict behavior (for overviews, see Greenhalgh, 1987; Pruitt & Carnevale, 1993; Thompson, 1990).

Complex Conflict Behavior

The interdependence concerns theory may be applied to the phenomenon of conglomerated conflict behavior by assuming that the behavioral components cannot be explained by a single degree of positive or negative goal interdependence. An important scientific leap forward might be made if it would be shown that a conflicting group member has multiple goal interdependencies with the other group members. As a consequence, this group member will also have more than one level of concern for one's own goals as well as more than one level of concern for the other group members' goals, simultaneously, sequentially, or even both. In theory, in polarized conflicts, and in almost every negotiation, each side will have multiple interdependencies and interests, not just one (Fisher & Ury, 1981; Roloff & Jordan, 1992; Thomas, 1992b). To cite Deutsch (1973, p. 21), "Most situations of everyday life involve a complex set of goals and subgoals." Also, multiple levels of concern for one's own and others' goals may originate from short-term and long-term perspectives (cf. Thomas, 1992). Those various interdependency-based goals are the cradle of multiple instantaneous or changing combinations of dual goal concern and subsequent components of conglomerated conflict behavior.

Consider the following example of concerns complexity in a Dutch municipal corporation in which a "conservative" mayor is both positively and negatively interdependent with more "progressive" local councilors. The mayor falls out with the councilors regarding a forbidden demonstration against the liberal policy of drug abuse. Given his conservative attitude, he is sympathetic to the ideal of a more preserving policy that the demonstration hopes to bring nearer. He has also developed some supportive concern for the opponents' plan to now use the ban on the demonstration as a propaganda stunt. At the same time, the mayor becomes highly concerned about loss of face when giving in by permitting the demonstration. Undoubtedly, this constellation of interdepencence-based goal concerns will motivate the mayor to create conglomerated conflict behavior. Through tacit coordination, the opponents' propaganda stunt might be facilitated by maintaining both ban and face, while valuable replacements for the demonstration might be negotiated. To support managers and other policymakers facing social problems, and their consultants, studies of the behavioral determinants in such complex conflict situations are urgently necessary.

Recapitulation

Although goal interdependence theory takes into account both structure and process when explaining cooperation and competition, it may be improved and extended by integrating it with the dual goal concern theory into an interdependence concerns theory. Positive goal interdependence tends to equalize the parties' levels of concern for one's own and others' goals, whereas negative goal interdependence tends to produce opposite levels of strong concern for one's own goals and weak concern for others' goals. Dual goal concern then explains the occurrence of avoiding, accommodating, compromising, problem solving, process controlling, resisting, issue fighting, and outcome fighting. The first tests of the integrated theory are encouraging, but its applicability to conglomerated conflict behavior is still in its infancy. As a consequence, we must be cautious with recommendations of particular conflict behavior.

PRESCRIPTIVE THEORIES OF CONFLICT BEHAVIOR

Ideally, a prescriptive theory is based on a solid explanatory theory that, in turn, is based on a solid descriptive theory. In addition, a good prescriptive theory is also based on empirical demonstrations of the surplus value of the recommended behavior. Hence, it is a pity that the majority of the prescriptive statements and models in the field of conflict management are still predominantly based on unsystematic observations, experience of many years, or even common sense. An apt illustration is Vroom and Yetton's (1973) well-known decision tree consisting of eight yes-or-no criterion questions and a set of decision rules to determine a leader's most desirable reaction to social conflict and other intragroup problems. In total, the tree's branches lead to 14 behavioral recommendations. Wall (1985, pp. 71–78) developed a similar tree with four ordered criterion questions to make the best choice from eight negotiation tactics. The criterion questions read: Is opponent engaging in inappropriate behavior? Is opponent contingently cooperative? Is future negotiation important? Does opponent have limited resources? And the negotiation options prescribed by the decision rules are conciliatory and reward tactics; threat and coercive tactics; soft, neutral, and tough posturing; and competitive debate.

We would like to contrast such decision aids, rules of thumb, and role prescriptions with the recommendations from the goal interdependence theory and the dual goal concern theory. These classic theories—the roots of our integrated interdependence concerns theory—do recommend courses of action based on empirical examinations of their effectiveness for the group. In the present context, *group effectiveness* refers to the extent to which the conflict behavior is producing desired outcomes for the conflicting group members together by overcoming the conflict issues, by improving the mutual relationship, or both (cf. Thomas, 1992b; Tjosvold, 1991; Van de Vliert et al., 1995).

Goal Interdependence Theory

From the theory's inception, Deutsch (1949) disseminated the message that positive interdependence elicits effective, constructive processes, whereas negative interdependence elicits ineffective, destructive processes. Over the years, considerable research has supported his corollary that conflict parties under circumstances of greater positive interdependence are more open-minded, feeling more motivated to understand others' arguments and desires, and reacting to the opponents in a more cooperative and deescalating way (Deutsch, 1973; Janssen et al., 1996; Johnson & Johnson, 1989; Johnson et al., 1981; Tjosvold, 1989, 1990).

The related recommendation has it that a group should be structured as much as possible in such a way that its group members need each other to be successful in their personal tasks, as in a good medical surgery team. This creation of functional complementarity, group remuneration, and the like, brings about clearly paramount, superordinate goals (Sherif, 1966), the realization of which offers the prospect of collective gain. Note that a superordinate goal goes beyond a common goal such as "each of us must produce as much as possible"; it is a common goal that the group members can only attain if they join their forces.

Implementation of positive goal interdependence is not altogether free of risks. It has been demonstrated to act ineffectively rather than effectively if the tasks of parties in a conflict are insufficiently differentiated so they do not really depend on one another (Brown & Wade, 1987), if group identity maintenance pressures exist that elicit groupthink and its aversive consequences (Turner & Pratkanis, 1994, 1998), if task conflict is not accompanied by person conflict, or vice versa (Janssen, Van de Vliert, & Veenstra, 1999) and if one of the parties in the conflict rather than a third party initiates the superordinate goal, this initiative giving a fresh impulse to hostilities (Johnson & Lewicki, 1969).

Another risk of employing positive goal interdependence as a design parameter of effective groups flows from the fact that the goal interdependence theory focuses on the relation between goals but neglects the levels of goal concern (Van de Vliert, 1998b). Promotive goal interdependence, that is, positive covariation of the group members' goals, is possible at both low and high levels of concern for both one's own and the opponent's goals (Janssen et al., 1996; Van de Vliert, 1997). Thus, relying on the theory, a lazy designer and technician who depend on each other for the realization of their facile goals would still be effecting a constructive conflict outcome. As this seems unlikely, it poses the theoretically interesting and practically important question whether positive goal interdependence stimulates group effectiveness only if members have at least moderately high task objectives.

Compared to the risky implementation of positive goal interdependence, the main prescription flowing from the related interdependence concerns theory stands out as more attractive. It reads that increases in concern for the opponent's goals deescalate the conflict and produce better substantive and relational outcomes (for empirical evidence, see Janssen & Van de Vliert, 1996). This alternative recommendation is less risky because it does not require the successful implementation of positive goal interdependence, and it does pay attention to the level of goal concern. In addition, it is a more parsimonious recommendation because it highlights concern for the opponent's goals whereas concern for one's own goals is left out of consideration completely.

Dual Goal Concern Theory

Blake and Mouton's (1964, 1970) seminal conflict management theory has generated four waves of prescriptive views. First, a one-best-way perspective stating that problem solving always serves the joint welfare best. Second, a contingency perspective asserting that each mode of conflict behavior is appropriate in some situations. Third, a time perspective suggesting that the contingency approach provides answers to the short-term question of how best to cope with the here and now, whereas the one-best-way approach deals with the longer term task of creating desirable future circumstances. Last, a complexity perspective proposing that conglomerated conflict behavior is needed to really optimize group effectiveness. We review these prescriptive frameworks in this order.

One-Best-Way Perspective.   Blake and Mouton (1970) stated that the high/high concurrence of the two concerns produces the most effective mode of conflict management: problem solving, also called the "fifth achievement." One decade later they even presented their dual goal concern theory as a one-best-style approach (Blake & Mouton, 1981, p. 441; for similar views, see Fisher & Ury, 1981; Pneuman & Bruehl, 1982).

Evidence exists both in favor of and against the standpoint that problem solving is the best way to handle conflict. Investigations of real-life superior–subordinate conflicts strongly suggest that integrative methods are both the most common and the most effective manners of conflict management (Barker, Tjosvold, & Andrews, 1988; Rahim, 1992; Renwick, 1977; Tjosvold, 1991; Volkema & Bergmann, 1989). More generally, it has also been documented that successful resolution not only removes the conflict issue, but also leads to greater group productivity, more creative and constructive outcomes (Butler, 1994; Jehn, 1995; Johnson, Johnson, & Smith, 1989; Rubin et al., 1994; Tutzauer & Roloff, 1988), trust and openness (Deutsch, 1973, 1980), attraction (Johnson et al., 1989), and depersonalization of future conflicts (Filley, 1975).

Arguments against the recommendation of problem solving, however, are that often insufficient opportunities for integration exist, that it is too time and energy consuming, and that unilateral openness and drawing attention to joint interests may escalate the conflict (Filley, 1975; Johnson & Lewicki, 1969; Walton, 1987). One illustration of this is the study by

Schweiger, Sandberg and Ragan (1986), who showed that the price of better but laborious solutions to the conflict may well be that the opponents fancy the idea of future cooperation less than before.

Contingency Perspective. A great number of authors have attacked the foregoing view, contending that there is no one best mode of conflict management. Instead, the answer regarding what is most successful can only be given in the light of situational realities (e.g., Axelrod, 1984; Gladwin & Walter, 1980; Rahim, 1992; Robbins, 1974; Thomas, 1977, 1992b). For example, experienced managers reported that it would be appropriate to adopt each mode of conflict behavior from the five-part taxonomy in a number of specific situations, including the following ones (Thomas, 1977): (a) avoiding when an issue is trivial, or more important issues are pressing, (b) accommodating to build social credits for later issues, especially when the present issue is more important to the opponent than to oneself, (c) compromising when goals are important but not worth the effort of more assertive modes, and under time pressure, (d) problem solving to gain commitment or to work through feelings that have interfered with a relationship, and (e) fighting when quick and decisive action is vital—that is, in emergencies—and when important but unpopular actions need implementing. Note that these prescriptions are either not or are hardly based on investigated explanations and effect evaluations of the conflict behaviors involved.

Time Perspective. Short-term wisdom may be long-term folly, and the other way around. By implication, short-term and long-term conflict management goals are not related to effectiveness in a predictable way. This fact has recently brought Thomas (1992a, 1992b) to the insight that the contingency perspective and the "problem-solving ethic" are reconcilable by taking two time horizons into account.

The contingency perspective supposedly focuses on coping with the immediate conflict situation emphasizing the best possible short-term outcomes. According to Thomas (1992a, 1992b), it does not move beyond the limitations of the current conditions and is relatively pragmatic in flavor. The one-best-way perspective of conflict resolution, on the other hand, supposedly focuses on the improvement of the social relations in the longer run. It emphasizes that contextual variables are changeable rather than given, and that the ideal functioning of the social system should be brought nearer by all manner of means.

Complexity Perspective. The one-best-way and contingency perspectives rest on three common presuppositions. First, a party to a conflict, at least within one cycle of transaction, uses only one pure mode of conflict behavior that is unrelated to other pure modes of conflict behavior. Second, this pure mode of conflict behavior is determined by one level of concern for one's own goals and one level of concern for others' goals. Third, as a rule, it is taken for granted that distinct modes of behavior only have a mutually independent influence on the substantive and relational outcomes of a conflict, and do not intermediate or moderate each other's impact on the effectiveness. The time perspective starts to introduce some complexity by focusing on behavioral sequentiality, still ignoring behavioral simultaneity.

In contrast, the complexity assumption proposed and discussed in this chapter holds, first of all, that conglomerated conflict behavior is very common and that its behavioral components are meaningfully interrelated rather than discrete. Furthermore, it is assumed that these behavioral components are a function of multiple goal concerns, including short- and long-term concerns for one's own and others' goals. Finally, we firmly believe that these behavioral components do intermediate and moderate each other's effectiveness.

As for intermediation, Van de Vliert et al. (1995) showed that problem solving is the most effective mode of police sergeants' and senior nurses' conflict behavior only if the other behavioral components are not controlled. If all behavioral components are simultaneously taken into consideration, process controlling is more rather than less effective than problem solving. The tentative order of increasing effectiveness of components of conglomerated conflict behavior is as follows: outcome fighting, avoiding, issue fighting, accommodating, compromising, problem solving, process controlling. It is worth noting that, quite paradoxically, the opposites of ineffective outcome fighting versus effective process controlling have more in common with each other than with any other behavioral component. Consequently, outcome fighting and process controlling stand out as a bad and a good alternative for getting one's way. To handle intragroup conflict more effectively, one should replace outcome fighting with process controlling.

Components of conglomerated conflict behavior also moderate each other's impact on the substantive and relational outcomes of the conflict. For example, in a recent field experiment in Dutch hospitals, Van de Vliert, Nauta, Euwema, and Janssen (1997) demonstrated that a larger component of problem solving is more effective, but especially so when combined with a larger component of outcome fighting (see Fig. 9.5). Interestingly, sex composition did not influence this interactive impact of problem solving and outcome fighting on the conflicting parties' joint effectiveness. The intriguing finding of the hospital study was replicated in a national development center of the police force, in a laboratory experiment, and among work dyads from industries, consultancy firms, and governmental institutions (Van de Vliert et al., 1999). Time and again, it could be shown that problem solving

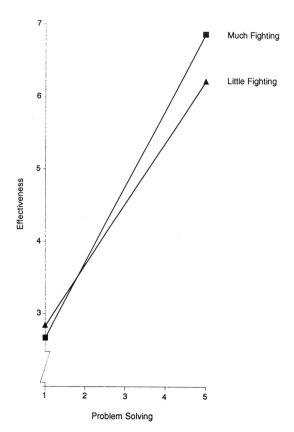

FIG. 9.5.   Effectiveness of conglomerated conflict behavior as an interactive function of the components of problem solving and outcome fighting.

and outcome fighting are frequently combined simultaneously and sequentially, and that the components of problem solving and outcome fighting especially enhance the parties' joint effectiveness in close conjunction with each other. The best substantive and relational outcomes for the organization appeared to be reached through outcome fighting followed by problem solving.

The last results seem to corroborate the alleged recommendability of *constructive controversy*, signifying that more controversial behavior within problem-solving groups evokes better ideas and more creative group decisions, more satisfaction, and more commitment to the implementations of the decisions (Amason, 1996; Amason & Schweiger, 1994; Cosier, 1978; Janis, 1982; Jehn, 1994, 1995; Johnson et al., 1989; Schweiger, Sandberg, & Rechner, 1989; Schwenk, 1990; Turner & Pratkanis, 1994, 1998; Van de Vliert & De Dreu, 1994; Walton, Cutcher-Gershenfeld & McKersie, 1994).

Recapitulation

Much too often, contingency frameworks and other prescriptive theories of conflict behavior rest on educated speculation or practical experience rather than on research-based descriptions, explanations, and effect evaluations. Although this critique does not apply to the goal interdependence theory and the dual goal concern theory, these paradigms have other weaknesses. Notably, the goal interdependence theory neglects the requirement of high levels of goal concern as a group design parameter, whereas the original dual goal concern theory focuses too narrowly on the one-best-way reaction of problem solving. Simultaneous or sequential conglomerations of problem solving and outcome fighting appear to be more recommendable than pure problem solving or fighting.

ADVANTAGES OF OUR VIEWPOINT

In the introduction, descriptive, explanatory, and prescriptive theories are defined as three qualitatively different approaches. In fact, they represent a metatheory that is simple, general, and accurate. Once this viewpoint is adopted, it is quite easy to interrelate rather than mix up the what, why, and how-to aspects of a phenomenon such as intragroup conflict behavior. For example, it immediately caught our eye that concern for one's own and others' goals, as well as integration and distribution, are often incorrectly used to describe group members' conflict behaviors in terms of behavioral causes or consequences. Conversely, good behavioral descriptors such as cooperation and competition were unmasked as being no good adjectives of behavioral predictors. It became similarly obvious that, to date, still too many prescriptive statements and models about effective conflict management lack adequate descriptive operationalization and explanatory empirical demonstration.

As an additional benefit, our approach reinforces the apt metaphor that, just like concrete building, theory building always comes in layers. Conceptually interrelated and empirically viable descriptors are needed to lay the foundation. Empirically supported rules of correspondence between the descriptors and their determinants or consequences are then needed to reach the level of explanation. Finally, a prescriptive theory recommending successful courses of action is valid and applicable only to the extent that it is based on a solid explanatory theory that, in turn, is based on a solid descriptive theory. Along these lines, we have developed and supported the intriguing proposition that conglomerated conflict behavior with both a large component of problem solving and a large component of outcome fighting is a recommendable course of action.

CONCLUDING PROPOSITIONS

The most important messages in this chapter on intragroup conflict behaviors may be summarized in the following seven propositions.

Viewpoint
1. The distinction between descriptive, explanatory, and prescriptive theories fosters scholarly progress and practical improvement.
Description
2. The dichotomy of cooperation and competition, the trichotomy of moving away–toward–against, and the typology of avoiding, accommodating, compromising, problem solving, and fighting, are interrelated in terms of their agreeableness and activeness.
3. A person's reaction to intragroup conflict is a complex simultaneous or sequential aggregation of various degrees of several interrelated behavioral components, referred to as conglomerated conflict behavior.
Explanation
4. Positive goal interdependence tends to equalize the parties' levels of concern for one's own and others' goals, whereas negative goal interdependence tends to produce opposite levels of strong concern for one's own goals and weak concern for others' goals.
5. A conflicting group member has multiple goal interdependencies and, consequently, multiple combined levels of concern for one's own and others' goals, which codetermine the degrees of occurrence of the behavioral components.
Prescription
6. The implementation of positive goal interdependence to enhance group effectiveness may be recommended only if at least moderately high levels of concern for one's own and others' goals are present.
7. Especially recommendable is conglomerated conflict behavior with both a large component of problem solving and a large component of outcome fighting.

REFERENCES

Amason, A. C. (1996). Distinguishing the effects of functional and dysfunctional conflict on strategic decision making: Resolving a paradox for top management teams. *Academy of Management Journal, 39*, 123–148.
Amason, A. C., & Schweiger, D. M. (1994). Resolving the paradox of conflict, strategic decision making, and organizational performance. *International Journal of Conflict Management, 5*, 239–253.
Axelrod, R. (1984). *The evolution of cooperation.* New York: Basic Books.

Bales, R. F. (1950). *Interaction process analysis: A method for the study of small groups.* Reading, MA: Addison-Wesley.

Barker, J., Tjosvold, D., & Andrews, I. R. (1988). Conflict approaches of effective and ineffective project managers: A field study in a matrix organization. *Journal of Management Studies, 25,* 167–178.

Bartunek, J. M., Kolb, D. M., & Lewicki, R. (1992). Bringing conflict out from behind the scenes. In D. M. Kolb & J. M. Bartunek (Eds.), *Hidden conflict in organizations: Uncovering behind-the-scenes disputes* (pp. 209–228). Newbury Park, CA: Sage.

Bisno, H. (1988). *Managing conflict.* Newbury Park, CA: Sage.

Blake, R. R., & Mouton, J. S. (1964). *The managerial grid.* Houston, TX: Gulf.

Blake, R. R., & Mouton, J. S. (1970). The fifth achievement. *Journal of Applied Behavioral Science, 6,* 413–426.

Blake, R. R., & Mouton, J. S. (1981). Management by grid principles or situationalism: Which? *Group and Organization Studies, 6,* 439–455.

Brown, R., & Wade, G. (1987). Superordinate goals and intergroup behavior: The effects of role ambiguity and status on intergroup attitudes and task performance. *European Journal of Social Psychology, 17,* 131–142.

Butler, J. K., Jr. (1994). Conflict styles and outcomes in a negotiation with fully-integrative potential. *International Journal of Conflict Management, 5,* 309–325.

Cosier, R. A. (1978). The effects of three potential aids for making strategic decisions on prediction accuracy. *Organizational Behavior and Human Performance, 22,* 295–306.

Cosier, R. A., & Ruble, T. L. (1981). Research on conflict-handling behavior: An experimental approach. *Academy of Management Journal, 24,* 816–831.

Daves, W. F., & Holland, C. L. (1989). The structure of conflict behavior of managers assessed with self- and subordinate ratings. *Human Relations, 42,* 741–756.

De Dreu, C. K. W., Nauta, A., & Van de Vliert, E. (1995). Self-serving evaluations of conflict behavior and escalation of the dispute. *Journal of Applied Social Psychology, 25,* 2049–2066.

De Dreu, C. K. W., & Van Lange, P. A. M. (1995). The impact of social value orientations on negotiator cognition and behavior. *Personality and Social Psychology Bulletin, 21,* 1178–1188.

Deutsch, M. (1949). A theory of cooperation and competition. *Human Relations, 2,* 129–151.

Deutsch, M. (1973). *The resolution of conflict: Constructive and destructive processes.* New Haven, CT: Yale University Press.

Deutsch, M. (1980). Fifty years of conflict. In L. Festinger (Ed.), *Retrospections on social psychology* (pp. 46–77). New York: Oxford University Press.

Filley, A. C. (1975). *Interpersonal conflict resolution.* Glenview, IL: Scott, Foresman.

Fisher, R., & Ury, W. (1981). *Getting to yes: Negotiating agreement without giving in.* London: Hutchinson.

Gladwin, T. N., & Walter, I. (1980). *Multinationals under fire: Lessons in the management of conflict.* New York: Wiley.

Glasl, F. (1980). *Konfliktmanagement: Diagnose und Behandlung von Konflikt in Organisationen* [Conflict management: Diagnosis and treatment of conflict in organizations]. Bern: Haupt.

Greenhalgh, L. (1987). Interpersonal conflicts in organizations. In C. L. Cooper & I. T. Robertson (Eds.), *International review of industrial and organizational psychology* (pp. 229–271). Chichester, England: Wiley.

Gulliver, P. H. (1979). *Disputes and negotiations: A cross-cultural perspective.* New York: Academic Press.

Hall, J. (1969). *Conflict management survey.* Conroe, TX: Teleometrics International.

Horney, K. (1945). *Our inner conflicts: A constructive theory of neurosis.* New York: Norton.

Janis, I. L. (1982). *Groupthink* (2nd ed.). Boston, MA: Houghton Mifflin.

Janssen, O., & Van de Vliert, E. (1996). Concern for the other's goals: Key to (de-)escalation of conflict. *International Journal of Conflict Management, 7,* 99–120.

Janssen, O., Van de Vliert, E., Euwema, M. C., & Stroebe, W. (1996). *How goal interdependence motivates conflict behavior.* Unpublished manuscript, University of Groningen, the Netherlands.

Janssen, O., Van de Vliert, E., & Veenstra, C. (1999). How task and person conflict shape the role of positive interdependence in management teams. *Journal of Conflict Management, 25,* 117–142.

Jehn, K. A. (1994). Enhancing effectiveness: An investigation of advantages and disadvantages of value-based intragroup conflict. *International Journal of Conflict Management, 5,* 223–238.

Jehn, K. A. (1995). A multimethod examination of the benefits and detriments of intragroup conflict. *Administrative Science Quarterly, 40,* 256–282.

Johnson, D. W., & Johnson, R. T. (1989). *Cooperation and competition: Theory and research.* Edina, MN: Interaction Book Company.

Johnson, D. W., Johnson, R. T., & Smith, K. (1989). Controversy within decision making situations. In M. A. Rahim (Ed.), *Managing conflict: An interdisciplinary approach* (pp. 251–264). New York: Praeger.

Johnson, D. W., & Lewicki, R. J. (1969). The initiation of superordinate goals. *Journal of Applied Behavioral Science, 5,* 9–24.

Johnson, D. W., Maruyama, G., Johnson, R. T., Nelson, D., & Skon, S. (1981). Effects of cooperative, competitive, and individualistic goal structures on achievement: A meta-analysis. *Psychological Bulletin, 89,* 47–62.

Kabanoff, B. (1987). Predictive validity of the MODE conflict instrument. *Journal of Applied Psychology, 72,* 160–163.

Katz, D., & Kahn, R. L. (1978). *The social psychology of organizations* (2nd ed.). New York: Wiley.

Kiesler, D. J. (1983). The 1982 interpersonal circle: A taxonomy for complementary in human transactions. *Psychological Review, 90,* 185–214.

Kramer, R. M., McClintock, C. G., & Messick, D. M. (1986). Social values and cooperative response to a simulated resource conservation crisis. *Journal of Personality, 54,* 576–592.

Lawrence, P. R., & Lorsch, J. W. (1967). *Organization and environment: Managing differentiation and integration.* Cambridge: Harvard University Press.

Lax, D. A., & Sebenius, J. K. (1986). *The manager as negotiator: Bargaining for cooperation and competitive gain.* New York: Free Press.

Lewicki, R. J., Weiss, S. E., & Lewin, D. (1992). Models of conflict, negotiation and third party intervention: A review and synthesis. *Journal of Organizational Behavior, 13,* 209–252.

Lind, E. A., & Tyler, T. R. (1988). *The social psychology of procedural justice.* New York: Plenum.

McClintock, C. G. (1976). Social motivations in settings of outcome interdependence. In D. Druckman (Ed.), *Negotiations* (pp. 49–77). Beverly Hills, CA: Sage.

McClintock, C. G., & Allison, S. (1989). Social value orientation and helping behavior. *Journal of Applied Social Psychology, 19,* 353–362.

McClintock, C. G., & Liebrand, W. B. G. (1988). The role of interdependence structure, individual value orientation, and other's strategy in social decision making: A transformational analysis. *Journal of Personality and Social Psychology, 55,* 396–409.

Mintzberg, H. (1979). *The structuring of organizations.* Englewood Cliffs, NJ: Prentice-Hall.

Nicotera, A. M. (1993). Beyond two dimensions: A grounded theory model of conflict-handling behavior. *Management Communication Quarterly, 6,* 282–306.

Orford, J. (1986). The rules of interpersonal complementarity: Does hostility beget hostility and dominance, submission? *Psychological Review, 93,* 365–377.

Orford, J. (1994). The interpersonal circumplex: A theory and method for applied psychology. *Human Relations, 47,* 1347–1375.

Pneuman, R. W., & Bruehl, M. E. (1982). *Managing conflict.* Englewood Cliffs, NJ: Prentice-Hall.

Prein, H. C. M. (1976). Stijlen van conflicthantering [Styles of conflict management]. *Nederlands Tijdschrift voor de Psychologie, 31,* 321–346.

Pruitt, D. G. (1981). *Negotiation behavior*. New York: Academic Press.

Pruitt, D. G., & Carnevale, P. J. (1993). *Negotiation in social conflict*. Buckingham, England: Open University Press.

Psenicka, C., & Rahim, M. A. (1989). Integrative and distributive dimensions of styles of handling interpersonal conflict and bargaining outcome. In M. A. Rahim (Ed.), *Managing conflict: An interdisciplinary approach* (pp. 33–40). New York: Praeger.

Putnam, L. L. (1990). Reframing integrative and distributive bargaining: A process perspective. In B. H. Sheppard, M. H. Bazerman, & R. J. Lewicki (Eds.), *Research on negotiation in organizations* (Vol. 2, pp. 3–30). Greenwich, CT: JAI.

Putnam, L. L., & Wilson, C. E. (1982). Communicative strategies in organizational conflicts: Reliability and validity of a measurement scale. In M. Burgoon (Ed.), *Communication yearbook* (Vol. 6, pp. 629–652). Beverly Hills, CA: Sage.

Putnam, L. L., & Wilson, S. R. (1989). Argumentation and bargaining strategies as discriminators of integrative outcomes. In M. A. Rahim (Ed.), *Managing conflict: An interdisciplinary approach* (pp. 121–141). New York: Praeger.

Rahim, M. A. (1983). *Rahim organizational conflict inventories*. Palo Alto, CA: Consulting Psychologists Press.

Rahim, M. A. (1992). *Managing conflict in organizations* (2nd ed.). Westport, CT: Praeger.

Renwick, P. A. (1977). The effects of sex differences on the perception and management of superior–subordinate conflict: An exploratory study. *Organizational Behavior and Human Performance, 19*, 403–415.

Robbins, S. P. (1974). *Managing organizational conflict: A nontraditional approach*. Englewood Cliffs, NJ: Prentice-Hall.

Roloff, M. E. (1976). Communication strategies, relationships, and relational change. In G. R. Miller (Ed.), *Explorations in interpersonal communication* (pp. 173–196). Beverly Hills, CA: Sage.

Roloff, M. E., & Jordan, J. M. (1992). Achieving negotiation goals: The "fruits and foibles" of planning ahead. In L. L. Putnam & M. E. Roloff (Eds.), *Communication and negotiation* (pp. 1–45). Newbury Park, CA: Sage.

Rubin, J. Z., Pruitt, D. G., & Kim, S. H. (1994). *Social conflict: Escalation, stalemate, and settlement*. New York: McGraw-Hill.

Ruble, T. L., & Thomas, K. W. (1976). Support for a two-dimensional model of conflict behavior. *Organizational Behavior and Human Performance, 16*, 143–155.

Schweiger, D. M., Sandberg, W. R., & Ragan, J. W. (1986). Group approaches for improving strategic decision making: A comparative analysis of dialectical inquiry, devil's advocacy, and consensus. *Academy of Management Journal, 29*, 51–71.

Schweiger, D. M., Sandberg, W. R., & Rechner, P. L. (1989). Experiential effects of dialectical inquiry, devil's advocacy, and consensus approaches to strategic decision making. *Academy of Management Journal, 32*, 745–772.

Schwenk, C. R. (1990). Effects of dialectical inquiry and devil's advocacy on decision making. *Organizational Behavior and Human Decision Processes, 47*, 161–176.

Sheppard, B. H. (1984). Third party conflict intervention: A procedural framework. In B. M. Staw & L. L. Cummings (Eds.), *Research in organizational behavior* (Vol. 6, pp. 141–190). Greenwich, CT: JAI.

Sheppard, B. H., Lewicki, R. J., & Minton, J. W. (1992). *Organizational justice: The search for fairness in the workplace*. New York: Lexington Books.

Sherif, M. (1966). *In common predicament*. Boston, MA: Houghton Mifflin.

Shockley-Zalabak, P. (1988). Assessing the Hall conflict management survey. *Management Communication Quarterly, 1*, 302–320.

Sternberg, R. J., & Dobson, D. M. (1987). Resolving interpersonal conflicts: An analysis of stylistic consistency. *Journal of Personality and Social Psychology, 52*, 794–812.

Sternberg, R. J., & Soriano, L. J. (1984). Styles of conflict resolution. *Journal of Personality and Social Psychology, 47,* 115–126.

Thomas, K. W. (1976). Conflict and conflict management. In M. D. Dunnette (Ed.), *Handbook of industrial and organizational psychology* (pp. 889–935). Chicago: Rand McNally.

Thomas, K. W. (1977). Toward multidimensional values in teaching: The example of conflict behaviors. *Academy of Management Review, 2,* 484–490.

Thomas, K. W. (1988). The conflict-handling modes: Toward more precise theory. *Management Communication Quarterly, 1,* 430–436.

Thomas, K. W. (1992a). Conflict and conflict management: Reflections and update. *Journal of Organizational Behavior, 13,* 265–274.

Thomas, K. W. (1992b). Conflict and negotiation processes in organizations. In M.D. Dunnette & L. M. Hough (Eds.), *Handbook of industrial and organizational psychology* (2nd ed., pp. 651–717). Palo Alto, CA: Consulting Psychologists Press.

Thomas, K. W., & Kilmann, R. H. (1974). *The Thomas–Kilmann conflict mode instrument.* Tuxedo, NY: Xicom.

Thompson, L. L. (1990). Negotiation behavior and outcomes: Empirical evidence and theoretical issues. *Psychological Bulletin, 108,* 515–532.

Tjosvold, D. (1989). Interdependence approach to conflict management in organizations. In M. A. Rahim (Ed.), *Managing conflict: An interdisciplinary approach* (pp. 41–50). New York: Praeger.

Tjosvold, D. (1990). The goal interdependence approach to communication in conflict: An organizational study. In M. A. Rahim (Ed.), *Theory and research in conflict management* (pp. 15–27). New York: Praeger.

Tjosvold, D. (1991). *The conflict-positive organization: Stimulate diversity and create unity.* Reading, MA: Addison-Wesley.

Tracey, T. J. (1994). An examination of the complementarity of interpersonal behavior. *Journal of Personality and Social Psychology, 67,* 864–878.

Turner, M. E., & Pratkanis, A. R. (1994). Social identity maintenance prescriptions for preventing groupthink: Reducing identity protection and enhancing intellectual conflict. *International Journal of Conflict Management, 5,* 254–270.

Turner, M. E., & Pratkanis, A. R. (1998). A social identity maintenance model of groupthink. *Organizational Behavior and Human Decision Processes, 73,* 210–235.

Tutzauer, F., & Roloff, M. E. (1988). Communication processes leading to integrative agreements: Three paths to joint benefits. *Communication Research, 15,* 360–380.

Van Lange, P. A. M. (1992). Rationality and morality in social dilemmas: The influence of social value orientations. In W. B. G. Liebrand, D. M. Messick, & H. A. M. Wilke (Eds.), *Social dilemmas: Theoretical issues and research findings* (pp. 133–146). Oxford: Pergamon Press.

Van de Vliert, E. (1990). Sternberg's styles of handling interpersonal conflict: A theory-based reanalysis. *International Journal of Conflict Management, 1,* 69–80.

Van de Vliert, E. (1997). *Complex interpersonal conflict behaviour: Theoretical frontiers.* Hove, England: Psychology Press.

Van de Vliert, E. (1998a). Conflict and conflict management. In P. J. D. Drenth, H. Thierry, & C. J. de Wolff (Eds.), *Handbook of work and organizational psychology, 2nd ed. Volume 3: Personnel psychology* (pp. 351–376). Hove, England: Psychology Press.

Van de Vliert, E. (1998b). Cooperation–competition theory raises more questions than it answers. *Applied Psychology: An International Review, 47,* 323–327.

Van de Vliert, E., & De Dreu, C. K. W. (1994). Optimizing performance by conflict stimulation. *International Journal of Conflict Management, 5,* 211–222.

Van de Vliert, E., & Euwema, M. C. (1994). Agreeableness and activeness as components of conflict behavior. *Journal of Personality and Social Psychology, 66,* 674–687.

Van de Vliert, E., Euwema, M. C., & Huismans, S. E. (1995). Managing conflict with a subordinate or a superior: Effectiveness of conglomerated behavior. *Journal of Applied Psychology, 80,* 271–281.

Van de Vliert, E., & Hordijk, J. W. (1989). A theoretical position of compromising among other styles of conflict management. *Journal of Social Psychology, 129,* 681–690.

Van de Vliert, E., & Kabanoff, B. (1990). Toward theory-based measures of conflict management. *Academy of Management Journal, 33,* 199–209.

Van de Vliert, E., Nauta, A., Euwema, M. C., & Janssen, O. (1997). The effectiveness of mixing problem solving and forcing. In C. K. W. De Dreu & E. Van de Vliert (Eds.), *Using conflict in organizations* (pp. 38–52). Thousand Oaks, CA: Sage

Van de Vliert, E., Nauta, A., Giebels, E., & Janssen, O. (1999). Constructive conflict at work. *Journal of Organizational Behavior, 20,* 475–491.

Van de Vliert, E., & Prein, H. C. M. (1989). The difference in the meaning of forcing in the conflict management of actors and observers. In M. A. Rahim (Ed.), *Managing conflict: An interdisciplinary approach* (pp. 51–63). New York: Praeger.

Volkema, R. J., & Bergmann, T. J. (1989). Interpersonal conflict at work: An analysis of behavioral responses. *Human Relations, 42,* 757–770.

Vroom, V. H., & Yetton, P. W. (1973). *Leadership and decision making.* Pittsburgh, PA: University of Pittsburgh Press.

Wall, J. A., Jr. (1985). *Negotiation: Theory and practice.* Glenview, IL: Scott, Foresman.

Walton, R. E. (1987). *Managing conflict: Interpersonal dialogue and third party roles.* Reading, MA: Addison-Wesley.

Walton, R. E., Cutcher-Gershenfeld, J. E., & McKersie, R. B. (1994). *Strategic negotiations: A theory of change in labor–management relations.* Boston, MA: Harvard Business School Press.

Walton, R. E., & McKersie, R. B. (1965). *A behavioral theory of labor negotiations: An analysis of a social interaction system.* New York: McGraw Hill.

Weider-Hatfield, D. (1988). Assessing the Rahim organizational conflict inventory-II (ROCI-II). *Management Communication Quarterly, 1,* 350–366.

Wilson, S. R., & Waltman, M. S. (1988). Assessing the Putnam–Wilson organizational communication instrument (OCCI). *Management Communication Quarterly, 1,* 367–388.

Chapter 10

Status Contests in Meetings: Negotiating the Informal Order

David A. Owens
Vanderbilt University

Robert I. Sutton
Stanford University

Meetings can be more than an occasion to do work. Schwartzman (1986) argued that meetings often become arenas where a group's status order is "played and displayed." This view of meetings has received little attention in research on behavior in organizations. In this chapter, we develop Schwartzman's observation. We describe the status organizing processes that occur in face-to-face groups and treat meetings as occasions for *status contests* (Maclay & Kneipe, 1972).

A variety of behavioral scientists have described meetings where participants seemed to be working toward enhancing their social standing rather than helping the group achieve some goal. For example, Bloch (1971) described the premeeting activities among members of the Merina Elders' council.

> The actual time of the meeting was always set three or four hours too early, and as for many Merina occasions, great skill was required by those who wanted to arrive at the right time, in the right place. Nobody wanted to arrive too early, but obviously it would not do to arrive too late. The influence of a person is at stake in manoeuvres of this kind, and his effectiveness at such a meeting depends on his appearing at the right time to give the impression that the meeting is starting because of his arrival. This involves a lot of waiting about in nearby houses and sending children to spy out the land and report back. [Then] as if by magic the raiamandreny [elders] all appear at once at a time little related to the originally appointed hour. (p. 48)

299

In *Street Corner Society*, Whyte (1943) observed how the bowling scores of a street corner gang reflected the group's internal status structure; high-status group members invariably earned the top scores. For example, during a bowling tournament, as one of the low-status gang members found himself in the lead after four frames, he inexplicably began to make mistakes.

> As mistake followed mistake, he stopped trying. Between turns he went out for drinks, so that he became flushed and unsteady on his feet. . . . His collapse was sudden and complete; in the space of a few boxes [turns] he had dropped from first to last place. (p. 20)

Later, when asked what might have happened had this bowler or any other low-status member remained in the lead, the two high-status gang leaders replied,

> We would have talked them out of it. We would have made plenty of noise. We would have been really vicious. . . . If they had won, there would have been a lot of noise. Plenty of arguments. We would have called it lucky—things like that. We would have tried to get them in another match and ruin them. We would have to put them in their places. (p. 21)

Similarly, Sutton and Hargadon (1996) described brainstorming sessions at a product development firm as status auctions. A brainstorm meeting was a gathering where design engineers selected ad hoc from the organization met to suggest creative solutions to a particular technical problem. Technical creativity was the most highly valued skill among the engineers studied and the brainstorm meeting was the place where this skill was displayed. As one designer put it, "It is a place to strut your stuff" (p. 696). The brainstorm consisted of a 1- to 2-hour session of originating and discussing potential solutions to the problem and ended with the group's facilitator asking, "Which ideas should we develop further?" The group then identified the best ideas and their originators. Whereas the facilitator may have treated this as weighing the myriad problem solutions, designers treated it as a tallying of the score. As one designer reported, "I like being one of the three or four people who came up with the creative ideas. If I am not, I sometimes spend a couple more hours afterwards to develop better ideas" (p. 707).

FIVE ASSUMPTIONS ABOUT STATUS CONTESTS

In each of these three examples, the status order of a group is displayed and negotiated in a face-to-face meeting. We propose that the following five assumptions are evident in each example and form a basis for thinking about status contests in meetings.

1. Status Orders Exist in Groups

That human groups form status orders is a finding evident throughout the behavioral sciences (e.g., Bales, 1951; Berger, Fisek, Norman, & Zelditch, 1977; Domhoff, 1967; Mills, 1957; Veblen, 1899; Warner, Meeker, & Eells, 1949; Weber, 1922/1980; see Wegener, 1992, for a review). Research has shown that individuals and groups assess one another's social status, ranking it on a scale from low to high. These individual assessments coalesce into a status order as members share them in the group. Sharing does not occur verbally; rather it proceeds as group members observe status-claiming behaviors in the group and reactions to those behaviors by other members. By seeing who defers to whom and who gets greater rewards for like effort, members can form a consensus of the group's status order. Bloch's Merina elders and Whyte's gang leaders both showed the understanding that their behavior in the group and the group's reactions to their behavior was symbolic of their place in the status order.

2. Individuals Actively Gain or Lose Status Within Status Orders

A person's value to a group is assessed by other members based on the possession of desirable characteristics (e.g., Bales, 1951; Berger et al., 1977; Fisek, 1974; Lenski, 1954). This assessment serves as the basis of the social status awarded to that person. If individual possession of valued characteristics can be controlled, a person can potentially manipulate his or her rank in the status order. Although some characteristics, for example sex and race, are immutable, others, like functional expertise or creativity, could be strategically acquired or expressed. Strategic expression of a previously hidden expertise can force the group to reassess the individual's value to the group. Environment and context also moderate an individual's value to the group by making personally held characteristics more or less critical in helping the group achieve its goals. In the example above, Sutton and Hargadon's (1996) designers worked overtime to increase their value to the group by generating better and more creative ideas. By doing so, they hoped to reverse status loss that may have occurred by not being acknowledged as a top idea generator for the group. Likewise, Whyte's low-status bowler threw the game as a way of decreasing his valuation and actively managing his status downward.

3. There Are Rewards and Costs for Gaining or Losing Status

Much sociological literature regards a reward of status to be the control of societally valued assets (e.g., Domhoff, 1967; Mills, 1957; Veblen, 1899). Social-psychological research, however, focuses on the control of a group's process and deference in communication from others as the desirable rewards. High-status group members are consistently found to be given more opportunities to participate, to initiate communication more often, to enjoy more opportunities to evaluate the group's output, and to have an overall greater influence on the group's decisions (Bales, 1951; see Berger, Rosenholtz, & Zelditch, 1980). Such influence over a group can offer both psychological and instrumental rewards; an individual's ego and social integration needs are satisfied while he or she is able to set the group's goals and to direct the group in how to meet them. In the example above, the Merina elders fought to keep their status because to lose it would have meant a loss of deference and control, or as Bloch put it, a loss of "effectiveness."

4. The Negotiation of Status in Face-to-Face Groups Is Patterned

The potlatches of the Kwakiutl Indians (e.g., Benedict, 1934) and the Cockfights of the Balinese (Geertz, 1973), are examples from a history of anthropological research that details behavioral patterns of status contests in preindustrial and industrial societies (e.g., Bourdieu, 1984; Maclay & Knipe, 1972). Regardless of which society, all show normative attitudes that prescribe appropriate status-claiming behaviors. These behaviors are invariably deeply ingrained, taken for granted, and treated as a routine (if occasionally annoying) aspect of group process. Whyte's high-status gang leaders in the previous example mirror this taken for granted attitude—without deliberation, they knew exactly how to respond to an untoward status bid by one of their subordinates. In the case of the Merina, all elders engaged in the status game in the same way causing the meeting to start late. As Bloch pointed out, this occurs "for many Merina occasions." The townspeople sanctioned this behavior as well by providing children for spying and nearby houses for hiding in.

5. Meetings Serve as a Venue and Occasion for Status Negotiations or Contests in Organizations

Whereas status is a property of the individual, the enactment of status involves the participation of a group. Status behaviors become meaningful when dominance and submission have been negotiated and all participants understand their place (Strauss, 1978). When an individual knows who is of higher status and who is of lower status, he or she can behave appropriately. But subjective assessments of the status of others may conflict between members of the group. Therefore, in order to communicate and resolve the conflicts, a forum facilitating the display and negotiation of status is required. The meeting provides one venue for that facilitation. The examples presented earlier reinforce the notion that an individual's rank in the status order is tenuous; but the individuals all seemed to understand that there was a time and place—the meeting—where they would properly work to manage it.

NEGOTIATING ORDER THROUGH MEETINGS

> A pet food manufacturer keeps 30 cats as a consumer panel. At the time of feeding, the cats cue up in a definite order, always the same. Only when a new cat enters is there some disorder: It tries to take a place in the queue and is bitten by every neighbor until it has found a place where henceforth it is tolerated. (Hofstede, 1980, p. 66)

The negotiation of a status order, or the coalescing of individually held rankings into a jointly held status structure, is facilitated by a forum and an occasion for its occurrence. The meeting is one such occasion. Conventional views of meetings see them as places to do the work of the organization and see overtly political behaviors as counter to the purpose of meetings. Yet Schwartzman (1986) suggested that perhaps "the opposite may be the case, that 'hidden agendas' are functional for the purpose of the meeting, because the purpose is to reconcile the formal with the informal system and to legitimate this merger as 'the business' of the organization" (p. 247). The negotiation of the status order can thus serve to resolve the inevitable conflicts that arise from the operation of two different systems—the formal and the informal—of authority and status.

The meeting provides an effective venue for a group to negotiate its status order. Meetings are social settings where group members can observe the clues that signal one another's status. These signals take the form of verbal acts such as interruption and physical acts such as gesture and posture. By seeing both individuals' behaviors and reactions to those behaviors by the group, a shared consensus about the shape of the status order can form. This consensus can also be contested and made subject to renegotiation by individuals in the meeting through strategic enactment of status-seeking behaviors. The meeting may be an appropriate place for such expressive behaviors because in a meeting, they can occur under the guise of legitimate instrumental organizational activity (Sutton & Hargadon, 1996). The meeting is not the only place where status contests take place; E-mail discussion groups, social gatherings, and any other venue where members can gather, enact status behaviors, and observe and react to the status displays of others are all likely venues and occasions (e.g., Sproull & Kiesler, 1986; Weisband, Schneider, & Connolly, 1995).

We borrow Goffman's (1969) term *the move* to indicate the basic element of the status-negotiating behaviors that occur in a status contest. A move is a patterned behavior enacted in response to a social situation. The negotiation process is a series of moves made by members in an attempt to manipulate the status structure of the group. Manipulations take the form of attempts to improve, sustain, or reduce the social standing of the self or of others in the group. Moves can be offensive or defensive, and are directed at particular targets or perceived challengers to an individual's status aims, or to the entire group audience. In ongoing groups, members can employ an array of strategies for status management.

Several strategies are evident in the examples presented earlier. Among the Merina Elders, status maintenance required an appearance at the start of the meeting and not before or after; the strategy was one of hide and wait. Whyte's (1943) gang leaders, on the other hand, discussed how they would have openly obstructed and discredited the performance of a lower status member had he done too well in the gang's bowling tournament. Sutton and Hargadon's (1996) engineer worked secretly to create valued ideas that would be brought to the attention of the group later.

Given the wide choice of strategies available and the myriad forms that moves can take during a status contest, our task is to provide a conceptual framework that describes the moves and the situations in which they may occur. We believe that there is an order to the status dynamics in the group, and we attempt to map it as follows. We start with an individual's first step toward status, that of joining a group as a newcomer. From the group's perspective, such a person typically has low status. This affects the types of moves that can be used to achieve the higher status that full membership brings. We argue that the low-status individual is likely to use moves that develop their integration in the group (Blau, 1964) and reinforce the status quo.

Once well integrated within a group, there is an increase in status for the individual. Less concerned with integration, this person need no longer constantly submit to others. But his or her status rank is still vulnerable to manipulation and must therefore be actively managed. Management is likely to take the form of moves directed at others of similar status; it is relative to these similar others that status is most easily gained and status loss most readily contested. The norms and goals of the group (and the embedding organization) will influence the choice of move used in this heavily contested terrain.

At the top of the hierarchy, we argue that yet a third set of dynamics affects status ordering. Maintaining the overall order in a stable state is a likely motivating force for an individual at this level. This insures his or her valued position. The high status of these individuals allows them to maintain stability through disproportionate control over group communication and decisions, but they also have more to lose should the system undergo radical change or collapse. Dominance moves—the most powerful of the move types—are likely to predominate as high-status individuals attempt to reify the status quo order, making clear to lower status members not only the state, but the currency of the status order as well. We now discuss each of these three dynamics and move types in greater detail.

GAINING ENTRY: INTEGRATION MOVES

Entry into a preexisting group can be difficult for a new member. This can occur if the group does not recognize that the newcomer possesses characteristics that the group values. In order to become an integrated member, the newcomer must make visible those characteristics. Doing so assures the newcomer a place in the established status structure, ensuring that he or she will be valued in a socially appropriate way (Goffman, 1959). The meeting is an important part of this integration process because it serves as the place where group members can see and acknowledge who is a member in good standing in the group.

As a first step toward status and an appropriate place in the group, newcomers may pursue integration through ingratiation or supplication moves. Ingratiation describes attempts to ply higher-status others with flattery and favors intended to induce liking (Jones & Pittman, 1982). Supplication, on the other hand, indicates the adoption of a peripheral or otherwise undesirable social role in the group (Jones, & Pittman, 1982). By using either of these approaches, an individual attempting integration presents little threat to the established status order of the group (Blau, 1964).

Ingratiation is invariably directed at high-status members of the group. When a newcomer directs flattering communications at high-status group members and defers to their communications, the existing status order is reinforced. As a result, increased liking of the newcomer by high-status members is likely to occur. This occurs because high-status group members have the most interest vested in the status order that the newcomer is reifying. For the newcomer, being positively valued by high-status members can translate into increased integration in the group. This is likely because high-status members have a greater ability to facilitate status increase by virtue of possessing greater influence over the group.

An example of an ingratiation move occurs during a meeting when an individual attributes the achievement of valued outputs by the group to a higher status group member. During a conversation at a meeting observed by one of us, a heretofore quiet low-status person suddenly spoke aloud to a high-status group member, "Pat, that was a great idea about switching those two parts." Although the idea in question had been a product of complex group interaction and consensus building, the low-status member openly attributed it to the high-status person. Although attributions of a leader's control over the group's effectiveness or outcome are common (Meindl, Ehrlich, & Dukerich, 1985), stating it during a meeting is an ingratiation move, one that reifies the status order. By making this move, a low-status individual may be trying to become recognized as an interactant with high-status members; this is also a measure status and integration (Bales, 1951).

Supplication or embracing a subdominant role in the group (Jones & Pittman, 1982) is another possible integrating strategy for a newcomer. If the role becomes an integral part of the group's process, an increase in integration of the role inhabitant will result (Gouran, 1982). Examples of the supplicant role are the joker, the critic, the conservative, the radical, or the chronic volunteer. Although not consciously valued, these roles are often invaluable for a group's functioning (Gouran, 1982; Jones & Pittman, 1982; Klapp, 1954). Individuals in these roles serve as tension reducers through joking and other forms of conflict reduction, as task-overflow helpers by taking on excess work within the group, or as reference points by constantly reasserting a position that the group must stay aware of. Individuals in these roles may also serve as embodiments of the group's standing norms.

In a supplicant role, an integration seeker is not necessarily powerless. For example, the "devil's advocate" role allows individuals to present dissenting views while remaining personally distanced from them. Opinions voiced by the devil's advocate are understood by the group to be a part of the individual's role. Similarly, the joker role may defuse tense situations for the group in relatively unvalued ways, yet the role also possesses license to render harsh criticism on individuals in the group when it is delivered from the strictured confines of the joker role.[1] In each case, supplicants may violate existing deference patterns and yet avoid being personally threatening to the status order of the group.

As status bids, integrating moves facilitate entry into a group by low-status individuals. By creating and managing the group's perception that he or she possesses valued characteristics, an individual may be welcomed into the group. Although these moves are more likely to be used by newcomers and low-status group members, integration moves can also be used by medium- and high-status members of a group with the effect of improved group cohesiveness. This occurs as members communicate mutual respect through the display of deference and express mutual liking through flattery and helping. Such moves help to maintain the integration that is necessary for

---

[1]The freedom of the joker to release tension and to present scathing criticism is impeccably depicted in Shakespeare's *King Lear.*

a group's existence, and that may enhance the group's performance in an organizational context as well (Ancona, Caldwell, & O'Reilly, 1992).

UNCERTAINTY AND VULNERABILITY: CONTESTING MOVES

The pressure to participate in the status game continues even after an individual is well integrated in a group and moves up in the status hierarchy. We predict that rather than ceasing status-seeking behaviors, as Blau (1964) has argued, or taking a fixed position in a stable status order as others believe (cf. Berger & Zelditch, 1985), a midstatus level individual will continue to make status moves. Indeed, common experience suggests that status moves are a regular occurrence, even in long-standing groups. Although individuals at this level enjoy greater control over their status and are now in a better position to move up the status ladder, they remain susceptible to losing status at the hands of the many others that coexist at a similar level in the group. At this level, the status order of the group will be the most volatile.

Mid-level individuals are likely to be concerned with the group's ability to achieve its goals or duties. At this level, members are fully vested in the group, and the group's goals (and the demands of the embedding organization) become salient as these affect the potential success and long-term survival of the group. Low-status newcomers, on the other hand, are less likely to be familiar with the group's norms, values, and environment; for them, the group's goals and external demands are less visible and therefore of less actionable consequence.

At an intermediate status level, concern about the group's task performance can be used by members as a basis for status moves. To achieve higher status, they can manipulate the group's perception of their individual possession of task performance skills or abilities. Such perceptions serve as a basis for status in task-performance groups (Berger et al., 1977; Fisek, 1974). These moves may be less effective in situations of high certainty where a group understands how to achieve success and survival. Under certainty, individuals are awarded status consistent with their ability to affect task performance (Pfeffer & Salancik, 1978). There is little basis to manipulate importance to the group. But in situations of high task uncertainty or ambiguity, failure in task performance becomes possible or likely and the group's existence may be threatened. In this case, an individual's ability to help the group is indeterminate and thus subject to strategic manipulation. If a person in this situation can generate perceptions in the group that he or she has the greatest expertise, power, or potential to help, then the group is likely to defer to his or her lead.

These moves are contestable though, because in a state of uncertainty, many midstatus level members may be in a position to create plausible appearances of possessing the expertise and the ability necessary to help the group. As various individuals attempt to lead the group one way or another through the uncertainty, they must implicitly and explicitly discredit each other's views in the attempt to make their own lead more plausible (e.g., Latour & Woolgar, 1979).

Contesting occurs in several ways. By *shifting frame* (Goffman, 1974), an individual convinces the group to accept an alternative definition of its situation or of the problem at hand. The new definition or frame for the group is one in which the move maker possesses more valued status characteristics than in the group's previous frame. For example, at a meeting of an interdisciplinary project team one of us observed, the group was trying to understand how to move forward with an ill-defined project. During a worried pause in the discussion, one member suddenly exclaimed, "Oh! This is a *marketing* problem, we learned how to handle this in *business school!*" By shifting the group's frame, the mover had redefined the problem into an area where he (apparently) possessed the expertise needed to solve it. This move implicitly demanded the group's deference to his pursuit of the problem solution.

A shift can also be accomplished through the use of technical language or jargon that frames the group's problem in terms unavailable to others in the group. This move not only blocks communication on the part of nonliterate members, but the certainty and precision that such language conveys implies a familiarity and dominion over the issues at hand (Rifkin, 1990).[2] In addition to enhancing the status of an individual, this move can give the group organizational legitimacy. Outsiders are likely to assume that if a group is making technical talk, then it is doing its rational sanctioned work.

Group members can also frame their advantages using the group's external environment as a referent. By calling attention to possessed characteristics that are valued outside of the group, an individual may manage to override the group's local status structure. Use of such a strategy is consistent with research findings showing that societally ascribed status characteristics such as gender, race, and ethnicity affect individuals' status in task-performance groups. The effect is noted even when these characteristics bear no reasonable relationship to task performance (Berger et al., 1977). Thus, characteristics like education, social class, salary, experience, or age may be introduced, effectively bolstering the credibility of an individual's communications and his or her status. For example, one of us observed an individ-

---

[2]The development of a technical language in a specific problem area implies that the discipline has dealt with this type of problem before and that it is therefore tractable by an individual possessing the appropriate expertise.

ual prefacing a comment to a group with "Back at *Harvard*, I knew this guy. . . ." This made clear her educational background when this information was not otherwise available or salient to the group. Conversational digressions in meetings such as telling stories of hobbies, former work experiences, and places visited are also moves of this form.

In the contestable middle of the status hierarchy, individuals can act in ways that threaten the established status order. By attempting to assert control over the group's direction, they contest the group's framing of its situation using moves that play against task-performance issues such as expertise or external performance and legitimacy demands. Particularly in ambiguous situations, these moves constantly question the group's movement and force it to continually reassess the direction it takes. This move behavior can help the group by focusing competitive energy toward activities, specifically task performance, for which the group is rewarded. Although these moves are most likely to be aimed at those similar others who also live in the middle of the status hierarchy, it is not only the status of these similar others that is at risk. By gaining control of the group's communications and activities, plausible claims of ownership of the group's successes can be generated at the expense of the group's high-status members. Although newcomers have little chance of upsetting the status order due to the vested interest and control of those in the middle and at the top of the hierarchy, mid-level members do have a chance to significantly alter the status quo.

ASSERTING DOMINANCE: CONTROL MOVES

At the top of the hierarchy, a third set of dynamics affects the types of status moves used. Individuals at the top of the hierarchy have the most invested in the established status order and are likely to act in ways that maintain the order. An upset of the status order threatens the rewards of status, both physical and psychological, that high-status individuals have privileged access to. Attempts to maintain the status quo by high-status individuals are likely to occur through control of the status-ordering processes of the group and through a constant reassertion of dominance over the group.[3]

We posit that high-status individuals assert control over the status-ordering process in order to manage the status attained by others lower in

---

[3]Dominance moves are those closest to raw assertions of power. We have in mind a particular type of dominance that occurs only through the possession of high social standing by the mover. Thus tyrants, invading armies, or formal authorities in organizations have the power to assert dominance over a group, but they earn little social status in the process. They have not participated through the value system, that is, reifying, challenging, or subverting it. Participation from within the group's value system is the basic requirement in our conception of status in a group.

the hierarchy. This prevents accumulations of status by individuals who might potentially threaten the existing status order. Those nearest the top of the order have an advantage in this effort; they have greater control over the process through which status is earned or lost (Berger & Zelditch, 1985). We view *control moves* at this level as attempts to initiate, block, or otherwise manage the flow of communication and activity in the group. By controlling the participation of others in the communication flow, an individual maintains influence and control over the group (Kelley, 1951).

Control over the group's status-organizing process is asserted most directly by encouraging or constraining the participation of particular group members in the group's communication and activity flow. Being able to address communications to the group marks an individual as an integrated member of the group. It also provides opportunities for the individual to make status moves. One individual's attempt to reframe the group's situation—thus threatening the status order—may be cut off, while the supplicant move of another member—a move that reifies the status quo—is encouraged. This behavior gives the high-status member control of both the status-ordering process and the currency with which status can be achieved in the group. For example, we observed a group meeting where one midstatus individual discussing one of the group's projects was interrupted by the high-status group leader. The leader then invited another individual, a well-known ingratiator in the group, to discuss his weekend fishing trip at great length. From a group effectiveness point of view, this behavior seems counterproductive for the group, but from the perspective of status management, it makes sense. The high-status leader was controlling communication access as well as the currency of status by his subordinates.

The moderation of other group members' participation occurs through both verbal and physical behaviors. Verbal interruption is the most obvious form of control. By breaking another individual's communications, an interrupter gains control over the rate, direction, and substance of conversational flow. This enables the interrupting individual to channel the group's focus and activity in a direction that can protect or reinforce his or her own social standing. As well, interruption is a self-provided opportunity to make another move. We expect simple interruption to be a common strategy by individuals at the highest status levels, because it takes advantage of the invariable deference given by lower status individuals to those of higher status, especially when the status differences are large.

Physical control strategies are subtler than verbal ones, yet they may be as common. In face to face meetings, these moves take forms such as dominance gestures or taking physical control of the communication media such as the chalk or whiteboard markers. Because most organizations proscribe inflicting physical harm, in line with societal norms, we are more likely to see dominance signaled by the dramatic gestures of high-status individuals. Aggressively shaking the head in disagreement, raising the voice, increasing gesticulation, and rolling the eyes skyward are all such gestures. These behaviors interrupt the flow of an interaction by ritually signaling the potential for harm to be inflicted by the perpetrator on his or her target during a dominance contest (Maclay & Knipe, 1972). Even where the signal is ritual, the effects are real. When facing such behavior from a high-status other, a low-status person will invariably stop whatever he or she is doing and defer.

These participation-control moves are the most simple or primal of the move strategies; they may be the sublimation of physical dominance strategies into the realm of complex communication.[4] If true, this notion underlines the importance of the relationship between communication and status in groups. This connection is the operative assumption for status theorists that build on the work of Bales (1951) and Kelly (1951), as do we. The importance of communication and its control also supports our thesis that meetings in organizations—where communication is the normative goal—are an important place to organize status.

Yet, another way of taking control of the group's communication channel is by gaining the group's attention. In the example at the outset of this chapter, the Merina Elder's council members sought the attention of others at the meeting by having the meeting start with their arrival. This was an important key to maintaining their influence. Nonetheless, high-status individuals can also use late entry to or early exit from a meeting to draw attention to themselves and away from the communications already underway in the group. Conspicuously entering late into a meeting that is already underway can disrupt the proceedings; this gives the intruder the opportunity to assert control over the group's communications as all attention focuses on him or her. The individual can also demand to be "brought up to speed" on the group's business, which he or she missed by virtue of being late. This new focus or activity for the group puts the latecomer at the center of the group's communications giving the mover an ideal opportunity to critique progress and to turn it to a new direction for action. As we have already discussed, evaluating the group's output and influencing its future direction are concomitants of possessing high status. Similarly, leaving a meeting early may be a move as well. When a high-status individual announces the "need" to leave early, an implicit (or explicit) demand is placed that important orders of business be handled forthright by the group, before this individual must leave. The mover thus preserves his or her power in the group by exercising control over the

---

[4]Dominance strategies of these types most closely resemble those observed by ethologists in dominance processes in animal groups (e.g., Ardrey, 1967; Schjelderup-Ebbe, 1935).

group's more important task efforts, ensuring that they are handled early in the meeting while he or she is still present.

The attention garnered by leaving early or arriving late to meetings can also be used to generate perceptions or attributions in the group that the mover is busy. Busyness is likely to be taken by the group as a sign of an individual's industriousness and their importance to others external to the group. The move may therefore be sanctioned even though late arrival or early departure can disrupt the performance of tasks on a group's meeting agenda.[5] Demands placed on a member from outside of the group—that is, having reasons for late arrival or early departure that transcend the needs of the group—can increase status by reflecting to the group the importance and integration of this individual within the larger organization.

In addition to arrival time, physical artifacts can be used to garner attention and signify status (Bourdieu, 1984; Mills, 1957; Veblen, 1899). They can also be used as props for moves made in meetings. Simple possession of certain props may have status value due to their high economic cost. Currently, items such as laptop computers, cellular phones, and to a decreasing extent, personal paging devices (beepers) indicate to a group that an individual is sufficiently valued that the organization has supplied this expensive, complicated, "efficiency-aiding" equipment to him or her. Or that the individual has the economic resources and rational need to purchase such an item on their own. By using such equipment during a meeting, for example allowing a pager to beep or a portable phone to ring, an individual is making a move. Just as for late arrival, the disruption of the group's process can position the mover to assert control over the group's communication flow. This occurs in addition to signaling the group that the mover has just received a message from outside of the group, a message that is so important that it cannot wait until the current meeting has ended.

The controlling moves used at the highest status level act to reinforce the existing status order. Because a person at this level possesses high status, he or she has more to lose if there are radical changes to the status order. Yet this individual also possesses greater control over the probable shape of the status order, as well as the currency with which it is shaped. Dominance-signaling moves are likely to be common at this level because they are more effective when emanating from high-status individuals. Dominance behaviors from low-status individuals are much less threatening. We note also that even though status confers rewards and perquisites to the individual possessing it, the responsibility for a group's success that comes with status can also be burdensome. It may be this burden that motivates some part of the

---

[5]Schwartzman (1989) noted that such "disruptions" might be functional for the group as they provide extra time for needed informal communication among other members of the group before and after the group's formal meeting.

actions undertaken by high-status individuals to control or dominate the group. Dominance moves may be reactions to the pressures of the situation and not simply ego-driven status acquisitiveness. By controlling the stability of the status order, a high-status individual can keep the group focused on task performance instead of allowing the group to expend energy or resources in incessant attempts to remodel the status hierarchy. As such, the move behavior can be instrumental to the group's greater good.

DISCUSSION

Our model of status management in workgroups in organizations describes the pressures that can drive move behaviors at three status levels.[6] At the lowest level of status, marginal membership and lack of integration within a group is a compelling force. This leads an individual to attempt integration within the group through ingratiation and supplication behaviors. These integrating moves can facilitate cohesiveness and mutual liking within the group. At intermediary levels of status, task concerns come to the fore and contestable moves that play on the group's uncertainty about its performance will predominate as the mechanism used to raise an individual's status within the group. These moves can also benefit the group by turning competitive energy toward the group's task-performance goals. At the highest levels of status, concern shifts to the control and stability of the status order. High-status individuals are aided in this task by the deference patterns inherent in status behaviors. Effects of these moves are to facilitate the group's task performance while maintaining the group's values. Controlling moves focus energy and attention in the group in directions that support the group's preexisting goal and value systems as embodied in the status order.

Revisiting the examples presented at the beginning of this chapter, we now interpret the actions of the protagonists using this conceptualization. When Whyte's (1943) low-status bowler purposely loses the game, this action makes him unthreatening to the group. Taking the supplicant role of "drunk," he aids his integration into the group by not threatening the status quo. Sutton and Hargadon's (1996) well-integrated engineer works after hours to prove task-based competence by providing new solutions to the group's problem while boosting his or her status with respect to otherwise similar engineers in the group. Finally, the Merina Elder's council members work hard to stage the reification of their status positions. Similarly, Whyte's gang leaders closely watched their low-status bowler, ready to

---

[6]Of course, any of these move types are liable to be used at any status level. But, we presume that the forces described create distinct pressures and situations that make the indicated move types more likely by the occupants of each of the three levels we have described.

control (or reverse) the rate of his progress through the status hierarchy in their group.

The conceptions of active status management that permeate our examples and model also deserve a bit of elaboration. There is a normative attitude in our culture that negatively sanctions the pursuit of status. Nevertheless, we argue that individuals must still actively engage in status management. In a group, a person's moves affect not only the status of the self, but they affect the status of others in the group as well. Although we are convinced that status orders in groups are not zero-sum structures, the basis for one individual's status can easily, if inadvertently, be undermined by the actions of others in the group. Inactive individuals may simply be displaced toward the bottom of the order as new values or goals for the group are negotiated or as new environments are encountered, and as the inactive individual is now found lacking in social or instrumental value to the group. Status management, even if ignored, affects all members of the group. Thus the Merina Elders, the gang leaders, and the engineers strive to actively manipulate their status so as not to have it manipulated for them by others.[7]

MEETINGS AS STATUS CONTESTS

The status contest is a social one and it requires a social setting in which to conduct it. We have argued that the meeting provides such a setting in organizations. By providing a place and a time to meet, the stage is set for the negotiation of order in a group. Meetings provide both the occasion and the physical necessities required for the display of an individual's status behaviors, for the observation of other members' status behaviors, and for the group to observe its collective reactions to all of these displays. The immedi-

---

[7]Whyte's low-status bowler adds a twist to this explanation because he appears to actively manage his status downward. This is interesting because although societal norms do not encourage the "tooting of our own horns," we certainly are not expected to torpedo our own progress either. It remains to be explained why well-integrated members at higher status levels might also actively *not* seek increased status aside from the supplicant role. This could be explained by arguing that Whyte's bowler, to take a concrete example, manages his status downward because he does not want the higher placed role and the responsibility to meet the expectations that come with it. Maintaining higher status comes with costs, especially in the highly contested terrain of the ambiguous middle of a group or organization's hierarchy. Krackhardt (1996) provided an analogous interpretation in his discussion of Simmelian ties. In his study, the protagonist Chris, by virtue of his central structural position in a social network, has the opportunity to step into a position of leadership over a group making a unionization drive. But instead of stepping up to lead, Chris unexpectedly quits the organization entirely, just before the big unionization vote. Krackhardt reasoned that Chris may not have been willing to take on the responsibilities such as depersonalizing and antagonizing existing friendships that the new role and increased status would have brought.

acy and integration fostered in a face to face meeting enables the formation of a consensus (even if fleeting and contestable) that facilitates the coordinated behaviors that reify a status order and make it real in its effects. Also, far from a simple game, status contests in meetings beget complexity as meetings for groups in organizations reoccur time after time. This admits the possibility of nontrivial strategy by individuals, and it encourages the formation of contextual norms regarding move behaviors within the group. We leave it to later empirical research to further verify these norms and the benefits or dysfunctions that status contests can bring.

REFERENCES

Ancona, D. G., Caldwell, D., & O'Reilly, C. (1992). Demography and design: Predictors of new product team performance. *Organization Science, 3*, 321–341.

Ardrey, R. (1967). *The territorial imperative.* London: Collins.

Bales, R. F. (1951). Channels of communication in small groups. *American Sociological Review, 16*, 461–468.

Benedict, R. (1934). *Patterns of culture.* New York: Mentor Books.

Berger, J., Fisek, M. H., Norman, R. Z., & Zelditch, M. J. (1977). *Status characteristics and social interaction.* New York: Elsevier.

Berger, J., Rosenholtz, S. J. & Zelditch, M. (1980). Status organizing process. *Annual Review of Sociology, 6*, 479–508.

Berger, J., & Zelditch, M. (1985). *Status, rewards, and influence.* San Francisco: Jossey-Bass.

Blau, P. M. (1964). *Exchange and power in social life.* New York: Wiley.

Bloch, M. (1971). Decision-making in councils among the Merina of Madagascar. In A. Richards & A. Kuper (Eds.), *Councils in action* (Vol. 6, pp. 29–62). Cambridge, England: Cambridge University Press.

Bourdieu, P. (1984). *Distinction: A social critique of the judgment of taste.* Cambridge, MA: Harvard University Press.

Domhoff, G. W. (1967). *Who rules America?* New Jersey: Prentice-Hall.

Fisek, M. H. (1974). A model for the evolution of status structures in task-oriented discussion groups. In J. Berger, T. L. Conner, & M. H. Fisek (Eds.), *Expectation states theory: A theoretical research program* (pp. 55–83). Cambridge, MA: Winthrop.

Geertz, C. (1973). *The interpretation of cultures.* New York: Basic Books.

Goffman, E. (1959). *The presentation of self in everyday life.* New York: Anchor Books.

Goffman, E. (1969). *Strategic interaction.* Philadelphia: University of Pennsylvania Press.

Goffman, E. (1974). *Frame analysis.* Boston: Northeastern University Press.

Gouran, D. S. (1982). *Making decisions in groups.* Glenview, IL: Scott, Foresman.

Hofstede, G. (1980). *Culture's consequences: International differences in work-related values.* Beverly Hills: Sage.

Jones, E. E., & Pittman, T. S. (1982). Toward a general theory of strategic self-presentation. In J. Suls (Ed.), *Psychological perspectives on the self* (pp. 231–262). Hillsdale, NJ: Lawrence Erlbaum Associates.

Kelley, H. H. (1951). Communication in experimentally created hierarchies. *Human Relations, 4*, 39–56.

Klapp, O. (1954). Heroes, villains and fools as agents of social control. *American Sociological Review, 19*, 57–62.

Krackhardt, D. (1996). *Groups, roles, and Simmelian ties in organizations.* Manuscript in preparation, Heinz School of Public Policy, Carnegie Melon University, Pittsburgh, PA.

Latour, B., & Woolgar, S. (1979). *Laboratory life: The social construction of scientific facts.* Beverly Hills, CA: Sage.

Lenski, G. E. (1954). Status crystallization: A non-vertical dimension of social status. *American Sociological Review, 19,* 405–414.

Maclay, G., & Knipe, H. (1972). *The dominant man: The pecking order in human society.* New York: Delacorte Press.

Meindl, J. R., Ehrlich, S. B., & Dukerich, J. M. (1985). The romance of leadership. *Administrative Science Quarterly, 30,* 78–102

Mills, C. W. (1957). *The power elite.* New York: Oxford University Press.

Pfeffer, J., & Salancik G. (1978). *The external control of organizations.* New York: Harper & Row.

Rifkin, W. D. (1990). *Communication between technical and nontechnical people: The negotiation of expert status.* Unpublished doctoral dissertation, Stanford University.

Schjelderup-Ebbe, T. (1935). Social behavior of birds. In C. Murchison (Ed.), *Handbook of social psychology* (pp. 947–972). Worcester, MA: Clark University Press.

Schwartzman, H. B. (1986). The meeting as a neglected social form in organizational studies. *Research in Organizational Behavior, 8,* 233–258.

Schwartzman, H. B. (1989). *The meeting: Gatherings in organizations and communities.* New York: Plenum.

Sproull, L., & Kiesler, S. (1986). Reducing social context cues: Electronic mail in organizational communications. *Management Science, 32,* 492–1512.

Strauss, A. L. (1978). *Negotiations: Varieties, contexts, processes, and social order.* San Francisco: Jossey-Bass.

Sutton, R. I., & Hargadon, A. (1996). Brainstorming groups in context: Effectiveness in a product design firm. *Administrative Science Quarterly, 41,* 685–718.

Veblen, T. (1899). *The theory of the leisure class.* New York: Macmillan.

Warner, W. L., Meeker, M., & Eells, K. (1949). *Social class in America, a manual of procedure for the measurement of social status.* Chicago: Science Research Associates.

Weber, Max. (1968). *Economy and society: An outline of interpretive sociology* (G. Roth & C. Wittich, Eds.; E. Fischoff, Trans.) New York: Bedminster Press. (Original work published 1922)

Wegener, B. (1992). Concepts and measurement of prestige. *Annual Review of Sociology, 18,* 253–280.

Weisband, S. P., Schneider, S. K., & Connolly, T. (1995). Computer-mediated communication and social information: Status salience and status differences. *Academy of Management Journal, 4,* 1124–1151.

Whyte, W. F. (1943). *Street corner society* (2nd ed.). Chicago: University of Chicago Press.

Part IV

INNOVATION
AND LEARNING

Chapter 11

Creativity in Groups and Teams

Paul B. Paulus,
Timothy S. Larey,
Mary T. Dzindolet,
University of Texas at Arlington

Developing new ideas is a key component of the success of large and small businesses. Many small businesses are founded on the basis of ideas of one or more individuals. Such businesses have accounted for most of the new jobs in the United States in the past few years. Some of these small businesses grow to be rather large, such as Nike and Microsoft. Yet, regardless of their size, companies are continually seeking a better idea than their competitors. Their continued survival depends on judicious selection of new directions, products, and programs. Much of the idea generation and decision making in organizations involves groups or teams. Teamwork and lateralization of the organization are trends in many organizations, motivated at least in part by a strong belief in the efficacy of groups or teamwork (Guzzo & Dickson, 1996; Hackman, 1990; Salas & Swezey, 1992; Schrage, 1995; Woodman, Sawyer, & Griffin, 1993).

There are many benefits of group interaction or teamwork. Group activities can build cohesiveness or team spirit, which in turn may be related to increased job motivation and morale. The shared decision making and responsibility of a team-based organization may lead to greater support or endorsement of organizational initiatives or programs. Groups can also take advantage of the shared expertise of the members. This may be particularly useful both in generating novel approaches and avoiding costly mistakes. These and other benefits of work groups have been championed both by practitioners and scholars (Cotton, 1993; Hackman, 1990; Levine & Tyson, 1990; Payne, 1990; Tjosvold, 1991; West, 1990; Zander, 1994). However, this perspective is in stark contrast to much research on the productivity of groups that suggests that group activities often suffer from a production loss (Shepperd, 1993). When the products of groups are compared with those of a similar number of individuals who perform in isolation, the performance of the subset of individuals (nominal groups) often may exceed that of the interactive groups. It appears to be much easier to demonstrate negative effects of group activities than positive ones (Buys, 1978). Of course, some activities require group involvement (e.g., athletic teams, juries, corporate boards) and in many cases, groups form or convene simply for the purpose of shared activity rather than productivity. Groups can also be effective in decision making tasks under certain conditions (Kerr, MacCoun, & Kramer, 1996; Larey, 1994)

In this chapter, we analyze the effectiveness of groups in generating ideas. Most of our thinking time is solitary, but often we are brought together in groups to share ideas and generate new ones. This is particularly likely when a group or organization is facing a problem or is in need of new ideas. Idea meetings may involve rather informal or unorganized sharing of ideas, they may be highly organized (Van de Ven & Delbecq, 1974), or even controlled by computers (Nunamaker, Dennis, Valacich, Vogel, & George, 1991). One popular technique to facilitate idea exchange involves the use of brainstorming rules (Osborn, 1957). These rules encourage individuals to generate large numbers of ideas in a nonevaluative atmosphere. Participants are instructed not to criticize or evaluate ideas as they are presented, to say whatever comes to mind, and to build on ideas generated by other group members. Osborn (1957, 1963) and others (e.g., Davis, 1986; Prince, 1970; Rawlinson, 1981; Rickards, 1993) have promoted this technique as being useful in generating large numbers of ideas as well as high quality ideas. Unfortunately, controlled laboratory research has not supported these claims. To the contrary, groups often generate only half as many ideas as similar numbers of solitary performers and do not generate higher quality ideas (Diehl & Stroebe, 1987; Larey & Paulus, 1999; Mullen, Johnson, & Salas, 1991).

What are the implications of these findings for idea generation or group creativity in organizations? One possibility is that work groups suffer the same production losses as those observed with laboratory groups. Moreover, because group members do not have appropriate baseline comparisons to evaluate their productivity, they may have the illusion that they are being very productive or creative even when their performance level is relatively low (Paulus & Asuncion, 1995; Stroebe, Diehl, & Abakoumkin, 1992). However, it is also possible that groups in organizational settings do not suffer productivity losses experienced by laboratory groups. Because most of the controlled studies have used ad hoc and untrained groups of students generating ideas on topics of little personal relevance, generalization to organizational settings may be unwarranted.

A third possibility is that interactive idea generation in both laboratory and work groups is effective under some conditions but not under others (Paulus, Brown, & Ortega, 1999). We evaluate each of these alternatives and the related theoretical processes and practical implications.

THE PRODUCTION LOSS PERSPECTIVE

Shortly after the publication of Osborn's book, empirical studies attempted to determine whether the claims for its effectiveness were warranted (Taylor, Berry, & Block, 1958). Some studies compared group brainstorming with nominal groups and others compared the effectiveness of different brainstorming procedures. Although brainstorming procedures in groups appear to lead to enhanced idea generation compared to other group procedures (Parnes & Meadow, 1959), comparisons of brainstorming groups with nominal groups have generally found production losses in interactive groups (Mullen et al., 1991). Interactive groups often generated only half as many ideas as nominals. Such losses are even found for groups composed of coworkers trained in group dynamics who are generating ideas on an issue of personal relevance (Paulus, Larey, & Ortega, 1995).

Much research has focused on discovering the basis for this production loss. One obvious problem with group brainstorming is that individuals have to share the idea-generating time and solitary performers do not. Because only group members must present their ideas one at a time, they have less time in which to express their ideas. Moreover, they may forget ideas as they wait their turn or decide that their ideas are no longer pertinent. It may also be difficult to generate ideas while others are sharing theirs. These potential problems with generating ideas in a group setting are termed *production blocking* (Diehl & Stroebe, 1987; Stroebe & Diehl, 1994). Studies by Diehl and Stroebe (1987, 1991) suggest that the critical factor in production blocking is the inability to present ideas as they are generated. The amount of time available and distraction by the performance of others do not seem to be as important.

In interactive groups, one's ideas and actions are exposed to the evaluative scrutiny of other group members. Even though the group members are instructed to refrain from critical reactions to ideas, group members may still be concerned about what other group members think of them and their contributions. This evaluative concern may inhibit the generation of ideas in groups and may be particularly true for those individuals who are quite sensitive to the potential reactions of others. For example, individuals who are high in social interaction anxiety are highly concerned about how others perceive or evaluate them (Leary & Kowalski, 1993). Camacho and Paulus (1995) examined nominal and interactive groups composed of either all high-interaction anxious or all low-interaction anxious individuals. In the nominal conditions, there was little difference in the performance of these two types of individuals. However, the performance of interactive groups of high-anxious individuals was much worse than that of groups composed of low-anxious individuals. Thus, it appears likely that part of the production loss in groups is due to social or cognitive inhibition experienced by high-anxious individuals.

It has been well established that individuals in groups may exert reduced effort or loaf when their performance is not individually monitored (Karau & Williams, 1993). This tendency to loaf may contribute to the productivity loss in groups when only a group product is obtained (Diehl & Stroebe, 1987). However, production loss in groups is also obtained when each person's performance in the group is individually monitored (e.g., Camacho & Paulus, 1995; Paulus & Dzindolet, 1993; Paulus et al., 1995). Another type of motivation loss, free riding, can account for production loss even when group members are individually accountable (Kerr & Bruun, 1983). When some group members are active contributors to the group product, other group members may feel less pressure to contribute their ideas and take a "free ride" on the active members' efforts. This type of pattern of distribution of effort is often observed in groups (Bales, 1970).

The research literature suggests that all three of these factors may play a role in the production loss of group brainstorming. Paulus and Dzindolet (1993) proposed that production blocking, evaluation apprehension, and free riding serve to establish a rather low level of initial performance in most idea-generating groups. The opportunity for social comparison in the group setting may lead to this low level of performance becoming somewhat of a normative standard for the group. That is, the fairly low rate of performance of most group members may be deemed as a socially appropriate or typical level. The resulting rather unambitious standard of performance may be maintained throughout the group session and in subsequent sessions (Paulus & Dzindolet, 1993). The social comparison process also results in a homogenization of performance in interactive groups, contrary to predictions of free riding. Furthermore, there is a tendency for the group performance or goals to go in the direction of the least productive group members (Camacho & Paulus, 1995; Larey & Paulus, 1995; Paulus & Dzindolet, 1993). The Paulus and Dzindolet (1993) social influence model is summarized in Fig. 11.1. This model depicts the role of social influence processes as one of maintaining low performance levels and moving in a downward direction. However, as discussed later in this chapter, this state of affairs is not inevitable. Procedures designed to reduce evaluation apprehension, free riding, and blocking should increase performance levels in groups. In addition, under some conditions, the social interaction might stimulate performance of group members in an upward direction.

PRODUCTIVITY LOSS SCENARIO

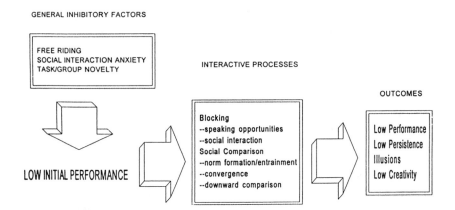

FIG. 11.1.   The social influence model of production loss in group brain-storming.

Perceptions and Illusions

Although there is empirical evidence for the role of various processes in the production loss in group brainstorming, there appears to be little subjective awareness of these processes. Individuals in groups report generally positive feelings and enjoyment of the group experience. There is no evidence of the negative affect that one would expect to be linked to the evaluative concerns or to the experience of blocking. Specific questions about evaluation apprehension, effort, and social influence do not yield different results for participants in individual and group conditions. Questions designed to tap the experience of blocking suggest that solitary performers find the task more difficult and frustrating than do group performers (cf. Camacho & Paulus, 1995; Paulus & Dzindolet, 1993). Although these patterns of findings may be used as evidence against the role of the hypothesized processes, it is likely that individuals are not aware of the subtle processes that play a role in group performance (Wilson, Laser, & Stone, 1982). Group processes may be too involved to allow for much simultaneous introspection.

In addition to the generally positive feelings associated with group activity, group members perceive their performance more favorably than do solitary performers (Homma, Tajima, & Hayashi, 1995; Paulus, Dzindolet, Poletes, & Camacho, 1993; Stroebe et al., 1992). This may partly be due to a generally positive bias toward group brainstorming that most bring to the session. The majority of individuals appear to believe that they would generate more ideas in a group than alone (Paulus et al., 1993; Paulus et al., 1995). This belief about the efficacy of groups may influence perceptions of actual performance in groups. Another factor in the favorable perception of group performance may be the tendency for individuals in groups to take credit for ideas that were actually generated by others (Stroebe et al., 1992). In one study, members of groups of four each took credit for 36% of the ideas generated (Paulus et al., 1993).

Social comparison processes may also contribute to the illusion of group productivity. When group members compare their performances, most group members will find that their performance is similar to that of other group members. The tendency for homogenization of performance in groups should enhance the perception of similarity. As a result, most group members may feel relatively satisfied with their performance in comparison to solitary performers who may be somewhat uncertain about the adequacy of their performance. Consistent with the social comparison interpretation, several studies have found that provision of information about performance of others enhances perception of performance (Paulus et al., 1993; Paulus, Larey, Putman, Leggett, & Roland, 1996).

The illusion of productivity observed in brainstorming groups has implications for other group contexts as well. The generally favorable perception of group activities and teamwork in organizations may also be based on illusions due to similar processes (e.g., preexisting biases, cognitive appropriation, social comparison). Although teamwork is very popular in organizations (Guzzo & Salas, 1995; Tjosvold, 1991), teams require considerable training (Swezey & Salas, 1992) and are effective only under certain conditions (Guzzo & Dickson, 1996; Hackman, 1990; Hitchcock & Willard, 1995; Levine & Tyson, 1990; Varney, 1989). Moreover, it is often difficult to separate the effects of teamwork from the influence of other variables that are likely to vary with the use of teams such as leadership style and compensation systems (Cotton, 1993; Levine & Tyson, 1990). Therefore, the effectiveness of a particular team's functioning may be difficult to judge for participants as well as scientific observers in the absence of appropriate comparisons with other teams or with comparable organizations that do not use teams. The illusion effects suggest that individuals may be quite satisfied with suboptimal team performance when such comparisons are not available (Cordery, Mueller, & Smith, 1991).

Conditions for Effective Brainstorming

Controlled research has clearly demonstrated that group brainstorming is not very effective. This is in stark contrast to the claims for its efficacy by practitioners. These claims may be due in part to the practitioners' illusion of productivity. Reports by Osborn and others of rates of productivity of group brainstorming indicate that those rates are about the same as rates obtained in laboratory groups (Paulus et al., 1995). So their perceptions of efficacy evidently have some illusory aspects. However, differences between the procedures used in experimental studies and those used by practitioners may account for some of the discrepancy between the research findings and the experiences reported by practitioners. Laboratory studies have not employed the types of procedures recommended by practitioners (e.g., Grossman, Rodgers, & Moore, 1989; Osborn, 1957; Rawlinson, 1981). Practitioners typically use facilitators to aid group members in following the brainstorming rules and in encouraging them to continue generating ideas during lulls. Professionals also tend to use group brainstorming after a session of writing ideas individually. This procedure would allow individuals to generate a large number of ideas that they can share with the group and may minimize the impact of various inhibitory processes (e.g., evaluation, free riding, blocking). Groups are often provided extensive training in brainstorming, and they may include several expert brainstormers who serve as pacesetters (Osborn, 1957). When groups start running low on ideas, they can be provided with breaks to "recharge" their idea generating capacity. This may involve the trying out of different roles or perspectives suggested by the facilitator (Prince, 1970).

What is the evidence for the effectiveness of these and other procedures designed to enhance group brainstorming? There is little controlled research that has addressed these issues. We have obtained some support for their efficacy in the course of our research studies. Trained facilitators can bring the performance of interactive groups to the level of nominal groups (Oxley, Dzindolet, & Paulus, 1996). Training groups to effectively follow the brainstorming rules enables them to generate almost as many ideas as nominal groups (Leggett, Putman, Roland, & Paulus, 1996). Providing brief 5-minute breaks during which individuals are reminded of the brainstorming rules also enhances group brainstorming significantly (Horn, 1993). In one study, we combined a number of practitioner-recommended procedures (e.g., breaks and prior solitary brainstorming) and techniques to reduce the illusion of productivity (e.g., the provision of a high group standard and instructions to keep track of the number of ideas generated) in one group condition. This condition led to significantly higher performance than a regular group brainstorming condition (Dzindolet & Paulus, 1995).

Evidence on the impact of the sequence of individual to group brainstorming is mixed. For example, in one study the individual brainstorming followed by group brainstorming yielded similar overall results as a group to individual sequence (Paulus et al., 1995). However, in a study that involved extensive training in brainstorming rules and longer brainstorming sessions (25 min. vs. 15 min.), the group to alone sequence enhanced productivity relative to the alone to group sequence (Leggett et al., 1996).

As we suggested earlier, some individuals may be better suited to group brainstorming than others. Low socially anxious individuals perform almost as well in interactive groups as in nominal groups (Camacho & Paulus, 1995). Those who strongly prefer working alone on tasks do better when they are brainstorming alone than those who strongly prefer working in groups. Those who prefer working in groups generate more total ideas in groups than low-preference individuals, but many of these ideas are repeats of ideas from other group members (Larey & Paulus, 1999). Interestingly, those who enjoy thinking or who have a high need for cognition (Petty & Cacioppo, 1982) do not generate more ideas than those who are low on this dimension, either alone or when exposed to ideas by others (Dosset, 1995).

Although brainstorming in groups may work well for some types of people and not for others, it is difficult in practice to pretest individuals to determine which type of idea generation or work setting would be best for them. However, it should be clear to supervisors and facilitators that individuals who do not perform well in one type of setting may excel in a different one. The senior author has noticed this whenever his classes are involved in various group activities. Students who have a rather mediocre record on prior exams may function very effectively in group settings. The types of social inclinations and cognitive skills required for effective group functioning may be quite different from those related to excellence in individualistic endeavors.

We have also discovered some factors that do not reduce the gap between individual and group brainstorming. These include brainstorming with friends or group "icebreaker" exercises (O'Conner, 1995), familiarity with the other group members, the use of a job relevant problem (Paulus et al., 1995), and prior experience on brainstorming tasks (Paulus & Dzindolet, 1993).

Electronic Brainstorming

We have outlined a number of ways in which production losses associated with group brainstorming can be significantly reduced. Another approach to overcoming the problems of group brainstorming involves the use of a computer-based group interaction paradigm (Gallupe, Bastianutti, & Cooper, 1991). This type of brainstorming is called electronic brainstorming and is part of group decision support systems that have been developed at many universities and in many organizations (Jessup & Valacich, 1993). Typically, groups ranging in size from 4 to 18 generate ideas simultaneously on individual computers. Throughout the session, brainstormers have access to the ideas generated by the other group members on one part of their screen. The ideas of the group are stored by a central computer. This enables the groups to evaluate the ideas at the end of the session. Studies have found that electronic brainstorming leads to enhanced performance relative to conventional brainstorming (Gallupe et al., 1991). This is typically attributed to the anonymity of the technology and the fact that group members can generate ideas simultaneously (no production blocking) (Nunamaker, Dennis, Valacich, & Vogel, 1991). However, electronic brainstormers do not perform better than nominal groups of oral brainstormers (cf. Paulus et al., 1995). Electronic brainstorming is a useful approach if one wants to give the brainstormers a sense of group involvement without the drawbacks of conventional group brainstorming.

Several studies have claimed that electronic brainstorming with large size groups actually leads to enhancement of performance relative to similar sized groups brainstorming individually (Dennis & Valacich, 1993). This type of finding is taken as evidence for a synergistic effect of group brainstorming. However, a detailed analysis of these studies suggests that the evidence for such an effect is rather weak (Paulus et al., 1995). For example, in one of the most extensive studies of this type (Valacich, Dennis, & Connolly, 1994), the overall level of idea generation was extremely low. It will require a number of additional studies with varied problems to determine whether there are indeed benefits of increasing group size with electronic brainstorming.

THEORETICAL BASES FOR GROUP SYNERGY OR CREATIVITY

Much of the research on group brainstorming is consistent with the notion that this type of group activity results in production losses. We have suggested that under some conditions and for some types of people, such production losses may be minimal. However, there is no compelling evidence for enhanced performance of interactive brainstorming relative to solitary brainstorming. This state of affairs is quite consistent with the literature on creativity. Most reviews conclude that high levels of creativity require long periods of isolation and that most creative achievements are the result of individual mental activity (Ochse, 1990; Simonton, 1988; Sternberg, 1988). In fact, the social science literature yields few citations of group creativity (Kasof, 1995; Paulus et al., 1999). Reviews on creativity generally ignore group processes or cite the fact that groups hinder creativity on the basis of the brainstorming literature (Amabile, 1983; Simonton, 1988; Sternberg & Lubart, 1996). However, there are those who feel that groups can be an important basis for creative contributions. Many scientific endeavors involve teams of scientists who join together to solve problems requiring diverse skills and knowledge domains. Some of the most important scientific developments come from such collaborations (Snyder, 1989). There are also a number of organizational scholars who emphasize the creative potential of groups (Hare, 1982; King & Anderson, 1990; Nystrom, 1979; Schrage, 1995; Woodman et al., 1993). They point out that group creativity depends on such factors as leadership, cohesiveness, communication patterns, motivation, member knowledge, and group composition.

There are a number of processes that could be related to enhanced creativity in groups. Osborn (1957) outlined four major ones—social reinforcement, social facilitation/stimulation, rivalry/competition, and mutual association. Social reinforcement is the positive reaction to ideas that individuals receive from their fellow brainstormers. This should motivate them to keep generating ideas. However, our observations of group interaction suggest that social reinforcement activity may actually distract or block the participants in the idea-generation process. Moreover, in groups, there is a tendency to reinforce or respond favorably to ideas that individuals have in common (Stewart & Stasser, 1995). So the reinforcement process may lead to a tendency to share common rather than uncommon or unique responses (Larey & Paulus, 1999). The positive feelings generated by shared social reinforcements may be partially responsible for the positive feelings and illusions about performance that characterize groups.

Much research suggests that simple behaviors may be facilitated in the presence of others (Zajonc, 1965, 1980). This may partly reflect some type of increased arousal or energization in group settings that in turn enhances well-learned or simple responses. Some types of brainstorming tasks (e.g., thinking up uses for a paper clip) may indeed be fairly simple in the early stages and could benefit from such arousal. Another basis for socially facilitated behavior is mimicry or matching of observed behaviors. Both humans and animals appear to have a strong tendency to repeat or match observed behaviors (Miller & Dollard, 1941; Zajonc, 1980). In the brainstorming context, individuals may match the rate of activity of other brainstormers (Paulus & Dzindolet, 1993) or the category of ideas being discussed (Larey & Paulus, 1999). Therefore, high rates of activity on the part of one group brainstormer should stimulate a high rate of activity on the part of other group members. This is of course exactly opposite to a prediction based on production blocking and downward comparison processes. We have obtained some evidence for the positive effects of social matching. Active brainstormers who generate a high number of ideas without taking up much time appear to stimulate idea generation in their partners (Dzindolet, 1992). However, in the typical group idea-sharing situation, much of the discussion may involve elaboration or digressions that may divert from a focus on the basic ideas and limit the amount of time available for idea generation. It seems likely that the potential stimulating effects of exposure to shared ideas is often counteracted by the production blocking experienced as one is trying to generate one's own ideas and the tendency to free ride.

Although the brainstorming instructions provide a nonevaluative context for idea generation, there still may be somewhat of a competitive atmosphere as individuals attempt to outdo each other in the number of ideas generated. Yet, in many groups, there may be little incentive for generating large numbers of ideas and there may be a tendency for downward comparison in which the low performers set the standard. Groups may even set low goals for themselves to avoid group failure in meeting their goal (Larey & Paulus, 1995). To counteract such downward matching tendencies, one could institute various procedures to increase rivalry or competition. Paulus and Dzindolet (1993) found that providing interactive groups with information about the potential performance of nominal groups greatly increased the performance of the interactive groups. In another study, providing brainstorming pairs information about each other's performance in one session enhanced their performance in the next session in comparison to pairs not provided such information (Paulus et al., 1993). The fact that interactive pairs generally perform about as well on brainstorming tasks as nominal pairs may be related to the fact that pairing is more likely to induce a tendency toward competition than groupings of four or more. A recent study examined the competition in groups of four in which all individuals brainstormed by typing ideas on computers (Paulus et al., 1996). Conditions varied whether individuals verbally shared these ideas and/or were asked to indicate the number of ideas they generated every 5 minutes. Comparison of ideas every 5 minutes enhanced performance relative to the other conditions. Thus, increased competitiveness in interactive groups may be one basis for enhanced idea generation relative to nominal groups.

Osborn (1957) assumed that idea generation in groups would result in much mutual association. That is, ideas by one group member could stimulate related ideas for the other group members. The mutual stimulation of ideas should greatly increase the range of ideas generated in groups compared to individuals. Unfortunately, there is little evidence for this type of process in brainstorming groups. Interactive groups not only generate fewer ideas than nominal groups, but their ideas also come from a smaller range of idea categories (Larey & Paulus, 1999). Research on electronic brainstorming also finds little evidence of cognitive stimulation from idea exposure (Connolly, Routhieaux, & Schneider, 1993). All the findings thus far suggest that it is difficult for individuals to process and reflect on information or ideas from others as they are generating theirs (see also Gilbert, Pelham, & Krull, 1988; Gurman, 1968; Lamm & Trommsdorff, 1973). Stimulating effects of group interaction may be most likely observed if one examines solitary performance after group interaction. The ideas presented in groups may serve as primes for ideas during subsequent private reflection periods (Leggett et al., 1996).

Benefits from group interaction are particularly likely for tasks that require diverse knowledge domains. It is difficult for one individual to have all of the expertise required for many tasks. Moreover, overlearning has been related to reduced creativity (Mednick, 1962; Ochse, 1990). Diverse groups enhance the potential for novel combinations of ideas. At least one study has provided some evidence for the positive role of diversity on group brainstorming (Stroebe & Diehl, 1994). However, too much diversity in a group may have detrimental effects (Jackson, May, & Whitney, 1995; Kirchmeyer, 1993). There may be both conflict among those with diverse perspectives and problems of communication if the groups do not overlap sufficiently in their linguistic or conceptual domains (Maznevski, 1994).

A Cognitive Theory of Group Creativity

One reason that studies do not clearly demonstrate the creative potential of groups may be the lack of established paradigms for the study of group creativity. Paulus and his colleagues have recently suggested a cognitive theory and paradigm for the study of group creativity (Brown & Paulus, 1996; Paulus et al., 1999). We briefly outline some of the major features of a cognitive theory of creativity consistent with some of the findings cited in this chapter.

One useful categorization of creativity for idea generation has been provided by Guilford (1967). Individuals can be creative by generating many ideas (fluency), ideas from a wide variety of domains or categories (flexibility), novel or unique ideas (originality), or by combining or modifying existing ideas (elaboration). From this perspective, creative groups should generate many ideas from a wide range of categories, generate a high number of unique ideas, and provide opportunities for elaboration of each others' ideas. Why does this not occur in brainstorming groups? One reason may be that groups in controlled studies tend to be fairly homogeneous in their knowledge or background for the problems used. In organizations and scientific teams, problem-solving groups are composed of individuals who have the diverse set of skills and knowledge required for problem solution. Moreover, these groups experience a mixture of individual and group working sessions depending on their needs. They may spend most of their time working on their particular area of responsibility but periodically may seek the counsel or expertise of other group members. Group meetings may be scheduled to share information, solve particular problems, or set group goals. We know of no controlled research that has evaluated the benefits of group interaction or teamwork in this context. There is evidence that groups can be useful in evaluating alternative courses of action or hypotheses based on information provided. Groups appear to be superior to the average individual in recognizing truth, rejecting errors, and in processing information (Kerr et al., 1996; Laughlin, Vanderstoep, & Hollingshead, 1991). Although groups may be less productive in generating ideas than nominal groups, interactive groups can be better at evaluating the output of the idea-generating process (e.g., its creativity or uniqueness, Larey & Paulus, 1999). It is also obvious that some tasks can only be done by groups (e.g.,team sports) or with individuals with a diverse set of skills. What is not clear is the extent to which creativity or idea-generation tasks that can be performed at both the individual or group level benefit from diversity.

Our model of cognitive creativity in groups makes a number of assumptions. Ideas related to a particular issue will fall into different cognitive categories that vary in depth (number of ideas). Some ideas will be more difficult to retrieve than others. At the level of groups, there is likely to be some overlap among the idea sets of the group members. The extent of overlap will depend on the extent to which the group members have similar experiences in relation to the problem. Similarly, groups will differ in the variety among their idea sets. This reflects the combined variety of experiences that group members may have had in regard to a particular problem. When the idea sets of the group members are combined conceptually, groups can vary in the overall depth of a particular idea or idea category, and in the degree to which this depth is dispersed over the idea space or is relatively narrow.

Individual idea generation should be a function of the size and diversity of the available idea set. However, individuals may differ in their motivation to access their ideas or their cognitive awareness of the potential set of ideas available. Thus individual performance can be increased by using procedures that increase motivation or awareness of the pool of available ideas. For example, Paulus and Dzindolet (1993) found that informing brainstormers of the large number of ideas that could be generated greatly increased the number of ideas generated. Similarly, providing a brief break during the brainstorming session can significantly increase the number of ideas generated (Horn, 1993). Toward the end of brainstorming sessions, participants typically reduce their rate of idea production significantly. Brief breaks during the session may give participants renewed motivation to tap their available ideas.

When group members share their ideas, a number of social processes may influence the rate of idea generation. The performance of group members can provide both social and cognitive stimulation. Social stimulation can take the form of a mutual matching of the rate of performance. Each group may converge to an "average" rate of performance based on their individual inclinations (Paulus & Dzindolet, 1993). An emphasis on performance of individual group members may lead to increased feelings of competition in groups and enhanced motivation to generate ideas (Paulus et al., 1996). Cognitive stimulation may involve priming of idea categories or stimulation of specific ideas in response to ideas presented in the group. When someone in the group presents an idea in a new category, this should stimulate other group members to generate additional ideas in this category. Group members can also act on ideas from others by modifying them or combining them with related ideas of their own.

From this perspective, groups have great potential for the production of creative ideas. The research cited in this chapter indicates that this potential is not typically met. Social loafing, social anxiety, blocking, and downward comparison have been suggested as potential reasons for this productivity loss. Another possibility is that it may be very difficult to process ideas generated by others while one is generating one's own (Grossman et al., 1989), hence the failure to find a cognitive impact of exposure to idea generation during electronic brainstorming (Connolly et al., 1993). Therefore, the potential benefit of cognitive stimulation provided by group interaction may be apparent only when individuals have solitary performance sessions following group interaction (Dossett, 1995). These sessions may allow individuals to effectively utilize the primes provided and integrate their ideas with the ideas presented. Therefore, group brainstorming may primarily a useful adjunct to solitary creative activities.

Cognitive benefits of social interaction may also be most evident for groups with diverse knowledge or idea structures. Such groups should enhance the chance that individuals will be primed to access unfamiliar or low-frequency domains or categories. Diverse groups should also increase the probability of unique combinations of ideas. However, high levels of diversity may increase the difficulty of communication if there is not sufficient cognitive overlap (Maznevski, 1994). For example, companies sometimes hire individuals to facilitate communication among engineers and computer programmers. These facilitators have a broad knowledge of both programming and engineering. High levels of diversity may also inhibit social interaction in general because most individuals appear to prefer interacting with those of similar cultural, philosophical, or intellectual background (Clore & Byrne, 1974; Jackson et al., 1995). There may also be a bias in groups to focus on shared ideas or expertise rather than on unique ideas or skills (Dennis, 1996; Stewart & Stasser, 1995). Facilitators, special training, or extended experience as a team (Watson, Kumar, & Michaelsen, 1993) may be required to enable groups to tap their full intellectual potential.

Creativity in Teams

Teamwork in organizations increasingly involves the exchange of knowledge among group members (McDermott, 1995). Many organizations and practitioners believe that teams have great creative potential, but it is recognized that teams often do not meet their potential (Boyett & Boyett, 1993; Guzzo & Salas, 1995; Hitchcock & Willard, 1995; McDermott, 1995; Robbins & Finley, 1995; Schrage, 1995). Teams may suffer from many of the same problems that we have discovered with ad hoc groups that interact only for short periods of time. Team members may loaf or free ride, inhibit the activity of other team members by critical or evaluative reactions, or block overall team productivity by engaging in counterproductive behavior (e.g., extensive socializing with other group members). Teams may converge to the level of performance of the least productive members, yet harbor illusions of their effectiveness. Knowledge teams may not effectively share their diverse range of knowledge among the team members (McDermott, 1995).

If teams indeed suffer from these types of problems, the various techniques that have been shown to increase effectiveness of brainstorming groups may be useful in enhancing teamwork. This would be particularly true with teams that are concerned about knowledge or information sharing. Of course, these techniques should be useful any time team members come together to generate ideas.

Teams should be kept to the minimal number of members required to do the task. This should minimize the potential for social loafing or free riding and limit the degree of production blocking when teams meet to share ideas. When individuals work as members of a team, some degree of individual accountability or competition may enhance motivation and limit the tendency to social loafing. It is important to set challenging goals to counteract the tendency toward downward comparison in performance matching and goal setting. When teams are involved in intense interactive activities, it is important to provide breaks at various times in this process. When the task involves idea generation, moving from group to individual sessions periodically may optimize the generation of unique ideas. The composition of the team is also important. Teams composed of individuals with complementary skills and areas of expertise enhance the chances of solving complex problems or generating novel ideas. Teams composed of individuals who are low in social anxiety and have a favorable attitude to group interaction are most likely to function at a high level. Trained facilitators and/or training teams in the process of idea sharing and collaboration appear to be important for effective teamwork. Finally, it would seem important for team members to understand the tendency for group members to have inflated perceptions of their performance. This may lead them to seek out objective indicators of team performance.

The strong faith in teamwork that pervades various cultures may often be based on illusory perceptions of their efficacy. Many group processes can contribute to teams performing significantly below their potential. However, with appropriate training and support (Hackman, 1990; Hitchcock & Willard, 1995; Swezey & Salas, 1992; Varney, 1989) and by using some of the insights from research on group creativity, it may be possible for teams to realize their synergistic potential.

SUMMARY

Contrary to the enthusiastic endorsement of group and team activities in organizations, controlled research has not provided much evidence for the efficacy of such groups or teams in tapping the creative potential of their group members. We have provided an analysis of the basis of such production losses in groups and have proposed some ways in which the creative potential of groups can be realized more fully. Future research will have to determine whether our speculations are well founded or merely a persistence of illusions about group effectiveness.

ACKNOWLEDGMENTS

Some of the research discussed and the preparation of this chapter were supported by a grant from the National Science Foundation.

REFERENCES

Amabile, T. M. (1983). *The social psychology of creativity*. New York: Springer-Verlag.
Bales, B. F. (1970). *Personality and interpersonal behavior*. New York: Holt, Rinehart & Winston.
Boyett, J. H., & Boyett, J. T. (1993). *Beyond workplace 2000*. Bergenfield, NJ: Penguin.
Brown, V., & Paulus, P. (1996). A simple dynamic model of social factors in group brainstorming. *Small Group Research, 27*, 91–114.
Buys, C. J. (1978). Humans would do better without groups. *Personality and Social Psychology Bulletin, 4*, 123–125.
Camacho, L. M., & Paulus, P. B. (1995). The role of social anxiousness in group brainstorming. *Journal of Personality and Social Psychology, 68*, 1071–1080.
Clore, G. L., & Byrne, D. (1974). A reinforcement-affect model of attraction. In T. L. Huston (Ed.), *Foundations of interpersonal attraction* (pp. 143–170). New York: Academic Press.
Connolly, T., Routhieaux, R. L., & Schneider, S. K. (1993). On the effectiveness of group brainstorming: Test of one underlying cognitive mechanism. *Small Group Research, 24*, 490–503.
Cordery, J. L., Mueller, W. S., & Smith, L. M. (1991). Attitudinal and behavioral effects of autonomous group working: A longitudinal field study. *Academy of Management Journal, 34*, 464–476.
Cotton, J. L. (1993). *Employee involvement*. Newbury Park, CA: Sage.

Davis, G. A. (1986). *Creativity is forever* (2nd ed.). Dubuque, IA: Kendall/Hunt.

Dennis, A. R. (1996). Information exchange and use in small group decision making. *Small Group Research, 27,* 532–550.

Dennis, A. R., & Valacich, J. S. (1993). Computer brainstorms: More heads are better than one. *Journal of Applied Psychology, 78,* 531–537.

Diehl, M., & Stroebe, W. (1987). Productivity loss in brainstorming groups: Toward the solution of a riddle. *Journal of Personality and Social Psychology, 53,* 497–509.

Diehl, M., & Stroebe, W. (1991). Productivity loss in idea-generating groups: Tracking down the blocking effect. *Journal of Personality and Social Psychology, 61,* 392–403.

Dossett, P. R. (1995). *Some effects of distraction, matching, and cognitive stimulation on individual brainstorming.* Unpublished master's thesis, University of Texas at Arlington.

Dzindolet, M. T. (1992). *An assessment of blocking and social influence processes in brainstorming.* Unpublished doctoral dissertation, University of Texas at Arlington.

Dzindolet, M. T., & Paulus, P. B. (1995, September). *Improving interactive brainstorming performance.* Presented at the meetings of the Society of Experimental Social Psychology, Washington, DC.

Gallupe, R. B., Bastianutti, L. M., & Cooper, W. H. (1991). Unblocking brainstorms. *Journal of Applied Psychology, 76,* 137–142.

Gilbert, D. T., Pelham, B. W., & Krull, D. S. (1988). On cognitive business: When person perceivers meet persons perceived. *Journal of Personality and Social Psychology, 54,* 733–739.

Grossman, S. R., Rodgers, B. E., & Moore, B. R. (1989, December). Turn group input into stellar output. *Working Woman,* 36–38.

Guilford, J. P. (1967). *The nature of human intelligence.* New York: McGraw-Hill.

Gurman, E. B. (1968). Creativity as a function of orientation and group participation. *Psychological Reports, 22,* 471–478.

Guzzo, R. A., & Dickson, M. W. (1996). Teams in organizations: Recent research on performance and effectiveness. *Annual Review of Psychology, 47,* 307–338.

Guzzo, R. A., & Salas, E. (Eds.). (1995). *Team effectiveness and decision making in organizations.* San Francisco: Jossey-Bass.

Hackman, J. R. (Ed.). (1990). *Groups that work (and those that don't): Creating conditions for effective teamwork.* San Francisco: Jossey-Bass.

Hare, A. P. (1982). *Creativity in small groups.* Beverly Hills, CA: Sage.

Hitchcock, D., & Willard, M. (1995). *Why teams can fail and what to do about it.* Chicago: Irwin.

Homma, M., Tajima, K., & Hayashi, M. (1995). The effects of misperception of performance in brainstorming groups. *The Japanese Journal of Experimental Social Psychology, 34,* 221–231.

Horn, E. M. (1993). *The influence of modality order and break period on a brainstorming task.* Unpublished honors thesis, University of Texas at Arlington.

Jackson, S. E., May, K. E., & Whitney, K. (1995). Understanding the dynamics of diversity in decision making teams. In R. A. Guzzo & E. Salas (Eds.), *Team effectiveness and decision making in organizations* (pp. 204–261). San Francisco: Jossey-Bass.

Jessup, L. M., & Valacich, J. S. (1993). (Eds.). *Group support systems.* New York: Macmillan.

Kasof, J. (1995). Explaining creativity: The attributional perspective. *Creativity Research Journal, 8,* 311–366.

Karau, S. J., & Williams, K. D. (1993). Social loafing: A meta-analytic review and theoretical integration. *Journal of Personality and Social Psychology, 65,* 681–706.

Kerr, N. L., & Bruun, S. E. (1983). Dispensability of member effort and group motivation losses: Free-rider effects. *Journal of Personality and Social Psychology, 44,* 78–94.

Kerr, N. L., MacCoun, R. J., & Kramer, G. P. (1996). Bias in judgment: Comparing individuals and groups. *Psychological Review, 103,* 687–719.

King, N., & Anderson, N. (1990). Innovation in working groups. In M. A. West & J. L. Farr (Eds.), *Innovation and creativity at work: Psychological and organizational strategies* (pp. 81–100). London, England: Wiley.

Kirchmeyer, C. (1993). Multicultural task groups: An account of the low contribution level of minorities. *Small Group Research, 24*, 127–148.

Lamm, H., & Trommsdorff, G. (1973). Group versus individual performance on tasks requiring ideational proficiency (brainstorming). *European Journal of Social Psychology, 3*, 361–387.

Larey, T. S. (1994). *Convergent and divergent thinking, group composition, and creativity in brainstorming groups.* Unpublished doctoral dissertation, University of Texas at Arlington.

Larey, T. S., & Paulus, P. B. (1995). Social comparison and goal setting in brainstorming groups. *Journal of Applied Social Psychology, 25*, 1579–1597.

Larey, T. S., & Paulus, P. B. (1999). Group preference and convergent tendencies in small groups: A content analysis of brainstorming performance. *Creativity Research Journal, 12*, 175–184.

Laughlin, P. R., Vanderstoep, S. W., & Hollingshead, A. B. (1991). Collective versus individual induction: Recognition of truth, rejection of error, and collective information processing. *Journal of Personality and Social Psychology, 61*, 50–67.

Leary, M. R., & Kowalski, R. (1993). The interaction anxiousness scale: Construct and criterion-related validity. *Journal of Personality Assessment, 61*, 136–146.

Leggett, K. L., Putman, V. L., Roland, E. J., & Paulus, P. B. (1996, April). *The effects of training on performance in group brainstorming.* Presented at the Southwestern Psychological Association, Houston.

Levine, D. I., & Tyson, L. D. (1990). Participation, productivity, and the firm's environment. In A. S. Blinder (Ed.), *Paying for productivity* (pp. 183–237). Washington, DC: The Brookings Institution.

Maznevski, M. L. (1994). Understanding our differences: Performance in decision making groups with diverse members. *Human Relations, 47*, 531–552.

McDermott, R. A. (1995, September). *The new knowledge worker: Unlocking the knowledge capital of your company.* Paper presented at the 1995 International Conference on Work Teams, Dallas, TX.

Mednick, S. A. (1962). The associative basis of the creative process. *Psychological Review, 69*, 220–232.

Miller, N. E., & Dollard, J. (1941). *Social learning and imitation.* New Haven, CT: Yale University Press.

Mullen, B., Johnson, C., & Salas, E. (1991). Productivity loss in brainstorming groups: A meta-analytic integration. *Basic and Applied Social Psychology, 12*, 3–23.

Nunamaker, J. F., Jr., Dennis, A. R., Valacich, J. S., & Vogel, D. R. (1991). Information technology for negotiating groups: Generating options for mutual gain. *Management Science, 37*(10), 1325–1346.

Nunamaker, J. F., Jr., Dennis, A. R., Valacich, J. S., Vogel, D. R., & George, J. F. (1991). Electronic meeting systems to support group work. *Communications of the ACM, 34*, 40–61.

Nystrom, H. (1979). *Creativity and innovation.* New York: Wiley.

Ochse, R. (1990). *Before the gates of excellence: The determinants of creative genius.* New York: Cambridge University Press.

O'Conner, F. C. (1995). *Does familiarity play a role in reducing the productivity gap in group brainstorming?* Unpublished honors thesis, University of Texas at Arlington.

Osborn, A. F. (1957). *Applied imagination* (1st ed.). New York: Scribner's.

Osborn, A. F. (1963). *Applied imagination* (2nd ed.). New York: Scribner's.

Oxley, N. L., Dzindolet, M. T., & Paulus, P. B. (1996). The effects of facilitators on the performance of brainstorming groups. *Journal of Social Behavior and Personality, 11*, 633–646.

Parnes, S. J., & Meadow, A. (1959). Effect of "brainstorming" instructions on creative problem-solving by trained and untrained subjects. *Journal of Educational Psychology, 50*, 171–176.

Paulus, P. B., & Asuncion, A. (1995). Creativity: Illusion and reality. *Creativity Research Journal, 8*, 397–403.

Paulus, P. B., Brown, V., & Ortega, A. H. (1999). Group creativity. In R. E. Purser & A. Montuori (Eds.), *Social creativity: Vol. 2* (pp. 151–176). Cresskill, NJ: Hampton.

Paulus, P. B., & Dzindolet, M. T. (1993). Social influence processes in group brainstorming. *Journal of Personality and Social Psychology, 64,* 575–586.

Paulus, P. B., Dzindolet, M. T., Poletes, G., & Camacho, L. M. (1993). Perception of performance in group brainstorming: The illusion of group productivity. *Personality and Social Psychology Bulletin, 19,* 78–89.

Paulus, P. B., Larey, T. S., & Ortega, A. H. (1995). Performance and perceptions of brainstormers in an organizational setting. *Basic and Applied Social Psychology, 17,* 249–265.

Paulus, P. B., Larey, T. S., Putman, V. L., Leggett, K. L., & Roland, E. J. (1996). Social influence process in computer brainstorming. *Basic and Applied Social Psychology, 18,* 3–14.

Payne, R. (1990). The effectiveness of research teams: A review. In M. A. West & J. L. Farr (Eds.), *Innovation and creativity at work: Psychological and organizational strategies* (pp. 101–122). London, England: Wiley.

Petty, R. E., & Caccioppo, J. T. (1982). The need for cognition scale. *Journal of Personality and Social Psychology, 42,* 116–131.

Prince, G. M. (1970). *The practice of creativity.* New York: Harper & Row.

Rawlinson, J. G. (1981). *Creative thinking and brainstorming.* New York: Wiley.

Rickards, T. (1993). Creative leadership: Messages from the front line and the back room. *Journal of Creative Behavior, 27,* 46–56.

Robbins, H. A., & Finley, M. (1995). *Why teams don't work: What went wrong and how to make it right.* Princeton, NJ: Peterson's/Pacesetter Books.

Schrage, M. (1995). *No more teams! Mastering the dynamics of creative collaboration.* New York: Currency Doubleday.

Shepperd, J. A. (1993). Productivity loss in performance groups: A motivation analysis. *Psychological Bulletin, 113,* 67–81.

Simonton, D. K. (1988). *Scientific genius: A psychology of science.* New York: Cambridge University Press.

Snyder, S. H. (1989). *Brainstorming: The science and politics of opiate research.* Cambridge, MA: Harvard University Press.

Sternberg, R. J. (Ed.). (1988). *The nature of creativity: Contemporary psychological perspectives.* Cambridge, England: Cambridge University Press.

Sterberg, R. J., & Lubart, R. J. (1996). Investing in creativity. *American Psychologist, 51,* 677–688.

Stewart, D. D., & Stasser, G. (1995). Expert role assignment and information sampling during collective recall and decision-making. *Journal of Personality and Social Psychology, 69,* 619–628.

Stroebe, W., & Diehl, M. (1994). Why groups are less effective than their members: On productivity losses in idea-generating groups. In W. Stroebe & M. Hewstone (Eds.), *European review of social psychology* (Vol. 5, pp. 271–303). London, England: Wiley.

Stroebe, W., Diehl, M., & Abakoumkin, G. (1992). The illusion of group effectivity. *Personality and Social Psychology Bulletin, 18,* 643–650.

Swezey, R. W., & Salas, E. (Eds.). (1992). *Teams: Their training and performance.* Norwood, NJ: Ablex.

Taylor, D. W., Berry, P. C., & Block, C. H. (1958). Does group participation when using brainstorming facilitate or inhibit creative thinking? *Administrative Science Quarterly, 3,* 23–47.

Tjosvold, D. (1991). *Team organization: An enduring competitive advantage.* New York: Wiley.

Valacich, J. S., Dennis, A. R., & Connolly, T. (1994). Idea generation in computer-based groups: A new ending to an old story. *Organizational Behavior and Human Decision Processes, 57,* 448–467.

Van de Ven, A., & Delbecq, A. (1974). The effectiveness of nominal, delphi, and interacting group decision making processes. *Academy of Management Journal, 17,* 314–318.

Varney, G. H. (1989). *Building productive teams: An action guide and resource book*. San Francisco: Jossey-Bass.

Watson, W. E., Kumar, K., & Michaelsen, L. K. (1993). Cultural diversity's impact on interaction process and performance: Comparing homogeneous and diverse task groups. *Academy of Management Journal, 36*, 590–602.

West, M. A. (1990). The social psychology of innovation in groups. In M. A. West & J. L. Farr (Eds.), *Innovation and creativity at work: Psychological and organizational strategies* (pp. 309–334). London, England: Wiley.

Wilson, T. D., Laser, P. S., & Stone, J. I. (1982). Judging the predictors of one's own mood: Accuracy and the use of shared theories. *Journal of Experimental Social Psychology, 18*, 537–556.

Woodman, R. W., Sawyer, J. E., & Griffin, R. W. (1993). Toward a theory of organizational creativity. *Academy of Management Review, 18*, 293–321.

Zander, A. (1994). *Making groups effective* (2nd ed.). San Francisco: Jossey-Bass.

Zajonc, R. B. (1965). Social facilitation. *Science, 149*, 269–274.

Zajonc, R. B. (1980). Compresence. In P. Paulus (Ed.), *Psychology of group influence* (pp. 35–60). Hillsdale, NJ: Lawrence Erlbaum Associates.

Chapter 12

Effects of Top Management Teams on the Organization of Innovation Through Alternative Types of Strategic Alliances

Kathleen M. Eisenhardt
Stanford University

Claudia Bird Schoonhoven
University of California, Irvine

Katherine Lyman
University of Missouri, Columbia

As Schumpeter (1942) described, successive waves of innovation continuously reshape the nature of competition among firms. Gales of creative destruction establish new market opportunities and demolish old ones, thereby shaping and transforming the competitive landscape. Empirical evidence confirms that innovation is extraordinarily critical for contemporary firms (Brown & Eisenhardt, 1995; Henderson & Cockburn, 1993; Jelinek & Schoonhoven, 1990). For example, a study (Eisenhardt & Tabrizi, 1995) of high-technology products demonstrates the importance of a rapid flow of innovative products to firm performance. The implication of this work is that the management of innovation is a central competence within firms, particularly among those operating in high-velocity environments where the pace of technical and competitive change is rapid, extreme, and unpredictable. Well-positioned and timed innovations can not only improve the competitive position of focal firms, but can also destroy the advantages of other firms (D'Aveni, 1994).

Yet, innovation is challenging to achieve. Innovation can be enormously costly, especially as the scale of the innovation process increases. It can be risky as well, particularly as the size of technology leaps grows. Many innovations require the synthesis of a variety of technologies. Yet, it is difficult for any one organization to always have adequate resident knowledge in every relevant technology. For example, multimedia, which combines telecommunications, video, and computer technologies, challenges the resources of even the most wealthy corporations. Moreover, it is unclear whether it is even wise to have complete technological skills given the rapid pace of innovation in many industries. Finally, given the critical role that industry standards play in locking in customer choices, social and political factors can be as central as technical ones in innovation (David, 1985).

One solution to the high costs and risks of innovation is to create technology alliances with other firms. Technology-acquisition alliances are partnerships between two or more organizations in which the focal firm trades resources such as cash, other technology, or marketing skills for the technological innovations of other firms. These alliances involve the personnel of the partner firms working together to transfer and adapt technical developments from one firm to another over time. Thus, these alliances provide firms with access to technology that they did not initially have and so may lessen the time, risk, and cost of developing innovations independently and in-house.

A second approach is to form joint product development alliances with other firms. These are partnerships in which two or more firms agree to combine engineering and other personnel to jointly create new products. As such, they require extensive interaction among the personnel of each firm, especially among engineers, often over a long period of time, in order to create innovations together. In comparison with technology alliances, the resulting relationship involves not only using the technical innovations of other firms, but also jointly creating new innovations and developing related products. Once again, these alliances provide firms with access to technology that they did not initially have, and so may lessen the time, risk, and cost of developing innovative products.

Finally, firms can go it alone. As others have observed, alliances have numerous drawbacks that can make innovation alone an attractive alternative. For example, alliances can have high transaction costs because of extreme uncertainty of dealing with another organization (Hennart, 1991; Williamson, 1991). Alliances can also reduce the revenue streams of innovations by forcing firms to share profits (e.g., Shan, 1990). Alliances can also be vehicles by which firms lose technological knowledge and other organizational competencies to other firms (e.g., Hamel, Doz, & Prahalad, 1989; Teece, 1987). They may also lull managers into overrelying on partners and so fail to develop important internal technical skills. Finally, alliances can be very difficult to implement successfully (e.g., Larson, 1992; Parkhe, 1993). Therefore, although alliances appear to have advantages, there are alternative ways in which firms organize innovation.

The purpose of this chapter is to explore the organization of innovation in new, technology-based firms. Specifically, we examine when young firms form technology-sharing and joint product development alliances and when they do not. Our theoretical lens is a resource-based view of alliance formation (Eisenhardt & Schoonhoven, 1996) that emphasizes how social factors, such as top management team attributes, and strategic factors, such as industry, affect alliance formation. By alliance, we mean "an organizational arrangement in which two or more organizations combine to pursue common interests" (Borys & Jemison, 1989, p. 324). Other authors have used alternative terms such as cooperative arrangements (Shan, 1990) and interorganizational linkages (Miner, Amburgey, & Stearns, 1990) to describe this cooperative phenomenon. For consistency, however, we use the term, strategic alliance, throughout the chapter.

We begin with a brief description of the resource-based view of alliance formation and the importance of specific alliance characteristics. We then develop a set of hypotheses surrounding when joint product development and technology alliances arise, and examine them using a longitudinal, event history model and a population of entrepreneurial new ventures in the U.S. semiconductor industry. We conclude with a discussion of the findings. After controlling for organizational effects, the data illustrate:

1. For product development alliances where firms collaborate closely to create new products, the social connections and social status of the top management team play a primary role in their creation, whereas the external environment plays a lesser, although significant role.

2. For technology-sharing alliances, only size of the founding top management team plays a role in their formation.

3. In both alliance types, however, the top management team plays a more prominent role than does the external environment.

The contribution of the chapter to the groups literature is insight into when top management teams have a significant effect on strategic alliance formation and when they do not. We also contribute to the innovation literature insight into how firms organize the innovation process using external relationships. We observe the conditions under which firms employ various types of innovation-related alliances, when they are less likely to do so, and how the alliance relationships relate to one another. Finally, the chapter contributes to a central debate in the organization and strategy literatures concerning firm (especially, top management team) versus industry effects (e.g., Finkelstein & Hambrick, 1996) by showing that *both* firm effects, including leadership (top management team) and industry factors (competition and market stage) contribute to alliance outcomes.

THEORETICAL BACKGROUND AND HYPOTHESES

Why do some young firms form alliances? One theoretical approach for understanding when strategic alliances form is transaction cost economics (e.g., Hennart, 1988, 1991; Pisano, 1990; Shan, 1990; Williamson, 1991). Transaction cost economics, however, was originally developed to contrast markets versus hierarchies, not to predict alliance formation. Not surprisingly then, the theory has a narrow emphasis on transaction cost efficiency as the motivation for such cooperation. Yet, strategic alliances arise for many other reasons such as to gain skills, mitigate risk, accelerate development time, and gain legitimacy, all of which go beyond efficiency motivations (e.g., Hamel et al., 1989; Larson, 1992; Stinchcombe, 1965). In addition, firm characteristics such as strategy, national background, and top management factors, which are not transaction characteristics, may also be relevant (Eisenhardt & Schoonhoven, 1996; Pisano, 1990; Shan, 1990). Thus, given the importance of strategic issues such as risk, timing, and legitimacy to innovation, transaction cost thinking is likely to be limited as a theoretical lens for understanding the organization of innovation through strategic alliances.

Resource-Based View of Alliance Formation

A broader perspective is a resource-based view of alliance formation. This approach rests on the assumption that firms are usefully viewed as bundles of resources (e.g., Penrose, 1959; Wernerfelt, 1984). These resources are the strengths or assets of firms and can be thought of as either tangible or intangible. Examples of such resources include technical know-how, management skills, and even reputation.

To adopt a resource-based view of alliance formation means that alliances are a central mechanism by which firms can acquire additional resources to bolster their competitive positions. That is, alliances are fundamentally resource-sharing relationships in which firms can gain a variety of resource advantages such as cost sharing, risk sharing, increased legitimacy, and fast development of new skills (Eisenhardt & Schoonhoven, 1996).

Strategic alliances are, therefore, likely to be formed by young firms in several situations. One is when firms have the resources necessary to create opportunities for alliance formation. That is, alliances, like all forms of cooperation, depend on having opportunities to ally. This observation highlights that alliance formation is also a social phenomenon (e.g., Dyer, 1992; Granovetter, 1992; Larson, 1992). Alliance formation is more likely when members of the top management team have a strong social position with potential partners outside of the firm. In these situations, firm members are more likely to be aware of alliance opportunities and are more likely to be known and respected by others. That is, alliances are likely to form when key personnel know about alliance opportunities and can reduce the risks of alliance formation such as poor implementation and appropriation of knowledge that we noted earlier (Dyer, 1992; Gulati, 1993). For example, when firms have numerous external contacts and relationships at high levels with potential partner firms, the likelihood of alliance formation is increased because of enhanced awareness of opportunities, mutual knowledge, and trust (Eisenhardt & Schoonhoven, 1996). In contrast, managers of firms that lack social resources may not know about opportunities, may have little information with which to assess the trustworthiness of potential partners, and may lack the status and reputation necessary to attract partners themselves. As a consequence, they may be forced to or may actually prefer to act autonomously.

Strategic alliances are also likely to form when firms need the additional resources that alliances can provide. This is likely to occur when firms are in vulnerable strategic positions such that they compete in difficult market situations or are undertaking resource-demanding strategies (e.g., Burgers, Hill, & Kim, 1993; Shan, 1990). For example, firms in highly competitive markets have vulnerable strategic positions because margins are low, and it is difficult to differentiate products. Alliances can provide resources to share costs, to gain differentiable product technologies, or to bind partners together so that their mutual legitimacy and market power are enhanced (e.g., Hamel et al., 1989; Hagedoorn & Schakenraad, 1990). On the other hand, when the external environment is munificent or strategies are not resource demanding, it is less attractive to cooperate. The drawbacks of strategic alliances, such as the time it takes to implement and the potential for technology leakage, may outweigh the advantages of interfirm cooperation in these situations. Young firms are likely to go it alone.

Thus, interfirm cooperation through strategic alliances is more likely to occur when firms are in strong social positions with the resources necessary to know, attract, and engage partners or when firms are in vulnerable strategic positions for which they need the resources that alliances can provide to compete effectively. This view highlights that alliances are both a social phenomenon associated with mutual knowledge, trust, and commitment (e.g., Larson, 1992; Ouchi, 1980) and an economic phenomenon associated with incentives to cooperate (e.g., Axelrod, 1984; Parkhe, 1993).[1]

Previous research on alliance formation supports this perspective. Kogut, Shan, and Walker (1992) found that social position was important

---

[1]A resource-based view of the firm assumes that the need for resources and the opportunity to acquire those resources are distinct concepts and independent variables in the theory. Thus, in this chapter we treat the two as independent, main effects when operationalized.

to alliance formation. Positions of firms within social networks of allianced firms affected future opportunities for alliance formation. Similarly, Gulati (1993) found that firms were more likely to ally with past partnering firms. Shan (1990) found that alliances were more common in situations where firms were in vulnerable strategic positions. Specifically, he found greater rates of alliance formation among biotechnology firms when competing in highly competitive markets that were new to the firm. Finally, Eisenhardt and Schoonhoven (1996) found that both vulnerable strategic position and strong social position related to alliance formation.

However, alliances are not all alike. So, although the existing literature is useful in framing the general conditions under which higher rates of alliance formation are likely, it is less useful in framing when specific types of alliances will occur. Yet, alliances do differ from one another, making some alliances more (or less) appropriate in particular situations. Although vulnerable strategic and strong social resource positions may influence rates of alliance formation, the specific features of alliances affect which types of alliances will actually occur.

In the specific case of innovation-related alliances, technology-sharing and joint product development alliances can provide resources to enhance the innovation process, and thus to improve the strategic position of the firm. But, the two alliance types have important differences. Technology alliances involve the gaining of specific pieces of knowledge in return for resources such as capital, other technology, or manufacturing capacity. Personnel from the partnering firms join together to transfer technical developments over time. The focal firm is then able to use the technical innovations of the partnering firms in its own innovation processes: The resource gains from these alliances are usually well targeted, well known in advance, and quickly achieved. In addition, given the specificity of these alliances, risks of inadvertent technology leakage and opportunism are modest.

In contrast, joint product development alliances involve combining engineers and other personnel from the partnering firms to work together in the innovation process. In these alliances, the outline of the product is typically known and the partners understand which resources each will provide. For example, in the Taligent alliance between IBM and Apple, Apple was to provide software expertise while IBM provided the marketing, managerial, and other technical skills in their alliance to develop a new operating system. In alliances like these, the partners pool their resources in the creation of innovations. Knowledge that is exchanged is often quite tacit, and the alliance itself requires close and extensive interaction among employees to create new knowledge and ultimately to transform this into new products. Given interfirm interaction this extensive, these alliances may require considerable effort to develop effective working relationships. Thus, the resource gains from joint product development alliances are less certain at the outset, less precise, and achieved more slowly. In addition, the risks of opportunism by one's partner and technology leakage are greater than for technology alliances. On the other hand, joint product development alliances provide substantial risk and cost-sharing benefits.

Overall then, there are key differences between technology and product development alliances. Technology alliances are useful when well-known resources are needed quickly. Joint product development alliances are better suited to situations where it is unclear what will be involved within the innovation process, when time pressures are modest, and when risk sharing, cost sharing, and legitimation are critical. These differences suggest several situations where one type of alliance might be favored over another. We turn now to these hypotheses.

HYPOTHESES

Top Management Teams—Social Connections and Status

We argued that technology alliances are suited to situations in which speed and flexibility are important whereas product development alliances are appropriate in situations for which uncertainty and risk-sharing are particularly relevant. However, alliance formation is also related to social position. Strong social position enables organizations to form alliances by capitalizing on resources such as status, reputation, and contacts that create opportunities for alliance formation (e.g., Heimer, 1992).

For many organizations, the characteristics of top management are particularly important for determining its social position (D'Aveni, 1990; Eisenhardt & Schoonhoven, 1996). Top managers often are the sources of leads to alliance partners and are the architects of the firm's alliance strategy. These executives are usually the principal negotiators of alliance deals and their rapport with executives of partnering firms is often central to the formation of alliances. So, the status, contacts, and reputation of top management are central to the creation of opportunities for alliance formation.

When top management of an organization is referenced, it is often assumed to be a single individual, the president, or the chief executive officer (Hackman, 1990). Increasingly, a growing body of research has suggested that the top management team may be a more important determinant of an organization's ability to adapt than the chief executive officer alone (e.g., Finkelstein & Hambrick, 1990; Tushman & Romanelli, 1985). As O'Reilly and colleagues noted (1993), it is this group that ultimately makes important decisions and resource allocations that help or hinder a firm. The top management team is the locus of overall responsibility for the organization, and it is here that "strategic leadership" resides (Hambrick, 1989). There is support for the conclusion that the top team rather than the top individual has the greatest effects on organizational functioning (e.g., Ancona, 1990; Hambrick & D'Aveni, 1992; Norburn & Birley, 1988). As a consequence, we conceptualize top management as the team of executives responsible for strategic leadership of an organization (Hambrick, 1989).

Although social position is important for creating alliance opportunities, it is less important for technology alliances than for product development ones. Technology alliances involve the focused exchange of specific resources for technical innovations. There is little joint innovation activity as the focal firm is using these outside technical developments for in-house innovation enhancement. Although personnel from the partnering firms must interact over time in order to convey and understand the technology, the potential for opportunism and inadvertent technology leakage is less in this type of exchange, because what is exchanged is relatively well specified a priori. In contrast, product development alliances require close interaction among engineers and other personnel from the partnering companies as these individuals engage in creating joint innovation and ultimately new product development. Here, tacit knowledge is often exchanged and the potential for technical leakage and opportunism is high. Given these differences in the potential for opportunism, social position is likely to be more important in providing opportunities for joint product development alliances than for technology alliances (Dyer, 1992; Gulati, 1993). Social resources such as status, connections, and reputation are likely to help mitigate the risks and implementation problems of alliances.

Several characteristics of top management teams are particularly important in signaling the social resources of firms. One is the number of previous industry employers of the top management team. Executive teams whose members have had several industry employers are likely to have extensive webs of connections to potential alliance partners. They are also likely to be able to assess the credibility of potential alliance partners and in turn, can be more readily assessed themselves by potential partnering organizations. Similarly, larger top management teams are likely to have greater social connections outside the organization. These factors help alleviate the negative aspects of product development alliances. We hypothesize the following.

Hypothesis 1. The rate of joint product development alliance formation increases with greater social connections (previous industry employers, size) of the top management team. The rate of technology alliance formation is not related to social connections (number of previous industry employers, team size).

A second, critical characteristic of top management teams is the relative status imported to the new venture based on the hierarchical level of jobs previously held by team members. Teams whose members have had high-level positions are more likely to know the dealmakers in potential partnering firms and to be known by them. In addition, even when the firm's executives do not have personal contacts at potential partnering firms, their previous job levels enhance the prestige, status, and perceptions of the quality of the firm. Therefore, high-level connections and status are important for providing opportunities for alliance formation, especially in the case of product development alliances where the opportunities for technology leakages, implementation problems, and opportunistic behaviors are high. On the other hand, because technology alliances involve more specific resources, social resources such as prestige, status, and reputation are less important for creating alliance opportunities.

Hypothesis 2. The rate of joint product development alliance formation increases with higher previous job levels of the top management team. The rate of technology alliance formation is not related to previous jobs levels of the top management team.

Environment—Market Stage and Competition

The above hypotheses relate to differences in the social connectedness and social status of top management teams, which differentially affect formation rates of technology-acquisition and joint product development alliances (Gulati, 1993; Kogut et al., 1992). We argued that a strong social position enables firms to form alliances by capitalizing on resources created by its top management team like status, reputation, and contacts, which create opportunities for alliance formation (e.g., Heimer, 1992). However, alliance formation is also related to the firm's strategic position in the external environment relative to competition.

One situation in which alliance type is relevant is the market stage of the industry in which a firm participates. As others have described (Hambrick, MacMillan, & Day, 1982; Porter, 1980), industries evolve through several stages or configurations of attributes. Initially, emergent markets arise. These markets are small, new, and characterized by a lack of product clarity (Anderson & Zeithaml, 1984). Successful technologies or market channels are often unclear as is the eventual direction of the market (Klepper & Graddy, 1990). It is also very difficult to forecast when these markets will blossom. They may take a long time, and for some, the market may never grow large. Whereas some firms may be successful in emergent markets, many are not (Tushman & Anderson, 1986). Given this competitive uncertainty, strategic position is precarious with a key challenge being the management of this uncertainty.

Joint product development alliances are well suited to emergent markets in several ways. They provide cost-sharing and knowledge resources from other firms (Miner et al., 1990). These extra resources are particularly important as it may take a long time for the market to become viable (Van de Ven & Polley, 1992). Joint product development alliances also provide risk sharing through the close cooperation among partners. Again, this is useful because of the potentially long time that it takes for the market to become viable and because it may never actually become viable. In addition, product development alliances may help to legitimate the market and the market approach of the focal firm by tying together the resources of several firms with a common product approach to building the market. In contrast, technology alliances are focused on specific technical developments. Because it is difficult to forecast exactly which technical developments are needed in emergent markets, technology alliances are likely to be of less use than are product development alliances.

On the other hand, technology-acquisition alliances are well suited for firms facing growth stage markets. These markets are characterized by rapid pace (Eisenhardt, 1989). Demand and competitive structure change quickly (Anderson & Zeithaml, 1984). There are often multiple options for how to compete, and multiple candidates for the dominant design (Porter, 1980; Tushman & Anderson, 1986). This means that competitive structure, technology, and market share are all volatile. Flexibility is important as it is essential to keep up with fleeting windows of opportunity. As Eisenhardt (1989) wrote, fast pace and quick moves are keys to success in such high-velocity environments.

Technology-acquisition alliances can enhance the strategic position of firms in growth stage markets by creating resource flexibility. Such alliances can help firms to avoid the inflexibility of fixed technical resources, and so enable firms to make adjustments to their technical knowledge as conditions change. Thus, technology alliances can help firms gain needed technical developments without having to invest in every relevant technology. Such alliances allow firms to gain options in various technologies and so to plug specific innovation holes. In addition, technology alliances are also attractive in growth stage markets because they do not require the time commitment of more involving types of alliances. For example, because of their implementation difficulties (e.g., Larson, 1992), joint product development alliances may be too slow and involve too much commitment for firms facing growth stage markets.

Eventually, markets mature. In contrast to the two previous market stages, mature markets are large and slow to change (Anderson & Zeithaml, 1984; Klepper & Graddy, 1990). Demand is approaching saturation. Standards and competitors are entrenched and market share is stable (Hambrick et al., 1982). Dominant designs and technologies are usually clear. Market share and competition are slow to change as well. In addition, firms may have built up viable technology resources over time that they may be reluctant to share in alliances. Thus, uncertainty, legitimation, speed, and flexibility are less relevant here than in emergent or growth stage markets. So, whereas the occasional technology or product development alliance might occur, innovation-related alliances are less likely to be formed at high rates in mature markets.

Hypothesis 3. The rate of product development alliance formation increases in emergent stage markets. The rate of technology alliance formation increases in growth stage markets.

Competition also plays a role in determining the strategic position of an organization. It is argued that increased competition renders a firm's strategic position vulnerable. Greater numbers of competitors create a number of problems for an organization, including price competition, reduced profit margins, and product duplications making it difficult for organizations to differentiate themselves from others. On the other hand, research has demonstrated that in markets with fewer competitors, profits are higher (e.g., Klepper & Graddy, 1990) and the probability of surviving is higher (Carroll & Hannan, 1989).

Hypothesis 4. The rate of joint product development alliances increases in highly competitive markets. The rate of technology alliance formation is not related to the number of competitors.

Organizational Controls: Innovation Strategy and Prior Alliances

Differences in firm strategy may also affect strategic position and so whether and which alliances are formed. Although there are multiple ways to conceptualize strategy (e.g., Miles & Snow, 1978; Porter, 1980), the most relevant for innovation-related alliances is in terms of the innovativeness of the technology (Boeker, 1989; Maidique & Patch, 1982). Firms can differ widely on this dimension. For example, in the semiconductor memory business, some firms compete using older NMOS/PMOS technology whereas others use moderately innovative CMOS technology and still others use pioneering flash, FERRAM, or wafer-scale integration technologies.

These different strategies affect the level and type of resources that firms need to compete effectively (Maidique & Patch, 1982). Technically innovative strategies require extensive competency in one and often several technologies, and so demand a high level of resources (Jelinek & Schoonhoven, 1993). For such strategies, it is often difficult to anticipate specific technical problems, and so to forecast when and if innovations will occur. It is rare for innovative technology to work initially, and it often takes a long time, if ever, for new technologies to become viable. So, resource levels are likely to be hard to predict. For such strategies, joint product development alliances can be particularly helpful to help spread the costs and risks of very uncertain innovation processes across firms. In addition, legitimacy issues are often important for firms that use pioneering innovation strategies. The commercial viability of new technology is often unclear and technical standards can evolve because of political or social reasons, not just superior technology (David, 1985). For example, Betamax was considered to be technically superior to VHS as a video recording format, and yet, for a variety of nontechnical reasons, VHS became the standard. Thus, legitimation is crucial for pioneering technology, and alliances can help firms gain that legitimacy and related market power by tying closely with other firms in product development alliances. In contrast, because the path of pioneering technologies is so uncertain, technology-sharing alliances may be too targeted, and they do not have the extensive legitimation advantages of product development alliances because no common product is involved in the relationship.

Other firms compete with moderately innovative strategies. These strategies may be associated with technologies that are new, but that are also more incremental, rather than pathbreaking (Maidique & Patch, 1982). Paths to commercial viability are clear, more certain, and often shorter for firms pursuing moderately innovative strategies (Schoonhoven, Eisenhardt, & Lyman, 1990). So, needed resources are more obvious, and probably limited in scale and scope. In addition, given the moderate level of innovation, there are more likely to be other firms pursuing a similar strategy and so there is more pressure to create innovations quickly to outflank competitors. Technology-sharing alliances are likely to be attractive in this situation because they allow firms to quickly plug resource holes with specific technical developments.

Less innovative strategies may also require fewer resources. The related technologies are usually well established and so require fewer resources to develop into commercially viable products. Moreover, there is also likely to be less relevant, technical innovation occurring and so there are fewer opportunities for innovation-related alliance formation. Because of the issues developed previously, we controled for innovation strategy.

Finally, the formation of technology and product development alliances may also be related to each other. One possibility is that they are complementary. If firms engage in one, then they would also be more likely to form the other. In this case, we would expect a positive correlation between the two. However, given that we have argued that these alliance types are more likely to occur in different situations (i.e., different strategies, markets, and top management teams), they are unlikely to be complementary. A more plausible argument is that they are unrelated to one other. In either case, number of prior alliances of both types were controlled for in the analysis (Eisenhardt & Schoonhoven, 1996).

METHODS

Population

The population studied was semiconductor firms founded between 1978 and 1985 in the United States. We then tracked these firms and their alliance relationships longitudinally through 1988 or until death of the young firm. A new semiconductor firm was defined as a single-business organization that was founded to participate in the merchant semiconductor industry. This definition excluded captive suppliers, electronic distributors, and custom design houses whose sole business was subcontracting their expertise to others.

We developed a master list of firms within this population from industry lists that are maintained by the Semiconductor Industry Association (SIA), the major trade association of the industry; Dataquest and Integrated Circuit Engineering, two of the principal market research firms specializing in the semiconductor industry; *Electronic News*, a weekly newspaper with a specialty section on the semiconductor industry; and Semiconductor Equipment and Materials Institute (SEMI), which follows the semiconductor industry for member companies. After eliminating duplicate entries across sources, we wrote to the chief executive of each firm asking for information about the company. Based on this information, nine firms were eliminated from further study because they did not meet the population definition.

The final population of firms was 102. We included every semiconductor company founded in the United States between 1978 and 1985, regardless of whether or not the firm subsequently failed. Ninety eight firms participated in the study, for a participation rate of 96%. These firms were engaged in a variety of specific product areas and were located throughout the United States.

Data Sources

We collected longitudinal, field data on semiconductor firms founded in the United States between 1978 and 1985 (inclusive), and on alliances formed (year and month) and the various covariates from the birth of the firm through 1988 or until the firm failed. Although such longitudinal and field-based designs are demanding, they do permit a fuller understanding of phenomena by capturing organization-level information such as detailed data about the top management team and firm characteristics that are usually unavailable from secondary sources.

We have focused this chapter on joint product development and technology-acquisition alliances. These alliances are both common and important in the semiconductor industry because they deal with the heart of technology-based ventures, innovation. *Joint product development alliances* are defined as interorganizational arrangements in which the partnering firms combine engineering and other personnel to jointly design a product or products new to both firms. Because a new product is being created, there is typically a very high degree of interaction among personnel, especially engineers, of both firms in order to create joint innovations and ultimately, products. *Technology-acquisition alliances* are defined as interorganizational arrangements in which the focal firm obtains technology from another firm in return for resources such as cash or other technology. Therefore, there is frequent interaction among personnel from the partnering firms in order to work together to transfer and adapt the technical developments or series of technical developments to the focal firm. Thus, the focal firm is able to transfer specific technical innovations from another firm to its in-house innovation processes.

We collected data from several sources. The first was a structured, confidential interview that we used to question the CEO, founders, and other key executives. We chose these informants based on their extensive knowledge of the firm's history. We conducted most of these interviews on site and in pairs, with one researcher asking questions while the other took notes and recorded responses. We also tape-recorded the interviews. These interviews lasted between 1 and 4 hours. We used follow-up phone calls to collect any incomplete data. We obtained the firm's financial history from a supplementary questionnaire that was completed by the firm's chief financial officer. These data were supplemented with information from a variety of sources including corporate backgrounders, press releases, business plans, and market research reviews. Finally, we gathered data on the market stage construct and the competition control variable from the Semiconductor Industry Association (SIA), Dataquest, and Integrated Circuit Engineering (ICE).

Measures

Most new ventures in the semiconductor industry are founded by groups rather than by single individuals (Boeker, 1989). The top management team was designated as those people identified as members of executive management in the structured interviews. Such individuals typically included the CEO and his or her direct reports (usually the heads of various functions), all of whom worked full-time for the firm in executive positions. Respondents were able to easily identify the top management teams in their firms as this designation is clear in firms and such individuals are frequently identified as members of the top management group in corporate documents such as annual business plans and press releases, and in corporate functions such as CEO staff meetings. In order to ensure highly accurate data, respondents also consulted corporate records when they were unsure of their recall regarding particular executives.

Number of Previous Semiconductor Employers. This measure was computed as the mean number of semiconductor industry firms for which members of the top management team had previously worked. The data on previous employers were obtained from the structured interviews and corporate records. This measure was coded monthly for the life of the firm. Changes occurred as top managers joined and left the firm, so the top management team was reconstituted as the team changes.

Mean Previous Job Title. We measured the mean previous job title by first recording the highest previous job title of each top management team member. These data were obtained from the structured interviews and corporate records. Job titles were coded by hierarchical level, ranging from 7, president or chief executive officer of a firm to 0, a nonmanagerial level. These data were coded monthly.

Team Size. Team size was measured as the number of executives who were designated in the structured interviews as members of the top management team (Eisenhardt & Schoonhoven, 1996). These individuals worked full-time for the firm in executive positions and were considered to be members of the CEO's staff. This measure was coded monthly.

Market Stage. We measured the market stage via several steps. First, using worldwide market research data from Dataquest and ICE as well as the advice of industry executives, we identified six broad markets (application-specific circuits, memory, logic, gallium arsenide, linear, and discrete) and segments within these markets. This gave us a highly accurate and refined view of the industry. For example, these distinctions allowed us to differentiate between the mature read-only memory (ROM) market; the high-growth, dynamic random access memory (DRAM) market; and the smaller and newer electrically erasable and programmable read-only-memory (EEPROM) market. Second, we then assigned firms to markets based on their products. When firms diversified, we assigned them into the broader market encompassing all product lines. The third step was to assign market stage designations to each market. We conceptualized market stage as a configuration variable, not a continuous one. Therefore, using dimensions consistent with our theoretical development of each market stage configuration, we categorized each market as emergent, growth, or mature for each year in the study. We defined emergent stage markets as new (less than 7 years old) and small (less than $100 million in sales, adjusted to 1988 dollars). Growth stage markets were large (more than $100 million in sales, adjusted to 1988 dollars), high growth (growth rate greater than 20% per year), and followed emergent markets. Mature stage markets were large (more than $100 million in sales, adjusted to 1988 dollars, low growth (growing at less than 20% per year), and followed growth markets. Specific market designations are reported in Table 12.1.

Following Cameron, Kim, and Whetten (1987), market stage designations were selected carefully through conversations with industry executives, reading market research reports, and natural breaks in the data. We

TABLE 12.1
Categorization of Market Stages

Market	Emergent	Growth	Mature
Semi-Custom (ASCI)	1978–1982	1983–1988	
Digital gate arrays	1978–1980	1981–1988	
Analog gate arrays	1978–1988		
Standard cells	1978–1982	1983–1988	
Programmable logic devices	1978–1982	1983–1988	
Silicon compilers	1981–1988		
Memory		1978–1988	
DRAM		1978–1988	
SRAM		1978–1988	
ROM		1978–1982	1983–1988
EPROM		1978–1984	1985–1988
EEPROM	1978–1985	1986–1988	
FERRAM	1985–1988		
Discrete			1978–1988
Optoelectronic components			1978–1988
Power field effect transistors			1978–1988
Other			1978–1988
Linear			
Gallium arsenide	1981–1988		1978–1988
Digital	1981–1988		
Analog	1982–1988		
Logic			
Microprocessors		1978–1988	
Microperipherals			1978–1988
Standard logic			1978–1988

confirmed these market stage designations by matching qualitative market descriptions (e.g., commercial viability) in market research reports with the theoretical descriptions of each market stage described earlier. For example, the linear market in 1986, which we had typed as mature, was termed "very mature" by Integrated Circuit Engineering (1987). The robustness of these cut points was examined by rerunning analyses using different values (e.g., market sizes from $80 to $150 million, rates of growth varying above and below 20%), with no difference in our results. Finally, the choice of market stage was empirically verified by examining the formation of alliances using market size, a continuous variable that was related to the stages. The dummy variable operationalization of market stage provided the better fit with the data and was, of course, more consistent with the underlying theoretical argument. Market stage was coded for each year a firm is in existence.

Number of Competitors. Using the market segments that were described in the market stage description, we measured the number of competitors using worldwide industry data from Dataquest, ICE, and, in a very few cases, confidential market research reports from firms in the study. These data were updated annually.

Controls

Founding Date. A number of authors have noted that alliance formation became more prevalent during the time period of the study (e.g., Hagedoorn & Schakenraad, 1991; Harrigan, 1988; Parkhe, 1993). We controlled for founding date by converting this date (month and year) to the number of months relative to January, 1978, the beginning of the study. Higher values, therefore, indicated younger firms.

Firm Size. We also controlled for firm size using total assets, a meaningful measure of firm size for new ventures. This was obtained from the financial questionnaire, completed by the firm's financial officer, and measured as assets at the end of year one after founding.

Innovation Strategy. As described earlier, innovation-based approaches appropriately capture strategy in technology-based firms such as semiconductor ventures (e.g., Boeker, 1989; Maidique & Patch, 1982). Therefore, our hypothesis and measures of strategy were related to innovation. Specifically, we used two measures. One was an objective measure, the minimum design feature size (in microns). The feature size was a physical measurement of the miniaturization of the line widths in the circuit designs used by semiconductor firms. Smaller feature sizes meant more innovative technology, because packing more circuits into a smaller area was the fundamental technical challenge within the industry. This was provided by the CEO, chief technical officer, or other key respondent during the structured interviews.

Innovation strategy was also measured using three questions that were answered by the CEOs or other key respondents during the structured interviews. The first question considered innovation through extensions to existing knowledge: "To what extent could you rely on existing knowledge to build the first product?" The second question captured innovation that occurs when technologies are combined: "To what extent did you synthesize existing knowledge to produce your first product?" The third question assessed the overall degree of technical innovation: "How difficult was it to produce your first product?" Respondents used a 0 to 10 scale to respond to these questions. A three-item index was developed by reverse coding the first question and computing the mean response to the three questions. The Cronbach alpha was .75. Given the persistence of strategy over time (e.g., Kimberly, 1980; Mintzberg & Waters, 1982), especially for young semiconductor firms (Boeker, 1989), this construct was measured at founding.

Cumulative Prior Alliances. The number of prior alliances were cumulated over the life of the firm, with separate measures for technology-acquisition and product development alliances. This control was coded monthly for each alliance type and increased when a firm entered into a new alliance of a given type.

Analysis and Dependent Measure

Our analytic technique was event history, which takes into account both the occurrence and timing of events (Allison, 1984; Tuma & Hannan, 1984). The multivariate model estimated the rate of alliance formation over the life of the firm. Firms that made few or no alliances of a given type, or that took a long time to establish an alliance, exhibited a low rate of alliance formation; firms that made many alliances and earlier in their history exhibited a higher rate. The effects of covariates in the model were evaluated in terms of their significant impact in raising or lowering the rate of alliance formation. We used a Cox proportional hazards model (Cox, 1972) incorporating time-varying covariates estimated by the statistical program TDA.

We identified technology and product development alliances in the structured interviews by asking respondents: "Does your firm have any formalized alliance agreements with other companies?" If yes, the respondent was then asked to confirm that the alliance was a product development or technology-acquisition alliance (using the previously given definitions), that the alliance was actually executed by the two partners, when the alliance was formed, and the name of the partner. The formation date was defined as the date (month, year) on which both parties agreed to the alliance. Almost all of the alliances involved the signing of a formal agreement and an associated press release. Therefore, a specific date was available and clear.

We also took several steps to ensure the accuracy of these data. First, recall was enhanced by the fact that these alliances were major, objective events for these young firms, were often accompanied by press releases, and typically involved our respondents among the top management negotiators. Thus, these data were important, objective, and well known to the respondents. Second, when respondents were unsure of information such as the exact month of formation, they consulted other sources to ascertain the correct information. Third, alliance data were gathered chronologically in order to facilitate the recall of informants as it is easier to recall information chronologically than when it is asked out of context. Finally, we were able to double-check the informants' responses for over 90% of the firms against various secondary data including press releases and business plans. There were no discrepancies regarding whether or not an alliance existed, a finding consistent with the significance of alliances within these young firms and with having very knowledgeable respondents. In approximately 10% of the alliances, there was a discrepancy concerning the exact date of formation that was cleared up in every case by further consultation with the informants and their consulting corporate archives.

Over 65% of the sample firms formed product development or technology alliances. All firms were included in the analysis until the end of observations in 1988 or, for the few firms that died, until their death. This amount of right censoring is routinely and robustly handled within event history analysis (e.g., Tuma & Hannan, 1984). There was no left censoring in these data as all firms were tracked from birth. The alliance partners included customers and firms in the computer, automotive, telecommunications, defense, aircraft, and other industries; major semiconductor merchant producers (e.g., Intel, National, Phillips, Toshiba); smaller semiconductor merchant producers, including other firms in our study (approximately 13% of the alliances); and a few miscellaneous and unnamed partners who remained anonymous. Joint product development alliances were more likely to involve customers whereas technology-acquisition alliances were more frequently formed with other semiconductor firms.

RESULTS

Table 12.2 displays the correlation matrix of all variables in the analysis. Table 12.3 displays results of the event history analyses for the formation of joint product development alliances (Model 1) and technology-acquisition alliances (Model 2).

TABLE 12.2
Correlation Matrix

Variables	1	2	3	4	5	6	7	8	9	10	11
1. Market stage—growth											
2. Market stage—emergent	-.51										
3. Feature size	.00	-.26									
4. Innovative scale	.00	.22	-.38								
5. Team size	.08	-.04	-.06	.00							
6. Number of industry employers	.18	-.18	.07	-.19	.11						
7. Mean previous highest job level	.06	-.16	.11	.02	-.27	-.15					
8. Founding date	-.09	.10	.05	-.05	-.15	.01	.18				
9. Firm size	-.03	-.03	.19	.04	.16	-.04	.08	.21			
10. Cumulative alliances—pd	-.03	.08	-.10	.17	.01	-.02	.14	.12	-.04		
11. Cumulative alliances—tl	.10	-.06	-.11	.10	.14	-.01	.05	-.18	-.06	.08	
12. Number of competitors	.22	-.32	.23	-.13	-.05	.09	.28	.11	.12	.09	.11

Note. N = 4,696 spells. Feature size is expressed in microns; founding date, in months; and size, in millions of dollars of assets.

TABLE 12.3
The Effects of Founding Top Management Team and External Environment
on the Rate of Alliance Formation (Cox Models)

	Alliance Type	
	Product Development Model 1	Technology-Acquisition Model 2
Organizational Controls		
Firm age	.03***	.00
	(.01)	(.01)
Firm size	.00	−.00
	(.00)	(.00)
Innovation strategy		
feature size in microns	−.15*	−.29**
	(.10)	(.17)
innovation scale	.12**	.15***
	(.06)	(.07)
Prior alliances–cumulative		
Product dev. alliances	.20	−.15
	(.16)	(.31)
Technology-sharing alliances	.33**	.21
	(.19)	(.23)
Hypothesized Constructs		
Top management team—social connections & status		
Social connections (prior industry employers)	.16**	.04
	(.06)	(.10)
Social connections (founding team size)	.10**	.06*
	(.05)	(.06)
Social status (prior job hierarchical level)	.13**	.09
	(.07)	(.09)
External environment—market & competition		
Market stage[a] (emergent)	.51*	—
	(.36)	—
Market stage (growth)	—	.04
	—	(.36)
Number of competitors	.01*	.00
	(.01)	(.01)
−2 Log likelihood (4694 spells)	−1558.2***	−1557.8***

Note. Standard errors are in parentheses.

[a]Dummy variables for which reference category is "other market stages"; emergent versus growth & mature, growth versus emergent and mature. In analyses not reported here, we tested the effect of all three market types but only one dummy was significant in a model, as reported above.

*p < .10. **p < .05. ***p < .01.

The first set of variables reported for both models in Table 12.3 contains organizational controls; the new venture's founding date, size, innovation strategy, and cumulative number of prior alliances of both types. Results for product development alliances (Model 1) show that younger new ventures, with more innovative strategies[2] and greater numbers of technology-sharing alliances are associated with *higher* rates of product development alliance formation. Organizational size and number of cumulative product development alliances were not significant.

For technology-acquisition alliances (Model 2), only the innovation strategy controls had a significant effect on the rate of strategic alliance formation. The more innovative the new firm's technology, the greater the rate of technology-acquisition alliances. We also found that firm age, size, and the cumulative number of joint product development alliances were not significantly associated with the rate of technology-acquisition alliance formation. The same was true for the cumulative number of technology alliances.

The remaining variables in both models provide results for the hypothesized constructs. Consistent with Hypothesis 1, Model 1 shows that top management teams with greater numbers of social connections (indicated by the mean number of prior industry employers and the founding team size) were significantly related to higher rates of product development alliances. As was argued in Hypothesis 2, the greater the social status the top management team brings to the new organization via higher level previous jobs, the higher the rate of product development alliances.

The next two coefficients express the impact of the external environment on alliance formation. Consistent with Hypothesis 3, firms competing in emergent markets have higher rates of joint product development alliances. In Hypothesis 4, it was predicted that in highly competitive markets, the rate of joint product development alliances would increase. Table 12.3 indicates that the coefficient for number of competitors in the external marketplace was significant and positive. These results support Hypothesis 4 for the formation of joint product development alliances.

Turning to Model 2 and results for technology-acquisition alliances, we hypothesized that neither social connections nor social status of the top management team would have a significant effect on this alliance type. The results were supportive of Hypothesis 1: The number of prior industry employers was not related and the size of the founding top management team was only marginally related to number of technology-acquisi-

---

[2]Minimum design features, measured in microns, indicate greater innovation with smaller values. Thus the negative coefficient indicates that less innovative design features (higher values) are associated with a lower rate of alliance formation. That is, .05 micron minimum feature designs are less innovative than .03 micron minimum feature designs.

tion alliances formed. There was no significant effect of the top management team's social status, as indicated by the mean prior job hierarchical level, on this second alliance type, as expected (Hypothesis 2).

With respect to the impact of the external environment, firms in growth stage markets did not have significantly higher rates of technology alliances form, (H_3), nor did the number of competitors influence technology-acquisition alliances (H_4).

Finally, the data in Table 12.3 show that more cumulative technology alliances were positively associated with higher formation rates of joint product development alliances. That is, the two types of alliances are interrelated but not reciprocally, with only technology-acquisition alliances influencing the formation of product development ones. Although cumulative prior alliances were entered as controls for both alliance types, the nonreciprocal nature of the results suggests that in order to obtain innovation benefits through the creation of joint product development alliances with others, new firms must first rely on the more targeted technology-acquisition alliances.

DISCUSSION

The purpose of this chapter is to explore the organization of innovation through strategic alliances and to compare the influence of the top management team with that of the external environment. We used a resource-based view of alliance formation to explore rates of innovation-related, strategic alliances within a population of entrepreneurial, semiconductor firms. There are several results.

First, top management characteristics differentially affected rates of innovation acquisition alliances. We found that firms with top management teams that were large and well connected through past industry employers and former high-level job positions formed joint product development alliances at higher rates. We argued that joint product development alliances were more vulnerable to implementation delays, opportunism, and technology leakages than were technology alliances. Therefore, the social position of top management teams would be important to mitigate these potential disadvantages of joint product development alliances. In contrast, we argued that top management team factors would be less relevant to technology alliances because they involve a more circumscribed relationship between the firms. Consistent with this view, the size of the top management team was marginally important, and the more status-oriented and reputation factors, such as number of previous industry employers and highest previous job levels, were not significantly related to technology alliances. That is, whereas the time resources and connections of larger teams matters somewhat, status and reputation factors are not relevant to technology alliances.

Second, market conditions also differentially affected the rates of alliance formation. Specifically, semiconductor ventures formed joint product development alliances at higher rates when they faced emergent stage markets. We argued that such situations would be particularly advantageous for product development alliances, because of the match between the high uncertainty of such markets and the risk-sharing and cost-sharing advantages of these alliances. In contrast, we found that technology alliances were unrelated to market stage. Or, in other words, firms formed technology alliances without apparent regard for whether the market was emergent, growth, or mature. Thus, it appears that joint product development alliances are a more specialized form of alliance whereas technology alliances are a more versatile form that firms use in a variety of industry conditions.

Third, the results indicate that the rates of formation of the two alliance types were interrelated. Technology acquisition alliances increased the rate of joint product development alliances although the converse was not true. This suggests that the experience of forming technology alliances may help firms learn how to execute the more involved joint product development alliances. It may also be the case that technology alliances are a way for firms to build their reputations for being good alliance partners, which then translates into opportunities for joint product development alliances at subsequent times. The interrelationship of these two alliance types could be fruitfully explored in future research.

Finally, it is worth noting that innovation strategy affected rates of formation for both technology acquisition and joint product development alliances, and in a similar fashion. Firms pursuing pioneering technology strategies were more likely to have higher formation rates for both types of alliances. This suggests that firms with innovative strategies are likely to use external relationships more aggressively than firms with less innovative strategies. In the semiconductor industry, new firms committed to a strategy of innovation aggressively pursued multiple avenues of innovation once they got their first products developed internally. This makes good sense intuitively because the torrid pace of innovation in the semiconductor industry places a premium on speed. These innovation leaders were demonstrably more active in their alliance behavior than other new semiconductor firms by acquiring technology externally and by creating new technology through joint development projects with others.

Overall, our findings suggest that rates of alliance formation are dependent on the interplay of alliance characteristics with top management team, strategy, and market factors that created needs and opportunities for alliance formation. Strong social positions led to alliance formation, but their importance varied with the type of alliance. Similarly, vulnerable strategic positions such as emergent markets and innovative strategies also lead to alliance formation, but the specific type depends on the characteristics of the alliance. In general, *technology alliances* are the versatile alliance form that firms use across a variety of market conditions and top management team configurations in order to gain technical know-how quickly. *Joint product development alliances* are more specialized such that firms use them in new markets and technologies where uncertainty, risk sharing, and legitimation are salient.

Finally, our results relate to a prominent debate within the strategy and organization's literatures (especially top management team). In these literatures there exists the industry versus firm debate. This study supports the view that both firm and industry conditions are important for predicting formation rates of strategic alliances. More significantly in this study, their importance varies with the type of alliance. Both industry (emergent market stage) and firm (top management team, innovation strategy, alliance history) were significant predictors of rates of joint product development alliance formation. In contrast, technology acquisition alliances were related to firm (innovation strategy, top management team size), *not* industry factors. We suggest, therefore, that the real issue is not whether the industry or firm is important—they obviously both matter—but rather the conditions under which is each important.

Second is the debate surrounding the relevance of transaction cost thinking (e.g., Perrow, 1986). Although we did not test transaction cost hypotheses, our results do relate to this theory. What we found was that pioneering technology (presumably the most valuable if there were leakages) was associated with higher, not lower, rates of alliance formation. So, although firms ran greater risks of leaking their technology "crown jewels," the strategic advantages of alliances for technically aggressive firms appeared to override these appropriability concerns. Similarly, emergent markets have very high uncertainty, and so, are situations in which alliances *are* avoided. Yet, here high rates of joint product development alliance formation were found. Again, strategic concerns seemed to outweigh transaction cost problems of these alliances. Future research could profitably explore these issues with a direct comparison with transaction cost predictions.

CONCLUSIONS

As we noted at the outset of the chapter, successive waves of innovation continuously reshape the competitive landscape by creating new opportunities and destroying the old (Schumpeter, 1942). Firms can succeed in the context of waves of innovation presumably by reacting to them, or perhaps more effectively, by anticipating and even creating them (Brown & Eisenhardt, 1997). Well-positioned and fast-paced innovations can, therefore, not only improve the competitive position of firms, but can also destroy the advantages of others (D'Aveni, 1994). Yet, innovations are difficult to achieve. The innovation process is often very costly and very risky for firms to undertake.

In this study, we examined the organization of innovation using strategic alliances. We argued that innovation-related, strategic alliances were alternative ways to organize innovation beyond simply in-house development. We have three principal conclusions. One is that top management teams play a crucial role in alliance formation, particularly when those alliances require extensive interfirm interaction. Two is that firms with pioneering technical strategies are more active alliance partners, who engage in both types of innovation-related alliances at higher rates than less technically aggressive firms. Third, technology and product development alliances play two distinct roles in the organization of innovation in their firms. Technology alliances are a versatile form used in a variety of contexts and are stepping stones to product development alliances. In contrast, product development alliances are a specialized alliance form that experienced, high-status top management teams use in new markets and with new technologies.

ACKNOWLEDGEMENTS

We would like to acknowledge, with thanks, the financial support of the School of Engineering, Stanford University, the Tuck Associates Program of the Amos Tuck School of Business, Dartmouth College, and the University of Missouri Department of Sociology. Data collection was supported by the U.S. Department of Commerce Economic Development Administration, Grant No. RED-870-G-86-15, and data analysis by the National Science Foundation Decision Risk and Management Science Program, Award No. 8911370 and the Alfred P. Sloan Foundation. We are thankful for these sources of support. A version of this paper was presented at the Academy of Management annual meetings, Cincinnati, Ohio, August, 1996.

REFERENCES

Allison, P. (1984). *Event history analysis: Regression for longitudinal event data*. Beverly Hills, CA: Sage.
Ancona, D. (1990). Top management teams: Preparing for the revolution. In J. Carroll (Ed.), *Applied social psychology and organizational settings* (pp. 99–128). Hillsdale, NJ: Lawrence Erlbaum Associates.

Anderson, C., & Zeithaml, C. (1984). Stage of the product life cycle, business strategy, and business performance. *Academy of Management Journal, 27,* 5–24.

Axelrod, R. (1984). *The evolution of cooperation.* New York: Basic Books.

Boeker, W. (1989). Strategic change: The effects of founding and history. *Academy of Management Journal, 32,* 489–515.

Borys, B., & Jemison, D. (1989). Hybrid arrangements as strategic alliances: Theoretical issues in organizational combinations. *Academy of Management Review, 14,* 234–249.

Brown, S., & Eisenhardt, K. (1995). Product development: Past research, present findings, and future directions. *Academy of Management Review, 20,* 343–378.

Brown, S., & Eisenhardt, K. (1997). The art of continuous change. *Administrative Science Quarterly, 42,* 1–34.

Burgers, W., Hill, C., & Kim, W. (1993). A theory of global strategic alliances: The case of the global auto industry. *Strategic Management Journal, 14,* 419–432.

Cameron, K., Kim, M., & Whetten, D. (1987). Organizational effects of decline and turbulence. *Administrative Science Quarterly, 32,* 222–240.

Carroll, G., & Hannan, M. (1989). Density delay in the evolution of organizational populations: A model and five empirical tests. *Administrative Science Quarterly, 34,* 411–430.

Cox, D. (1972). Regression models and life-tables. *Journal of the Royal Statistical Society, 34,* 187–220.

D'Aveni, R. (1994). *Hypercompetition.* New York: Free Press.

David, P. (1985). Clio and the economics of QWERTY. *American Economic Review, 75,* 332–337.

Dyer, J. (1992). *Between markets and hierarchies: Towards a comprehensive theory of "hybrid" or "network" forms of governance.* Manuscript in preparation, University of California at Los Angeles.

Eisenhardt, K. (1989). Making fast strategic decisions in high velocity environments. *Academy of Management Journal, 32,* 543–576.

Eisenhardt, K., & Schoonhoven, C. B. (1996). Strategic alliance formation in entrepreneurial firms: Strategic needs and social opportunities for cooperation. *Organization Science, 2,* 136–150.

Eisenhardt, K., & Tabriti, B. (1995). Accelerating adaptive processes: Product innovation in the global computing industry. *Administrative Science Quarterly, 40,* 84–110.

Finkelstein, S., & Hambrick D. (1990). Top management team tenure and organizational roles. *Administrative Science Quarterly, 35,* 484–503.

Granovetter, M. (1992). Problems of explanation in economic sociology. In N. Nohria & R. Eccles (Eds.), *Networks and organization: Structure, form, and action* (pp. 25–56). Boston, MA: Harvard Business School Press.

Gulati, R. (1993). *The dynamics of alliance formation.* Unpublished doctoral dissertation, Harvard University, Cambridge, MA.

Hackman, R. (1990). *Groups that work and those that don't: Creating conditions for effective teamwork.* San Francisco: Jossey-Bass.

Hagedoorn, J., & Schakenraad, J. (1990). *Technology cooperation, strategic alliances and their motives: Brother, can you spare a dime, or do you have a light?* Manuscript in preparation, MERIT, Maastricht, Netherlands.

Hambrick, D. (1989). Guest editor's introduction: Putting top managers back in the strategy picture. *Strategic Management Journal, 10,* 5–15.

Hambrick, D., & D'Aveni, R. (1992). Top team deterioration as part of the downward spiral of large corporate bankruptcies. *Management Science, 38,* 1445–1446.

Hambrick, D., MacMillan, I., & Day, D. (1982). Strategic attributes and performance in the BCG matrix—A PIMS-based analysis of industrial product businesses. *Academy of Management Journal, 25,* 510–531.

Hamel, G., Doz, Y., & Prahalad, C. (1989, January/February). Collaborate with your competitors and win. *Harvard Business Review*, 133–139.

Harrigan, K. (1988). Joint ventures and competitive strategy. *Strategic Management Journal, 9*, 141–158.

Heimer, C. (1992). Doing your job and helping your friends: Universalistic norms about obligations to particular others in networks. In N. Nohria & R. Eccles (Eds.), *Networks and organizations: Structure, form, and action* (pp. 118–142). Boston, MA: Harvard Business School Press.

Henderson, R., & Cockburn, I. (1993). *Measuring core competence: Evidence from the pharmaceutical industry*. Manuscript in preparation, MIT, Cambridge, Mass.

Hennart, J. (1988). A transaction costs theory of equity joint ventures. *Strategic Management Journal, 9*, 361–374.

Hennart, J. (1991). The transaction costs theory of joint ventures: An empirical study of Japanese subsidiaries in the United States. *Management Science, 37*, 483–497.

Integrated Circuit Engineering. (1987). *Status 1986: A report on the integrated circuit industry*. Scottsdale, AZ: Author.

Jelinek, M., & Schoonhoven, C. B. (1990). *The innovation marathon*. Oxford, England: Basil Blackwell.

Kimberly, J. (1980). Initiation, innovation, and institutionalization in the creation process. In J. Kimberly & R. Miles (Eds.), *Organizational life cycle* (pp. 134–160). San Francisco: Jossey-Bass.

Klepper, S., & Graddy, E. (1990). The evolution of new industries and the determinants of market structure. *The RAND Journal of Economics, 21*, 27–44.

Kogut, B., Shan, W., & Walker, G. (1992). The make-or-cooperate decision in the context of an industry network. In N. Nohria & R. Eccles (Eds.), *Networks and organizations: Structure, form, and action* (pp. 348–365). Boston, MA: Harvard Business School Press.

Larson, A. (1992). Network dyads in entrepreneurial settings: A study of the governance of exchange relationships. *Administrative Science Quarterly, 37*, 76–104.

Maidique, M., & Patch, P. (1982). Corporate strategy and technological policy. In M. Tushman & W. Moore (Eds.), *Readings in the management of innovation* (pp. 273–285). Marshfield, MA: Pitman.

Miles, R., & Snow, C. (1978). *Organizational strategy, structure, and process*. New York: McGraw-Hill.

Miner, A., Amburgey, T., & Stearns, T. (1990). Interorganizational linkages and population dynamics: Buffering and transformational shields. *Administrative Science Quarterly, 35*, 689–713.

Mintzberg, H., & Waters, J. (1982). Tracking strategy in an entrepreneurial firm. *Academy of Management Journal, 25*, 465–499.

Norburn, D., & Birley, S. (1988). The top management team and corporate performance. *Strategic Management Journal, 9*, 225–237.

Ouchi, W. (1980). Markets, bureaucracies, and clans. *Administrative Science Quarterly, 25*, 124–141.

Parkhe, A. (1993). Strategic alliance structuring: A game theoretic and transaction cost examination of interfirm cooperation. *Academy of Management Journal, 36*, 794–829.

Penrose, E. (1959). *The theory of the growth of the firm*. New York: Wiley.

Perrow, C. (1986). *Complex organizations*. New York: Random House.

Pisano, G. (1990). The R&D boundaries of the firm: An empirical analysis. *Administrative Science Quarterly, 35*, 153–176.

Porter, M. (1980). *Competitive strategy: Techniques for analyzing industries and competitors*. New York: Free Press.

O'Reilly, C. A., III, Snyder, R. C., & Boothe, J. N. (1993). Effects of executive team demography on organizational change. In G. P. Huber & W. H. Glick (Eds.), *Organizational change and redesign: Ideas and insights for improving performance* (pp. 53–82). New York: Oxford University Press.

Schoonhoven, C. B., Eisenhardt, K., & Lyman, K. (1990). Speeding products to market: Waiting time to first product introductions in new firms. *Administrative Science Quarterly, 35,* 177–207.

Schumpeter, J. (1942). *Capitalism, socialism, and democracy.* New York: Harper & Row.

Shan, W. (1990). An empirical analysis of organizational strategies by entrepreneurial high-technology firms. *Strategic Management Journal, 11,* 129–139.

Stinchcombe, A. L. (1965). Social structure and organizations. In J. G. March (Ed.), *Handbook of organizations* (pp. 142–193). Chicago: Rand McNally.

Tuma, N., & Hannan, M. (1984). *Social dynamics: Models and methods.* Orlando, FL: Academic Press.

Tushman, M., & Anderson, P. (1986). Technological discontinuities and organizational environments. *Administrative Science Quarterly, 31,* 439–465.

Tushman, M., & Romanelli, E. (1985). Organizational evolution: A metamorphosis model of convergence and reorientation. In B. M. Staw & L. L. Cummings (Eds.), *Research in organizational behavior* (Vol. 7, pp. 172–222). Greenwich, CT: JAI.

Van de Ven, A., & Polley, D. (1992). Learning while innovating. *Organization Science, 3,* 92–116.

Wernerfelt, B. (1984). A resource-based view of the firm. *Strategic Management Journal, 5,* 171–180.

Williamson, O. (1991). Comparative economic organization: The analysis of discrete structural alternatives. *Administrative Science Quarterly, 36,* 269–296.

Chapter 13

Group Learning in Organizations

Linda Argote
Carnegie Mellon University

Deborah Gruenfeld
Charles Naquin
Northwestern University

Interest in the topic of group learning has increased markedly in recent years. Several theoretical pieces have been written on groups as information-processing systems (e.g., Klimoski & Mohammed, 1994; Larson & Christensen, 1993; Levine & Moreland, 1991; Wegner, 1986). A growing body of empirical research has examined how groups distribute and share information and combine their individual inputs into a collective product.

Interest in the topic of organizational learning has also increased dramatically. Numerous academic articles have appeared recently on the topic (Argote & Epple, 1990; Huber, 1991; Levitt & March, 1988). Books and articles on organizational learning have also proliferated in the business and popular press (e.g., Senge, 1990).

Although the increased interest in the topics of group and organizational learning occurred at the same time, the two streams of work have generally moved in parallel, with little crossover between them. The current chapter aims to integrate research on both group and organizational learning to arrive at a richer understanding of how groups learn in organizational contexts.

Each stream of research has much to offer this undertaking. Research on group learning, which focuses primarily on internal group processes, provides rigorous theoretical models of how knowledge is stored, retrieved, shared, and combined at the group level of analysis. These studies have provided valuable information about important group functions, such as socialization, influence, and communication.

Research on organizational learning provides insights into external group processes, including how groups learn from other groups. The organizational learning literature also illuminates how knowledge changes over time in groups. And it provides information about how organizational factors, such as an organization's technology or its structure, affect the acquisition and retention of knowledge by groups.

The contribution of these two literatures to understanding group learning in organizations derives in part from the methods the studies generally employ. Most studies of group learning have been laboratory studies, whereas most studies of organizational learning have been field studies. When one studies group learning in the laboratory, one can design experiments to disentangle various theoretical models more readily than one can in the field. One is also able to capture group processes in the controlled setting of the laboratory more readily than one can in the field.

By contrast, when one studies groups in context rather than in controlled laboratory situations, one can analyze how the performance of those groups depends on relationships with other groups or with the external environment. Further, when one focuses on studying learning by real groups, one is confronted with the important problem of how groups retain knowledge over time, especially in the face of membership change (see Arrow & McGrath, 1995). And one begins to see how organizational factors such as technology or structure interact with psychological factors to affect group learning. By integrating the literature on group learning with the literature on organizational learning, we hope to arrive at a richer understanding of how groups learn in organizational contexts.

Our focus is on acting groups in organizational contexts. By acting groups, we mean collections of individuals who are engaged in interdependent activities (Argote & McGrath, 1993). A new product development team, the staff of a hospital emergency room, and a university tenure committee are examples of acting groups in context.

We define group learning in terms of both the processes and outcomes of group interaction. As a process, group learning involves the activities through which individuals acquire, share, and combine knowledge through experience with one another. Evidence that group learning has occurred includes changes in knowledge, either implicit or explicit, that occur as a result of such collaborations. It is important to note that the processes through which group learning is manifested include, but are not limited to, synchronous communications, such as direct conversations, meetings, and simultaneous project work. The processes can also involve asynchronous interchanges such as iterative adjustments by interdependent employees' of one another's work products, which occur sequentially in time, yet without explicit discussion, corroboration, or agreement.

Learning at the group level should also be distinguished from individual learning. Group-level theory in general requires at least two major shifts in thinking, when compared with individual-based explanations for behavior in organizations. Both derive from the notion that a group is a system. From a systems perspective, social behavior is both interdependent and dynamic. That is, group behavior is embedded in both a social and a temporal context (McGrath & Gruenfeld, 1993). Members of work groups must coordinate with the actions of others, and in doing so, will have an impact on others in the system whether they intend to or not. Furthermore, these patterns of coordination and interdependence change over time (Argote & McGrath, 1993; McGrath, 1991).

A MODEL OF GROUP PROCESSES IN ORGANIZATIONAL CONTEXTS

To capture these characteristics of group learning, we draw on a metatheoretic conception of groups that makes the interdependency and dynamism of group activity concrete. The model suggests that groups in organizations accomplish their work through recurring cycles of four major sets of processes (Argote & McGrath, 1993). Groups come into being and establish themselves through *construction* (C) processes. They do their work via *operations* (O) processes. *Reconstruction* (R) processes are those by which groups have an impact on (i.e., change) themselves. Groups stay interconnected with, have effects on, and are affected by other parts of the organization through *external relations* (E) processes. These CORE processes are conceived not as a series of stages that unfold in a fixed sequence over the group's life span. Rather, they represent different aspects of an acting group's "stream of behavior," with some temporal ordering but with much overlap and recycling.

Construction

Construction processes refer to activities involved in the initial establishment of a work group. These activities involve selecting, organizing, and fitting together members, tools, and purposes from the embedding context (i.e., from the organizational environment). Construction entails both the *acquisition* of members, purposes, and tools to form the group as a system, and their *adaptation* to one another.[1]

---

[1]It is beyond the scope of this paper to review the large literature on the use of technology by groups and organizations. Recent reviews of this literature can be found in Kiesler and Sproull (1992), McGrath and Hollingshead (1994), and Orlikowski (1992).

Acquisition involves the recruitment of people, the establishment of purposes, and the appropriation of tools from the embedding system. Adaptation as used here is closely related to what Poole and colleagues refer to as "adaptive structuration" (DeSanctis & Poole, 1994; Poole & Roth, 1989a, 1989b). This refers to the processes by which a social unit brings about changes in the people, tools, and purposes of which it is composed so that those people can use those tools to attain those purposes. Members are socialized or "trained." Technologies are implemented, and often modified in the process. Purposes are elaborated into plans—laid out in terms of tasks, steps, schedules, and assignments. Much of such socialization, implementation, and planning is tacit, rather than deliberate or explicit.

Operations

Operations processes refer to the activities of the group as it carries out its purposes. Operations processes can involve three modes of activity—technical problem solving, conflict resolution, and execution (McGrath, 1991). *Technical problem solving* involves collective cognitive activity, including the formation of representations of the situation, the problem and its potential solutions, effective information acquisition, processing, and exchange. *Conflict resolution* involves both informational and normative influence processes, recognition of differing perspectives, values, and interests, and the operation of consensus building (and destroying) mechanisms (for a review see McGrath, 1984). *Task execution* processes, especially those involving complex motor performances, often require relatively precise coordination of action in time, space, and content. Operations processes also include internal control of group activity. This entails monitoring and managing the coordination required for effective task performance, managing the conflicts that arise among group members, and monitoring the quality of the group's products in relation to its purposes.

Reconstruction

We distinguish here, on the one hand, between modifications of the members, tools, and purposes as they are acquired from the embedding context *in order to do* a project properly (i.e., the construction and operations processes already described), and, on the other hand, modifications of the people, tools, and purposes *as a consequence of having done* a project (i.e., the reconstruction processes considered here). These processes refer to how the group uses its own activities and experience as a basis for modifying itself.

The reconstruction processes include aspects of what has been referred to as "organizational learning" (Argote & Epple, 1990; Levitt & March, 1988). We call these knowledge-embedding processes. There are three kinds: (a) changes in the people (accumulation of tacit and explicit knowledge and skills by group members as a function of doing the project in context); (b) changes in the tools (modifications in hardware and software resulting from their having been used to do the project, and documentation of those modifications); and (c) changes in the project plan or structure (modifications in the differentiation of steps and tasks, division of labor, scheduling, and assignments resulting from the project's execution). These embedding processes show up when one is dealing with a group that has some meaningful history and continuation over time.

External Relations

These processes refer to how the group relates to the organizational and environmental context within which it is embedded. This involves monitoring the external environment with respect to members, tools, and purposes, and managing potential changes in relations between the group and those aspects of that environment. A group's performance and success is affected by its relations with many individuals and groups both inside and outside the organization (Ancona, 1990; Gladstein, 1984). These extragroup relations are carried out by one or more members of the focal group. External relations refer to the group's reaching out to external sources.

We can view external relations, too, as having three subprocesses: monitoring and managing relations between the group and other groups and individuals in the embedding system that could potentially provide resources/obstacles for the group; monitoring and managing relations between the group and the tools, rules, and resources that exist in the embedding system and are potentially available to be appropriated by, or pose potential obstacles to, the group; and monitoring and managing relations between the group and purposes in the embedding system that pose potential changes in opportunities or demands for the group. In other words, these subprocesses involve the relationship of the group to the larger organization's members, tools, and purposes.

Research on the processes and outcomes of group learning in organizations can be organized in terms of these four processes. Work bearing on each of these is now discussed in turn.

CONSTRUCTION PROCESSES

Construction processes involve the acquisition of members, purposes, and tools and their mutual adaptation to each other. In this section, we integrate findings about construction processes that are relevant for understanding group learning in organizational contexts. Key findings are drawn from research on group member selection, group composition, socialization, training, and group planning.

Member Selection

Knowledge can be built into a group through the process of member selection. For example, cross-functional teams and task forces are typically composed by assigning employees with diverse functional backgrounds to a single work group. The premise underlying these types of group structures is that they allow employees to pool their diverse knowledge and viewpoints, thereby facilitating group learning.

Indeed, groups whose members are diverse with regard to background and perspective outperform groups with homogeneous members on tasks requiring creative problem solving and innovation, and on some intellective problem-solving tasks (Jackson, 1992). Theoretically, this occurs when coworkers experience cognitive conflict in the absence of pressure to conform or defer to a dominant viewpoint, and respond by revising fundamental assumptions and by generating novel insights (Damon, 1991; Levine & Resnick, 1993; Nemeth, 1992). As a result, groups with heterogeneous composition generate more arguments (Smith, Tindale, & Dugoni, 1996), apply a greater number of strategies (Nemeth & Wachtler, 1983), detect more novel solutions (Nemeth & Kwan, 1987), and are better at integrating multiple perspectives (Gruenfeld, 1995a; 1995b; Peterson & Nemeth, 1996) than groups without conflicting perspectives.

Learning in work groups can also be affected by the extent to which group members have prior relationships with one another (Gruenfeld, Mannix, Williams, & Neale, 1996). It is interesting to note that in many work groups, members of the same social networks often have access to the same sources of information (Burt, 1992). Hence, groups whose members have access to different social networks, independent of their individual knowledge and skills, may be more likely to learn through interaction than groups whose members' social ties are redundant (Granovetter, 1973). The transfer of knowledge among groups can also be facilitated when the group in which learning initially occurs is composed of members with social ties to a diverse array of external constituents.

These considerations suggest that groups composed of members who do not know one another well are more conducive to learning through the importing and exporting of information. However, member familiarity can have positive consequences for the internal dynamics of group learning. For example, group members who have become familiar through training (Liang, Moreland, & Argote, 1995), prior work together (Goodman & Leyden, 1991; Kim, 1997), or through interaction prior to working together (cf. Levine & Moreland, 1990) possess more knowledge about one another's skills, perspectives, and interpersonal styles than group members who are less well acquainted. This superior metaknowledge should reduce the process losses that often accompany group work by unfamiliar members (Hackman, 1992). For example, knowledge of members' roles and areas of unique expertise can facilitate coordination of effort and improve the use of specialized information because members know where knowledge resides in the group (Liang, Moreland, & Argote, 1995; Northcraft & Neale, 1993; Wittenbaum & Stasser, 1996). In addition, member familiarity can reduce the tendency to conform and suppress unusual or politically sensitive information (Carver & Scheier, 1981; Sanna & Shotland, 1990).

Recent studies of familiarity and friendship support these ideas. Gruenfeld et al. (1996) showed that groups whose members were familiar outperformed groups of strangers when members possessed a diverse array of knowledge. In contrast, groups of strangers outperformed groups of friends when the knowledge members held was redundant. This is consistent with the finding that groups of friends are better at applying conflict management strategies to suit the task at hand than are groups of strangers, whose conflict management approaches are less sophisticated (Shah & Jehn, 1993).

Rulke (1996) explicitly examined the selection strategy leaders used to select members for management game teams. She contrasted the effect on performance of selecting members for their general competence versus selecting for specialized expertise. Results indicated that selecting members on the basis of their general competence improved team performance. Rulke (1996) interpreted these results as indicating that shared knowledge and group cognitive integration may be more important to cross-functional management teams than specialized expertise.

Member Socialization and Training

In addition to selecting members with certain characteristics, knowledge can also be built into a group through socialization and training. In their review of the group socialization literature, Levine and Moreland (1991) concluded that research on socialization and training has focused too much on task knowledge about individual jobs and too little on social knowledge about the work group and the organizational contexts. Social knowledge includes knowledge about group culture, structure, and norms as well as knowledge about other group members, including their particular capabilities. Similarly, Feldman (1989) argued that effective task performance depends on social as well as individual task knowledge.

The arguments advanced by Levine and Moreland (1991) and by Feldman (1989) suggest that group training may be a more effective strategy for promoting certain kinds of group learning than individual training. Consistent with this suggestion, Liang, Moreland, and Argote (1995) and Moreland, Argote, and Krishnan (1996) found that group training improved group members' task allocations, coordination, and trust, and these factors in turn led to a higher quality product. These studies are discussed in more detail under the "reconstruction" process because knowledge was acquired about the group as a result of doing the task.

Group Planning

In addition to selecting, socializing, and training people, group learning can be affected by the initial planning and design of group work. Planning for individual work includes identifying resources and the acts to be performed, deciding how to perform those acts, anticipating when specific acts need to be performed in relation to other aspects of the work process, and determining which cues to monitor while performing the task. Planning for group work involves strategizing for the coordination of group member activities. This includes how subtasks should be delegated, the timing of individual contributions, and their integration (Weingart, 1992).

Groups do not usually engage in spontaneous planning behavior; rather, they focus on completing the task (Hackman, Brousseau, & Weiss, 1976). Paradoxically, this tendency is exacerbated when task goals are especially challenging (Weingart, 1992) because the arousal associated with fear of failure increases the probability that the group will perform its dominant response (Easterbrook, 1959; Geen & Gagne, 1977; Huber, 1985). Groups are more likely to engage in planning when the task is complex (Weingart, 1992) and coordination requirements are great (Weldon & Weingart, 1993).

Planning and setting goals for group tasks is generally associated with better performance than is performing in the absence of specific plans or goals. However, planning prior to the task is often not enough. Preplanning is generally geared toward attaining the overall task objectives (LeBreton & Henning, 1961), rather than anticipating all of the possible contingencies that might be encountered along the way. Therefore, groups often need to engage in planning on-line, during performance, in response to changing task demands and feedback about the effectiveness of strategies in use (Faludi, 1973; Friedmann, 1966). Planning that occurs as a consequence of having done the task is discussed under the "reconstruction" process.

Conclusion

Group learning through construction processes involves the design and implementation of group structures that embed and link sources of unique and complementary knowledge and expertise. This is primarily accomplished through strategic group composition (see Moreland & Levine, 1996, for a review). On balance, heterogeneous groups and groups whose members have ties to different social networks are likely to be better at learning than groups lacking these features. These compositional factors must also be reinforced by organizational support systems that facilitate the flow of information within and between groups (Hackman, 1990). These include physical settings that encourage face-to-face interaction, as well as electronic communication technologies, and systems that reward and train employees for sharing information and insights (Mohrman, Cohen, & Mohrman, 1995).

OPERATIONS PROCESSES

Constructing groups for the purpose of learning does not in and of itself insure that learning will occur. As noted earlier, group members must be encouraged to share their unique knowledge and insights in order for the collective to benefit. In addition, once the diverse contributions of individuals have been recognized, groups must be able to use these contributions to improve performance. That is, the group must operate on the knowledge obtained in order for learning to occur.

Considerable research has been done on how groups share and combine knowledge and how they develop new knowledge as a result of their interactions. In this section, we integrate research findings about operations processes that are relevant for understanding group learning. These findings are drawn from research on group remembering, collective induction, knowledge sharing, social decision schemes, minority influence, emergent knowledge, divergent thinking, and integrative complexity.

Sharing of Knowledge

One potential advantage of a group is the integration of each individual's unique knowledge into a collective group-level knowledge that is greater than that of any single member. However, this advantage is dependent on the degree to which the knowledge of individuals within the group can be effectively shared, or pooled, during group discussion. This integration of information, at a group level of analysis, involves a social process among group members. Retrieval and discussion of information is dependent on both an individual's memory and the social interaction within the group that influence whether or not an individual contributes recalled information to the collective group knowledge (Larson & Christensen, 1993).

Research on "group" (Hartwick, Sheppard, & Davis, 1982) or "collaborative" remembering (Clark & Stephenson, 1989) is relevant for understanding the sharing of knowledge within groups. Clark and Stephenson (1989) defined collaborative remembering as the negotiation of a joint account of an experience with others. Clark and Stephenson identified several empirical regularities about collaborative remembering. First, groups generally recall more information than individuals (see also Hill, 1982, for a review). Second, groups are generally more accurate than individuals. Third, groups are better than individuals at reducing reconstructive errors, errors that involve material that was consistent with what happened but that did not actually happen.

Hinsz (1990) also found that groups performed better than individuals on memory recognition tasks. Several processes were found to contribute to the superior performance of groups over individuals. First, pooling of information contributed to the superior performance of groups because groups had access to a wider pool of information than individuals. Second, because groups made fewer errors than individuals, error correction contributed to the superior performance of groups over individuals. Third, the greater ability of groups to determine what they could and could not recognize correctly also appeared to contribute to their superior memory.

In addition to memory recognition tasks, groups are also better than individuals at collective induction tasks. Collective induction is a group's search for descriptive, predictive, and explanatory generalizations, rules, and principles (Laughlin & Hollingshead, 1995). The two basic processes of induction involve hypothesis generation and evaluation. Hypothesis generation is the providing of a tentative explanation for some observed phenomenon. Hypothesis evaluation is the testing of that hypothesis through observation or experimentation. This sequence, generation and evaluation, is a cycle that continues until a correct hypothesis is generated. Examples of groups that use collective induction include research, trouble-shooting, and auditing teams.

In general, groups are found to be superior to individuals for inductive tasks, and their superiority stems from the advantage of groups in evaluating hypotheses proposed by individuals. Using a rule induction task in which subjects propose and evaluate hypotheses for the correct pattern to a sequence of playing cards, groups were better than individuals at recognizing a correct hypothesis once it was proposed by one or more group members (Laughlin & Futoran, 1985; Laughlin & McGlynn, 1986; Laughlin & Shippy, 1983). Groups, however, were not found to be better than individuals in developing new hypotheses: Groups did not achieve a correctly induced hypothesis that none of the members could have achieved alone. Thus, the superiority of collective induction over individual induction is due to the superior hypothesis evaluation by groups and not due to the generation of a superior hypothesis itself.

However, the extent to which the best hypotheses of individual members will become available to the group depends on the probability that individuals will pool their unique ideas. In fact, research shows that groups are more likely to pool and discuss the ideas that they have in common than they are to consider and operate on those that are unique to individual members (for a review see Wittenbaum & Stasser, 1996). An information-sampling model proposed by Stasser and Titus (1985, 1987) predicts that the probability that a piece of information will be mentioned during group discussion increases with the number of members who already know about it. Consequently, shared information is said to have a sampling advantage as it is more likely to be mentioned and discussed than unshared information.

Factors Affecting Sharing of Knowledge Within Groups

How information is distributed within a group influences how information is shared in group discussion. Information can be distributed so that it is shared by all or by only a certain portion of the group. A hidden profile (Stasser, 1988) is a profile of information distribution that is often used in exploring the effectiveness of a group in integrating information. A hidden profile describes a situation in which the information is distributed such that group members have different pieces of information, yet if all the information is pooled together and discussed, an optimal solution is available. This superior solution is hidden from each group member individually. In general, Stasser and his colleagues (Stasser & Titus, 1985) found that decision-making groups tend to fail in discovering a hidden profile. Common information is more likely to be shared than unique information. Factors demonstrated to affect the sharing of information by groups are now reviewed.

Information Load and Distribution. The discussion of an item of information by a group is dependent on an individual recalling that item of information. The recall of an item has been shown to be influenced by the amount of information that an individual has to remember or information load, and how the information is distributed within a group or the percentage of shared and unshared information. Stasser and Titus (1987) explored these factors and found that groups with low information loads and a high percentage of unshared information most effectively recalled unshared information in group discussion.

Group Size. Stasser and Titus (1987), and Stasser, Taylor, and Hanna (1989) found that the sampling advantage of shared information increases as group size increases. The larger the group, the more likely it is to discuss shared information.

Expert Roles. How information is distributed among the members of a group, and knowledge of that distribution, affects the social processes involved in retrieval and integration of information. It has been demonstrated that a group's awareness of the distribution of expert knowledge decreases the sampling advantage of shared information. Expert roles also provide a social validation for information that is relevant to their domain of expertise.

Stasser, Stewart, and Wittenbaum (1995) and Stewart and Stasser (1995) found that transactive memory systems, where individuals possess a meta-knowledge of who knows what in addition to their own content knowledge, can affect group discussion. The effect of these memory systems, however, is dependent on the extent to which members are knowledgeable of each others' areas of expertise. Groups with assigned expert roles mentioned and repeated more unshared information than groups without expert roles. In addition, Stasser, Stewart, and Wittenbaum (1995) found that groups with expert roles were more likely than groups without expert roles to find a hidden profile and make correct decisions.

Expert roles within a group can also provide social validation of unshared information. One explanation for the failure of a group to discuss unshared information, even if it is mentioned, is that social validation of an item of information is necessary before a group accepts it. Social validation occurs when the accuracy of the information introduced by one member is confirmed by another group member. Recognized expertise has been shown to provide this social validation. Group members are more likely to accept and remember information that is contributed by a recognized expert (Stewart & Stasser, 1995).

Nature of Task.   The nature of the task has been shown to affect the sharing of information in groups. In particular, the extent to which a task has a "demonstrably" correct answer affects group information sharing (Gigone & Hastie, 1993; Stasser & Stewart, 1992). Laughlin and Ellis (1986) proposed four conditions of demonstrability. First, consensus on a system of rules must exist in the group. Second, the group must believe that there is sufficient information to solve the task. Third, group members must be able to recognize and accept a correct answer when it is proposed. Fourth, the knowledgeable group member must be able to demonstrate the correctness of the answer.

Tasks can be classified on a continuum that is anchored by intellective and judgmental tasks. Intellective tasks are those for which there is a demonstrably correct solution, such as a math problem. Judgmental tasks are those for which there is not a demonstrably correct answer, such as a jury decision. The results of several studies have indicated that the number of group members necessary for a group to reach a collective decision decreased as the demonstrability of the appropriateness of the decision increased (Laughlin & Ellis, 1986).

Stasser and Stewart (1992) found that the perception of a demonstrably correct solution promoted discussion and the integration of unshared information. Conversely, the lack of a demonstrable answer promoted consensus building. In a similar vein, Gigone and Hastie (1993) showed that group judgments tended to use an implicit or explicit averaging rule to combine individual preferences into a group consensus.

Structuring Group Discussion. One potential variable that can increase the amount of unshared information discussed in a group is structuring the discussion to facilitate information disclosure. Contradictory results, however, have emerged from studies exploring this factor. Stasser, Taylor, and Hanna (1989) found that structuring discussion actually increased the tendency to discuss more shared than unshared information. In contrast, Larson, Foster-Fishman, and Keys (1994) found that having groups plan a decision-making strategy and providing group training on decision-making skills increased the amount of both shared and unshared information and altered the flow of information such that shared and unshared information were mentioned at an even pace.

Summary. In sum, characteristics of the group's composition, its structure, and its task affect whether unshared information will be shared. Information is most likely to be shared in groups when: (a) group members are not burdened with exceptionally high information loads, (b) diversity of opinion exists in the group, (c) group members are perceived as having special expertise, (d) groups are relatively small in size, and (e) tasks are perceived as having a demonstrably correct answer such as making a diagnosis.

Combining Information

Once information is shared by individual group members, it must somehow be combined into a group product. The social interactions that take place to sort through alternatives and form a group decision is called a social decision scheme (Davis, 1973). A *social decision scheme* is a rule or procedure— either implicit or explicit, formal or informal—that converts individual preferences into a single group response. Thus, a social decision scheme is a model of the social processes by which a group develops a solution.

Laughlin and Ellis (1986) proposed that groups use different social decision schemes depending on the task's demonstrability of correctness. The results of several studies, when viewed as a collection, demonstrate that the number of group members that is necessary and sufficient for a collective group decision increases as the demonstrability of the group response decreases. A majority-wins decision scheme best fits judgmental tasks without a demonstrably correct answer such as in mock juries (Davis, Kerr, Atkin, Holt, & Meek, 1975; Davis, Kerr, Stasser, Meek, & Holt, 1977; Kerr et al., 1976; see Davis 1980, and Penrod & Hastie, 1979, for reviews). Simple majority is the best-fitting social decision scheme for judgmental tasks without demonstrable correct answers such as betting (Cvetkovich & Baumgardner, 1973; Davis, Kerr, Sussmann, & Rissman, 1974; Kerr, Davis, Meek, & Rissman, 1975; Lambert, 1969, 1976; Zaleska, 1976, 1978). An equiprobability social decision scheme, in which the collective group decision is equally likely among the proposed alternatives regardless of the number of members favoring a particular alternative, best fits judgmental tasks without demonstrably correct answers (Davis, Hornik, & Hornseth, 1970; Zajonc, Wolosin, Wolosin, & Sherman, 1968; see Davis, 1982, for a review). Truth-supported wins, in which two correct members are needed for a correct group response, is the best-fitting social decision scheme for intellective tasks with nonobvious demonstrably correct answers, such as tests of world knowledge (Laughlin & Adamopoulos, 1980, 1982; Laughlin, Kerr, Davis, Halff, & Marciniak, 1975; Laughlin, Kerr, Munch, & Haggarty, 1976). A truth-wins social decision scheme, in which a single correct member is necessary and sufficient for a correct group response, is best fitting for intellective tasks with an obvious demonstrably correct answer (Laughlin & Ellis, 1986). A combination of majority and truth-supported wins social decision scheme best fits a collective induction task, which is intermediate on the continuum of tasks between intellective and judgmental ones (Laughlin & Futoran, 1985; Laughlin & Shippy, 1983).

Creating Solutions: Learning Through Minority Influence

When learning does occur in groups, it is often in response to the influence of an outsider, a marginal member, or some other representative of minority opinion (Levine & Moreland, 1985; Levine & Russo, 1987). Sometimes groups are persuaded by a minority to adopt the specific opinions and changes advocated (Maass & Clarke, 1983; Mugny, 1982). Other times, the presence of a minority initiates unintended changes in the perceptions of group members (Moscovici & Lage, 1978; Moscovici & Personnaz, 1980), or the structure and dynamics of the group (Levine & Moreland, 1985). What are the conditions that enable this to occur?

Source Characteristics.   Some group members are simply more likely to adopt the role of a change agent than others. Individuals who belong to and identify simultaneously with two or more groups, either by personal preference or by organizational design, are often especially cognizant of the trade-offs associated with how each group does business

(Meyerson & Scully, 1995). Such individuals, who could be characterized as marginals or boundary spanners, may have both the insight and the motivation to initiate change in the groups to which they belong.

Once a person has decided to enact an influence attempt, the degree to which it will have an impact depends most importantly on the source's credibility. For example, the size of the minority plays an important role (Tanford & Penrod, 1984). To begin with, a lone dissenter is more likely to conform to the majority than to express his or her deviance (Asch, 1956). Furthermore, a single minority member can be dismissed as an aberrant outlier more easily than a minority with some social support (Penrod & Hastie, 1980), which might in and of itself make the majority view appear questionable (Morris & Miller, 1975).

The credibility of a minority member also depends on the consistency with which his or her position is held over time (Moscovici, 1976, 1980, 1985). However, the appearance of rigidity interferes with the impact of minority influence (Mugny & Papastamou, 1976); hence, a minority who gradually distances him or herself from the majority is more persuasive than one who begins association with the majority as a staunch dissenter (Levine, Saxe, & Harris, 1976). Similarly, although minority advocates of extreme positions tend to be more influential than those of moderate positions because they seem more confident (Levine & Ranelli, 1978), the appearance of flexibility appears to be a critical mediator of this effect (Maass & Clarke, 1984).

A minority advocate's credibility also depends on the extent to which he or she appears to have the interests of the group at heart. For this reason, "double minorities," who both hold an unusual viewpoint and possess common features that make them appear to have personal interest in the outcome they are advocating, are less influential than minorities who appear less self-interested and hence, more trustworthy (Eagly, Wood, & Chaiken, 1978).

Finally, minority advocates of a position that is "demonstrably correct" are often able to convert the rest of the group with the sheer "truth" of their argument (Laughlin, 1988). Minority opinions that are consistent with the prevalent cultural trends (e.g., Zeitgeist) tend to have greater influence than those that seem less progressive (Kruglanski, 1989; Vinokur & Burnstein, 1978).

Impact on Group Beliefs. A group's reactions to minority influence can vary from polarization against the minority position (Tindale, Davis, Vollrath, Nagao, & Hinsz, 1990) to private acceptance of it (Moscovici, 1980; for reviews, see Kruglanski & Mackie, 1990; Levine, 1989). As noted earlier, minority influence can also enhance group creativity and lead to improved problem solving, without directly affecting the majority's outcome preferences (Nemeth, 1992).

Although the targets of minority influence are unlikely to conform in public, they are sometimes privately persuaded. For example, minority influence has led to changes in majority opinion about abortion (Perez & Mugny, 1986), perceptions of color (Moscovici, Lage, & Naffrechoux, 1969), and the outcomes of jury deliberation (Nemeth & Wachtler, 1983). This latent belief change or "conversion" is generally attributed to majority members' attempts to understand the apparent commitment of the minority (Moscovici, 1985) in the face of overwhelming normative and informational influence. This persistence suggests that the deviant position being advocated must be worth reconsidering.

Smith et al. (1996) found that a vocal minority acted as a "rein" on the extremity of majority opinion about whether English should be established as the official language of the United States. This finding stands in contrast to a previous study by Tindale et al. (1990) in which minorities had a polarizing effect on the majority. This difference, they argued, appears to depend on the nature of the task. The groups in Tindale et al. (1990) were required to reach consensus, whereas those in Smith et al. were simply instructed to have a discussion. On the basis of this difference, the authors concluded that minority influence may be more powerful when the presence of opposing opinions does not prevent the group from accomplishing its goal—that is, when the group's objective is to *learn*, rather than to merely perform.

Creating Solutions: Emergent Knowledge

An interesting aspect of group learning involves how group members, through collaboration, are able to generate knowledge and insights that no individual had to begin with. This creative, synergistic aspect of group learning has received considerable attention from researchers of cognitive development (Garton, 1992; Murray, 1983), and some European social psychologists (Doise & Mugny, 1984; Perret-Clermont, Perret, & Bell, 1991). However, despite some important contributions (for a review see Nemeth, 1992), investigations of emergent knowledge in groups have not been widely embraced by mainstream experimental social psychologists (Levine & Resnick, 1993).

The work that has been done indicates that social interaction, particularly when it involves the resolution of cognitive conflict, can lead to deep conceptual restructuring and to the emergence of novel insights. For example, peer interactions among children who are equally naive but who have different responses to the same problem can lead to mastery of new cognitive skills after a single interaction (Perret-Clermont et al., 1991). In addition, problem-solving groups in which members disagree often outperform groups without vocal dissenters on tasks requiring creativity (Nemeth, 1986;

Nemeth & Kwan, 1987) and the integration of multiple viewpoints (Peterson & Nemeth, 1996).

The development of emergent knowledge in groups appears to depend largely on two factors: (a) the presence of conflict among collaborators' viewpoints, and (b) the context in which conflict occurs (Damon, 1991; Levine & Resnick, 1993). Cognitive change is unlikely to occur in the absence of alternative viewpoints; hence, some degree of diversity in opinions is required (Nemeth, 1986). However, not all responses to conflict in groups involve cognitive change (Kruglanski & Mackie, 1990; Levine, 1989). When members experience pressure to accept one alternative and dismiss the others, they are unlikely to think beyond what is given (Damon, 1991; Peterson & Nemeth, 1996). Learning in such settings is more likely to resemble modeling, imitation, or conformity than the development of emergent knowledge (Rogoff, 1986; Tetlock, 1981, 1983). In contrast, when members are motivated to be accurate and are not constrained by time or pressure to accept a given solution, they are more likely to change strategies, integrate alternatives, and generate new ideas as a consequence (Damon, 1991; Nemeth, 1986; Piaget, 1932/1965). The impact of these conditions on collaborative learning has been observed in several domains of research.

Divergent Thinking.   Work by Charlan Nemeth and her colleagues demonstrates how conflict can stimulate the generation of knowledge in groups (for a review see Nemeth, 1992). On a variety of problem-solving tasks, groups in which a single member proposed unusual and even incorrect solutions outperformed groups in which no such deviance occurred. Groups affected by the presence of a vocal deviant detected more novel solutions, attempted a greater number of problem-solving strategies, and produced more original arguments and associations to words than groups without a vocal minority (Nemeth & Kwan, 1987; Nemeth & Wachtler, 1983). Furthermore, once a group has experienced this type of activity, these performance advantages generalize to subsequent, unrelated tasks when minority influence is not present (Smith, Tindale, & Dugoni, 1996).

Theoretically, these enhanced problem-solving abilities are a consequence of "divergent thinking," which occurs when group members encounter an unusual idea in the absence of social pressure to accept it (Nemeth, 1986). Arguments presented by a lone dissenter are typically perceived as inaccurate; consensus is often equated with truth. Hence, group members are motivated to reject a deviant's proposal, rather than to accept it, and respond by dismissing the proposed alternative and searching for additional ones. To do this effectively, group members are forced to reconceptualize their own position and its relation to the problem itself. Hence, divergent thinking occurs when conflict in groups is initiated by a vocal minority.

However, when the source of conflict is a majority member, divergent thinking does not occur. The targets of majority influence experience pressure to conform and therefore think "convergently," focusing exclusively on reasons to accept the position proposed by the majority. Hence, the presence of multiple perspectives in groups does not necessarily lead to the generation of emergent knowledge. The motivation to defer to a majority can limit cognitive flexibility and the tendency to think beyond what is given even when the majority itself presents multiple viewpoints. This was demonstrated in a recent study in which both majority members and minority members taught subjects to use multiple perspectives in a task requiring attention to both the meaning of a word and the color in which it was printed. Whereas subjects taught by majority members learned to use both perspectives one at a time, those taught by minority members learned to use both perspectives simultaneously, by switching back and forth between them (Peterson & Nemeth, 1996).

In sum, knowledge can emerge in groups when members recognize multiple perspectives and are able to use them simultaneously to gain conceptual leverage on the problem at hand. Maintaining the validity of multiple perspectives, especially when they are in conflict, typically requires understanding how they are related to one another (Peterson & Nemeth, 1996; Tetlock, 1986). However, this type of integrative reasoning is much more challenging than simply deciding whose individual idea is best, and therefore occurs much less often (Laughlin, VanderStoep, & Hollingshead, 1991; Levine & Resnick, 1993).

Integrative Complexity.   The development of multidimensional and integrative thinking in groups has also been the focus of recent research on integrative complexity (Gruenfeld, 1995a; Gruenfeld & Hollingshead, 1993). Decision makers exhibiting low integrative complexity tend to rely on a single, fixed view of the world, from which good and bad are easily discernable (e.g., "Conflict in groups should be avoided at all cost"). High integrative complexity corresponds to the acceptance of multiple worldviews and the value conflict that comes with understanding the trade-offs among them (e.g., "Conflict in groups can be threatening to members' relationships, but it is necessary for effective problem solving").

Consistent with Nemeth's work, integrative complexity in decision-making groups appears to depend on both the presence of conflict and the social structure in which it is embedded. An archival analysis of Supreme Court opinions showed that majority opinions written on behalf of a nonunanimous Court displayed greater integrative complexity than those written on behalf of a minority, or when the Court was unanimous (Gruenfeld, 1995a). In addition, subjects assigned to majority factions in nonunanimous laboratory groups experienced an increase in integrative complexity, whereas those assigned to minority factions and unanimous groups experienced a decrease in integrative complexity, after participating in a group decision task (Gruenfeld, 1995b).

Similarly, decision makers whose preferences are incompatible with those of the audience to which they are accountable merely conform to those preferences, whereas accountability to an audience with unknown preferences tends to increase decision makers' integrative complexity (Tetlock, Skitka, & Boettger, 1989).

However, the development of integrative complexity has also been observed in continuing work groups where neither conflict nor pressure to conform was induced experimentally. In one study (Gruenfeld & Hollingshead, 1993), 22 groups of 3–4 members each worked together over a 13-week period on a variety of group tasks. Group members, who were college students in an organizational psychology class, wrote essays each week (first as individuals, and then as a group) analyzing their performance on that week's task. The integrative complexity expressed in these documents provided a running account of the group's emerging knowledge about itself, and the complexity of those accounts was related to group performance: Groups exhibiting relatively high levels of intregrative complexity over time outperformed low complexity groups on intellective problem-solving tasks.

Both individual and group essays on group performance became more integratively complex over time. With increased experience and expertise, group members became increasingly likely to generate complex and integrative insights about the group's process–performance relationship (see also Cummings, Schlosser, & Arrow, 1995). However, expressions of knowledge about the group differed in their complexity as a function of whether the account was written in collaboration with other members, or by a single group member working alone.

Initially, the integrative complexity of group essays resembled that of the average individual essay, and was significantly lower than that expressed by the most integratively complex group member. This pattern is consistent with prior research on individual versus group performance on cognitive tasks (Hill, 1982). However, during the second half of the semester, the level of group complexity increased at a greater rate than either the average or highest individual level, until it was significantly greater than that of the average individual and statistically equivalent to that of the highest group member. This suggests that the integrative complexity of knowledge that emerges through group collaboration can be distinguished from that of the knowledge generated and remembered by the individual group member, and that the integrative complexity of a group can become greater than that of its individual members. Furthermore, the extent to which groups generate complex emergent knowledge is related to their performance: Groups exhibiting relatively high levels of integrative complexity over time also performed better than low complexity groups on cooperative group problem-solving tasks.

The emergence of complex knowledge in these groups was also affected by changes in their working conditions (Gruenfeld, Hollingshead, & Fan, 1995). During two separate periods, groups experienced changes in their communication technology (face-to-face versus computer-mediated), and their membership (one old member was replaced by one new member in each group for a 2-week period). Each time, the average level of group integrative complexity rose to a previously unobserved level, and never returned to the earlier, lower level. Interestingly, however, group integrative complexity rose only after familiar working conditions were restored. These findings indicate that the development of integrative complexity at the group level can be encouraged through exposure to alternating periods of experience and change, followed by time to reflect on the difference.

These findings were replicated in a second longitudinal study, which also provides an indication as to when the development of integrative complexity is most likely to occur. Cummings et al. (1995) found that the explanations presented by groups who wrote using collaborative computer software were more integratively complex than those presented by groups working face-to-face because they were composed by a greater number of authors who presented a greater proportion of unique ideas.

In sum, the data from these longitudinal studies suggests that emergent knowledge can be stimulated in groups for which the resolution of conflict is not a primary objective. Groups whose main objective is to learn from one another become better at identifying and integrating multiple perspectives over time even when conflict is not structurally imposed. Similarly, Smith et al. (1996) argued that groups will be most likely to consider the alternative perspectives of individual members when the presence of opposing opinions does not prevent the group from accomplishing its goal. When a group must reach consensus with regard to a single, unidimensional outcome, the presence of alternative perspectives reduces efficiency. In contrast, when a group collaborates for the purpose of learning or having an interesting discussion, alternative perspectives make the task more interesting.

The longitudinal studies differ from prior research on emergent knowledge in groups in an additional way, by examining collaborations among peers of equal status, rather than members of majority and minority factions. Research in cognitive development indicates that "discovery learning" (Damon, 1991), which requires radical shifts in previous operating assumptions, is more likely to occur through peer collaborations than through coaching or guided instruction by experts (Rogoff, 1986). In contrast to expert–novice collaborations in which respect tends to be unilateral, collaborations among peers tend to involve an active exchange of ideas between equal partners who need not defer to one another's intellectual authority (Piaget, 1932/1965).

In sum, these authors suggest that the nature of the interaction is more important than the relationship per se. The combination of equality and mutual respect, balanced discourse, and neither too much nor too little conflict, is optimal for the development of emergent knowledge through collaboration (Damon, 1991).

Group Biases

Although groups are usually better than the "average" individual and sometimes better than the "best" individual, on occasion, groups make disastrous decisions (e.g., see Janis, 1972) or persist in defensive routines that prevent them from learning (Argyris, 1992). Studies comparing the use of biases by groups and individuals generally find that groups amplify tendencies evident at the individual level (Tindale, 1993). For example, in their comparison of the use of base-rate and individuating information by groups and individuals, Argote, Devadas, and Melone (1990) found that groups were more biased than individuals when the individuating information was perceived as very informative, and less biased than individuals when the individuating information was perceived as less so (see also Argote, Seabright, & Dyer, 1986, and Nagao, Tindale, Hinsz, & Davis, 1985).

Understanding when groups cancel biases and when they amplify them is an important issue for group learning. Several recent theoretical advances have been aimed at integrating the literature on "groupthink" or on group biases and thereby provide insights into this issue. Turner, Pratkanis, Probasco, and Leve (1992) tested a social identity maintenance perspective on groupthink. Kerr, MacCoun, and Kramer (1996) used a social decision scheme approach to specifying conditions under which group decisions are more or less biased than individuals. These theoretical advances are promising.

Conclusion

Composing groups of knowledgeable individuals does not guarantee group learning. Knowledge that is privately held by individual members will remain latent unless it is made public and thereby becomes accessible to others. This can occur through direct communication, public documentation, overt demonstration, and the like. Furthermore, the individual contributions of group members, once acknowledged, must be processed, or operated on, by others. For example, facts and ideas must be combined, and or chosen among, so that the group can converge on a single "best" alternative that permits coordinated actions.

RECONSTRUCTION PROCESSES

Reconstruction processes involve modifications in group members, tools, and purposes that result from the group's experience. In this section, we integrate research findings about reconstruction processes that are relevant for understanding group learning. Findings are drawn from research on group planning, group learning, transactive memory, and repositories of group knowledge.

Evidence of group learning is often invisible until the group has reconstructed itself, its work processes, or products to accommodate new information. The change process can be initiated by a single individual who introduces or imposes new insights and values, but it is often the result of true collaboration and involves emergent ideas or structures that no one individual could have produced alone.

Groups can experience changes in structure, dynamics, and performance in response to initiatives, or anticipated initiatives, by individual members (Levine & Moreland, 1985; Levine & Resnick, 1993). A group's receptivity to these types of innovation can be affected by its developmental stage (Gersick, 1988) and the role transitions the group is currently undergoing (Levine & Moreland, 1985). For example, groups may change important characteristics in order to attract desirable new members, and newcomers often unintentionally change norms, patterns of status, and interaction among old-timers, as well as the group's ability to attain its goals. In addition, groups are more likely to revisit and evaluate current strategies, and attempt to initiate change at and around the midpoint of the group's work together than in either of the phases immediately prior to or following the midpoint (Gersick, 1989; Gersick & Hackman, 1990).

Group Planning

In addition to group learning that is enacted by tensions between the group and its individual members (Levine & Moreland, 1985; Levine & Resnick, 1993), learning in groups can also occur as a consequence of the passage of time (see also Gruenfeld & Hollingshead, 1993; McGrath, Arrow, Gruenfeld, Hollingshead, & O'Connor, 1993), and in response to feedback about past performance (Gersick, 1989; Hackman & Morris, 1975; Ocasio, 1995). Such effects have been observed with regard to group-planning activities.

A major reason for the positive impact of planning on group performance is that setting group goals is associated with the tendency to change strategies when necessary. It seems that although difficult goals may interfere with group-planning prior to the task, they actually increase the tendencies to change strategies (Weingart & Weldon, 1991), reorganize materials and working space, and discuss who should do what, when, and where during task execution (Weldon, Jehn, & Pradhan, 1991). All of these strategy change activities were associated with superior group performance. Furthermore, the level of group-planning was correlated with reports of the extent to which the group's strategy changed.

Once a group strategy has been adopted, it is not often revised easily. Even when feedback indicates that a particular strategy or plan is no longer optimal, groups can be slow to change their routines (Gersick & Hackman, 1990; Staw, Sandelands, & Dutton, 1981). Groups may ignore changes in the environment that render their goals obsolete (Staw & Boettger, 1990). Alternatively, evidence of failure may increase attention and effort with regard to the activities implicated, but this often leads to more focused execution of preestablished plans, rather than change in strategy (Gersick & Hackman, 1990; Gladstein & Reilly, 1985; Staw et al., 1981).

The extent to which evidence of failure actually leads to change can also depend on the group's dynamics and structure. For example, Ocasio (1995) proposed that the reactions of top management teams to economic adversity depend on the level of group cohesiveness, the equivalence of consequences for individual members, and the viability of emergent coalitions in the group. The experience of economic adversity in organizations, he argued, leads to a narrowing of attention (cf. Zajonc, 1965). In cohesive top management teams, this will lead to stability in, and centralization of control by, the dominant political coalition. Economic adversity can have a negative impact on cohesion, however, if its effects appear to have worse consequences for some individuals than others. Under these circumstances, group reactions to adversity can include changes in the structure of participation in decision making, increased group turnover, and changes in the composition of political coalitions. Turner (1988) found that how groups reacted to threat depended on the existing degree of centralization of their communication structures. In particular, the degree of centralization, the degree of threat, and the nature of the performance cues groups received interacted to affect the speed but not the quality of group performance.

Groups are also more susceptible to major transformations in their standard operating procedures during certain stages of group development than others (Gersick, 1989; see also Levine & Moreland, 1985, on innovation, discussed earlier). Gersick found that groups do engage in spontaneous self-reflection and often undergo a major transition in their approach toward their work at the midpoint of their life cycle (Gersick, 1989). In her research on task forces and student project teams, two basic approaches to this midpoint transition were observed. One major approach involved summarizing previous work, declaring it complete, and picking up a next subtask. The second approach groups used was to drop plans and activities that didn't seem to be working in the first phase of their work together and to identify—mostly through unsystematic means—a new purpose or objective at which to target their renewed efforts.

Gersick's work suggests that there are certain times during which efforts to help a group plan, reflect, strategize, and learn will be more useful than others. Her punctuated equilibrium model of group development suggests that groups are most likely to benefit from help planning at their first meeting, help reflecting and restrategizing at the midpoint, and help drawing conclusions and embedding knowledge during remembrance, after the task has been completed.

Transactive Memory

Another kind of knowledge that groups generate as they gain experience is knowledge of who is good at what. Wegner (1986) developed the concept of transactive memory to describe this kind of knowledge and its distribution. According to Wegner, as social systems gain experience, members acquire knowledge about the collective as well as knowledge of how to perform their individual tasks. Members learn who is good at what, whom to trust, and how to coordinate and communicate with one another. Thus, members acquire metaknowledge that enables them to access a much wider pool of information than they themselves possess.

Liang et al. (1995) used Wegner's concept of transactive memory to investigate the effect of training on group performance. In an initial study, the researchers compared the performance of groups whose members were trained individually to that of groups whose members were trained together. Groups whose members were trained together exhibited better recall and made fewer errors than groups whose members were trained apart.

The superior performance of groups in the group training condition seemed to be due to the operation of a transactive memory system. Groups whose members were trained together exhibited greater specialization or role differentiation, seemed to trust one another to a greater extent, and were better coordinated than groups whose members were trained individually. Further, the transactive memory variable was found to mediate the relationship between training and group performance (Baron & Kenny, 1986).

A subsequent study included two additional conditions to investigate whether the superior performance of subjects trained as a group was due to enhanced group development or to the acquisition of generic strategies for working in a group (see Moreland et al., 1996). One condition in which subjects were trained as individuals and then given a team-building exercise was added to investigate further whether the superior performance of subjects trained as a group was due to enhanced group development. The performance of subjects in this individual training plus team-building condition was inferior to that of subjects trained as a group and comparable to that of subjects who only received individual training. Thus, enhanced group development did not lead to superior group performance whereas transactive memory systems did.

Another condition was added to the second study in which subjects were trained in one group and performed in another. The performance of subjects who were trained in this condition was comparable to the performance of subjects in the individual training condition and the individual training plus team-building condition and inferior to that of subjects who trained and performed in the same group. Thus, it is not experience working with any group that drives the superior performance of group-trained subjects but rather experience working with particular group members that leads to the creation of transactive memory systems.

Hollenbeck et al. (1995) also found that experience improved group performance in their study of decision-making hierarchical teams. Further, much—but not all—of the effect of experience on performance was mediated by its effect on three core variables: team informity (the degree to which the team is informed about the decision), staff validity (the extent to which members' judgments are accurate), and hierarchical sensitivity (the degree to which the leader effectively weights group members' judgments in arriving at the decision). Experience improved these three core variables, which in turn improved group performance. In a second study, Hollenbeck et al. (1995) found that teams that had an incompetent member and those low in cohesiveness performed more poorly than their counterparts. Similar to the previous results, much—but not all—of the effect of cohesion and competence on decision accuracy was mediated by the three core variables.

Embedding Knowledge

Recent evidence suggests that knowledge acquired through group learning may decay or depreciate (Argote, Beckman, & Epple, 1990). In order for groups to minimize decay and to retain knowledge, knowledge acquired through task performance must be captured and embedded in a repository or "retention bin."

Discussions of group or organizational memory converge on several key repositories of collective knowledge (Argote, 1996; Levitt & March, 1988; Starbuck, 1992; Walsh & Ungson, 1991). Researchers generally agree that collective knowledge resides in individual employees, in the structure of the group or organization, and in its technology.

Knowledge Embedded in Individuals. We turn now to a discussion of research on the extent to which knowledge is embedded in individuals. Engeström, Brown, Engeström, and Korstinen (1990) provided an example of a medical clinic where knowledge was embedded primarily in one individual who was an administrator. Few documents existed. Other employees with significant knowledge of the clinic had retired or transferred. The administrator hoarded knowledge and did not pass it on to his subordinates. Engeström et al. (1990) argued that when the administrator retires, knowledge will be lost from the system.

What effect will turnover have on group learning and performance? Studies of the effect of turnover on learning and productivity gains provide insights into the extent to which knowledge is embedded in individuals because if knowledge is embedded primarily in individual group members, their turnover should affect group learning. One study in this vein investigated the effect of turnover of direct production workers in World War II shipyards (Argote et al., 1990). Results indicated that the rate of new hires and the rate of separations did not appear to affect the productivity of the yards. The shipyards were large organizations with formalized and specialized structures (Lane, 1951). Jobs were designed to be low in skill requirements so that inexperienced workers could become proficient quickly. These conditions at the shipyards may have buffered them from the effects of turnover.

Consistent with this suggestion about why turnover may not have mattered in the shipyards, the effect of turnover has also been shown to depend on how groups are structured. Devadas and Argote (1995) found that groups that were low in structure were not able to absorb the effects of turnover, whereas groups high in structure were. Factors contributing to the poor performance of groups in the low structure, turnover condition included their continual need to keep reorganizing around the skills of new members, their difficulty accessing knowledge, and the loss of critical knowledge they experienced when members left the group. Similarly, in a simulation study, Carley (1992) found that whereas teams learned better and faster than hierarchies, hierarchies were less affected by turnover than teams.

The effect of turnover on group learning has also been found to depend on the complexity of the task (Argote, Insko, Yovetich, & Romero, 1995). Differences in the performance of no turnover versus turnover groups were found to increase over time, and the increase in the performance gap was greater for the simple than for the complex task. The lesser impact of turnover on the complex task appeared to be due to the greater frequency of innovations that occurred on the complex task. The departure of experienced group members appeared less costly on the complex task because some of their knowledge was no longer relevant, due to innovations that had occurred.

The effect of turnover has also been shown to depend on the performance of departing members (Argote, Epple, Rao, & Murphy, 1995). In particular, the loss of high performing members was shown to hurt a truck plant's productivity, whereas the loss of poor performers did not have a significant effect on the plant's productivity.

These studies of the effect of turnover have primarily focused on turnover of workers engaged in direct production activities. Virany, Tushman, and Romanelli (1992) examined turnover of executives as a mechanism for organizational learning and adaptation in a study of minicomputer firms. The researchers suggested that executive change facilitates learning and adaptation by changing the knowledge base and communication processes of the executive team. Results indicated that turnover of the chief executive officer and turnover in the executive team were positively associated with organizational performance. Thus, in the turbulent minicomputer industry, executive change may have served as a means for bringing in new knowledge.

Taken together, these studies suggest conditions under which turnover is most likely to affect group learning. Results indicate that turnover affects learning when: (1) Departing members are exceptional performers (e.g., see Argote, Epple, et al., 1995); and (2) When the organizations, or the positions departing members occupy, are low in structure and constraints (e.g., Carley, 1992; Devadas & Argote, 1995; Virany et al., 1992). Whereas turnover of high-performing direct production workers in a manufacturing plant negatively affected the plant's productivity, turnover of executives in the turbulent minicomputer industry had a positive effect on performance. The former effect may have reflected the cost of the loss of individuals who had critical knowledge embedded in them whereas the latter may have reflected the benefit of incorporating individuals with new knowledge into the organizations. Turnover may be harmful on well-understood tasks and helpful on uncertain tasks where innovations can occur.

Knowledge Embedded in Structure and Technology. Knowledge can also be embedded in a group's structure, routines, or standard operating procedures. Nelson and Winter (1982) discussed routines, as repositories of knowledge at the organizational level of analysis (see Cyert & March, 1963; March & Simon, 1958, for earlier discussions). Gersick and Hackman (1990) developed the concept of routines at the group level of analysis.

Empirical evidence indicates that knowledge acquired through task performance can be embedded in supraindividual routines. For example, Cohen and Bacdayan (1994) found that the behavior of dyads displayed indicators of the operation of routines. In particular, performance became more reliable and faster over time. Different dyads evolved different routines that were stable over time (see also Weick & Gilfallan, 1971). Dyads persisted in using their routines, even when more effective approaches existed.

In a related vein, Epple, Argote, and Murphy (1996) took advantage of a naturally occurring experiment to evaluate the extent to which knowledge became embedded in the organization versus in individual workers (see also

Epple, Argote, & Devadas, 1991). A manufacturing plant added a second shift almost 2 years after the first shift had been in operation. Although the second shift was composed of predominantly new employees, knowledge acquired during the period of operating with one shift carried forward quite rapidly to both shifts of the two-shift period. The second shift achieved a level of productivity in 2 weeks that it had taken the first shift many months to achieve. This suggests that knowledge acquired during the period of one-shift operation had been embedded in the organization's structure or technology because both shifts used the same structure and technology, whereas the workers were different on the two shifts.

Several of the studies discussed previously are also relevant for an analysis of knowledge embedded in organizational structures or supraindividual routines. For example, Carley (1992) and Devadas and Argote (1995) found that hierarchies or highly structured groups were less affected by turnover than groups low in structure. A significant component of the knowledge of these groups was embedded in their structure, which mitigated the effect of turnover.

Conclusion

Once knowledge is obtained and used by groups, its implications often lead to change. Changes in a group's composition, plans, norms, and routines often correspond to changes in their understandings about themselves; hence, such changes provide compelling evidence that learning has occurred. The locus of a group's revisions can also indicate how knowledge is being embedded. When knowledge is embedded primarily in people, turnover can have powerful effects through which knowledge is either lost or enhanced. When knowledge is embedded in either the group task or structure, groups are likely to become simultaneously more stable and less flexible. Embedding knowledge in technology or structure facilitates its persistence over time and its transfer to other groups.

EXTERNAL RELATIONS PROCESSES

Finally, a critical aspect of group learning in organizations involves the transfer of knowledge gained at the group level to other groups that might also benefit (Cohen & Leventhal, 1990; Darr, Argote, & Epple, 1995; Miner & Haunschild, 1995). Contrary to expectations, improvements achieved by individual work groups do not always translate into organizational outcomes. For example, a subset of production teams may experience improvements in quality and efficiency, yet the organization may show no corresponding gains in profits or market share (Rousseau, 1991). In this section, we review literature on knowledge transfer and external relations strategies.

There are several conditions that must be met for effective knowledge transfer to occur. Often the most critical lessons and insights are tacit within their group of origin (Nonaka & Takeuchi, 1995). Because tacit knowledge is not easily articulated, it poses particular challenges to transfer. One mechanism for transferring tacit knowledge is to convert it to explicit knowledge through detailed observation and apprenticeships (Nonaka, 1991). Once tacit knowledge is converted to explicit, it can be transferred to other groups through verbal communication media. Another mechanism for transferring tacit knowledge across groups is to move personnel possessing the tacit knowledge to another group. Research has shown that individuals who acquire tacit knowledge about one task are able to transfer their knowledge to similar tasks, even if they remain unable to articulate their knowledge (Berry & Broadbent, 1984, 1987).

Groups must also be motivated to make their insights available to others and others must be motivated to receive the insights (Szulanski, 1994) for effective knowledge transfer to occur. This requires incentives that encourage information exchange with parties outside the group's social and temporal boundaries, including other groups working on similar projects who might be viewed as competitors, and management groups at the supervisory level.

To accomplish these knowledge transfer objectives, groups can adopt a variety of external relations strategies (Ancona, 1990). For example, groups that are primarily interested in exporting information might adopt an "informing" strategy, which involves maintaining an internal focus and simply informing outsiders of the nature of group outcomes. Alternatively, groups might adopt a "parading" strategy if their objective is to maximize visibility and contact vis-à-vis outsiders without actually involving them in their task activities. In contrast, groups that adopt a "probing" strategy actively solicit information from external groups and incorporate the knowledge obtained into their products.

Transferring Knowledge

Many mechanisms exist for transferring knowledge across groups. For example, training can be provided to the members of the "recipient" group or they can be given opportunities through apprenticeships and the like to observe experts at the "donor" site. Communication can be fostered between members of donor and recipient groups. Moving experienced personnel to the recipient group is a powerful mechanism for transferring knowledge (e.g., see Galbraith, 1990). Providing documents, blueprints, technology, and product prototypes to the recipient group can also facilitate knowledge transfer. These mechanisms map onto typologies of where knowledge is embedded in a social system: its people, its technology, or its structure (e.g., see Argote, 1996; Starbuck, 1992). Thus, knowledge can be transferred by moving people, technology, or structure to the recipient group or by "modifying" the people (e.g., through training), technology, and structure of the recipient group.

Evidence on transfer of knowledge across groups is now reviewed. When knowledge acquired in one group affects another (either positively or negatively), transfer of knowledge occurs. Our focus is on knowledge transfer across groups within the same organization or system of organizations. Thus, we do not focus on studies of "spillovers" of knowledge across competitors (e.g., see Irwin & Klenow, 1994). Our focus is also on studies that show performance consequences of knowledge transfer.

Groups that are part of some superordinate relationship such as membership in the same organization or franchise or chain are more likely to exhibit knowledge transfer than those lacking such a superordinate relationship. Darr et al. (1995) analyzed transfer of knowledge in 35 fast food franchises in a geographical area. Some stores were single store franchises, whereas others were part of multistore networks with the same owner. Mechanisms for transfer of knowledge existed. All of the stores produced the same product and were franchised from the same parent company. Materials and equipment were procured from a central agency. Meetings were held regularly for store owners to share information. A consultant from the parent company visited the stores regularly to transfer knowledge. Results indicated that store experience and franchise experience were significant predictors of productivity, whereas the experience of stores in different franchises was not significant. Thus, transfer of knowledge occurred across stores within the same franchise but not across stores in different franchises.

Similarly, Baum and Ingram (1995) found that Manhattan hotels benefitted from their own direct experience and the experience of hotels that were related to them through belonging to the same chain. Hotels benefitted from the experience of hotels in different chains in the industry up to the time of the focal hotel's founding but not thereafter.

Darr (1994) examined whether fast food stores in Great Britain were more likely to learn from stores that were similar to themselves versus those that were dissimilar. Darr (1994) found that stores were more likely to learn from stores following a similar than a dissimilar strategy. Thus, knowledge transferred across stores using a similar strategy.

The repository in which knowledge is embedded also affects the ease of its transfer. Knowledge embedded in structure or technology is more amenable to being transferred than knowledge embedded in individual workers. Zander and Kogut (1995) found that capabilities that could be codified in documents and software and those that could be readily taught to new workers transferred more readily than capabilities not easily codified or taught. Argote and Darr (in press) found that knowledge embedded in routines or technology was more likely to transfer outside the organization of origin than knowledge embedded in individuals. Epple, Argote, and Murphy (1996) found that embedding knowledge in technology or structure was a very effective way to facilitate knowledge transfer at a truck assembly plant.

Groups are most likely to learn from each other at particular times in their development such as early in their life cycle. In a study of knowledge transfer in World War II shipyards, Argote et al. (1990) found that shipyards that began production later were more productive initially than those with earlier start dates. Once shipyards began production, however, they did not benefit further from production experience at other yards. Thus, transfer occurred at the start of production but not thereafter. Similarly, Baum and Ingram (1995) found that knowledge transferred across hotels in different chains up to the time of the focal hotel's founding but not after it had been in operation.

Researchers are beginning to understand transfer of knowledge across groups. Although transfer is difficult to achieve, the benefits of transferring knowledge across groups or organizational units are large. For example, in the study of transfer of knowledge across pizza stores, single-store franchises that could not benefit from knowledge acquired by other stores in the same franchise were less productive and more likely to go out of business that stores in multistore franchises (also see Adler, 1990, and Irwin & Klenow, 1994, for further discussions of the benefits of transfer).

Conclusion

Importing knowledge from other groups is a powerful mechanism for group learning. Groups seem particularly open to benefitting from knowledge acquired by other groups at certain points in their development such as when they begin operation. Groups seem most likely to learn from other groups that are similar to themselves or that are part of some superordinate organizational relationship. Cognitive, motivational, and social factors all affect the ease of transferring knowledge across groups. A theme that emerges from most studies of knowledge transfer is the importance of personnel movement and personal contacts. The former facilitates the transfer of tacit as well as explicit knowledge whereas the latter is a richer communication medium that permits the transfer of more information.

DISCUSSION

Our review of the large literature relevant for understanding group learning in organizations indicates that we know more about the operations and
construction processes than about the reconstruction and the external relations or transfer processes. In part, this might reflect what is easiest to
observe from a social science perspective. The sharing, combining, and creating of knowledge can be accomplished in the context of a single meeting
or psychological experiment. The on-going and dynamic activities that
characterize reconstruction and external relations are more temporally diffuse and are therefore more difficult to capture using experimental social
science methods.

We would like to encourage more research on these latter processes, especially on the knowledge transfer process. We believe that the issue of the
transfer of knowledge is an extremely important practical problem. Whether
or not a group is able to learn from other groups has a major impact on its
productivity and survival prospects. The transfer process is also important
theoretically. Indeed, it arguably assumes aspects of the other processes
because in order to understand how to transfer knowledge, one has to understand aspects of acquiring and retaining it.

Another special challenge facing the study of group learning in organizations is that the topic requires theoretical and methodological shifts across
levels of analysis. In fact the tensions between individual versus group, and
between group versus organizational level goals and understandings are
necessary for learning in organizations to occur. As noted by Damon (1991):

> Any paradigm that assumes a one-way, deterministic relation between col-
> lective and individual knowledge construction is overly simplistic. Individu-
> als often need to separate themselves from groups in order to seek truth,
> and groups often learn from individuals who have separated themselves in
> just this way. (p. 392)

The same argument holds for the groups embedded in organizations.

It is also important to note that studies of these different sets of processes are misleading in their implication that the aspects of group learning
captured in research occur in isolation from one another. Most groups in
organizations need to manage their constructon, operations, reconstruction, and external relations activities simultaneously, in sequence if not in
tandem.

When one looks across the core processes of group learning, interesting
tensions or trade-offs emerge. Structures that promote acquiring knowledge
may not be good for retaining knowledge. For example, Carley (1992)
found that teams learned better and faster than hierarchies whereas hierar-

chies retained knowledge better, especially in the face of member turnover, than teams. Similarly, structures that promote acquiring knowledge by groups may not be good for transferring knowledge across them (Argote, 1995). For example, Adler and Cole (1993) argued that the autonomous work groups once used by Volvo that emphasized learning at individual or group levels failed to foster learning at the level of the organization. The autonomous work groups did not emphasize standardization and knowledge transfer, and thereby, may have inhibited organizational learning.

Embedded within cycles of these activities is a trade-off between phases of discovery and implementation, which require different group management strategies. Discovery learning in groups requires creativity and capitalizing on minority influence both within and across groups to challenge basic assumptions, question established processes, and disrupt norms and standard operating procedures. When the products of discovery are to be implemented, new insights must be diffused across groups through standardization and coordinated action, which requires building consensus through majority influence, as well as controlling social categorization and conflict between groups.

Research is needed on how these tensions and trade-offs across the group learning processes are managed. Can organizations be designed to simultaneously promote the acquisition and retention and transfer of knowledge? Or are there temporal, environmental, and task conditions that would favor fostering one learning process over the other?

On a more personal note, we are tremendously impressed by the richness and rigor of research on group learning in organizations. Several recent trends in research on group learning seem particularly promising. The first is the increasing use of longitudinal research designs where groups are analyzed over time. The second is the expanding emphasis on understanding group processes. The third is the growing number of studies that examine how changes in membership, technology, or structure affect group learning and performance. Changes in these factors approximate more closely the conditions under which "real" groups learn in organizational contexts. Thus, analyzing how group learning takes place in the face of changing membership, technology, or structure provides a more realistic picture of group learning. Further, studying the effects of these changes on group learning advances theory about the reconstruction process and the effects of embedding knowledge in these different repositories. Finally, the very recent trend of examining how groups learn from other groups is also particularly promising. We hope these trends continue. We think they will greatly enrich our understanding of how groups learn in organizational contexts.

Our primary goal in writing this chapter (and indeed a major goal of the volume) was to integrate the social psychological research on group learning with the organizational research. Because this was an "uncertain" task, we constructed a group of "diverse" members representing each of these two perspectives. We hope that the diverse membership enhanced the quality of the product (cf. Jackson, 1992). We also aimed to promote retention of knowledge by embedding the diverse literature on group learning in the CORE framework. Hopefully, the publicaton of the chapter in the Turner volume will facilitate transfer of knowledge to those interested in group learning in organizations.

ACKNOWLEDGMENTS

We wish to thank Karen DeCamp and Fernando Olivera for their help preparing the manuscript.

REFERENCES

Adler, P. S. (1990). Shared learning. *Management Science, 36*, 939–957.

Adler, P. S., & Cole, R. E. (1993, Spring). Designed for learning: A tale of two auto plants. *Sloan Management Review, 34*, 85–94.

Ancona, D. G. (1990). Outward bound: Strategies for team survival in an organization. *Academy of Management Journal, 33*(2), 334–365.

Argote, L. (1995, August). *Group versus organizational learning*. Paper presented at the Academy of Management meetings, Vancouver, Canada.

Argote, L. (1996). Organizational learning curves: Persistence, transfer and turnover. *International Journal of Technology Management, 11*, 759–769.

Argote, L., Beckman, S. L., & Epple, D. (1990). The persistence and transfer of learning in industrial settings. *Management Science, 36*, 140–154.

Argote, L., & Darr, E. (in press). Repositories of knowledge in franchise organizations: Individual, structural and technological. In G. Dosi, R. Nelson, & S. Winter (Eds.), *Nature and dynamics of organizational capabilities*. Oxford, UK: Oxford University Press.

Argote, L., Devadas, A., & Melone, N. (1990). The base-rate fallacy: Contrasting process and outcomes of group and individual judgment. *Organizational Behavior and Human Decision Processes, 46*, 296–310.

Argote, L., & Epple, D. (1990). Learning curves in manufacturing. *Science, 247*, 920–924.

Argote, L., Epple, D., Rao, R., & Murphy, K. (1995, October). *The acquisition and depreciation of knowledge in manufacturing: Turnover and the learning curve*. Paper presented at INFORMS, New Orleans, LA.

Argote, L., Insko, C. A., Yovetich, N., & Romero, A. A. (1995). Group learning curves: The effects of turnover and task complexity on group performance. *Journal of Applied Social Psychology, 25*, 512–529.

Argote, L., & McGrath, J. E. (1993). Group processes in organizations: Continuity and change. In L. L. Cooper & I. T. Robertson (Eds.), *International review of industrial and organizational psychology* (Vol. 8, pp. 333–389). New York: John Wiley.

Argote, L., Seabright, M. A., & Dyer, L. (1986). Individual versus group use of base-rate and individuating information. *Organizational Behavior and Human Decision Processes, 38*, 65–75.

Argyris, C. (1992). *On organizational learning.* Cambridge, MA: Blackwell Business.

Arrow, H., & McGrath, J. E. (1995). Membership dynamics in groups at work: A theoretical framework. *Research in Organizational Behavior, 17,* 373–411.

Asch, S. (1956). Studies of independence and conformity: I. A minority of one against a unanimous majority. *Psychological Monographs, 70*(9; Whole No. 416), 1–70.

Baron, R. M., & Kenny, D. A. (1986). The moderator–mediator variable distinction in social psychological research: Conceptual, strategic, and statistical considerations. *Journal of Personality and Social Psychology, 51,* 1173–1182.

Baum, J. A. C., & Ingram, P. (1995, October). *Population-level learning in the Manhattan hotel industry, 1898–1980.* Paper presented at INFORMS meetings, New Orleans, LA.

Berry, D. C., & Broadbent, D. E. (1984). On the relationship between task performance and associated verbalizable knowledge. *Quarterly Journal of Experimental Psychology, 36A,* 209–231.

Berry, D. C., & Broadbent, D. E. (1987). The combination of explicit and implicit learning processes in task control. *Psychological Research, 49,* 7–15.

Burt, R. S. (1992). *Structural holes: The social structure of competition.* Cambridge, MA: Harvard University Press.

Carley, K. (1992). Organizational learning and personnel turnover. *Organization Science, 3,* 20–46.

Carver, C., & Scheier, M. (1981). The self-attention-induced feedback loop and social facilitation. *Journal of Experimental Social Psychology, 17,* 545–568.

Clark, N. K., & Stephenson, G. M. (1989). Group remembering. In P. B. Paulus (Ed.), *Psychology of group influence* (2nd ed., pp. 357–391). Hillsdale, NJ: Lawrence Erlbaum Associates.

Cohen, M. D., & Bacdayan, P. (1994). Organizational routines are stored as procedural memory: Evidence from a laboratory study. *Organization Science, 5,* 554–568.

Cohen, W. M., & Levinthal, D. A. (1990). Absorptive capacity: A new perspective on learning and innovation. *Administrative Science Quarterly, 35,* 128–152.

Cummings, A., Schlosser, A., & Arrow, H. (1995). Developing complex group products: Idea combination in computer-mediated and face-to-face groups. *Computer Supported Cooperative Work, 4,* 229–251.

Cvetkovich, G., & Baumgardner, S. R. (1973). Attitude polarization: The relative influence of discussion group structure and reference group norms. *Journal of Personality and Social Psychology, 26,* 159–165.

Cyert, R. M., & March, J. G. (1963). *A behavioral theory of the firm.* Englewood Cliffs, NJ: Prentice-Hall.

Damon, W. (1991). Problems of direction in socially shared cognition. In L. B. Resnick, J. M. Levine, & S. D. Teasley (Eds.), *Perspectives on socially shared cognition* (pp. 384–397). Washington, DC: American Psychological Association.

Darr, E. (1994). *Partner similarity and knowledge transfer in English franchise organizations.* Unpublished doctoral dissertation, Graduate School of Industrial Administration, Carnegie Mellon University, Pittsburgh, PA.

Darr, E., Argote, L., & Epple, D. (1995). The acquisition, transfer and depreciation of knowledge in service organizations: Productivity in franchises. *Management Science, 41,* 1750–1762.

Davis, J. H. (1973). Group decision and social interaction: A theory of social decision schemes. *Psychological Review, 80,* 97–125.

Davis, J. H. (1980). Group decision and procedural justice. In M. Fishbein (Ed.), *Progress in social psychology* (Vol. 1, pp. 157–229). Hillsdale, NJ: Lawrence Erlbaum Associates.

Davis, J. H. (1982). Social interaction as a combinatorial process in group decision. In H. Brandstatter, J. H. Davis, & S. Stocker-Kreichgauer (Eds.), *Group decision making* (pp. 27–58). London: Academic Press.

Davis, J. H., Hornik, J. A., & Hornseth, J. P. (1970). Group decision schemes and strategy preferences on a sequential response task. *Journal of Personality and Social Psychology, 15,* 397–408.

Davis, J. H., Kerr, N. L., Atkin, R. S., Holt, R., & Meek, D. (1975). The decision processes of 6- and 12- person juries assigned unanimous and 2/3 majority rules. *Journal of Personality and Social Psychology, 32,* 1–14.

Davis, J. H., Kerr, N. L., Stasser, G., Meek, D., & Holt, R. (1977). Victim consequences, sentence severity, and decision processes in mock juries. *Organizational Behavior and Human Performance, 18,* 346–365.

Davis, J. H., Kerr, N. L., Sussmann, R., & Rissman, A. K. (1974). Social decision schemes under risk. *Journal of Personality and Social Psychology, 30,* 248–271.

DeSanctis, G., & Poole, M. S. (1994). Capturing the complexity in advanced technology use: Adaptive structuration theory. *Organization Science, 5,* 121–147.

Devadas, R., & Argote, L. (1995, May). *Collective learning and forgetting: The effects of turnover and group structure.* Paper presented at Midwestern Academy of Management Meetings, Chicago, IL.

Doise, W., & Mugny, G. (1984). *The social development of the intellect.* Oxford, England: Pergamon Press.

Eagly, A. H., Wood, W., & Chaiken, S. (1978). Causal inferences about communicators and their effect on opinion change. *Journal of Personality and Social Psychology, 36,* 424–435.

Easterbrook, J. A. (1959). The effect of emotion on cue utilization and the organization of behavior. *Psychological Review, 66,* 183–201.

Engeström, Y., Brown, K., Engeström, R., & Korstinen, K. (1990). Organizational forgetting: An activity–theoretical perspective. In D. Middleton & D. Edwards (Eds.), *Collective remembering* (pp. 139–168). London: Sage.

Epple, D., Argote, L., & Devadas, R. (1991). Organizational learning curves: A method for investigating intra-plant transfer of knowledge acquired through learning by doing. *Organization Science, 2,* 58–70.

Epple, D., Argote, L., & Murphy, K. (1996). An empirical investigation of the micro structure of knowledge acquisition and transfer through learning by doing. *Operations Research, 44,* 77–86.

Faludi, A. (1973). *Planning theory.* New York: Pergamon.

Feldman, D. C. (1989). Socialization, resocialization, and training. In I. L. Goldstein (Ed.), *Training and development in organizations* (pp. 121–182). San Francisco, CA: Jossey-Bass.

Friedmann, J. (1966). The institutional context. In B. M. Gross (Ed.), *Action under planning.* New York: McGraw-Hill.

Gailbraith, C. S. (1990). Transferring core manufacturing technologies in high-technology firms. *California Management Review, 32,* 56–70.

Garton, A. F. (1992). *Social interaction and the development of language and cognition.* Hillsdale, NJ: Lawrence Erlbaum Associates.

Geen, R. G., & Gagne, J. J. (1977). Drive theory of social facilitation: Twelve years of theory and research. *Psychological Bulletin, 84*(6), 1267–1288.

Gersick, C. (1988). Time and transition in work teams: Toward a new model of group development. *Academy of Management Journal, 312*(1), 9–41.

Gersick, C. (1989). Marking time: Predictable transitions in task groups. *Academy of Management Journal, 32*(2), 274–309.

Gersick, C., & Hackman, J. R. (1990). Habitual routines in task-performing groups. *Organizational Behavior and Human Decision Processes, 47,* 65–97.

Gigone, D., & Hastie, R. (1993). The common knowledge effect: Information sharing and group judgment. *Journal of Personality and Social Psychology, 65,* 959–974.

Gladstein, D. L. (1984). Groups in context: A model of task group effectiveness. *Administrative Science Quarterly, 29,* 499–517.

Gladstein, D. L., & Reilly, N. P. (1985). Group decision making under threat: The tycoon game. *Academy of Management Journal, 28,* 613–627.

Goodman, P. S., & Leyden, D. P. (1991). Familiarity and group productivity. *Journal of Applied Psychology, 76,* 578–586.

Granovetter, M. (1973). The strength of weak ties. *American Journal of Sociology, 78,* 1360–1379.

Gruenfeld, D. H. (1995a). Status, ideology and integrative complexity on the U. S. Supreme Court: Rethinking the politics of political decision making. *Journal of Personality and Social Psychology, 68*(1), 5–20.

Gruenfeld, D. H. (1995b). *Divergent thinking, accountability, and integrative complexity: Public versus private reactions to majority and minority status.* Unpublished manuscript, Kellogg Graduate School of Management, Northwestern University, Evanston, IL.

Gruenfeld, D. H., & Hollingshead, A. B. (1993). Sociocognition in work groups: The evolution of group integrative complexity and its relation to task performance. *Small Group Research, 24*(3), 383–405.

Gruenfeld, D. H., Hollingshead, A. B., & Fan, E. T. (1995, May). *Integrative complexity in work groups: The effects of continuity and change.* Presented at the Annual Meeting of the Midwestern Psychological Association, Chicago, IL.

Gruenfeld, D. H., Mannix, E. A., Williams, K. Y., & Neale, M. A. (1996). Group composition and decision making: How member familiarity and information distribution affect process and performance. *Organizational Behavior and Human Decision Processes, 67*(1), 1–15.

Hackman, J. R. (Ed.). (1990). *Groups that work (and those that don't): Creating conditions for effective teamwork.* San Francisco: Jossey-Bass.

Hackman, J. R. (1992). Group influences on individuals in organizations. In M. D. Dunnette & L. M. Hough (Eds.), *Handbook of industrial and organizational psychology* (Vol. 3, pp. 199–267). Chicago: Rand McNally.

Hackman, J. R., Brousseau, K. R., & Weiss, J. A. (1976). The interaction of task design and group performance strategies in determining group effectiveness. *Organizational Behavior and Human Performance, 16,* 350–365.

Hackman, J. R., & Morris, C. G. (1975). Group tasks, group interaction process, and group performance effectiveness: A review and proposed integration. In L. Berkowitz (Ed,), *Advances in experimental social psychology* (Vol. 8, pp. 45–99). New York: Academic Press.

Hartwick, J., Sheppard, B. L., & Davis, J. H. (1982). Group remembering: Research and implications. In R. A. Guzzo (Ed.), *Improving group decision making in organizations* (pp. 41–72). London: Academic Press.

Hill, G. W. (1982). Group versus individual performance: Are N + 1 heads better than one? *Psychological Bulletin, 91,* 517–539.

Hinsz, V. (1990). Cognitive and consensus processes in group recognition memory performance. *Journal of Personality and Social Psychology, 59,* 705–718.

Hollenbeck, J. R., Ilgen, D. R., Sego, D. J., Hedlund, J., Major, D. A., & Philips, J. (1995). Multilevel theory of team decision making: Decision performance in teams incorporating distributed expertise. *Journal of Applied Psychology, 80,* 292–316.

Huber, G. P. (1991). Organizational learning: The contributing processes and the literatures. *Organization Science, 2,* 88–115.

Huber, V. L. (1985). Effects of task difficulty, goal setting and strategy on performance of a heuristic task. *Journal of Applied Psychology, 70,* 492–504.

Irwin, D. A., & Klenow, P. J. (1994). Learning-by-doing spillovers in the semiconductor industry. *Journal of Political Economy, 102,* 1200–1227.

Jackson, S. (1992). Team composition in organizations. In S. Worchel, W. Wood, & J. Simpson (Eds.), *Group process and productivity* (pp. 138–176). London: Sage.

Janis, I. L. (1972). *Victim of groupthink.* Boston: Houghton Mifflin.

Kerr, N. L., Atkin, R. S., Stasser, G., Meek, D., Holt, R., & Davis, J. H. (1976). Guilt beyond a reasonable doubt: Effects of concept identification and assigned decision rule on the judgments of mock jurors. *Journal of Personality and Social Psychology, 34,* 282–294.

Kerr, N. L., Davis, J. H., Meek, D., & Rissman, A. K. (1975). Group position as a function of member attitudes: Choice shift effects from the perspective of social decision scheme theory. *Journal of Personality and Social Psychology, 31,* 574–593.

Kerr, N. L., MacCoun, R. J., & Kramer, G. P. (1996). Bias in judgment: Comparing individuals and groups. *Psychological Review, 103,* 687–719.

Kiesler, S., & Sproull, S. (1992). Group decision making and communication technology. *Organizational Behavior and Human Decision Processes, 52,* 96–123.

Kim, P. H. (1997). When what you know can hurt you: A study of experiential affects on group discussion and performance. *Organizational Behavior and Human Decision Processes, 69,* 165–177.

Klimoski, R., & Mohammed, S. (1994). Team mental model: Construct or metaphor? *Journal of Management, 20,* 403–437.

Kruglanski, A. W. (1989). Motivations for judging and knowing: Implications for causal attributions. In E. T. Higgins & R. M. Sorrentino (Eds.), *Handbook of motivation and cognition: Foundations of social behavior* (Vol. 2, pp. 333–368). New York: Guilford.

Kruglanski, A. W., & Mackie, D. M. (1990). Majority and minority influence: A judgmental process analysis. In W. Stroebe & M. Hewstone (Eds.), *European review of social psychology* (Vol. 1, pp. 229–261). London: Wiley.

Lambert, R. (1969). Extremisation du comportement de prose de risque en groupe et modele majoritaire [The extremization of risk-taking behavior in groups and majority models]. *Psychologie Française, 14,* 113–125.

Lambert, R. (1976). Situations of uncertainty: Social influence and decision processes. In H. Brandstatter, J. H. Davis, & H. Schuler (Eds.), *Dynamics of group decisions* (pp. 53–66). Beverly Hills, CA: Sage.

Lane, F. C. (1951). *Ships for victory: A history of shipbuilding under the U.S. Maritime Commission in World War II.* Baltimore, MD: Johns Hopkins Press.

Larson, J. R., Jr., & Christensen, C. (1993). Groups as problem-solving units: Toward a new meaning of social cognition. *The British Psychological Society, 32,* 5–30.

Larson, J. R., Foster-Fishman, P. G., & Keys, C. B. (1994). The discussion of shared and unshared information in decision making groups. *Journal of Personality and Social Psychology, 67,* 446–461.

Laughlin, P. R. (1988). Collective induction: Group performance, social combination processes, and mutual majority and minority influence. *Journal of Personality and Social Psychology, 54,* 254–267.

Laughlin, P. R., & Adamopoulos, J. (1980). Social combination processes and individual learning for six-person cooperative groups on an intellective task. *Journal of Personality and Social Psychology, 38,* 941–947.

Laughlin, P. R., & Adamopoulos, J. (1982). Social decision schemes on intellective tasks. In H. Brandstatter, J. H. Davis, & S. Stocker-Kreichgauer (Eds.), *Group decision making* (pp. 81–102). London: Academic Press.

Laughlin, P. R., & Ellis, A. L. (1986). Demonstrability and social combination processes on mathematical intellective tasks. *Journal of Experimental Social Psychology, 22,* 177–189.

Laughlin, P. R., & Futoran, G. C. (1985). Collective induction: Social combination and sequential transition. *Journal of Personality and Social Psychology, 48,* 608–613.

Laughlin, P. R., & Hollingshead, A. B. (1995). A theory of collective induction. *Organizational Behavior and Human Decision Processes, 61,* 94–107.

Laughlin, P. R., Kerr, N. L., Davis, J. H., Halff, H. M., & Marciniak, K. A. (1975). Group size, member ability, and social decision schemes on an intellective task. *Journal of Personality and Social Psychology, 31,* 522–535.

Laughlin, P. R., Kerr, N. L., Munch, M. M., & Haggarty, C. A. (1976). Social decision schemes of the same four-person groups on two different intellective tasks. *Journal of Personality and Social Psychology, 33*, 80–88.

Laughlin, P. R., & McGlynn, R. P. (1986). Collective induction: Mutual group and individual influence by exchange of hypotheses and evidence. *Journal of Experimental Social Psychology, 22*, 567–589.

Laughlin, P. R., & Shippy, T. A. (1983). Collective induction. *Journal of Personality and Social Psychology, 45*, 94–100.

Laughlin, P. R., VanderStoep, S. W., & Hollingshead, A. B. (1991). Collective versus individual induction: Recognition of truth, rejection of error, and collective information processing. *Journal of Personality and Social Psychology, 61*(1), 50–67.

LeBreton, P. P., & Henning, D. (1961). *Planning theory.* Englewood Cliffs, NJ: Prentice-Hall.

Levine, J. M. (1989). Reactions to opinion deviance in small groups. In P. B. Paulus (Ed.), *Psychology of group influence* (2nd ed., pp. 187–231). Hillsdale, NJ: Lawrence Erlbaum Associates.

Levine, J. M., & Moreland, R. L. (1985). Innovation and socialization in small groups. In S. Moscovici, D. Mugny, & E. van Avermaet (Eds.), *Perspectives on minority influence* (pp. 143–169). Cambridge, England: Cambridge University Press.

Levine, J. M., & Moreland, R. L. (1991). Culture and socialization in work groups. In L. B. Resnick, J. M. Levine, & S. D. Teasley (Eds.), *Perspectives on socially shared cognition* (pp. 257–279). Washington, DC: American Psychological Association.

Levine, J. M., & Ranelli, C. J. (1978). Majority reaction to shifting and stable attitudinal deviates. *European Journal of Social Psychology, 8*, 55–70.

Levine, J. M., & Resnick, L. B. (1993). Social foundations of cognition. *Annual Review of Psychology, 44*, 585–612.

Levine, J. M., & Russo, E. M. (1987). Majority and minority influence. In C. Hendrick (Ed.), *Review of personality and social psychology* (pp. 13–54). Beverly Hills, CA: Sage.

Levine, J. M., Saxe, L., & Harris, H. J. (1976). Reaction to opinion deviance: Impact of deviate's direction and distance of movement. *Sociometry, 39*, 97–107.

Levitt, B., & March, J. G. (1988). Organizational learning. *Annual Review of Sociology, 14*, 319–340.

Liang, D. W., Moreland, R., & Argote, L. (1995). Group versus individual training and group performance: The mediating role of transactive memory. *Personality and Social Psychology Bulletin, 21*, 384–393.

Maass, A., & Clark, R. D., III. (1983). Internalization versus compliance: Differential processes underlying minority influence and conformity. *European Journal of Social Psychology, 13*, 197–215.

Maass, A., & Clarke, R. D., III. (1984). Hidden impact of minorities: Fifteen years of minority influence research. *Psychological Bulletin, 95*, 428–450.

March, J. G., & Simon, H. A. (1958). *Organizations.* New York: Wiley.

McGrath, J. E. (1984). *Groups: Interaction and performance.* Englewood Cliffs, NJ: Prentice-Hall.

McGrath, J. E. (1991). Time, interaction and performance (TIP): A theory of small groups. *Small Group Research, 22*, 147–174.

McGrath, J. E., Arrow, H., Gruenfeld, D. H., Hollingshead, A. B., & O'Connor, K. M. (1993). Groups, tasks and technology: The effects of experience and change. *Small Group Research, 24*(3), 405–420.

McGrath, J. E., & Gruenfeld, D. H. (1993). Toward a dynamic and systematic theory of groups: An integration of six temporally enriched perspectives. In M. M. Chemers & R. Ayman (Eds.), *The future of leadership research: Promise and perspective* (pp. 217–244). Orlando, FL: Academic Press.

McGrath, J. E., & Hollingshead, A. B. (1994). *Groups interacting with technology.* Thousand Oaks, CA: Sage.

Meyerson, D., & Scully, M. (1995). Tempered radicalism and the politics of ambivalence and change. *Organization Science, 6*, 585–600.

Miner, A., & Haunschild, P. (1995). Population level learning. *Research in Organizational Behavior, 17*, 115–166.

Mohrman, S. A., Cohen, S. G., & Mohrman, A. M., Jr. (1995). *Designing team-based organizations: New forms of knowledge work*. San Francisco: Jossey-Bass.

Moreland, R., Argote, L., & Krishnan, R. (1996). Socially shared cognition at work: Transactive memory and group performance. In J. L. Nye & A. M. Brower (Eds.), *What's social about social cognition? Research on socially shared cognition in small groups* (pp. 57–84). Newbury Park, CA: Sage

Moreland, R. L., & Levine, J. M. (1996). The composition of small groups. In E. J. Lawler, B. Markovsky, C. Ridgeway, & H. Walker (Eds.), *Advances in group processes* (Vol. 9, pp. 237–280). Greenwich, CT: JAI.

Morris, W. N., & Miller, R. S. (1975). Impressions of dissenters and conformers: An attributional analysis. *Sociometry, 38*, 327–339.

Moscovici, S. (1976). *Social influence and social change*. London: Academic Press.

Moscovici, S. (1980). Toward a theory of conversion behavior. In L. Berkowitz (Ed.), *Advances in experimental social psychology* (Vol. 13, pp. 209–239). New York: Academic Press.

Moscovici, S. (1985). Social influence and conformity. In G. Lindzey & E. Aronson (Eds.), *The handbook of social psychology* (3rd ed., Vol. 2, pp. 347–412). New York: Random House.

Moscovici, S., & Lage, E. (1978). Studies in social influence IV: Minority influence in a context of original judgments. *European Journal of Social Psychology, 6*, 365–380.

Moscovici, S., Lage, E., & Naffrechoux, M. (1969). Influence of a consistent minority on the responses of a majority in a color perception task. *Sociometry, 32*, 365–379.

Moscovici, S., & Personnaz, B. (1980). Studies in social influence V: Minority influence and conversion behavior in a perceptual task. *Journal of Experimental Social Psychology, 16*, 270–282.

Mugny, G. (1982). *The power of minorities*. New York: Academic Press.

Mugny, G., & Papastamou, S. (1976). Pour une nouvelle approache de l'influence minoritaire: Les determinants psychosociaux des stratégies d'influence minoritaires [Towards a new approach of minority influence: Psychosocial determinants of the strategies of minority influence]. *Bulletin Psychologie, 30*, 573–579.

Murray, F. B. (1983). Learning and development through social interaction and conflict: A challenge to social learning theory. In L. Liben (Ed.), *Piaget and the foundation of knowledge* (pp. 231–247). Hillsdale, NJ: Lawrence Erlbaum Associates.

Nagao, D. H., Tindale, R. S., Hinsz, V. B., & Davis, J. H. (1985). Individual and group biases in information processing. In R. S. Tindale & D. H. Nagao (Co-chairs), *Cognitive factors in small group processes*. Symposium conducted at the American Psychological Association Annual Convention, Los Angeles, CA.

Nelson, R. R., & Winter, S. G. (1982). *An evolutionary theory of economic change*. Boston: Belkman Press.

Nemeth, C. J. (1986). Differential contributions of majority and minority influence. *Psychological Review, 93*, 23–32.

Nemeth, C. J. (1992). Minority dissent as a stimulant to group performance. In S. Worchel, W. Wood, & J. A. Simpson (Eds.), *Group process and productivity* (pp. 95–111). Newbury Park, CA: Sage.

Nemeth, C. J., & Kwan, J. L. (1987). Minority influence, divergent thinking and detection of correct solutions. *Journal of Applied Social Psychology, 17*, 786–797.

Nemeth, C. J., & Wachtler, J. (1983). Creative problem solving as a result of majority and minority influence. *European Journal of Social Psychology, 13*, 45–55.

Nonaka, I. (1991, November–December). The knowledge-creating company. *Harvard Business Review*, pp. 96–104.

Nonaka, I., & Takeuchi, H. (1995). *The knowledge-creating company.* New York: Oxford University Press.

Northcraft, G. B., & Neale, M. A. (1993). Negotiating successful research collaboration. In J. K. Murnighan (Ed.), *Social psychology in organizations: Advances in theory and research* (pp. 204–224). Englewood Cliffs, NJ: Prentice-Hall.

Ocasio, W. (1995). The enactment of economic adversity: A reconciliation of theories of failure-induced change and threat-rigidity. *Research in Organizational Behavior, 17,* 287–331.

Orlikowski, W. J. (1992). The duality of technology: Rethinking the concept of technology in organizations. *Organization Science, 3,* 398–427.

Penrod, S., & Hastie, R. (1979). Models of jury decision making: A critical overview. *Psychological Bulletin, 86,* 462–492.

Penrod, S., & Hastie, R. (1980). A computer simulation of jury decision making. *Psychological Review, 87,* 133–159.

Perez, J., & Mugny, G. (1986). Induction experimentale d'une influence minoritaire indirecte [Experimental implication of indirect minority influence]. *Cahiers de Psychologie Sociale, 32,* 15–24.

Perret-Clermont, A., Perret, J., & Bell, N. (1991). The social construction of meaning and cognitive activity in elementary school children. In L. B. Resnick, J. M. Levine, & S. D. Teasley (Eds.), *Perspectives on socially shared cognition* (pp. 41–62). Washington, DC: American Psychological Association.

Peterson, R. S., & Nemeth, C. J. (1996). Focus versus flexibility: Majority and minority influence can both improve performance. *Personality and Social Psychology Bulletin, 22*(1), 14–23.

Piaget, J. (1965). *The moral judgment of the child.* New York: Free Press. (Original work published in 1932)

Poole, M. S., & Roth, J. (1989a). Decision development in small groups IV: A typology of decision paths. *Human Communications Research, 15,* 323–356.

Poole, M. S., & Roth, J. (1989b). Decision development in small groups V: A test of a contingency model. *Human Communications Research, 15,* 549–589.

Rogoff, B. (1986). Adult assistance of children's learning. In T. E. Raphael (Ed.), *The contexts of school-based literacy* (pp. 86–110). New York: Random House.

Rousseau, D. M. (1991). Teamwork inside and out. *Business Week ADVANCE Executive Brief, 3,* pp. 1–23.

Rulke, D. L. (1996, August). *Cognitive integration or social integration: A simulated investigation of member selection strategy and cross-functional management team performance.* Paper presented at the meeting of the Academy of Management, Cincinnati.

Sanna, L. J., & Shotland, R. L. (1990). Valence of anticipated evaluation and social facilitation. *Journal of Experimental Social Psychology, 26,* 82–92.

Senge, P. M. (1990). *The fifth discipline: The art and practice of the learning organization.* New York: Currency Doubleday.

Shah, P. P., & Jehn, K. A. (1993). Do friends perform better than acquaintances: The interaction of friendship, conflict, and task. *Group Decision and Negotiation, 2*(2), 149–166.

Smith, C. M., Tindale, R. S., & Dugoni, B. L. (1996). Minority and majority influence on freely interacting groups: Qualitative versus quantitative differences. *British Journal of Social Psychology, 35*(1), 137–149.

Starbuck, W. H. (1992). Learning by knowledge-intensive firms. *Journal of Management Studies, 29,* 713–740.

Stasser, G. (1988). Computer simulation as a research tool: The DISCUSS model of group decision making. *Journal of Experimental Social Psychology, 24,* 393–422.

Stasser, G., & Stewart, D. (1992). The discovery of hidden profiles by decision making groups: Solving a problem versus making a judgment. *Journal of Personality and Social Psychology, 63,* 426–434.

Stasser, G., Stewart, D., & Wittenbaum, G. M. (1995). Expert roles and information exchange during discussion: The importance of knowing who knows what. *Journal of Experimental Social Psychology, 31*, 244–265.

Stasser, G., Taylor, L. A., & Hanna, C. (1989). Information sampling in structured and unstructured discussion of three and six person groups. *Journal of Personality and Social Psychology, 57*, 67–78.

Stasser, G., & Titus, W. (1985). Pooling of unshared information in group decision making: Biased information sampling during discussion. *Journal of Personality and Social Psychology, 48*, 1467–1478.

Stasser, G., & Titus, W. (1987). Effects of information load and percentage of shared information on the dissemination of unshared information during group discussion. *Journal of Personality and Social Psychology, 53*, 81–93.

Staw, B. M., & Boettger, R. D. (1990). Task revision: A neglected form of work performance. *Academy of Management Journal, 33*, 534–559.

Staw, B. M., Sandelands, L. E., & Dutton, J. E. (1981). Threat-rigidity effects in organizational behavior: A multilevel analysis. *Administrative Science Quarterly, 26*, 501–524.

Stewart, D. D., & Stasser, G. (1995). Expert role assignment and information sampling during collective recall and decision making. *Journal of Personality and Social Psychology, 69*, 619–628.

Szulanski, G. (1996). Exploring internal stickiness: Impediments to the transfer of best practice within the firm. *Strategic Management Journal, 17*, 27–43.

Tanford, S., & Penrod, S. (1984). Social influence model: A formal integration of research on majority and minority influence processes. *Psychological Bulletin, 95*, 189–225.

Tetlock, P. E. (1981). Pre- to post-election shifts presidential rhetoric: Impression management or cognitive adjustment? *Journal of Personality and Social Psychology, 41*, 207–212.

Tetlock, P. E. (1983). Accountability and complexity of thought. *Journal of Personality and Social Psychology, 45*, 74–83.

Tetlock, P. E. (1986). A value pluralism model of ideological reasoning. *Journal of Personality and Social Psychology, 50*, 819–827.

Tetlock, P. E., Skitka, L., & Boettger, R. (1989). Social and cognitive strategies of coping with accountability: Conformity, complexity, and bolstering. *Journal of Personality and Social Psychology, 57*, 632–641.

Tindale, R. S. (1993). Decision errors made by individuals and groups. In N. J. Castellan (Ed.), *Individual and group decision making* (pp. 109–124). Hillsdale NJ: Lawrence Erlbaum Associates.

Tindale, R. S., Davis, J. H., Vollrath, D. A., Nagao, D. H., & Hinsz, V. B. (1990). Asymmetrical social influence in freely interacting groups: A test of three models. *Journal of Personality and Social Psychology, 58*, 438–449.

Turner, M. E. (1988). *Threat: Assessments and consequences for work group performance.* Unpublished doctoral dissertation, Carnegie Mellon University, Pittsburgh, PA.

Turner, M. E., Pratkanis, A. R., Probasco, P., & Leve, C. (1992). Threat, cohesion, and group effectiveness: Testing a social identity maintenance perspective on groupthink. *Journal of Personality and Social Psychology, 63*, 781–796.

Vinokur, A., & Burnstein, E. (1978). The effects of partially shared persuasive arguments on group-induced shifts: A group-problem-solving approach. *Journal of Personality and Social Psychology, 29*, 305–325.

Virany, B., Tushman, M. L., & Romanelli, E. (1992). Executive succession and organization outcomes in turbulent environments: An organizational learning approach. *Organization Science, 3*, 72–91.

Walsh, J. P., & Ungson, G. R. (1991). Organizational memory. *Academy of Management Review, 16*, 57–90.

Wegner, D. M. (1986). Transactive memory: A contemporary analysis of the group mind. In B. Mullen & G. R. Goethals (Ed.), *Theories of group behavior* (pp. 185–205). New York: Springer-Verlag.

Weick, K. E., & Gilfallan, D. P. (1971). Fate of arbitrary traditions in a laboratory microculture. *Journal of Personality and Social Psychology, 17,* 179–191.

Weingart, L. R. (1992). Impact of group goals, task component complexity, effort, and planning on group performance. *Journal of Applied Psychology, 77,* 682–693.

Weingart, L. R., & Weldon, E. (1991). Processes that mediate the relationship between a group goal and group member performance. *Human Performance, 4,* 33–54.

Weldon, E., Jehn, K. M., & Pradhan, P. (1991). Processes that mediate the relationship between a group goal and improved group performance. *Journal of Personality and Social Psychology, 61,* 555–569.

Weldon, E., & Weingart, L. R. (1993). Group goals and group performance. *British Journal of Social Psychology, 32,* 307–334.

Wittenbaum, G. M., & Stasser, G. (1996). Management of information in small groups. In J. L. Nye & A. M. Brower (Eds.), *What's social about social cognition? Research on socially shared cognition in small groups* (pp. 3–28). Thousand Oaks, CA: Sage.

Zajonc, R. B. (1965). Social facilitation. *Science, 149,* 269–274.

Zajonc, R. B., Wolosin, R. J., Wolosin, M. A., & Sherman, S. J. (1968). Individual and group risk taking in a two-choice situation. *Journal of Experimental Social Psychology, 4,* 89–106.

Zaleska, M. (1976). Majority influence on group choices among bets. *Journal of Personality and Social Psychology, 33,* 8–17.

Zaleska, M. (1978). Some experimental results: Majority influence on group decisions. In H. Brandstatter, J. H. Davis, & H. Schuler (Eds.), *Dynamics of group decisions* (pp. 53–66). Beverly Hills, CA: Sage.

Zander, U., & Kogut, B. (1995). Knowledge and the speed of the transfer and imitation of organizational capabilities: An empirical test. *Organization Science, 6,* 76–92.

Part V

LIABILITIES FOR GROUPS

Racial Bias in Organizations: The Role of Group Processes in Its Causes and Cures

John F. Dovidio
Colgate University

Samuel L. Gaertner
University of Delaware

Betty A. Bachman
Siena College

The Civil Rights Legislation of the 1960s left a profound legacy on race relations in the United States. Before this legislation, racial discrimination that restricted the economic and educational opportunities of Blacks was not only customary in parts of the country but also legally permissible. Since the 1960s, social and economic indicators and the perceptions of both Whites and Blacks reflect significant improvements in the well-being of Blacks (Dovidio & Gaertner, 1986). In addition, the expressed racial attitudes of Whites have become consistently more positive, tolerant, and accepting. Negative stereotyping of Blacks has declined (Davis & Smith, 1996; Devine & Elliot, 1995; Dovidio & Gaertner, 1986; Karlins, Coffman, & Walters, 1969), and Whites' acceptance of Blacks across a range of formal (e.g., work) and informal (e.g., social) settings is at an unprecedented high (Dovidio, Brigham, Johnson, & Gaertner, 1996; Schuman, Steeh, & Bobo, 1985). By 1972, 97% reported that they supported equal employment opportunities for Blacks. White America is also becoming more accepting of Black leaders. In 1958, the majority of Whites reported that they would not be willing to vote for a well-qualified Black presidential candidate; in 1994, over 90% said that they would (Davis & Smith, 1996). Thus, over the past three decades, social norms and mores have also changed dramatically.

Nevertheless, despite these profound social changes, racial disparities persist. America remains "two nations" (Hacker, 1995), with continuing and sometimes increasing gaps between Blacks and Whites in social, economic, and personal well-being. Symptoms of racial tension, which erupted in the

1960s, are reappearing. As the 1990s began, riots in Miami, Tampa, New Jersey, Washington, DC, and Los Angeles, and more recently in St. Petersburg, reflected large-scale racial violence. In the first 6 months of 1996, there were 27 suspicious fires across the South, presumed to be racially motivated arson (Morganthau, Carroll, Klaidman, Miller, & Brant, 1996). The majority of Blacks in America today have a profound distrust for the police and legal system, and about a third are overtly distrustful of Whites in general (Anderson, 1996). Middle-class Blacks are very worried about the future for Blacks and for the nation (Hochschild, 1995).

This chapter examines one factor that contributes to racial bias in the workplace. We propose that, whereas the Civil Rights Legislation has been substantially successful at addressing "old-fashioned," overt forms of racism, a contemporary form of racism—aversive racism—has evolved that is more subtle but that may be as insidious as the traditional form. We consider the nature of contemporary racial attitudes among Whites, exploring evidence of subtle bias. Then we illustrate how understanding the dynamics of subtle bias, and particularly the group processes involved, can help to guide the development of organizational, interpersonal, and intergroup strategies to eliminate this bias.

Aversive racism involves forms of discrimination that are more subtle than old-fashioned overt expressions. This discrimination is often unintentional and unconscious, and the mechanisms involved often may become divorced from personal decision making, residing in policies that reflect institutional racism. The impact on Blacks (as well as other people of color) is profound, however. Like the old-fashioned form, aversive racism contributes to the restriction of personal and economic opportunities of Black Americans and helps to maintain a status quo that has traditionally benefitted White Americans. As a consequence, aversive racism may produce greater bias—although still subtle and rationalizable—against higher status African Americans, who directly or symbolically threaten the traditional role relationship between White and Black Americans. The aversive racism framework thus offers a psychological explanation and a mechanism that underlies the "glass ceiling" phenomenon frequently observed in industry and government.

Across organizations as diverse as the armed forces, federal government, and Fortune 1000 companies, there is evidence of greater racial disparities at higher status levels. In addition, these patterns have persisted over the last 10 years. Within the Navy, for example, Blacks represent 13% of the force, but only 5% of the officers and 1.5% of the admirals. Furthermore, these differences cannot be accounted for by vastly different backgrounds. A recent study by the General Accounting Office found that, over a recent 5-year period, the success rate of Blacks who qualified for promotions was systematically below the rate of Whites across all of the military services. The disparities in promotion rates tended to increase with higher ranks for enlisted personnel and up through ranks equivalent to Major for officers (Hudson, 1995). Patterns of disparities for various segments of federal employees also demonstrate that Blacks are generally less well represented in higher grades (e.g., GS 16–18) than in lower grades. Furthermore, these disparities have remained relatively stable across time. A recent Department of Labor survey of Fortune 1000 companies provided independent evidence of the glass ceiling effect for minorities in industry. Representations of minorities consistently decline with higher occupational status. Fewer than 1% of the top-level executives in Fortune 1000 industrial and Fortune 500 service forms are Black. Independent research reveals that not only are Blacks promoted less frequently than Whites, they have less access to training and development opportunities (Greenhaus, Parasurman, & Wormley, 1990). Black managers are more likely than are White managers to be dissatisfied with their rate of advancement and prospects for advancement (Cox & Nkomo, 1991; Morrison, 1992; Ragins, 1995).

A U.S. Bureau of the Census study (Bennett, 1992) further confirmed substantial income disparities between Black and White men. In 1990, Black men with a high school education earned $5,828 less per year than White men with comparable education ($16,554 vs. $ $22,382). The gap was even larger ($7,940) between college educated Black and White men ($30,766 vs. $38,706). These gaps did not occur between Black and White women. With a high school degree, Black women made only $333 less than their White counterparts, and with a college degree, they made $3,210 more. Still today, Black males must work about 16 months to earn a salary equivalent to what a White male earns in one year (Oliver & Shapiro, 1998). A recent report by the Economic Policy Institute concluded that the wage gap in recent years "interestingly . . . grew faster for those Black males with more education" (McClain, 1995, p. A11). In 1995, although 24.5% of Blacks surveyed felt that their economic opportunities have been increasing, almost twice that many (46.6%) believed that their economic opportunities have been decreasing, and this difference was even greater (21.4% vs. 50.0%) for more highly educated Blacks (*Black Enterprise*, 1995, p. 66).

Thus, across a range of settings, we see consistent patterns of disparities in occupational advancement and income. Disparities between Blacks and Whites, particularly for men, in representation and compensation increase with higher levels of status. We acknowledge that the glass ceiling effect can occur for a wide range of reasons and that the leap from laboratory to organizations is a large one. Nevertheless, we propose that the aversive racism framework can enhance our understanding about how and why these effects occur and how discrimination can persist despite increasingly positive expressions of Whites' racial attitudes.

CONTEMPORARY RACIAL ATTITUDES

Whereas traditional forms of prejudice are direct and overt, contemporary forms are indirect and subtle. Aversive racism (see Dovidio & Gaertner, 1991; Dovidio, Mann, & Gaertner, 1989; Gaertner & Dovidio, 1986; Kovel, 1970) has been identified as a modern form of prejudice that characterizes the racial attitudes of many Whites who endorse egalitarian values, who regard themselves as nonprejudiced, but who discriminate in subtle, rationalizable ways. The work on aversive racism considers primarily Whites' attitudes toward Blacks. Elsewhere we have demonstrated the generalizability of these processes to attitudes toward Latinos (Dovidio, Gaertner, Anastasio, & Sanitioso, 1992) and women (Dovidio & Gaertner, 1983).

Aversive Racism and Ambivalence

According to the aversive racism perspective, many people who consciously and sincerely support egalitarian principles and believe themselves to be nonprejudiced also unconsciously harbor negative feelings and beliefs about Blacks (as well as about other historically disadvantaged groups). Thus, the attitudes of aversive racists are not univalently positive or negative; they are ambivalent. In contrast to traditional research that focused on the *psychopathological* aspects of prejudice, we suggest that biases related to *normal* human functioning may also predispose a person to develop racial prejudice. In particular, racial biases may be based in part on almost unavoidable cognitive (e.g., informational processing biases that result when people are categorized into ingroups and outgroups; see Hamilton & Trolier, 1986), motivational (e.g., personal or group interest), and sociocultural processes (e.g., social learning; see Gaertner & Dovidio, 1986).

Cognitive factors relate to how people process information. Hamilton and Trolier (1986), for example, reviewed how the simple and arbitrary categorization of people into groups produces ingroup favoritism (see also Brewer, 1979). The mere categorization of people into distinct groups is sufficient to arouse intergroup bias. That is, even without actual contact, members of each group generally have more favorable regard for members within their own group than they have for members of other groups. Greater belief similarity to the self is also attributed to ingroup members (Stein, Hardyck, & Smith, 1965), and belief similarity is a powerful determinant of interpersonal attraction (Byrne, 1971). In addition, people are more likely to be helpful and cooperative and to exercise greater personal restraint in their use of limited common resources when they are interacting with ingroup members than with others (Hornstein, 1976; Kramer & Brewer, 1984; Piliavin, Dovidio, Gaertner, & Clark, 1981; Schroeder, Penner, Dovidio, & Piliavin, 1995).

Motivational factors involve the satisfaction of basic needs. At the individual level, for example, needs for self-esteem can promote the derogation of outgroups in order to improve one's subjective well-being (Wills, 1981) and achieve a sense of "positive distinctiveness" for oneself and one's group (Tajfel & Turner, 1979; Turner, 1987). At the societal level, economic competition that threatens to alter the traditionally subordinate status of Blacks relative to Whites fosters discrimination of Whites against Blacks (Wilson, 1980). Practices and policies that threaten the traditional status of Whites relative to Blacks may produce negative reactions even among people who truly believe that they are nonprejudiced.

Social and cultural factors can also contribute to Whites' negative feelings toward Blacks. The sociocultural approach focuses on the transmission of cultural values through normal socialization. Prejudice is a tradition in the United States. From a sociological perspective, the structure of society tends to perpetuate prejudice and discrimination. Specifically, the institutional racism framework proposes that beliefs about relative status and power become embedded in social roles and norms (see Feagin & Feagin, 1978). These beliefs, in turn, help to maintain the social, educational, political, and economic advantages that Whites have over Blacks.

Nevertheless, in a nation founded on the principle that "all men [sic] are created equal," there are strong forces that promote racial equality. Norms of fairness and equality have had great social, political, and moral impact on the history of the United States. The prevalence of these egalitarian norms has been clearly demonstrated in experimental (e.g., Roese & Jamieson, 1993; Sigall & Page, 1971) and survey (e.g., Kluegel & Smith, 1986) research. Whereas the forces that support prejudice often involve fundamental psychological processes, the factors promoting egalitarianism often involve higher order, more complex, and abstract social, moral, and religious principles.

The feelings of aversive racists toward Blacks are characterized by mildly negative feelings, such as fear, disgust, uneasiness, and indifference, that tend to motivate avoidance rather than intentionally destructive or hostile behavior, which instead is more likely to characterize the traditional, old-fashioned form of racism. Relative to the more overt, traditional racists (see Kovel, 1970), aversive racists do not represent the open flame of racial hatred nor do they usually intend to act out of bigoted beliefs or feelings. Instead, bias is expressed in subtle and indirect ways that do not threaten the aversive racist's nonprejudiced self-image.

Manifestations of Aversive Racism

The aversive racism framework helps to identify when discrimination against Blacks and other minority groups will or will not occur. The ambivalence involving both positive and negative feelings that aversive racists experience creates psychological tension that leads to behavioral instability. Thus, unlike the consistent and overt pattern of discrimination that might be expected from old-fashioned racists, aversive racists sometimes discriminate (manifesting their negative feelings) and sometimes do not (reflecting their egalitarian beliefs).

Because aversive racists consciously recognize and endorse egalitarian values—they truly want to be fair and just people—they will not discriminate in situations in which they recognize that discrimination would be obvious to others and themselves. Specifically, we propose that when people are presented with a situation in which the appropriate response is clear, in which right and wrong is clearly defined, aversive racists will not discriminate against Blacks. Wrongdoing would be obvious and therefore would directly threaten their nonprejudiced self-image. However, because aversive racists still possess negative feelings, these negative feelings will eventually be expressed, but they will be expressed in subtle, indirect, and rationalizable ways. Discrimination will occur when appropriate (and thus inappropriate) behavior is not obvious or when an aversive racist can justify or rationalize a negative response on the basis of some factor other than race. Under these circumstances, aversive racists may discriminate but in a way that insulates them from having to confront the possibility that their behavior was racially motivated.

In addition, because aversive racists may be very guarded about behaving in anti-Black ways, their biases may be more likely manifested as pro-White rather than as anti-Black behaviors (i.e., ingroup favoritism rather than outgroup derogation). Brewer's (1979) analysis of the intergroup literature suggests that bias due primarily to social categorization largely reflects ingroup favoritism rather than outgroup rejection. From this perspective, the racial biases of aversive racists rest partially on a failure to expand their circle of inclusion beyond Whites when considering the ingroup/outgroup status of people of color. Nevertheless, the consequences of bias due to pro-ingroup motivations are not necessarily less disadvantageous than bias driven by anti-outgroup intentions. For example, in terms of ultimate consequences, the failure of minority applicants to obtain employment because someone else enjoyed ingroup ties to a personnel director is not that different than if the personnel director refused to hire minority applicants outright (Gaertner et al., 1997). Thus, interpersonal and intergroup forces in prejudice tend to converge for aversive racists.

Consistent with the aversive racism perspective, other theories of contemporary racism and sexism also hypothesize that bias is currently expressed more subtly than in the past. One such approach is symbolic racism theory (Sears, 1988) or modern racism (McConahay, 1986) theory. According to symbolic racism theory, negative feelings toward Blacks that Whites acquire early in life persist into adulthood but are expressed indirectly and symbolically, in terms of opposition to busing or resistance to preferential treatment, rather than directly or overtly, as in support for seg-regation. McConahay (1986) further proposed that because modern racism involves the rejection of traditional racist beliefs and the displacement of anti-Black feelings onto more abstract social and political issues, modern racists, like aversive racists, are relatively unaware of their racist feelings. Swim, Aikin, Hall, and Hunter (1995) extended these notions to contem-porary prejudice toward women. However, whereas symbolic and modern racism are subtle forms of contemporary racism that seem to exist among political conservatives, aversive racism seems to be more strongly associated with liberals. Across a number of paradigms, we have found consistent empirical support for this framework (see Gaertner & Dovidio, 1986).

EMPIRICAL EVIDENCE

In this section of the chapter, we consider implications of our framework for Whites' evaluations of and interactions with Blacks in situations relevant to the workplace. In particular, we explore the subtleties of the manifestations of aversive racism and the motivation of Whites to maintain their relative status with Blacks.

Subtle, Rationalizable Bias

The bias of aversive racists may be subtle, but its effects can be profound. In one of the early tests of our framework (Gaertner & Dovidio, 1977), we tried to take advantage of a naturally occurring event and model it in the labo-ratory. The event was the Kitty Genovese incident, which occurred in New York City in 1964. Kitty Genovese was returning home one evening. As she entered the parking lot of her building, a man drove up, jumped out of his car, and began to stab her. She screamed. Lights went on in her building. The brutal attack continued for 45 minutes, but no one intervened or even called the police. After the attack, the assailant calmly got into his car and drove away. When the police arrived a short time later, they found that there had been 38 witnesses to the incident.

How could it happen that none of these people helped, either directly or indirectly? One explanation that psychologists have developed concerns the bystander's sense of responsibility (Darley & Latané, 1968). When a person is the only witness to an emergency, that bystander bears 100% responsibil-ity for helping and 100% of the guilt and blame for not helping. The appro-priate behavior in this situation, helping, is clearly defined. If, however, a person witnesses an emergency but believes that somebody else is around who can help or will help, then that bystander's personal responsibility is less clearly defined. Under these circumstances, the bystander could rationalize not helping by coming to believe that someone else will intervene. Of course, if everyone believes that someone else will help, no one will intervene. Research on the behavior of Whites with White victims demonstrates consistent support for this "diffusion of responsibility" phenomenon (Darley & Latané, 1968; see also Schroeder et al., 1995). This is presumably what occurred in the Kitty Genovese incident.

To test our hypotheses about subtle discrimination, we modeled a situation in the laboratory after a classic experiment by Darley and Latané (1968). The situation we created was a serious accident, not a stabbing, in which the victim screamed for help. Like Darley and Latané (1968), we led some of our subjects to believe that they would be the only witness to this emergency, whereas we led others to believe that there would be two other people present in this situation who heard the emergency as well. As a second dimension, we varied the race of the victim. In half of the cases, the victim was White; in the other half of the cases, the victim was Black. The participants in the study were White, as were the other two people who were sometimes presumed to be present.

We predicted that when people were the only witness to the emergency, aversive racists would not discriminate against the Black victim. In this situation, appropriate behavior is clearly defined. To not help a Black victim could easily be interpreted, by oneself or others, as racial bias. We predicted, however, that because aversive racists have unconscious negative feelings toward Blacks, they would discriminate when they could justify their behavior on the basis of some factor other than race—such as the belief that someone else would help the victim. Specifically, we expected that Blacks would be helped less than Whites only when White bystanders believed that there were other witnesses to the emergency.

The results of the study supported our predictions. When White bystanders were the only witness to the emergency, they helped very frequently and equivalently for Black and White victims. There was no evidence of old-fashioned racism. In contrast, when White bystanders were given an opportunity to rationalize not helping on the basis of the belief that one of the two other witnesses could intervene, they were less likely to help, particularly when the victim was African American. When participants believed that there were two other bystanders, they helped the Black victim half as often as they helped the White victim (38% vs. 75%). If this situation were real, the White victim would have died 25% of the time; the Black victim would have died 62% of the time. As we hypothesized, the nature of the situation determines whether discrimination does or does not occur.

This subtle bias can also influence less dramatic but still very consequential outcomes in personnel decisions. In one experiment, students were asked to provide input on a prospective faculty member. White subjects listened to a tape recording of a lecture presumably given by a Black or White applicant (manipulated with a photograph) seeking a position at their university. After listening to the lecture, subjects were quizzed on the content. The quizzes were allegedly graded. Actually, subjects were randomly assigned positive feedback (scores of 87% or better), negative feedback (scores of 63% or worse), or no feedback. Before the conclusion of the session, subjects completed teaching evaluation questionnaires.

Overall, students who received negative feedback rated the professor lower for the position than did those who received no feedback or positive feedback. In addition, students who received the negative feedback rated the Black teacher significantly lower than the White teacher. In contrast, students who received no feedback did not discriminate against the Black candidate, whereas subjects who received positive feedback tended to rate the Black teacher more positively than the White teacher. Overall, participants in this study seemed to use an "indirect attitudinal process" whereby information about the other person's race differentially enhanced the salience and potency of nonrace-related elements, in this case the teacher's effectiveness, that would justify a negative response even if a White person were involved.

Because of its subtlety, indirectness, and unintentionality, aversive racism may contribute to the distrust that Blacks have toward Whites. The interracial behavior of aversive racists is more variable than that of old-fashioned racists who express their antipathy openly and directly. Aversive racists sometimes discriminate and sometimes do not—often depending on the strength of norms defining appropriate behavior in a situation. Thus, from the perspective of a Black person, the behavior of an aversive racist may be seen as inconsistent and disingenuous, and thus undeserving of one's trust. Perhaps as a consequence of this distrust, compared to Whites, Blacks are less responsive to feedback—positive and as well as negative—from Whites (see Major & Crocker, 1993). When they are interacting with Whites who are aware of their race, they tend to discount negative feedback as being racially biased and positive feedback as overcompensation in an effort to appear nonprejudiced—both manifestations of aversive racism. As a consequence, in work settings, Blacks may benefit less from feedback than Whites. In addition, aversive racists may be less likely to offer open and honest feedback to Blacks than to Whites. In particular, they may avoid giving negative feedback because they are particularly sensitive to maintaining a nonprejudiced image and avoiding any attributions of racial bias. As a result, aversive racists may provide less valuable feedback to Blacks than to Whites as well. The consequences of aversive racism therefore extend beyond the initial behavior of a White person to a Black person to influence the fundamental nature of interracial interaction for both Blacks and Whites.

Status and Bias

Whereas the expression may be more subtle, the consequence of aversive racism is comparable to that of old-fashioned racism—the perpetuation of a system that provides Whites advantaged status relative to Blacks and other minorities. Relatedly, Jackman and Muha (1984) argued that "dominant social groups routinely develop ideologies that legitimize and justify the status quo, and the well-educated members of these dominant groups are the most sophisticated practitioners of their group's ideology" (p. 751). Thus, we further investigated the relationship between status and bias in the context of an important decision for our subjects (Kline & Dovidio, 1982). We recruited subjects to help us make admissions decisions for their university. Subjects were presented with information about an applicant whose qualifications were systematically varied. Some subjects evaluated a poorly qualified applicant, one who would be perceived as having little chance for admission. Other participants rated a moderately qualified candidate, who had a modest chance of admission. The rest judged a highly qualified applicant with credentials identified by the Admissions Office as highly competitive for acceptance. In addition, the race of the applicant was manipulated by a photograph attached to the file. The central question concerned how this picture would affect subjects' admissions decisions.

Discrimination against the Black applicant occurred, but it did not occur equally in all conditions. Participants rated the poorly qualified Black and White applicants equally low. Perhaps because both White and Black applicants with these credentials were rated as well below the standard for admission, there was little motivation to discriminate. However, participants did show some bias when they evaluated the moderately qualified White applicant slightly higher than the comparable Black candidate. Discrimination against the Black applicant was most apparent, though, when the applicants were highly qualified. This bias seemed to reflect a pro-ingroup bias. Although White subjects evaluated the highly qualified Black applicant very positively, they judged the highly qualified White applicant—with exactly the same credentials—as even better.

This study also included individual items that contributed to the overall evaluative score—scaled according to how directly they related to the information presented in the applicant's transcript. The less directly related the item was to the transcript information, the greater the bias. These results are consistent with the findings in organizational settings that Whites tend to evaluate Blacks less favorably than Whites on subjective dimensions of work performance (Cox & Nkomo, 1986; Kraiger & Ford, 1985) and support Goddard's (1986) observation in applied settings that "vague, ill-defined, subjective criteria lend themselves to all kinds of biased judgments" (p. 34).

Once again, it is important to note that although the expression of aversive racism may be subtle, the consequences are serious. Aversive racism, like more blatant forms, may contribute to the restriction of opportunity for Blacks and other minorities. Affirmative action, for example, is a federal policy originally designed to insure fair treatment to historically disadvantaged minorities. Consistent with the aversive racism framework, resistance to affirmative action is not commonly expressed directly but rather mainly as concerns about individual freedom or about unfair and biased distribution of rewards (often referred to, for example as reverse discrimination). Nevertheless, although common protests by Whites regarding affirmative action seem to express mainly the concern that qualified Whites will be disadvantaged relative to less qualified Blacks, it is possible that the reversal of the traditional role relationship, in which Whites occupy positions of superior status, represents the primary threat to Whites. Thus, the purpose of another study was to investigate the possibility that the generally articulated issue of relative competence is a rationalization in which a nonracial factor, competence, is used by Whites to object to affirmative action programs that increase the likelihood that they will be subordinated to minority groups (Dovidio & Gaertner, 1981).

White male undergraduates were introduced to a Black or White male confederate who was presented as either the subject's supervisor or subordinate. In addition, the confederate was described as being higher or lower than the subject in an intellectual ability that was relevant to the dyad's task. The dependent measure was an incidental helping task, picking up pencils that the confederate "accidentally" knocked to the floor.

Overall, participants helped Black partners more than White partners. The effect of race, however, was moderated by status and ability. Specifically, the results indicated that relative status, rather than relative ability, was the primary determinant of helping behavior toward Blacks. Black supervisors were helped less than Black subordinates, whereas White supervisors were helped somewhat more than White subordinates. Relative ability, in contrast, did not affect prosocial behavior toward Blacks. In general, high- and low-ability Blacks were helped equally as often, whereas high-ability White partners were helped more frequently than were low-ability White partners. Thus, ability, not status, was instrumental in determining helping toward Whites, but status, not ability, was the major factor influencing prosocial behavior toward Blacks. Given that there were no significant effects involving subjects' self-reports of prejudice, it seems that even well-intentioned Whites will respond negatively to a Black supervisor compared to a Black subordinate, regardless of apparent qualifications.

How could people in this experiment rationalize not responding positively to competent Blacks? Subjects' postexperimental evaluations of their partners revealed that their behaviors may have been mediated by perceptions of relative intelligence (competence). Although subjects' ratings indicated that they accepted high-ability White partners as being somewhat more intelligent than themselves, the ratings revealed that subjects described even high-ability Black partners as significantly less intelligent than themselves. Blacks may be regarded as intelligent, but not as intelligent as Whites. It therefore appears that although Whites may accept that a Black person is intelligent on an absolute dimension, White subjects are reluctant to believe that a Black person is higher or equal in intelligence compared to themselves. We subsequently replicated these findings in terms of bias against White women and demonstrated similar dynamics in sexism (Dovidio & Gaertner, 1983).

We have described a considerable amount of research to illustrate how aversive racism operates at the personal level. Organizations are complex, however; there are many different factors involving decisions that occur in organizations. As a consequence, we can never say that because disparities exist, racism is the cause. But, where racism exists, disparities will exist. Thus, we suggest that by understanding some of the fundamental causes of discrimination and disparity, individuals and organizations will be better equipped to combat bias and to understand resistance to programs designed to address the consequences of racism.

COMBATTING SUBTLE BIAS

The subtle processes underlying discrimination can be identified and isolated under the controlled conditions of the laboratory. However, in organizational decision making in which the controlled conditions of an experiment are rarely possible, these processes present a significant challenge to the equitable treatment of members of disadvantaged groups. Krieger (1995), in the *Stanford Law Review*, identified one particular challenge for organizations and the legal system: "Herein lies the practical problem. . . . Validating subjective decisionmaking systems is neither empirically nor economically feasible, especially for jobs where intangible qualities, such as interpersonal skills, creativity, and ability to make sound judgments under conditions of uncertainty are critical" (p. 1232). In addition, to the extent that legal proof of discrimination requires the demonstration that race is the determining factor and that the actions were intentional, the biases of aversive racists are immune to legal prosecution. Aversive racists discriminate only when other, nonrace-related factors can justify their negative treatment of Blacks, and their biases are normally unconscious and unintentional— factors that may make these behaviors immune to successful legal prosecution (Krieger, 1995). Because of its pervasiveness, subtlety, and complexity, traditional techniques for addressing racism are unlikely to be successful in combatting the adverse effects of aversive racism for diversity within organizations, as well.

Challenges to Traditional Approaches to Organizational Change

Traditional approaches to achieve and manage diversity successfully in organizations have taken several tacts. Programs have been developed to change employees' attitudes and enhance intercultural sensitivity. "Bottom-up" actions and initiatives for diversity are typically the preferred vehicle for change in many organizations. Other organizations have worked to establish culture-neutral and color-blind climates to support equal opportunity. We acknowledge that approaches that emphasize changing attitudes, bottom-up or "grass-roots" initiative for change, and color-blind equal opportunity can have some positive impact on race relations and racial diversity in organizations and be effective for combatting the traditional form of racism. However, aversive racism is like a virus that has mutated into a new form that may be particularly resistant to these traditional "cures."

Changing Attitudes. Attempts to change attitudes directly through training and education that, for example, emphasize the immorality of prejudice and illegality of discrimination will not be effective for aversive racists because aversive racists *already* know that prejudice is bad, and they are aware that discrimination is both morally and legally wrong. The problem is that they do not understand that they *themselves* are prejudiced or recognize when they are discriminating. Consequently, plans for managing diversity, like that adopted by the Xerox Corporation (Sessa, 1992), that focus directly on achieving balanced workforce goals and make changing attitudes secondary—and an assumed by-product of daily experience with genuine diversity—will be more successful, in both the short- and long-run, for addressing the consequences of aversive racism than programs focusing primary on improving racial attitudes and enhancing interracial understanding (Alderfer, 1992; Gottfredson, 1992).

Bottom-Up Versus Top-Down Initiatives. The role of volunteerism versus strong leadership represents one of the main dilemmas for developing diversity programs and is a dilemma that is "endemic to all programs of organizational change" (Gottfredson, 1992, p. 292). Volunteer and grass-roots approaches to managing diversity have the virtue of considering a particularly broad range of issues, can generate a sense of ownership, commonly minimize backlash, and represent desired strategies for producing change (DeLuca & McDowell, 1992). Nevertheless, they may not address and undermine directly enough the structural and institutional barriers created by aversive racism. Fine (1995) concluded that "when diversity initia-tives are decentralized, they often fail to transform the organizational cul-ture. . . . Diversity initiatives require time and money, both important and unusually scarce organizational resources that are controlled by senior man-agement" (pp. 133–134). The negative impact of aversive racism for Blacks (as well as for other traditionally disadvantaged groups) is more pro-nounced at higher levels of status within organizations. Thus, it is the peo-ple who occupy the positions of highest status and power within organiza-tions who may be most threatened by further progress of Blacks and other underrepresented groups, yet, ironically who also have the greatest poten-tial to initiate change.

Although bottom-up change is often preferred to large-scale top-down change for enduring results (Kanter, 1983), top-down change may be uniquely suited to combatting aversive racism, for which behaviors need to be brought in line with conscious ideals. Kanter's (1977; see also Kanter, Stein, & Jick, 1992) structuralist perspective, for example, proposed that gender differences in access to structural forms of power cause behavioral differences between the sexes. Ragins (1995) further argued that "the effec-tive management of diversity requires significant and inclusive change in cultural, structural, and behavioral domains" of organizations (p. 94). How-ever, Jackson (1992) found that many senior executives were insulated from the changing world and were not sensitive to the increasing diversity of their workforce. Others were aware of the strategic importance, but offered a range of justifications for not taking action. As Jackson (1992) reported, one interviewee explained, "I don't really want to raise awareness of an issue until I have solutions—I'm looking for solutions first" (p. 6). In contrast, senior officials in other organizations have successfully implemented initia-tives for achieving diversity. Xerox, for example, ties its managers' evalua-tions and compensation directly to how successfully they contribute to achieving balanced workforce goals.

Although organizational culture, structure, and behavior is critically shaped and supported by the power holders of the organization (Ragins, 1995; Schein, 1985), Kanter et al. (1992) observed that there are limitations to such actions in making enduring change and that isolated single efforts are likely to fail because organizations are systems and change "needs to be seen as rooted in myriad features, and ultimately is an expression of the organization's character" (p. 7). Achieving and managing diversity cannot be successful without the support and involvement of senior managers (Loden & Rosener, 1991), but the work of creating a new culture must occur throughout the organization (Fine, 1995). Employees need to understand why the present state of diversity within the organization is unsatisfactory and why enhancing diversity (1) reflects a valid conceptual framework, (2) is tied operationally to the organization's critical goals and strategic plans,

(3) is based on a thorough understanding of the actual situation, and (4) involves and empowers people throughout the organization (Kanter et al., 1992). Thus, although "bold stroke" leadership, which involves a rapid time frame and high leader control, may be necessary initially to attack the barriers created by aversive racism, change needs to be supported and sustained by "long-march" strategies that are longer term, that include initiatives throughout the organization, that involve top-level initiatives but not commands. Long-march approaches are more effective at changing organizational habits and culture (Kanter et al., 1992). Aversive racism is unconscious and habitual, and its forces are embedded in institutional and cultural biases.

Color-Blind Versus Culture Conscious. Another dilemma for organizations is whether to adopt a more traditional color-blind, equal opportunity approach to fostering diversity or to initiate more active interventions that are often associated with affirmative action. Using a color-blind approach avoids the resentment frequently generated by treating people differently, often seen as "preferentially." Gottfredson (1992) observed:

> Many members of nonpreferred groups resent what they perceive to be reverse discrimination and come to believe that members of preferred groups cannot succeed without preferences. On the other hand, members of preferred groups resent the implication that they cannot compete on their merits and do not deserve their successes. (p. 289)

Also, performance standards may generally be seen to decline within the organization. Thus, some companies (e.g., Coopers & Lybrand; see DeLuca & McDowell, 1992) have chosen not to establish special programs for traditionally underrepresented groups, and other companies (e.g., Pepsi; see Fulkerson & Schuler, 1992) have stressed the importance of a culture-neutral climate (e.g., developing shared values and a common vocabulary) within the organization (Gottfredson, 1992).

While acknowledging the potential problems, the aversive racism perspective suggests that a more active approach to supporting diversity is needed. People automatically categorize others on the basis of race; it may not be possible to be color-blind in our society. Furthermore, because people fundamentally categorize others by race and racism still exists—even among well-intentioned people—offering equal opportunity in principle does not insure equal opportunity in practice. Bias occurs, but in subtle and indirect, but persistent, ways.

In addition to combatting potential biases *against* Blacks and other historically underrepresented groups, active policies that explicitly recognize diversity and difference can help to compensate for the traditional advantages *for* White men in terms of informal networks and mentoring that help them succeed within the organization (Ragins, 1995). Providing greater support to one group, even in the absence of discrimination against other groups, can undermine efforts to achieve diversity successfully within an organization. Also, as Ferdman (1995) noted, recognition of cultural differences and different needs and values of groups is essential because group differences are real. For example, job performance appraisals that include the use of self-evaluations may disadvantage persons of Chinese origin, who score lower than most Americans because they tend to understate their contributions consistent with modesty norms in Chinese culture (Farh, Dobbins, & Cheng, 1991). Being color-blind typically involves seeing people as the same—and implicitly as White. It is inherently biased against members of minority groups because it suggests the superiority of being White and undermines the potential benefits of heterogeneity and diversity in achieving the organization's objectives (Ruderman, Hughes-James, & Jackson, 1996).

In summary, approaches for dealing with the traditional form of racism are generally not effective for combatting the consequences of aversive racism. Changing attitudes directly does not work; aversive racists already consciously endorse egalitarian, nonprejudiced views. Relying on well-intentioned volunteer or grassroots initiatives are not likely to be successful by themselves; aversive racists are well intentioned, but their subtle and indirect resistance to Blacks is manifested most strongly at the highest levels of the organization. Aiming to provide equal opportunity may not be successful; aversive racists are not color-blind and as a consequence, bias can continue to occur at the personal level or in terms of policies that subtly disadvantage Blacks, fail to provide Blacks the support that Whites receive, or neglect to capitalize on the benefits of diversity for the organization. Thus, new strategies and techniques, beyond those used for traditional forms of bias, need to be developed and implemented to address this contemporary form of bias.

Alternative Approaches

Strategies for combatting the effects of contemporary forms of racism can capitalize on the forces that contribute to the ambivalence that aversive racists experience. First, aversive racists have good intentions and are consciously motivated to be nonprejudiced. It may thus be possible to harness these good intentions in constructive ways that will produce more positive behavior that can ultimately alter the unconscious feelings that aversive racists harbor. Second, by understanding how normal processes contribute to the negative racial feelings of aversive racists, some of these principles, such as social categorization and ingroup favoritism, can be redirected to create more genuinely accepting and inclusive behaviors and attitudes.

Social Norms and Self-Image. Strategies to eliminate the consequences of aversive racism can capitalize on aversive racists' desire to conform to prevailing norms and to be sincerely committed to being nonprejudiced. However, the traditional approach of emphasizing social norms that proscribe the avoidance of negative behavior toward Blacks and other people of color are not likely to be effective for addressing manifestations of aversive racism. Aversive racists have already internalized these norms and are very guarded about overtly or intentionally discriminating against people of color. Instead, Pettigrew argued that to address the motivations underlying contemporary forms of bias, it is as important to establish positive norms for proactively pursuing equality as it is to strengthen exiting norms against discrimination. These norms may be internalized as an important aspect of organizational citizenship and, at the very least, can produce significant compliance. For instance, across a number of years in the U.S. Army, among candidates identified as qualified, the officer promotion rates of minorities were consistently lower than rates for Whites. Concerned about these disparities, the Army set as an explicit goal for promotion boards in 1991 and 1992 that women and minorities be promoted at a rate no lower than the overall service rate. The promotion boards achieved these objectives in a way that was unprecedented in any previous year. As Sessa (1992) concluded, "To manage diversity effectively, a corporation must value diversity; it must have diversity; and it must change the organization to accommodate diversity and make it an integral part of the organization" (p. 37).

Supportive of the importance of establishing positive norms, corporate research has revealed that the recognition of the value of diversity by top management and higher administration is a key factor for successfully achieving corporate equality (Hitt & Keats, 1984; Marino, 1980). Allstate Insurance, for example, made corporate diversity a high priority in 1976, initiating a voluntary diversity program that exceeded federal affirmative action requirements. From 1975 to 1995, it increased its representation of Black white-collar workers from 9.5% to 14.8%, a rate of increase that is more than double the rate of increase for all other corporations (Annin, 1995). Thus, the development of positive social norms is essential for eliminating the impact of aversive racism. Conversely, allowing the development of norms within groups that encourage, or simply permit, discrimination can allow the bias of aversive racists as well as of old-fashioned racists to flourish.

Because aversive racists are motivated by their good intentions, making them aware of unconscious negative feelings may also have important benefits. Devine and Monteith (1993), for instance, found that people who reported that they were relatively nonprejudiced felt guilty when they became aware of discrepancies between their potential behavior toward minorities (i.e., what they would do) and their personal standards (i.e, what they should do). These emotional reactions, in turn, motivate people subsequently to control their potentially biased responses and behave more favorably in future interracial interactions (Monteith, 1993). Along these same lines, a complementary strategy would be to accentuate positive behaviors toward Blacks associated with the recognition of common ingroup identity, as well as inhibiting negative feelings. Trying to inhibit negative reactions could produce more perfunctory and tokenistic behaviors. The well-intentioned attitudes of aversive racists may thus be harnessed productively to eliminate the prejudicial aspects of their attitudes and behavior.

However, strategies that focus on the interpersonal and intrapersonal aspects of aversive racism, such as making people sensitive to their racial biases, may not be sufficient. Strategies that engineer the structure of group interactions may be necessary to combat effectively the fundamental basis of some of the motivations involved in aversive racism. We have argued in this chapter that aversive racism may be rooted, in part, in fundamental, normal psychological processes. One such process is the categorization of people into ingroups and outgroups, "wes" and "theys." People respond systematically more favorably to others whom they perceive to belong to their group than to different groups. Thus, changing the basis of categorization from race to an alternative dimension can alter who is a "we" and who is a "they," undermining a contributing force to aversive racism.

Social Identity. In recent years, we have attempted to reduce intergroup bias within the framework of the common ingroup identity model by changing group members' cognitive representations from different groups to one group (Gaertner, Dovidio, Anastasio, Bachman, & Rust, 1993; Gaertner, Rust, Dovidio, Bachman, & Anastasio, 1994). The common ingroup identity model is based on the social categorization approach to intergroup behavior (Brewer, 1979; Brown & Turner, 1981; Tajfel & Turner, 1979). The model proposes that intergroup bias and conflict can be reduced by influencing the ways in which group members conceive of group boundaries. Previous research has demonstrated that techniques that decrease the salience of intergroup boundaries, such as individuating members of the outgroup by revealing variability in their opinions (Wilder, 1978) or personalizing interactions on the basis of more intimate, personally relevant information (Brewer & Miller, 1984; Miller, Brewer & Edwards, 1985), reduce bias towards members of other groups.

The common ingroup identity model proposes that *re*categorization, in contrast to the *de*categorization approaches described earlier, may also provide an effective strategy for reducing intergroup bias. Recategorization is not designed to reduce or eliminate categorization but rather to structure a definition of group categorization in ways that reduce intergroup bias and conflict. Specifically, we hypothesize that if members of different groups are induced to conceive of themselves as a single group rather than as two separate groups, attitudes toward former outgroup members will become more positive through processes involving pro-ingroup bias (Brewer, 1979; Mullen, Brown, & Smith, 1992; Tajfel & Turner, 1979). Categorization of a person as an ingroup member rather than as an outgroup member has, for example, been demonstrated to produce greater perceptions of shared beliefs (Brown, 1984; Brown & Abrams, 1986; Hogg & Turner, 1985; Stein et al., 1965; Wilder, 1984); to facilitate empathic arousal, whereby a person's motivational system becomes coordinated to the needs of another (Hornstein, 1976; Piliavin et al., 1981); to enhance memory for positive information about others (Howard & Rothbart, 1980); and to reduce blame for an accident or other negative outcomes (Wang & McKillip, 1978). Thus, by redefining original outgroup members as ingroup members, the cognitive and motivational processes that initially contributed to intergroup bias and conflict may be redirected toward establishing more positive intergroup relations. In application, recategorization from different, potentially competing groups to one group can be achieved by calling attention to existing common superordinate group memberships (e.g., their common organizational or unit identity) or by introducing new factors (e.g., common goals or fate) that are perceived to be shared by members.

The common ingroup identity model is presented schematically in Fig. 14.1. On the left, situational factors and interventions, such as similarity and interdependence, are hypothesized to influence cognitive representations of the memberships (center) as one group (recategorization), as two groups (categorization), or as separate individuals (decategorization). Within the model, intergroup cognition involved in social categorization is the critical mediator of subsequent intergroup attitudes and behavior. Recategorization reduces bias by extending the benefits of ingroup favoritism to former outgroup members. Attitudes and behavior toward these former outgroup members thus become more favorable, approaching those toward ingroup members. Decategorization, in contrast, reduces favoritism toward original ingroup members as they become perceived as separate individuals rather than members of one's own group.

Consistent with this model, we have found evidence that aspects of intergroup contact that are designed to promote an inclusive one-group representation, rather than a representation of two groups, decreases intergroup bias. In one study (Gaertner, Mann, Murrell, & Dovidio, 1989), members of two original subgroups who shared a common group name, were cooperatively interdependent, and were spatially integrated perceived themselves

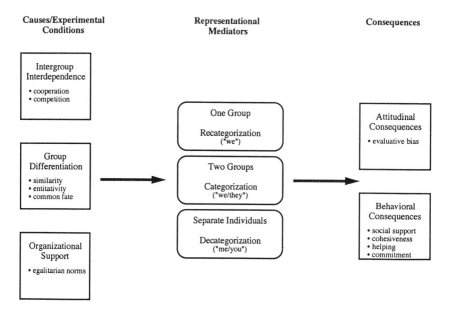

FIG. 14.1. The common ingroup identity model: The hypothesized effects of social and environmental influences on recategorization and on subsequent intergroup attitudes and behaviors.

more like one group, felt less like two groups, and exhibited lower levels of intergroup bias than did members who retained their subgroup names, were competitively interdependent, and were segregated spatially. There were two additional aspects of the findings that were directly supportive of the model. Bias was reduced primarily by more positive evaluations of outgroup members; also, the impact of the manipulations on increasing positive evaluations of outgroup members and decreasing bias was mediated by group representations. Other research has indicated that spatial arrangements that influence perceptions of entitativity (i.e., perceptions of groupness; Gaertner & Dovidio, 1986; see Campbell, 1958) and factors identified by the contact hypothesis, such as cooperation (Gaertner, Mann, Dovidio, Murrell, & Pomare, 1990) as well as perceptions of equal status, supportive norms, and interpersonal interaction (Gaertner et al., 1994), also improve evaluations of outgroup members and decrease intergroup bias by changing members' representations of the aggregate from two groups to one group.

Recategorization of different groups into one group may be a particularly powerful and pragmatic strategy for combatting subtle forms of bias. Creating the perception of a common ingroup identity not only reduces the likelihood of discrimination based on race but also increases the likelihood of positive interracial behaviors. People are more helpful toward ingroup members (Kramer & Brewer, 1984; Piliavin et al., 1981) and apply different and more generous standards of morality, justice, and fairness to ingroup members than to outgroup members (Opotow, 1990).

We have demonstrated, for instance, that creating a common ingroup bond facilitates interracial helping. We conducted a field experiment at the University of Delaware football stadium before a football game between the University of Delaware and Westchester State University (Gaertner et al., 1997). Black and White student experimenters, wearing signature hats to indicate their apparent university affiliation, approached White fans whose clothing similarly revealed school symbols, colors, or names. The experimenters asked these fans to participate in an interview of "food preferences." The dependent measure was whether the fan agreed to participate in the interview. We predicted that potential bias against Black experimenters would be eliminated when the fan and the experimenter shared a common group identity—the same university affiliation.

The results were generally consistent with the hypotheses, but not exactly what we expected. Although the presence or absence of common university identity did not affect compliance with a White interviewer (43% vs. 40%) and White fans did not significantly discriminate against Blacks when they did not share a common identity (36% vs. 40%), they did comply significantly more frequently with a Black interviewer when they shared common university identity than when they had different university affiliations (59% vs. 36%). Thus, as expected, making an alternative, common identity salient produced more positive and helpful behavior by Whites toward Blacks.

The development of a common ingroup identity does not necessarily require people to forsake their subgroup identity. As Ferdman (1995) noted, every individual belongs to multiple groups. For example, Rodriguez-Scheel (1980) found that Chicanos in Detroit chose nonethnic categories, such as religion, occupation, and family related, as often as ethnic labels to describe themselves. Indeed, it is often undesirable or impossible for people to relinquish their ethnic or racial subgroup identities. However, this may have beneficial rather than detrimental effects on the reduction of intergroup prejudice. It is possible for people to conceive of two groups (for example, parents and children) as operating interdependently with the context of a superordinate (family) entity. The dual identity in which members' subgroup and superordinate group identities are salient simultaneously (e.g., African American) may be particularly likely to permit the positive benefits of contact to generalize to outgroup members not present in the contact situation. In contrast to a purely one-group representation, the dual identity maintains the associative link to these additional outgroup members (see Anastasio, Bachman, Gaertner, & Dovidio, 1997). Consistent with this reasoning, we have found that in a multiethnic high school, those students who reported a dual identity (e.g., Korean Americans) had more positive intergroup attitudes than those who reported a separate group identity (e.g., Koreans; Gaertner et al., 1994). The simultaneous recognition of distinct and common aspects of identity may provide the effective balance for producing favorable and generalizable intergroup attitudes.

Structuring situations to foster a common ingroup identity can also be an useful strategy for addressing other forms of intergroup bias and conflict within organizations. The dynamics and the interventions are readily applicable to situations in which people could view other groups as competitors but they need not see them this way. For instance, marketing and production units in organizations may perceive their groups as competitors for internal resources; however, they may alternatively conceive of their groups as interdependent units of a superordinate organization working cooperatively toward a common goal.

We have recently found evidence that the principles underlying the common ingroup identity model may apply to relations and outcomes in corporate mergers (Bachman, Gaertner, Anastasio, & Rust, 1993; Mottola, Bachman, Gaertner, & Dovidio, 1997). Corporate mergers are quite common. Nearly 6,000 mergers occurred in 1995, involving a total value of $388 billion (M&A Almanac, 1996). However, they often are not successful. Over 65% of mergers do not meet original expectations (McCann & Gilkey, 1988), and it is estimated that between 50% and 80% are financial failures (Marks & Mirvis, 1986). Social and personnel issues contribute significantly to the problems that develop in the merged organizations. Merging two previously separate organizations frequently results in low levels of commitment to the merged organization among members of both the acquired and acquiring organizations (Schweiger & Weber, 1989).

In one study (Bachman et al., 1993; see also Bachman, 1993), we conducted a survey of banking executives who had participated in corporate mergers. Our interest was in examining the responses of members of the organizations to postmerger integration. We hypothesized that the presence of favorable contact conditions (e.g., equal status and positive interdependence between the merging groups; see Allport, 1954) would reduce threat and promote a common ingroup identity, in part by providing assurances to members that their premerger group would not be disadvantaged as a consequence of the merger. Consistent with these expectations, the results revealed that more favorable perceptions of the contact conditions were associated with lower levels of threat and more unified perceptions of the merged organization. These factors, in turn, predicted higher levels of organizational commitment, greater job satisfaction, and lower turnover intentions. Thus, the manner in which organizations structure the conditions of postmerger integration can greatly enhance members' positive responses to the merged organization and to each other.

Furthermore, a second study (Mottola et al., 1997) demonstrated that manipulating conditions of integration in terms of broad merger patterns can shape the development of a common identity, which can in turn influence employee commitment to the merged organization. In this simulated merger situation, the way the merger was described was systematically varied to represent an "absorb" pattern, in which one organization's culture disappears as employees are completely assimilated into the acquiring organization; a "blend" pattern, in which portions of each organization's culture remains identifiable; and a "combine" pattern, in which the merged organization borrows certain aspects from both companies and creates a new culture that is essentially different than either of the premerger organizations' cultures (see Schoennauer, 1967).

As expected, the absorb pattern produced the lowest expectations of positive contact between members of the two organizations and the weakest perceptions of organizational support; the combine pattern created the highest expectations of positive contact and support. Expectations of positive contact and organizational support then related to the extent to which respondents perceived a common ingroup identity. As suggested by the common ingroup identity model, a common ingroup identity was associated with lower levels of threat, which in turn predicted greater levels of organizational commitment. Thus, understanding the general dynamics of intergroup relations within organizations can facilitate the development of strategies and interventions that can reduce bias and encourage productive interaction between members of diverse groups—either racial or corporate.

CONCLUSION

Contemporary forms of racism are more subtle than the original form and thus are more difficult to detect and combat. The Civil Rights legislation of the 1960s made overt racial discrimination illegal and, as a consequence, norms of egalitarianism have become stronger. In part because of compliance with these norms and in part because of genuine internalization, fewer Whites than ever before are expressing prejudice and bias overtly. However, subtle types of bias are still prevalent. One type, aversive racism, develops out of the ambivalence that many Whites experience between (1) a sincere commitment to egalitarian norms and a nonprejudiced self-image, and (2) negative feelings and beliefs about Blacks (or other minority groups), often harbored unconsciously, that are based on almost unavoidable cognitive, motivational, and sociocultural influences. As we illustrated in the present chapter, the bias of aversive racists is expressed in indirect and rationalizable ways. However, although the bias may be subtle, the consequences are systematic and significant. We acknowledge that all bias is not subtle, and that old-fashioned racism is still a critical issue in the United States. Nevertheless, the more subtle and sophisticated forms of racism are more likely to characterize the racial attitudes of well-educated Whites in positions of leadership and power (Jackman & Muha, 1984).

Although prejudice and subtle bias may be conceived of as interpersonal or broad social issues, we propose that group processes can play a fundamental role in contributing to and thus ultimately in combatting subtle bias. Aversive racism is rooted partially in the primary categorization of people as ingroup or outgroup members on the basis of race. Thus, bias and discrimination often take the shape of ingroup favoritism rather than outgroup derogation. Consequently, new strategies to address aversive racism and other forms of intergroup bias may be focused on harnessing the motivations underlying intergroup bias and redirecting them to reduce bias by encouraging alternative forms of social categorization, making "them" part of "us." The common ingroup identity model proposes that the influence of various factors (e.g., cooperation vs. competition, proximity, common fate) may operate, at least in part, through a common process—the cognitive representation of the groups as one group, separate groups, or separate individuals. Strategies that promote a onegroup representation reduce bias as the forces of ingroup favoritism are applied to former outgroup members. Consistent with this perspective, cooperative interdependence on racially heterogeneous "teams" is one of the most effective ways of reducing racial bias (Aronson, Blaney, Stephan, Sikes, & Snapp, 1978; Slavin, 1985).

Group-based interventions may also be easier to implement effectively in work situations. Attempts to enhance people's awareness of their potential for prejudice may meet with personal denial. Aversive racists sincerely believe that they are not prejudiced. Attempts to institute policies to establish positive norms of egalitarianism may meet with reactance and resistance if they threaten the status of Whites. For example, although about three fourths of Whites support affirmative action *in principle*, typically about three fourths resist the implementation of any particular affirmative action program *in practice* (Dovidio et al., 1989). Group-based interventions, which do not threaten an individual's self-image and are less overtly proscriptive, may produce significant changes in attitudes and behavior without arousing reactance. Cooperatively interdependent groups can be created as problem-solving teams, with the reduction of bias being an important but implicit objective.

In addition, the processes and programs developed to address racial bias can be modified and extended to address other types of intergroup bias within an organization. Interventions designed to induce a common ingroup identity can be used to reduce conflict between work groups (e.g., marketing and production groups) that might ordinarily see themselves as separate and perhaps competing units. As we demonstrated earlier, the development of a common ingroup identity may be a critical mediator of the success of corporate reorganizations.

In conclusion, although racial prejudice may be seen as an individual problem or a general social ill, contemporary forms of bias may be based, in part, on group and intergroup processes. These processes are fundamental to social interaction and thus to organizations. Knowledge of the dynamics of racial bias and strategies to combat it may therefore facilitate an understanding of other types of group relations within organizations. Future research might consider the most effective ways for senior management to initiate fundamental organizational change to embrace and value diversity that minimizes backlash and the adverse effects of perceived preferential treatment. We have found, for instance, that focusing people on issues of macrojustice (e.g., how policies might be considered fair within the broader context of past injustice) or common goals (e.g., how policies can contribute to achieving collective goals), rather than on selfinterest or the facts of a particular case, can increase support for affirmative action (Dovidio & Gaertner, 1996). In terms of group processes, future work might examine ways of making the benefits of a common ingroup identity more generalizable and enduring. For example, the development of a common ingroup identity can be encouraged by emphasizing the similarity and common goals of members within an organization while simultaneously recognizing racial and cultural differences. The emphasis on similarity would be expected to create a common ingroup identity, which would improve attitudes toward people directly involved; the simultaneous emphasis on difference would establish a link between members present and other members of their racial or ethnic group, which would provide an avenue for generalization to occur. Thus, emphasizing similarity and difference simultaneously may be more beneficial than focusing on either exclusively. An enhanced theoretical understanding of group processes as a contributing cause of bias and the identification of the psychological processes involved are critical for identifying appropriate "cures" and implementing pragmatic strategies for reducing conflict and bias across a range of groups and issues.

ACKNOWLEDGEMENTS

Preparation of this chapter was facilitated by NIMH Grant MH 48721. We are grateful for the helpful comments and suggestions offered by Marlene Turner.

REFERENCES

Alderfer, C. P. (1992). Changing race relations embedded in organizations: Report on a long-term project with the XYZ Corporation. In S. E. Jackson & Associates (Eds.), *Diversity in the workplace: Human resources initiatives* (pp. 138–166). New York: Guilford.

Allport, G. W. (1954). *The nature of prejudice*. Cambridge, MA: Addison-Wesley.

Anastasio, P. A., Bachman, B. A., Gaertner, S. L., & Dovidio, J. F. (1997). Categorization, recategorization, and common ingroup identity. In R. Spears, P. J. Oakes, N. Ellemers, & S. A. Haslam (Eds.), *The social psychology of stereotyping and group life* (pp. 236–256). Oxford, England: Basil Blackwell.

Anderson, J. (1996, April 29, May 6). Black and blue. *New Yorker*, pp. 62–64.

Annin. P. (1995, April 3). The corporation: Allstate saw the light when it started following the money. *Newsweek*, *125*(14), 32–33.

Aronson, E., Blaney, N., Stephan, C., Sikes, J., & Snapp, M. (1978). *The jigsaw classroom*. Beverly Hills, CA: Sage.

Bachman, B. A. (1993). *An intergroup model of organizational mergers*. Unpublished doctoral dissertation, Department of Psychology, University of Delaware, Newark.

Bachman, B. A., Gaertner, S. L., Anastasio, P. A., & Rust, M. C. (1993, April). *When corporations merge: Organizational identification among employees of acquiring and acquired organizations*. Paper presented at the annual meeting of the Eastern Psychological Association, Crystal City, VA.

Bennett, C. E. (1992). *The Black population of the United States: March 1991* (1992 Current Population Reports, Series P-20, No. 464). Washington, DC: U.S. Bureau of the Census.

Black Enterprise. (1995, August). *26*, p. 66.

Brewer, M. B. (1979). In-group bias in the minimal intergroup situation: A cognitive–motivational analysis. *Psychological Bulletin*, *86*, 307–324.

Brewer, M. B., & Miller, N. (1984). Beyond the contact hypothesis: Theoretical perspectives on desegregation. In N. Miller & M. B. Brewer (Eds.), *Groups in contact: The psychology of desegregation* (pp. 281–302). Orlando, FL: Academic Press.

Brown, R. J. (1984). The effects of intergroup similarity and cooperative vs. competitive orientation on intergroup discrimination. *British Journal of Social Psychology*, *21*, 21–33.

Brown, R. J., & Abrams, D. (1986). The effects of intergroup similarity and goal interdependence on intergroup attitudes and task performance. *Journal of Experimental Social Psychology*, *22*, 78–92.

Brown, R. J., & Turner, J. C. (1981). Interpersonal and intergroup behavior. In J. C. Turner & H. Giles (Eds.), *Intergroup behavior* (pp. 33–64). Chicago, IL: University of Chicago Press.

Byrne, D. (1971). *The attraction paradigm*. New York: Academic Press.

Campbell, D. T. (1958). Common fate, similarity and other indices of the status of aggregates of persons as social entities. *Behavioral Science*, *3*, 14–25.

Cox, T., & Nkomo, S. M. (1986). Differential performance appraisal criteria: A field study of Black and White managers. *Group & Organization Studies*, *11*, 101–119.

Cox, T., & Nkomo, S. M. (1991). A race and gender-group analysis of early career experience of MBAs. *Work and Occupations*, *18*, 431–446.

Darley, J. M., & Latané, B. (1968). Bystander intervention in emergencies: Diffusion of responsibility. *Journal of Personality and Social Psychology*, *8*, 377–383.

Davis, J. A., & Smith, T. W. (1994). *General social surveys, 1972–1996: Cumulative codebook*. Chicago: National Opinion Research Center.

DeLuca, J. M., & McDowell, R. N. (1992). Managing diversity: A strategic "grass-roots" approach. In S. E. Jackson & Associates (Eds.), *Diversity in the workplace: Human resources initiatives* (pp. 227–247). New York: Guilford.

Devine, P. G., & Elliot, A. J. (1995). Are racial stereotypes really fading? The Princeton Trilogy revisited. *Personality and Social Psychology Bulletin, 21*, 1139–1150.

Devine, P. G., & Monteith, M. J. (1993). The role of discrepancy-associated affect in prejudice reduction. In D. M. Mackie & D. L. Hamilton (Eds.), *Affect, cognition, and stereotyping: Interactive processes in intergroup perception* (pp. 317–344). Orlando, FL: Academic Press.

Dovidio, J. F., Brigham, J. C., Johnson, B. T., & Gaertner, S. L. (1996). Stereotyping, prejudice, and discrimination: Another look. In N. Macrae, C. Stangor, & M. Hewstone (Eds.), *Foundations of stereotypes and stereotyping* (pp. 276–319). New York: Guilford.

Dovidio, J. F., & Gaertner, S. L. (1981). The effects of race, status, and ability on helping behavior. *Social Psychology Quarterly, 44*, 192–203.

Dovidio, J. F., & Gaertner, S. L. (1983). The effects of sex, status, and ability on helping behavior. *Journal of Applied Social Psychology, 13*, 191–205.

Dovidio, J. F., & Gaertner, S. L. (1986). Prejudice, discrimination, and racism: Historical trends and contemporary approaches. In J. F. Dovidio & S. L. Gaertner (Eds.), *Prejudice, discrimination, and racism* (pp. 1–34). Orlando, FL: Academic Press.

Dovidio, J. F., & Gaertner, S. L. (1991). Changes in the nature and expression of racial prejudice. In H. Knopke, J. Norrell, & R. Rogers (Eds.), *Opening doors: An appraisal of race relations in contemporary America* (pp. 201–241). Tuscaloosa, AL: University of Alabama Press.

Dovidio, J. F., & Gaertner, S. L. (1996). Affirmative action, unintentional racial biases, and intergroup relations. *Journal of Social Issues, 52*(4), 51–75.

Dovidio, J. F., Gaertner, S. L., Anastasio, P. A., & Sanitioso, R. (1992). Cognitive and motivational bases of bias: The implications of aversive racism for attitudes toward Hispanics. In S. Knouse, P. Rosenfeld, & A. Culbertson (Eds.), *Hispanics in the workplace* (pp. 75–106). Newbury Park, CA: Sage.

Dovidio, J. F., Mann, J. A., & Gaertner, S. L. (1989). Resistance to affirmative action: The implication of aversive racism. In F. A. Blanchard & F. J. Crosby (Eds.), *Affirmative action in perspective* (pp. 83–102). New York: Springer-Verlag.

Farh, J., Dobbins, G. H., & Cheng, B. (1991). Cultural relativity in action: A comparison of self-ratings made by Chinese and U. S. workers. *Personnel Psychology, 44*, 129–147.

Feagin, J. R., & Feagin, L. B. (1978). *Discrimination American style: Institutional racism and sexism.* Englewood Cliffs, NJ: Prentice-Hall.

Ferdman, B. M. (1995). Cultural identity and diversity in organizations: Bridging the gap between group differences and individual uniqueness. In M. M. Chemers, S. Oskamp, & M. A. Costanzo (Eds.), *Diversity in organizations: New perspectives for a changing workplace* (pp. 37–61). Thousand Oaks, CA: Sage.

Fine, M. G. (1995). *Building successful multicultural organizations: Challenges and opportunities.* Westport, CT: Quorum Books.

Fulkerson, J. R., & Schuler, R. S. (1992). Managing world-wide diversity at Pepsi-Cola International. In S. E. Jackson & Associates (Eds.), *Diversity in the workplace: Human resources initiatives* (pp. 248–278). New York: Guilford.

Gaertner, S. L., & Dovidio, J. F. (1977). The subtlety of white racism, arousal, and helping behavior. *Journal of Personality and Social Psychology, 35*, 691–707.

Gaertner, S. L., & Dovidio, J. F. (1986). The aversive form of racism. In J. F. Dovidio & S. L. Gaertner (Eds.), *Prejudice, discrimination, and racism* (pp. 61–89). Orlando, FL: Academic Press.

Gaertner, S. L., Dovidio, J. F., Anastasio, P. A., Bachman, B. A., & Rust, M. C. (1993). The common ingroup identity model: Recategorization and the reduction of intergroup bias. In W. Stroebe & M. Hewstone (Eds.), *European review of social psychology* (Vol. 4, pp. 1–26). New York: Wiley.

Gaertner, S. L., Dovidio, J. F., Banker, B. S., Rust, M. C., Nier, J. A., Mottola, G. R., & Ward, C. M. (1997). Does racism necessarily mean anti-blackness? Aversive racism and pro-whiteness. In M. Fine, L. Powell, L. C. Weis, & L. M. Wong (Eds.), *Off white readings on race, power, and society* (pp. 167–178). New York: Routledge.

Gaertner, S. L., Mann, J. A., Dovidio, J. F., Murrell, A. J., & Pomare, M. (1990). How does cooperation reduce intergroup bias? *Journal of Personality and Social Psychology, 59,* 692–704.

Gaertner, S. L., Mann, J., Murrell, A., & Dovidio, J. F. (1989). Reducing intergroup bias: The benefits of recategorization. *Journal of Personality and Social Psychology, 57,* 239–249.

Gaertner, S. L., Rust, M. C., Dovidio, J. F., Bachman, B. A., & Anastasio, P. A. (1994). The contact hypothesis: The role of a common ingroup identity on reducing intergroup bias. *Small Groups Research, 25,* 224–249.

Goddard, R. W. (1986, October). Post-employment: The changing current in discrimination charges. *Personnel Journal, 65,* 34–40.

Gottfredson, L. S. (1992). Dilemmas in developing diversity programs. In S. E. Jackson & Associates (Eds.), *Diversity in the workplace: Human resources initiatives* (pp. 279–305). New York: Guilford.

Greenhaus, J. H., Parasurman, S., & Wormley, W. M. (1990). Effects of race on organizational experiences, job performance, evaluations, and career outcomes. *Academy of Management Journal, 33,* 64–86.

Hacker, A. (1995). *Two nations: Black and white, separate, hostile, unequal.* New York: Ballantine.

Hamilton, D. L., & Trolier, T. K. (1986). Stereotypes and stereotyping: An overview of the cognitive approach. In J. F. Dovidio & S. L. Gaertner (Eds.), *Prejudice, discrimination, and racism* (pp. 127–163). Orlando, FL: Academic Press.

Hitt, M. A., & Keats, B. W. (1984). Empirical identification of the criteria for effective affirmative action programs. *Journal of Applied Behavioral Science, 20,* 203–222.

Hochschild, J. L. (1995). *Facing up to the American dream: Race, class, and the soul of the nation.* Princeton, NJ: Princeton University Press.

Hogg, M. A., & Turner, J. C. (1985). Interpersonal attraction, social identification and psychological group formation. *European Journal of Social Psychology, 15,* 51–66.

Hornstein, H. A. (1976). *Cruelty and kindness: A new look at aggression and altruism.* Englewood Cliffs, NJ: Prentice-Hall.

Howard, J. M., & Rothbart, M. (1980). Social categorization for in-group and out-group behavior. *Journal of Personality and Social Psychology, 38,* 301–310.

Hudson, N. (1995, December 4). Study: Races differ in promotion rates. *Navy Times,* p. 8.

Jackman, M. R., & Muha, M. J. (1984). Education and intergroup attitudes: Moral enlightenment, superficial democratic commitment, or ideological refinement? *American Sociological Review, 49,* 751–769.

Jackson, S. E. (1992). Preview of the road to be traveled. In S. E. Jackson & Associates (Eds.), *Diversity in the workplace: Human resources initiatives* (pp. 3–12). New York: Guilford.

Kanter, R. M. (1977). *Men and women of the corporation.* New York: Basic Books.

Kanter, R. M. (1983). *The change masters: Innovation for productivity in the American corporation.* New York: Simon & Schuster.

Kanter, R. M., Stein, B. A., & Jick, T. D. (1992). *The challenge of organizational change: How companies experience it and leaders guide it.* New York: Free Press.

Karlins, M., Coffman, T. L., & Walters, G. (1969). On the fading of social stereotypes: Studies in three generations of college students. *Journal of Personality and Social Psychology, 13,* 1–16.

Kline, B. B., & Dovidio, J. F. (1982, April). *Effects of race, sex, and qualifications on predictions of a college applicant's performance.* Paper presented at the annual meeting of the Eastern Psychological Association, Baltimore.

Kluegel, J. R., & Smith, E. R. (1986). *Beliefs about inequality: American's views of what is and what ought to be.* New York: Aldine de Gruyter.

Kovel, J. (1970). *White racism: A psychohistory.* New York: Pantheon.

Kraiger, K., & Ford, J. K. (1985). A meta-analysis of ratee effects in performance ratings. *Journal of Applied Psychology, 70*, 56–65.

Kramer, R. M., & Brewer, M. B. (1984). Effects of group identity on resource use in a simulated commons dilemma. *Journal of Personality and Social Psychology, 46*, 1044–1057.

Krieger, L. H. (1995). The content of our categories: A cognitive bias approach to discrimination and equal employment opportunity. *Stanford Law Review, 47*, 1161–1248.

Loden, M., & Rosener, J. B. (1991). *Workforce America! Managing employee diversity as a vital resource.* Homewood, IL: Business One Irwin.

M & A Almanac. (1996). *Mergers and Acquisitions, 30*, 37.

Major, B., & Crocker, J. (1993). Social stigma: The consequences of attributional ambiguity. In D. M. Mackie & D. L. Hamilton (Eds.), *Affect, cognition, and stereotyping* (pp. 345–370). San Diego, CA: Academic Press.

Marks, M. L., & Mirvis, P. (1986, Summer). Merger syndrome: Stress and uncertainty. *Mergers and Acquisitions*, 50–55.

Marino, K. E. (1980). A preliminary investigation into behavioral dimensions of affirmative action compliance. *Journal of Applied Psychology, 65*, 346–350.

McCann, J. E., & Gilkey, R. (1988). *Joining forces: Creating and managing successful mergers and acquisitions.* New Jersey: Prentice-Hall.

McClain, J. D. (1995, April 30). Blacks still lag in pay and job opportunities. *Syracuse Herald American*, p. A11.

McConahay, J. B. (1986). Modern racism, ambivalence, and the modern racism scale. In J. F. Dovidio & S. L. Gaertner (Eds.), *Prejudice, discrimination, and racism* (pp. 91–125). Orlando, FL: Academic Press.

Miller, N., Brewer, M. B., & Edwards, K. (1985). Cooperative interaction in desegregated settings: A laboratory analog. *Journal of Social Issues, 41*, 63–75.

Monteith, M. (1993). Self-regulation of prejudiced responses: Implications for progress in prejudice-reduction efforts. *Journal of Personality and Social Psychology, 65*, 469–485.

Morganthau, T., Carroll, G., Klaidman, D., Miller, M., & Brant, M. (1996, June 24). Fires in the night. *Newsweek, 127*(26), 29–32.

Morrison, A. M. (1992). *The new leaders: Guidelines on leadership diversity in America.* San Francisco: Jossey-Bass.

Mottola, G. R., Bachman, B. A., Gaertner, S. L., & Dovidio, J. F. (1997). How groups merge: The effects of merger integration patterns on expectations of organizational commitment. *Journal of Applied Social Psychology, 27*, 1335–1358.

Mullen, B., Brown, R., & Smith, C. (1992). Ingroup bias as a function of salience, relevance, and status: An integration. *European Journal of Social Psychology, 22*, 103–122.

Oliver, M. L., & Shapiro, T. M. (1998). The racial asset gap. In L. A. Daniels (Ed.), *The state of Black America 1998* (pp. 15–36). Washington, DC: The Urban League.

Opotow, S. (1990). Moral exclusion and injustice: An introduction. *Journal of Social Issues, 46*(1), 1–20.

Pettigrew, T. F. (1994, October). *Education and policy.* Paper presented at University of Massachusetts Conference on Racism, Amherst, MA.

Piliavin, J. A., Dovidio, J. F., Gaertner, S. L., & Clark, R. D., III. (1981). *Emergency intervention.* New York: Academic Press.

Ragins, B. R. (1995). Diversity, power, and mentorship in organizations. In M. M. Chemers, S. Oskamp, & M. A. Costanzo (Eds.), *Diversity in organizations: New perspectives for a changing workplace* (pp. 91–132). Thousand Oaks, CA: Sage.

Rodriguez-Scheel, J. (1980). *An investigation of the components of social identity for a Detroit sample.* Unpublished manuscript, Occidental College, Psychology Department, Los Angeles, CA.

Roese, N. J., & Jamieson, D. W. (1993). Twenty years of bogus pipeline research: A critical review and meta-analysis. *Psychological Bulletin, 114*, 363–375.

Ruderman, M. N., Hughes-James, M. W., & Jackson, S. E. (Eds.). (1996). *Selected research on work team diversity.* Washington, DC: American Psychological Association.

Schein, E. H. (1985). *Organizational culture and leadership.* San Francisco: Jossey-Bass.

Schoennauer, A. W. (1967, January–February). Behavior patterns of executives business in acquisitions. *Personnel Administrator, 30,* 27–31.

Schroeder, D. A., Penner, L. A., Dovidio, J. F., & Piliavin, J. A. (1995). *Psychology of helping and altruism: Problems and puzzles.* New York: McGraw-Hill.

Schuman, H., Steeh, C., & Bobo, L. (1985). *Racial attitudes in America: Trends and interpretations.* Cambridge, MA: Harvard University Press.

Schweiger, D. M., & Weber, Y. (1989). Strategies for managing human resources during mergers and acquisitions: An empirical investigation. *Human Resource Planning, 12,* 69–86.

Sears, D. O. (1988). Symbolic racism. In P. A. Katz & D. A. Taylor (Eds.), *Eliminating racism: Profiles in controversy* (pp. 53–84). New York: Plenum Press.

Sessa, V. I. (1992). Managing diversity at the Xerox Corporation: Balanced workforce goals and caucus groups. In S. E. Jackson & Associates (Eds.), *Diversity in the workplace: Human resources initiatives* (pp. 37–64). New York: Guilford.

Sigall, H., & Page, R. (1971). Current stereotypes: A little fading, a little faking. *Journal of Personality and Social Psychology, 18,* 247–255.

Slavin, R. E. (1985). Cooperative learning: Applying contact theory in desegregated schools. *Journal of Social Issues, 41,* 45–62.

Stein, D. D., Hardyck, J. A., & Smith, M. B. (1965). Race and belief: An open and shut case. *Journal of Personality and Social Psychology, 1,* 281–289.

Swim, J. K., Aikin, K. J., Hall, W. S., & Hunter, B. A. (1995). Sexism and racism: Old-fashioned and modern prejudices. *Journal of Personality and Social Psychology, 68,* 199–214.

Tajfel, H., & Turner, J. C. (1979). An integrative theory of intergroup conflict. In W. G. Austin & S. Worchel (Eds.), *The social psychology of intergroup relations* (pp. 33–48). Monterey, CA: Brooks/Cole.

Turner, J. C. (1987). *Rediscovering the social group: A self-categorization theory.* New York: Basil Blackwell.

Wang, H., & McKillip, J. (1978). Ethnic identification and judgements of an accident. *Personality and Social Psychology Bulletin, 4,* 296–299. Wilder, D. A. (1978). Reduction of intergroup discrimination through individuation of the out-group. *Journal of Personality and Social Psychology, 36,* 1361–1374.

Wilder, D. A. (1984). Predictions of belief homogeneity and similarity following social categorization. *British Journal of Social Psychology, 23,* 323–333.

Wills, T. A. (1981). Downward comparison principles in social psychology. *Psychological Bulletin, 90,* 245–271.

Wilson, W. J. (1980). *The declining significance of race* (2nd ed.). Chicago: University of Chicago Press.

Chapter 15

The Dilemma of Threat: Group Effectiveness and Ineffectiveness Under Adversity

Marlene E. Turner
San Jose State University

Todd Horvitz
University of California, Santa Cruz

Threats pose a paradox for groups and teams. Sometimes, threats can spur extraordinary group achievements. Yet, frequently, threats can produce disastrous consequences that can endanger the very existence of the group and innocent bystanders. Groups in organizational settings can be called on to resolve a breathtaking array of decision situations that can be considered threatening. For example, management teams may need to respond to product tampering, employee sabotage, employee violence, dangerous product failures, toxic spills, natural disasters, and host of other hazards. On a more mundane level, groups may need to respond to extreme competitive pressures (both internal and external to the organization), negative publicity, and takeover and acquisition attempts. Yet, our understanding of just what makes groups effective and ineffective under these conditions is indeed only quite rudimentary.

In this chapter, we attempt to provide an overview of the various literatures relevant to understanding how groups perform under external threat. To do so, we examine the major theoretical streams that consider group effectiveness under threatening conditions. In doing so, we limit our discussion to perspectives that specifically treat group effectiveness under threat. We discuss the limited empirical research that has been conducted on the topic and present some theoretical propositions that draw on this work. Along these lines, we attempt to specify the consequences of threat for performance. We do not attempt to build a full-range model of group effectiveness. Rather, we are concerned with a fine-grained analysis of the effects of threat on group-decision performance. Finally, we propose interventions that may be useful in enhancing the performance of groups operating under threat. First, however, we discuss the meaning of threat.

WHAT IS THREAT?

Like the concept of stress, threat can assume many different guises. For example, we can say that a group experiences a threat (a stimulus) or feels threatened (a response). The literature on threat documents that this multiplicity of meaning is further reflected in the operationalizations of threat. Threat has been defined as financial adversity, product tampering, natural disasters, loss of esteem, loss of status, extreme time pressure, and so forth.

For the purposes of this chapter, we define threat as an external circumstance that involves potential loss for the group. There are several important features about this definition. First, we are concerned with only with external threats. Threats that originate from inside the group are likely to have a number of quite different consequences than those we discuss here. Second, by incorporating the notion of loss, we encompass threats that may involve both tangible (such as money, resources, or physical health) and intangible (such as esteem or status) losses. Third, this definition underscores the importance of the probabilistic nature of the loss. Fourth, this definition acknowledges that perceptions of threat can vary considerably across groups. Clearly, groups will differ on the extent to which they will perceive a given situation as potentially involving loss.

The Experience of Threat: What Makes Groups Perceive Situations as Threatening?

Lazarus and Folkman (1984) presented the most developed model of threat appraisal. According to their approach, the perceptual process is categorized into primary and secondary appraisal. Primary appraisal refers to the process by which a given situation is determined to be threatening. Factors that influence this process include beliefs about the importance of the situation, level of control, the degree of novelty, uncertainty, duration, and ambiguity. Secondary appraisal refers to the process by which coping options are determined. This process includes an evaluation of the available coping options, the efficacy of those options, and the likelihood that the options can be employed.

This model implies that appraisals of threat are complex interactions between, in our case, the group and the situation in which it finds itself. According to the model, groups are more likely to experience threat when the situation is important, novel, uncertain, imminent, ambiguous, and of long duration, and when coping responses are unavailable, are ineffective, or cannot be implemented (see Tomaka, Blascovich, Kelsey, & Leitten, 1993, for empirical evidence regarding this model).

Group appraisals of threat, then, can vary considerably depending on both the situational characteristics and the resources of the members. This in turn allows for an enormous variability in group responses to threat and, in particular, group performance under threatening conditions. The following sections detail theoretical statements that attempt to capture the complex influences on group effectiveness when members experience threat.

Theoretical Statements of Group Effectiveness Under Threat: A Review of the Literature

At least seven theoretical perspectives regarding the effects of threat on performance have been advanced. These include (a) the inverted-U hypotheses, (b) attentional capacity explanations, (c) threat-rigidity effects, (d) groupthink, (e) crucial decision theories, (f) crisis management, and (g) self-handicapping. In the following sections, we briefly examine each theoretical stance and review the empirical literature pertinent to each perspective.

The Inverted-U Hypothesis

Interest in performance under threat has been notable since the early part of the 20th century. One of the classic formulations, typically termed the Yerkes–Dodson law (Yerkes & Dodson, 1908), posited an inverted-U relationship between threat and performance. As the level of threat increased to an optimal level, performance was predicted to likewise increase. As the level of threat exceeded this optimal level, performance was expected to decrease. This proposition was tested using rats who performed a visual discrimination task under varying levels of shock (see Yerkes & Dodson, 1908). The inverted-U relationship was observed only when the task was complex but not when it was simple. Although this hypothesis is intuitively plausible when thinking about group and even individual performance under threat, recent reviews of the literature reveal little support for this relationship (see Lazarus & Folkman, 1984). For example, Kohn (1954) manipulated three levels of threat (using an electric shock manipulation) and found only a direct negative effect of stress on performance. Isenberg (1981) induced three levels of time pressure as threat and found little evidence of a quadratic effect on decision accuracy in a discrimination task. As time pressure increased, the number of correct responses decreased whereas the number of incorrect responses increased and then decreased. Moreover, quadratic effects on efficiency measures were not significant. Turner, Pratkanis, Probasco, and Leve (1992), in an internal analysis, found no quadratic effects of perceived threat on decision accuracy. Thus, the inverted-U hypothesis has received very little empirical support.

Attentional Capacity Explanations

A second set of propositions suggests that threat should have a direct, negative effect on performance. Although a variety of explanations has been offered, most rely on the notion of impaired attentional capacity to clarify why threat might have such adverse consequences (Easterbrook, 1959; Kahneman, 1973; Keinan, 1987; Mogg, Mathews, Bird, & Macgregor-Morris, 1990; Wickens, 1984). According to this perspective, threat induces arousal, which takes up attentional and cognitive capacity. This in turn results in impaired performance. Driskell and Salas (1996) suggested that a range of literature demonstrates that threat results in impaired performance. Indeed, some empirical evidence substantiates this perspective. For example, Lanzetta, Wendt, Langham, and Haefner (1956) observed that groups under threat (operationalized as an evaluation test) were more inefficient and made poorer use of group member resources than groups not under threat. Likewise, Rempel and Fisher (1997) found that threat resulted in decrements in group problem-solving effectiveness.

Empirical research on time pressure as threat is generally interpreted in light of the attentional capacity explanation. Time pressure threats are expected to take up attentional capacity and thereby at least hamper performance speed and perhaps also impair performance accuracy. Research frequently finds that a time pressure threat can slow performance (Katchmar, Ross, & Andrews, 1958; Moffitt & Stagner, 1956; Murphy, 1959; Turner, 1992; Turner et al., 1992). However, effects of time pressure on decision accuracy appear quite equivocal. Time pressure has resulted in more stereotypic (and thus less accurate) judgments (Kruglanski & Freund, 1983) and shorter, less original, and less creative group-task products (Kelly & McGrath, 1985). However, time pressure has also failed to significantly impair performance accuracy (Janz, Colquitt, & Noe, 1997; Katchmar et al., 1958; Moffitt & Stagner, 1956; Turner, 1992).

The attentional capacity perspective cannot, by itself, satisfactorily explain a relatively large body of work demonstrating that threat can actually improve performance. For example, some research fails to observe any decrements in the performance of groups operating under threat (Lanzetta, Haefner, Langham, & Axelrod, 1954; Worchel & Shackelford, 1991). In contrast, other research shows that threat may have facilitatory effects on performance (Drabek & Haas, 1969; Kruglanski & Freund, 1983; Turner et al., 1992).

Threat-Rigidity Effects

One of the most influential explanations of the effects of threat on group performance is the threat-rigidity hypothesis (Staw, Sandelands, & Dutton, 1981). This perspective suggests that a threat to the vital interests of an entity will result in various forms of rigidity, including centralization of structure, restriction in information processing, routinization, formalization, and repeated reliance on dominant or well-learned responses. According to this perspective, rigidity may have either functional or dysfunctional consequences for the group. When the threat involves a major change in the environment or in known causal relations, the rigidity is predicted to be ineffective. In other words, well-learned responses are predicted to be inappropriate. However, when, the threat does not involve a major environmental change, the rigidity may well be functional because it can motivate the production of well-learned responses that are appropriate for coping with the threat.

Empirical research directly testing the threat-rigidity hypothesis has been limited and largely equivocal. In a laboratory experiment using a management strategy simulation game, Gladstein and Reilly (1985) obtained partial support for this perspective. They found that threat restricted information processing, as predicted by threat-rigidity perspectives. However, contrary to threat-rigidity predictions, threat did not increase centralization of authority. Argote, Turner, and Fichman (1989) found perceptions of threat to be associated with greater centralization of communication structures but not to be associated with any decrements in performance. D'Aunno and Sutton (1992), in a direct test of the threat-rigidity hypothesis, found that decreases in the total budgets of drug abuse treatment organizations were associated with more rigid use of existing procedures, reductions in work force, and competition among organization members. Decreases in the number of different funding sources were associated with more autocratic decision making, reductions in the workforce, and competition among members. Indirect support from the model can be derived from studies that examine responses to financial adversity. Cameron, Kim, and Whetten (1987) demonstrated that stable or declining university revenues are associated with greater resistance to change and greater stagnation. Similarly, studies of organization responses to financial adversity likewise document constriction in information processing and restriction in participatory decision making (e.g., D'Aveni & MacMillan, 1990; Hall & Mansfield, 1971; Pfeffer & Leblebici, 1973). In many of these studies, performance proved an elusive variable. Frequently it was either impossible to measure (due to ambiguity about outcomes, for example) or it was inextricably confounded with financial adversity itself.

Other work provides similarly equivocal support for the fully specified threat-rigidity effects. Cameron, Freeman, and Mishra (1993) found that automobile manufacturing organizations undergoing downsizing employed three general strategies; workforce reduction, organizational change, and systemic strategies focusing on changing organizational culture, values, and attitudes. Moreover, they found that firms were likely to engage in several, if not all, of these types of responses. Of the three, only the workforce reduction tactic would be consistent with the threat-rigidity hypothesis. The other tactics involve novel strategies that deviate from the well-learned responses predicted by the threat-rigidity model. Evidence from political science likewise questions a strict interpretation of the threat-rigidity hypothesis. In a review of the literature on governmental policymaking groups' decision making under threat and crisis. Hart, Rosenthal, and Kouzmin (1993) suggested that groups may exhibit a variety of responses including informal decentralization, formal decentralization, decision paralysis, and decision avoidance.

Other evidence from both laboratory and field settings suggests that responses to threat may be more varied than the threat-rigidity model might predict. Hamblin (1958) found that leadership in groups under threat was more unstable than in groups in nonthreatening conditions. Lanzetta et al. (1954) demonstrated that threat resulted in less autocratic behavior, greater variability, and more requests of information and opinions. Lanzetta (1955) observed that threatened groups exhibited more equalitarian behavior than did nonthreatened groups. Driskell and Salas (1991) observed that group leaders and members became more receptive to information provided by others. Drabek and Haas (1969) found that group activity became more shared under simulated threat and performance rates increased. In examining responses to financial adversity, Ocasio (1995) postulated that such conditions can lead either to threat-rigidity effects or failure-induced change. Ocasio suggested that change is likely to be adopted when it is well learned, congruent with core beliefs of decision makers, and favorable to the interests of decision makers.

In sum, threat-rigidity effects do indeed seem to characterize some group responses to threatening situations. However, it is clear that threat-rigidity effects may be elusive under certain conditions and that other interpretations are needed to explain the full range of group behavior under threat.

Groupthink

Although frequently not associated with decision making under threat, the groupthink model in fact assigns threat a central role. Interestingly, the majority of empirical work examining group effectiveness under threatening conditions has been conducted by groupthink researchers. Janis's classic formulation (Janis, 1972, 1982) as well as his more recent reformulation (see, for example, Janis, 1989) hypothesized that decision-making groups are most likely to experience groupthink when they are highly cohesive, insulated from experts, perform limited search and appraisal of information, operate under directed leadership, and experience conditions of high stress or threat with low self-esteem and little hope of finding a better solution to a pressing problem than that favored by the leader or influential members.

When present, these antecedent conditions are hypothesized to foster the extreme consensus-seeking characteristic of groupthink. This in turn is predicted to lead to two categories of undesirable decision-making processes. The first, traditionally labeled symptoms of groupthink, include illusion of invulnerability, collective rationalization, stereotypes of outgroups, self-censorship, mindguards, and belief in the inherent morality of the group. The second, typically identified as symptoms of defective decision making, involve the incomplete survey of alternatives and objectives, poor information search, failure to appraise the risks of the preferred solution, and selective information processing. Not surprisingly, these combined forces are predicted to result in extremely defective decision-making performance by the group.

Empirical Research on Groupthink. Recent reviews of groupthink research draw three major conclusions regarding the state of the groupthink theory. First, case and laboratory research rarely document the full constellation of groupthink effects. For example, although Tetlock (1979) and Janis (1972, 1982) provided some support for the full groupthink model, both recent and classic case analyses demonstrate that groupthink can occur in situations where only a limited number of antecedents can be discerned (see, for example, Hart, 1990; Longley & Pruitt, 1980; Raven, 1974; for reviews see Aldag & Fuller, 1993; Park, 1990). Other studies suggest that groupthink is not apparent when even most of the antecedents conditions exist (e.g., Neck & Moorhead, 1992). Likewise, laboratory studies, although they have experimentally manipulated only a few groupthink antecedents, rarely provide supporting evidence for the full groupthink model (see, e.g., Callaway & Esser, 1984; Callaway, Marriott, & Esser, 1985; Flowers, 1977; Leana, 1985). For example, laboratory experiments as well as analyses of both the Nixon White House (Raven, 1974) and the Challenger space shuttle decision (Esser & Lindoerfer, 1989) found little evidence for the traditional conception of cohesion as mutual attraction (see Callaway & Esser, 1984; Callaway et al., 1985; Flowers, 1977; Fodor & Smith, 1982; Leana, 1985). Despite its prominence in most groupthink case studies, threat, as operationalized in laboratory experiments, has rarely had any consequences for any group decision-making outcomes or processes (see Callaway & Esser, 1984; Callaway et al., 1985; Flowers, 1977; Fodor & Smith, 1982; Leana, 1985). Thus, when laboratory experiments find evidence for groupthink, it tends to be partial—

for example, finding that directive leadership does limit discussion but that this does not interact with cohesion and ultimately does not affect other decision processes.

Second, and perhaps most critically for our purposes here, few experimental studies have documented the end result and the hallmark of groupthink: the low quality, defective decisions. For example, studies investigating the effects of cohesion and leadership style showed no adverse effects on performance (Flowers, 1977; Fodor & Smith, 1982; Leana, 1985). Studies investigating the effects of social cohesion and discussion procedures (e.g., restricted vs. participatory discussion) similarly provided no evidence of impaired decision performance under groupthink conditions (Callaway & Esser, 1984; Callaway et al., 1985; Courtwright, 1978).

A third conclusion drawn from groupthink research is that questionable support has been provided for the causal sequences associated with the original model. No research has supported the hypothesized links among the five antecedents, the seven groupthink symptoms, and the eight defective decision-making symptoms in either a "strict" sense (whereby groupthink processes should occur only when all the antecedent conditions are present) or in an "additive" sense (whereby groupthink processes should be more pronounced as the number of antecedent conditions increases). However, some evidence has been found for a particularistic approach that suggests that groupthink outcomes will depend on the unique situational properties invoked by the particular set of antecedent conditions found in each groupthink situation.

Taken together, these findings have fostered a variety of evaluations regarding the viability of the groupthink theory. For example, Fuller and Aldag (1998) argued that the limited evidence for the complete groupthink theory offsets any potential usefulness of the model. A second view of groupthink suggests that the nature of the empirical evidence warrants a more fine-grained analysis of both the groupthink concept and the theoretical underpinnings of the model. In short, this perspective holds that groupthink needs to be reformulated in significant ways before attaining its purported usefulness. Whyte (1998) used the concept of collective efficacy to help explain the failure of cohesion as a key antecedent variable. Similarly, Kramer (1998) suggested that other motivations, such as the motivation to maintain political power, may produce groupthink in the governmental arena. One model that has recently been developed and subjected to empirical tests is the social identity maintenance model of groupthink.

Groupthink as Social Identity Maintenance. Turner and Pratkanis (1994, 1995, 1998a) proposed a model of groupthink as social identity maintentance (SIM) that underscores the importance of meaningful threat as a core antecedent of groupthink. The social identity maintenance perspective underscores the prominence of the group's social construction of its internal processes and external circumstances. According to this approach, group members actively attempt to maintain and even enhance their evaluations of the group and its actions. Groupthink then becomes a process of concurrence seeking that is directed at maintaining a shared positive view of the functioning of the group. In other words, the group attempts to protect its collective identity, especially under conditions of threat. The SIM perspective both converges with and diverges from traditional conceptualizations of groupthink. It shares with these models the notion that groupthink is fundamentally a process by which group members seek to secure concurrence and by virtue of that, mutual acceptance as bona fide group participants. Yet, it differs from these models in crucial ways. Most importantly, it suggests that this process is undertaken to maintain and reinforce the positive image of the group. Further, it proposes that groupthink will occur under identifiable, specific conditions and it provides some insights into the process by which those antecedent conditions produce both groupthink and its consequences. The SIM model proposes that groupthink occurs when members attempt to maintain a shared positive image of the group. Two assumptions underlie this notion. Most simplistically, group members must develop a positive image of the group. Second, that image must be questioned by a collective threat. These two conditions, then, are essential for the development of groupthink as social identity maintenance. The model suggests that two antecedents of groupthink, threat and cohesion as social identity maintenance, are especially critical.

How do groups develop a positive image? One route involves the interplay of self-categorization processes and social identity maintenance and thus involves the second important condition of the SIM model. According to this perspective (J. C. Turner, 1981), group members must categorize themselves as a group (e.g., Kennedy men, Nixon White House) rather than, say, as a set of unique individuals. In other words, members must perceive the group as indeed having a social identity. The SIM model suggests that groups who do not meet this precondition will be unlikely to develop groupthink as social identity maintenance. In short, simply drawing together a group of individuals (despite their level of mutual attraction) will be insufficient to produce this form of groupthink. Note that the SIM perspective diverges from some traditional approaches that define cohesion in terms of mutual attraction (e.g., Lott & Lott, 1965) but is consistent with the notion of cohesion as pressure to maintain the group (Cartwright & Zander, 1953). Categorization has three consequences for groupthink. When categorization occurs, the group tends to develop positive views of the group (J. C. Turner, 1981). Categorization leads groups to seek positive distinctiveness for the ingroup and to exhibit a motivational bias for positive collective self-esteem (J. C. Turner,

1981, 1982). Thus, we see that members tend to develop a positive image of the group and, importantly, are motivated to protect that image. Categorization also serves as the basis on which cohesion operates by reinforcing similarities between the individual and other members and by making the group identity salient. Finally, and most importantly, categorization provides the basis upon which the collective threat operates.

The second condition, a collective threat, is particularly relevant to this chapter. According to the SIM model, threat is the catalyst for the intragroup processes that promote the concurrence seeking and defective decision making that are the hallmarks of the groupthink phenomenon. It is critical that the threat be collective in nature. A threat to an individual member of the group is not likely to engender the groupthink-like consequences that a collective threat will. For example, a threat to a single member may result in the dismissal of that member in order to maintain the group's image. And, for social identity maintenance pressures to operate, this collective threat should also question or attack the positive image of the group.

In instances where the collective identity is threatened, the group tends to focus on those cues that can help maintain the shared positive image of the group that is invoked by social categorization. Thus, the overriding task of the group becomes image protection or even enhancement. Under certain circumstances, this can have detrimental consequences for group functioning. This is especially the case when high cohesion coupled with a social identity exacerbates identity protection motivations.

Experimental research on the SIM model has provided reasonable support for its predictions. Turner et al. (1992) found that group decision effectiveness was interactively affected by cohesion (manipulated using a social identity approach) and threat (manipulated using a collective identity threat). Group solution quality was poorer in the high threat, high cohesion (the groupthink treatment) and the low threat, low cohesion treatments than in the high threat, low cohesion and the low threat, high cohesion. Interestingly, threat by itself served to enhance performance. For the first time, this research documented in the laboratory the impaired decision making that is the ultimate consequence of groupthink and demonstrated the prominence of cohesion as social identity and of collective threat that incorporates group consequences. Finally, this work shows that groups do construct their self-evaluations so that they indeed project a positive image.

In sum, research on groupthink has provided only equivocal support for the full model. Moreover, this work has once again demonstrated the seemingly paradoxical effects of threat on performance: Groups performed more effectively at times and less effectively at other times under threat. Further, research on the social identity maintenance model has demonstrated that the usefulness of the groupthink model rests on the selected conceptualizations of key antecedents—including threat—and on the specifications of the unique properties of the situation fostering groupthink processes.

Crucial Decision Making

Building on his groupthink model, Janis (1989) developed a model of crucial policy decision making that proposes four types of decision-making responses to a threatening situation. Janis proposed that decision makers may use cognitive decision rules, affiliative decision rules, egocentric decision rules, or vigilant problem solving. The first three refer to simplistic strategies whereas the fourth type refers to a more complex type of tactic. Cognitive rules involve relying on simplistic strategies for decision making and the use of a few simple decision rules. Cognitive rules include the use of decision-making heuristics, historical analogies, and limited information search and evaluation. Affiliative decision rules are strategies designed to cope with the threat in ways that will not adversely affect the decision makers' relationships with important others. Examples of these include methods to avoid punishment, rigging meetings to suppress opposition, and groupthink. Egocentric or self-serving rules are rules that give priority to satisfying decision makers' own personal goals or needs. Vigilant problem solving refers to processes that involve careful formulation of the problem, gathering of sufficient information, rigorous evaluation and reappraisal of alternatives, and thoughtful selection of the decision alternative.

For situations that are of little importance, Janis proposed that decision makers will be likely to use one or more of the first three rules when situations are perceived to involve threats of little importance. Under such conditions, decision quality may indeed be relatively high because heuristic or simplistic processing may actually contribute toward identifying a correct response to the situation. In contrast, the use of a vigilant problem-solving strategy may be ineffective as it requires considerable resources that might be more effectively used elsewhere.

Predictions regarding strategy use are more complex when situations involve serious threat. Under those conditions, the nature of the constraints that are deemed to be important determine the type of decision rule used. For example, when time is limited, cognitive rules are likely to come into play. When a need to maintain power or to secure acceptability of a decision in an organization is primary, affiliative rules are likely to be used. Egocentric rules are likely to be used when emotional stress of decisional conflict is present or when a strong personal motive such as greed or desire for fame exists. Janis suggested that each of these strategies is likely to result in poor quality decision making. When the pressures associated with the three simplistic strategies are absent or are at a low level, vigilant problem solving may be used and is likely to result in high-quality decision making.

Like the groupthink model, this model is intuitively appealing as it captures a wide array of decision phenomena in an engaging way. But, also like the groupthink example, a number of concerns can be raised about the model. First, some ambiguity exists regarding the conceptualization of key constructs. Second, the processes that underlie the causal relations between antecedents and outcomes are frequently left largely unspecified. Third, and perhaps most importantly, the core assumptions of the model seem untenuous. For example, the model suggests that hypervigilant problem solving is likely only when constraints favoring more simplistic strategies are absent or are manageable. Yet, threat inherently encompasses many of these constraints. Thus, most threatening situations do not appear to conform to these requirements.

Not surprisingly, few empirical studies have examined the propositions of this relatively recent model. It is likely, however, that the theoretical and conceptual ambiguity surrounding the model will hamper research efforts—much as in the case of the groupthink model (see Turner & Pratkanis, 1998b, for a discussion of this issue).

Crisis Management

Most definitions of crisis incorporate some notion of threat (e.g., Dutton, 1986; Jackson & Dutton, 1987; Pearson & Clair, 1998; Quarantelli, 1988; Shrivastava, Mitroff, Miller, & Miglani, 1988). Yet, despite this centrality of threat, crisis management theories frequently pay little more than lip service to the potential consequences of threat for effective decision making under crisis conditions (Rosenthal, Charles, 't Hart, Kouzmin, & Jarman, 1989). Pearson and Clair (1998) presented a model of crisis management that suggests that the effectiveness of that process is affected by executive perceptions about risk, the environmental context (industry regulations and institutional practices), individual and collective responses (including shattered assumptions, impaired cognitive and behavioral responses, eroded social structure), and planned and ad hoc responses (such as team vs. individual response, information dissemination, etc.).

Mitroff, Pearson, and colleagues (1993, 1996) presented a multistage model of responding to crisis. They suggested that effective responses to crisis are more likely if the organization has prepared for crises and if the management team is adequately trained. They further suggested that crises are more likely to be effectively managed if (a) detection activities are undertaken (i.e., identifying the precise nature of the crisis, any warning signals, and the causes), (b) damage and containment activities are pursued (i.e., recalling products, shifting manufacturing facilities, etc.), (c) communication with the media is effectively handled (including information dissemination and image management). Postcrisis phases include recovery plans (to resume normal business operations) and learning processes (to mitigate or avoid future crises). Suggestions for effective management include securing executive buy-in, developing shared models of crisis awareness, and the development of crisis scenarios and responses.

Rosenthal et al. (1989) advocated a move away from typology approaches (e.g., conceptualizing crises by their forms such as product tampering, product spoilage, employee violence, equipment malfunctions, and so forth) and advocate examining the characteristics of crises. They highlighted three crucial attributes that may potentially prove important in determining responses to crisis: the degree of threat, uncertainty, and urgency associated with the situation.

Thus, crisis management advocates tend to highlight the crucial importance of preparation and practiced responses. However, the implications of this line of research for understanding group effectiveness under threat are, at this time, limited. First, models of crisis management pay insufficient attention to intragroup processes and their relation to performance and other outcomes. Second, as Quarantelli (1988) noted, empirical evidence regarding effective crisis management is scant. Third, the conceptual entanglement of crisis and outcome effectiveness tends to obscure any causal relations that might be discerned in the various research streams.

Self-Handicapping

Research that suggests that when faced with a threat to self-esteem, people are likely to self-handicap—that is, they seek to protect against potential failure by actively setting up circumstances or by claiming certain attributes or characteristics (such as reduced effort or alcohol or drug consumption) that may be blamed for poor performance (Frankel & M. L. Snyder, 1978; Higgins, 1990; Jones & Berglas, 1978; Miller, 1976; C. R. Snyder, 1990; M. L. Snyder, Smoller, Strenta, & Frankel, 1981). Although this results in poor performance on the task, failure on the task does not reflect poorly on self-esteem because it can be attributed to a volitional self-handicapping.

This perspective has been relatively ignored in the literature on groups and particularly regarding group behavior under threat. Yet, it appears to have explanatory usefulness. For example, Turner et al. (1992) demonstrated that groups can indeed demonstrate self-handicapping tendencies under threat. They found that groups subjected to a collective identity threat performed significantly better when provided with a potential excuse for poor performance than did groups also subjected to this type of threat but not provided with such an excuse. The excuse thus allowed groups to blame potential failure on this external situation rather than the group itself. Thus, groups had little need to engage in self-handicapping processes under threat when this face-saving excuse was available. It appears likely then that threat can indeed induce self-protection mechanisms in groups.

STEPS TOWARD AN INTEGRATION: THE PERFORMANCE CUE HYPOTHESIS

What are the implications of these diverse perspectives for understanding the consequences of threat for group effectiveness? On the one hand, we see a staggering array of theoretical perspectives. Further obscuring the picture are the highly equivocal empirical findings: Threat has enhanced, impaired, and left untouched group effectiveness. On the other hand, certain commonalities emerge that may provide some preliminary clues toward developing an integrative approach to group effectiveness under threat.

The Cognitive Consequences of Threat

Threat appears to have two reliable effects on decision processing. First, it serves to focus attention. Note that this does not necessarily mean that attention is diminished. Rather, it implies that threat directs attention toward certain cues and away from other cues. Second, that attention is directed toward what can be termed threat-relevant cues (as demonstrated by research on the social identity maintenance model and on the focusing effects of threat discussed earlier). These cues are those that assist in dealing with the threat—however that may be defined by the group in question. Thus, threat-relevant cues do not necessarily encompass information that particularly enhances performance. Instead, these are cues that, in the perception of the group, are relevant for handling or coping with the threat. A variety of empirical work substantiates these predictions. Wachtel (1968) demonstrated that threat directs attention toward cues that are relevant for task accomplishment. Cues not relevant to the task were less likely to be attended. Similarly, Kohn (1954) found that recall of task-irrelevant details became significantly poorer under threat. Mogg, Mathews, Bird, and Macgregor-Morris (1990) observed that subjects under threat likewise tended to allocate attention to threat-relevant information.

The Motivational Consequences of Threat

From our review, we suggest that threat also appears to reliably affect the motivational responses of the group. Threat appears to stimlate self-protective responses from the group, as evidenced by research on self-handicapping and the social identity maintenance model of groupthink. Thus, at least part of the group's effort is directed toward safeguarding the group and maintaining emotional equanimity. However, the exact nature of these efforts can vary dramatically. For example, as we have seen, some groups appear to be spurred toward greater achievements whereas others appear to engage in self-handicapping processes.

The Intervening Role of Performance Cue

What are the implications of these cognitive and motivational consequences for group effectiveness? We suggest that two interdependent effects occur. First, threat appears to focus group members' attention on the threat and on the consequences of that threat for the group. Second, we suggest that the nature of the performance cue associated with the threatening situation will critically impact how groups perform. We define a performance cue as the fundamental assumptions that a group makes about how to appropriately respond to a threat. Thus, how the group interprets the requirements of the threatening situation becomes paramount in determining how that group responds.

Threats appear to vary in the type of performance cues that they invoke. What are the types of cues that may occur under threat? An examination of the literature suggests that several types are common. First, threats appear to invoke strong self-protection mechanisms by groups. Thus, in these instances, the overriding concern of the group becomes maintenance of the group and of a positive view of the functioning of the group.[1] Second, threats may invoke performance quality requirements. That is, the threat demands high quality decision making. Third, the threat may demand speed of response. In other words, rapid decision making becomes the primary concern.

How might groups respond to threats involving these types of cues? Let us first examine threats that stimulate self-protection mechanisms. An example of this type of threat would be a threat to the identity of the group. Unchecked, this type of threat is likely to induce the group to focus on threat-relevant activities and goals. In this case, the goal of the group is transformed from the pursuit of effective functioning to the maintenance, protection, and even enhancement of the threatened image. Not surprisingly, when the task is complex and uncertain, this focusing of attention detracts from the decision-making process to such an extent that performance is impaired. Empirical evidence supports this view. When groups focus on self-protection (in the absence of other cues), performance does seem to be impaired (e.g., Turner & Pratkanis, 1998; Turner et al., 1992).

---

[1]This perspective will not be the case if members do not perceive the group as a means of handling the threat. When members do not perceive the group in this fashion, the group tends to disband (see Argote et al., 1989). For the purposes of this chapter, we are of course primarily concerned with collective threats that necessarily encompass the entire group.

Now let us consider a threat with a quality performance requirement. For example, in this type of threat, accurate performance is demanded in order to adequately deal with the threatening situation. Under those conditions, the group tends to focus on producing a high quality decision. In this case, we see that effective functioning of the group tends to be the central goal. And, consequently, performance tends to improve. Once again, empirical results tend to support this view. Kruglanski and Freund (1983) found that individuals performed more effectively when threat incorporated a quality requirement. Groups appear to do the same (see Turner, 1992; Turner & Pratkanis, 1998b).

Threats may also emphasize speed of response. Under these situations, the overriding concern of the group becomes the rapid production of a decision. In practice, these threats actually appear to take at least two different forms, with each form having very different consequences for quality. When threats incorporate a difficult deadline (that is, the deadline exerts extreme time pressure on the group), performance quality (in the absence of other interventions) tends to suffer. Under these conditions, the group tends to focus on swiftly making a decision. This in turn tends to exacerbate premature closure processes within the group. Procedures that limit the amount of time spent on a task provide an upper bound on the amount of decision evaluation that can occur. It is possible that threat may merely serve to slow decision processing (as a result of taking up attentional capacity through the focusing of attention) rather than necessarily decreasing the amount of solution evaluation (Turner, 1992). If threat does slow processing, it follows that, in a given time period, threatened groups will be able to engage in less evaluation than will nonthreatened groups. It may be this decreased evaluation, caused by time limits rather than by threat itself, that serves to impair decision quality. In contrast, when threats emphasize producing a response as rapidly as possible, performance quality may not greatly suffer. These threats appear to have an implicit quality cue (not surprisingly) that causes groups to focus on both speed and quality. Once again, empirical results appear to substantiate this view. Kruglanski and Freund (1983) observed that time deadlines produced more stereotypic (and thus poorer quality) judgments. Turner (1992) found that groups under threat performed more slowly than did groups working in nonthreatening conditions but also found that groups told to work as rapidly as possible did so at no loss of performance quality as compared to groups told to work as accurately as possible (see also Landy, McCue, & Aronson, 1969).

Thus, in sum, it appears that the unique situational properties invoked by the threatening circumstances have significant impacts on group responses. We suggest that the implicit or explicit performance cues inherent in the threatening situation have dramatic effects on group decision quality. This variability of outcomes moreover helps explain the paradoxical findings with regard to group effectiveness under threat. In the following section, we examine interventions designed to ameliorate the negative consequences of threat for group performance.

INTERVENTIONS FOR ENHANCING GROUP EFFECTIVENESS UNDER THREAT

What then can be done to ensure that groups perform effectively under threat? Our perspective suggests that the threat-relevant performance cues are crucial to designing effective interventions. Threat induces groups to focus their attention and direct their efforts toward those cues—whatever they might be. When those cues do not favor or signal effective functioning, the performance of the group is likely to suffer because attention is directed away from the decision-making process. Clearly then, interventions must redirect that focus of attention, when appropriate, away from such goals as identity protection or meeting deadlines and toward goals that facilitate high quality performance. The following sections review three categories of interventions that may be useful in that regard: (a) interventions designed to help groups cope with threat per se, (b) cognitive processing interventions, and (c) self-protection interventions.

Stress Training Interventions

Stress Inoculation Training. Stress inoculation training or stress exposure training involves training individuals to effectively cope with stress by gradually exposing them to successively higher levels of stress while simultaneously teaching effective coping skills (Johnston & Cannon-Bowers, 1996). Typical skills include thought restructuring, problem solving, and physiological reaction control. Johnston and Cannon-Bowers concluded that this type of training can be quite effective in enhancing performance. However, this type of training can also be problematic in implementation. First, it is likely to be expensive. Second, it is not clear to what extent the training can generalize across stressors (Keinan & Friedland, 1996). Thus, training for one type of threat may not provide resources for coping with other types of threat. Similarly, training for one type of task may not generalize to other types of tasks. Thus, although this form of training may be useful, it may be limited in its applications to either extremely high risk endeavors or to teams that consistently face threatening situations.

Cognitive Processing Interventions

Generally, the objective of these interventions is to direct the focus of the group's attention toward effective problem solving or decision making. The following tactics vary in their obtrusiveness and in complexity of implementation. Thus, groups who are less inclined to respond well to more structured interventions might still benefit from the more subtle tactics.

Structured Discussion Principles

Maier (1952) presented extensive research demonstrating the efficacy of structured discussion in enhancing group effectiveness. These techniques provide recommendations for establishing procedures for clarifying responsibility, analyzing the situation, framing the question or decision, gathering information, structuring consideration of alternatives, frequently soliciting further suggestions, providing evaluation, and so forth. The goal of these recommendations is to delay solution selection and to increase the problem-solving phase. These interventions attempt to prevent premature closure on a solution and to extend problem analysis and evaluation. These recommendations can be given to the group in a variety of ways. One method is to provide training in discussion principles either for the group leader only or for all members. This approach may work well when there is sufficient time, resources, and motivation to complete such a program. A second method is simply to expose group members to these recommendations. For example, groups may be given guidelines that emphasize the recognition of all suggestions but continued solicitation of solutions, the protection of individuals from criticism, keeping the discussion problem centered, and listing all solutions before evaluating them. M. E. Turner and Pratkanis (1994) found that highly cohesive, threatened groups (i.e., groups in groupthink conditions) given these types of structured decision guidelines produced significantly higher quality decisions than did highly cohesion, threatened groups not given these guidelines.

A second approach to structured discussion is the constructive controversy approach developed by Tjosvold (see, for example, Tjosvold, 1991, 1995). Under this approach, the superordinate cooperative goal of effective performance is coupled with specific mechanisms ensuring that issues are explored thoroughly, diverse opinions are stimulated, and opposing ideas are sought and integrated into a final solution. Specific tactics include the establishment of norms favoring the expression of opinions, doubts, and uncertainty, the consultation of relevant sources (including those who are likely to disagree), the implementation of constructive criticism of ideas rather than people, and the integration of solutions rather than the use of zero-sum choice procedures (see Tjosvold, 1991, 1995, for further details and a persuasive review of the supporting evidence).

A third approach useful in orchestrating group discussions can be adapted from the dispute resolution arena. Fisher, Kopelman, and Schneider (1996) provided a particularly detailed list of tactics designed to integratively resolve conflict. Fisher et al. recommended that parties follow certain guidelines that enable the: (a) exploration of partisan perceptions, (b) analysis of perceived choices, (c) generation of fresh ideas, and (d) implementation of a solution. Although initially designed to resolve rather than stimulate conflict, these tactics can be readily adapted to achieve opinion diversity in situations where groups might experience groupthink stemming from SIM pressures. For example, the analysis of perceived choices would entail the systematic appraisal of the consequences (including personal, political, organizational, interpersonal, and so forth) of proposed action plans for stakeholders. Particularly useful are the recommendations for generating and considering new alternatives. These tactics include a methodical evaluation of the problem, the causes, general approaches, and specific action plans in light of precise criteria such as goals, options, legitimacy, commitments, and so on that are fully spelled out before the decision process begins. The implementation of a solution likewise involves both a detailed analysis of the preferred recommendation and the solicitation of constructive criticism. We suggest that this general approach might be particularly useful for groups operating under groupthink conditions when it is accompanied by the simultaneous reinforcement of a superordinate goal and the reduction or channeling of emotions stemming from social identity pressures.

Establishment of Procedures for Protecting Minority Opinions. These procedures are critical in situations where premature closure or extreme convergence is likely. The protection of minority opinions may be one method of facilitating the evaluation and subsequent adoption of more effective solutions. These strategies can be relatively easy to implement. Simple exposure to minority opinions may increase the cognitive resources devoted to the task as well as the search and evaluation of novel solutions (Nemeth, 1992; Nemeth & Staw, 1989; Peterson & Nemeth, 1996). Maier and Solem (1952) found that groups simply instructed to encourage discussion and participation of all members produced significantly better decisions than did groups without those instructions.

Use of Directed Decision Aids. At least three procedures have been designed to structure the decision itself. First, the developmental discussion technique is a decision aid designed to direct the evaluation into logical steps and into positive action channels. This technique is particularly useful in the development and exploration of ideas, the analyses of barriers and conditions interfering with actions, and for solving problems for which group members have adequate skills but tend to form judgments on an impressionistic basis. The technique involves the solicitation of all opinions and the systematic appraisal of objectives and alternatives (cf. Maier & Hoffman, 1960a, for specific guidelines). A second strategy for structuring or directing the evaluation process is called the "two column method." This technique requires that all aspects of the situation be listed, that advantages and disadvantages of each aspect be considered and rated, and that there be systematic appraisals of methods for securing the advantages and minimizing the disadvantages (cf. Maier, 1952, 1963). Finally, one simple technique that may be especially useful when group members operate under time pressure or are resistant to more structured methods is to require groups to identify a second solution or decision recommendation once the first has been submitted. In short, this technique tends to enhance the problem-solving and idea-generation phases of the discussion and can significantly enhance performance quality (Maier & Hoffman, 1960b).

Interventions Designed to Reduce Self-Protection Mechanisms

Threat can also induce groups to primarily engage in strategies designed for self-protection, such as self-handicapping. Thus, the goal of these types of interventions is to redirect that focus again toward problem solving and effective functioning.

Provide an Excuse or Face-Saving Mechanism for Potential Poor Performance

One method of reducing the need for groups to engage in self-protection strategies is to provide an excuse for potential poor performance. M. E. Turner et al. (1992) found that groups operating under an identity threat (i.e., experiencing a collective threat to a group identity) who were given an excuse for poor performance performed significantly better than groups working under similar conditions without such an excuse.

The Risk Technique. A second effective strategy for reducing pressures toward identity protection is an application of the risk technique (Maier, 1952). The risk technique is a structured discussion situation designed to facilitate the expression and reduction of fear and threat. The discussion is structured so that group members talk about dangers or risks involved in a decision and delay discussion of any potential gains. The process emphasizes a reaction to or reflection of the underlying content of the risks associated with a particular decision or situation. Following this discussion of risks is a discussion of controls or mechanisms for dealing with the risks or dangers. Research with this technique has demonstrated its usefulness in clarifying and reducing fears and threats with a variety of groups including factory workers, students, and managers (cf. Maier, 1952).

Multiple Role-Playing Procedures. This process can be accomplished through two procedures. First, group members may assume the perspectives of other constituencies with a stake in the decision. A second approach focuses on the internal workings of the group. Each member can be asked to assume the role or perspective of another group member. This approach facilitates the confrontation of threats and rationales for decisions (cf. Maier, 1952) and allows the development of multiple perspectives. Fisher et al. 1996) recommended that parties adopt perspectives of themselves, of others involved in the situation, and of neutral observers, and explore each party's objectives, interests, and current positions or favored recommendations.

Guidelines for Effectively Implementing Interventions

Turner and Pratkanis (1997, 1998a) suggested that simply implementing interventions may prove threatening for a group. In some instances, groups may perceive these interventions as further questioning their capability to effectively function. This in turn would exacerbate perceptions of threat and direct the focus of attention toward self-protection. Turner and Pratkanis suggested three strategies that would be useful in overcoming these concerns: (a) Make the intervention early in the situation before the threat effects consume the group, (b) introduce strategies that can reduce, obviate, or redirect identity protection motivations (as discussed earlier), and (c) link the intervention strategy to the group in a supportive rather than threatening way.

CONCLUSION

Our understanding of how groups function under threat is still in its infancy. There appear to be several reasons for this. First, group research is notoriously difficult to conduct. Second, conditions of threat tend to exacerbate this difficulty. Meaningful operationalizations of threat in laboratory settings are troublesome to design and implement. Experimental realism is difficult to achieve. Respondents do not like to admit that they feel threatened and thus manipulation checks are extremely problematic. Field settings are likewise troublesome. Organizations are frequently loathe to allow researchers to observe groups cope (or not) with threatening situations. Retrospective reports by participants regarding behavior under threat may not be trustworthy.

Clearly, then, crucial research questions regarding group effectiveness under threat abound. From a theoretical standpoint, a number of conceptual formulations have been inadequately tested. Research needs to address the specific components of threat (such as the attendant performance cue) and examine how those components affect group performance. We suggest that research should focus on fine-grained approaches to understanding group behavior under threat. A number of extraordinarily complex models have been proposed. Yet, our current lack of detailed knowledge of how unique situational properties of threat affect intragroup processing and decision making obscures the usefulness of such models. Thus, we believe that research should focus on articulating the properties of threat and detailing the underlying processes that link those properties with group performance. In this way, we can gain richer insights into how groups function under threat and how to prevent the destructive consequences of threat.

ACKNOWLEDGMENTS

Financial support to the first author was provided by the College of Business, San Jose State University. We thank Anthony R. Pratkanis for helpful comments on this chapter

REFERENCES

Aldag, R. J., & Fuller, S. R. (1993). Beyond fiasco: A reappraisal of the groupthink phenomenon and a new model of group decision processes. *Psychological Bulletin, 113*, 533–552.

Argote, L., Turner, M. E., & Fichman, M. (1989). To centralize or not to centralize: The effects of uncertainty and threat on group structure and performance. *Organizational Behavior and Human Decision Processes, 43*, 58–74.

Callaway, M. R., & Esser, J. K. (1984). Groupthink: Effects of cohesiveness and problem-solving procedures on group decision making. *Social Behavior and Personality, 12*, 157–164.

Callaway, M. R., Marriott, R. G., & Esser, J. K. (1985). Effects of dominance on group decision making: Toward a stress-reduction explanation of groupthink. *Journal of Personality and Social Psychology, 4*, 949–952.

Cameron, K. S., Freeman, S. J., & Mishra, A. K. (1993). Downsizing and redesigning organizations. In G. P. Huber & W. H. Glick (Eds.), *Organizational change and redesign* (pp. 19–65) New York: Oxford University Press.

Cameron, K. S., Kim, M. U., & Whetten, D. A. (1987). Organizational effects of decline and turbulence. *Administrative Science Quarterly, 32*, 222–240.

Cartwright, D., & Zander, A. (1968). *Group dynamics* (3rd ed.). New York: Harper & Row.

Courtwright, J. A. (1978). A laboratory investigation of groupthink. *Communication Monographs, 45*, 229–246.

D'Aunno, T., & Sutton, R. I. (1992). The responses of drug abuse treatment organizations to financial adversity: A partial test of the threat-rigidity thesis. *Journal of Management, 18*, 117–131.

D'Aveni, R. A., & MacMillan, I. C. (1990). Crisis and the content of managerial communication: A study of top managers in surviving and failing firms. *Administrative Science Quarterly, 35*, 634–657.

Davis, J. H. (1969). *Group performance*. Reading, MA: Addison-Wesley.

de Dreu, C., & Van de Vliert, E. (Eds.). (1997). *Using conflict in organizations*. London: Sage.

Drabek, T. E., & Haas, J. E. (1969). Laboratory simulation of organizational stress. *American Sociological Review, 34*, 223–238.

Driskell, J. E., & Salas, E. (1996). *Stress and human performance*. Mahwah, NJ: Lawrence Erlbaum Associates.

Dutton, J. E. (1986). The processing of crisis and non-crisis strategic issues. *Journal of Management Studies, 23*, 501–517.

Dutton, J. E., & Jackson, S. J. (1987). Categorizing strategic issues. *Academy of Management Review, 12*, 76–90.

Easterbrook, J. A. (1959). The effect of emotion on cue utilization and the organization of behavior. *Psychological Review, 66*, 183–201.

Esser, J. K., & Lindoerfer, J. S. (1989). Groupthink and the space shuttle Challenger accident: Toward a quantitative case analysis. *Journal of Behavioral Decision Making, 2*, 167–177.

Fisher, F., Kopelman, E., & Schneider, A. K. (1996). *Beyond Machiavelli: Tools for coping with conflict*. New York: Penguin.

Flowers, M. L. (1977). A laboratory test of some implications of Janis's groupthink hypothesis. *Journal of Personality and Social Psychology, 35*, 888–896.

Fodor, E. M., & Smith, T. (1982). The power motive as an influence on group decision making. *Journal of Personality and Social Psychology, 42*, 178–185.

Frankel, A., & Snyder, M. L. (1978). Poor performance following unsolvable problems: Learned helplessness or egotism? *Journal of Personality and Social Psychology, 36*, 1415–1423.

Fuller, S. R., & Aldag, R. J. (1998). Organizational Tonypandy: Lessons from a quarter century of groupthink phenomenon. *Organizational Behavior & Human Decision Processes, 73*, 163–184.

Gladstein, D., & Reilly, N. (1985). Group decision making under threat: The tycoon game. *Academy of Management Journal, 28*, 613–627.

Hall, D., & Mansfield, R. (1971). Organizational and individual response to stress. *Administrative Science Quarterly, 16*, 533–547.

Hamblin, R. L. (1958). Leadership and crises. *Sociometry, 21*, 322–335.

Hart, P., 't, Rosenthal, U., & Kouzmin, A. (1993). Crisis decision making: The centralization thesis revisited. *Administration and Society, 25*, 12–45.

Higgins, R. L. (1990). Self-handicapping: Historical roots and contemporary approaches. In R. L. Higgins, C. R. Snyder, & S. Berglas (Eds.), *Self-handicapping: The paradox that isn't* (pp. 1–35). NY: Plenum.

Isenberg, D. (1981). Some effects of time-pressure on vertical structure and decision-making accuracy in small groups. *Organizational Behavior and Human Performance, 27*, 119–134.

Janis, I. L. (1972). *Victims of groupthink*. Boston: Houghton Mifflin.

Janis, I. L. (1982). *Groupthink: Psychological studies of policy decisions and fiascoes* (2nd ed.). Boston: Houghton Mifflin.

Janis, I. L. (1989). *Crucial decisions: Leadership in policymaking and crisis management.* New York: Free Press.

Janz, B. D., Colquitt, J. A., & Noe, R. A. (1997). Knowledge worker team effectiveness: The role of autonomy, interdependence, team development, and contextual support variables. *Personnel Psychology, 50,* 877–904.

Johnston, J. H., & Cannon-Bowers, J. A. (1996). Training for stress exposure. In J. E. Driskell & E. Salas (Eds.), *Stress and human performance* (pp. 223–256). Mahwah, NJ: Lawrence Erlbaum Associates.

Jones, E. E., & Berglas, S. (1978). Control of attributions about the self through self-handicapping strategies. *Personality and Social Psychology Bulletin, 4,* 200–206.

Kahneman, D. (1973). *Attention and effort.* Englewood Cliffs, NJ: Prentice-Hall.

Katchmar, L. T., Ross, S., & Andrews, T. G. (1958). Effects of stress and anxiety on performance of a complex verbal coding task. *Journal of Experimental Psychology, 55,* 559–564.

Keinan, G. (1987). Decision making under stress: Scanning of alternatives under controllable and uncontrollable threats. *Journal of Personality and Social Psychology, 49,* 638–644.

Keinan, G., & Friedland, N. (1996). Training effective performance under stress: Queries, dilemmas, and possible solutions. In J. E. Driskell & E. Salas (Eds.), *Stress and human performance* (pp. 257–277). Mahwah, NJ: Lawrence Erlbaum Associates.

Kelly, J. R., & McGrath, J. E. (1985). Effects of time limits and task types on task performance in interaction in four person groups. *Journal of Personality and Social Psychology, 49,* 395–407.

Kohn, H. (1954). The effects of variations in intensity of experimentally induced stress situations upon certain aspects of perception and performance. *Journal of Genetic Psychology, 85,* 289–304.

Kramer, R. M. (1998). Revisiting the Bay of Pigs and Vietnam decisions twenty-five years later. *Organizational Behavior and Human Decision Processes, 73,* 236–271.

Kruglanski, A., & Freund, T. (1983). The freezing and unfreezing of lay-inferences: Effects on impressional primacy, ethnic stereotyping and numerical anchoring. *Journal of Experimental Social Psychology, 19,* 448–468.

Landy, D., McCue, K., & Aronson, E. (1969). Beyond Parkinson's Law: III. The effect of protractive and contractive distractions on the wasting of time on subsequent tasks. *Journal of Applied Psychology, 53,* 236–239.

Lanzetta, J. (1955). Group behavior under stress. *Human Relations, 8,* 29–52.

Lanzetta, J., Haefner, D., Langham, P., & Axelrod, H. (1954). Some effects of situational threat on group behavior. *Journal of Abnormal Psychology, 49,* 445–453.

Lanzetta, J., Wendt, G., Langham, P., & Haefer, D. (1956). Effects of an "anxiety-reducing" medicine on group behavior under threat. *Journal of Abnormal and Social Psychology, 51,* 103–113.

Lazarus, R. S., & Folkman, S. (1984). *Stress, appraisal, and coping.* New York: Springer.

Leana, C. R. (1985). A partial test of Janis' groupthink model: Effects of group cohesiveness and leader behavior on defective decision making. *Journal of Management, 11,* 5–17.

Longley, J., & Pruitt, D. G. (1980). Groupthink: A critique of Janis's theory. In L. Wheeler (Ed.), *Review of personality and social psychology* (Vol. 1, pp. 74–93). Beverly Hills, CA: Sage.

Lott, A. J., & Lott, B. E. (1965). Group cohesiveness as interpersonal attraction: A review of relationships with antecedent and consequent variables. *Psychological Bulletin, 64,* 259–309.

Maier, N. R. F. (1952). *Principles of human relations.* New York: Wiley.

Maier, N. R. F. (1963). *Problem-solving discussions and conferences.* New York: McGraw-Hill.

Maier, N. R. F., & Hoffman, L. R. (1960a). Using trained "developmental" discussion leaders to improve further the quality of group decisions. *Journal of Applied Psychology, 44,* 247–251.

Maier, N. R. F., & Hoffman, L. R. (1960b). Quality of first and second solution in group problem solving. *Journal of Applied Psychology, 44,* 278–283.

Maier, N. R. F., & Solem, A. R. (1952). The contribution of a discussion leader to the quality of group thinking: The effective use of minority opinions. *Human Relations, 5,* 277–288.

Miller, R. T. (1976). Ego involvement and attribution for success and failure. *Journal of Personality and Social Psychology, 34,* 901–906.

Mitroff, I., & Pearson, C. (1993). *Crisis management.* San Francisco: Jossey-Bass.

Mitroff, I., Pearson, C., & Harrington, L. K. (1996). *The essential guide to managing corporate crises.* New York: Oxford University Press.

Moffitt, J., & Stagner, R. (1956). Perceptual rigidity and closure as functions of anxiety. *Journal of Abnormal and Social Psychology, 52,* 354–357.

Mogg, K., Mathews, A., Bird, C., Macgregor-Morris, R. (1990). Effects of stress and anxiety on the processing of threat stimuli. *Journal of Personality and Social Psychology, 59,* 1230–1237.

Murphy, R. (1959). Effects of threat of shock, distraction and task design on performance. *Journal of Experimental Psychology, 58,* 134–141.

Neck, C. P., & Moorhead, G. (1992). Jury deliberations in the trial of U. S. v. John DeLorean: A case analysis of groupthink avoidance and an enhanced framework. *Human Relations, 45,* 1077–1091.

Nemeth, C. J. (1992). Minority dissent as a stimulant to group performance. In S. Worchel, W. Wood, & J. A. Simpson (Eds.), *Group process and productivity* (pp. 95–111). Newbury Park, CA: Sage.

Nemeth, C. J., & Staw, B. M. (1989). The tradeoffs of social control and innovation in groups and organizations. In L. Berkowitz (Ed.), *Advances in experimental social psychology* (Vol. 22, pp. 175–210). New York: Academic Press.

Ocasio, W. (1995). The enactment of economic adversity: A reconciliation of theories of failure-induced change and threat-rigidity. *Research in Organizational Behavior, 17,* 287–331.

Park, W. (1990). A review of research on groupthink. *Journal of Behavioral Decision Making, 3,* 229–245.

Pearson, C. M., & Clair, J. A. (1998). Reframing crisis management. *Academy of Management Review, 23,* 59–76.

Peterson, R. S., & Nemeth, C. J. (1996). Focus versus flexibility: Majority and minority influence can both improve performance. *Personality and Social Psychology Bulletin, 22,* 14–23.

Pfeffer, J., & Leblebici, H. (1973). The effects of competition on some dimensions of organizational structure. *Social Forces, 52,* 268–279.

Quarantelli, E. L. (1988). Disaster crisis management: A summary of research findings. *Journal of Management Studies, 25,* 373–385.

Raven, B. H. (1974). The Nixon group. *Journal of Social Issues, 30,* 297–320.

Rempel, M. W., & Fisher, R. J. (1997). Perceived threat, cohesion, and group problem solving in intergroup conflict. *International Journal of Conflict Management, 8,* 216–234.

Rosenthal, U., Charles, M. T., & Hart, P., 't (Eds.). (1989). *Coping with crises: The management of disasters, riots, and terrorism.* Springfield, IL: Thomas.

Shrivastava, P., Mitroff, I., Miler, D., & Miglani, A. (1988). Understanding industrial crises. *Journal of Management Studies, 25,* 285–303.

Snyder, C. R. (1990). Self-handicapping processes and sequelae. In R. L. Higgins, C. R. Snyder, & S. Berglas (Eds.), *Self-handicapping: The paradox that isn't* (pp. 107–150). New York: Plenum.

Snyder, M. L., Smoller, B., Strenta, A., & Frankel, A. (1981). A comparison of egotism, negativity, and learned helplessness as explanations for poor performance after unsolvable problems. *Journal of Personality and Social Psychology, 40,* 24–30.

Staw, B., Sandelands, L., & Dutton, J. (1981). Threat-rigidity effects in organizational behavior: A multi-level analysis. *Administrative Science Quarterly, 26,* 501–524.

Stein, A. A. (1976). Conflict and cohesion: A review of the literature. *Journal of Conflict Resolution, 20,* 143–172.

Tetlock, P. E. (1979) Identifying victims of groupthink from public statements of decision makers. *Journal of Personality and Social Psychology, 37,* 1314–1324.

Tjosvold, D. (1991). *Team organization: An enduring competitive advantage.* Chichester, England: Wiley.

Tjosvold, D. (1995). Cooperation theory, constructive controversy, and effectiveness: Learning from crisis. In R. A. Guzzo & E. Salas (Eds.), *Team effectiveness and decision making in organizations* (pp. 79–112). San Francisco: Jossey-Bass.

Tomaka, J., Blascovich, J., Kelsey, R. M., & Leitten, C. L. (1993). Subjective, physiological, and behavioral effects of threat and challenge appraisal. *Journal of Personality and Social Psychology, 65,* 248–260.

Turner, J. C. (1981). The experimental social psychology of intergroup behavior. In J. C. Turner & H. Giles (Eds.), *Intergroup behavior* (pp. 66–101). Chicago: University of Chicago Press.

Turner, J. C. (1982). Towards a cognitive redefinition of the social group. In H. Tajfel (Ed.), *Social identity and intergroup relations* (pp. 15–40). Cambridge, England: Cambridge University Press.

Turner, M. E. (1992). Group effectiveness under threat: The impact of structural centrality and performance set. *Journal of Social Behavior and Personality, 7,* 511–528.

Turner, M. E., & Pratkanis, A. R. (1994). [Effects of structured decision aids on decision effectiveness under groupthink]. Unpublished raw data.

Turner, M. E., & Pratkanis, A. R. (1997). Mitigating groupthink by stimulating constructive conflict. In C. de Dreu & E. Van de Vliert (Eds.), *Using conflict in organizations* (pp. 53–71). London: Sage.

Turner, M. E., & Pratkanis, A. R. (1998a). A social identity maintenance model of groupthink. *Organizational Behavior and Human Decision Processes, 73,* 210–235.

Turner, M. E., & Pratkanis, A. R. (1998b). Twenty-five years of groupthink theory and research: Lessons from the evolution of a theory. *Organizational Behavior and Human Decision Processes, 73,* 105–115.

Turner, M. E., & Pratkanis, A. R. (1995). Social identity maintenance prescriptions for preventing groupthink: Reducing identity protection and enhancing intellectual conflict. In E. van de Vliert & C. K. de Dreu (Eds.), *Optimizing performance through conflict stimulation* [Special issue]. *International Journal of Conflict Management, 5,* 254–270.

Turner, M. E., Pratkanis, A. R., Probasco, P., & Leve, C. (1992). Threat, cohesion, and group effectiveness: Testing a social identity maintenance perspective on groupthink. *Journal of Personality and Social Psychology, 63,* 781–796.

Wachtel, P. L. (1968). Style and capacity in analytic functioning. *Journal of Personality, 36,* 202–212.

Wickens, C. D. (1984). Processing resources in attention. In R. Parasuraman & D. R. Davis (Eds.), *Attention and performance* (Vol. 4, 63–102). London: Academic Press.

Worchel, S., & Shackelford, S. L. (1991). Groups under stress: The influence of group structure and environment on process and performance. *Personality and Social Psychology Bulletin, 17,* 640–647.

Whyte, G. (1998). Recasting Janis's groupthink model: The key role of collective efficacy in decision fiascoes. *Organizational Behavior and Human Decision Processes, 73,* 185–209.

Yerkes, R. M., & Dodson, J. D. (1908). The relation of strength of stimulus to rapidity of habit formation. *Journal of Comparative and Neurological Psychology, 18,* 459–482.

Chapter 16

Collective Corruption in the Corporate World: Toward a Process Model

Arthur P. Brief
Robert T. Buttram
Tulane University

Janet M. Dukerich
University of Texas at Austin

In a recent court case, Beech-Nut Nutrition Corporation, at one time the second largest baby food manufacturer in the United States, pleaded guilty to charges of selling adulterated apple juice during a period from 1981 to 1983. The plea was based on the "collective knowledge" of its employees that its juice was impure (Welles, 1988). Beech-Nut purchased "apple concentrate" from Interjuice Trading Corporation at 20% below market price. Later, it was proven the "concentrate" contained no juice at all; in fact, it was a "100% fraudulent chemical cocktail." Beech-Nut continued to market the baby food as "100% fruit juice" even after suspicions regarding the concentrate were raised within the company. And, to avoid having part of their inventory seized by New York State authorities, Beech-Nut transported this inventory to New Jersey in the dead of night. Eventually, this same inventory was sold in foreign markets.

The Beech-Nut case is not an isolated one. For example, the Cordis Corporation recently pleaded guilty to charges of deliberately marketing defective products. The products in question were pacemakers. Also, consider the actions taken recently against the Proctor & Gamble Company. More than a quarter century ago, the Food and Drug Administration (FDA) ruled consumers are misled by the word "fresh" on the labels of products that, in fact, are made from concentrates. Nevertheless, Proctor & Gamble, until recently, labeled its orange juice from concentrate as Citrus Hill *Fresh* Choice. The firm ignored early warnings from the FDA and finally dropped the word fresh from the label only after the agency seized several thousand cases of the product ("Proctor & Gamble: On a Short Leash," 1991).

Finally, consider the woes of the Northrop Corporation, a major defense contractor. In recent years, Northrop has been investigated repeatedly by the U.S. Department of Justice (see Harris, 1989; Harris & Pasztor, 1989.) One recent case focused on the firm's alleged attempts to obtain inside information about competitor's bids on Navy contracts. In another case, Northrop was charged with falsifying test results for flight-data transmitters used in the guidance systems of air-launched cruise missiles. Falsified test results were at the crux of yet another case, this one involving the stabilization systems for the Navy's Harrier jet fighter.

Aside from the fact that they all depict instances of ethically questionable corporate practices, the above cases are alike in two important respects. First, the acts of corruption depicted required a collective effort. For example, no one person produces a deceptive advertisement (e.g., portraying reconstituted orange juice as fresh); many hands would have had to be involved. That is, the problem being addressed is one of aggregate wrongdoing, not just that of a single individual in the corporation.

Second, the cases appear to be similar because in each, it can be assumed the corruption was officially sanctioned. (In this context, we are using the verb "sanction" to mean to endorse or to condone.) Because a collective was involved in each of the acts, it can be presumed that some authority figure in the corporation was least aware of the corruption. What cannot be inferred from the cases is the nature of the official sanctions. Approval or consent may have been either implicit or explicit. A direct order to engage in a corrupt practice represents explicit sanctioning; and, the creation of a corporate climate emphasizing results without regard to means is an example of implicit sanctioning. These distinctions, although often subtle, will be detailed somewhat further later. For now, the important point is that the corruption with which we are concerned is sanctioned officially.

In sum, the above cases characterize a not uncommon problem that has significant negative consequences for individuals, corporations, and the larger society: The problem of sanctioned corporate corruption. Such corruption is officially ordered or condoned, is engaged in by a collective of employees, and is ethically questionable. It is a problem to which inadequate attention has been paid, both by managers and academics. Most treatments of unethical behavior in the workplace have focused on the individual, addressing why a person might behave unethically or how such behavior may be inhibited (e.g., Fritzche & Becker, 1984; Hegarty & Sims, 1978; Posner & Schmidt, 1984; Trevino & Youngblood, 1990). The purpose of this chapter, therefore, is to draw attention to the problem of sanctioned, collective actions by attempting to describe the processes that result in such corporate corruption.

In the remainder of this chapter, three processes are described: *sanctioning*—the implicit or explicit endorsement of a corrupt corporate practice by an authority figure who likely has engaged in amoral reasoning; *compliance*—the initial obedience of organizational members to the authorization to engage in a corrupt practice; and *institutionalization*—the means by which the collective wrongdoing becomes part and parcel of everyday organizational life. Together, our descriptions of these processes tell a story about how an ethically questionable practice can become woven into the fabric of an organization. We deal with how the practice surfaces (sanctioning), how people at first react to it (compliance), and how it becomes a routine for them (institutionalization). Thus, for a given practice, we see the processes as temporally ordered, but, in a fluid way. That is, we suspect sanctioning to bleed into compliance and compliance into institutionalization, resulting in what would appear to be overlapping processes.

Although our characterizations of the three processes were influenced by various studies of organizations and behaviors in them, much of our discussion was inspired by a seemingly foreign body of research. That body of research is concerned with collective violence (e.g., the Nazi Holocaust and the Mai Lai massacre). It is this literature that deals most with the legitimization of moral disengagement (e.g., Arendt, 1964; Ball-Rokeach, 1972; Bandura, 1990a; 1990b; Kelman & Hamilton, 1989); and, it is such disengagement that we argue is the root cause of sanctioned corporate corruption. Following the descriptions of the processes, the chapter closes with an exploration of the ways in which sanctioned corruption may be fought. These speculations focus on creating a climate for "functional disobedience."

SANCTIONING

In the fall of 1991, a federal grand jury indicted the Rockwell International Corporation on charges of over billing NASA for work done on the space shuttle program. The indictment contended that a particular manager instructed some employees to "fix the numbers" and to "soak the shuttle." If proven to be the case, the Rockwell manager's behavior could be interpreted as a direct order to employees to engage in a morally questionable practice, that is, as an explicit form of the official sanctioning of corporate corruption. Alternatively, the manager might have led his subordinates to over bill NASA without issuing a direct order, by creating a climate in which employees believed such acts were condoned or expected, if not explicitly encouraged by management. Ultimately, the employees may have believed that they would be rewarded for engaging in the behavior.

The case of the Leslie Fay Companies, which recently were rocked by an accounting scandal (Strom, 1993), provides an example of this implicit sanctioning. According to company insiders, Donald F. Kenia, (Leslie Fay's controller), made a practice of providing divisional controllers with quarterly or monthly figures for the profits their divisions were expected to show. Divisional controllers, in turn, juggled their numbers as necessary in order to meet these bottom-line figures. Although Kenia may not have issued explicit orders to doctor the books, it would not be surprising if divisional controllers got the message that such behavior was accepted, if not expected at Leslie Fay.

As Yeager (1986) pointed out, in such results-oriented environments "[t]he implicit message received from the top may be that much more weight is attached to job completion than to legal or ethical means of accomplishment" (p. 110). Such authorization is typified by an emphasis on ends and a disregard for means. Consider the explanation given by a cashier upon being discovered as an accomplice to embezzlement: "There is no doubt that I juggled the books, but I was under orders to balance the books *no matter what means*" (Passas, as cited in Cressey, 1953, p. ; see Clinard, 1983, for additional illustrations).

Thus, the difference between explicit and implicit sanctioning may be rather subtle. The literature on organizational climate (e.g., Kopelman, Brief, & Guzzo, 1990; Victor & Cullen, 1988) suggests a combination of factors that may lead employees to see management as condoning a corrupt practice. These factors are the setting of very high standards of performance, lavishly rewarding employees for meeting those standards or harshly punishing them for failing to do so, and, making it clear that management is disinterested in the methods, procedures, or other means employees use to accomplish the standards.

Regardless of the form of sanctioning, or its pervasiveness in a corporation, one is led to question why a manager would choose to order or encourage his or her subordinates to engage in a morally questionable practice. For an answer to this question, we look to the literatures on moral reasoning and ethical decision making. As will be shown, it is our position that it is unfair to label most managers who sanction corrupt practices as immoral individuals; rather, their decisions to sanction typically can be described as *amoral*.

Sanctioning as a Result of Amoral Reasoning

People can be thought of as engaging in moral reasoning when they are confronted with a decision that requires a choice between two or more important values (e.g., Kohlberg, 1976). For example, if a person holds dear both the values of "equality" and "a comfortable life" (Rokeach, 1968) and is confronted with the question "Should taxes be raised to aid the poor?", then it can be said the person's answer to this question is a product of moral reasoning (Tetlock, 1986). However, when the decision does not evoke conflicting value standards, then moral reasoning is not engaged. We believe that corporate officials experience little or no value conflict when deciding to sanction many morally questionable activities. The amoral reasoning that leads to the decision to sanction corrupt acts results from an adherence to an integrated value system that places corporate success above all other concerns.

The value system we see as supporting sanctioned corruption is one dominated by three interests—the self, the corporation, and the public. As McCoy (1985) described it, corporate officials have inherited the belief that the realization of these potentially incompatible values, in fact, can be achieved simultaneously by pursuing the interests of the corporation. That is, by managing to enhance the health of the corporation, self- and public interests also are served. Thus, corporate interests dominate in this mutually compatible set of evoked values.

The rise of self-, corporate, and public interests as a mutually compatible set of values widely held by America's corporate officials has been associated with the economic teachings of Adam Smith, the 18th century Scottish moral philosopher (e.g., Canterbery, 1976; Friedman & Friedman, 1979; McCoy, 1985). Representative of Smith's ideas is the concept of the "invisible hand" that leads individuals, in pursuit of their own interests, to promote, unintentionally but frequently, the interests of society. The entrepreneurs of the 18th century took this and other of Smith's ideas as justification for their complete freedom to pursue their self-interests, for by doing so, they not only benefitted themselves but also society at large.

These early capitalists, as well as their 20th century counterparts, often overlooked the fact that Smith wrote of the pursuit of self-interests *enlightened* by an altruistic conscience as a means of deterring undesirable social behaviors. This oversight is evident, for example, in Milton Friedman's assertion that "few trends could so thoroughly undermine the very foundations of our free society as the acceptance by corporate officials of a social responsibility other than to make as much money for their stockholders as possible" (1962, p. 9). Commenting on Friedman's position, McCoy (1985) observed Smith's views "are distorted and rendered incomprehensible when reduced to laissez-faire economic dogma" (p. 103). Scott and Hart (1989) argued that, by accepting the domination of corporate interests, managers have abandoned the obligations of moral autonomy. Thus, a subscription to the "organizational imperative," as Scott and Hart called it, may cause corporate officials to overlook some of the ethical implications of their business decisions. Following Kolberg (1976), these decisions are most appropriately characterized as arising from an amoral reasoning process.

Our emphasis on the amorality of corporate official reasoning in choosing to sanction a corrupt practice should not be taken as a failure to recognize alternative explanations. Explicit orders, implicit encouragement, or tacit approval of a corrupt practice, in fact, may be a product, for example, of ignorance or evil. We assume, however, that corporate officialdom is reflective of the larger society; and, we cannot accept the notion that society is largely sinful or wicked. Thus, the possibility remains that the sanctioning of corporate corruption is best viewed as an *amoral* act.[1]

Regardless of the underlying reasons for the official authorization of a corrupt practice, such sanctioning serves to define the situation so as to absolve lower organizational participants of the responsibility to make personal moral choices (Kelman & Hamilton, 1989). Later, we detail why this is so—why, for very different reasons, a subordinate's initial response to a superior's directive to engage in a corrupt practice may be as devoid of moral considerations as the superior's decision to issue the directive in the first place.

COMPLIANCE

When a group of Rockwell employees are told by their supervisor to "soak the shuttle," why might they comply? The answer to this question can be found in a diverse set of writings. For example, Hannah Arendt (1964), based on her philosophical observations of Eichmann's trial for his role in the Final Solution, wrote:

> [it is] the nature of every bureaucracy . . . to make functionaries and mere cogs in the administrative machinery out of men. . . . Eichmann acted fully within the framework of the kind of judgment required of him: He acted in accordance with the rule, examined the order issued to him for its "manifest" legality . . . he did not have to fall back upon his "conscience." (pp. 289, 293)

The research of psychologist Stanley Milgram (1974) provides another example of *obedience to authority*, the answer we see to the compliance question. Milgram, after observing his subjects' compliance with instructions to deliver an ostensibly harmful electric shock to another human being, wrote:

> Obedience does not take the form of a dramatic confrontation of opposed wills or philosophies but is embedded in a larger atmosphere where social relationships, career aspirations, and technical routines set the dominant tone. Typically, we do not find a heroic figure struggling with conscience, nor a pathologically aggressive man ruthlessly exploiting a position of power, but a functionary who has been given a job to do and who strives to create an impression of competence in his work. (p. 187)

---

[1]Employing reasoning different from ours, Gioia (1992), in analyzing the Ford Motor Company's decision to market the Pinto with a potentially lethal design flaw, reached a similar conclusion regarding the amoral nature of sanctioning.

We explore further Arendt's and Milgram's ideas suggesting that lower level participants in a corporation comply with an official authorization to engage in a corrupt practice largely and simply because the authorization is seen as legitimate. Before proceeding, however, two points need to be made.

First, we want to emphasize again that we are treating compliance as a group-level phenomenon. Even though one may attempt to explain it by evoking individual-level decision-making processes (as Hamilton & Sanders, 1992, have recently have done), "compliance" is defined here as the initial obedience of a collective of employees to an official authorization to engage in a corrupt practice.[2]

Second, we wish to acknowledge the parallels between the discussion that follows and one recently offered by Hamilton and Sanders (1992). These authors, in attempting to explain organizational crimes of obedience, employed various criticisms of classical models of rational choice to assert that corporate officials frame situations for subordinates so that they do not engage in the calculus of an individualistic, rational actor; rather, the subordinates are led to see these situations as not entailing a choice but as ones demanding the fulfillment of role requirements and obligations. This explanation for compliance is not inconsistent with the following one. As will be seen, however, our explanation is distinct, perhaps complimentary, emphasizing the effects of legitimate authority in corporate settings.

The Role of Legitimate Authority

To pursue further the role of authority in explaining the process of collective compliance, a definition of the construct is needed. For this, we principally draw from the early writings of Herbert Simon (1945). Simon asserted:

> "authority" may be defined as the power to make decisions which guide the actions of another. It is a relationship between two individuals, one "superior," the other "subordinate." The superior frames and transmits decisions with the expectation that they will be accepted by the subordinate. The subordinate expects such decisions, and his conduct is determined by them. (p. 125; Also, see Simon, 1951)

Following the lead of Tead (1929) and Stene (1940), Simon further differentiated authority from other kinds of influence by noting that subordinates hold in abeyance their own critical faculties for choosing between

---

[2]For alternative and broader views of compliance, see, for example, Cialdini (1993) and Pratkanis and Aronson (1992).

alternatives and use the formal criterion of the receipt of a command or signal as their basis for choice. Moreover, he recognized Friedrich's (1937) "rule of anticipated reactions" that implies subordinates may and are expected to ask themselves "How would my superior wish me to behave under these circumstances?" Thus, the implementation of authority requires no a priori command; and, therefore, Simon's description of authority refers to the consequences of both previously identified forms of sanctioning, implicit and explicit.

Although the previous paragraph addresses what is an "authority relation" (Dubin, 1958/1987), it is not concerned with when and why subordinates are obedient. There are numerous answers available to the "why" question. Milgram (1974), for example, provided a biological answer. He reasoned that a potential for obedience is the prerequisite for a social organization that enables a species to deal with its environment and maintain internal harmony. Given the enormous survival value of such an organization, a capacity for obedience to hierarchical authority is bred into the organism through the extended operation of evolutionary processes.

Other scholars have focused on subordinates' tendencies to view their superiors as legitimate authorities, and therefore deserving of unquestioning obedience. Following Kelman and Hamilton (1989), authority refers to an officeholder's claim that he or she has the right to give orders by virtue of his or her position and only becomes legitimate when his or her subordinates accept that claim. Often subordinates perceive the authority of their superiors as legitimate because superiors have the power at their disposal to punish disobedience. Some even treat such coercive power as a defining characteristic of legitimacy (Stinchcombe, 1968). But, other bases for legitimacy are readily identifiable.

Some of these other bases have been isolated by Dubin (1958/1987):

> The sense of legitimacy may rest on a belief in the need for order that results from the exercise of authority. It may also rest on a belief that the exercise of authority has some legal justification—that the decision maker is simply fulfilling his legal right in issuing orders. Finally, this sense of legitimacy may be grounded in a moral belief. For example the decision maker may be viewed as having a moral obligation to his employer, or to the company stockholders, to exercise authority in keeping the work organization going. (p. 35)

This latter reason identified by Dubin is consistent with the arguments advanced by Scott and Hart (1989) that hierarchical obedience is seen as necessary to enhance organizational health and such well-being is what gives rise to good for individuals and society.

Of course, obedience to authority has its limits, even when that authority is viewed as legitimate. For example, subordinates may be unable to obey because they do not understand an order, lack the ability to comply, or have received a countervailing order from an authority perceived as more legitimate (e.g., Barnard, 1938; Kelman & Hamilton, 1989). In addition, some orders may be so blatantly pernicious that a subordinate may be unable to accept them. To use the language of Barnard (1938), such orders would fall outside a subordinate's "zone of indifference."

How wide is the average subordinate's "zone of indifference?" Which orders will a subordinate find acceptable and which not? The current literature provides few answers to this crucial question. Barnard's answer is typical. He merely asserted that the greater the inducements offered the subordinate, the wider the range of orders that subordinate will find acceptable. Barnard reasoned that although personal considerations (e.g., personal values) influence a person's decision to accept or reject a job offer, once the offer is accepted, such considerations will not determine the content of the person's organizational behaviors; rather, those behaviors will be determined by the demands of efficiency.

Barnard's thinking is echoed in the observations of other scholars. For example, Simon (1945) asserted that "the employee sign[s] a blank check, so to speak in entering upon his employment" (p. 116). Thus, Simon viewed the behavior patterns of subordinates as being governed by the criterion to follow those behavior alternatives that are selected for them by their superiors. The motivation for using such a criterion of obedience he saw as "the price of retaining [a] position, securing a higher salary or other advantages" (p. 133). Similarly, Arendt (1978, p. 232) asserted that the employee, "For the sake of his pension, his life insurance, the security of his wife and children [is] prepared to do literally anything." Finally, consider the results of Hornstein's (1986) study of managerial courage. Hornstein found that, even among corporate officials, acceptance of one's boss's authority is the norm and, in part, also a product of financial considerations. His results show that managers who have children (and consequently face heavy financial burdens) are particularly unlikely to challenge their superiors on any issue.

Although many contemporary organizational scholars seek to explain variance in the organizational behaviors of individuals, the previous arguments suggest initial reactions of subordinates to a superior's authorization to engage in a corrupt practice may be invariant, with subordinates collectively complying under many, if not most, conditions. The reason offered for such compliance was that the legitimate authority of hierarchically superior corporate officials creates a high potential for obedience across subordinates to "orders" regarding their understood job duties. Berkowitz (1983), in reviewing the social psychology literature on compliance, concluded, "Probably more than any other factor, *collective approval*—the agreement of the group members—legitimates the pattern of dominance and subordination in the group" (p. 180).

Thus, as we previously noted, obedience is not a result of "a heroic figure struggling with conscience" (Milgram, 1974, p. 187); rather, it is a group-level phenomenon that is a product of legitimate authority. It is inappropriate, therefore, to view a subordinate's initial reaction to a superior's authorization of a corrupt practice as the consequence of a moral reasoning process in which the subordinate deliberately considers the ethical implications of the sanctioned behavior.

Division of Labor and Moral Disengagement

Thus far, we have focused on legitimate authority as a factor promoting initial collective compliance. However, there are other characteristics of organizations that can contribute to initial compliance, such as the division of labor within an organization. We suggest (as have others) that the division of a task into many discrete subtasks has the effect of limiting the discretion of subordinates. As Kelman (1973) stated:

> Not only does this arrangement result in a diffusion of responsibility, but it reduces the amount and limits the scope of decision making that is necessary. . . . At each point, the only decisions that generally have to be made are operational ones. *There is no expectation that the moral implications will be considered at any of these points, nor is there any opportunity to do so.* (p. 47, italics added)

It is clear that, under such circumstances, initial collective compliance can be viewed as almost automatic. The following section of this chapter explores similar arrangements that contribute not only to initial compliance, but also to ongoing corporate corruption. In discussing this process, we show further the amoral nature of collective participation in corrupt practices.

INSTITUTIONALIZATION

Our analysis to this point has been restricted to single, initial acts of compliance on the part of an organizational collective. Yet, history is replete with examples of collective wrongdoing that take the form of protracted, repetitive cycles of routinized activity (or inactivity), the impact of which, although sometimes delayed or gradual, is cumulative and nonetheless devastating (e.g., the Nazi Holocaust, the Challenger disaster, etc.). Business organizations are by no means immune to this phenomenon. As Clinard and Quinney (1973) noted over two decades ago, ". . . the nation's leading corporations are committing destructive acts against man and nature. Specifically, all of this is being done systematically and repeatedly, rather than randomly and occasionally. The crimes are being committed *as a standard operating procedure*" (p. 212, italics added).

How do such insidious cycles of routinized wrongdoing come into being? Why do they continue? In the sections that follow, we describe several mechanisms by which initial acts of collective compliance, rather than remaining single, isolated incidents, may become woven into the fabric of everyday organizational life.

When Functional Rationality Is King

One circumstance under which collective wrongdoing may become institutionalized is when the members of the offending organization simply persist in their adherence to directives that, on their surface, carry no obvious moral or ethical implications. Consistent with Kelman's (1973) view, Bandura (1990b) observed that

> most enterprises require the services of many people, each performing fragmentary jobs that seem harmless in themselves. The fractional contribution is easily isolated from the eventual function, especially when participants exercise little personal judgement in carrying out a subfunction that is related by remote, complex links to the end result. (p. 36)

Bandura went on to note that, after activities have been assigned to such programmed subfunctions, attention shifts from the meaning of what one is doing to the details of the job at hand. That is, the practice becomes routinized, a product of habitual or mechanical engagement. Attention to the details of the job and wanting to look good to one's superiors drives the employee further and further away from any potential moral consideration of the consequences of his or her actions.

An example of this can be found in the case of Fawn Hall who, in 1987, testified before a congressional committee regarding her role in the Iran-Contra affair. In her testimony, Hall admitted to altering and destroying official government documents at the direction of her superior, Oliver North. Hamilton and Sanders (1992) described the proceedings as follows:

> [Hall] provided illustrations of the way in which illegal actions become routinized and integrated into one's daily work. When asked whether she realized the significance of altering official documents, she replied, "That was my job, and I wasn't reading or trying to find out what his [North's] motives were or what he was trying to hide." And in response to a question probing her awareness of the nature of the documents she was shredding, Hall responded, "I really didn't notice, sir. *I was just purely doing my job*." (p. 51, italics added)

Another illustration of this phenomenon can be found in Denny Gioia's (1992) description of his experience as Field Recall Coordinator for the Ford Motor Company. As Recall Coordinator, Gioia's responsibilities included the collection and analysis of information regarding possible problems with Ford vehicles, information critical to making responsible decisions regarding the necessity of vehicle recall. Gioia recalled opening several new files shortly after his tenure as Recall Coordinator began:

> One of these new files concerned reports of Pintos "lighting up" (in the words of a field representative) in rear-end accidents. There were actually very few reports. . . . Was there a problem? Not as far as I was concerned. *My cue for labeling a case as a problem either required high frequencies of occurrence or directly-traceable causes.* I had little time for speculative contemplation on potential problems *that did not fit a pattern that suggested known courses of action* leading to possible recall. (pp. 381–382, italics added)

Later, after having viewed first-hand the crumpled, burned remains of a Pinto at a Ford recall station, Gioia called for a department-level review of the Pinto case. According to Gioia:

> [A]fter the usual round of discussion about criteria and justification for recall, everyone voted against recommending recall—including me. *It did not fit the pattern of recallable standards.* . . . *It was a good business decision, even if people might be dying.* (1992, p. 382, italics added)

Both Hall's and Gioia's descriptions support the argument that organizational inhabitants tend to act as functionaries, intent on fulfilling their roles and adhering to the rules associated with those roles. This is consistent with the views of numerous authors (e.g., Alford, 1990; Bandura, 1990a, 1990b; Hall, 1977; Jackall, 1988; Kelman, 1973; Kelman & Hamilton, 1989) who argued that, under conditions of highly standardized, highly routinized work, attention narrows on what earlier organizational theorists (e.g., Mannheim, 1940; Weber, 1922/1978) called "formal" or "functional" rationality. Moreover, under these conditions, a focus on rule adherence and effective task performance often is associated with ignoring the ethical implications of one's actions. As Jackall (1988) stated, "In bureaucratic settings, which are institutionalized paradigms of functional rationality, technique and procedure tend to become ascendant over substantive reflection about organizational goals . . . one person's hysteria and cause for moral outrage [becomes] another's familiar and somewhat dull routine" (pp. 76, 194).

Thus, in an organization where work roles are narrowly defined and highly standardized, there exists the potential for the mindless, mechanized production of wrongdoing on a grand scale. Darley offered the following vivid description of the process as it unfolded during the Nazi Holocaust:

> When death, like cars or chairs, is produced on assembly lines, each individual eventually concentrates on the microrequirements of his or her part of the process; the eventual outcome is rarely thought of. A group of police in a city round up the Jews and take them to a stadium. Later an army contingent takes them to the boxcars. A railroad worker throws the switches that bring the train to one or another subdestination on the way to the concentration camp. The fact of the eventual deaths is so remote that no participant finds it salient. Each person doing a subtask does so in a routinized way; it is only the final assembly of those subtasks that is horrible, and no individual "sees" that final solution. (p. 210)

Darley's chilling portrait of collective iniquity is consistent with our portrayal of corporate corruption as a product of amoral reasoning. Is it plausible, however, to assert that the ultimate effects of organizational wrongdoing invariably will be cloaked in a web of apparently banal functions and routines? Although it may be plausible to suggest a railroad worker continued a role in the Final Solution out of ignorance of its ultimate consequences, clearly such a claim cannot be made for the concentration camp executioner. More generally, we believe members of corrupt organizations sometimes are *not* blinded by the segmented, routine nature of tasks and *do* see the consequences of their actions.

Such conscious malfeasance is illustrated in accounts of standard operating procedures employed with the intent of excluding certain categories of people from the internal environment of an organization. According to one recently filed class-action complaint, employees of the Holiday Spa health-club chain were instructed to engage in racially discriminatory practices such as "offering prospective black members only the highest-priced membership options, identifying prospective black customers in spa records with codes, such as DNWAM ('Do Not Want As Member'), and denying or giving only cursory tours of the facilities to blacks" (Abramson & Lambert, 1989). Plaintiffs alleged that such discriminatory policies were in place at Holiday Spas in Atlanta, Baltimore, Boston, Philadelphia, and Washington, DC. Obviously, employees who engaged in these appalling and surprisingly formalized practices must have been aware of the inequities engendered by their actions.

Thus, it is apparent that ongoing collective wrongdoing is possible, even when the members of the collective possess knowledge of the actual or potential consequences of their behaviors. Although rules and routines may help to distract people from the ethical implications of their actions, we argue that additional forces often come into play, forces that support organizational inhabitants repeating their morally questionable behaviors. Consistent with social constructionist theory, (e.g., Berger & Luckmann, 1967; Salancik & Pfeffer, 1978), we argue that blatant wrongdoing can become institutionalized through the *collective interpretation* of "ethically loaded" activities. Such a socially constructed reality provides an interpretation of wrongdoing that justifies, in the minds of organizational members, its continuation. These members, thereby, become participants in a moral microcosm that likely could not survive outside the organization. This idea is consistent with Jackall's (1988) observation that people are capable of relying on one set of ethical standards in the workplace and a wholly inconsistent set when away from work, thereby segmenting their moral lives.[3] In the following section we explore somewhat further how moral microcosms within organizations become socially constructed.

The Emergence of a Culture for Ethical Deviance

A number of theorists (e.g., Baucus, 1989, 1994; Darley, 1992; Finney & Lesieur, 1982; Kramer, 1982; Sutherland, 1949/1983) have noted the likelihood that a deviant ethical culture will emerge in an organization where wrongdoing is commonplace; a culture that supports continued wrongdoing on the part of the collective. As Baucus (1994) suggested,

> once employees engage in illegal activities, deviant norms and values develop around such behavior, and wrongdoing becomes part of the firm's culture. . . . Corporate culture may encourage illegality by creating conditions that predispose employees to commit wrongdoing. Shared values, norms, and beliefs can influence an otherwise moral individual to engage in questionable or illegal activities. Industry and corporate culture also perpetuates illegality, reinforcing wrongdoing, and resulting in repeated violations. (pp. 711–712)

Under such conditions, behaviors that might easily be defined as noxious by an outsider may be redefined as harmless or even desirable by those imbedded within the culture for deviance.

An example of such reframing of reality can be found in Sutherland's (1983) seminal work on white-collar crime. Sutherland reported the dismay experienced by a newcomer upon his initial exposure to the fraudulent practices common in the used-car business. In the words of the new insider:

> The thing that struck me as strange was that all these people were proud of their ability to fleece customers. They boasted of their crookedness and were admired by their friends and enemies in proportion to their ability to get away with a crooked deal: It was called shrewdness. (p. 243)

---

[3]See also Welch's (1994) discussion of how individuals separate their personal agendas from the organization's agenda.

Such recasting of unethical behavior in a more favorable light can be accomplished in a variety of ways. For example, all manner of organizations engage in what Bandura (1990a, 1990b) called "euphemistic labeling"; the use of emotionally sterile or positively valenced terminology to describe morally troublesome activities or events. As Jackall (1988) described it:

> [I]n the textile industry, cotton dust becomes an "air-borne particulate" and byssinosis or brown lung a "symptom complex." In the chemical industry, spewing highly toxic hydrogen fluoride into a neighboring community's air is characterized as a "release beyond the fence line." The nuclear power industry, . . . is, of course, a wonderland of euphemisms. For example, the "incident" at Three Mile Island in March 1979 was variously called an "abnormal evolution" or, perhaps better, a "plant transient." (p. 136)

According to Bandura, the application of such hygienic language "provides a convenient device for masking reprehensible activities or even conferring a respectable status upon them. Through convoluted verbiage, destructive conduct is made benign and those who engage in it are relieved of a sense of personal agency" (1990b, p. 31).[4] Thus, euphemistic labeling likely will have an impact on the meanings organizational inhabitants assign to ethically ambiguous behavior, thereby perpetuating a collective culture tolerant of pernicious activity.

In addition to the use of euphemistic labeling, a culture for ethical deviance may be encouraged when members of the organization offer elaborate rationales or justifications for untoward behavior within the group. Consider the remarks offered by Ray Danner, the Chief Executive Officer of Shoney's, in response to charges that he promoted discriminatory employment practices in the restaurant chain. "In looking for anything to identify why is this unit under-performing," Danner said, "in some cases, I would have probably said that this is a neighborhood of predominantly white neighbors, and we have a considerable amount of black employees and this might be a problem" (Watkins, 1993, p. 427). The implicit endorsement of racial discrimination inherent in this statement appears to have been lost on Danner. Instead, from the perspective of the restaurateur, considering race when making employment decisions is completely justified as a "business necessity." No doubt statements such as this are seized upon by the members of corrupt organizations as means for "making sense" of their continued compliance with pernicious directives.[5]

---

[4]See Diener, Dineen, Endresen, Beaman, and Fraser (1975) for laboratory evidence in support of this assertion.

[5]For more on the effects of business justifications on promoting organizational wrongdoing, see Buttram, Brief, Elliott, Reizenstein, and McCline (1994) and Reizenstein and Brief (1995).

Finally, organization-wide tolerance of harmful acts may be promoted by depictions of the victims of wrongdoing as unworthy of compassion, if not worthy of their fate. Bandura and his colleagues argued (e.g., Bandura, 1990a, 1990b) and demonstrated (Bandura, Underwood, & Fromson, 1975) that normal inhibitions against aggression and injurious behavior are dramatically reduced when the potential victims are psychologically divested of their human qualities. One of the most ghastly examples of such "dehumanization" emerges from Lifton's (1986) analysis of the psychological states experienced by doctors involved in the extermination of the Jews in Nazi Germany. According to Lifton, one Nazi doctor justified his role in this way: "My Hippocratic oath tells me to cut a gangrenous appendix out of the human body. The Jews are the gangrenous appendix of mankind. That's why I cut them out" (Lifton, 1986, p. 232).

Similar, but obviously less ghastly, examples of dehumanization and denigration are contained in accounts of wrongdoing in business organizations. For example, during his investigation of alleged racial discrimination at Shoney's restaurants, attorney Tommy Warren learned that job applications submitted by Black applicants were routinely coded with an "A" standing for "Ape" (Watkins, 1993). Likewise, recent allegations of employment discrimination brought against the Olde Discount Corporation, (a Detroit-based brokerage firm), indicate that managers in this company openly used derogatory terms such as "broads" and "monkeys" to refer to women and Blacks respectively (Antilla, 1995). The extent to which such conceptions permeate an organization's culture surely has implications for the degree of harm done *and* for the tendency for such harmdoing to persist.

Of course, dehumanization need not take such a blatant and derogatory form. Let us return briefly to the Ford Pinto case described earlier. One of the more startling revelations surrounding the case involved the methods used by Ford executives to reach a conclusion regarding the necessity of improving the safety of the Pinto's fuel tank (Dowie, 1977; Gioia, 1992). Specifically, Ford officials undertook a cost-benefit analysis wherein the cost of redesign ($11 per vehicle times 12,500,000 vehicles) was compared to the estimated savings that would accrue from preventing 180 deaths, (each valued at $200,000), 180 burn injuries, (each valued at $67,000), and 2,100 burned cars, (each valued at $700). It was precisely on this callous calculus that Ford officials based their decision *not* to institute a production fix (Gioia, 1992).

The preceding illustration reminds us of Kelman's observation that "[t]hose who participate as part of the bureaucratic apparatus increasingly come to see their victims as bodies to count and enter into their reports, as faceless figures that will determine their productivity rates and promotions" (1973, p. 50). The Pinto case clearly illustrates how the conversion of human beings into "faceless figures" can contribute to the institutionalization of a

morally troublesome decision process. At Ford, people became cost esti-
mates.

Creating the Evil Automaton

A passage from Sutherland's (1983) analysis of white-collar crime nicely
summarizes the institutionalization process as we have described it thus far:

> As a part of the process of learning practical business, a young man with ide-
> alism and thoughtfulness for others is inducted into white collar crime. In
> many cases he is ordered by managers to do things which he regards as
> unethical or illegal, while in other cases he learns from those who have the
> same rank as his own how they make a success. He learns specific techniques
> of violating the law, together with definitions of situations in which those
> techniques may be used. Also, he develops a general ideology. This ideolo-
> gy grows in part out of the specific practices and is in the nature of gener-
> alization from concrete experiences, but in part it is transmitted as a gener-
> alization by phrases such as "We are not in business for our health,"
> "Business is business," and "No business was ever built on beatitudes."
> These generalizations, whether transmitted as such or constructed from
> concrete practices, assist the neophyte in business to accept the illegal prac-
> tices and provide rationalizations for them. (p. 245)

Implicit in Sutherland's description, (and as yet underemphasized in
our discussion), is the notion that institutionalized wrongdoing may perpetuate itself, more or less automatically, as a by-product of the socialization process in organizations. That this might happen can be explained in
terms of what we know about the binding nature of behavioral commitment (see, for example, Darley, 1992; Kelman, 1973; and Staub, 1989).

First, consider the likelihood that a newcomer to a corrupt organization
will engage in some initial act of wrongdoing, however minor (e.g., misleading a customer as to the terms of a warranty.) This act may represent an
unthinking response to the request of a superior or a deliberate response to
conformity pressures brought to bear by peers and associates (see Berkowitz,
1983). The damaging consequences of the act might not be fully recognized
until after the fact. Once these consequences have been recognized, however, a progressive social psychological process is initiated, a process that will
tend to propel the newcomer in the direction of accepting and perhaps even
embracing the ideology (i.e., values and beliefs) that sustains ethical
deviance within the organization. As Kelman (1973) described the process:

> [once the newcomer] has taken the initial step, he is in a new psychological and
> social situation in which the pressures to continue are quite powerful. . . . Many
> forces that might originally have kept him out of the situation reverse direction
> once he has made a commitment . . . and now help to keep him in the situa-

tion. For example, concern about the criminal nature of the action, which might originally have inhibited him from becoming involved, may now lead to deeper involvement in efforts to justify the action and to avoid negative consequences. (p. 46)

The notion that novice wrongdoers will be confronted with "pressures to persist" is consistent with a body of research on the escalation of commitment (e.g., Brockner & Rubin, 1985; Staw, 1981). This research demonstrates that decision makers who commit themselves to a course of action tend to add resources in support of that action in suboptimal ways in order to justify their initial decision. They throw "good" money after "bad." Thus, people may tend to repeat their participation in corrupt practices simply to demonstrate to others (and to themselves) that their initial involvement was legitimate.

Such self-justification mechanisms are critical to our conception of the socialization process in corrupt organizations. If we assume that the newcomer is aware that he or she has committed a wrong *and* (as virtually all of us do), seeks to maintain a positive self-image, then this newcomer will likely cast about for something that will allow him or her to justify the wrongdoing. In an organization with a well-developed culture for ethical deviance, that justifying "something" will be the culture itself—those socially constructed values and beliefs that collectively define reality for members of the organization. Importantly (and consistent with dissonance theory, Festinger, 1957; Festinger & Carlsmith, 1959), we assert our newcomer will *internalize* these values and beliefs in an attempt to maintain consistency between his or her attitudes and behaviors.[6] Through this process of internalization, new inhabitants of corrupt organizations themselves become corrupt, thus perpetuating a culture for ethical deviance and the wrongdoings this culture has produced.

Some readers may wish to argue with our assertion that engaging in morally questionable behaviors will arouse dissonance and produce attitude change among the members of a complex organization. They might point, for example, to findings showing that dissonance arousal and associated attitude change are minimal under conditions where coercive pressure is applied to induce behavior inconsistent with attitudes (see Cooper & Fazio, 1984; Festinger & Carlsmith, 1959). It may be argued that the inhabitants of an organization, (and, in particular, an employing organization) are limited in their discretion with respect to the behaviors in which they engage. Thus, these limits on discretion may eliminate the need to reconcile discrepancies between organizational behaviors and personal attitudes.

---

[6]See Kelman (1958) on the distinctions among compliance, identification, and internalization.

We propose a counterargument. First, following the lead of Simon (1945), we believe that, within limits, people can be viewed as choosing whether or not to accept a job offer and, correspondingly, the role requirements and obligations that go along with it.[7] Second, we believe, consistent with much theorizing elsewhere (e.g., Goffman, 1967; Henslin, 1967; Langer, 1975; Taylor & Brown, 1988), that people possess a strong functional tendency to view themselves as in control of their own lives, as confronting options, and as making choices. Thus, subordinates will tend to view their organizational behaviors not as acts of compliance, but as reflections of their own choice processes. They will view themselves as independent actors, not as mere pawns in the workplace.

These arguments are consistent with Staub's (1989) observations concerning the link between behavior and moral reasoning. Staub asserted that

> even if initially there is some external pressure, it often becomes difficult to experience regular participation in an activity as alien. People begin to see their engagement in the activity as part of themselves. . . . People come to see themselves as agents and begin to consider and elaborate on the reasons for their actions. . . . If there is harm to others, progressively the victims' well-being and even lives will lose value in their eyes. In other words, people observe their own actions and draw inferences, both about those affected by them and about themselves. . . . Further actions consistent with their changing views of themselves become likely. (p. 80)

More forceful is Darley's (1992) account of the production of evildoers in corrupt organizations. According to Darley,

> the essence of the process involves causing individuals, under pressure, to take small steps along a continuum that ends with evildoing. Each step is so small as to be essentially continuous with previous ones; after each step, the individual is positioned to take the next one. *The individual's morality follows rather than leads.* Morality is retrospectively fitted to previous acts by rationalizations involving "higher goods," "regrettable necessities," and other rationalizations. . . . One way of characterizing these mental adjustments is as a neutralization or even a positive valuation of actions that are generally regarded as morally reprehensible. This tells us how the person will continue to act vis-a-vis those actions. *That individual will autonomously and independently continue to harm others.* (pp. 208, 210, italics added)

The implications of Darley's account are obvious and frightening: Once a newcomer has been successfully initiated into a deviant ethical culture,

---

[7]Our use of the phrase "within limits" recognizes that some individuals, because of the financial pressures they experience, may not feel they freely chose their jobs (e.g., Doran, Stone, Brief, & George, 1991).

he or she possesses the capacity for autonomous wrongdoing. There is no need for elaborate monitoring and control (Eisenhardt, 1989; Williamson, 1975) to insure continued compliance by the collective, for the members of the collective offer no ethical objection to the corrupt organizational practices. Rather, in the context of institutionalized wrongdoing, the organization becomes populated with wrongdoing automatons, each of whom adds a quantum of momentum to the plodding machine that is the corrupt organization.

In the preceding pages, we described how collective wrongdoing may become institutionalized. We argued that an emphasis on functional rationality may promote mindless obedience on a large scale and over an extended period of time. We also described how a culture for ethical deviance may emerge wherein morally questionable behavior is reframed or reinterpreted in more sanitary terms. Finally, we asserted that the socialization process in corrupt corporations has the capacity to produce inherently corrupt individuals, thereby perpetuating organizational wrongdoing. In the concluding section of this chapter we suggest approaches for hindering such collective wrongdoing.

HINDERING COLLECTIVE WRONGDOING

The preceding sections of this chapter were disturbing, both to research and to write. We hope they have been disturbing to read as well. If they have, then the reader may recognize, as we have, the similarities among the organizational machinery of the Holocaust, firms engaging in collective wrongdoing, *and* economically effective business organizations. We contend that the most troublesome of these similarities is an obedient workforce. Without a workforce ready, willing, and able to follow directives from above, the Holocaust could not have occurred, firms could not engage in collective wrongdoing, and, no business could survive in the marketplace. Regarding this last assertion, Katz (1964) and others observed that organizational survival is dependent on employees reliably performing their assigned roles, doing what management expects of them. Thus, one possible solution to collective wrongdoing in the corporate world is to encourage disobedience; however, this medicine, if not carefully administered and monitored, could kill the patient, the business enterprise. It is to this dilemma that we principally turn in considering the prevention of collective wrongdoing.

Not only is the substantive content of this section different from what has preceded, so is its flavor. Whereas our message thus far has been pessimistic, we now intend to share our, albeit constrained, optimism that the emergence of collective wrongdoing in corporations can be hindered. Moreover, whereas our previous analysis has been descriptive, we now shift to a more prescriptive mode. Our prescriptivelike statements, however, should not be taken as recommended courses of managerial action; rather, they most appropriately are viewed as propositions suggestive of potential interventions.[8]

A "Lesson" From Social Psychology

We have been concerned with the compliance of a collective to a directive from above to do wrong. Organizational members who openly question or otherwise attempt to resist such directives are likely to be in the minority. Can such a relatively small group, (perhaps even a lone dissenter), turn an organization away from wrongdoing? Considerable social psychological evidence suggests this might be possible (e.g., Berkowitz, 1983; Wolfe, 1985).

Minorities have been found to exert influence on majorities if the following conditions are met (Baron & Byrne, 1991; Moscovici, 1985): First, the dissenters must not waffle in their opposition; they must be consistent. However, the dissenters also must avoid appearing rigid or dogmatic. Finally, to the degree that the dissenters can frame their opposition as consistent with current social trends (e.g., as conservative at a time of growing conservatism), they will be more successful in their attempts to sway the majority, assuming their beliefs and attitudes are seen as generally in-line with those of majority group members.

As we will see, the above conditions in no way guarantee that the dissenters, in fact, will be able to sway the organization away from doing wrong. But, minority resistance per se can be functional. It can cause members of the majority to think more about the directive in question; and, such thinking may lead some to consider previously unrecognized moral implications of their actions (Nemeth, 1986).[9]

The problem with the social psychological literature on minority influence is that it does not attend to the realities of organizational life portrayed in the previous sections of this chapter. The open questioning of directives from above and other forms of resistance are unlikely to be tolerated in many modern organizations. Denise Perryman, a former waitress for the Denny's restaurant chain, learned this the hard way. Black customers, according to plaintiff's attorneys, were forced to pay in advance at as many as 150 to 200 Denny's restaurants in California, Florida, Illinois, Maryland, Ohio, Oklahoma, and Oregon (Kohn, 1994). When Perryman disobeyed the order to collect from Black customers in advance, she was fired.

Thus, it is a fallacy to place the burden of preventing collective wrongdoing solely on the shoulders of organizational dissenters. They may not

---

[8]For more on this distinction, see Brief and Dukerich (1991).
[9]For more on the benefits of dissent in organizations, see Nemeth and Staw (1989).

surface; and, if they do, they likely will not succeed (e.g., Near & Miceli, 1995). The organization itself, its structure, roles, and norms, must be altered before such principled dissent (Graham, 1986) can be expected to operate. Thus, the organization must be the focus of attempts to hinder collective wrongdoing. We now turn to this focus.

Changing Organizations

Managers and scholars alike have given very little attention to promoting *disobedience* among organizational members. Rather, they have devoted a tremendous amount of energy to understanding how to promote compliance through such mechanisms as goal setting, performance appraisal/feedback, and incentive compensation. Again, this devotion to compliance is understandable, for organizational survival is dependent on members dependably performing their assigned roles—on doing what they are told to do (Katz, 1964). Thus, much of what we have to say about promoting disobedience is highly speculative. Moreover, our speculations are limited to a certain type of noncompliance that we call "functional disobedience." Functional disobedience is a response to explicit or implicit instructions from above that are interpreted as requiring one to engage in some unsavory practice. Minimally, this response entails openly questioning the legitimacy of the interpreted instructions. Such questioning might lead to discussions with the authority figure thought to have issued the orders and/or to acts of insubordination.

Structure, Roles, and Norms.   Building on the ideas of Kelman and Hamilton (1989) and Brief et al.'s (1995) translation of them, we envision an organization out of the ordinary; one that could promote functional disobedience. In combination, the structure, roles, and norms characteristic of this organization would be different than those of most firms.

Structurally, authority in the organization should be dispersed. By dispersed authority, we do not mean decentralized authority, whereby decision making is delegated down the hierarchy to particular individuals or groups for specific issues. Although decentralization is not incompatible with dispersion, it is not synonymous.

Dispersed authority is somewhat akin to the checks and balances built into the Constitution of the United States. It entails the approval of organizational policies, practices, and procedures by two or more independent parties. For example, in an attempt to avoid discriminatory personnel practices, the methods and procedures used for making hiring and promotion decisions would require approval of such decisions by both a line and a human resources executive. Such dispersion of authority at least opens the door for lower level participants to question directives received from one party by giving them the opportunity to appeal to the other. Dispersion of authority may be less efficient than locating a decision with one all power-ful manager; but, as we have shown, such a concentration of authority can be hazardous.

Let us now turn to the issue of roles. As we have already suggested, the roles of organizational members traditionally have involved being "loyal"; and, often this loyalty has been defined as servitude to one's boss (e.g., Jackall, 1988). Redefining the role of the loyal organizational member to encompass faithfulness not only to the organization but also to its various stakeholders (e.g., its customers) provides a broader basis for judging the ethical implications of one's actions than exists when one enacts the role of "dutiful underling." Policies and practices that "put the customer first" (e.g., Saturn Corporation's recent owner "homecomings") may help organizational members to consider their obligations to others, and may cause them to disobey orders from above that are in conflict with the welfare of various organizational stakeholders. This is consistent with Kelman's (1973) speculation that the individualization of potential victims, (in our case customers, stockholders, and other stakeholders), may serve to activate moral restraints against violent or harmful behavior.[10]

What about norms? Particularly among managers, the norm in many organizations is to display support for instructions from above; individual concerns with those directives remain unspoken (see Janis, 1972). Alternatively, a norm of honest and open discourse among peers supports the critical discussion of instructions from above, thereby facilitating the articulation of misgivings, the reinforcement of doubts, and analyses of how to respond. The social psychological literature on conformity and compliance is clear; there is strength in numbers (e.g., Berkowitz, 1983). Without a norm supportive of peer discourse, those who are troubled by the course of organizational events probably will not discover like-minded others and likely will go along obediently with the group. Although norms are attributes of groups (e.g., Hackman, 1992), a group's processes and outcomes are sensitive to the organizational context in which it is embedded (e.g., Guzzo & Shea, 1992). Thus, a norm of honest and open discourse among peers can be encouraged at the level of the organization (see Janis, 1972, and Harvey, 1974). We suggest methods for accomplishing this in the following paragraphs.

Creating a Climate for Functional Disobedience. Recall, we noted that it is the simultaneous combination of dispersed authority, broad definitions of loyalty, and norms supportive of peer discourse that is character-

---

[10]Staw and Boettger (1990) also provided some empirical support for this, demonstrating that accountability pressures associated with a role can lead people to revise their tasks at work.

istic of the extraordinary organization capable of cultivating functional disobedience. A single tactic (e.g., broadening the definition of a loyal employee) is unlikely to work. The forces that exist in most modern organizations to maintain obedience are multiple and self-reinforcing, and will likely overpower any single-faceted attempt to encourage dissent.[11]

Thus, a systemic approach must be taken in order to foster functional disobedience. This argument is consistent with the literature on organizational climate (e.g., Schneider, Brief, & Guzzo, in press; Schneider, Guzzo, & Brief, 1992) that tells us that a combination of factors is necessary to create what Schneider and Rentsch (1988) called a "sense of the imperative." In the current case, that imperative is to do no wrong. In addition to the three factors already described, (i.e., dispersed authority, loyalty broadly defined, and norms of open discourse), the climate literature (Schneider et al., in press) points to additional facets of organizations that are likely to require attention if an imperative to do no wrong is to be realized. These facets include goal emphasis, means emphasis, reward orientation, task support, and socioemotional support (Kopelman et al., 1990).

If an organization is to promote functional disobedience effectively, then the goal of disobeying morally questionable orders must be emphasized by management, methods and procedures for accomplishing this goal must be visibly in place, employees must be rewarded for functional disobedience, support (e.g., training) for accomplishing this goal must be readily available, and, employees generally must feel their personal welfare is protected by management. How to formulate and implement each of these changes clearly is beyond the scope of this chapter. But, there are some clues available about how to proceed.

For instance, to establish support for accomplishing the functional disobedience goal, Gioia (1992) recommended training people to engage in "script-breaking" when they encounter task cues that have ethical overtones. The idea is to sensitize people to tasks that demand moral reasoning rather than the presumably rational application of organizational routines. In this way, according to Gioia, work scripts can become equipped with decision nodes that tell the actor "now think." Such training may be essential for individuals to see the ethical implications of the tasks they are asked to perform. Jones (1991) made a similar argument, noting that the moral intensity of an issue needs to be recognized before moral reasoning and moral behavior are engaged.

Of course, organizational members are unlikely to persist in script breaking if they find it unrewarding to do so. As Darley (1994) pointed out, a subordinate who engages in functional disobedience, (or, as Darley called it,

---

[11]See Clinard (1983) for descriptions of the near intractability of institutionalized corporate wrongdoing.

"constructive" or "creative disobedience"), and who is "called on the carpet" for having done so, is unlikely to engage in further disobedience. Rather, this individual, assuming he or she remains in the organization, is likely to obey orders literally and even reflexively in the future. The subordinate who receives managerial support for his or her functional disobedience, on the other hand, can be expected to engage in further disobedience should legal or ethical standards dictate.

Remember, the organizational climate literature tells us that *all* of the ingredients specified (i.e., goal emphasis, means emphasis, reward orientation, etc.) must be present in order to create in the minds of organizational members the belief that functional disobedience is a valued behavior; without this belief, dissent will be a very low base-rate phenomenon. Moreover, and again in line with Kelman and Hamilton (1989), we believe the other facets of an organization's structure, roles, and norms described earlier are important too. If these do not occur simultaneously with a change in climate, functional disobedience is unlikely. To do everything we have suggested, and to do it right, is a monumental challenge. But, not to try, with deeds rather than words, is to accept a high risk for collective wrongdoing, because the forces supportive of blind obedience are inherent in all organizations.

CONCLUDING THOUGHTS

We have covered much territory, some of which has been mapped previously—some not. Much of the scenery was not pretty, some of it even ugly. But ugliness is a fact of organizational life. By admitting this fact, however, we do not accept it as unalterable. We, as organizational scholars, have much to contribute to beautifying the landscape. We sincerely hope that this chapter, at least in some small way, has encouraged you to dig in and help with the effort.

REFERENCES

Abramson, J., & Lambert, W. (1989, November 14). Bally unit's spas face new bias charges. *The Wall Street Journal*, p. B5.

Alford, C. F. (1990). The organization of evil. *Political Psychology, 11*, 5–27.

Antilla, S. (1995, April 26). Young white men only, please. *The New York Times*, pp. C1, C3.

Arendt, H. (1964). *Eichmann in Jerusalem*. New York: Penguin.

Arendt, H. (1978). *The Jew as pariah*. New York: Grove Press.

Ball-Rokeach, S. J. (1972). The legitimization of violence. In J. F. Short, Jr., & M. E. Wolfgang (Eds.), *Collective violence* (pp. 101–111). Chicago: Atherton.

Bandura, A. (1990a). Mechanisms of moral disengagement. In W. Reich (Ed.), *Origins of terrorism: Psychologies, ideologies, theologies, states of mind* (pp. 161–191). Cambridge, England: Cambridge University Press.

Bandura, A. (1990b). Selective activation and disengagement of moral control. *The Journal of Social Issues, 46*, 27–46.

Bandura, A., Underwood, B., & Fromson, M. E. (1975). Disinhibition of aggression through diffusion of responsibility and dehumanization of victims. *Journal of Research in Personality, 9*, 253–269.

Barnard, C. I. (1938). *The functions of the executive*. Cambridge, MA: Harvard University Press.

Baron, R. A., & Byrne, D. (1991). *Social psychology*. Boston: Allyn & Bacon.

Baucus, M. S. (1989). Why firms do it and what happens to them: A reexamination of the theory of illegal corporate behavior. In L. E. Preston (Ed.), *Research in corporate social performance and policy* (Vol. 11, pp. 93–118). Greenwich, CT: JAI.

Baucus, M. S. (1994). Pressure, opportunity and predisposition: A multivariate model of corporate illegality. *Journal of Management, 20*, 699–721.

Berger, P. L., & Luckmann, T. (1967). *The social construction of reality*. Garden City, NY: Anchor.

Berkowitz, L. (1983). Imitation, conformity, and compliance. In B. M. Staw (Ed.), *Psychological foundations of organizational behavior* (pp. 170–190). Oakland, NJ: Scott, Foresman.

Brief, A. P., & Dukerich, J. M. (1991). Theory in organizational behavior. Can it be useful? In B. M. Staw & L. L. Cummings (Eds.), *Research in organizational behavior* (Vol. 13, pp. 327–352). Greenwich, CT: JAI.

Brief, A. P., Reizenstein, R. M., Buttram, R. T., Pugh, S. D., Elliott, J. D., McCline, R. L., & Vaslow, J. B. (1995). *The new racism in corporate America*. Manuscript submitted for publication.

Brockner, J., & Rubin, J. Z. (1985). *Entrapment in escalating conflicts: A social psychological analysis*. New York: Springer-Verlag.

Buttram, R. T., Brief, A. P., Elliott, J. D., Reizenstein, R. M., & McCline, R. L. (1994, August). *Releasing the beast: A study of compliance with orders to use race as a selection criterion*. Paper presented at the National Academy of Management Meetings, Dallas, TX.

Canterbery, E. R. (1976). *The making of economics*. Belmont, CA: Wadsworth.

Cialdini, R. B. (1993). *Influence: Science and practice* (3rd ed.). Glenview, IL: Scott, Foresman.

Clinard, M. B. (1983). *Corporate ethics and crime*. Beverly Hills, CA: Sage.

Clinard, M. B., & Quinney, R. (1973). *Criminal behavior systems: A typology* (2nd ed.). New York: Holt, Rinehart.

Cooper, J., & Fazio, R. H. (1984). A new look at dissonance theory. In L. Berkowitz (Ed.), *Advances in experimental social psychology* (Vol. 17, pp. 229–266). New York: Academic Press.

Cressey, D. R. (1953). *Other people's money: A study in the social psychology of embezzlement*. Glencoe, IL: The Free Press.

Darley, J. M. (1992). Social organization for the production of evil. *Psychological Inquiry, 3*, 199–218.

Darley, J. M. (1994). *Constructive and destructive obedience and disobedience and a taxonomy of principal–agent relationships*. Manuscript submitted for publication, Princeton University.

Diener, E., Dineen, J., Endresen, K., Beaman, A. L., & Fraser, S. C. (1975). Effects of altered responsibility, cognitive set, and modeling on physical aggression and deindividuation. *Journal of Personality and Social Psychology, 31*, 328–337.

Doran, L. I., Stone, V. K., Brief, A. P., & George, J. M. (1991). Behavioral intentions as predictors of job attitudes: The role of economic choice. *Journal of Applied Psychology, 76*, 40–45.

Dowie, M. (1977). How Ford put two million firetraps on wheels. *Business and Society Review, 23*, 46–55.

Dubin, R. (1987). *The world of work*. New York: Garland Publishing Inc. (Original work published 1958)

Eisenhardt, K. M. (1989). Agency theory: An assessment and review. *Academy of Management Review, 14*, 57–74.

Festinger, L. (1957). *A theory of cognitive dissonance*. Evanston, IL: Row Peterson.

Festinger, L., & Carlsmith, J. M. (1959). Cognitive consequences of forced compliance. *Journal of Abnormal and Social Psychology, 58*, 203–210.

Finney, H. C., & Lesieur, H. R. (1982). A contingency theory of organizational crime. In S. B. Bacharach (Ed.), *Research in the sociology of organizations* (Vol. 1, pp. 255–299). Greenwich, CT: JAI.

Friedman, M. (1962). *Capitalism and freedom*. Chicago: University of Chicago Press.

Friedman, M., & Friedman, R. (1979). *Free to choose*. New York: Harcourt Brace.

Friedrich, C. J. (1937). *Constitutional government and politics*. New York: Harper & Bros.

Fritzche, D. J., & Becker, H. (1984). Linking management behavior to ethical philosophy. *Academy of Management Journal, 27*, 166–175.

Gioia, D. A. (1992). Pinto fires and personal ethics: A script analysis of missed opportunities. *Journal of Business Ethics, 11*, 379–389.

Goffman, E. (1967). *Interaction ritual: Essays on face-to-face behavior*. Garden City, NY: Doubleday.

Graham, J. W. (1986). Principled organizational dissent: A theoretical essay. In B. M. Staw & L. L. Cummings (Eds.), *Research in organizational behavior* (Vol. 8, pp. 1–52). Greenwich, CT: JAI.

Guzzo, R. A., & Shea, G. P. (1992). Group performance and intergroup relations in organizations. In M. D. Dunnette & L. M. Hough (Eds.), *Handbook of industrial and organizational psychology* (Vol. 3, pp. 269–314). Palo Alto, CA: Consulting Psychologists Press.

Hackman, J. R. (1992). Group influences on individuals in organizations. In M. D. Dunnette & L. M. Hough (Eds.), *Handbook of industrial and organizational psychology* (Vol. 3, pp. 199–268). Palo Alto, CA: Consulting Psychologists Press.

Hall, R. D. (1977). *Organizations: Structure and process*. Englewood Cliffs, NJ: Prentice-Hall.

Hamilton, V. L., & Sanders, J. (1992). Responsibility and risk in organizational crimes of obedience. In B. M. Staw & L. L. Cummings (Eds.), *Research in organizational behavior* (Vol. 14, pp. 49–90). Greenwich, CT: JAI.

Harris, R. J., Jr. (1989, April 12). Northrop indicted on federal charges of falsifying tests on weapons parts. *The Wall Street Journal*, p. A4.

Harris, R. J., Jr., & Pasztor, A. (1989, April 13). Pentagon plans to suspend Northrop unit. *The Wall Street Journal*, p. A4.

Harvey, J. B. (1974, Summer). The Abilene paradox: The management of agreement. *Organizational Dynamics*, pp. 17–34.

Hegarty, W. H., & Sims, H. P. (1978). Some determinants of unethical decision behavior: An experiment. *Journal of Applied Psychology, 63*, 451–457.

Henslin, J. M. (1967). Craps and magic. *American Journal of Sociology, 73*, 316–330.

Hornstein, H. A. (1986). *Managerial courage*. New York: Wiley.

Jackall, R. (1988). *Moral mazes: The world of corporate managers*. New York: Oxford University Press.

Janis, I. L. (1972). *Victims of groupthink: A psychological study of foreign-policy decisions and fiascos*. Boston: Houghton-Mifflin.

Jones, T. M. (1991). Ethical decision making by individuals in organizations: An issue-contingent model. *Academy of Management Review, 16*, 366–395.

Katz, D. (1964). The motivational basis of organizational behavior. *Behavioral Science, 9*, 131–146.

Kelman, H. C. (1958). Compliance, identification, and internalization: Three processes of attitude change. *Journal of Conflict Resolution, 2*, 51–60.

Kelman, H. C. (1973). Violence without moral restraint: Reflections on the dehumanization of victims and victimizers. *Journal of Social Issues, 29*, 25–61.

Kelman, H. C., & Hamilton, V. L. (1989). *Crimes of obedience*. New Haven, CT: Yale University Press.

Kohlberg, L. (1976). Moral stages and moralization: The cognitive developmental approach. In T. Lichona (Ed.), *Moral development and behavior* (pp. 31–53). New York: Holt, Rinehart & Winston.

Kohn, H. (1994, November 6). Service with a sneer. *The New York Times Magazine*, pp. 43–47.

Kopelman, R. E., Brief, A. P., & Guzzo, R. A. (1990). The role of climate and culture in productivity. In B. Schneider (Ed.), *Organizational climate and culture* (pp. 282–318). San Francisco: Jossey-Bass.

Kramer, R. C. (1982). Corporate crime: An organizational perspective. In P. Wickman & T. Dailey (Eds.), *White-collar and economic crime* (pp. 75–94). Lexington, MA: Lexington.

Langer, E. J. (1975). The illusion of control. *Journal of Personality and Social Psychology, 32,* 311–328.

Lifton, R. J. (1986). *The Nazi doctors.* New York: Basic Books.

Mannheim, K. (1940). *Man and society in an age of reconstruction.* London: Paul, Trench, Trubner & Co., Ltd.

McCoy, C. S. (1985). *Management of values: The ethical differences in corporate policy and performance.* Boston: Pitman.

Milgram, S. (1974). *Obedience to authority.* New York: Harper & Row.

Moscovici, S. (1985). Social influence and conformity. In G. Lindzey & E. Aronson (Eds.), *Handbook of social psychology* (pp. 347–412). New York: Random House.

Near, J. P., & Miceli, M. P. (1995). Effective whistle-blowing. *Academy of Management Review, 20,* 679–708.

Nemeth, C. J. (1986). Differential contributions of majority and minority influence. *Psychological Review, 93,* 23–32.

Nemeth, C. J., & Staw, B. M. (1989). The tradeoffs of social control and innovation in groups and organization. In L. Berkowitz (Ed.), *Advances in experimental social psychology* (Vol. 22, pp. 175–240). San Diego: Academic Press.

Passas, N. (1990). Anomie and corporate deviance. *Contemporary Crises, 14,* 157–178.

Posner, B. Z., & Schmidt, W. H. (1984). Values and the American manager: An update. *California Management Review, 26,* 202–216.

Pratkanis, A., & Aronson, E. (1992). *Age of propaganda: The everyday use and abuse of persuasion.* San Francisco: Freeman.

Proctor & Gamble: On a short leash. (1991, July 22). *Business Week,* p. 76.

Reizenstein, R. M., & Brief, A. P. (1995). *Just doing business: Compliance and racism as explanations for unfair employment discrimination.* Unpublished manuscript, Tulane University, New Orleans, LA.

Rokeach, M. (1968). *Beliefs, attitudes, and values.* San Francisco: Jossey–Bass.

Salancik, G. R., & Pfeffer, J. (1978). A social information processing approach to job attitudes and task design. *Administrative Science Quarterly, 23,* 224–253.

Schneider, B., Brief, A. P., & Guzzo, R. A. (in press). Creating a climate and culture for sustainable organizational change. *Organizational Dynamics.*

Schneider, B., Guzzo, R. A., & Brief, A. P. (1992). Climate for productivity. In W. K. Hodson (Ed.), *Maynard's industrial engineering handbook* (pp. 2.21–2.40). New York: McGraw-Hill.

Schneider, B., & Rentsch, J. (1988). Managing climates and cultures: A futures perspective. In J. Hage (Ed.), *Futures of organizations* (pp. 181–200). Lexington, MA: Lexington.

Scott, W. G., & Hart, D. K. (1989). *Organizational values in America.* New Brunswick, NJ: Transaction Publishers.

Simon, H. A. (1945). *Administrative behavior.* New York: The Free Press.

Simon, H. A. (1951). A formal theory of the employment relationship. *Econometrica, 19,* 293–305.

Staub, E. (1989). *The roots of evil: The origins of genocide and other group violence.* Cambridge, England: Cambridge University Press.

Staw, B. M. (1981). The escalation of commitment to a course of action. *Academy of Management Review, 6*, 577–587.

Staw, B. M., & Boettger, R. D. (1990). Task revisions: A neglected form of work performance. *Academy of Management Journal, 33*, 534–559.

Stene, E. O. (1940). An approach to a science of administration. *American Political Science Review, 34*, 1124–1137.

Stinchcombe, A. (1968). *Constructing social theories.* New York: Harcourt Brace.

Strom, S. (1993, February 11). Sorting out the mess at Leslie Fay. *The New York Times*, pp. C1, C6.

Sutherland, E. H. (1983). *White collar crime: The uncut version.* New Haven, CT: Yale University Press. (Original work published 1949)

Taylor, S. E., & Brown, J. D. (1988). Illusion and well-being: A social psychological perspective on mental health. *Psychological Bulletin, 103*, 193–210.

Tead, O. (1929). *Human nature and management.* New York: McGraw-Hill.

Tetlock, P. E. (1986). A value pluralism model of ideological reasoning. *Journal of Personality and Social Psychology, 50*, 819–827.

Trevino, L. K., & Youngblood, S. A. (1990). Bad apples in bad barrels: A causal analysis of ethical decision-making behavior. *Journal of Applied Psychology, 75*, 378–385.

Victor, B., & Cullen, J. B. (1988). The organizational bases of ethical work climates. *Administrative Science Quarterly, 33*, 101–112.

Watkins, S. (1993, October 18). Racism du jour at Shoney's. *The Nation*, pp. 424–428.

Weber, M. (1978). *Economy and society: An outline of interpretive sociology* (G. Roth & C. Wittich, Eds.; E. Fischoff et al., Trans.). Berkeley, CA: University of California Press. (Original work published 1922)

Welch, D. D. (1994). *Conflicting agendas.* Cleveland, OH: The Pilgrim Press.

Welles, C. (1988, February 22). What led Beech-Nut down the road to disgrace? *Business Week*, pp. 124–128.

Wolfe, S. (1985). Manifest and latent influence of majorities and minorities. *Journal of Personality and Social Psychology, 43*, 899–908.

Williamson, O. (1975). *Markets and hierarchies: Analysis and antitrust implications.* New York: The Free Press.

Yeager, P. C. (1986). Analyzing corporate offenses: Progress and prospects. In J. Post (Ed.), *Research in corporate social performance and policy* (Vol. 8, pp. 93–120). Greenwich, CT: JAI.

Chapter 17

The Importance of the Individual in an Age of Groupism

Edwin A. Locke
Diana Tirnauer
Quinetta Roberson
Barry Goldman
University of Maryland

Michael E. Latham
University of Minnesota

Elizabeth Weldon
Hong Kong University of Science

We offer this chapter as an antidote to the "group frenzy" that has seized the business world. We begin by showing evidence of this frenzy. Then, we demonstrate the critical role played by individuals in groups from the points of view of the need for group member ability, the role of individual champions in organizational change, and the importance of whistleblowers. Next, we document the dangers of groups, including conformity, social loafing, and groupthink. We conclude by reiterating the importance of independent thought on the part of each individual and make some recommendations for the design of effective groups.

GROUPISM

This is the age of groupism. Groups and teams are everywhere. There are cross-functional teams, product teams, new product teams, project teams, customer teams, service teams, sales teams, task teams, process improvement teams, quality control teams, natural work teams, cost-reduction teams, financial teams, and self-managed teams. Some MBA programs are even focused around student teams.

Don't get us wrong—there are legitimate reasons for using teams or groups, three in particular:

1. *Knowledge.* Other things (such as intelligence, experience, and effort) being equal, teams possess more knowledge than individuals—or more precisely, five knowledgeable individuals can know more than one, especially when each has expertise in a different field or specialty.

2. *Action Capability.* An effective group of people can accomplish tasks no individual could accomplish alone, for example, build a skyscraper, play a symphony, run a factory.

3. *Coordination.* A team can be a useful way to coordinate the activities of individuals so that tasks get done more efficiently and effectively.

But in recent years, the emphasis on groups and teams has gone far beyond any rational assessment of their practical usefulness. We are in the age of groupomania. Teams have become endowed with almost mystical qualities. It is as though putting people into a team endows them with superhuman capacities and makes them virtually omnipotent. Teams, it is implied, will cure almost any organizational disease, solve any problem, achieve any goal. But of course, they do not. Why has this occurred? Somewhere along the way, something important has been forgotten.

What has been forgotten is that teams are composed of individuals. We are not entering into a sociological debate concerning whether teams are more than the sum of their members. Our point is more fundamental. It is a metaphysical fact that groups and teams are composed of separate, sovereign, individuals whose brains are not interconnected. There is no superorganism called a group apart from its individual members. Take away the parts and the whole is gone. Although group members may stimulate and inspire one another, they do not automatically endow each other with the knowledge or intelligence that none of them possesses, skills that none of them has, or moral virtues that all of them lack.

But you would never know this from reading recent articles on this subject. As a case in point, consider a recent article in *Fortune* magazine that glorifies teams (Labich, 1996). Seven high performing teams are described; the Navy Seals, the Dallas Cowboy offensive line, the Tokyo String Quartet, the University of North Carolina women's soccer team, the Massachusetts General Hospital emergency-trauma team, the Boots and Coots international firefighting team (hellfighters), and the Childress stock-car racing team. We quote in full the author's conclusions about what makes them all successful (Labich, 1996):

> We are talking here about teamwork at a rarefied level, a swarm of people acting as one. These folks have checked their self-interest back in the garage somewhere and moved to another zone. It's a state in which team members—be they musicians, commandos, or athletes—create a collective ego,

one that gets results unattainable by people merely working side by side. It's all about humility, of course. Is that why it's such a scarce thing in the business world? (p. 99)

In sum, the author is saying that effective teams are not composed of individuals with skills, values, minds, and egos, but of egoless, humble, ciphers who, by some unnamed process, merge into a superorganism with an ego of its own.

The article is striking for the way this conclusion ignores the story's own content. Let's take a look at the facts the author mentioned in the same article. First, the team members in question are brilliantly talented. The Navy Seals are initially selected based on extremely rigorous criteria and then put through a hellish training regimen that only 30% of this elite group gets through. The Dallas Cowboy line (in 1966) consisted of five huge (300 lbs. or more), hard-working and highly trained individuals, who their coach claimed were the best he had ever had (several were all pro's). The members of the Tokyo String Quartet are all skilled enough to be virtuoso soloists. The North Carolina women's soccer coach puts the members through ferocious practices and posts the performance of each individual player on every practice drill each week. The Mass. General team consists of experts in several medical specialties. The Boots and Coots hellfighter team is so selective that they refuse to hire anyone they have not known for years and trained extensively. (Only the Childress team denigrates skill, seemingly because most of the team activities do not require a high skill level.)

Does Labich expect us to believe that these teams would still be highly effective if its members were not incredibly able, hard-working, and trained to an extraordinarily high level of skill? Does he think an offensive line consisting of untrained, 200-pound, lazy wimps who worked very smoothly together could carry the Cowboys to a super bowl victory? Michael Schrage (1995, p. 88), the author of an article in another business publication, *Forbes ASAP*, got it right when he said, "A collaboration of incompetents, no matter how diligent or well-meaning, cannot be successful." (See Cannon-Bowers, Tannenbaum, Salas, & Volpe, 1995, for an acknowledgment of the critical role of member competencies in team performance.)

Second, consider the issue of humility. Are the Cowboy linemen really humble, simply because they do not boast and seek the limelight? Quoting from Labich, ignoring his data once again (1996, p. 94), " [One linemen] says he and his colleagues are especially proud that opponents have been able to penetrate their protective curtain and dump quarterback Troy Aikman on his fanny only about once per game this season." Does Labich believe that these linemen would be just as effective if they were not proud of their achievements—that is, if they did not personally care how well they performed? Does he expect us to believe that the Navy Seals are not personally proud of being good enough to be accepted into one of the most elite military units in the world? Does he think that it is not in the self-interest of each member of the NC women's soccer team to work hard and cooperate so that they can win the national championship?

The inadequacy of team spirit or team cohesion alone in fostering good performance was revealed in an article on the recent Olympic games (Schrof, 1996). U.S. team coaches stressed team cohesion more than ever before, but some of the most cohesive teams did very poorly (e.g., men's soccer, women's volleyball). The men's soccer coach explicitly rejected the concept of the "hotshot superstar" in favor of players who could lift team spirits. Apparently, they failed to also lift team scoring. Ability aside, psychologist Roberta Kraus, who worked with several Olympic teams, argued that too much of a team focus can be damaging motivationally. "Players who have lost their individuality inside the team become weaknesses because they don't have a sense of their unique role. That means they tend to hesitate and not assert themselves when their particular abilities are called for" (as cited in Schrof, 1996, p. 54). Even articles that discuss team "troubles" hardly mention the significance of the individual members (e.g., Dumaine, 1994).

We believe that the basic requirements of team effectiveness are thinking members of high skill and ability who passionately want to excel, succeed, and win. In short, they are the same as the requirements for successful individual performance. The added requirement in the case of groups is that group members have to cooperate, that is, coordinate their activities. But the reason for doing this is egoistic—they cannot perform the requisite tasks effectively or at all unless they work together.

Consider the following example. Imagine a basketball player, Pete, who is a very good ball handler and passer, plays defense well, and rebounds effectively. But he is not a very good shooter, averaging only about 6–8 points a game. If Pete is rational, which means that he recognizes his limitations, yet wants to take the actions needed to win, he will play within himself, using his strengths and avoiding his weaknesses. Rather than taking a lot of shots, he will set up plays for others and pass the ball to them so that they can score. Conventionally, Pete would be called an "unselfish" player, because he does not try to score a lot of points. But the truth is exactly the opposite. Trying to score a lot would, in fact, be egoless and irrational, because it would risk losing the game and thereby undermine his own goal. It would be a contradiction to claim that he wants to win and then take actions that make it impossible. By passing, playing tough defense and rebounding, Pete is being selfish in relation to his own goal. If Pete wants to be a solo star, he should change to another sport like tennis.

Our goal in this chapter is to bring a rational perspective to bear on the issue of the role of the individual in the group. First, we demonstrate the importance of the individual in the group by demonstrating the impact of individual ability on group performance, discussing the role that individual product and process champions play in innovation, the significance of the whistle-blower, and the role of the individual in resisting conformity pressures. In each case, we show that the individual hero is important to group success. Then, we describe the negative effects of overemphasizing team processes and underemphasizing individual processes in groups with specific reference to social loafing and groupthink.

THE IMPORTANCE OF THE INDIVIDUAL

Team Member Ability

Because groups are composed of individuals, it should not be surprising to find that member ability and knowledge strongly affect group performance. Steiner (1972) observed that group productivity depends on the relevant resources of the individual group members, and the distribution of these resources among the group's members. In addition, both the general and specific abilities of individuals have been found to be consistently related to total group performance (Davis, 1969). Substantial research has documented this relationship (Haythorn, 1968; Heslin, 1964; Shaw, 1976; Steiner, 1972).

In a series of recent studies using the NASA "Moon Survival," Bottger and Yetton (Bottger & Yetton, 1988; Yetton & Bottger, 1982, 1983) showed the impact of group member ability on group decisions. They found that group problem-solving quality depended on the task knowledge of the individual group members. Yetton and Bottger (1982) found that a "best-member strategy" in which the group adopts the individual decision of its best member as its own decision consistently produced a better result than consensus methods of problem solving. Although a best-member strategy assumes that group members have accurate information about the relative expertise of its members, given such information, a best-member strategy will outperform the group average. In addition, Yetton and Bottger (1982) discovered that group consensus rarely produced decisions that are superior to those of the group's best member. Other studies have found similar results (Libby, Trotman, & Zimmer, 1987; Miner, 1984). Watson, Sharp, and Michaelsen (1991) also found that best-member scores on a problem-solving task were significant contributors to group decision-making effectiveness. However, over time, the best predictor of group effectiveness changed from the best-member score to the average member score.

In another study, Yetton and Bottger (1983) analyzed the effects of member task skills on the relationship between group size and group performance for both simulated and interacting groups. They found that although adding members to a group of optimal size produced marginal contributions to group performance, such contributions were greater for high-ability members than for low-ability members. In a later study, Bottger and Yetton (1988) found that the knowledge of the group's *two* best members was significantly correlated with group performance. A more recent study by Ganster, Williams, and Poppler (1991) supported this finding.

Tziner and Eden (1985) analyzed the impact of member competence on group performance in 3-person tank crews performing routine military field tasks requiring coordination between crew members. By experimentally manipulating crew composition across three levels of individual ability and motivation, Tziner and Eden were able to uncover both additive and interactive crew composition effects. Overall, the researchers found that group performance was strongly affected by average member ability. In addition, Tziner and Eden (1985) observed a three-way interaction between the ability levels of the three crew positions. High-ability individuals were found to contribute more to crew performance when working with two other high-ability individuals, compared to some combination of both high- and low-ability crew mates. Homogeneously high-ability groups surpassed the expected level of group performance, based on individual member ability; in contrast, crews composed entirely of low-ability members fell significantly below the predicted level of performance.

In a similar vein, in a study of 2-person teams, Laughlin and Johnson (1966) found that the performance of a person working with a partner of comparable or greater ability improved relative to his own performance when working alone, whereas the performance of a person working with a partner of lesser ability did not improve. Extending Laughlin and Johnson's experiment to a comparison of individuals and 3- or 4-person groups, Laughlin, Branch, and Johnson (1969) and Laughlin and Branch (1972) found that group problem solving on a complementary task was directly related to the number of high-ability individuals in the group, as low- and medium-ability members impeded group performance. A later study on the performance of groups of mixed ability replicated these findings (Laughlin, 1978).

With respect to the issue of group versus individual performance, we would expect the literature to show contingent results because a group has a greater potential amount of knowledge and yet, may not always utilize it due to process losses. The literature, in fact, shows mixed results (Hill, 1982), but still reveals the importance of the individual group members. Graham and Dillon (1974) examined the reliability of individual member productive-thinking ability and the relative productivity of a group composed of both low- and high-performing individuals. Groups composed of individuals who were highly productive when working alone on the brainstorming task performed better than groups composed of members with low individual brainstorming productivity. This finding was replicated by Shaw and Ashton

(1976), who found that the number of successful groups on a problem-solving task was proportional to the number of individuals in the sample who could successfully complete a similar task when working alone.

Task Moderators.   Although the abilities of individuals who constitute a group are powerful determinants of group performance, the impact of high-versus low-ability group members depends on the task. Steiner (1972) argued that task characteristics are critical. According to Steiner, a disjunctive task is one in which the group's individual members may produce different solutions, but the group may only offer a single solution as its final product. On this type of task, the ability of a group's most competent member is most predictive of group performance (Steiner, 1972). In contrast, a conjunctive task requires that all group members adequately perform each aspect of the task. For this type of task, the ability of a group's least able member is a stronger predictor of the group's performance (Gill, 1979; Steiner, 1972). In support of the latter hypothesis, O'Brien and Owens (1969), found that group productivity on a conjunctive task was correlated with both the average ability of the group and the ability of the group's least able member.

Kabanoff and O'Brien (1979) analyzed the performance of leader–subordinate groups that were required to complete a creative verbal task under various cooperation structures. Overall, the performance of groups with high-ability members was superior to that of groups composed of low-ability members. However, Kabanoff and O'Brien (1979) found a significant interaction effect between group leader ability and task organization, such that groups with high-ability leaders performed better than groups with low-ability leaders under a noncollaborative task structure, whereas leader ability had no effect on group performance under a collaborative task structure.

In sum, considerable research has shown that the skills of individual group members are critical determinants of group success. Furthermore, observations of military tactical decision-making teams confirm that member competencies are critical to effective team performance (McIntyre & Salas, 1995). In general, groups perform better when they are composed of high-ability group members and high-ability leaders, and the interactive effects of working with group members of comparable or higher ability on a task are significant. However, the relationship between member ability and group performance is moderated by task contingencies so that the ability of the group's least able member is more predictive of group performance on a conjunctive or collaborative task, whereas the ability of the group's most competent member is more predictive of group performance for a disjunctive or noncollaborative task.

A note is in order here concerning the relation between team diversity and team effectiveness. Research on the effects of group heterogeneity on group performance and effectiveness has been conducted with respect to various compositional dimensions (see Cox, 1993; Haythorn, 1968; Mann, 1959). A review of this literature by Jackson, May, and Whitney (1995) concluded that with respect to performance, the relationship between team diversity or heterogeneity and performance is complex, variable, and not easily explainable by existing theories. Part of the problem here is that no one has asked or answered the question; heterogeneous with respect to what? We would suggest that the effect of team heterogeneity would be impossible to predict without taking into account, among other factors, the skills and abilities of the individual members in relation to what the task requires. For example, an effective cross-functional team may require members who have widely different types of knowledge and expertise, whereas an effective new product engineering team may require members with similar or overlapping knowledge and skills. Therefore, we suggest that the effects of group diversity on team effectiveness do not exist in a vacuum; the consideration of the roles of both member ability and task contingencies are important factors in this complex relationship.

Champions of Product and Process

The possession of outstanding ability is not the only way that an individual can make a group—or an organization—more effective. Passionate individuals play critical roles in bringing about organizational innovation. In an increasing number of industries, continual innovation is essential to competitive success as the competitive environment changes in rapid and complex ways (Peters & Waterman, 1982).

Several studies show that a product or process champion who promotes a particular innovation within the organization is essential to successful innovation (Burgelman, 1983a; Howell & Higgins, 1990; Madique, 1980; Quinn, 1979; Schon, 1963). In his seminal work on product champions, Schon (1963, p. 84) found that "[t]ypically, one man [sic] emerges as champion of the idea. It is characteristic of champions that they identify with the idea as their own." Similarly, in his field study of internal corporate venturing, Burgelman (1983a, p. 241) found that "the motor of corporate entrepreneurship resides in the autonomous strategic initiatives of individuals at the operational levels in the organization," so that individuals are the driving engine behind successful innovations.

Similary, Kanter (1983, 1989) found that innovation in established companies often begins with the ideas and passions of a single individual at the "grass roots" of a company. When companies do not support the initiatives of such enterprising individuals, they may become "Lone Rangers"—an innovator who is "half outlaw as well as hero" (Kanter, 1983, p. 100). These individuals pursue their ideas without the support of the company, and sometimes break company rules and redirect resources to demonstrate the viability of their innovation. However, in the consistently innovative companies, such as Ohio Bell, Kodak, and 3M, these behaviors were considered legitimate activities, and individual champions received the resources required to pursue innovative ideas. Obviously, these projects could not ultimately succeed without the support and contribution of many members of the company. However, these innovations began with single individuals who had both a creative idea and the initiative and persistence to push for "their" project.

Two more recent studies support these findings. In a study of a successful organizational change program at a major food company, Locke, Kristof, and Nagle (1996) found that the program was led not by the CEO, but almost entirely by a small number of individuals at lower levels. The program, which the company called CPI, for continuous process improvement, was moved forward by a few executives at the VP level and by a few plant managers with the agreement of but not much support from the CEO. These "process champions" were motivated by a common conviction that changing to a CPI culture was essential to the company's survival. To create this culture, these champions promoted increased communication, training, goal setting, appraisal, team formation, and reward over a period of several years. These actions led to a new culture, millions of dollars in savings, and a noticeable increase in employee morale.

In another study, Weldon (1995) studied changes to products, services, and work procedures produced by members of empowered work groups. These groups had the authority to change the way they did their work to increase efficiency, safety, quality, and customer satisfaction. Results showed that a champion was important to the success of most group innovations. In fact, individual group members were the most common source of innovative ideas for change, compared to group discussion, ideas from the team leader, and suggestions from people outside the group. In addition, the actions of individual team members played an important role in the development and implementation of many ideas. When the source of the idea and development and implementation were considered together, individual efforts (rather than the team working together as a group) played an important role in 50% of all changes.

Studies also show that individual champions typically feel a strong sense of psychological ownership (Pierce, Rubenfeld, & Morgan, 1991) and responsibility for the innovation's success. Field and case studies find that successful champions are usually individuals who spontaneously push particular innovations for which they feel a great deal of personal passion (Burgelman, 1983b; Peters & Waterman, 1982; Peterson & Berger, 1971; Schon, 1963). For example, Steve Jobs felt strongly that a computer should be fun and was the driving force behind the MacIntosh computer. He procured the resources required to complete the project, helped solve problems when they arose, and acted as team cheerleader when morale ebbed. Similarly, Jack Welch championed a new plastic through the GE bureaucracy, because he believed the tremendously strong material could be a big business for GE. He bootlegged resources, conducted surreptitious customer satisfaction tests, and solicited the favor of upper level managers who could help him succeed. In each case, the champion felt strongly about his idea and was willing to invest time and energy to make sure it could succeed.

As these examples show, individual heroes are essential to innovation and change. These heroes feel a strong commitment to the organization and to the group project, and they are willing to invest their own time and energy to support that commitment. Without these committed individuals, risky innovations would rarely succeed in formal organizations.

Whistle-Blowing

Sometimes individuals can only bring about needed organizational change by going outside regular organizational channels—often a great risk to their careers. An example is whistle-blowing.

Whistle-blowing refers to the "unauthorized" disclosure of information about unethical or illegal organizational actions by an organizational member (e.g., see Vinten, 1994). Such disclosures are made outside the official chain of command, usually to an external source such as a newspaper or TV journalist.

Considering the huge number of people employed in the United States, some 123 million, whistle-blowing is a rare event. Between 1989 and 1995, there were only 530 cases reported in the newspapers (Brewer & the U.S. Department of Agriculture, as cited in Near & Micell, 1996). Seventy percent of these were in the public sector. This figure clearly understates the number of cases but, even if this figure is multiplied by a factor if 100, it is obvious that the number of whistle-blower cases is still small.

Here are some case examples.

Paula Coughlin and Tailhook

"It was an outrage—that's what it comes down to—it was a crime."—Paula Coughlin

Ms. Coughlin was an admiral's aide when she complained to the Navy that she was sexually harassed at the Tailhook Association's convention of naval aviators at the Las Vegas Hilton in September, 1991 (Noble, 1994). An investigation by the Pentagon concluded that 83 women there were assaulted or harassed by drunken aviators. Following Ms. Coughlin's lead, 80 women made similar assertions and a handful also filed a civil lawsuit. The incident received so much attention that, during June, 1992, she was called to the White House to brief President Bush on it: "He started to cry," she recalled "and said he was really upset" reminding her that he had a daughter who was also 31 (the same age as Coughlin). The women claimed they were groped and fondled as they were forced down a gauntlet of dozens of drunken sailors. Ms. Coughlin resigned from the Navy in 1994, citing unrelenting pressure from the filing of her complaint. She eventually reached a settlement with the Tailhook Association, an organization for military aviators (earlier, she prevailed in her civil litigation against the Hilton Hotels). She sued Tailhook for failing to properly supervise the convention. "It was an outrage," she recalled "that's what it comes down to—it was a crime."

Zalman Magid and the San Diego County Mental Health Center

"There are some people who don't like to make waves."—Dr. Zalman Magid

Beginning in 1984, a series of negligent deaths occurred at the San Diego County Mental Health Center (Glazer & Glazer, 1989). These deaths included a suicide victim who was denied admission after being brought to the hospital by the police following an earlier suicide attempt that same day; a drug overdose; and an inmate killed at the hands of his undermedicated psychotic roommate. Zalman Magid was the staff psychiatrist for 6 years when he was approached by two staff colleagues, who were upset with the quality of patient care and increase in patient deaths. Dr. Magid wrote a letter of complaint to the Board of Medical Quality Assurance, in which he outlined a pattern of neglect. After the state initiated an investigation, Dr. Magid was pressured by hospital administrators to withdraw his letter. "I decided not to do this," he recalled, "because I felt that I had done the right thing." Dr. Magid asserted that while the mutual support of others was helpful, "when it came down to the nitty gritty, their support alone was not sufficient." He believed it was, in the final analysis, his beliefs and values that sustained him through the most difficult periods. "Because of [my beliefs and values] I felt it was extremely important for me to act. If I did not act, there was a good likelihood that other people would die. According to Jewish law, if one knows that a death is likely to occur and one does nothing to prevent it or warn others, then . . . one is morally responsible for the ensuing death." Surprisingly, he found Jewish community leaders unresponsive to his pleas for help when the hospital began to retaliate against him by reassigning him to a nonmedical position. "There are some people who don't like to make waves," he explained. Later, in an effort to destroy his credibility, he was charged with trumped-up allegations of negligence. Investigations by both California and federal authorities eventually supported Dr. Magid's claims and led to sanctions against the hospital.

Charles Varnadore and Oak Ridge National Laboratory

"What they did borders on attempted murder, knowingly putting a cancer patient with a suppressed immune system in there."—lawyer for Charles Varnadore

Oak Ridge National Laboratory is a government nuclear laboratory in Tennessee that is run by Martin Marietta Energy Systems. Charles Varnadore, a 50-year-old mechanic, worked at the lab since 1974 (Wald, 1992). In 1989, he had an operation for colon cancer followed by 52 weeks of chemotherapy. After chemotherapy, he returned to work and began complaining about the way in which contaminated soil samples were treated in disregard of safety procedures. The effect of this treatment was to allow toxic chemicals in the samples to escape into the environment. The Energy Department confirmed that this was a repeated problem at Oak Ridge. When he received an unsatisfactory response from his superiors, Varnadore aired his complaints on CBS News during March, 1991. During this same month, the American Medical Association released a study indicating that workers at Oak Ridge who were exposed to very low levels of nuclear radiation for many years had a leukemia death rate 63% higher than the general population. Soon thereafter, Varnadore was transferred to a room containing radioactive waste. In September he was moved to another room which contained mercury, radioactive materials and asbestos. His lawyers called the rooms "indoor waste dumps." In 1993, an administrative law judge at the Department of Labor agreed that Oak Ridge managers had indeed retaliated against him for his whistle-blowing.

Naoto Kan and the Japanese Health Ministry

"Japan's staid political system doesn't often breed whistleblowers. But that hasn't stopped Naoto Kan."—Wall Street Journal (March 4, 1996)

Soon after his appointment as Health Minister in 1996, Naoto Kan publicly disclosed his own ministry's role in facilitating the spread of AIDS in Japan (Hamilton, 1996). He disclosed that officials of the Health Ministry insisted for 2 years beginning in 1983 that untreated blood products were safe, notwithstanding official evidence to the contrary and the availability of heat-treating technology. Worse still, he then released "smoking gun" documents whose existence the Ministry had denied for years. During this 2-year period, nearly 40% of Japan's estimated 5,000 hemophiliacs contracted the AIDS virus through transfusions. One week after his disclosure he issued a public apology, as current Health Minister, to the 1,800 or so Japanese hemophiliacs who contracted HIV, the precursor to AIDS, from blood products: "Until now, the government's responsibility has never been clear. I apologize for inflicting such heavy damage on so many people." Prosecutors have recently announced an investigation into charges of criminal negligence at the Health Ministry and in the pharmaceutical industry based on Minister Kan's charges.

Vil Mirzayanov and the Russian Chemical Weapons Program

"As long as work continues on new kinds of toxic substances, I will continue fighting whether I am arrested again or not."—Vil Mirzayanov.

Vil Mirzayanov wrote a 1992 newspaper article disclosing a top-secret Soviet chemical-weapons program (Efron, 1994). He was subsequently charged with disclosing state secrets, but the charges were dropped in 1994. Mirzayanov, a chemist, wrote that the head of the Soviet chemical weapons program lied in 1987 when he presented as complete the chemical arsenal shown to international observers. In fact, he said that the toxic gas that Mirzayanov's lab helped develop was loaded into aviation bombs and strategic missiles but was not on the list sent to international inspectors. In dropping the case against him, Mirzayanov said the prosecutor has shown that the "time has come in this country when such dangerous activities as development and manufacture of chemical weapons can be countered by legal means."

Although there has been only limited research on the general topic of whistle-blowing, and little meaningful agreement among researchers as to individual traits of whistle-blowers, these examples show that the price for whistle-blowing can be quite high and suggest that only individuals with a strong sense of morality are usually willing to pay that price. Glazer and Glazer (1989, p. 97) noted that "only those employees who have a highly developed alternative belief system [i.e., philosophy] can withstand the intense pressure to conform." Similarly, Jos, Tompkins, and Hays (1989, p. 557) concluded that "[i]t is also clear that those who are willing to blow the whistle are not only committed to certain values but that they are capable of *acting* on this sense of obligation even when there are strong organizational and situational pressures to the contrary."

Considering that whistle-blowing threatens the reputation of the entire organization and thus may pit one person, in effect, against thousands, and that retaliation against whistle-blowers is common (Near, Ryan, & Micelli, 1995), it is obvious that such actions require great personal courage. When whistle-blowing rights an egregious wrong, the individual group member is, in fact, a hero.

THE DANGERS OF GROUPS (AND HOW TO LIMIT THEM)

The topics discussed in the previous section all show the importance of the individual. In this section, we consider three ways that overemphasizing the team at the expense of the individual can produce negative consequences for the group. That is, overemphasizing team processes, team cohesion, team identity, and team performance at the expense of individual thinking, individual performance, individual identity, and individual motivation can produce dysfunctional results.

Conformity

It is well known that groups pressure people to conform to their expectations and that very frequently people do conform—often contrary to their own beliefs and values and even contrary to objective facts (Kiesler & Kiesler, 1969). This holds true in family groups, organizational groups, and even countries. However, several caveats are in order here. First, it is important to distinguish social habits (e.g., dress, forms of greeting, types of food) from basic values. Conforming to social habits is technically conformity, but it is trivial as compared to basic values (e.g., religion, philosophy). Cohesive groups whose values are corrupt (i.e., evil) can cause enormous harm both to themselves and to others (e.g., death squads working for dictators, terrorist organizations, criminal gangs).

Second, behavioral compliance may or may not indicate actual conformity, that is, going along with the group against one's own judgment. Compliance that contradicts one's own beliefs is conformity. Deutsch and Gerard (1955) called such conformity behavior "normative influence," and found it to be greatest among groups that exert pressure to conform to group judgment on individuals who are uncertain about the correctness of their own judgment. However, groups may actually persuade one or more of their members that a certain course of action is right (Deutsch & Gerard, 1955; Hogg & Turner, 1987). With this type of influence, an individual is persuaded to accept information by factual evidence and rational argument (Deutsch & Gerard, 1955). In such case, going along with the group represents conviction, not conformity. (Of course, many people join groups because they already agree with the groups' values.)

This brings us to a third, very critical point. Group conformity is not inevitable—that is, it is not preprogrammed by our genes and compelled by our social environment. Every individual with a normal brain has the power to identify the group's values and opinions, to appraise their validity, and to decide whether or not to go along. These choices stem from the faculty of volition, that is, the choice to focus one's mind on facts and logic or let it drift at the mercy of sensations of the moment, emotions, or the demands of others (Binswanger, 1991; Locke & Kristof, 1996; Peikoff, 1991). Everyone, of course, does not exercise their faculty of volition, or more precisely, does not exercise it to the same degree. Thus, in the conformity literature, one finds that, although conformity is common, it is not inevitable.

To begin this review, we must note that firm conclusions about the incidence of conformity cannot be drawn from studies in which there are no objective facts to consider. A case in point is the "autokinetic" effect that involves perceptions of movement of a light in a dark room (Sherif, 1935, 1936). Sherif noted that "a single point of light cannot be localized definitely, because there is nothing in reference to which you can locate it." The effect (which involves the experience of seeing the light move) "takes place even when the person looking at the light knows perfectly well that the light is not moving" (Sherif, 1936, p 92). Although individuals do conform to group opinion on this task (see also Allen, 1965), this is not very meaningful, because one opinion is as good (or bad) as another.

In contrast, the famous experiments by Asch (1952) are better tests. Here, the subjects matched lines of varying lengths to a standard line. In this case, the correct match was directly perceivable. That is, there was an objectively correct answer. When the group (consisting of precoached stooges) deliberately chose the wrong match (i.e., one that was longer or shorter than the standard line), 33% of the subjects went along. Because 7% of the subjects made matching errors in a control group, the net conformity effect was 26%.

Crutchfield modified Asch's experiments to eliminate the necessity of a real confederate majority by confining subjects to independent cubicles (Krech & Crutchfield, 1958). The "group" majority was simulated using a switchboard with lights that supposedly represented other members' opinions. Subjects observed stimuli similar to Asch's line-judging task, and also performed simple arithmetic problems and answered questions about social issues. Although each individual thought he or she was the last of 5 group members to answer the questions, in actuality, the lights were controlled by the experimenter to show strong consensus among the other 4. When matching lines, as many as 30% of the subjects conformed to the false group consensus. In situations of greater ambiguity, such as with solutions to insoluble mathematical problems, conformity was as high as 80%. Again, this is not a very meaningful test, because there were no right answers.

The results of these experiments at first glance may seem compelling; both Crutchfield and Asch found approximately 30% conformity when there was an objective and correct answer. However, to put this in perspective, 70% of subjects did not conform.

Several studies have looked at conformity in real life rather than lab settings. These studies tend to involve cases where more important issues were at stake. In one study, conformity and attitudes toward the group were studied among community residents who had joined a local housing council (Festinger, Schachter, & Back, 1968). In this research, the committees under study addressed uncontroversial and only moderately important issues. Results showed that the attractiveness of the group and communication among members were important predictors of conformity. In groups where individuals were attracted to the group and communication was "good," conformity to norms was as high as 90%. In more unattractive groups with "poor" communication, conformity to norms was as low as 30%. What is not clear here, however, is the degree to which the members actually agreed with the group. For example, high communication among members in the more attractive group could result in more rational persuasion. This would produce rational agreement rather than conformity.

The incidence of conformity appears to be even lower when important issues are involved. Burdick and McBride (cited in Festinger, 1957; cf. Allen, 1965) studied high school students' opinions about curfew regulations. Students' private opinions were assessed through written "discussions." Subjects were then shown other written opinions (manipulated by the experimenters) about the curfew regulations. Some subjects were tempted to change their opinion by being offered rewards for doing so. The experimenters also attempted to coerce others into changing their opinions through physical threats. Results showed only a net change of 16% toward the group norm in the reward group and 10% in the threat group (Festinger, 1957; c.f. Allen, 1965). These results suggest that people are not as likely to change opinions or behaviors when important issues are involved, even when threats and rewards are offered.

Another field study produced similar results. This was the famous bank wiring room at the Hawthorne Works of the Western Electric Company (Roethlisberger & Dickson, 1956). This room contained 14 technical, administrative, and supervisory employees. The group was observed and its output and activities recorded over approximately a 6-month period. The group established strong informal norms regarding proper behavior; 1) do not produce too much; 2) do not produce too little; 3) do not squeal on fellow workers; and 4) do not act officious. There were strong social and professional pressures against anyone who did not conform to these norms. For example, a worker might be ostracized socially, might not receive help when needed, or might be "binged" (hit with a hard blow to the upper arm) if he violated the group norms. Despite this pressure, all the norms were still violated. In fact, 4 out of the 14 workers went against them in some fashion on a regular basis. Although other group members may have been rationally convinced of the validity of these norms, this was not determined. The implications are that despite repercussions, individuals may choose to deviate from established group norms.

Resistance to conformity pressures takes distinct forms. An individual may consider the group norm and deliberately rebel against it (e.g., hippies who refuse to wash their clothes), which is labeled "anticonformity." This is actually a type of conformity, because the anticonformists' behavior is still based on the group's behavior. A true "independent" either does not consider the group norm at all (divorced from rational arguments) when rendering an opinion or taking action, or considers and rejects the group position because it is not convincing (Allen, 1965; Hogg & Turner, 1987; Nail & Ruch, 1992; Stricker, Messick, & Jackson, 1970; Willis, 1965).

There have been several personality traits associated with independent action against group conformity pressure. (We will not discuss situational variables here.) The following traits have been shown to influence an individual's tendency to resist conformity pressures; *high self-esteem* (Bernheim, 1994; Costanzo, 1970; Hogg & Turner, 1987; League & Jackson, 1964; Locke, McClear, & Knight, 1996; cf. Kiesler & Kiesler); *conviction* (Asch, 1952); *self-confidence* (Krech & Crutchfield, 1958); *intelligence* (Krech & Crutchfield, 1958); *originality*, as measured through thought process assessment and problem solving ability (Krech & Crutchfield, 1958); and *ego strength* (the ability to cope despite stressful situations; Krech & Crutchfield, 1958). In addition, in some studies women have been found to be more conforming than men (Bond & Smith, 1996; Krech & Crutchfield, 1958). However, Eagly's meta-analysis (1978) found that when contemporary sex-role differences were controlled (e.g., it was not socially acceptable for women pre-1970 to speak out in a group, etc.), conformity behavior differences dissipated. Also, when topics empirically shown to be of more interest to men than to women (e.g., economic information, political information, etc.) were controlled for, again, there were no significant differences in conformity behaviors between men and women.

Of course, there are benefits of group pressure to conform (see Milgram, 1965a). For example, when the group is right and the individual is wrong (e.g., a family that tries to persuade their child not to engage in criminal activity), group pressure serves a useful purpose. If a person violates valid group norms (e.g., be honest and do your fair share of the work), the group is right to ostracize and even dismiss him or her from the group. On the other hand, history reveals many cases where the group was wrong and the individual was right. Virtually every great scientific and technological discovery in history was made in the face of overwhelming opposition and skepticism from the general public and even the "experts" (for example, the Wright brothers in their first flight). Overall, the basic issue is: What are the reasons for the group's views and are the arguments rationally convincing?

In summary, although conformity is common, it is probably not as pervasive as social psychologists assume. First, it is sometimes mislabeled. People may act in conjunction with the group because they have been rationally persuaded. This is not conformity. Second, in most studies, some or many people did not conform. Even in Milgram's (1965a, 1965b) studies where pressure to conform was exerted by prestigious scientists, anywhere from 30% to 70% of the participants resisted complete conformity (i.e., giving the most extreme shock), and in Asch's experiment, 70% did not conform. Third, conformity is reduced when important issues are involved.

But, of course, all these studies yield only journalistic (i.e., statistical) data. Observing what people on the average do does not prove that they had to act as they did. As noted earlier, people possess the faculty of volition (Peikoff, 1991) and thus can choose whether or not to exercise their power of reason and act accordingly.

Social Loafing

Overemphasis on the group at the expense of the individual can also reduce individuals' incentive to contribute their effort to a group or organizational outcome. In a now classic experiment Latané, Williams, and Harkins (1979) instructed subjects to shout as loudly as possible, both individually and with others. Without the subjects' knowledge, the experimenters measured the subjects' individual performance in both the individual and group conditions. Results showed that individual performance was substantially lower in the group setting when compared to the individual setting. Latané et al. (1979) named this reduction of individual effort in a collective setting "social loafing". Subsequent research has shown that social loafing occurs across a wide variety of tasks and populations (Hardy & Latané, 1988; Karau & Williams, 1993).

When group outcomes are emphasized, individuals see less connection between their own contributions (time, effort, and skills) and the recognition and rewards they receive (Karau & Williams, 1993). Thus, when group rather than individual outcomes and accountability are emphasized, group members have less incentive to work hard. The lack of individual incentives can contribute to social loafing in at least three ways; 1) the free-rider effect, 2) the "sucker" effect, and 3) felt dispensability.

Free Riding. In some situations, social loafing derives from a desire to free ride on the effort of others. When a group task makes individual contributions anonymous, and rewards are shared equally, group members can reduce their own individual effort but still enjoy an equal share of the results (Albanese & Van Fleet, 1985; Olson, 1965). Thus, social loafing occurs when group members believe that their own contributions cannot be identified (Harkins & Jackson, 1985; Williams, Harkins, & Latané, 1981). Under these conditions, group members can reduce their effort and free ride on that of others.

The "Sucker" Effect. When conditions allow group members to take a free ride, many group members may assume that other group members will do so. Rather than be a "sucker" (Kerr, 1983) who contributes more than others, people reduce their effort to match the low level expected from others (Jackson & Harkins, 1985; Schnake, 1991). They reduce their efforts because people dislike inequitable situations where group members share equal rewards but make unequal contributions (Adams, 1965). Given the limited options available to a group member, reducing one's effort is often the easiest way to restore perceived equity, and this action produces social loafing.

Felt Dispensability. In some cases, social loafing results from feelings of being dispensable. Group members may feel dispensable when more able group members are available to accomplish the task, less able group members will cause the group to fail (Kerr & Bruun, 1983), or their efforts are redundant because they duplicate the contribution of others (Weldon & Mustari, 1988). When group members feel dispensable, they often reduce their effort.

Although these three explanations involve different psychological dynamics, they share a common foundation: 1) individual group members are concerned with the impact of their personal contributions on group performance; 2) group members expect some return on their effort; and 3) group work often weakens the link between individual effort, contributions to group success, and individual outcomes (Karau & Williams, 1993; Sheppard, 1993). Failure to deal with these issues may result from a focus on the group at the expense of the individual that groupism promotes.

To reduce or eliminate social loafing, the importance of individual psychological processes must be recognized. Individual group members must see a clear connection between their individual effort and the attainment of valued outcomes (Sheppard, 1993). In some contexts, this may be achieved by structuring the task so that each individual's contribution is identifiable (Williams et al., 1981) and rewarded or punished. Alternatively, converting a group task to individual tasks may solve the problem (Sheppard, 1993). In other situations, individual group members must be convinced that their contributions are important and unique (Harkins & Petty, 1982). Under the conditions that recognize individual concerns and incentives, group members will be less likely to loaf.

Therefore, it is clear that a concern for individual psychological processes and individual motivation are essential to group success. Although effective group processes (e.g., group interaction, group spirit, and group cohesion) are important, they are not sufficient to produce beneficial results.

Groupthink

Groupthink is a mode of thinking group members engage in when group consensus is considered (explicitly or implicitly) to be more important than rational, independent thinking. Symptoms of groupthink include the illusion of group invulnerability, rationalization, the (false) assumption of the group's morality, stereotyping of opposing groups, pressure on dissident members, self-censorship by members, the illusion of group unanimity, and the emergence of mind guards to key opposing viewpoints from the group. Groupthink leads to faulty group decision making and has been asserted to underlie many of history's notoriously bad decisions. For example, Janis and Mann (1977) suggested that groupthink contributed to Neville Chamberlain's decision to appease Hitler during 1937 and 1938, despite repeated warnings that appeasement would not stop him; President Kennedy's decision to launch the Bay of Pigs invasion of Cuba despite information indicating that the invasion would be unsuccessful; and President Johnson's decision to escalate the war in Vietnam despite information that the war could not be won.

In his original analysis, Janis (1982) suggested that groupthink is produced by a set of conditions that include group cohesion, insulation from outside information, unstructured decision-making processes, overly directive leadership, and high stress due to external threat, which lead to a strong desire for consensus, which produces faulty decision processes. Group members fail to consider a range of alternative actions, they ignore alternative goals, minimize actual risks, engage in biased information processing, and fail to produce a contingency plan.

Although subsequent research has not provided strong support for all of Janis's hypotheses (see Aldag & Fuller, 1993 for a review), at least two of these factors, external threat and group cohesion, seem to play an important role, although the nature of cohesion differs somewhat from that described by Janis. The strong mutual attraction of group members and resulting esprit de corps described by Janis seem to be less important than a strong desire to maintain a favorable group image because group members identify with the group. That is, a positive image of the self depends at least in part on a positive image of the group. In a laboratory study designed to test the effects of these two factors, Turner, Pratkanis, Probasco, and Leve (1992) showed that groups made up of individuals who identified with the group and who hoped to maintain a shared positive view of the group produced faulty decisions when working under threatening, stressful conditions. Raven's (1974) analysis of the Watergate cover-up and Esser and Lindoerfer's (1989) analysis of the space shuttle Challenger accident also show the importance of these effects.

Thus, a strong emphasis on the group and strong identification with the group may contribute to poor group decisions. Although procedures designed to structure the group decision making may mitigate these effects (Aldag & Fuller, 1993; Neck & Moorhead, 1995; Sims, 1992), it is clear that the organization's culture must encourage individuals to maintain a strong sense of personal identity to promote critical, independent thinking.

CONCLUSIONS

As we have shown, group success often depends on the heroic efforts of individual members. Effective groups are composed of individuals with a high degree of task relevant knowledge and ability, strong values and goals, and the willingness and courage to think for themselves. These individuals are most able to stand up to group conformity pressures, blow the whistle when the organization commits immoral acts, and champion organizational change. We have also shown that groupism can encourage loafing and undermine rational thinking processes. These pernicious effects are best remedied by recognizing the importance of individual psychological processes and individual contributions to the group.

Our emphasis on the individual is not idle chatter. Recently, the CEO of Honda had to rid the company of excess "consensus management which he found slow and unfocused, [and under which] no hard decisions were made" (Taylor, 1996, p. 96). He began by stressing the need for more individual initiative.

Consider next the following story, told recently, in confidence, to one of the authors.

> As a consultant to an airline manufacturer, I was helping to troubleshoot a system that would test part of the avionics (i.e., electronics) for their new aircraft. The test system was not working and for 2 weeks they had had a large team studying the test system, but they could not figure out what was wrong with it. I spent 3 days analyzing how the system was built, and then told the committee chairman that in 2 hours I could test the system performance, because I now understood where the system would fail first. He laughed and said, "You mean to tell me that all these engineers have been studying this problem for 2 weeks and all by yourself you are going to characterize the system performance in 2 hours?" I said, "Yes," and I did.
>
> The problem was that each engineer saw a small part of the problem but no single mind had studied the problem as a whole, that is, the total system. They had 32 channels of information but, because of a faulty design, no more than two could work at the same time. This meant that some of the avionics could not be fully tested by the system. (In an actual airplane, if the avionics were to malfunction, it would lead to disaster.) Well, this discovery started a panic. So what did they do? They made another team of these same engineers, and they brainstormed ideas at random and then voted on how to fix the system! In disgust and horror, I said to the team leader, "You don't really think this is going to work do you?" He admitted that they had no clue as to what to do, but said at least everyone felt they had participated! Finally, one member of the team, who seemed to have some real understanding of what the problem was, took over the project, selected his own small team of knowledgeable people, and fixed it. Who knows what went on in other units? I know that once the whole avionics system and all backups went dead during a test flight and they never could explain it. If this is the way they characteristically analyze problems, I don't ever want to fly in this airplane.

This striking example illustrates an important principle: A team working on a complex problem is helpless unless one or more individual members grasps the system (nature of the problem) as a whole. Simply throwing a large number of minds (i.e., a team) at the problem will not necessarily produce effective results. It reminds us of the oft-told tale of the team of blindfolded men feeling the different parts of an elephant; each thought the part that he perceived was the whole. The proper resolution is that at least one member has to remove his blindfold and perceive the entire animal. On complex tasks, this has to be a person of exceptional ability and knowledge.

Now let us consider the issue of motivation. Our position is that groups do not become effective by destroying the egos of their individual members. An individual with no ego, that is, no motive power, will not be of any use to anyone. An individual with no ego will not be concerned with blowing the whistle to expose wrongdoing; will not be concerned with innovation; and will not be motivated to contribute to group performance. Therefore, *what the group needs to do is to harness the egos of its members in order to achieve a common goal that is personally valued by each member.* To be motivated, each member must be convinced that the goal has personal significance. For example, in a sports team, this goal is winning, which leads to personal satisfaction. In a work team, it is success in solving some problem, which contributes to company success, which in turn aids job security and future opportunity. Therefore, a key task of team and organizational leaders is to show members why working for a group or organizational goal is in their self-interest. Sometimes this is as simple as giving a convincing, rational explanation for the goal in question, or linking rewards to performance.

Linking rewards to performance is crucial. In every team, there are some members who contribute more than others and some who contribute less. Naturally, members resent free riders who get the same rewards as everyone else. At the same time, members who contribute more than others resent not getting the recognition they deserve. Although some group advocates believe that every group member should be rewarded equally to maintain group "solidarity," solidarity at the expense of justice is self-defeating. Unfortunately, it is not easy to collect objective information about individual contributions to the team. This problem remains to be solved in most organizations (Murphy & Cleveland, 1995). Although this is not a full treatise on group effectiveness, we suggest the following guidelines in the design and operation of effective groups.

1. For groups or teams to be maximally effective, each should have members with high ability and task-relevant skills and knowledge.

2. Group members should be convinced that attaining the group goal is in their own self-interest; there should be an integration of individual and group interests.

3. Each group member should take personal responsibility for thinking independently and completing specific tasks, and should be encouraged by the group to do so.

4. At least one group member (or else an outside party) should have responsibility for the "big picture" to insure that the separate parts of the

group task fit together and that the work of one group is integrated with that of other groups.

Of course, teams whose members are both able and motivated do not inevitably succeed. There can be many reasons for this: The problem, as given, may be unsolvable; there may not be adequate support (e.g., resources) from outside the group; the time allowed may be too short; the means for implementing the solution may not be provided; the team goal may be unclear; or there may be personality conflicts among the members. Furthermore, team members may not possess the needed team management skills to effectively coordinate individual efforts. This latter problem is usually resolvable through training, however.

On the other hand, we believe that there are certain individuals who are incapable of working in peer groups. We are not referring here to individuals who are neurotic or totally blind to the basic requirements of group functioning (e.g., for taking turns when speaking), although such people do exist. Rather, there are some people whose knowledge, ability, confidence, ambition, energy, and passion are so overwhelming—so much greater than everyone else's—that they can only function as loners or as leaders. And it is better that they do. Groups would destroy them—or vice versa. Ayn Rand (1943/1993) called these people "Prime Movers"—people who move civilization forward through their own power and genius:

> The great creators—the thinkers, the artists, the scientists, the inventors—stood alone against the men of their time. . . . Every great new invention was denounced. . . .But the men of unborrowed vision went ahead. They fought, they suffered and they paid. But they won. . . .
>
> The creators were not selfless. It is the whole secret of their power—that it was self-sufficient, self-motivated, self-generated. A first cause, a fount of energy, a life force, a Prime Mover. The creator served nothing and no one. He had lived for himself. . . .
>
> Men have been taught that it is a virtue to agree with others. But the creator is the man who disagrees. Men have been taught that it is a virtue to swim with the current. But the creator is the man who goes against the current. Men have been taught that it is a virtue to stand together. But the creator is the man who stands alone. . . .
>
> The creator—denied, opposed, persecuted, exploited—went on, moved forward and carried all humanity along on his energy. (p. 678–682)

Yes, we need to use some teams and groups in the management of organizations. But we should not forget that they are composed of individuals and that, at root, organizations rise and fall as a result of the thinking (or nonthinking) of individual minds.

REFERENCES

Adams, J. S. (1965). Inequity in social exchange. In L. Berkowitz (Ed.), *Advances in experimental social psychology* (Vol. 2, pp. 267–299). New York: Academic Press.

Albanese, R., & Van Fleet, D. D. (1985). Rational behavior in groups: The free-riding tendency. *Academy of Management Review, 10*, 244–255.

Aldag, R., & Fuller, S. R. (1993). Beyond fiasco: A reappraisal of the groupthink phenomenon and a new model of group decision processes. *Psychological Bulletin, 113*, 533–552.

Allen, V. L. (1965). Situational factors in conformity. In L. Berkowitz (Ed.), *Advances in experimental social psychology* (Vol. 2, pp. 133–175). New York: Academic Press.

Asch, S. E. (1952). *Social psychology.* New Jersey: Prentice-Hall.

Bernheim, B. D. (1994). A theory of conformity. *Journal of Political Economy, 102*, 841–877.

Binswanger, H. (1991). Volition as cognitive self-regulation. *Organizational Behavior and Human Decision Processes, 50*, 154–178.

Bond, R., & Smith, P. B. (1996). Culture and conformity: A meta-analysis of studies using Asch's (1952b, 1956) line judgment task. *Psychological Bulletin, 119*, 111–137.

Bottger, P., & Yetton, P. (1988). An integration of process and decision scheme explanations of group problem solving performance. *Organizational Behavior and Human Decision Processes, 42*, 234–249.

Breckler, S. J., & Greenwald, A. G. (1986). Motivational facets of the self. In R. M. Sorrentino & E. T. Higgins (Eds.), *Handbook of motivation and cognition* (Vol. 1, pp. 145–164). New York: Guilford.

Burgelman, R. A. (1983a). A process model of internal corporate venturing in the diversified major firm. *Administrative Science Quarterly, 28*, 223–244.

Burgelman, R. A. (1983b). Corporate entrepreneurship and strategic management: Insights from a process study. *Management Science, 29*, 1349–1364.

Cannon-Bowers, J., Tannebaum, S., Salas, E., & Volpe, C. (1995). Defining competencies and establishing team training requirements. In R. Guzzo & E. Salas (Eds.), *Team effectiveness and decision-making in organizations* (pp. 333–380). San Francisco, CA: Jossey-Bass.

Costanzo, P. R. (1970). Conformity development as a function of self-blame. *Journal of Personality and Social Psychology, 14*, 366–374.

Cox, T., Jr. (1993), *Cultural diversity in organizations.* San Francisco, CA: Berrett Koehler.

Davis, J. (1969). *Group performance.* Reading, MA: Addison-Wesley.

Deutsch, M., & Gerard, H. B. (1955). A study of normative and informational social influences upon individual judgment. *Journal of Abnormal and Social Psychology, 51*, 629–636.

Dumaine, B. (1994, September 5). The trouble with teams. *Fortune,* pp. 86–92.

Eagly, A. H. (1978). Sex differences in influenceability. *Psychological Bulletin, 85*, 86–116.

Efron, S. (1994, March 12). Chemical arms whistle-blower cleared. *Los Angeles Times.*

Esser, J. K., & Lindoerfer, J. S. (1989). Groupthink and the space shuttle Challenger accident: Toward a quantitative case analysis. *Journal of Behavioral Decision Making, 2*, 167–177.

Festinger, L. (1957). *A theory of cognitive dissonance.* Evanston, IL: Row, Peterson.

Festinger, L., Schachter, S., & Back, K. (1968). Operation of group standards. In D. Cartwright & A. Zander, *Group dynamics: Research and theory* (3rd ed., pp. 152–164). New York: Harper & Row.

Ganster, D., Williams, S., & Poppler, P. (1991). Does training in problem solving improve the quality of group decisions. *Journal of Applied Psychology, 76*, 479–483.

Gill, D. (1979). The prediction of group motor performance from individual member abilities. *Journal of Motor Behavior, 11*, 113–122.

Glazer, M., & Glazer, P. (1989). *The whistle blowers.* New York: Basic Books.

Graham, W., & Dillon, P. (1974). Creative supergroups: Group performance as a function of individual performance on brainstorming tasks. *Journal of Social Psychology, 93*, 101–105.

Hamilton, D. P. (1996, March 4). Tokyo minister bares mistakes in AIDS policy. *The Wall Street Journal*, p. B1.

Hardy, C. J. & Latané, B. (1988). Social loafing in cheerleaders: Effects of team membership and competition. *Journal of Sport and Exercise Psychology, 10*, 109–114.

Harkins, S. G., & Jackson, J. M. (1985). The role of evaluation in eliminating social loafing. *Personality and Social Psychology Bulletin, 11*, 575–584.

Harkins, S. G., & Petty, R. E. (1982). Effects of task difficulty and task uniqueness on social loafing. *Journal of Personality and Social Psychology, 43*, 1214–1229.

Haythorn, W. (1968). The composition of groups: A review of the literature. *Acta Psychologica, 28*, 97–128.

Heslin, R. (1964). Predicting group task effectiveness from member characteristics. *Psychological Bulletin, 62*, 248–256.

Hill, G. (1982). Group versus individual performance: Are N+1 heads better than one? *Psychological Bulletin, 91*, 517–539.

Hogg, M. A., & Turner, J. C. (1987). Social identity and conformity: A theory of referent information influence. In W. Doise & S. Moscovici (Eds.), *Current issues in European social psychology* (Vol. 2, pp. 139–182). Cambridge, England: Cambridge University Press.

Howell, J. M., & Higgins, C. A. (1990). Champions of technological innovation. *Administrative Science Quarterly, 35*, 317–341.

Jackson, J. M., & Harkins, S. G. (1985). Equity in effort: An explanation of the social loafing effect. *Journal of Personality and Social Psychology, 49*, 1199–1206.

Jackson, S., May, K., & Whitney, K. (1995). Understanding the dynamics of diversity in decision-making teams. In R. Guzzo & E. Salas (Eds.), *Team effectiveness and decision-making in organizations* (pp. 204–261). San Francisco, CA: Jossey-Bass.

Janis, I. L. (1982a). *Groupthink*. Boston: Houghton-Mifflin.

Janis, I. L., & Mann, L. (1977). *Decision making: A psychological analysis of conflict, choice and commitment*. New York: The Free Press.

Jos, P., Tompkins, M., & Hays, S. (1989, November–December). In praise of difficult people: A portrait of the committed whistleblower. *Public Administration Review*, pp. 552–560.

Kabanoff, B., & O'Brien, G. (1979). Cooperation structure and the relationship of leader and member ability to group performance. *Journal of Applied Psychology, 64*, 526–532.

Kanter, R. M. (1983). *The change masters: Innovation for productivity in the American corporation*. New York: Simon & Schuster.

Kanter, R. M. (1988). *When giants learn to dance: Mastering the challenge of strategy, management, and careers in the 1990s*. New York: Simon & Schuster.

Karau, S. J. & Williams, K. D. (1993). Social loafing: A meta-analytic review and theoretical integration. *Journal of Personality and Social Psychology, 65*, 681–706.

Kerr, N. L. (1983). Motivation losses in small groups: A social dilemma analysis. *Journal of Personality and Social Psychology, 45*, 819–828.

Kerr, N. L., & Bruun, S. (1983). Dispensability of member effort and group motivation losses: Free-rider effects. *Journal of Personality and Social Psychology, 44*, 78–94.

Kiesler, C. A., & Kiesler, S. B. (1969). *Conformity*. Reading, MA: Addison-Wesley.

Krech, D., & Crutchfield, R. S. (1958). *Elements of psychology*. New York: Knopf.

Labich, K. (1996, February 19). Elite teams get the job done. *Fortune*, pp. 90–99.

Latané, B., Williams, K., & Harkins, S. (1979). Many hands make light the work: The causes and consequences of social loafing. *Journal of Personality and Social Psychology, 37*, 822–832.

Laughlin, P. (1978). Ability and group problem solving. *Journal of Research and Development in Education, 12*, 114–120.

Laughlin, P., & Branch, L. (1972). Individual versus tetradic performance on a complementary task as a function of initial ability level. *Organizational Behavior and Human Performance, 8*, 201–216.

Laughlin, P., Branch, L., & Johnson, H. (1969). Individual versus triadic performance on a unidimensional complementary task as a function of initial ability level. *Journal of Personality and Social Psychology, 12*(2), 144–150.

Laughlin, P., & Johnson, H. (1966). Group and individual performance on a complementary task as a function of initial ability. *Journal of Experimental Social Psychology, 2*, 407–414.

League, B. J., & Jackson, D. N. (1964). Conformity, veridicality, and self-esteem. *Journal of Personality and Social Psychology, 68*, 113–115.

Libby, R., Trotman, K., & Zimmer, I. (1987). Member variation, recognition of expertise, and group performance. *Journal of Applied Psychology, 72*, 81–87.

Locke, E. A., & Kristof, A. L. (1996). Volitional choices in the goal achievement process. In P. M. Gollwitzer & J. A. Bargh (Eds.), *The psychology of action: Linking cognition and motivation to behavior* (pp. 365–384). New York: Guilford.

Locke, E. A., Kristof, A., & Nagle, B. (1996). *Using process champions to promote successful organizational change.* Unpublished manuscript, University of Maryland, College of Business & Management.

Locke, E. A., McClear, K., & Knight, D. (1996). Self-esteem and work. In C. L. Cooper & I. T. Robertson (Eds.), *International review of industrial and organizational psychology* (Vol. 11, pp. 1–32). Chichester, England: Wiley.

McIntyre, R., & Salas, E. (1995). Measuring and managing team performance: Lesson from complex environments. In R. Guzzo & E. Salas (Eds.), *Team effectiveness and decision-making in organizations* (pp. 9–45). San Francisco, CA: Jossey-Bass.

Madique, M. A. (1980). Entrepreneurs, champions, and technological innovations. *Sloan Management Review, 21*, 59–76.

Mann, R. (1959). A review of the relationships between personality and performance in small groups. *Psychological Bulletin, 56*, 241–270.

Milgram, S. (1965a). Liberating effects of group pressure. *Journal of Personality and Social Psychology, 1*, 127–134.

Milgram, S. (1965b). Some conditions of obedience and disobedience to authority. In I. D. Steiner & M. Fishbein (Eds.), *Current studies in social psychology* (pp. 243–262). New York: Holt, Rinehard.

Miner, F. (1984). Group versus individual decision making: An investigation of performance measures, decision strategies, and process losses/gains. *Organizational Behavior and Human Performance, 24*, 73–92.

Mulvey, P., Veiga, J., & Elsass, P. (1996). When teammates raise a white flag. *The Academy of Management Executive, 10*, 40–49.

Murphy, K. R., & Cleveland, J. N. (1995). *Understanding performance appraisal: Social, organizational, and goal based perspectives.* Thousand Oaks, CA: Sage.

Nail, P. R., & Ruch, G. L. (1992). Social influence and the diamond model of social response: Toward an extended theory of informational influence. *British Journal of Social Psychology, 31*, 171–187.

Near, J. P., & Miceli, M. P. (1996). Whistle-blowing: Myth and reality. *Journal of Management, 22*, 507–526.

Near, J. P., Ryan, B., & Miceli, M. P. (1995). Results of a human resource management "experiment": Whistle-blowing in the federal bureaucracy, 1980–1992. *Proceedings of the 1995 Annual Meeting of the Academy of Management* (Vancouver), 369–373.

Neck, C., & Moorhead, G. (1995). Groupthink remodeled: The importance of leadership, time pressure and methodical decision-making procedures. *Human Relations, 48*, 537–557.

Noble, K. B. (1994, October 5). Woman tells of retaliation for complaint on tailhook. *New York Times.*

O'Brien, G., & Owens, A. (1969). Effects of organizational structure on correlations between member abilities and group productivity. *Journal of Applied Psychology, 53*, 525–530.

Olson, M. (1965). *The logic of collective action: Public goods and the theory of groups.* Cambridge, MA: Harvard University Press.

Peikoff, L. (1991). *Objectivism: The philosophy of Ayn Rand.* New York: Dutton.

Peters, T. J., & Waterman, R. H. (1982). *In search of excellence: Lessons from America's best-run companies.* New York: Harper & Row.

Peterson, R. A., & Berger, D. G. (1971). Entrepreneurship in organizations: Evidence from the popular music industry. *Administrative Science Quarterly, 16,* 97–106.

Pierce, J. L., Rubenfeld, S. A., & Morgan, S. (1991). Employee ownership: A conceptual model of process and effects. *Academy of Management Review, 16,* 121–144.

Rand, A. (1943/1993). *The fountainhead.* New York: Signet. (Original work published 1943)

Raven, B. H. (1974). The Nixon group. *Journal of Social Issues, 30,* 297–320.

Roethlisberger, F. J., & Dickson, W. J. (1956). *Management and the worker: An account of a research program conducted by the Western Electric Company, Hawthorne Works, Chicago.* Cambridge, MA: Harvard University Press.

Quinn, J. B. (1979). Technological innovation, entrepreneurship, and strategy. *Sloan Management Review, 20,* 19–30.

Schnake, M. (1991). Equity in effort: The "sucker effect" in co-acting groups. *Journal of Management, 17,* 41–55.

Schon, D. A. (1963, March–April). Champions for radical new inventions. *Harvard Business Review, 41,* 77–86.

Schrage, M. (1995, June 5). The rules of collaboration. *Forbes ASAP,* p. 88.

Schrof, J. (1996, August 5). Team chemistry set. *U.S. News & World Report,* pp. 53–56.

Shaw, M. (1976). *Group dynamics: The psychology of small group behavior* (2nd ed.). New York: McGraw-Hill.

Shaw, M., & Ashton, N. (1976). Do assembly affects occur on disjunctive tasks? *Bulletin of the Psychonomic Society, 9,* 469–471.

Sheppard, J. A. (1993). Productivity loss in performance groups: A motivational analysis. *Psychological Bulletin, 113,* 67–81.

Sherif, M. (1935). A study of some social factors in perception. *Archives of Psychology, 27,* 187.

Sherif, M. (1936). *The psychology of social norms.* New York: Harper & Brothers.

Sims, R. R. (1992). Linking groupthink to unethical behavior in organizations. *Journal of Business Ethics, 11,* 651–662.

Steiner, I. (1972). *Group processes and productivity.* New York: Academic Press.

Stricker, L. J., Messick, S., & Jackson, D. N. (1970). Conformity, anticonformity, and independence: Their dimensionality and generality. *Journal of Personality and Social Psychology, 16,* 494–507.

Taylor, A., III. (1996, September 9). The man who put Honda back on track. *Fortune,* 92–100.

Turner, M. E., Pratkanis, A., Probasco, P., & Leve, C. (1992). Threat, cohesion, and group effectiveness: Testing a social identity maintenance perspective on groupthink. *Journal of Personality and Social Psychology, 63,* 781–796.

Tziner, A., & Eden, D. (1985). Effects of crew composition on crew performance: Does the whole equal the sum of its parts? *Journal of Applied Psychology, 70,* 85–93.

Vinten, G. (1994). *Whistle blowing: Subversion or corporate citizenship?* New York: St. Martin's Press.

Wald, M. L. (1992, February 5). Nuclear laboratory whistle-blower is disciplined for questioning a test. *The New York Times,* p. A16.

Watson, W., Sharp, W., & Michaelsen, L. (1991). Member competence, group interaction, and group decision making: A longitudinal study. *Journal of Applied Psychology, 76,* 803–809.

Weldon, E. (1995, May). *Strategy formation in empowered work teams.* Paper presented at the annual meeting of the Society for Industrial and Organizational Psychology, Orlando, FL.

Weldon, E., & Mustari, E. L. (1988). Felt dispensability in groups of coactors: The effects of shared responsibility and explicit anonymity on cognitive effort. *Organizational Behavior and Human Decision Processes, 41,* 330–351.

Williams, K. D., Harkins, S., & Latané, B. (1981). Identifiability as a deterrent to social loafing: Two cheering experiments. *Journal of Personality and Social Psychology, 40*, 303–311.

Willis, R. H. (1965). Conformity, independence, and anti-conformity. *Human Relations, 18*, 373–388.

Yetton, P., & Bottger, P. (1982). Individual versus group problem solving: An empirical test of a best-member strategy. *Organizational Behavior and Human Performance, 29*, 307–321.

Yetton, P., & Bottger, P. (1983). The relationships among group size, member ability, social decision schemes and performance. *Organizational Behavior and Human Performance, 32*, 145–159.

Author Index

Subject Index